1990

Performance Practices
in
Classic Piano Music

Music: Scholarship and Performance

Thomas Binkley, General Editor

PERFORMANCE PRACTICES IN CLASSIC PIANO MUSIC

Their Principles and Applications

SANDRA P. ROSENBLUM

INDIANA UNIVERSITY PRESS
BLOOMINGTON AND INDIANAPOLIS

Quotations from *The Collected Correspondence and London Notebooks of Joseph Haydn,* edited and translated by H. C. Robbins Landon, © 1959 by Barrie and Rockliff, are used with the permission of Barrie and Jenkins, an imprint of Century Hutchinson Ltd.

Quotations from Carl Philipp Emanuel Bach, *Essay on the True Art of Playing Keyboard Instruments,* translated and edited by William J. Mitchell, originally published by Cassell & Co. Ltd., are used with the permission of Cassell & Co. Ltd., Macmillan Publishing Company, and W. W. Norton & Company, Inc. Copyright 1949 by W. W. Norton & Company, Inc. Copyright renewed 1976 by Alice L. Mitchell.

Quotations from *The Letters of Beethoven,* translated and edited by Emily Anderson, © 1961; and from *The Letters of Mozart and His Family,* translated and edited by Emily Anderson, 2d ed., edited by A. Hyatt King and Monica Carolan, © 1966, are used with the permission of Macmillan Press Ltd.

Quotations from Carl Czerny, *On the Proper Performance of all Beethoven's Works for the Piano,* © 1970 by Universal Edition A. G. Wien, all rights reserved, are used by permission of European American Music Distributors Corporation, sole U. S. agent for Universal Edition.

Quotations from *Thayer's Life of Beethoven,* revised and edited by Elliot Forbes, are used with the permission of Princeton University Press. Copyright 1949, © 1964, rev. ed. 1967 by Princeton University Press.

Quotations from Leopold Mozart, *A Treatise on the Fundamental Principles of Violin Playing,* translated by Editha Knocker, 2d ed., © 1951, are used with the permission of Oxford University Press.

Manufactured in the United States of America

Library of Congress Cataloging-in-Publication Data

Rosenblum, Sandra P., 1928–
    Performance practices in classic piano music.

    (Music—scholarship and performance)
    Bibliography: p.
    Includes index.
    1. Piano—Performance. 2. Music—History and criticism—18th century. 3. Music—History and criticism—19th century. I. Title. II. Series.
ML705.R67 1988   786.3'041   87-45437
ISBN 0-253-34314-3

1   2   3   4   5   92   91   90   89   88

To the composers whose works inspired this inquiry

Be patient with all that is unsolved . . .
and try to love the questions themselves. . . .

—RAINER MARIA RILKE
Briefe an einen jungen Dichter
[Letter of 16 July 1903]

CONTENTS

PLATES AND CHARTS

FOREWORD

Performance Practices in Classic Piano Music is a book long overdue. It is a natural outgrowth of the "urtext" phenomenon—the desire to know, insofar as that is possible, a composer's intentions and to try to execute those intentions faithfully. In the fall of 1957, when I began to work with a new teacher, I had never heard the word "urtext." Grete Hinterhofer, then in her late fifties, was very excited by the fact that editions were starting to appear that represented as closely as possible what composers had originally set down, without corrections or additions of expressive markings.

Grete Hinterhofer had been a child prodigy in Vienna, along with Rudolf Serkin, and she often recounted in a colorful way tales of concert life during the early years of the century. She believed that concert life had "improved" since those years. At that time, not only did pianists play Beethoven sonatas with whatever expressive devices they felt to be appropriate ("personal" interpretations, they were called), but the programs themselves consisted largely of works later viewed as second-rate or "unworthy" (one of her big numbers as a young concertizing pianist was a lengthy *Rosenkavalier* paraphrase). As the century progressed, however, there seemed to be an ever greater desire to understand what Beethoven had really wanted, to be a transmitter of his ideas, rather than simply to use his works as vehicles for self-expression. Thus, how important these new "clean" and reliable editions seemed and, indeed, how very necessary they were in achieving these new goals!

Since the 1950s "urtexts" have virtually wiped out all other editions; those old "edited" versions seem to be totally a thing of the past. The proliferation of these urtexts seems a bit hard to understand at times; in the case of the Mozart piano sonatas there are now five current ones in addition to the old *Gesamtausgabe* reprinted by Kalmus. One cannot help but wonder which text is more "ur" than the others (for there are, to be sure, minor differences among them). What have been the "advances" in Mozart playing as a direct result of these "better" editions? Or can we call the change in style an "advance" at all?

The question is at the very least debatable. Not every musician and critic feels that performance has unequivocally changed for the better in the last 50 years. Some would argue that most players of today may be more faithful to the text, but those of the past played with more imagination and flair. And while it may be true that the older players indulged in self-expressive whims, their performances seemed more interesting and varied than the more "sober" and "correct" (are they, really?) versions we so commonly hear now. The truth is that most players today are not as faithful to the text as they might think, for it may well be that they do not really know how to *read* the text. I believe that most eighteenth-century musicians would find their playing of that repertory a bit cool and bloodless.

I met Grete Hinterhofer some years later, just after Paul Badura-Skoda had brought out the reprint of Czerny's *On the Proper Performance of all Beethoven's Works for the Piano,* a work that figures prominently in the present book. I told her how excited I had been by many of Czerny's suggestions. She dismissed the whole thing with a wave of the hand: "Look what he says about the second movement of the Beethoven Opus 10, No. 3, for example. According to Czerny one should accelerate and slow down in all kinds of places not marked by Beethoven—typical nineteenth-century excesses! If Beethoven had wanted that he would have marked it." Were she alive today she would learn so much from Sandra Rosenblum's book! Musical notation can convey quite specific ideas, but these ideas vary from period to period and from composer to composer, and without help in deciphering them the "ur"-est of urtexts is of little value. The Viennese Classic period in particular is incredibly rich in source information; D. G. Türk, Leopold Mozart, C. P. E. Bach, and Quantz tell us in great detail *how to read the notation;* without such information the music cannot be rendered properly, and it can lose a great deal of its expressivity and passion. For every one of these sources calls for expressivity and passion; that is the point of music making: to stir the listener!

In Türk's *Klavierschule* the chapter on performance is divided into two sections: Execution and Expression. In the section on Expression Türk tells us that the greatest performer is the one who understands the music in its deepest sense and is able to transmit this sense to the listener in the most direct manner. But the chapter on Execution is almost five times as long; here we read in infinite detail how the musical language expresses itself through heavy and light, long and short, dark and light, etc. The ubiquitous slurs in Mozart are the soul of his expression, yet they are almost totally missing in virtually every modern performance. With the five urtext editions of the Mozart sonatas, is there a single performance that slurs the opening bars of K. 332/i as Mozart so specifically and carefully requested? Not only Grete Hinterhofer, but every other teacher I had, would have advised a smoother "long line" for those measures, and yet every eighteenth-century source tells us that they *must* be set off from each other: they are expressive, but independent! If one observes these slurs, a "lilting" rhythm appears, which is absolutely essential to the *real* long line of the movement.

It seems clear that the "early instrument" movement has begun to have some effect on the playing of this repertory on modern instruments. No one will deny the effect the harpsichord has had on the playing of Bach on the modern piano, even by those players who disdain the harpsichord. A similar kind of influence is being felt for this later repertory, since late eighteenth-century and early nineteenth-century pianos have different expressive capabilities than their later counterparts (the more rapid decay after the initial attack, for example, means more diminuendo in an appoggiatura, and the greater the difference between the first and second note of an appoggiatura, the greater the expressivity).

It is my firm belief that a thorough acquaintance with the performance practices of the Viennese Classic period can bring forth a new generation of players. Far more drama, wit, and passion will be heard in this repertory, with more varied performances than those to which we are accustomed. We have urtexts, we have original instruments, and here at last in Sandra Rosenblum's detailed and insightful study we have information on the language itself: each is indispensable and dependent on the others.

MALCOLM BILSON
Ithaca, New York

PREFACE:
ABOUT PERFORMANCE PRACTICES

Performance and teaching indicated the need and provided the stimulus for this book. The research, carried on during more than a decade, has informed my own playing and has helped me fulfil more completely the responsibility of teaching others. The ideas presented here attempt to guide musicians toward performances in which Classic piano music speaks directly, each piece in its own tongue and with all the expressivity that its composer might have desired. Such stylistically appropriate performances are, of necessity, based on contemporary information.

Musical notation has never been able to convey all the information essential for such performance. The score is at best a good clue to the composer's creative spirit. The body of knowledge known as "performance practices" helps fill the void between the score and the performance. More specifically, performance practices refer to the characteristics of notation and the conventions of performance in different periods, in different countries, and for different composers, including those customs so commonly understood that they were not notated, as well as the niceties that proved too subtle to notate. Familiarity with these conventions provides a framework for interpretation and guidelines to the many choices available within a style, to the kinds and degree of freedom that prevailed, to the extent performances can vary within stylistic limits, and to the existence of ambiguous areas.

At its best and most exciting, performance is the completion of the creative process, revealing the fullness of the composer's legacy. When the composer-performer relationship involves an attempt at similarity of viewpoint, the performer is the co-creator of a work of art. Such involvement means trying to ascertain the composer's intentions, not to duplicate performances of the past but rather to understand and to remain within the framework of the composer's style while creating a performance that has conviction and spontaneity.

For numerous questions of performance there is no single answer, just as there is no single interpretation for a musical composition. Problems that are incapable of complete solution with our present knowledge give rise to varying responses. In other areas of performance the known limits allow greater breadth of choice than we might expect—or even wish.

My purpose is to provide historical information and practical assistance in applying that information to the shaping of interpretation, all with respect for musicality and the individual composition at hand. With so many different subject areas considered, it is likely that readers will disagree with particular details or conclusions. This volume is but a stepping-stone, written to stimulate discussion and thought that will inevitably lead to new discoveries and greater knowledge. The process of learning is ongoing; the search enriches the performance.

SANDRA P. ROSENBLUM
Belmont, MA

ACKNOWLEDGMENTS

No book of this scope results solely from the effort of a single individual. Beyond my own research, this study has benefited from the work of others in performance practices and related fields, all of which has been filtered through my own understanding and point of view. These scholars are acknowledged in the course of the volume.

The list of persons who lent assistance is lengthy, but I would first single out two to whom I wish to express a special debt of gratitude. William S. Newman of Chapel Hill, North Carolina, gave unstintingly of his wisdom, musical expertise, and professional contacts. His thoughtful comments on the first version of this study, incisive questions, suggestions, and unwavering support encouraged me to produce the volume in its present form.

Max Rudolf of Philadelphia, one of the musicians to whom Professor Newman introduced me, also made unique contributions. Through an extensive correspondence he shared generously his extraordinary musical knowledge, insightful comments, and keen criticism on numerous topics both broad and detailed. His unusual scholarly command of eighteenth- and nineteenth-century German and Italian enriched my understanding of numerous passages and sharpened the nuance of many of my translations.

For the privilege of playing fortepianos, both original instruments and replicas, I am grateful to G. Norman Eddy and Ruth Eddy of Cambridge, Massachusetts; to Owen Jander of Wellesley, Massachusetts; to Barbara Lambert and D. Samuel Quigly, former and present keepers of the instrument collection in the Museum of Fine Arts, Boston; to Gerhard Stradner, curator of the instrument collection in the Kunsthistorisches Museum, Vienna; and to the Music Department of Wellesley College.

The libraries listed below have very kindly granted permission for me to base musical examples on primary sources in their collections. The location of the primary source designated for each figure is cited in the following section, "Sources of Figures." Particular appreciation and thanks go also to those persons mentioned here for their assistance in gathering information and checking details and for their countless courtesies and special attention. These include, alphabetically by institution, Sieghard Brandenburg, Beethoven-Archiv and Beethoven-Haus; Benediktinerstift, Göttweig; Marian Zwiercan, Biblioteka Jagiellońska; François Lesure, Bibliothèque Nationale; Peter A. Ward Jones, Bodleian Library; Ruth Bleeker and Dianne Ota, Boston Public Library; Hugh Cobbe, O. W. Neighbour, and J. A. Parkinson, British Library, Music Library; Conservatorio di Musica "Giuseppe Verdi," Milan; James Cassaro, Cornell University Music Library; Deutsche Staatsbibliothek, Berlin; Ruth Watanabe and Mary Davidson, Sibley Music Library of the Eastman School of Music; Fitzwilliam Museum; Forschungsbibliothek, Gotha; Otto Biba and Peter Riethus, Archiv of the Gesellschaft der Musikfreunde; Michael Ochs, Holly Mockovak, Larry Mowers, John Howard, and the entire staff of the Eda Kuhn Loeb and Isham Memorial Music Libraries of Harvard University; Houghton Library, Harvard University; Jon Newsom and William C. Parsons, Library of Congress, Music Division; Nationale Forschungs- und Gedenkstätten, Weimar; Jean Bowen, Susan T. Sommer, and the entire staff of the Music Division of The New York Public Library at Lincoln Center; Günter Brosche, Joseph Gmeiner, and Rosemary Hilmar, Österreichische Nationalbibliothek; J. Rigbie Turner, The Pierpont Morgan Library, New York; Royal College of Music, London; Rudolf Elvers and

Joachim Jaeneke, Staatsbibliothek Preussischer Kulturbesitz, Berlin; Stiftelsen Musik-kulturens Främjande, Stockholm; Peggy Daub and Wallace Bjorke, University of Michigan, Music Library; Suzanne Egleston, Rachel Frew, and William Meredith, Music Library of the University of North Carolina at Chapel Hill; Wiener Stadt- und Landesbibliothek; Victor Cardell, Music Library, Yale University.

Grateful acknowledgment is also here made to Bärenreiter-Verlag, Kassel, for granting permission to base identified figures on texts of the *Neue Mozart Ausgabe* (*NMA*), the Hallesche Händel Ausgabe, and a facsimile from the *Neue Bach-Ausgabe;* to G. Henle Verlag, Munich, for granting permission to base identified figures on texts of the *Beethoven Neue Ausgabe* (*BNA*), the *Joseph Haydn Werke* (*JHW*), and the *Stichvorlage* of Beethoven's Op. 47; to "Les Heures Claires," Paris, for permission to base two figures on the published facsimile of Beethoven's Op. 57 (originally published by H. Piazza Editions d'art); to Laaber-Verlag, Cologne, for permission to base two figures on a sonata in Ernest T. Ferand, *Improvisation in Nine Centuries of Western Music* (1961, originally published by Arno Volk Verlag); to the British Library for permission to publish quotations from its copy of Johann Nepomuk Hummel's *A Complete Theoretical & Practical Course of Instruction on the Art of Playing the Pianoforte* (London: Boosey, 1829); to Century Hutchinson Publishing Group Ltd., London, for permission to publish quotations from *The Collected Correspondence and London Notebooks of Joseph Haydn*, translated and edited by H. C. Robbins Landon (1959, originally published by Barrie and Rockliff); to European American Music Distributors Corp., Valley Forge, Pennsylvania, for permission to publish quotations from Carl Czerny's *On the Proper Performance of all Beethoven's Works for the Piano*, edited by Paul Badura-Skoda (Universal Edition A. G. Wien, 1970); to Macmillan Press Ltd., of London, for permission to publish quotations from *The Letters of Beethoven*, translated and edited by Emily Anderson (1961), and from *The Letters of Mozart and His Family*, translated and edited by Emily Anderson, 2d ed., edited by A. Hyatt King and Monica Carolan (1966); to Cassell & Co. Ltd., of London, and W. W. Norton and Co. and Macmillan Publishing Co., both of New York, for permission to publish quotations from Carl Philipp Emanuel Bach's *Essay on the True Art of Playing Keyboard Instruments*, translated and edited by Donald W. Mitchell (1949); to Oxford University Press, London, for permission to publish quotations from Leopold Mozart's *A Treatise on the Fundamental Principles of Violin Playing*, translated and edited by Editha Knocker, 2d ed. (1951); and to Princeton University Press, Princeton, New Jersey, for permission to publish quotations from *Thayer's Life of Beethoven*, revised and edited by Elliot Forbes (rev. ed., 1967).

Others whom I thank for their kindnesses in answering my queries are Derek Adlam (Nottinghamshire, England), George J. Buelow (Indiana University, Bloomington), Emily Clark (Newberry Library), Etienne Darbellay (Versoix, Switzerland), Vera Deak and Robert Evansen (Brandeis University Library), Kenneth Drake (University of Illinois), Georg Feder and Sonja Gerlach (Haydn-Institut), Raymond Haggh (University of Nebraska), Cynthia A. Hoover (Smithsonian Institution), Douglas P. Johnson (University of Virginia), John Koster (New Bedford, Massachusetts), Richard Kramer (SUNY at Stony Brook), Hans-Werner Küthen (Beethoven-Archiv), Laurence Libin and Stewart Pollens (Metropolitan Museum of Art, New York), Paula Morgan (Princeton University Library), Virginia Pleasants (London, England), Audun Ravnan (University of Nebraska), Robert E. Smith (Somerville, Massachusetts), and Mimi Tashiro (Stanford University Library).

My appreciation goes to the Bunting Institute of Radcliffe College for a two-year grant that provided for the early work on this volume. Susan S. Adams and Ronald A. Richardson most graciously assisted with translations from German and French respectively. Mildred Freiberg and Elfrieda Hiebert lent encouragement, enthusiasm, and suggestions that were invaluable during the long process of research and writing. My daughter, Laurie Rosenblum, and former students John Blacklow, Lara Jordan, Nancy Reynolds, and Lauren Shohet helped with numerous tasks, including proofreading, occasional typing, and preparing musical examples. My son, Bruce, handled many problems of word processing. The typing and retyping of the entire manuscript several times was expertly done by Elizabeth Duncan, to whom I owe much for her mastering my word-processing program, her sharp eye, and her unending good humor. Finally, thanks go to my husband, Louis, for his ability to reorganize and shorten sentences and for his enduring patience during the many periods of intensive work on this project.

SOURCES OF FIGURES

I wish to thank the libraries and other owners for access to this material and for their kind permission to base my figures on these sources. Figures not listed are readily available in facsimiles or other publications or are from sources owned by the author.

Beethoven-Haus, Bonn
   Figures 3.11 (Sammlung H. C. Bodmer, Mh5), 4.15 (Sammlung H. C. Bodmer, Mh7; facs., Bonn, 1954), 4.25 (Sammlung H. C. Bodmer, Mh5), 4.26 (Sammlung H. C. Bodmer, Mh6), 5.30 (BH 61), 6.20 (facs., Bonn, 1978), 9.6 (BH 62), 9.12 (Aut., Sammlung H. C. Bodmer, BMh 3), 9.14 (facs., Vienna: Universal, 1921).
Benediktinerstift, Göttweig, Austria
   Figure 5.12a.
Biblioteka Jagiellońska, Kraków
   Figures 3.20, 5.38, 5.39, 7.20, 7.24, 7.51, 7.74.
Bibliothèque Nationale, Paris
   Figures 3.12, 5.19 (Aut.), 5.20 (Aut.), 6.2, 7.21 (OE), 7.68, 7.108, 8.15, 8.19.
Bodleian Library, Oxford; courtesy of the Curators
   Figures 4.5, 4.6, 9.20, 9.21.
Boston Public Library; courtesy of the Trustees
   Figures 3.5 (OE), 5.23, 7.15, 7.57, 10.13.
British Library, London, Music Library
   Figures 3.6, 3.24, 3.25, 4.1, 4.7, 4.10, 4.11, 4.14, 4.19, 4.21, 4.27, 5.9a, 5.10a, 5.11, 5.17, 5.19 (OE), 5.20 (OE), 5.26, 5.27, 5.31, 5.44a, 6.5, 6.6, 6.7, 6.10, 6.11, 6.12, 6.13, 6.15, 6.16, 6.17, 6.18, 6.19, 6.21, 7.11, 7.25, 7.26, 7.85 (Hirsch Collection), 7.90, 7.99, 7.112, 7.126, 8.6, 8.7, 8.14, 8.18, 9.10, 9.19 (OE), 9.22 (OE), 10.3 (OE), 10.5.
Conservatorio di Musica "Giuseppe Verdi," Milan
   Figure 4.2.
Cornell University, Music Library
   Figure 7.19.
Deutsche Staatsbibliothek, Berlin/DDR, Musikabteilung
   Figures 5.3, 7.10, 7.29.
Eastman School of Music, Sibley Music Library
   Figure 3.4.
Fitzwilliam Museum, Cambridge, England; by permission of the Syndics.
   Figure 3.14.
Forschungsbibliothek, Gotha
   Secondary source for Figures 7.53, 7.123, 7.124b (all from Ms. p. 27a).
Gesellschaft der Musikfreunde, Vienna, Archiv
   Figures 4.13, 4.16, 4.20, 5.45a, 6.22, 6.23, 6.24, 7.47, 7.75, 7.81, 7.87b and c, 7.107a, 8.4, 9.8, 9.18.
Harvard University, Eda Kuhn Loeb Music Library
   Figures 3.17b, 8.3.
Harvard University, Houghton Library
   Figures 5.1, 5.5, 7.44, 7.71.

Harvard University, Isham Memorial Library
    Figures 5.8a, 7.28.
G. Henle Verlag, Munich
    Figure 5.21.
Library of Congress, Music Division
    Figures 3.2, 3.7, 3.8, 3.17a, 3.18, 3.19, 4.8, 4.9, 4.12, 4.22, 5.7, 5.12b, 5.29, 5.33, 5.44b,
    5.46, 6.1, 6.3, 6.4, 7.12, 7.13, 7.17, 7.30, 7.32, 7.45, 7.46, 7.52, 7.62, 7.72, 7.87d, 7.89,
    9.9.
Nationale Forschungs- und Gedenkstätten, Weimar
    Figures 7.102, 8.5 (Aut.).
New York Public Library at Lincoln Center; Astor, Lenox, and Tilden Foundations;
    Music Division
    Figures 3.1, 3.10, 3.15, 4.3, 4.4, 4.18, 5.6, 5.16, 5.18, 5.22, 5.28, 5.36, 5.37, 5.40, 5.43,
    6.25, 7.8, 7.14, 7.22, 7.23, 7.31, 7.33, 7.34, 7.37, 7.56b, 7.60, 7.61, 7.63, 7.64, 7.65, 7.67,
    7.76, 7.77, 7.86, 7.87a, 7.105, 7.106, 7.109, 7.110, 7.113, 7.120, 8.5 (OE), 8.8, 9.11, 9.12
    (OE), 10.12 (OE), 10.14.
Österreichische Nationalbibliothek, Vienna, Musiksammlung
    Figures 3.9 and 4.23 (S. H. Beethoven 73); 3.13, 5.47, 7.35 and 7.36 (S. H. Beethoven
    56); 4.17 (S. H. Beethoven 188); 7.38 (MS 40.188); 7.43 and 7.122 (S.m. 9822); 7.103
    (S. H. Haydn 856); 7.111 (Mus. Hs. 16.447); 9.7 (MS 40.225).
Pierpont Morgan Library, New York
    Figures 3.5 (Aut., Mary Flagler Cary Music Collection); 5.25; 5.41 and 7.3 (Robert
    Owen Lehman Collection, on deposit); 7.66; 7.88 (Dannie and Hettie Heineman
    Collection); 7.119 (Robert Owen Lehman Collection, on deposit).
Royal College of Music, London
    Figures 9.19, 9.22, and 10.3 (all three from the edition "for the Author").
Collection of William H. Scheide, Princeton, New Jersey
    Figure 10.12 (Aut.).
Staatsbibliothek Preussischer Kulturbesitz, Berlin, Musikabteilung
    Figures 5.42; 7.50; 7.53 (Mus. ms. 10119); 7.82; 7.83; 7.92; 7.104; 7.123 and 7.124
    (Mus. ms. 10119).
Stiftelsen Musikkulturens Främjande, Stockholm
    Figures 3.3, 7.16.
University of Michigan, Ann Arbor, Music Library
    Figures 7.5, 7.49, 7.54, 7.95a and c, 7.100, 7.125, 10.4.
University of North Carolina at Chapel Hill, Music Library
    Figure 4.24.
Wiener Stadt- und Landesbibliothek
    Figures 5.14, 7.4, 7.6, 7.7, 7.18, 7.27, 7.48, 7.84, 7.93a, 8.21.
Yale University, Music Library
    Figures 5.15, 7.39, 7.96, 7.101, 8.20.

INTRODUCTION:
USING THIS BOOK

This book was written for serious piano students, for performers—professional and amateur, for piano and fortepiano teachers, for students of performance practices, and as a resource for scholars. Each person can use it differently, according to his or her purpose and level of interest. Some may look for specific musical examples or for information on particular topics; others may read for general guidance or for conclusions without necessarily following all the detail; still others will find that the discussion and conclusions gain in significance through the details. Documents from the Classic period share the view that expressive performance is the result of attention to detail.

In addition to providing historical information necessary for stylistically appropriate performance—one based on contemporary evidence and well-founded stylistic considerations—the discussions in this volume furnish examples of decision making, of the application of principles, and of research methods. The documentation also supplies references that can serve as springboards for further reading or research. Throughout the text I have tried to leave a clear impression of which statements are from verifiable sources and which are my own opinions. My suggestions should be viewed as those of one musician, to be used, modified, or set aside.

The primary sources for this study, as for all research on performance practices, include chiefly composers' holographs and sketches, first and selected early editions, and certain contemporary manuscript copies; the contemporary instruments; theoretical sources, teaching books, letters, and diaries of the period; and, lastly, articles, reviews, and other information from contemporary periodicals and books. The Viennese, German, and English fortepianos I have played are described at the end of chapter 2.

As many musical examples as possible have been included in the text, particularly from compositions that pianists may not have in their libraries. However, when reading large sections of text it would be helpful to have at hand the Sonatas of Haydn, Mozart, and Beethoven in credible modern editions. Frequent reference is also made to Clementi's Sonatas Opp. 7/3 and 13/6, to Mozart's Rondo K. 485 and Adagio K. 540, and to Beethoven's Bagatelle Op. 119/2. Reference to music not contained in this volume is always based on the texts listed in the Selected Bibliography or named in the general discussion. The need for using musical texts based on the best source or combination of sources is implicit throughout.

The figures included are based on the source(s), identified in the captions, that would yield as authentic a reading as possible. A few examples for which the best sources were not readily available are based on recent scholarly editions whose editors used those sources. The directions of certain stems, occasional placement of notes between the staves, some uses of accidentals, and the C clefs (in Emanuel Bach's *Versuch über die wahre Art das Clavier zu spielen* and *Sechs Sonaten . . . mit veränderten Reprisen,* the first edition of Türk's *Klavierschule,* Haydn's Sonatas up to about Hob. XVI/26, an infrequent Mozart autograph, and Figures 5.1, 5.2, 5.3, 5.5 and 5.8a) have been modernized; otherwise I have retained the original notational forms, some of which may look unusual in modern engraving. In particular, beams that may relate to accentuation or articulation, the placement of pedal indications, the spacing of verbal directions (*crescendo, calando,* etc.), and the slurring of ornaments to their main notes (where it exists) have been adhered to as closely as possible. The English fingering, + to 4, has also been retained in the figures from Cramer's Etudes, Clementi's Sonatinas Op. 36, and Hüllmandel's Andante.

In the figures, broken slurs and ties (e.g., Figs. 5.18, 5.28c) and anything enclosed in brackets (Fig. 4.23b) are editorial additions based solely on the composer's own directions in analogous passages. Brackets also enclose the tempo heading, instrument names in scores, and time signature when a figure begins in mid-movement. Parentheses enclose an occasional addition from a valued secondary source.

In using the Hoboken numbers for Haydn's Piano Sonatas I have omitted the category numeral XVI; thus, an identification that would normally read "Hob. XVI/50" is "Hob. 50" in this volume. The original Köchel numbers, by which many of Mozart's works are still more commonly known, are used in the text. The revised numbers, according to the seventh edition of Köchel's *Verzeichnis,* are included in the Index, e.g., K. 310/300d.

I have often used "piano" as a generic term in titles of works, in the text, and where instruments are labeled in the figures. This avoids the confusion of terminology described in "The Piano's Ultimate Triumph" (chap. 1). For simplicity I have used only "Sonata" in the titles of the many piano sonatas discussed.

Translations of texts whose titles are cited in their original languages are my own unless otherwise credited. If the English title of a translated text is cited in a note, the quotation is from that volume. When several sources are cited in a note to support a statement, they are often in chronological rather than alphabetical order.

Specific pitches are denoted according to the following system (the whole note F's indicate the keyboard compass of five-octave fortepianos):

ABBREVIATIONS

AMZ	*Allgemeine musikalische Zeitung*
anon.	anonymous
Aut.	autograph
BGA	*Beethoven's Werke: Vollständige . . . Ausgabe (Gesamtausgabe; Complete Edition)*
BNA	Beethoven, *Werke: neue Ausgabe . . . (New Edition)*
Bro	Broder edition of the Mozart *Sonatas*
ca.	*circa*
col.	column
comp.	composed in
ed.	edition; edited by; editor
enl.	enlarged
f.	folio
facs.	facsimile
fig.	figure
fn.	footnote
HE	Henle Edition
Hob.	Hoboken, for Anthony van Hoboken, whose system of numbering is used for Haydn's compositions. Roman numerals designate categories of works (e.g., XV for keyboard trios; XVI for keyboard sonatas, although XVI is omitted in this volume). Arabic numerals give an approximate chronological order within each group. (Some works are now known to be misplaced.) See Hoboken, *Haydn: Thematisch-bibliographisches Werkverzeichnis.*
HSU	Haydn, *Complete Piano Sonatas,* published by Schott/Universal (formerly Universal)
JHW	Haydn, *Werke*
L	left hand
m. (mm.)	measure(s)
ms.	manuscript
MGA	*Mozart's Werke . . . Gesammtausgabe (Complete Edition)*
MGG	*Die Musik in Geschichte und Gegenwart*
NG	*The New Grove Dictionary of Music and Musicians*
NGMI	*The New Grove Dictionary of Musical Instruments*
NMA	Mozart, *Neue Ausgabe . . . (New Mozart Edition)*
n. (nn.)	end note(s)
n.p.	no pagination
OC	*Oeuvres complettes (Complete Works)*
OE	original (1st) edition
p. (pp.)	page(s)

p.n.	plate number
pt.	part
pub.	published in or by
R	right hand
r	recto (front side of double page)
rep.	reprint
rev.	revised
ser.	series
SU	Schott/Universal
T	both hands
trans.	translated by, translator
v	verso (back side of page)
var.	variation
WoO	without opus number, as indexed in Kinsky and Halm, *Das Werk Beethovens*
Wq.	For Alfred Wotquenne, whose numbering is used for Carl Philipp Emanuel Bach's compositions. See his *Thematisches Verzeichnis der Werke von Carl Philipp Emanuel Bach* (Leipzig: Breitkopf & Härtel, 1905).
WU	*Wiener Urtext* (*Vienna Urtext Edition,* pub. Schott/Universal; formerly Universal)

Compositions, movements, and measure numbers are identified as follows: Beethoven's Sonata Op. 31/2/i/93–94 signifies the second Sonata of Op. 31, first movement, measures 93–94; Op. 33/6/1–8 signifies the sixth Bagatelle of Op. 33, measures 1–8; K. 540/12 signifies measure 12 of Mozart's Adagio K. 540.

CHAPTER

1

Background
for the Study

Point of View

The goal of historically founded performance practices is to reveal each composition to its fullest in a manner at once consonant with the composer's expectations (as best we can discern them) and satisfying to the performer and the audience. For the music of the Classic period the most effective approach to this goal is gained from a chronological point of view: that is, by perceiving the newer style(s) of performance as having evolved gradually from the late Baroque and early Classic styles rather than as a premature and incomplete version of nineteenth-century Romantic pianism. Classic performance practices grew naturally from changes in musical styles and in the pianos themselves. Throughout the period, treatment of dynamics, touch, accentuation, articulation, ornaments, tempo, and rhythm, along with the new element of pedaling, responded to the developments in idioms and instruments.

In the context of this volume, the styles of performance regarded as "Classic" include the varied practices that appear to have been prevalent among knowledgeable performers from about the mid-1770s or 1780 to the early 1820s, the span of time generally regarded as the "mature" Classic period. Performance practices from the late Baroque (roughly 1690 to about 1730–1740) and early Classic (ca. 1730–1735 to ca. 1775)[1] periods are described where that discussion will assist understanding of the Classic practices. This chapter will provide background for the study of performance practices by tracing briefly the invention and gradual acceptance of the piano as a new keyboard instrument; by considering some influences on performance specific to the period; by observing relevant changes in the musical scores; and by discussing the relationships of four Classic composers to keyboard performance and to the new instrument. Then, before beginning with performance practices, chapter 2 will describe the characteristics and growth of the typical pianos for which the music of the Classic period was composed.

So much attention to the early piano, or "fortepiano," is not intended to imply any limitation of performance to an "authentic" instrument, nor does playing such an instrument of itself guarantee a fine performance. Knowledge of the playing qualities and sounds of the fortepiano helps one comprehend the intimate relationship between the instrument and its music. While playing original instruments or authentic replicas is greatly to be encouraged, at the least as a freeing experience and an important way of understanding the music intended for them, economic factors will, for the foreseeable future, preclude widespread availability of such pianos. Additionally, personal taste—or prejudice—makes it difficult for some to accept performance of the Classic repertoire on a fortepiano. This is particularly the case with those who view the modern instrument as an improvement over earlier forms rather than as a relatively recent member of a family that counts among its generations many distinguished members. Nevertheless, the number of fortepianos played in concerts and recordings and available in academic institutions and museums is growing substantially, making their sound more readily accessible to serious students of the Classic style. The understanding gained from hearing and playing these instruments leads to a fuller comprehension of the music itself, hence to a more penetrating performance on any piano. Some questions about performance are resolved by the fortepiano. Some of the instrument's qualities that project the unique character of Classic keyboard music are easily translated into performance on the modern piano when the performer knows how the music interacts with the instrument of its time.

INVENTION AND GRADUAL ACCEPTANCE OF THE PIANO

The Musical Need

The invention, development, and acceptance of a musical instrument with a new expressive potential may be the result of many interrelated factors, but chief among them is usually a musical need. From the early Baroque era, when dynamic contrast and accentuation became more important in instrumental performance, musicians had been intrigued by the idea of a keyboard instrument that could produce both a substantial sound and flexible dynamics. The harpsichord was considered ideal but for its dynamic inflexibility.

Of the instruments in use, only the clavichord, in which a small piece of brass hits the string when a key is depressed, could produce immediate dynamic variation controlled by the player's touch, including *crescendos, decrescendos,* and accents. Because the metal piece, called a tangent, remains in contact with the string until the key is released, the player could also introduce an *affettuoso* vibrato, or *Bebung,* by alternately increasing and decreasing the pressure on the key. Although some larger clavichords were especially well suited to the *empfindsamer* (highly sensitive) *Stil* of the eighteenth century, most produced only a delicate tone, ranging from extremely soft to barely *mezzo-forte,* which limited its use to solo playing and accompaniment of lieder in the home.

The organ and the harpsichord were capable of the robust tone needed for use with other instruments or in public functions, but their methods of tone production prohibited graduated dynamic variation. In the organ a change in the predetermined air flow would alter the pitch rather than the dynamic level of the sound; in the harpsichord the plectra would pluck the strings only when the predetermined force was reached.[2] A change of tone color or quantity of sound could be achieved on single-manual (keyboard) organs and harpsichords only by changing, adding, or deleting sets of pipes or strings, or, on the harpsichord, by applying one of several muting devices to the strings by use of a hand stop on the front of the case. On instruments with two manuals the player could preset different tone colors and move from one to the other at appropriate places in the music. Any such change of sound produces an immediate contrast, known as "terrace," or block, dynamics and applicable only on an architectural scale.

Another factor in the emergence of the piano was the new musical style developing in the mid-eighteenth century, which had started in Italy in the 1730s. Its melodies—simpler, often lyrical or tuneful, and of a periodic nature—demanded nuance and dynamic inflection. There were isolated experiments with swell mechanisms for the organ in the eighteenth century, but the swell pedal was not perfected and used widely for another hundred years. From the late 1750s in France and the early 1760s in England—well before the piano became widely used—some harpsichords were built with knee- or foot-operated mechanisms for producing *crescendos*.[3] But, inevitably, the growing need for dynamic expression led to the success of the instrument in which dynamic flexibility was inherently easy rather than an afterthought.

Cristofori's Invention

Around 1600 Hans Haiden of Nuremburg invented a way to bow harpsichord strings in an effort to make the sound more variable.[4] However, by 1700[5] Bartolommeo Cristofori, keeper of instruments at the Medici court in Florence, had solved the problem more directly: he had the strings of a harpsichord hit with hammers rather than plucked. The harder a key was depressed, the faster the hammer rose and the louder the sound. In a prescient account of this invention, written in 1711, Scipione Maffei called the instrument "gravicembalo col piano e forte" (harpsichord with soft and loud).[6]

Maffei provided a colorful description of the musical need, the instrument itself, and the reasons for its slow acceptance:

> It is known to every one who delights in music, that one of the principal means by which the skillful in that art derive the secret of especially delighting those who listen, is the piano and forte in the theme and its response, or in the gradual diminution of tone, little by little, and then returning suddenly to the full power of the instrument; which artifice is frequently used and with marvellous effect, in the great concerts of Rome, to the incredible delight of such as enjoy the perfection of art. Now, of this diversity and alteration of tone, in which instruments played by the bow especially excel, the harpsichord is entirely deprived, and it would have been thought a vain endeavour to propose to make it so that

it should participate in this power. Nevertheless, so bold an invention has been
... executed ... by Signor Bartolommeo Cristofali [*sic*]. ... The production of
greater or less sound depends on the degree of power with which the player
presses on the keys, by regulating which, not only the piano and forte are heard,
but also the gradations and diversity of power, as in a violoncello. Some professors have not given to this invention all the praise it deserves; because, in
the first place, they did not see how much ingenuity was required to overcome
the difficulty, ... and, secondly, because it appeared to them that the tone of
such an instrument was more soft and less distinct than the ordinary ones; but
this is a feeling produced by first impressions of the clearer sound we have on
other harpsichords; but in a short time the ear so adapts itself, and becomes so
charmed with it, that it never tires, and the common harpsichord no longer
pleases; and we must add that it sounds yet more sweet at some distance. It
has further been objected to this instrument, that it has not a powerful tone,
and not quite so loud as other harpsichords. To this may be answered, first,
that it has more power than they imagine, if any one who wishes and knows
how to use it will strike the keys briskly; and, secondly, he should consider the
object, the attainment of which has been so greatly desired, and not in a point
of view for which it was not intended.

   This is properly a chamber instrument, and it is not intended for church
music, nor for a great orchestra. ... It is certain that, to accompany a singer,
and to play with one other instrument, or even for a moderate concert, it
succeeds perfectly; although this is not its principal intention, but rather to be
played alone, like the lute, the harp, viols of six strings, and other most sweet
instruments. But, really, the great cause of the opposition which this new instrument has encountered is the general want of knowledge of how, at first, to
play it; because it is not sufficient to know how to play perfectly upon instruments with the ordinary fingerboard, but, being a new instrument, it requires
a person who understanding its capabilities, shall have made a particular study
of its effects, so as to regulate the measure of force required on the keys and
the effects of decreasing it, also to choose pieces suited to it for delicacy, and
especially for the movement of the parts, that the subject may be heard distinctly
in each.[7]

Maffei championed the attributes of the new instrument and probably credited it with more flexibility of tone and a better action than it had. From what
we can tell now, it seems that the sound of the piano in its early decades was
really not very different from, or as strong as, the sound of the harpsichord.
A way had to be found to increase the tension on the strings, for in order to
produce a full and controllable sound, strings that are struck have to be under
more tension than strings that are plucked. Because of its undistinguished
sound and problems with its action, the piano remained in the shadow of the
harpsichord until approximately the mid-1770s. Through the eighteenth century and well beyond, the history of the piano is one of continual invention
and change in an effort to enlarge its sound and make its action more responsive
and reliable.

The Piano's Ultimate Triumph

Italian interest in Cristofori's invention seems to have been limited. However, Maffei's article appeared in German in Johann Mattheson's *Critica musica* of 1725, and Cristofori's action was taken up by Gottfried Silbermann, a renowned organ and clavichord builder. Although Johann Sebastian Bach is said to have criticized a Silbermann piano of the 1730s for its heavy touch and weak treble, he apparently approved of Silbermann's improved instruments, on which he played at the court of Frederick the Great in 1747[8] and on which he conceived the unique three-part Ricercar from the *Musical Offering,* probably as a piece for piano.[9]

Emanuel Bach, employed by the king, stated his opinion of these instruments in Part I of his *Essay,* published in 1753.

> The more recent pianoforte [in the German, *Forte piano*], when it is sturdy and well built, has many fine qualities, although its touch must be carefully worked out, a task which is not without difficulties. It sounds well by itself and in small ensembles.[10]

By 1762 and the publication of Part II of the *Essay,* Bach was more accepting of the new instrument.

> The fortepiano and clavichord provide the best accompaniments in performances that require the most elegant taste. . . . [Those instruments] enjoy great advantages over the harpsichord and organ because of the many ways in which their volume can be gradually changed.[11]

By 1773 Bach wrote from Hamburg that Friederici's square pianos (*Fortbiens*) "are very good and I will sell many of them."[12] In 1780 this champion of the clavichord would publish the first of his important collections "für Kenner und Liebhaber" (for connoisseurs and amateurs) identified specifically for the fortepiano.

During the mid-eighteenth century an occasional composer wrote keyboard solos intended for the piano. The twelve *Sonate da Cimbalo di piano e forte* Op. 1, by Lodovico Giustini di Pistoia, published in Florence in 1732, may be the earliest such pieces. Although many of the changes between *forte* and *piano* would have been possible on a double-manual harpsichord, such sequences as *for[te], più forte; for., pia[no], più pia.* over six measures; *for.* (in the previous measure) shaded to *pia.* on the second of two consecutive trilled notes; and *più pia.* to taper a phrase ending are clearly indications for the *crescendos* and *decrescendos* possible on the piano.[13]

Johann Gottfried Eckard's *Six Sonates pour le clavecin* Op. 1, were published in Paris in 1763, five years before the piano appeared there in a public concert. In spite of the titling "pour le clavecin" (for the harpsichord), Eckard's frequent dynamic changes, graduated dynamics, use of *mf* and *mp,* and above all, his *Avertissement* inside the volume, leave no doubt as to his preferred instrument. Eckard wrote:

I have tried to make this work generally suitable for the harpsichord, the clavichord and the forte & piano [*sic*]. It is for this reason that I have felt obliged
to indicate the soft and the loud so frequently, which would have been useless
if I had had only the harpsichord in mind.[14]

Casual reference to keyboard instruments on title pages, in holographs, in
articles, and in letters was common well into the 1790s and beyond, only in
part because of the lack of a widely recognized name for the new instrument.
The names *pianoforte* and *fortepiano* came into use first in central and north
Germany in the 1740s, but they were not used with any consistency until near
the end of the century. In south Germany and Austria those names were used
only occasionally even in the third quarter of the century, and in Italy not
until the 1790s.[15] Rather, the instrument was variously called *cimbalo di piano
e forte, cembalo di martellati, cembalo, clavicembalo, clavecin, instrument,
Flügel, Clavier, Hammerclavier, Hammerflügel*, or *hammer harpsichord*.[16] Eckard, who knew Emanuel Bach's *Essay*,[17] may have been responsible for introducing the new name in France via the *Avertissement* quoted above.[18]

Haydn, Mozart, and their contemporaries still used *Clavier* or *Cembalo* as
a generic term for keyboard instrument in holographs of and references to
works for which the piano was unquestionably intended.[19] For example, Mozart
wrote "Cembalo" to indicate the piano part in the holographs of the Concerto
K. 450 and Fig. 7.17. In more specific usage of the time, *Cembalo* meant
harpsichord unequivocally; for many—especially north German—writers, a
Clavier was a clavichord.[20] Unfortunately, writers were often inconsistent or
unwittingly confusing (see p. 27).

Titles of printed editions frequently read "pour le Clavecin ou Piano-Forte,"
or the like. In works that have a differentiated piano style, for example, Beethoven's solo keyboard sonatas from Op. 2, such titling was presumably intended to avoid limiting sales by stating a preferred instrument, or conversely,
to try to reach as broad a market as possible. Op. 14, published by Mollo of
Vienna in 1799, is the first of Beethoven's solo keyboard sonatas titled specifically "pour le Piano-Forte" in the original edition. Yet Opp. 26 and 27,
published by Cappi of Vienna in 1802, revert to "pour le Clavecin ou Forte-
Piano" and "per il Clavicembalo o Piano-Forte" respectively,[21] indications for
the damper pedal in those sonatas notwithstanding! The holograph of Op. 26,
one of the few autograph sources for Beethoven's early keyboard works, carries
the title (on an inside leaf) "Sonate pour le Pianoforte."[22] Was the composer
consulted, and if so, did he agree to the change? Simrock's "Editiou [*sic*] tres
correcte" of Beethoven's Op. 31[23] as well as Nägeli's first edition of those
sonatas were titled for piano, but Cappi's reprint was again "pour le Clavecin
ou Piano-Forte." The reasons for these indications were certainly not musical.
In a word, the instruments named on printed title pages may be misleading
in determining composers' preferred instruments.[24] To avoid confusion I have
often used simply the generic "piano" in titles and text.

Although in the 1760s the piano was still considered an instrument for use
primarily in private circles, it had begun to appear in the relatively new but

increasingly frequent public concerts. A recently recovered document indicates that one Johann Baptist Schmid [Schmidt?] played a concert on a "Fortipiano" in Vienna's Burgtheater as early as 1763.[25] In London on 16 May 1767 Mr. Dibdin accompanied Miss Brickler at her Benefit Concert in Covent Garden "on a new Instrument call'd a Piano Forte."[26] A solo appearance followed at a benefit for Mr. Fischer on 2 June 1768, in which Johann Christian Bach played a Zumpe square piano,[27] perhaps performing a sonata from his Op. 5, which was published in the same year. The piano also appeared during that year in at least one program of the important Concert spirituel in Paris[28] and in a concert in Dublin.[29]

During the 1770s the piano was used in some orchestral and opera performances. An official pianist, a nephew of the well-known Dr. Burney, was appointed to Drury Lane Theatre in 1770; Griffith Jones was given this office at Covent Garden a few years later.[30] Michael Kelly reports that in Dublin both Italian and Irish opera companies were conducted "at the pianoforte" in 1779. In Rome in that year it was "customary for the composer of an opera, to preside at the pianoforte" for its first three performances. Pianos were used in Parma and Venice in 1780. Understandably, practice remained mixed; the harpsichord was still the continuo instrument in 1781 at the royal theatre in Vienna[31] and in the King's Theatre (the Italian opera) in London.[32]

Clementi, who was one of the King's Theatre harpsichordists in the later 1770s, also played the harpsichord in his few solo appearances in 1775, 1778, and early 1779. His first public appearance as a pianist, according to the concert program, took place on 23 April 1779,[33] approximately four years after he had moved to London from the estate of Peter Beckford in rural Dorset. On that occasion he played a "Duet upon the Piano Forte" with Mr. Dance.

During the mid-1770s the piano was also used for concertos in public concerts—important recognition considering the popularity of the genre. In 1776 all of Johann Christian Bach's concerto performances in London were on the new instrument, and there were similar performances in that city by other pianists during the decade.[34] On 22 October 1777, in the concert hall of Count Fugger of Augsburg, Mozart gave a program on the fortepiano that included his Concerto for Three Keyboards (*Claviere*) K. 242, the Concerto K. 238, one of his symphonies, and two or three of his pieces for solo piano. The event produced at least one newspaper announcement indicating keen anticipation, and an admiring review explained that the Concerto for Three Keyboards could be programed because "Herr Stein happened to have three instruments of the kind ready." The review, in the *Augsburgische Staats- und Gelehrten Zeitung* of 28 October 1777, goes on:

> Everything was extraordinary, tasteful and admirable. . . . the rendering on the fortepiano so neat, so clean, so full of expression, and yet at the same time extraordinarily rapid, so that one hardly knew what to give attention to first, and all the hearers were enraptured. One found here mastery in the thought, mastery in the performance, mastery in the instruments, all at the same time.[35]

Mozart's appearances as a pianist continued, and a "Piano Forte" was featured "completely alone" on 3 April 1781 in his first public concert after settling in Vienna.[36] On 12 March 1785 Leopold Mozart wrote to his daughter from Vienna, where he was visiting Wolfgang:

> It is impossible for me to describe the rush and bustle. Since my arrival your brother's fortepiano has been taken at least a dozen times to the theatre or to some other house. He has had a large fortepiano pedal made, which stands under the instrument and is about two feet longer and extremely heavy. It is taken to the Mehlgrube every Friday and has also been taken to Count Zichy's and to Prince Kaunitz's.[37]

Altogether, it appears that during the 1780s the piano indeed won its place as the preeminent keyboard instrument,[38] although the harpsichord remained in use to some extent, especially for continuo parts.[39] The practice of having a keyboard instrument accompany the orchestra died slowly during the last part of the eighteenth century and the early part of the nineteenth; the choice of instrument varied according to local circumstances. Interestingly, in London in 1791 the newspapers announced that Haydn would "preside at the harpsichord" during performances of his symphonies;[40] however, Charles Burney, an astute observer of musical life in Europe, specifically noted Haydn at the pianoforte during those concerts.[41] Was the reference to the harpsichord made out of habit, or was there a change of plan? The year 1797 saw the inception in London of the *Pianoforte Magazine,* which contained pieces for amateur players and coupons redeemable for a piano.[42] In 1799 the recently established but esteemed Paris Conservatoire appointed François Boieldieu its first professor of piano and began to award a prize for piano rather than harpsichord.[43]

SOME INFLUENCES ON PERFORMANCE

He who performs a composition so that its inherent affect (character, etc.) is expressed (made perceptible) to the utmost even in every single passage, and that the tones become, so to speak, a language [*Sprache*] of the feelings, of him one says that he has a good execution. Good execution, therefore, is the most important, yet at the same time the most difficult aspect of music making.

—DANIEL GOTTLOB TÜRK[44]

The principal object of music is the expression of passionate feelings. . . .

—HEINRICH CHRISTOPH KOCH[45]

Music and Rhetoric

These two quotations present several themes that are central to eighteenth-century musical thought and performance. The ideas suggest that Classic music owes the roots of some of its attitudes toward expression to Baroque ideals; but, as the Classic style matured, it shaped these attitudes to its own needs. The passage from Türk's *Klavierschule,* the most comprehensive book on keyboard performance practice in the late eighteenth century,[46] refers to "inherent affect," a concept of Baroque origin. Türk compares the expressive execution of music to the delivery of ideas through the spoken word; and he implies that this "important, yet ... difficult" expressive execution should move the listener, a sentiment stated more boldly by Koch.

Türk draws repeatedly on analogies between rhetoric and music as he discusses clarity, punctuation, accentuation, and other aspects of "good execution."[47] In describing the forms of instrumental music he ranks the sonata first among pieces written for the keyboard, comparing it to the ode in poetry. Consequently, the sonata

> presumes ... much power of invention and a lofty—I would almost want to say musical-poetic—flight of thoughts and of expression. . . . Every emotion and passion can be expressed in it. Indeed, the more expressive a sonata is, the more the composer is heard, as it were, to speak in tones. . . .[48]

The theme of music as speech, as "a language of the feelings," recurs frequently in writings of the period. "The whole [art of] music is based on the power ... of inarticulate tones to express ... the language of the feelings without words . . . ," wrote Kirnberger in Sulzer's *Allgemeine Theorie der schönen Künste.*[49] Koch quoted from the same encyclopedia in his *Lexikon:*

> The essence of melody exists in expression. It must always depict a passionate feeling or a mood. Everyone who hears it must imagine that he is hearing the speech of a man who is absorbed by a certain feeling. . . .[50]

Rhetoric, which may be most simply defined as the art of expressive discourse, originated in the ancient Greek and Roman descriptions of oratory. Rediscovery of Quintilian's *Institutio oratorio* in 1416 provided an important source for the "growing union between rhetoric and music" in the sixteenth century.[51] Rhetoric interested Baroque musicians and theorists for two main reasons: It provided concepts of temporal form and some applicable descriptive vocabulary; and its avowed purpose was to move the "affections" (emotions) of the listener.

The association of music with rhetorical principles was a fundamental part of Baroque aesthetics that eventually supported the rise of purely instrumental music. In *Der vollkommene Capellmeister* of 1739, a principal source, Johann Mattheson explored the relationship between rhetoric and music at many levels, from the philosophic to the smallest rhythmic segments, the poetic meters (iamb, trochee, etc.), which he called "tone-feet" in music.[52] Using the vocabulary of syntax and punctuation he compared the hierarchies of grammatical and melodic structure to the level of paragraph and musical "section," with special attention to the importance and clarification of the smaller segments of phrases (*Einschnitte*).[53]

Another major aspect of Baroque musical practice that arose from the association of rhetoric and music was the "doctrine of the affections."[54] The affections, often referred to as passions or sentiments, were treated as emotional abstractions: states of mind, feelings, and reactions characteristic of man in a universal sense, such as love, anger, sadness, and so on. The affections were thus the content of music. During the seventeenth and the early eighteenth centuries most pieces, movements, or sections of a long work contained only a single affection and moved with unbroken stride until its expression was complete.

With the waning of the Baroque and the emerging of the *galant* style in the 1730s to 1750s, and throughout the changing musical currents of the rest of the century, rhetorical concepts and the affections continued to inform musical practice to varying, although gradually lessening, degrees. The *galant* (i.e., mainly homophonic Classical) style,[55] with its changing and contrasting elements and moods, could no longer host the doctrine of the affections in the Baroque sense. Therefore after 1750 the affections gradually lost "their objective quality as rationalized emotional states" that unified each piece; instead, they frequently represented more subjective emotions of the composer.[56] Emotions were not static, but subject to change and fluctuation, argued Johann Nikolaus Forkel. He rationalized the contrast that was part of the new instrumental style by suggesting that "music expresses the 'multiple modifications' of feeling through multiple modifications of musical expression. . . ." This "allowed for, indeed required, the specifically musical elements of affective contrast and compositional interest and variety."[57] By the end of the century, when Koch reiterated that the goal of music was "the expression of passionate feelings,"[58] the idea seems to have implied a turning from the universal affections to more individual, pre-Romantic self-expression.

Empfindsamkeit (Sensibility)

Around the middle of the eighteenth century musicians in north Germany turned the expressive ideals of rhetorical theory to a more intensely expressive musical style. According to Quantz,

> The orator and the musician have, at the bottom, the same aim . . . , namely to make themselves masters of the hearts of their listeners, to arouse or still their passions, and to transport them now to this sentiment, now to that.

> Good execution must be *expressive, and appropriate to each passion [Leiden-schaft] that one encounters.* . . . The performer of a piece must seek to enter into the principal and related passions that he is to express. And since in the majority of pieces one passion constantly alternates with another, the performer must know how to judge the nature of the passion that each idea contains, and constantly make his execution conform to it. Only in this manner will he do justice to the intentions of the composer. . . .[59]

The north German school, of which Koch and Quantz were members, cultivated the *empfindsamer Stil* (highly sensitive style), in which intimate and very moving—sometimes sentimental—expression was the goal. This music, a variation of the widespread *galant* style, may display fragmented melodic lines, expressive leaps, rhythmic diversity, unexpected rests, ambiguous or dissonant harmony, frequent dynamic change, and considerable ornamentation. Such characteristics accommodate rapid changes of mood, which enhance the personal quality of the expression. Repeated reference to the feelings (*Empfindungen*) in Classic music criticism may result in part from the ultimate absorption of the *empfindsamer Stil* into the musical language of mature Classicism.

Other north Germans whose writings reflect this sensibility include Marpurg, Kirnberger, and Schulz.[60] J. A. P. Schulz's description of the sonata in Sulzer's *Allgemeine Theorie der schönen Künste,* a very widely read encyclopedia, emphasizes the potential expressive and rhetorical qualities of that form. Schulz's description influenced Türk's writing on the sonata (p. 9 above); and the final sentence of the following extract from Schulz's contribution is also quoted in Koch's article:

> Sonata. An instrumental piece of two, three or four successive movements of different character. . . .
>
> In no form has instrumental music a more appropriate opportunity than in the sonata to display its power to depict feelings without words. The symphony [and] the overture have a more specifically determined character. The form of a concerto seems designed more to give an able player opportunity to be heard with the accompaniment of many instruments than to be used for strong emotions. Beyond these and the dances, which also have their own character, there remains in instrumental music only the form of the sonata, which can assume all characters and every expression. In a sonata the composer can intend to express a monologue in tones of sorrow, distress, pain, or tenderness, or of delight and joy; or [he can intend] to carry on a sentimental dialogue in merely impassioned tones among similar or contrasting characters; or [he can] simply depict powerful, stormy, or contrasting emotions, or pleasing emotions flowing along easily and gently.[61]

The most admired proponent of *Empfindsamkeit,* for which a large clavichord (secondarily a fortepiano) was an ideal vehicle, was Emanuel Bach. Charles Burney attributed Bach's "fine vocal taste in composing lessons" to the influence of Hasse's operas, of which Frederick the Great was inordinately fond.[62] Curiously, Bach never wrote any operas, but he absorbed the influence of recitative and dramatic vocal settings into his keyboard music. He often shaped melodies pitchwise and rhythmically to sound like emotional speech or recitative, which occasionally occurs *per se,* as in the Andante of the first "Prussian" Sonata Wq. 48/1/ii (mm. 3–9 [beat 1] and 12–15 [beat 1]). According to Schulz, the keyboard sonatas of Emanuel Bach were "so communicative [*sprechend*] that one believes he is perceiving not tones but an understandable language that sets and keeps our imagination and feelings in motion."[63]

Thus, within the sonata style—as distinguished from the contrasting symphonic style, which expressed "the grand, the ceremonious, and the sublime"[64] in a more splendid, less personal way—music should speak as declamation, not merely in the "figurative sense of 'speaking to the heart' but in the sense of an actual discourse."[65] This is Arnold Schering's interpretation of the eighteenth-century ideal that instrumental music should imitate vocal music and of the frequent advice to "sing" on the keyboard. Schering emphasized that from Mattheson and Marpurg

> until the aesthetic of the young Romanticism, a communicative [*sprechende*] music and a communicative performance on instruments is clearly considered ideal. . . . One spoke of the principle of discourse [*das redende Prinzip*] in music or . . . of "notes that speak" [*tons parlants*].[66]

In eighteenth-century writing the keyboardist is repeatedly urged "especially to hear skilled singers; in that way one learns to think in terms of singing. . . ."[67] What was meant was *not* singing as "a cantabile, melodious connecting of melody notes," but as "a musical declamation in accordance with rhetorical principles."[68] This would include projection of Mattheson's incises (*Einschnitte*) and tone feet as a singer projects clauses and words. (See chap. 3, pp. 92–93 and chap. 5, pp. 158–164.)

How much of this north German *Empfindsamkeit*, with its heightened rhetorical cast, reached Vienna, where Italian influence and the *galant* style reigned? Undated descriptions of Haydn's early encounters with Emanuel Bach's "first six sonatas" and his *Essay* have been widely quoted since their appearances in the biographical accounts of Georg August Griesinger and Albert Cristoph Dies respectively, both published in 1810.[69] A. Peter Brown's sleuth-like sifting of these rather vague reports leaves enough residue to indicate that Haydn may well have purchased Bach's *Essay* soon after publication of Part II in 1762, when both parts apparently first became available in Vienna and Part II could have answered as "the newest and best . . . textbook of theory."[70]

Brown's dissection of Griesinger's reference to Bach's "first six sonatas" questions the identity of the sonatas and the chronology of the report. If "first" means first published, it would refer to the six "Prussian" Sonatas, Wq. 48, which appeared in 1742, were procurable in Vienna by 1756,[71] and include movements of a decidedly "sensitive" bent. The possibility of Haydn's acquaintance with this set, with Wq. 49, the "Württemberg" Sonatas, or with Wq. 62/4, 5, 9, 16—also available in Vienna in the 1750s, might relate to the sudden appearance among his sunny early keyboard sonatas of the more passionate slow movement of Hob. 2, possibly composed "about 1760."[72] If, however, "first six sonatas" means those published specifically as Op. 1, then it would apply only to later works: either to an unauthorized Parisian print of sonatas from Wq. 62 and 65, published in 1761 and sold in Vienna by an agent who also sold "other publications that Haydn owned, works by Marpurg, Mattheson, Fux, and Kirnberger"; to *Six sonates . . . à l'usage des dames*, Wq. 54 (pub. 1769?); or to the first set of *Kenner und Liebhaber* Sonatas, Wq. 55 (pub. 1779).[73] Fortunately Haydn's friend Abbé Maximilian Stadler cast a more general light on the possible influence of *Empfindsamkeit* on Viennese music. According to his report, Haydn had heard the "masterpieces of Hasse" while still "a boy" and later studied "foreign 'products' such as those of C. P. E. Bach, etc." From Stadler's information Brown concludes that "the study of Emanuel Bach was not unfashionable in Vienna among Haydn's circle," plausibly in the 1760s.[74]

But it was not necessarily only through the influence of "foreign products" that rhetorical principles might have been propagated in Vienna. In support of the concept that a "rhetorical" performance is appropriate for some of Haydn's works, Eva Badura-Skoda has stated that there are also Viennese sources of the eighteenth century, most preserved only in manuscript, that discuss "many of the same topics as the North German theorists."[75] In 1770 Johann Friedrich Daube, a theorist trained largely in south Germany, who was living in Vienna, urged composers "to consider carefully the rules of oratory."[76] The work from which that quotation comes, *Der musikalische Dillettant* (1770–1773), is "a remarkably original contribution to a doctrine of composing expressly oriented to the Classical style."[77] Indeed, the "awakening of self-expression in music" is regarded by Max Rudolf as concomitant with a larger "sensitivity," "an all-embracing emotional longing [that] prevailed . . . in human behavior patterns" as well as in the arts through much of the eighteenth century.[78]

Sturm und Drang (Storm and Stress)

Sturm und Drang is a term adopted by music historians from a German literary movement of the 1770s. Théodore de Wyzewa related the term to a period in Haydn's artistic development, from about 1766 to the early 1770s, during which Haydn produced a series of aggressively expressive works.[79] Later *Sturm und Drang* was used in differing ways, to an extent that it is now regarded with some degree of discomfort by many musicians.[80]

Differentiation of the passionate expression characteristic of so-called *Sturm und Drang* music from that of the *Empfindsamkeit* may properly be regarded as a matter of degree and orientation. A description of *Sturm und Drang* music would include—in addition to a heightening of "sensitive" characteristics—an increase in minor keys, syncopation, propulsive rhythms, chromaticism, abrupt changes, and the use of instrumental recitative. "Stormy passions" (*stürmender Leidenschaften*)[81] represent a bolder, perhaps more popular, kind of expression than the intimate leanings of sensibility. The two currents coexisted and were finally subsumed into the universal language of mature Classicism.

Opera seria provided a natural home for musical *Sturm und Drang,* not only in somber or fiery arias in minor keys but also, more importantly, in the obbligato (orchestrally accompanied) recitative during which some of the intense feelings were dramatized by the actor and the orchestra. Capping a long series of operas, Gluck's tragic masterpiece *Orfeo ed Euridice,* performed in Vienna in 1762, "helped feed the subsequent wave of *Sturm und Drang* pathos in Viennese symphonists."[82] Thus, in writing more emotionally outspoken works in minor keys from the mid-1760s to the early 1770s (along with works in other moods and styles), Haydn used a current idiom to expand his own range of expression. In 1772, coincidental with the peak of Haydn's stylistic explorations, the young Mozart completed his opera *Lucio Silla* for performance in Milan. Several sections show the stylistic characteristics of *Sturm und Drang*,[83] which Mozart developed further in *Zaide* and *Idomeneo*, reflections, perhaps, of his visits to Mannheim and Paris in 1777 and 1778.[84]

Haydn and Mozart

In individual ways, the keyboard music of Haydn and Mozart reflects the eighteenth-century currents of *Empfindsamkeit* and *Sturm und Drang*. Works that stand out among Haydn's larger-scale sonatas of ca. 1767 to ca. 1771 include the moving Adagio of Hob. 46 in A-flat major—the first Adagio sonata movement since Hob. 3; the truly "sensitive" first movement of Hob. 44 in C minor; and the forcefully emotional Sonata in C minor Hob. 20. The later Sonata in E minor Hob. 34 opens with a return to *Sturm und Drang*, followed by an Adagio that is a model of musical discourse. The lighthearted third movement, played "innocentemente," resolves the tension.

Mozart's Sonata K. 309, composed in Mannheim in 1778, mirrors the predilection for dynamic nuance, contrasts, and *crescendos* characteristic of the "Mannheim school." The second movement is also noted by Stanley Sadie for its "aura of 'sensibility.' "[85] The passionate Sonata in A minor K. 310 is Mozart's first in a minor key. Its composition in Paris during the summer of 1778 may reflect the popularity there of the stormy keyboard styles of Eckard and Schobert. Somewhat later, in his Fantasy K. 397, Mozart shifted among varying degrees of changing emotions, creating a highly rhetorical and volatile setting.[86]

Beethoven and the Rhetorical Spirit

Beethoven made the acquaintance of Bach's *Essay* and some of his compositions in Bonn under his teacher Christian Gottlob Neefe, who had "partly educated himself from the textbooks of Marpurg and C. P. E. Bach"[87] and who remained a dedicated admirer of Emanuel Bach's works. By roughly 1790 Beethoven had begun to consult Mattheson's *Der vollkommene Capellmeister* at least for its information on double counterpoint;[88] between 1790 and 1794 or 1795 he also consulted Kirnberger's *Kunst des reinen Satzes* in relation to three specific issues.[89] Whether his interest in the 1790s might have led him to any of the extensive sections in those volumes that deal with rhetorical-musical concepts is not known. However, there is evidence that Beethoven referred to *Der vollkommene Capellmeister* again in 1802 and at other times during his life specifically in relation to text setting.[90] He also owned Daniel Webb's *Betrachtungen über die Verwandschaft der Poesie und Musik* (Leipzig: Schwickert, 1771),[91] originally published in English as *Observations on the cor-*

respondence between poetry and music (London, 1769). (For Beethoven's notes
on poetic feet, see p. 100.) His more general reading included works by Goethe,
Schiller, Klopstock, Herder, and other contemporaries; a number of Shake-
speare's plays (in German); and books by Greek and Roman writers, such as
Homer, Plato, Aristotle, and Horace, some of which may have been concerned
with oratory.[92]

During his youth in Bonn, Beethoven would have heard performances that
incorporated elements of a rhetorical style. In Neefe's important report of 2
March 1783 on musicians active in Bonn, we read that Kapellmeister Mattioli,
previously a successful opera conductor,

> is a man full of fire, of lively temperament and fine feeling. . . . He was the first
> to introduce accentuation, instrumental declamation, careful attention to forte
> and piano, [and to] all the degrees of light and shade in the orchestra of this
> place.[93]

In 1788 Beethoven became a violist in this orchestra, which later astonished
Junker with the effectiveness of its dynamics and accentuation.[94] Neefe also
described the singing of the niece of the Elector, Countess von Hatzfeld: "She
declaims recitatives admirably and it is a pleasure to hear her arias *di parlante.*"[95] Admittedly, that description relates to music with a text. But the
Countess also "plays the fortepiano very brilliantly and in playing gives way
completely to her emotions."

Beyond his exposure to the north German musical rhetoric, Beethoven
inherited the vast accomplishments of Haydn and Mozart. They had created
a style in which the several currents of early Classicism were absorbed into a
mature language with a variety of characteristic figures and manners of expression.[96] They had also successfully fused individual expressivity with formal
elegance. Thus, right from Beethoven's Opp. 1 and 2, his works are enriched
with the full range of ideas and styles of expression of a universal language
presented within controlled forms. And if ever music was to carry out the
function of words, it is in the opening and Arioso of his Sonata Op. 110/iii.

Beyond Beethoven

References to a rhetorical style of performance continued into the nineteenth century. A finely drawn description of Dussek's "splendid" playing in
Prague in 1802, penned by Wenzel J. Tomášek in the 1840s, includes such a
comment: "His truly declamatory style, especially in cantabile movements,
remains the ideal for every artistic performance—something that no pianist
after him has attained."[97] Nor are these references limited to central European
sources. An anonymous review of "Mr. Cramer's Concert" in the *Harmonicon*
of July 1823 reads like our earlier comments by Schulz, Türk, and Koch:

> Of Mr. [Johann Baptist] Cramer's talents, there is but one opinion, which
> was so well expressed, three or four years ago, in a daily paper, that we . . .

reprint it as the concluding part of this notice. "As a performer on the pianoforte, Cramer is unrivalled. . . . His brilliancy of execution is astonishing; but
this quality . . . amounts to little or nothing in the general estimate of such
merits as his in taste, expression, feeling, the power that he possesses of almost
making the instrument speak a language. . . . those who love to have their
sympathies awakened by the 'eloquent music' which this instrument may be
made to '*discourse,*' . . . such persons should seize every opportunity that is
afforded them of hearing Cramer" . . . [italics added].[98]

THE MUSICAL SCORE

Changes in the Classic Era

During the second half of the eighteenth century many threads in the evolv-
ing fabric of music led composers to include in their scores an increasing
number of directions for performance. There were several reasons for this good
fortune. Underlying the development of both the *galant* style and the *Empfindsamkeit* was the departure from the Baroque ideal of a single affection.
The resulting musical contrast, as well as the intimate and sometimes kaleidoscopic expression of the *empfindsamer Stil,* required that composers provide
guidance if performers were to realize, according to Kirnberger, "the accurate
expression of the feelings and passions in all their particular shadings" and
fine nuances.[99] Such expression was "the noblest if not the sole merit of a
completed composition."[100]

In addition to directions for tempo, articulation, dynamics, and, later, pedaling, the maturing Classic style required more-refined coordination of dynamics and articulation with thematic material and formal events. Early reference to this basic aspect of the style occurs in at least two articles by Schulz
in the first edition of *Allgemeine Theorie.* He stressed that "the few signs with
which the composer describes the execution of single notes or phrases," such
as slurs, strokes or dots, *forte* and *piano,* etc., "must be observed as exactly as
possible because *for certain movements they are as essential as the notes themselves* . . . [italics added]." The performer must bring out the "principal notes,"
phrases, and periods and must provide more or less shading as a more or less
important section appears.[101] Schulz was explicit regarding the coordination
or concinnity[102] of elements to enhance an event when he wrote that a *crescendo*
"introduced along with a rising and increasingly expressive melody, is of the
greatest effect."[103]

The acceptance of the piano was a response to these musical needs. Although capable of great subtlety, the clavichord was too quiet; the harpsichord,
on the other hand, was by then regarded as colorless. Burney referred to it as
"monotonous" in 1772;[104] Schulz called it "one of the most incomplete instruments" in 1774;[105] and Vogler wrote in 1778 that "no forte and piano, and
above all no shadow and light can be produced on it; thus it entertains the
music lover just as little as it arouses the sensibilities."[106] The expressive po-

tential of the increasingly popular piano allowed composers to become more explicit in indicating the needs of the music. Beyond its dynamic capabilities, during the 1780s the developing instrument attained an improved singing tone, an action that favored sensitive articulation, a mechanism (knee lever or pedal) that raised the dampers independently of the fingers, and one or more such mechanisms to mute the sound and alter the tone color (see chap. 2).

Along with the new refinements of the Classic style and the expressive potential of the piano, there was, as noted earlier, a progressive development of creative individuality. All three factors increased the need for composers to edit their music and for performers to receive this information. Growing subtlety in the use of dynamics, articulation, and tempo was too much a part of the basic concept to be left to chance. Beethoven made this clear in his now famous letter of August 1825 to Karl Holz concerning the copy of his Quartet Op. 132:

> Obligatissimo—... the marks p $<$ $>$ etc. etc. have been horribly neglected and frequently, very frequently, inserted in the wrong place. No doubt, haste is responsible for this. For God's sake please impress on Rampel to copy everything exactly as it stands. ... Sometimes the $<$ are inserted intentionally after the notes. For instance, ♪♪. The slurs should be exactly as they are now. It is not all the same whether it is like this ♪♪ or like this ♪♪....[107]

Finally, changing economic conditions toward the end of the eighteenth century brought about the rapid rise of a middle class, among whom it became fashionable to have at least a small square piano for domestic music making.[108] Considerable expansion of music publishing, wider dissemination of music, and an increase in both amateur performance and public concerts all followed naturally. No longer were performances of composers' works limited by manuscript copies made within their own circles, where their performance styles might be understood even if the details were not written down. No longer did composers have any control over who played their music. More-careful editing was the best way to influence how it was played.

More-Recent Developments

The nineteenth and twentieth centuries witnessed significant changes in musical and performance styles. During the same period, publication of the Classic repertoire proliferated, overseen by numerous performer-editors increasingly remote from, or completely unaware of, the original performance customs appropriate to the music. These editors added freely to the texts with no thought to the possible incompatibility of their recommendations with the instruments and music of an earlier time. Dynamics were styled, pedal was applied, tempos were determined, and ornaments were realized, all in ways suited to a later temper. Such additions were most often made without any differentiation between the composer's own editing and the later accretions.

During the second half of the nineteenth century a more historically oriented approach began to stir. Breitkopf & Härtel published their "kritisch durchgesehene" (critically revised) editions of the works of Beethoven (*BGA*) and Mozart (*MGA*), a giant step forward for their time. Gustav Nottebohm's studies of Beethoven's sketches, completed autographs, and first editions resulted in his publishing numerous corrections to editions of Beethoven's works, including the *BGA*.[109] Hans Bischoff was a leader among the new critical editors. His editions of the keyboard works of Handel, J. S. Bach, Clementi, Mozart, and Schubert, published during the 1880s and 1890s, were forerunners of today's "urtext-performance" editions. Bischoff's publications of Bach's works are still available and very useful; they include variant readings from identified sources, and the editorial suggestions are printed in clearly differentiated small type.[110] More recently, the continuing search for original materials in the libraries, old estates, and monasteries of Europe has yielded better sources for many works. The desire to come closer to the music of earlier periods has gradually led to texts purged of intermediary material and to wide acceptance of the idea that a reliable text is a prerequisite for a stylistically appropriate performance.

Today we benefit from the renewed source study and publication of updated *urtext* (original text) editions. Although various types of urtext editions have evolved, when possible, most editors attempt to present what a composer might have considered his final or preferred version of a work (any expected improvised embellishments aside), with some degree of variant readings included.[111] The scholarly complete works, such as the *JHW, NMA,* and *BNA,* present variants from the important primary and secondary sources, occasionally in the main text but more commonly in a separate critical report (*kritischer Bericht*). Urtext editions intended for practical use may include only variants that the editor considers of special significance, with or without a brief critical report. Some of these editions contain occasional, historically based suggestions for performance, though whether such editorial comment belongs in an urtext is questioned by many. Strictly speaking, an urtext should not contain editorial fingerings either, since they also influence interpretation. Yet the trend toward urtext-performance editions convenient for use by teachers and students is breaking down this barrier in all but the most scholarly publications.

The ranking of sources for an urtext (among the autograph, a copy used for engraving, the first edition, a corrected edition, etc.) will vary not only from composer to composer but frequently from work to work, depending on the extant material for each and on how much contact the composer might have had with the first or another early edition (e.g., see chap. 5, n. 50). The final reading may also depend on the editor's interpretation of details within a single source or on the relative importance given to comparative sources. Thus, there can be more than one "urtext" reading of a single composition even when the different editors work with the same sources. (Several kinds of differences in editorial readings will figure in later chapters.) A trustworthy edition generally presents information about its sources in the prefatory material or in a critical report.

THE COMPOSERS AND THEIR PIANISM

What were the relationships of Haydn, Mozart, Clementi, and Beethoven to keyboard performance? When did each turn to the new instrument?

Haydn

Unlike many composers who wrote a considerable amount of keyboard music, Haydn was not an unusually gifted keyboard performer. The relatively scarce descriptions of his playing leave the impression that he was a serviceable and effective performer who appeared in public most often as a keyboardist for an orchestra or for a singer.[112] Samuel Wesley's report of Haydn's playing in London on 2 March 1792 supports that impression. The passage described consists of sixteenth-note broken chords for the right hand, each contained within an octave.

> His Performance on the Piano Forte, although not such as to stamp him a first-rate artist upon that Instrument, was indisputably neat and distinct. In the Finale of one of his Symphonies [No. 98] is a Passage of attractive Brilliancy, which he has given to the Piano Forte, and which the Writer of this Memoir remembers him to have executed with the utmost Accuracy and Precision.[113]

Nonetheless, composition for keyboard alone, with other instruments, or with voice was important to Haydn throughout his life. Further, as we shall see below and in chapter 2, he was keenly aware of the individual characteristics of pianos by different makers, and his compositions of the 1790s witness his response to the English instruments he encountered during his London visits.

It has not been determined with any certainty when Haydn first composed for the fortepiano, when he finally abandoned the harpsichord, and whether he ever intended the clavichord as the preferred performance instrument for any of his sonatas. Although it was very much favored in north Germany, the clavichord seems to have been little used for performance in Austria, causing many to suppose that it served Haydn, also, primarily for practice, teaching, and composing. Only recently has support been voiced for the possibility that some of his early "instructional" sonatas as well as some from ca. 1767 to ca. 1774 may have been conceived for the clavichord.[114] Opinions also vary with respect to the real differences between harpsichord and fortepiano (or clavichord) idioms in the 1770s, the proper approaches to the problem of differentiation, and the interpretation of relevant information. For example, the presence of "pianistic" dynamics in Hob. 18, 20, and 29 (all probably dating from ca. 1771–1774) belies the complexity of the issues concerned with differentiation of instrumental idiom and general stylistic development during that decade. Those issues may be even more forcefully demonstrated in a sonata such as Hob. 32, which lacks dynamics but contains an eclectic collection of keyboard textures.[115]

Another difficulty in determining Haydn's preferred instrument for particular works is the paucity of information regarding the early history of the fortepiano in south Germany and Austria and its possible presence at Esterháza, where Haydn lived from 1766 to 1790. Early acquisition of a piano for that lavish establishment would have provided Haydn access before he owned one. According to H. C. Robbins Landon,

> "G F. von R." [Rotenstein] . . . informs us that he was at Esterháza for the visit of the Empress Maria Theresa in 1773, and on the second day "there was a *grand table* and a musical concert, *auch liess sich ein Musikus auf einem Pianoforte hören"* [at which] a musician was even heard on a pianoforte.[116]

The apparent presence of a piano in 1773 makes me wonder whether there might have been one as early as 1771, the year in which Haydn wrote at least the exposition (with many dynamics) and sketches for the rest of the first movement of his Sonata in C minor, Hob. 20, as well as the Finale to m. 130. The dynamic shadings and the accents in this work require a touch-sensitive instrument (see Fig. 3.12); but the sizable, often implied *crescendos* and above all the sustained tension and drive in some sections suggest to me performance on a fortepiano rather than on even a well-built, substantial clavichord. We cannot be at all certain that there was a piano at Esterháza by 1771. Yet, Eva Badura-Skoda writes that in the Acta Musicalia documents of the Esterházy family, there are several notes from the 1760s "concerning the purchase of strings for keyboard instruments and expenses for repair and tuning, e.g., of 'den dreien Instrumenten oder Flügln.' . . ."[117] This ambiguity about the proper name for "the three instruments" is reminiscent of the general uncertainty, noted earlier, about a name for the fortepiano. (The use of *Flügl* as piano also appears below in one of Haydn's letters.) At this time we can only conclude that irrespective of his personal preferences Haydn's sonatas were probably played on whatever instrument was available.

At last, from 1788 on Haydn's letters dispel any doubt about the instrument intended. They also contain ample evidence of Haydn's sensitivity to both the differences among various makes of pianos and the increasing difficulty of some of his compositions for piano. Thus in a letter of 26 October 1788 to the Viennese publisher Artaria, Haydn wrote, "In order to compose your three *Clavier* sonatas particularly well, I was compelled to buy a new Fortepiano."[118] (Note his generic use of *Clavier*.) This letter seems to be the earliest record of his having owned a piano, but I interpret "new Fortepiano" as a replacement for another Haydn had owned, perhaps by the time he wrote the Sonatas Hob. 40–42, which are replete with pianistic textures and dynamic marks and are his first published specifically "pour le Pianoforte" (by Bossler in 1784[119]).

In 1789 Haydn wrote to Artaria about the Fantasia in C major, Hob. XVII/4:

> In an inspired hour I composed a wholly new *Capriccio* [sic] for the fortepiano which, on account of its taste, uniqueness, and careful construction will quite

certainly be received with complete approval from professional and nonprofessional alike. It is only one movement, rather long, but not all too difficult. . . .[120]

The following exchange of letters between Haydn and Marianne von Genzinger relates to the Sonata in E-flat major, Hob. 49. On 27 June 1790 Haydn wrote:

> Your grace will no doubt have received the new *Clavier* Sonata by now. . . .
> Three days ago I had to play this Sonata at Mademoiselle Nannette's in the presence of my most gracious Prince. At first I doubted that I would receive any applause because of its difficulty, but was soon convinced of the contrary since I received a gold tobacco-box as a gift. . . . It's only a pity that Your Grace doesn't own a fortepiano by Schanz, since everything is better expressed on it.
> . . . Your Grace might give your small piano [*Flügl*], which is still quite good, to Fräulein Peperl and buy yourself a new fortepiano. . . . I know I ought to have composed this Sonata for your kind of *Clavier,* but I found this impossible because I am no longer accustomed to it.[121]

In answer to a return letter, he wrote again on 4 July 1790:

> I am simply delighted that my Prince intends to give Your Grace a new fortepiano, all the more so since I am in some measure responsible for it: . . . now the purchase . . . consists in Your Grace choosing one to fit your touch and suit your fancy. It is quite true that my friend Herr Walther [*sic*] is very celebrated, . . . but . . . speaking frankly, sometimes there is not more than one instrument in ten which you could really describe as good, and apart from that they are very expensive. I know Herr von Nikl's fortepiano: it's excellent, but too heavy for Your Grace's hand, and one can't play everything on it with the necessary delicacy. Therefore I should like Your Grace to try one made by Herr Schanz, his fortepianos are particularly light in touch and the mechanism very agreeable. A good fortepiano is absolutely necessary . . . and my Sonata will gain double its effect by it.[122]

Frau von Genzinger responded on 11 July 1790:

> I like the Sonata very much, but there is one thing which I wish could be changed (if by so doing it does not detract from the beauty of the piece), and that is the passage in the second part of the Adagio, where the hands cross over; I am not used to this and thus find it hard to do. . . .[123]

Frau von Genzinger's difficulty notwithstanding, Haydn's writing for the piano remained for the most part well within the framework of common late eighteenth-century technical demands.

Mozart

Mozart, Clementi, and Beethoven were considered outstanding soloists in their prime. The voluminous correspondence of the Mozart family not only attests to Wolfgang's prowess as a performer but also reveals his concerns about the piano and his approach to numerous technical and expressive aspects of pianism. The letters of 1777–1778 from Augsburg and Mannheim are especially rich in information.

Mozart's keen appraisal of the instruments of Johann Andreas Stein, in a letter presumably written on 17 October 1777 from Augsburg, indicates his previous familiarity with the piano as well as some of the problems that had slowed its acceptance.

> This time I shall begin at once with Stein's pianofortes. Before I had seen any of his make Späth's claviers had always been my favourites. But now I much prefer Stein's, for they damp ever so much better than the Regensburg instruments. When I strike hard, I can keep my finger on the note or raise it, but the sound ceases the moment I have produced it. In whatever way I touch the keys, the tone is always even. It never jars, it is never stronger or weaker or entirely absent; in a word, it is always even. . . . His instruments have this special advantage over others that they are made with escape action. Only one maker in a hundred bothers about this. But without an escapement it is impossible to avoid jangling and vibration after the note is struck. When you touch the keys, the hammers fall back again the moment after they have struck the strings, whether you hold down the keys or release them. . . . He guarantees that the sounding-board will neither break nor split. . . . The device too which you work with your knee is better on his than on other instruments. I have only to touch it and it works; and when you shift your knee the slightest bit, you do not hear the least reverberation. . . . When I told Herr Stein that I should very much like to play on his organ, he was greatly surprised and said: "What? A man like you, so fine a clavier-player, wants to play on an instrument which has no douceur, no expression, no piano, no forte, but is always the same?"[124]

Although it is uncertain which keyboard instrument Mozart might have intended for many of his works composed between 1774 and 1777, there seems to be no doubt that all his solo keyboard sonatas and all his works for keyboard after 1777 (with the possible exception of the Concerto for Two Keyboards K. 365, comp. 1779) were written for the fortepiano.[125] If nothing else, the frequency of dynamic indications—including *crescendo* and *decrescendo*—in the first six Sonatas K. 279–284, written between January and March 1775 in Munich, provides strong evidence of their intended instrument. In view of the small number of dynamics in many later works, it would seem that Mozart was playing to the particular advantage of the still novel instrument on which he performed in competition in Munich (see p. 24).

Comments on the playing of numerous musicians and students emphasize the importance Mozart attached to a singing cantabile, expressive dynamics, accurate sightreading, appropriate fingering, proper finger position, and fluent playing. He criticized inordinate speed, inaccuracy, uncalled-for changes of tempo, incorrect *rubato* (p. 379), and exaggeration of either physical movement or musical expression, to name just a few.[126] In a letter of 26 November 1777 from Mannheim, he made short shrift of one well-known musician: "Sterkel came in. He played five duets, but so fast that it was hard to follow them, and not at all clearly, and not in time."[127]

Mozart's description of the playing of Maria (Nannette) Stein, daughter of the instrument maker, is devastating of the young lady but instructive for us. It was penned in Augsburg on 23–24 October 1777, a week after Mozart had written glowingly of Stein's pianos.

> Anyone who sees and hears her play and can keep from laughing, must, like her father, be made of stone. For instead of sitting in the middle of the clavier, she sits right up opposite the treble, as it gives her more chance of flopping about and making grimaces. She rolls her eyes and smirks. When a passage is repeated, she plays it more slowly the second time. If it has to be played a third time, then she plays it even more slowly. When a passage is being played, the arm must be raised as high as possible, and according as the notes in the passage are stressed, the arm, not the fingers, must do this, and that too with great emphasis in a heavy and clumsy manner. But the best joke of all is that when she comes to a passage which ought to flow like oil and which necessitates a change of finger, she does not bother her head about it, but when the moment arrives, she just leaves out the notes, raises her hand and starts off again quite comfortably—a method by which she is much more likely to strike a wrong note. ... she will not make progress by this method—... [or] acquire great rapidity, since she definitely does all she can to make her hands heavy. Further, she will never acquire the most essential, the most difficult and the chief requisite in music, which is, time, because from her earliest years she has done her utmost not to play in time. Herr Stein and I discussed this point for two hours at least and I have almost converted him, for he now asks my advice on everything.[128]

Admiration was showered generously on Mozart's own playing in press notices and comments of his peers, not to speak of reports in the family letters. One laudatory review from 1777 has been cited on p. 7. Michael Kelly reported on an evening in Vienna about 1781:

> [After a concert, Mozart] favoured the company by performing fantasias and capriccios on the pianoforte. His feeling, the rapidity of his fingers, the great execution and strength of his left hand, particularly, and the apparent inspiration of his modulations, astounded me.[129]

And a year before Mozart's death Gerber wrote, "That he still ranks among the best and most skillful of our keyboard players [Klavierspieler] now living will be believed without any reminder from me."[130]

Beethoven's comments, from a later time, have a different ring. Some were passed on by Czerny:

> In later years Beethoven also told me that he had heard Mozart play several times and that, since the fortepiano was still in its infancy in his time, Mozart had become accustomed to a style of playing on the more commonly used harpsichord that was in no way suited to the fortepiano. Later I made the

acquaintance of several people who had studied with Mozart, and found that their way of playing confirmed this remark.[131]

Czerny also mentioned Beethoven's impressions to Otto Jahn in 1852:

> Beethoven said . . . that he had heard Mozart play; [Mozart] had a delicate but choppy touch, with no legato, which Beethoven at first found very strange, since he was accustomed to treat the pianoforte like an organ.[132]

Another opinion may be added to Beethoven's. Herr Saust, who had heard Mozart play, told A. J. Hipkins that "Mozart had no remarkable execution on the instrument, and that, for instance, he would not have compared as a virtuoso with Dussek."[133]

The difference in attitude toward Mozart's playing between his own contemporaries and later critics (Beethoven and Saust) reflects an evolutionary change in musical and performance styles and the gradualness of adaptation to the fortepiano. Mozart carried over to the easy action of the early Viennese piano much of the fleet, often nonlegato style of the harpsichord. Beethoven could have heard Mozart play only during his brief visit to Vienna in the spring of 1787, when he met Mozart and "perhaps had a few lessons from him."[134] By this time Mozart had owned his Walter fortepiano for several years and was widely recognized as a pianist. However, the comments of the aging Beethoven were made from the vantage of improved instruments, increasingly varied use of the slur, and a more highly developed legato cantabile style. (See "The Language of the Slur" in chap. 5, especially pp. 171–172.)

Clementi

Clementi's accomplishments, unlike those of Haydn, Mozart, and Beethoven, centered mainly around the keyboard. By the later 1780s Clementi was the pianist with "the greatest international reputation,"[135] yet his conversion to the new instrument had come later than Mozart's. The first achievements that brought Clementi to the attention of the musical world seem to have been the publication, announced on 15 June 1779,[136] and his subsequent performances on the harpsichord of the solo Sonatas Op. 2. Surprisingly, the flamboyant virtuosity demanded by these works, whose double-note passages and rapid octaves greatly extended the contemporary concepts of keyboard technique, was conceived when the composer was still—as far as can be known—primarily a harpsichordist.[137] With the sole exception of his appearance as a duet partner at the piano in April 1779, until near the end of 1781, all of Clementi's performances for which the instrument is recorded were on the harpsichord. The one bit of evidence that Clementi was playing both harpsichord and piano in 1781 is that Broadwood shipped both instruments to him in May of that year while he was still in Paris.[138]

Mozart, on the other hand, had played a piano in competition with Herr von Beecke as early as 1775 in Munich.[139] As we have seen, by the time of his arrival in Augsburg in 1777 he understood the instrument and played it extraordinarily well by contemporary standards. Thus when Clementi unexpectedly met Mozart face to face on 24 December 1781 for a competition at the Viennese court, Mozart was unquestionably the more-experienced pianist.

Mozart reacted sharply to the tremendous technical skill exhibited by his opponent. Clementi was a mere "mechanicus" who excelled in showing off double thirds and sixths but who played without "a farthing's worth of taste or feeling," he wrote his family in two successive letters.[140] Mozart may have felt discomfort in the face of a stronger technician and of changing keyboard styles; yet Clementi's description of his own playing, as recalled in 1829 by his student Ludwig Berger, leaves the impression that Mozart's comments were justified to an extent. In 1806 Berger asked Clementi whether he had treated the instrument in his present style at the time of the competition. Clementi

answered in the negative, adding that, in those early days he still preferred to display his talents by brilliant execution, especially in double-note passages, which were not customary before him, and in improvisations; only later did he adopt the more cantabile and refined style of performance by listening attentively to singers celebrated at the time, and also through the gradual perfection particularly of the English pianos, whose earlier faulty construction virtually precluded a cantabile, legato style of playing.[141]

Clementi's impression of Mozart's playing, as retold by Berger, was more generous.

I had never until then heard anyone perform with so much spirit and grace. I was truly astounded by an Adagio and several of his extemporized variations, for which the Emperor chose the theme. . . . [142]

In spite of his late start, Clementi became a pioneer in cultivating many of the piano's technical and expressive possibilities. Undoubtedly influenced by the musical environment during his extended sojourns in Paris and Vienna in 1780–1782,[143] possibly influenced by Mozart's playing, perhaps aided by his own early training as an organist,[144] and encouraged by the improving tone of available fortepianos (see p. 39), he developed an expressive legato style of composition and performance for which he and his followers, the "London pianoforte school," become widely known. He (and they in turn) greatly extended the variety of textures and sonorities used in writing for the piano.

Although many of Clementi's earlier works display a more neutral style, several aspects of his Sonatas Op. 7, composed in Vienna in 1782, suggest strongly that they were intended only for the piano, Artaria's "Pour le Clavecin ou Pianoforte" notwithstanding. Striking among such characteristics beyond the refined, frequently changing dynamics, are the singing legato lines of the first and second movements (see also p. 165). Reviews in Cramer's *Magazin der Musik* of two concerts in London during March 1784 reflect the change in Clementi's playing: "Mr. Clementi played a sonata on the pianoforte and everyone had to admit that his execution displayed matchless facility and expression." Two weeks later his playing displayed "fine taste, delicacy, and great dexterity."[145]

A report from Bern in the *Magazin der Musik* of 11 December 1784 is more vivid:

> If you look at his fast passages in octaves for one hand, you would not believe that they could be executed neatly; but he always plays far more than is written—even such things as octave trills—and each note is very distinct from the others. [He plays] with such inimitable rapture, [with] continuous *crescendo* and *diminuendo*, barely perceptible *lentando* and *rubando*, etc., that it would be impossible to express all of this on paper.
>
> For certain passages he has his own fingering; he plays chain trills marvelously, even with [such fingerings as] 3-1, 4-2, 5-1. I have never heard anyone play the sonatas of Domenico Scarlatti as he does. Before [hearing him] I only half knew them.[146]

The unidentified writer was equally impressed with Clementi's "complete knowledge" of the "mechanical and physical" properties of fortepianos by a number of specific makers. "Clementi finds shortcomings and their causes that elude a hundred others...."[147] Evidently he had his own ideas about piano construction well before he became a maker.

Apparently Clementi had given up his career as a virtuoso pianist by around 1790.[148] Still, some impressions recorded in 1810 demonstrate that his mature pianism met the most exacting of eighteenth-century musical standards: to excel "equally in the *adagio* and the *allegro*," with all the artistic as well as technical mastery that that implied. (We will shortly see that same phrase applied to the playing of Beethoven in 1791.)

> Clementi ... is regarded as the greatest pianist who has ever lived. ... He excels equally in the *adagio* and the *allegro*. ... He improvised in a manner to make one believe that [the music] had been written out.[149]

Although his achievements are not as well known as those of Haydn, Mozart, and Beethoven, Clementi ranks as a versatile and highly influential figure in the history of keyboard music. In addition to being a composer, a virtuoso pianist, and a sought-after teacher, he was a conductor, a knowledgeable music publisher,[150] an innovative and successful piano manufacturer,[151] and an astute businessman. He influenced the writing of several composers, including Beethoven, who held Clementi's sonatas in high esteem. Through his concertizing, teaching, and published works, including his *Introduction to the Art of Playing on the Pianoforte* and *Gradus ad Parnassum*, Clementi passed on to a whole new generation of pianists his ideals of performance, which emphasized, in addition to legato technique, fluency in a new range of technical challenges and fingering based on musical needs. The *Introduction* was used widely in Europe and the United States and was plagiarized liberally in other keyboard tutors of the period;[152] the *Gradus* and the sonatas were taught and studied by many important pianists of the first half of the nineteenth century.[153]

Beethoven

Beethoven became known to the musical world of the 1790s not as a composer but as a virtuoso pianist and improviser. He was completely in command of the fortepiano and was already forging the performance style for his as yet unwritten works. (See "Beethoven's Exercises and Other Fragments" in chap. 6.) Fortepianos had been made in Bonn at least since early in 1783 and had probably been played there before then. On 2 March 1783 Neefe sent a report containing a vivid picture of musical life in Bonn to Cramer's *Magazin der Musik*. Countess von Hatzfeld "plays the fortepiano very brilliantly"; Herr von Mastiaux owns "a large pyramid-shaped piano [*Hammerclavier*]"; an "able mechanic," Gottlieb Friederich Riedlen, who arrived "not long ago," builds "especially good instruments with newly invented hammers. . . ."[154] This article also contains the earliest printed mention of Beethoven, who "plays the *Clavier* very skillfully and with power. . . ."[155] Unfortunately, Neefe used "Clavier" so inconsistently in this extensive report that one cannot tell if he meant keyboard instruments, the clavichord, or the piano. Nonetheless, it would appear that by this time Beethoven had played the clavichord,[156] organ, harpsichord, and presumably the piano.[157] His "Kurfürsten" Sonatas WoO 47, composed in ?1783,[158] could have been performed on a large clavichord, although with considerably less effect than on a fortepiano. Those compositions show that Beethoven was thoroughly familiar with the use of such dynamic indications as *pp, ff* (hardly for a clavichord), *cres.*, and *f* for an accent as well as for a full sound (see "Indications for Accents" in chap. 3). On his return from a short trip to Vienna in 1787, Beethoven, like Mozart before him, visited Stein's piano shop in Augsburg.[159] The following year Count von Waldstein gave Beethoven one of Stein's instruments, of which there were already a number in Bonn.[160]

Fortunately, Karl Junker recorded his impressions of Beethoven's extemporizing in 1791, four years before the completion of the Trios and Sonatas of Opp. 1 and 2.

> The greatness of this amiable, light-hearted man, as a virtuoso, may in my opinion be safely estimated from his almost inexhaustible wealth of ideas, the altogether characteristic style of expression in his playing, and the great execution which he displays. I know, therefore, no one thing which he lacks, that conduces to the greatness of an artist. I have heard Vogler upon the pianoforte . . . have often heard him, heard him by the hour . . . , and never failed to wonder at his astonishing execution; but Bethofen [*sic*] in addition to the execution, has greater clearness and weight of idea, and more expression—in short, he is more for the heart—equally great, therefore, as an *adagio* or *allegro* player. . . . His style of treating his instrument is so different from that usually adopted, that it impresses one with the idea, that by a path of his own discovery he has attained that height of excellence whereon he now stands.[161]

Beethoven moved to Vienna in November 1792. The *Jahrbuch der Ton-kunst von Wien und Prag* of 1796 states that he "is universally admired for his unusual speed and for the extraordinary difficulties that he executes with so much ease." His playing also "distinguishes itself through precision, feeling, and taste. . . ."[162] Little wonder that Beethoven's expectations for pianism surpassed those of Haydn and Mozart right from his Opp. 1 and 2, both completed just a year earlier.

Reichardt reported on Beethoven's performance in a concert of 22 December 1808:

> Eighth Piece: A new Fortepiano Concerto [the Fourth] of enormous difficulty, which Beethoven performed astonishingly well in the fastest possible tempos. The Adagio, a masterpiece of beautifully developed melody, he truly sang on his instrument with a profound melancholy that also touched me deeply.[163]

The impression of a tremendously fast tempo for the first movement, an Allegro moderato in common time, may have been created as much by the prevalence of passage-work in sixteenth-note triplets and 32d notes—twice as fast as any in Beethoven's earlier concertos with the exception of Op. 37/iii—as by the tempo itself.

In 1839 Carl Czerny published three volumes of his *Complete Theoretical and Practical Piano Forte School,* much of which was a reflection of the musical values and pianistic training he had acquired as Beethoven's student and long-time associate. In a chapter entitled "On the Peculiar Style of Execution most Suitable to Different Composers and Their Works," he described Beethoven as a pianist

> who enriched the Piano-forte by new and bold passages, by the use of the pedals, by an extraordinary characteristic manner of execution, which was particularly remarkable for the strict Legato of the full chords, and which therefore formed a new kind of melody;—and by many effects not before thought of. His execution did not possess the pure and brilliant elegance of many other Pianists; but on the other hand it was energetic, profound, noble, and particularly in the Adagio, highly feeling and romantic.[164]

Czerny amplified this picture with other comments: "Beethoven's playing was notable for its tremendous power, character, unheard-of bravura and facility. . . ."[165] "No one matched him in the speed of his scales, double trills, leaps, etc. (not even Hummel)."[166] But Friedrich Starke wrote of a more ethereal aspect of technique and sound:

> in this fantasy [improvisation] he arrived at a floating [*schwebendes*] manner of playing in which the tones were only whispered in a *ppp* and yet, at the same time, every one could be heard.[167]

These descriptions of Beethoven's playing at its best share an admiration for his technical prowess, his unique handling of the instrument, and his pro-

found expressivity, traits naturally reflected in his pieces for piano. But Beethoven's increasing devotion to composition around the turn of the century
and the consequent neglect of practicing, exacerbated in turn by his gradual
loss of hearing, subsequently led to more mixed or openly critical comments.
Cherubini characterized Beethoven's playing as "rough."[168] Clementi's evaluation, apparently based on some occasions in 1807, was that Beethoven's
playing "was not polished, and was frequently impetuous, like himself, yet it
was always full of spirit."[169] Moscheles's impressions of Beethoven's performance at the premiere of the "Archduke" Trio on 11 April 1814 are recorded
in his diary:

> Aside from its spirit, his playing satisfied me less [than the new Trio], for it
> had neither clarity nor precision; yet I observed many traces of a great pianism,
> which I had long recognized in his compositions.[170]

In May 1814 Beethoven played in another performance of the Trio. Except as
accompanist for "Adelaide" in January 1815, it was his last public appearance
as a pianist.[171]

Beethoven's preoccupation with the expression of mood or character pervaded not only his pianism but his teaching as well. Otto Jahn reported the
comment of Countess Giulietta Gallenberg (née Guicciardi):

> Beethoven was her teacher.—He allowed her to play his compositions, but was
> endlessly severe until the interpretation was correct in the very smallest de-
> tails.[172]

Ferdinand Ries left a colorful description of a lesson with the master:

> When Beethoven gave me a lesson he was, I might also say, unnaturally patient.
> ... Thus he often would have me repeat a single number ten or more times.
> In the Variations in F major, Op. 34, ... I was obliged to repeat almost the
> entire final Adagio variation seventeen times; and even then he was not satisfied
> with the expression in the small cadenza, though I thought I played it as well
> as he did. ... When I left out something in a passage, a note or a skip, which
> in many cases he wished to have specially emphasized, or struck a wrong key,
> he seldom said anything; yet when I was at fault with regard to the expression,
> the *crescendi* or matters of that kind, or in the character of the piece, he would
> grow angry. Mistakes of the other kind, he said, were due to chance; but these
> last resulted from want of knowledge, feeling or attention.[173]

Czerny's Observations on Beethoven Performance

As this volume progresses, Czerny's observations and comments will assume increasing importance for the performance of Beethoven's works. Of the
sizable group of musicians from whose knowledge we will benefit, Czerny had
the longest and closest association with the composer. At "about ten years"
of age,[174] probably during the winter of 1800–1801,[175] Czerny began piano les-

sons with Beethoven. Although regular lessons were discontinued "after some time,"[176] in 1805 Beethoven wrote Czerny an unusual testimonial, including mention of his "extraordinary progress on the pianoforte" and his "marvelous" memory.[177] The talented student remained thereafter in the composer's close musical circle. Czerny heard Beethoven play frequently and knew his playing in its prime. It was to Czerny that Beethoven turned for the first performance of the "Emperor" Concerto in Vienna in 1812, when he no longer played regularly in public.[178] He also entrusted to Czerny the instruction of his beloved nephew, Karl. Although some of Czerny's statements and suggestions in *Proper Performance* were undoubtedly affected by the lapse in time and changes in taste between the 1820s and the 1840s, Czerny remains an important witness to the "proper" performance of Beethoven's piano music.[179] He was respected as such by his contemporary Ignaz Moscheles,[180] who himself had firsthand knowledge of Beethoven's own interpretations;[181] by the great Beethoven scholar Gustav Nottebohm (see pp. 329 and 336–337); and by Johannes Brahms.[182]

2

THE FORTEPIANO
CIRCA 1780–1820

GENERAL CHARACTERISTICS OF CONSTRUCTION

"The large fortepiano surpasses all others [keyboard instruments] in cost as well as in excellence" wrote Abbé Vogler in 1778.[1] Three-quarters of a century after its invention, the early piano had gained widespread use and was rapidly superseding both the harpsichord and the clavichord. The instruments of that time were quite different in construction, touch, and tone from what we know as the piano today. Because their actions and sound qualities evolved with the keyboard idioms of the Classic era, the instruments and the music are particularly well suited to each other in many ways. It is therefore important to distinguish between the early piano and its descendant, the pianoforte, in both name and substance.

Some musicians now reserve the name *fortepiano* for the comparatively light wooden instrument that existed through the Classic era and beyond, prior to the widespread adoption of a substantial iron frame and felt-covered hammers toward the middle of the nineteenth century.[2] While this distinction is not strictly a historical one—English sources from the 1760s on used *fortepiano* and *pianoforte* interchangeably—it is widely understood and useful.

Actually, there was no such thing as *the* fortepiano, for the instruments not only differed with locale but were changing quickly everywhere. Nevertheless, all Classic fortepianos shared a number of characteristics that differentiate them from modern pianofortes and account for some of the qualities of the music written for them. (The important differences between Viennese and English instruments are discussed later in this chapter.[3])

In Germany the building of fortepianos began during the first half of the eighteenth century. Gottfried Silbermann used Cristofori's model, while other makers, including Johann Socher, invented less-complicated actions.[4] In London the craft was established during the 1760s by a group of immigrants who left their native Saxony as a result of the Seven Years' War. Several, of whom the best known is Johann Christoph Zumpe, are thought to have been apprentices of Silbermann.[5] The early history of fortepiano building in Vienna has not been well traced, but by the 1780s that city had emerged as a leading center of production with a tradition distinct from that of Johann Andreas Stein in Augsburg, south Germany.[6]

Fortepianos were made primarily in two shapes. Rectangular instruments called "square" pianos were very popular with the burgeoning middle class, for whom so many tutors were written. Wing-shaped "grand" pianos resembled large harpsichords and were sometimes built into the cases of the older instruments. Both shapes had a far lighter construction throughout and a much easier touch than the modern piano. The resulting tone was incisive and clear, albeit considerably smaller, more transparent, and shorter-lived than that to which we are now accustomed.

The frames of all the early instruments were fragile structures built entirely of wood within a wooden case. The keyboard compass before the 1790s was generally five octaves, sometimes four and a half. A five-octave range, from FF to f^3, remained the most usual on the Continent into the first few years of the nineteenth century.

At first the strings were thin and not overspun, except for overspun bass strings, which came into use in the last quarter of the eighteenth century.[7] Double-stringing was common in the five-octave instruments, but some makers used triple-stringing from around b^1 or c^2 to the top in an effort to gain more tone. Small wooden hammers were covered with leather, usually deerskin, and its hardness or softness was a determining factor in the quality of sound of each instrument. In line with the light construction, the keys were narrower, the key dip was considerably shallower, and the action was much lighter than those of modern pianofortes. According to measurements made by Malcolm Bilson, a Viennese piano of Mozart's time had a key dip of "about 3 millimeters and it takes roughly 10–15 grams to get it down," whereas our modern piano has a key dip of "about 9 millimeters and it takes roughly 55 grams [about 2 ounces] to push it down."[8] Many instruments had mechanisms to raise and lower the dampers and to effect other tonal changes (see "Mutations," below).

Such were the pianos played by Mozart, by Clementi until the 1790s, by Haydn until his London visits, and by Beethoven until 1803, although he probably had an instrument with the treble notes f-sharp^3 and g^3 by around 1800. (Specific aspects of tone, actions, and "mutations" are discussed below.) The works of Mozart and Haydn fit gracefully within the five-octave range. Rarely are we aware of the limitations of range in Mozart's works. In the Sonata K. 333/i his artful veering away from g^3 in the recapitulation (mm. 143 ff.) provides an unexpectedly climactic phrase extension before the return to the anticipated thematic material.[9] Haydn wrote above f^3, to a^3, only in the Sonata Hob. 50, composed for English instruments during or after his second trip to London in 1794–1795.[10] After the turn of the century Clementi wrote for a range of five and a half octaves, FF to c^4. He also added the new high notes, along with pedal signs and other changes, when he revised some of his earlier works, such as the Sonatas Op. 13/4–6 and the Sonatinas Op. 36.[11]

Beethoven wrote f-sharp[3] in the Sonata Op. 14/1/i/41, composed in 1798, although he carefully but obviously omitted that note at Op. 14/2/i/43. In the Concerto Op. 15/i/172 (originally comp. 1795), he wrote an f[3] that has since been interpreted as f-sharp[3] by analogy with the recapitulation—the lack of a sharp in the holograph, in the first edition by Mollo (1801), and in the reprint by Simrock notwithstanding.[12] It is impossible to know whether the presence of the f-sharp[3] in Op. 14/1 and the lack of a sharp in Op. 15/i/172 were slips of the pen or were intentional.[13] The fortepiano by Walter that Czerny observed in Beethoven's apartment around 1800—"the best [make] of its time"[14]—probably had the additional top notes, since Beethoven wrote to g[3] without reservation in the earliest notated sections of the Third Concerto Op. 37, which date from shortly before April 1800.[15] Nevertheless, he generally avoided them in music published before 1804, presumably for commercial reasons. If we play one of these five-octave instruments (shown in Plate Ia) we gain a "Classic" sense of the highness and lowness of their outside notes, which later acquired a different character as the range expanded at both ends.

EXPANSION OF KEYBOARD COMPASS AND INSTRUMENT SIZE

Changes in Range and Construction

In 1791 Broadwood of London built a five-and-a-half octave piano with a range of FF to c[4] at the request of Jan Ladislav Dussek, "which being liked, [Johann Baptist] Cramer Junior had one."[16] In 1794 that firm built its first six-octave instrument, also for Dussek.[17] Its range was the typical English six octaves of CC to c[4], while the Viennese six-octave range, which Streicher was building by 1803,[18] was FF to f[4]. Other firms also made instruments of five and a half and six octaves. The Smithsonian Institution owns a number of pianos built between about 1795 and 1800 with the compass of FF to c[4]; among them are squares by Charles Albrecht of Philadelphia, Longman and Broderip of London, and another unnamed English maker, and a grand by Érard of Paris.[19] The Kunsthistorisches Museum also has a grand piano with that range built around 1795 by Ferdinand Hofmann of Vienna.[20]

Although the early six-octave instruments were undoubtedly considered special, fortepianos "with additional keys" quickly became fashionable, apparently earlier in England than on the Continent. A review of Dussek's "Grand Concert[o] militaire" in *AMZ* of 6 August 1800 indicates that in some places the composer had placed "small notes over the system" so that the player could use the higher notes of "the pianos of a full six octaves *that are now very common in England*" [italics added].[21] Beyond the requests of composer-performers such as Dussek, another impetus for enlarging the keyboard compass may have been the growing popularity of duets. The genre seems to have been in fashion by 1779, when Clementi played a duet in public on the fortepiano and had his Three Duets Op. 3 published.[22] Around 1800 interest in playing four-hand arrangements of orchestral music surfaced. The increasing range of the orchestra also required five and a half or six octaves to encompass the parts.[23]

Typically, English grands were triple-strung throughout, including those of only five octaves.[24] This significant departure from Continental practice, in which usually only instruments of larger compass were triple-strung, produced more tone and, coupled with the rapid expansion of range in the 1790s, presumably suggested strengthening the frame. Around 1800 English makers introduced long iron braces into their grands to help them withstand the greater string tension; during the 1820s Broadwood and the French firm of Pleyel used enough metal bracing to form something like a partial frame.[25] The more conservative Viennese makers used iron bracing only from about 1835 on.[26]

In addition to the increasing number, thickness, and tension of the strings and the growing bulk of the instrument, many other factors, including the size of the hammer, determined the quantity of sound produced. The size of the hammer increased as the wooden core became larger and as the number of layers of leather increased from one to five or more in this rapidly developing instrument. A larger hammer, in turn, provided more striking area, which yielded more tone. Therefore the tendency was to increase the size of the hammer as instruments grew larger and more solid in the quest for greater sonority. A very beautiful six-octave Broadwood of 1816 that I have heard has hammer coverings that vary from seven layers in the bass; to six, then to five in mid-range; and to four in the upper treble.[27]

Beethoven's Extension of Range

The continuous growth of the piano during the life of Beethoven is reflected more accurately in his written use of the keyboard compass than in the three documented and extant instruments that he had after the Walter. (Of other pianos that he apparently had for varying periods of time there are tantalizing hints and sometimes a name, but little else.) No evidence has been found that Beethoven ever specifically requested additional notes of any builder; having his works published limited their compass to what he knew was generally available on Viennese instruments. However, his own piano(s) may not have had all the required notes for certain pieces.

In one instance, Beethoven wrote notes not available on his Walter for the premiere of the Concerto Op. 37 on another piano. It is likely that the Walter, on which he started to compose Op. 37, extended to g^3. However, he sketched a cadenza for the first movement of that work that demands a treble range to c^4 and was probably penned "not much earlier" than the date of the concert, 5 April 1803.[28] That was well before the arrival, in autumn 1803, of his Érard piano, with a treble that reached to c^4 (and with pedals rather than knee levers). Beethoven must have anticipated introducing the Concerto on an instrument that extended to five octaves and a fifth—a range he might also have used as he filled out the incomplete piano solo in performance, although the text notated at the time does not exceed g^3. Incidentally, he left evidence of having sketched and played beyond the range of his own known instrument. Since the Concerto, with its top notes to c^4 in the second and third movements, was not published until November 1804,[29] it is probable that Beethoven completed its composition and extended the written treble after the arrival of the Érard; Hans-Werner Küthen suggests June to July 1804, when the solo part would have had to be prepared for Ferdinand Ries's performance on 19 July 1804.[30] It is interesting that Beethoven did not enlarge the range of the first movement.

In 1807 Beethoven prepared a piano transcription of his Violin Concerto Op. 61, the range of which, AA to c^4, would have fit instruments of both Viennese and London manufacture. The transcription was made at the request of Muzio Clementi, whose music publishing and piano manufacturing businesses stood to profit from such arrangements. Interestingly, Beethoven's cadenzas for this concerto, which have been dated ?1809,[31] reach to f^4, the top of the Viennese six-octave range; but this exceeds the English six octaves, which stopped at c^4 and added notes in the bass. Beethoven's Trios Op. 70, composed in 1808, span six full octaves—FF (also as EE-sharp) to f^4, as does the Sonata Op. 81a, composed in 1809–1810. We are not certain what other instrument(s) besides his Érard Beethoven may have had between 1807 and the end of 1810 or whether any encompassed six octaves. In a letter of 6 May 1810 to Johann Andreas Streicher, he alluded to having a "worn out" instrument by that maker.[32] In September Beethoven complained to Streicher that his French piano was "quite useless," and in mid-November he reminded Streicher of his promise of an instrument by the end of October.[33] We can only wonder whether Streicher and his wife, Nannette, leading builders and good friends of Beethoven, loaned him a six-octave piano during this period[34] and what other unknown or undescribed pianos he might have had as he further extended the range of his compositions.[35]

In Op. 101, composed in 1816, Beethoven lowered the bass range to EE. Perhaps it was the newness of this note that occasioned the printing of "Contra E" at its first entry (i/223) in the original edition. With the completion of the "Hammerklavier" Sonata in 1818 he had expanded the keyboard range as far as he would, down to CC. The resulting six octaves and a fourth, CC–f^4, had become more common "after about 1816."[36] Thus, by the time Beethoven received a gift of a Broadwood piano in 1818—the next instrument documented after his Érard—its six-octave compass of CC to c^4 was of no particular advantage to him. In 1826, after virtually all his composing for piano was done, Beethoven received a Graf piano with the range of CC to f^4 that encompassed his entire *oeuvre*.[37] Although Streicher had built a piano with seven octaves by 1816,[38] and although Érard began to produce seven-octave grands with a range of CC to c^5 in 1823 or 1824,[39] six and six and a half octaves remained the more common sizes through the 1820s.

The Problem of "Note Restoration"

The history of the gradual extension of the keyboard bears on the practice of "restoring" a rare treble note in Mozart's music, or occasionally completing

Clementi's or Beethoven's octaves or melodic shapes—as shown analogously in another key, where a shortage of notes forced the composer to adopt obvious alterations. The Duet Sonata K. 521 illustrates the kind of missing note that Mozart chose not to camouflage or capitalize on, as he did in K. 333/i (mentioned above). At i/70 the Primo needs g^3—at least if the player thinks that this measure should match m. 211 in the recapitulation, where three successive beats start on a^2, c^3, and e-flat^3 (followed by a rest). In m. 70 those same beats start on c-sharp^3, e^3, and e^3 again.

A common occurrence in Beethoven's sonatas is the lack of a top or bottom note of an octave, such as the g-flat^3 in Op. 10/1/i/128 (compare with m. 120), or the EE's in Opp. 2/3/ii/26 and 90/i/214. Pianists today usually complete these octaves and others, believing that Beethoven would have done the same had the notes been generally available on the current pianos. The octave is needed at Op. 10/1/i/128 to avoid a melodic hole. Presumably for this reason, that g-flat was added in the important copy of Beethoven's works that Mathias Swarz made for Tobias Haslinger between 1818 and 1821.[40] However, the mentioned EE's do not appear in that copy. In his famous edition of Beethoven's Sonatas, Artur Schnabel specifically directed that the EE in Op. 90/i/214 not be added.[41] Indeed, if the simultaneous E's in m. 210 are played as the lines imply, the upper e as the conclusion of the quiet melody and only the E *forte*, then by analogy the single written E in m. 214 can stand on its own. Nevertheless, the EE is suggested by an "8" printed below E in the first state of the Haslinger edition of this sonata, part of the projected *Gesamtausgabe* begun in 1828. (For the historical importance of Haslinger's incomplete *Gesamtausgabe*, see "Metronomizations of Beethoven's Sonatas in the Haslinger *Gesamtausgabe*, . . ." in chap. 9.)

There are several places in the "Archduke" Trio where it would seem natural to play the octave E and EE after the other octaves, but there is only one suggestion to this effect in the holograph. At iii/164, beneath E, there is an "8" that is realized in the first edition (Steiner, 1816) to make the octave. Unfortunately, because of the considerable interval between the completion of this Trio on 26 March 1811 and its publication in September 1816 we are uncertain when the 8 might have been entered, at least until there has been further study of the entire manuscript.[42] (Compare Fig. 5.25, comp. 1812, pub. Steiner, July 1816 without additional EE's.)

In Clementi's Sonata Op. 7/3/iii (pub. 1782, rev. and pub. 1790–1795?[43]), adding the bottom notes to continue the bass octaves in mm. 77–79 would alter the balance of sound that was deliberately changed after the initial octaves in m. 76. Although Clementi used the "additional notes" between f^3 and c^4 freely, he never notated the bass notes below FF in spite of the fact that pianos with a range of CC to c^4 were not uncommon in England by around 1800. His restraint, like Beethoven's, must have been commercially motivated.

Restoration becomes considerably more problematic when it involves reshaping a theme, supposedly as Beethoven would have written it had the extra notes been available. Would he have made both Op. 14/2/i/43 and its equivalent m. 170 in the recapitulation exactly the same had f-sharp³ been available for m. 43? His solution at Op. 14/1/i/135–136, where the expected melodic continuation emerges from the alto, adds unexpected subtlety and a change of tone color. Had Beethoven wanted an exact repetition of mm. 44–45 he could have kept mm. 134–135 in the same octave as m. 130, just as he did in the exposition. In this same movement Schnabel and Claudio Arrau also refrain from playing the three EE's in mm. 152–154, conceivably because that many would give the bass a heavy sound alien to Beethoven's piano and to the passage.[44] Additionally there are melodic situations, such as those at Opp. 14/2/i/102 and 31/2/iii/189–192, where Beethoven's solution of note repetition in lieu of unavailable notes creates increased tension. This aesthetic effect would be lost if those passages were "restored" to match earlier measures in their movements.

As for the opinions of Beethoven's contemporaries, Czerny and Schindler argued against altering the master's texts. Czerny stated merely that in pieces "written for the five-octave instruments of former times, the attempt to employ the sixth octave ... is always unfavorable...."[45] Schindler pointed to the characteristic sound of each octave of the piano as a reason for not tampering with the texts; but he mentioned elsewhere that when, around 1816, Beethoven considered preparing a new edition of his piano works, one of the reasons for doing so was to take advantage of the extended keyboard.[46] In connection with the consideration of a new edition in 1824, Streicher wrote to Beethoven about reshaping passages for the extended keyboard in order to increase sales, not for aesthetic reasons.[47] Few musicians today are prepared to act in Beethoven's stead.

As fortepianos expanded from the five-octave instrument that is often considered the "Classic" piano, their actions became more resistant and their overall size and weight grew. The change from five to six octaves was particularly significant, for with the attendant growth in structure, the weight of the instrument approximately doubled.[48] Reflecting these changes in construction, the tone quality became increasingly sonorous and longer-lasting, characteristics that in turn enhanced legato playing and the "singing" sound. Thus, the instruments of different sizes for which Beethoven composed also differed in other respects that may have been more important than keyboard compass itself: those of tone and touch.

TONE AND TOUCH

In 1801 Andreas Streicher wrote an owner's manual on the playing and care of fortepianos. It reveals the aesthetic ideals of an important piano teacher and builder, some of which also reflect on the differences between Viennese and English instruments.

Streicher stressed that the performer should have "an instrument on which he can play in a *light, singing, polished,* and *expressive* manner" and "that he be acquainted exactly with the mechanical capabilities of the instruments, so that he not demand of it that which it cannot deliver. . . ." Fortepianos "*that have little flexibility in tone, where the keyboard action is very hard, and in which the action does not support the movement of the fingers* [are] inferior to other instruments in *expressive playing.*" Streicher's goal was that an artist "with proper feeling" play an instrument

> *that produced all degrees of loudness and softness of tone, even in the finest nuances, the keyboard of which was made in such a manner that the player didn't even think of the mechanical action, and on which you could with the greatest of ease produce everything (play a fast staccato, sing, and allow the tone simply to die away). . . .*[49]

Notice his concern with the way in which sounds are left.

Tones on the fortepiano, Streicher continued, "should resemble as much as possible the tone of the best wind instruments." Under the hands of an artist

> the keyboard is like a soft pliable mass out of which he can produce tones in any manner he wishes. . . . his tone always remains beautiful *since he tries to produce his forte and fortissimo more through full chords than through single notes.*[50]

Although the more massive construction of the pianoforte produces a considerably larger and longer-lived sound than that of the fortepiano, the sound of the earlier instrument possesses certain qualities that are especially appropriate for Classic music. Fortepiano tone is silvery and rich in overtones. The decisive, bright sound of the initial attack decays rapidly. These qualities give the tone good definition, making it perfectly suited to the textural clarity of the contemporary music, both solo and ensemble. In an articulate style the rapid decay allows a player more flexibility in using the space between notes to shape dynamic and articulative change. The familiar problems of balance that we encounter playing Classic chamber music on modern instruments do not arise when the fortepiano is allied with instruments of its own time.

The manner of fortepiano construction also produced marked natural differences in color between the bass, middle, and treble registers that would be anathema on a modern instrument. Such differences sharpen the distinctions between parts of the musical texture and enhance polyphonic passages. The bass is sonorous and dark but remains clear, avoiding the woolly quality of the pianoforte. Low trills and closely spaced bass chords sound well on the fortepiano. When pushed, the bass can also growl. The middle register produces a warm singing tone. The treble, which begins at c^2 or a little higher, tends toward dryness and, in my experience, varies more among instruments in its effects than do the other registers. It is sometimes flutelike, but it can also sound metallic and very penetrating. On some instruments, including the Broadwood grand of 1804 that I have played, the dryness of the treble requires an adjustment in touch to produce a convincing legato: in that upper range it may be essential for the fingers to overlap on successive notes, while in the lower registers a fine legato is produced by lifting the finger from the key when the next one is played.[51]

Particularly important elements in the tone quality of any piano are the precise striking point of the hammer on the string and the equalization of string tension. On the suggestion of his friend Muzio Clementi,[52] who was not yet a builder himself, John Broadwood sought scientific advice for those technical problems. Around 1788 Broadwood divided the bridge to achieve equal tension through all the strings. At the same time he located the striking point at approximately one-ninth of the vibrating length of the string (with some latitude in the treble), thus suppressing the more dissonant harmonics.[53] These innovations produced a fuller singing tone, "more even throughout its compass and, above all, with increased dynamic flexibility."[54] Presumably they were among the improvements in English instruments to which Clementi referred when reflecting on his adoption of "the more cantabile [*gesangvolleres*] and refined style" (above, p. 25).

Fortepianists needed, above all, delicacy and lightness of touch to play the new instrument well and to interpret the music of the period. Along with tonal clarity, the shallow key dip and light actions formed a perfect vehicle for the nonlegato, the short slurs, the ornamentation, and the fleet passage-work that are such important elements of Classic music. The fortepiano responds best to a touch that relies primarily on a finger technique similar to that needed by a harpsichord or clavichord player (see "Point of View" in chap. 6). Applied skillfully, such a technique brings out the subtlest gradations of color and articulation, with innumerable degrees of detached sound. Modern pianists fortunate enough to hear or to play a fortepiano gain insight into its performance characteristics, its advantages and limitations, and through these into the musical styles and performance practices of the Classic era. This awareness encourages more effective presentation of the subtleties of style and sound on whichever instrument may serve as the performing medium: fortepiano or pianoforte.

"MUTATIONS": HAND STOPS, LEVERS, AND PEDALS

"Mutations" (*Veränderungen*) or changes of tone color, also called stops—an integral part of the organ and the harpsichord—were provided for the early piano as a matter of course. Some were familiar; others were new means to mold or alter the sound. The devices that operated these mutations were at first hand "stops" (knobs), then knee levers, and finally pedals.

Hand stops, placed in the case above or to the side of the keyboard, were adapted from those used to change registration on the organ and the harpsichord. Since one hand had to be free to activate and release a stop (unless an assistant was present), it could be used only for broadly scaled effects. Knee levers mounted in the case beneath the keyboard[55] overcame this problem, but their comfortable and efficient use depended on the player's having legs of sufficient length, especially from the knee down. Lifting the heel causes the knee to raise the lever. (In Plate Ia the bottom edge of the levers is just visible beneath the front rim of the case in the center.) If there are more than two levers running parallel to the keyboard, the player may have difficulty finding the correct one; for this reason some builders used only two levers and a hand stop to achieve three changes. Other builders placed knee levers at right angles to the keyboard. The more convenient pedal was introduced in England in the 1770s and was patented by John Broadwood in 1783.[56]

The fortepiano was the first keyboard instrument to have a mechanism independent of the keys designed specifically for raising the dampers from the strings. Gottfried Silbermann adopted the hand stop to raise and lower the dampers by the 1740s;[57] the far more flexible and effective knee lever appeared on fortepianos by the 1770s. Virtually all makes had a stop, lever, or pedal for this purpose by the last quarter of the eighteenth century.[58] Regardless of the mechanism, when the dampers are raised the strings are free to vibrate sympathetically with any notes that are played. The reinforced overtones impart a glow or richness to the sound. This increased resonance also improves the sustaining of the sound. On some fortepianos the damper-raising mechanism was divided so that bass and treble dampers could be worked independently of each other. (See discussion of "split" damper mechanisms on p. 135.) Another arrangement, which Mozart had on his Walter, was one lever that raised all the dampers and another that raised just those in the treble, usually from around c^1 up.

English and French builders adopted the pedal during the 1780s and 90s, German and Viennese builders generally not until the early years of the nineteenth century and then apparently only for instruments of six octaves or more. (But see below, chap. 4, n.9.) Because few Viennese pianos from those years seem to have survived, precise dating for the adoption of pedals in Vienna is not possible. With one early exception, all the extant pianos by Graf have pedals; yet the "earliest known signed and dated Viennese action" piano with a damper pedal instead of a knee lever is a Streicher from 1811.[59]

In addition to the damper-raising mechanism, most fortepianos had at least one additional stop to mute the sound or otherwise alter the tone color. Some had two or three; a few had as many as five. The only softening device that has survived is imprecisely called the *una corda* (one string) pedal or sometimes the soft pedal or *Verschiebung* ("shifting" pedal). It has been used in varying forms since Cristofori applied it in 1722,[60] and it is found on all modern grand pianos. The name *una corda* remains from instruments of the eighteenth century to around the late 1830s[61] whose mechanisms moved the action far enough to the side so that even in trichord construction the hammer struck only one string. With the pedal depressed only partially the hammer could also strike two strings (as it does in the triple-strung section of the modern grand piano when fully depressed), making it possible for Beethoven to request *una corda, due corde,* and *tre corde* in the Andante con moto of the Piano Concerto No. 4, and *poi a poi tutte le corde* (gradually all the strings) in the Fugue of Op. 110 and in other works. When the *una corda* is activated, sympathetic vibration of the unstruck strings adds to the change of sonority (see also pp. 141–142).

A much-favored sound, especially on Viennese fortepianos, was that produced by the "moderator," otherwise known as the "piano" or "céleste" stop. This device consists of a wooden batten to which is attached a strip of leather or cloth. The unattached edge of the material may be cut into a series of tongues. A lever or pedal moves the batten forward, interposing the material between the hammers and the strings. The weakened impact of the hammers reduces the vibrating energy of the strings, which diminishes the overtones. This muted sound is tender and melancholy on some fortepianos, noticeably quieter than the *una corda.* The "double moderator" or "pianissimo" pedal was so constructed that if the batten was moved farther forward, either by depressing the same pedal more or by a second pedal, the hammer struck a thicker or double layer of material, producing an even softer sound, as if from a distance.[62]

The "lute" stop (*Lautenzug*) consists of a wooden batten covered with leather or cloth. When it is made to press against the strings by moving a lever or pedal, the vibrations are partially blocked, shortening the duration of the notes. The sound is dry, soft, and distinct, similar to the effect produced by the lute or buff stop on a harpsichord. Not surprisingly, two early pianists expressed opposing points of view about the appropriate use of this pedal. Louis Adam suggested that it be used only in rapid passages and where the notes ought to be played distinctly,[63] thus using the dry sound to its best advantage; Daniel Steibelt wrote that it must not be used alone, but always in combination with the damper pedal,[64] which offsets the dryness to some degree.

The somewhat less quiet and dry sound of the "harp" stop is produced by allowing a fringe of wool or silk, again attached to a strip of wood, to mingle with the strings.[65] The "bassoon" stop produces a raucous sound by placing a wooden batten covered with parchment across the strings. Percussion effects also existed for use in the Turkish and military music that was popular at the end of the eighteenth and early in the nineteenth centuries.

Adam, Steibelt, and Friedrich Starke each developed signs that they used in their pedagogical compositions to indicate the several pedals. Neither those signs nor indications for any pedal other than the damper and the *una corda* attained currency, for aside from the moderator, the rest were short-lived. Schubert called for the moderator in the holograph of "Morgenlied" (1820) with "Durchaus mit dem pianissimo" (Throughout with the pianissimo).[66] Whether or how frequently any composers expected that *pp* would serve as an indicator for either the *una corda* or the moderator remains a moot question.[67] Occasionally in the nineteenth century *sordino* or *con sordini* may have signaled the lute stop or the moderator (see chap. 4, n. 54).

Some firms would fit a custom-built fortepiano with the levers or pedals preferred by the buyer.[68] National preferences also played some role in the

PLATE I. Two fortepianos played for this study.
a. Anton Walter, Vienna, ca. 1795. Viennese action. Length 221.5 cm; width 102.5 cm. Courtesy of Sammlung alter Musikinstrumente, Kunsthistorisches Museum, Vienna.

pedals used. English grand pianos usually had only the damper pedal—sometimes divided—and the *una corda* (as in Plate Ib); while square pianos frequently had lute and divided damper controls,[69] since the shifting of the *una corda* was not compatible with their construction. Adam and Steibelt both describe French grand pianos fitted with four pedals. Adam lists the lute,

b. Muzio Clementi & Co., London, ca. 1805. English grand action. Length 277.4 cm; width 106.2 cm. Courtesy of Mr. and Mrs. G. Norman Eddy, Cambridge, Massachusetts.

damper, *céleste* (moderator), and *una corda* pedals placed in that order (with the damper pedal on the left side).[70] Steibelt includes the bassoon pedal instead of the *céleste*.[71] Continental pianos usually had a lute pedal and/or a moderator,[72] and they frequently had more pedals than did the English instruments. The pedals on Beethoven's three extant pianos, by makers in as many countries, fit these generalizations. His Érard had the four pedals described by Adam;

his Broadwood had the typical English damper (in this case divided) and *una corda* pedals; and his Graf—made especially for him—had *una corda,* moderator, and damper pedals,[73] a characteristic Viennese arrangement.

The number of mutations designed to quiet the sound of the fortepiano invites some speculation. It is true that each produced tone of a different timbre, yet the presence on the same piano of lute, moderator, and *una corda* pedals might also indicate that the need to augment the availability of soft sounds by mechanical means was a consideration. Although one of the advantages of the fortepiano over the harpsichord was its ability to play loud and soft with both quick and graduated changes, on early fortepianos the degree of contrast was limited—on the *forte* side by light construction and on the *piano* side by the easy action that hampered good control. On some it was (and is still) difficult to achieve a sound between *piano* and *forte,* as suggested by contemporary references to the lack of "mezzotints."[74] This shortcoming explains in part the rarity of the designations *mp* and *mf* in music of the period (see chap. 3). It must also have taken time for keyboard players accustomed to the other instruments to develop a touch that took full advantage of the dynamic possibilities afforded by the fortepiano. In spite of Streicher's expressed aversion to the moderator and lute stops, along with the other mutations that he considered "merely childish amusement,"[75] their use at once carried on the familiar and enhanced the availability of "piano e forte" for inexperienced players until the improved construction of the instrument allowed better contrast and control solely through the action and the player's touch. In Czerny's opinion this development did not happen until the 1820s, when the hammer covering was also substantially refined.

> And finally, in the period from 1820 to 1830 the all-important leathering of the hammer heads was brought to a degree of perfection (especially by the Viennese *Clavier* [!] makers) such that through touch alone one could draw a great number of shadings of tone from each key and could suddenly gain an entirely new aspect of piano playing. It was possible to execute the most delicate *pianissimos without any mechanical mutation* [italics added] while in all *octaves* the more powerful touch produced not only a great strength [*Stärke*] but to some extent a completely different type of sound.[76]

ENGLISH VERSUS VIENNESE FORTEPIANOS

Actions and Sounds

London became a center of fortepiano manufacturing, competing with Germany and Austria—or more specifically, Vienna—during the 1780s. The essential difference between the two styles of instrument, indeed the root from which certain other differences sprang, lay in the physical relationship between the key and its hammer. In the German-Viennese action, known as the *Prellmechanik,* the shank of the hammer was connected directly with its own key through a wooden fork (Fig. 2.1). When the key was depressed, the tail of the hammer shank caught on an overhanging rail and the hammer was thrown up to strike the strings. This mechanism, coupled with the general lightness of construction, produced an action of hair-trigger speed and an alert, dancelike sound. An escapement was added in the early 1770s, probably by Johann Andreas Stein,[77] to prevent the hammers from restriking the strings. Leather dampers that wedged between the strings worked swiftly, cutting off the sound with a crispness that further defined the ethos of the instrument and the music of the Viennese composers.

In the English action, the hammer, instead of being connected to its key, was hinged at its tail to a common rail, necessitating a pusher or jack near the back of the key to set the hammer in motion.[78] This principle, sometimes known as the *Stossmechanik*[79] (Fig. 2.2), descended from the Cristofori-Silbermann action. It was propagated in England by a group of German immigrant builders familiar with Silbermann's instruments.[80]

The more complex English action produced a deeper key dip, a heavier touch, and slower note repetition than did the Viennese action. English builders also used slightly wider keys, thicker strings, larger hammers made with more layers of leather, and a carefully selected striking point. These features, coupled with the expansion of the keyboard compass, triple-stringing, and introduction

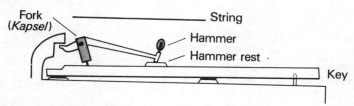

Fig. 2.1. Principle of the *Prellmechanik* (without escapement). The hammer pivots in the wooden fork connected directly to its key.

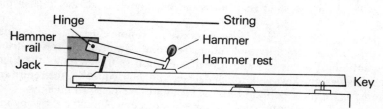

Fig. 2.2. Principle of the *Stossmechanik* (without escapement). The hammer, activated by a jack attached to the key, pivots on its hinge in the hammer rail. In the English development of the *Stossmechanik,* the hammer points away from the player and does not rest on the key.

of iron braces mentioned earlier, led to the development of a sturdier instrument in which the construction, both internal (frame and action) and external (case and stand), was more robust than that of the German-Viennese pianos (see Plate Ib). Finally, the dampers of the English grands, made of a coarse woven cloth that rested lightly on the strings, did not damp quickly, permitting further reverberation before the tone stopped. The advantages of these instruments were a fuller, more sonorous tone and a more extended dynamic range. By modern standards the touch of these English pianos is still shallow and light, and the tone is small; yet their differences from the Viennese pianos are immediately clear to anyone familiar with both types. These differences were sufficient to help the "London pianoforte school," including Clementi, Field, Dussek, Cramer, and Pinto, develop the broad cantabile style of performance with which it was identified. (See "Legato . . . Described in Tutors," in chap. 5, and n. 27.)

On the other hand, the lighter construction, transparent bell-like sound, and more responsive action and damping of the German-Viennese instruments are ideal for the music of Haydn, Mozart, and Beethoven, which depends so much for its effectiveness on two-note slurs and other short articulative groupings. Not surprisingly, the pianists of the Viennese school became known for the clarity, articulative precision, and fluency of their playing. Hummel, a pupil of Mozart and an outstanding representative of the Viennese style of playing, described astutely the important characteristics of both kinds of instruments:

> Piano-fortes, generally speaking, are constructed on two different plans, the *German* or *Vienna*, as it is termed, and the *English;* the former is played upon with great facility as to touch, the latter with considerably less ease. Other modes of construction are compounded of these two. . . .
>
> It cannot be denied but that each of these mechanisms has its peculiar advantages. The German piano may be played upon with ease by the weakest hand. It allows the performer to impart to his execution every possible degree of light and shade, speaks clearly and promptly, has a round, fluty tone, which in a large room contrasts well with the accompanying orchestra, and does not impede rapidity of execution by requiring too great an effort. These instruments are likewise durable, and cost but about half the price of the English pianoforte.
>
> To the English construction however, we must not refuse the praises due, on the score of its durability and fullness of tone. Nevertheless this instrument does not admit of the same facility of execution as the German; the touch is much heavier, the keys sink much deeper, and, consequently, the return of the hammer upon the repetition of a note, cannot take place so quickly.
>
> Whoever is yet unaccustomed to these instruments, should not by any means allow himself to be discomposed by the deep descent of the keys, nor by the heaviness of the touch; only let him not hurry himself in the time, and let him play all quick passages and runs with the usual lightness of finger; even passages which require to be executed with strength, must, as in the German instruments, be produced by the power of the fingers, and not by the weight of the arms; for as this mechanism is not capable of such numerous modifications as to degree

of tone as ours, we gain no louder sound by a heavy blow, than may be produced by the elasticity of the fingers.

In the first moment, we are sensible of something unpleasant, because in forte passages in particular, on our German instruments, we press the keys quite down, while here, they must be only touched superficially, as otherwise we could not succeed in executing such runs without excessive effort and double difficulty. As a counterpoise to this however, through the fullness of tone in the English pianoforte, the melody receives a peculiar charm and harmonious sweetness.

In the mean time, I have observed that, powerfully as these instruments sound in a chamber, they change the nature of their tone in spacious localities; and that they are less distinguishable than ours, when associated with complicated orchestral accompaniments; this, in my opinion, is to be attributed to the thickness and fullness of their tone.[81]

Significantly, from the 1790s there was a close relationship between English and French piano building that resulted in large measure from the presence in London of Sébastien Érard during the French Revolution. In 1792 he founded a London branch of the French-based Érard firm, which had been building square pianos similar to Zumpe's since 1780.[82] Érard's first grand piano, built around 1796 in Paris,[83] had a modified English action. Beethoven, who was used to the Viennese instruments, apparently always had difficulty playing the piano given to him by Érard in spite of at least two attempts to have its heavier action altered.[84]

Attempts to Modify the Viennese Action

From the outset of the nineteenth century—as the changing music for piano required more power to express its content, as a new breed of touring pianists strove toward greater virtuosity and dazzling effects, and as more concerts took place in public halls with larger orchestras—some Viennese makers tried to meet the requests for instruments with a heavier action, which would provide a bigger tone and allow better control of dynamics. Yet outright adoption of the English action did not seem an appropriate route at this time. The firm of Breitkopf & Härtel was unable to sell the Broadwood pianos imported as a trial in 1803.[85] Considerable correspondence between Härtel and Streicher, who supplied Härtel's Viennese instruments, records their attempts to assess and meet the demands of the market. Streicher felt strongly that the general public would not adapt to the difficulties of the English action if it were used; rather, "at least nine-tenths of the keyboard amateurs will have to give up their playing."[86]

A contemporary description of Nannette Streicher's instruments in 1796, before any attempted adjustments, draws attention to the crucial points.

The third great master, or rather mistress [of piano building], is Madame Streicher [Nannette Stein] ... the daughter of the famous instrument maker Stein of Augsburg. ... Her instruments do not have the strength of Walter's, but they are unequalled in balance of sound, [its] purity, ... sweetness, and softness. The tones are not aggressive but mellow, the handling [of the action] requires a light touch, elastic finger work, and a sensitive heart.[87]

As a result of strenuous efforts to satisfy the continuing requests of Breitkopf & Härtel and of Beethoven, Streicher was able to write in June 1805 that his firm's new instruments were "second to no other in strength of tone."[88] That year he added to the options of range and "mutations" previously available to purchasers[89] a choice of "two kinds" of instruments: the usual double-strung instrument with a "weaker tone," and one with a "strong" tone in which triple-stringing in the treble went along with alterations that made the action some-what heavier.[90] He also added the *una corda*. A letter of 11 March 1806, in which Streicher belatedly assured Härtel that he "has always ... preferred" the tone of the English and French pianos, reveals further progress in the development of his ideal:

> Along with Clementi and Dussek, I find this tone best suited to large-scale and particularly public performance. ... I have sought to combine this tone with our customary action and if I may trust ... the opinions of our best local pianists and amateurs, I have been rather successful. ...[91]

Around 1806 Breitkopf & Härtel began to manufacture its own pianos, evidently also with an action that afforded improved control of dynamics. In a concert on 8 May 1807 in Leipzig, Dussek "introduced" one of these instruments "for the first time."

> The instrument found the deserved applause of all the listeners, especially because of its beautiful singing tone and because of the great advantage that its tone could be modified more sensitively than one is used to hearing, even with the products of the most acclaimed German masters.[92]

In a letter of 7 February 1809 from Vienna, Reichardt reported on Streicher's later attempts to bring some of the advantages of the English instruments to his own, still without adopting the English action.

> Streicher has abandoned the softness, the too easy yielding [of the touch], and the bouncing roll of the other Viennese instruments, and, on Beethoven's advice and request, has given his instruments more resistance and elasticity so that the virtuoso who performs with strength and conviction has more control over the instrument for sustaining and supporting [the tone?] and for sensitive pressing and release [of the keys]. By these means he has given his instruments a greater and more varied character, so that more than any other instruments they will satisfy every virtuoso who seeks more than superficial glitter in performance.[93]

With time, builders made the Viennese action even heavier in an effort to provide the qualities sought. But with these changes the action lost its sensitivity, one of its main advantages.[94] Inevitably the continuing search for a more powerful instrument gained an increasing number of adherents for the English action, which had materially improved since the 1820s with the adoption of the double escapement. In May 1840 the piano factory of Breitkopf & Härtel placed an advertisement in the *Allgemeine Musikalische Zeitung* for "its new Concert Piano with English Mechanism."[95] Testimonials by Mendelssohn and Liszt emphasized the instrument's suitability for public performance because of the strength and fullness of its tone. Ultimately, as Steinway, Bechstein, and other makers recognized its advantages, a modified form of the English action prevailed, becoming the basis for the grand pianos that we play today. However, the altered Viennese action was not abandoned until 1909, when Bösendorfer stopped offering it as an option in its grands.[96]

FOUR CLASSIC COMPOSERS AND THEIR FORTEPIANOS

Composer-Performers and Piano Makers

Composer-performers of the Classic period were generally knowledgeable about the kinds of fortepianos available. Often they had direct contact with instrument makers, as has already been reported in relation to Clementi (before he himself became a maker), Mozart, Dussek, and Beethoven. Feedback between composer-performers and makers encouraged experimentation in design that ultimately led to improvements in the instruments. In Haydn's case, acquaintance with the English fortepianos of the 1790s altered both his pianistic allegiance and his compositional sonorities (see below).

Beethoven maintained contact with the Stein-Streicher family throughout his years in Vienna. His letters to them contain reactions to pianos and piano playing;[97] requests for borrowing, maintenance, or alteration of instruments;[98] and more mundane requests of Nannette Streicher for help in finding rooms or dealing with servants. In a letter of 6 May 1810 Beethoven urged Andreas Streicher "to ensure that the instruments do not wear out so quickly. . . . You know that my sole object is to promote the production of good instruments."[99] The allegiance of a composer, his use of an instrument, or even a word of interest might be of subsequent commercial value and was often sought by builders.[100]

Haydn, Mozart, and Clementi

Haydn and Mozart wrote comfortably for available fortepianos. By their mature years each had an instrument with which he was pleased. For Mozart it was a five-octave Walter acquired between 1782 and 1785.[101] This piano is now in Salzburg in the house in which he was born. It has two knee levers to work the dampers, of which the right one raised only those in the treble,[102] and a moderator operated by a knob in the middle of the case above the keyboard. Subsequently Mozart had it equipped with a pedal board that he used for improvisatory playing (n. 9). Haydn's favored instrument—unfortunately no longer extant—was a five-octave Schanz purchased in 1788, which Haydn described in 1790 as "particularly light in touch" and with a "very agreeable" mechanism. He had recently sent Marianne von Genzinger his Sonata in E-flat major Hob. 49, during the writing of which he had obviously been inspired by the tone and handling of his Schanz (see Haydn's letters, p. 21 above).

The differences between the Walter and the Schanz pianos, as described in the *Jahrbuch der Tonkunst von Wien und Prag* of 1796, complement their different uses by Mozart and Haydn.

> [Walter's] fortepianos have a full, bell-like tone, a precise response [*deutlichen Anspruch*] and a strong, resonant bass. . . .
> The tone [of Schanz's fortepianos] is not as strong as that of Walter's, but it is just as clear and generally more agreeable; they are also easier to handle because the keys do not fall as deep nor are they as wide as [those of] the former. . . .[103]

The writer added that for pianists fond of "a powerful sound," those who play with a "rich tone, extremely fast," and those who attempt "the most ticklish runs and the fastest octaves," he would recommend a Walter.[104] For Mozart's frequent public appearances, often with orchestra, a Walter was the appropriate choice, while Haydn's more intimate use of the piano was well served by the Schanz, at least for a while.

During his two London visits in 1790–1791 and 1794–1795, Haydn became enamored of the English grand pianos, and they influenced the compositions he wrote for them. He returned to Vienna in 1795 with a Longman and Broderip grand that had a five-and-a-half octave compass, from FF to c^4, and pedals rather than knee levers.[105] His last three Sonatas Hob. 50–52 and the late Piano Trios Hob. XV/27–29, of which all but Hob. 51 were written for the gifted Theresa Jansen Bartolozzi of London, are among the works that demonstrate his response to the assets of the English instruments. Beyond writing to a^3 in the virtuosic Hob. 50, Haydn utilized more variable and often fuller textures in those works and exploited the broader dynamic range available. A comparison of the Adagio themes of the two great Sonatas in E-flat major Hob. 49 and 52 reveals the more expansive writing inspired by the sonority of the English fortepianos. Other instrument-related characteristics include bolder contrast of registers and subtler use of dynamic indications, including the accent sign >, which had not previously appeared in his keyboard works.

In the spring of 1801, after which his verified writing for piano consisted only of accompaniments for folk song arrangements and possibly for his own last German songs (these dates are uncertain), Haydn was given an Érard grand piano. Horst Walter suggests that it might have resembled Beethoven's Érard of 1803, with a range up to c^4 and four pedals: lute, damper, moderator, and *una corda.*[106]

Clementi was a partner in a piano manufacturing firm that made some of the finest English instruments. Letters written to his partner Collard from the

Continent between 1803 and 1808 indicate that Clementi was genuinely concerned about maintaining the quality of their pianos;[107] his care is not surprising
if one recalls the report on Clementi from Bern (in Cramer's *Magazin der
Musik* of 11 December 1784, in chap. 1). Ignaz Moscheles, a leading pianist of
his time, preferred Clementi's pianos to others until about 1831, when for the
first time he played an Érard instead of a Clementi at his annual London
concert.[108] The music of Haydn, Mozart, and Clementi suits the capabilities
of the fortepianos they had and sounds well on those instruments.

Beethoven

The music of Beethoven demands greater sonority and expressive range
than that of his predecessors. Rochlitz recognized these needs when he reviewed the Sonatas of Opp. 26 and 27 in June 1802. After acknowledging
Beethoven's unusually perceptive understanding of the piano shown in the
writing and performance directions of Op. 27/2, he observed that "a very good
instrument is required if one wants a certain satisfaction in performing many
of his movements—for example, the entire first movement of No. 3" [Op. 27/
2].[109] When Beethoven composed that sonata he was probably using his Walter
piano.

Beethoven's comments and repeated communications to Streicher about
his Érard indicate dissatisfaction with this piano from the start, principally
because of its heavy action. By the time Beethoven received the Broadwood,
a number of his works needed treble notes beyond its keyboard compass, its
action may well have been heavier than he liked,[110] and his already seriously
impaired hearing must have prevented him from appreciating its special tonal
qualities. He enjoyed the "honor of the gift"[111] but later stated that his "London
instrument" did not achieve what was expected of it.[112] By 1826, when Beethoven received the Graf piano with quadruple-stringing from D to f^4 [113] and
a resonator,[114] even these features were insufficient to penetrate his deafness.[115]
These three instruments are now in the Kunsthistorisches Museum, Vienna,
the National Museum, Budapest, and Beethoven-Haus, Bonn, respectively.

Although Beethoven's supposed preference for the Broadwood has frequently been stated, William Newman's detailed reexamination of all available
information led to the conclusion that in spite of some deficiencies, Beethoven's lifelong preference was for the pianos of the Stein-Streicher family.[116] In
part as a by-product of his interest in the developing instrument, Beethoven
also complained about pianos and sought improvements in them all his life.
Was he truly dissatisfied with the instrument even when he could hear it, or
was he merely searching, as in his composing, for the best that was possible?
Opinions differ on this. But perhaps two of Beethoven's late comments have
been wrongly interpreted as representing his life-long attitude rather than his
reflections in the mid-1820s, when presumably he had new compositional ideas
in mind. In 1824, the year in which he completed the Bagatelles Op. 126—his
last significant piano works—Beethoven spoke to the harp maker Johann An-

dreas Stumpff of "the inadequacy of the grand piano, on which, in its present state, one could not play with strength and effectiveness."[117] And in 1826 he remarked to Karl Holz, referring specifically to his own "last"—and in his opinion best—sonatas for piano: "It is and remains an inadequate instrument."[118]

For the continually expanding conceptual and emotional realms of his music, and for the "characteristic and impassioned energy [of his playing], alternating with all the charm of smooth and connected cantabile,"[119] Beethoven explored each larger instrument as it came along in order to gain greater keyboard range, sound, and expressivity. How would he have felt about Streicher's altered pianos, or instruments of other eminent makers, such as Graf, had he been able to hear them fully? To a large extent his sound ideal was in his head then. Beethoven utilized every piano to its fullest, pushing it as far as possible. Struggle with the medium is inherent in some of his greatest works and should not always be concealed from the listener.

Instruments Played for This Study

For many years I have had the great good fortune of being welcome to play the fortepianos, both original instruments and replicas, owned by the individuals and institutions included in the list below. To the persons involved I owe a substantial debt of gratitude, for my ideas on performance practices could only have developed through the firsthand experience of playing the Classic repertoire on the instruments of the Classic period. From this experience I began to understand the intimate relationship between the actions and sounds of the instruments and the musical material. The main instruments I played are described briefly below, grouped according to place of origin in chronological order. All but those otherwise identified are grand pianos.

Viennese Instruments

Ca. 1785. Replica of an instrument by Anton Walter; built by Philip Belt. Original in the Kunsthistorisches Museum, Vienna. Range $FF-g^3$, five octaves and two notes; $FF-a^1$ double-strung, the rest triple-strung. Three knee levers operate the dampers, a moderator, and a bassoon stop. Wellesley College, Wellesley, Massachusetts.

Ca. 1795. Anton Walter. Range $FF-g^3$, five octaves and two notes; $FF-a^1$ double-strung, the rest triple-strung. Key dip ca. 3 mm. Two knee levers operate the dampers and a moderator. Kunsthistorisches Museum, Vienna. Catalog No. 23. Plate Ia.

Ca. 1780–1790s. Replica of Viennese style; built by Thomas McCobb. Range $FF-g^3$, five octaves and two notes; $FF-c^2$ double-strung, the rest triple-strung. One knee lever operates the dampers.

Ca. 1802–1805. Square piano by Caspar Katholnik. Range $FF-g^3$, five octaves and two notes; $FF-E$ single-strung, the rest double-strung. Two knee levers operate the dampers and a moderator (now missing). Mr. and Mrs. G. Norman Eddy, Cambridge, Massachusetts.

Ca. 1810. Replica of an anonymous Viennese instrument in the style of Conrad Graf; built by Robert E. Smith. Original owned by Mrs. Paul Harvey of Chicago. Range FF–f⁴, six octaves; triple-strung throughout. Three pedals: double moderator, moderator, damper. Owen Jander, Wellesley, Massachusetts.

Ca. 1815. Anonymous, Viennese school. FF–f⁴, six octaves; FF–e double strung, the rest triple-strung. Five knee levers (perpendicular to the keyboard) operate the *una corda,* bassoon stop, moderator, dampers, and dampers and moderator together. Museum of Fine Arts, Boston. Accession No. 1982.178.

1819. Matthäus Andreas Stein (son of Johann Andreas Stein of Augsburg; see n. 34). Range FF–f⁴, six octaves; triple-strung throughout. Key dip ca. 4 mm. Two pedals: *una corda,* damper. Resonance board. Kunsthistorisches Museum, Vienna.[120] Catalog No. 32.

Ca. 1830. Conrad Graf. Range CC–g⁴, six octaves and a fifth; CC–EE double-strung, the rest triple-strung. Key dip ca. 5 mm. Four pedals: *una corda,* bassoon, moderator, damper. Kunsthistorisches Museum, Vienna. Catalog No. 35.

German Instruments

1784. Replica of an instrument by Johann Andreas Stein, Augsburg. Original in the Toledo Art Museum, Ohio. Range FF–f³, five octaves; FF–d-sharp² double-strung, the rest triple-strung. A pair of knee levers operates the dampers in tandem; the levers may also be operated individually as "split" damper mechanisms.

Ca. 1795. Replica of an instrument by Louis Dulcken, Munich; built by Philip Belt. Original in the Smithsonian Institution, Washington, DC. Range FF–g³, five octaves and two notes; double-strung throughout. A pair of knee levers operates the dampers in tandem; the levers may also be operated individually as "split" damper mechanisms.

English Instruments

1791. Square piano by John Broadwood. Range F–f³, five octaves, double-strung throughout. No pedals or levers. Mr. and Mrs. G. Norman Eddy, Cambridge, Massachusetts.

Ca. 1800. Square piano by John Astor. Range FF–c⁴, five octaves and a fifth; double-strung throughout. Two pedals: damper and "swell" (raises a small section of lid line with the keyboard to the player's right). Museum of Fine Arts, Boston. Accession No. 63.3051.

1804. John Broadwood. Range FF–c⁴, five octaves and a fifth; triple-strung throughout. Two pedals: *una corda,* damper. Museum of Fine Arts, Boston. Accession No. 1967.1233.

Ca. 1805 (based on the range). Muzio Clementi & Co. Range FF–c⁴, five octaves and a fifth; triple-strung throughout. Two pedals: *una corda,* damper. Mr. and Mrs. G. Norman Eddy, Cambridge, Massachusetts. Plate Ib.

Ca. 1810–1812. Muzio Clementi & Co. Range CC–c⁴, six octaves; CC–FF double-strung, the rest triple-strung. Three pedals: *una corda* on the left, damper on the right; the function of the middle pedal has not been identified. Wellesley College, Wellesley, Massachusetts.

Personal Observations

The opportunity to play Viennese fortepianos of successive decades in the Kunsthistorisches Museum in Vienna was of tremendous advantage. The development and growth of the pianos became strikingly clear as I went from one to another. Changes in the action (of which the gradually deepening key dip and the additional weight needed to depress a key were just two symptoms); increases in the number and thickness of the strings; and enlargement of the keyboard compass, the hammers, and the body of the instrument were among the more obvious physical signs of growth. These changes and others had a palpable effect on the amount of sound, the timbre, and the sustaining power of each bigger and heavier instrument, thereby entailing compensatory changes in execution as I went from the five-octave Walter of 1795 to the six-octave Stein and then to the Graf of six octaves and a fifth, built in 1830, which might be classed as an early Romantic instrument.[121] The sound of pedaled passages changed noticeably as the tone became richer and longer-lived, so that some of Beethoven's more "dissonant" pedal markings had to be adjusted on the larger instruments. (See chap. 4, pp. 125, 131.)

One final consideration that must be dealt with here is the realization that we cannot know exactly how the authentic instruments sounded when they were new, for they are now close to 200 years old and have been restored. Time makes itself felt in the original materials through aging and in the newer ones through technological change. For example, wood dries out, requiring either lighter stringing, lower pitch, or some other change. On the other hand, present-day builders have only recently learned to draw wire for stringing according to an early process in order to approximate the tonal qualities of the original. For these reasons, even if we were able to compare old and new pianos side by side, we could not know exactly how close the sound of a replica might be to that of the original instrument when it was made. The replica of a Walter built around 1785, which I know well, is an instrument of dulcet quality; one of the surprises for me at the Kunsthistorisches Museum was how much quieter and gentler was the tone of an original Walter built in 1795.

We will not explore further the possible reasons for such tonal or other differences. Suffice it to say that whatever the known or unknown differences between original instruments—as we know them now and as they may have been—and their replicas, these differences become insignificant in contrast to those between fortepianos and modern pianofortes. The early instruments, old or new, afford us the best way of penetrating the spirit of the contemporary repertoire. They reward an empathic player with insights beyond expectation.

CHAPTER

3

DYNAMICS AND ACCENTUATION

PLAYING CLASSIC PERIOD MUSIC ON A MODERN GRAND PIANO

The difference in volume between the fortepiano and the modern pianoforte influences our interpretation of the Classic repertoire. A crude but serviceable comparison can be formulated by imagining each general level of sound on today's instrument to be roughly the equivalent of one level louder on the fortepiano. A full *mezzo-forte* or a restrained *forte* on a modern grand might approximate a full *forte* on an early instrument (irrespective of the differences in timbre); a *piano* might be close to an earlier *mezzo-piano*. The volume levels of stringed and wind instruments used in the Classic era were of similar scale.

Two basic approaches to interpreting Classic music on a pianoforte offer a starting point from which each pianist can ponder possible alternatives. The first is to play a modern instrument on its own terms, using its dynamic palette as the music suggests. This attitude assumes that everything is relative within its own framework and that in expanding to the tonal scale of the modern piano a piece will still retain something close to its inherent character, at the same time taking advantage of the more sonorous quality of the later instrument. Still, I believe that at least in the compositions of Haydn, Mozart, and Clementi, some part of the *forte* and *fortissimo* must be withheld so that the sheer loudness and thicker sonority do not mask the music's delicate features.[1]

The second approach is to scale down the dynamics of the modern instrument approximately as described above. With appropriate tempo and touch, such a *forte* in the music of Mozart, Haydn, and their contemporaries can sound energetic, loud, and round without being as heavy or weighty as in the music of Schumann or Brahms. Because from the arrival of Beethoven's Érard in the fall of 1803 his instruments exceeded the size and volume of those for which Mozart's and most of Haydn's music was written, and because some of Beethoven's music seems to anticipate the power of even later instruments, the volume used in playing his works on the pianoforte is extended beyond that used for the works of his predecessors. The trick in all of this music is to make a *fortissimo* sound as if it were being played as loudly as possible in order to suggest the excitement generated by an instrument extended to its limits, as each of these composers' instruments would have been in certain outbursts and climaxes. Since it seems inappropriate to utilize fully the forcefulness of the modern piano in much of this repertoire, some Classic pieces may actually sound grander on the smaller fortepiano with its dynamic range fully extended. Clementi's Sonata Op. 7/3, full of *fortissimos, sforzandos,* and dramatic rhetoric, is one such work.

To highlight design and reveal meaning is the essence of interpretation, and that essence can be realized in more ways than one. The choice depends in some measure on the way the performer relates to the style and feel of a particular piece. Dynamic usage is also influenced by the size of the concert hall and the instrument available. For example, a pianist who scales down the dynamics of a Mozart sonata on a powerful Steinway grand might decide to utilize more of the sound of an intimate Bechstein instrument. It is important that the performer not feel inhibited in handling dynamics, for such discomfort will dampen the vigor and joy of the interpretation. Similarly, the energy and impact of the dynamics must be sufficient to engage twentieth-century listeners, for we do not hear with eighteenth-century ears.

Robert Donington has differentiated between historical authenticity and essential authenticity.[2] Historical authenticity is the use of all available knowledge for any performance, which for Classic keyboard music would require a fortepiano of the type available to the composer, tuned at low pitch. Essential authenticity is the use of such knowledge and musicianship as are necessary to reveal the inherent character of a piece and to produce an aesthetically appealing performance with or without an authentic instrument.[3] The criteria of essential authenticity seem to me the more important. The cause is not authenticity *per se,* but effectiveness of interpretation. A reading that brings out the finesse and detail of the Classic repertoire can be musicianly and ultimately effective. Play Mozart on a modern piano, but do not modernize it. Project dynamic relationships, tempos, articulation, pedaling, and ornamentation that are congruous with the composer's concept.

Finally, there is an important difference between the bass registers of early and modern pianos. The clearly defined, bright tone of the fortepiano was never thick, even in the bass. Thus in the Classic repertoire it seems best to try to mitigate the kind of muddy sound often produced in the low register of the modern grand. Bass chords in close position can be a particular problem in the music of Clementi and Beethoven (e.g., Beethoven's Op. 2/2/i/160 and Op. 10/1/i/22). They are best managed by using little or no pedal and by lightening the inner notes and giving prominence to the outer ones, especially the bottommost.

NOTATION AND INTERPRETATION OF DYNAMIC INDICATIONS

Introduction

Türk gave dynamics a primary role in performance alongside articulation and tempo.

[In addition to studying and learning to apply] the expression of every feeling and passion in the most careful way, . . . I also consider . . . indispensable to express . . . 1) the appropriate degree of loudness and softness, 2) the detaching, sustaining, and slurring of notes, 3) the correct tempo.[4]

In spite of the growing importance of dynamic variability in early Classic and Classic music and its compelling role in the improvement and adoption of the fortepiano, some keyboard music of the Classic period contains relatively few dynamic marks, some none at all. Often broad stretches are marked just *piano* or *forte*, reminiscent—at least in appearance and sometimes in practice—of the "terraced" dynamics prevalent in Baroque harpsichord music. From the evidence of notated dynamics and theorists' advice, we can learn to judge where and what kinds of indications may have remained unwritten, including those that indicate dynamic level as well as those that suggest graduated change. These judgments depend in part on observed relationships between dynamics and form. As the Classic period progressed, the vocabulary of indications broadened. This provides more information, but leaves us, approximately 200 years later, with other questions of usage and interpretation.

Dynamics may be classed as absolute, relative, or gradual. Accordingly, *forte, piano,* and other terms that indicate specific "areas of sound" are absolute (see "The Scope of *Piano* and *Forte*" below). *Espressivo, più forte,* some accent indications, and other terms whose actual levels are determined by their immediate environment are relative. For example, realizations of *sf* or *più forte* can vary within the same piece or movement, depending on whether the indication is in a softer or louder context. Certain indications, such as *fp*, function as absolute in some contexts and relative in others, as we shall see. *Crescendo, diminuendo, mancando,* and similar terms are gradual.

Both written and unwritten dynamics in this repertoire deserve thoughtful realization. Classic period meanings of dynamic indications, specific uses by individual composers, ways of providing missing indications, when and when not to introduce graduated dynamics, and the use of dynamic accents are among the considerations important to this area of performance practices. Expressive portrayal of the affect is the goal; attention to detail is the means.

Orientation to Composers' Notation and Unfamiliar Terms

Haydn's early keyboard sonatas, composed mainly for harpsichord, contain no dynamic indications. Although sporadic markings appear in a small number of movements written between the late 1760s and 1774 (Hob. 46/i, 18/i, 20/i and iii, 22/i, 29/i), it was not until Hob. 35–39, published in 1780 with Hob. 20, that Haydn began to put at least a few dynamics (albeit sometimes not half a dozen) into most movements. However, from Hob. 40–42, published in 1784,[5] to his last sonatas there is a general increase in the number and subtlety of the indications.[6] In contrast, the first six sonatas of Mozart, written to exploit the fortepianos he found in Munich in the winter of 1775, are replete with dynamic signs, in some movements only *p* and *f,* in others more varied. The autograph of Sonata K. 280 contains about 227 indications, including a number marked individually for the right- and left-hand parts. Surprisingly, in some of his late compositions Mozart was content with sparse (or no) dynamic indications but was painstakingly thorough with articulation signs (e.g., Rondo K. 485, comp. 1786; Sonata K. 570, comp. 1789). Overall, Haydn wrote fewer performance indications of any kind than did Mozart, perhaps in part because Haydn grew up a generation earlier. Sometimes his directions are in passages of an unusual bent, where he may have felt it necessary to specify his intentions; a majority of the passages in which he left the dynamics open are probably those that were to be played according to understood practice.

Clementi's earliest keyboard works are also sparsely marked, primarily with *p* and *f,* possibly reflecting in part his continued performances on the harpsichord (see p. 24). The pieces of Opp. 5 and 6, published in 1780 or 1781 in Paris, begin to show more varied dynamics, while the Sonatas of Opp. 7–10, composed between December 1781 and May 1782 in Vienna,[7] contain the range (*pp* to *ff*) and a variety of indications characteristically appropriate to the fortepiano. These include frequent shading with *cresc., dim., sf,* and occasionally *mf,* the last of which Mozart and Beethoven used only rarely in their works for piano solo (e.g., Mozart, Adagio K. 540; Beethoven, Op. 2/2/iv/148) but which Mozart used more often in other media (e.g., sonatas for piano and violin, string quartets). In later works Clementi used *dolce, espressivo* (p. 60), *rinforzando, perdendosi,* and many other terms. *Mezzo* for *mezzo-piano* is notable because *mp* was used not at all in piano music by Haydn or Mozart and apparently only once by Beethoven (at Op. 111/i/22–23). Clementi's relatively greater use of *mp* and *mf* may have resulted from the heavier, somewhat more controllable action of the English fortepianos, as well as from their more sonorous tone and extended dynamic range, all of which made it easier to obtain those middle sounds.

Beethoven's dynamic marks are not only more numerous but more varied, subtler, more extreme, and sometimes more sharply contrasted than those of Haydn, Mozart, and Clementi. Conspicuous are his increasingly long *crescendos* and *decrescendos* and such special effects as *subito piano* immediately following a *crescendo,* often termed the "Beethoven *piano.*" Not as conspicuous but highly interesting is the distribution of absolute soft and loud dynamics in Beethoven's 32 piano sonatas. Of 9,297 indications of all types, approximately 24 percent are absolute soft dynamics (*mp, p, pp, ppp*) and 15 percent are absolute loud (*mf, f, ff*), yielding the surprising statistic that Beethoven suggested only two-thirds as many absolute loud as absolute soft sounds.[8] He used *pp* frequently, sometimes for surprisingly long stretches (e.g., Piano Trio Op. 1/2/iv/132b–139b, with *calando* following the *pianissimo*). In addition, he used other directions that generally imply some level of soft sound, such as *dolce, espressivo, sanft, mezza voce,* and *teneramente.*

We think of Beethoven as a composer who amplified the loud sonorities, but he stretched the softer ones as well. Although he wrote specific indications only for the damper and *una corda* pedals, his obvious interest in soft sounds has made me wonder how much he might have experimented with the moderator (and perhaps the lute pedal) on his Érard piano, received in 1803, when his hearing was still relatively good. A related but probably unanswerable question is whether he (or any other composer) ever intended the markings *pp* and *pianissimo,* by which the double moderator was sometimes known, to indicate either moderator or double moderator.

Among the indications added to the palette of dynamics or used more frequently by Beethoven than by his contemporaries are *ppp* (his first use for fortepiano is in Op. 53/iii/400), *più crescendo, crescendo poco a poco, leggiermente, teneramente,* and *ben marcato.* These and other instructions demonstrate his increasing interest in finely shaded dynamics and may imply the possibility of (or desire for) exercising greater control over the action and sound of the growing Viennese fortepiano. (Was the *ppp* in Op. 53 inspired by his recently arrived Érard, with its *una corda* pedal in addition to the moderator?) Beethoven also enhanced the subtlety of his directions by using indications in more exacting ways. *Sf* or *rinf.* may cap a written *crescendo* (Op. 126/5/29, Plate V) and may sometimes be followed by a short *decrescendo* hairpin, even where that would have been understood according to Classic conventions. At the *sf* in Op. 22/ii/16, for example, both the strong-to-weak rhythmic configuration and the resolution of the dissonant G-flat would have mandated a tapered sound to the F. Very often short hairpin signs facing each other provide detailed inflection for just three or four notes (e.g., Op. 2/1/i/27–30; Op. 106/iii/134).

One specific comparison in the use of dynamics that reflects in part a changing musical style is that approximately 86 percent of Mozart's 2,244 indications in the eighteen[9] piano sonatas and the Fantasy K. 475 are absolute, compared with only 39 percent of Beethoven's. Of the remainder of Beethoven's marks, approximately 26 percent are gradual and 35 percent are relative. With this carefully directed shading, his dynamics gained a considerably more active role in shaping a composition.

Some of the dynamic indications Beethoven wrote are properly instrumental or vocal effects that are not literally available to the pianist. Op. 7 has several. Figure 3.1 shows a pattern in which he presumably imagined an increase of sound during the time of the first chord, a natural effect for wind and stringed instruments.[10] In m. 39 of this Largo a *crescendo* hairpin lies between two octave chords, the first a half note marked *piano,* the second a dotted eighth marked *sf.* The same markings in conjunction with two chords

Fig. 3.1. Beethoven, Sonata Op. 7/ii (OE Artaria), mm. 11–12.

[Largo con gran espressione]

are repeated at iv/62–63. These *crescendos* are not possible on any piano. In all three examples, raising the dampers at the right instant between the chords (and lowering them for the *decrescendo* in Fig. 3.1) provides merely the slightest hint of the suggested effect. But some believe that performers who imagine and play the notes as though the piano could make the *crescendo* enhance the effect by approaching the keys with a different gesture (perhaps creating a different tone?) from one used by those who readily acquiesce to reason. Such markings, products of the composer's inner ear, demonstrate Beethoven's proclivity to "psychological" performance directions. The *cresc.* under a single held e^3 at Op. 14/1/ii/62 is another aural image.

Some dynamic marks of the Classic period may be unfamiliar. These include *mezzo* for "mezzo piano, or poco P, . . . rather soft";[11] *sotto voce,* "in an undertone, therefore soft";[12] *pia.* and *for.* for *piano* and *forte,* and *fmo* for *ff. Dolce*[13] and *espressivo* were sometimes used instead of *p* to indicate a particularly expressive soft execution. When Clementi published the first English edition of Op. 7 in the early 1790s, he substituted *espressivo* several times, and *dolce* once, where *piano* had been in the Viennese edition of 1782. In the opening of the Adagio of Beethoven's Trio for Piano, Clarinet or Violin, and Cello Op. 11, the accompaniment, in the piano, is marked *p;* the melody, played by the cello, is marked *con espressione.* When melody and accompaniment return in different instruments at m. 9, the dynamic indications move with their respective parts.

The somewhat ambiguous *pf* had two meanings according to Türk: *poco forte,* a little loudly; or *più forte,* louder.[14] *Poco forte* can indicate either an increase or a decrease in sound, depending on whether it is preceded by *p* or by *f. Più forte* can only indicate an increase in sound. Türk presents the need for choice in the Twelve Pieces at the end of his *Klavierschule.* In No. 3 *pf* appears on relatively long notes coupled with Ten., all within a quiet context. Türk refers the reader to page 337, example e, where it becomes clear that in the third piece *pf* indicates an accent, as *poco forte,* "a little loudly." In No. 6 *pf* appears at the beginning of a phrase after four measures of *piano,* suggesting that the new phrase be louder, *più forte.* Fortunately, *poco* and *più* were often spelled out.

The Scope of *Forte* and *Piano*

Basic *forte* and *piano* indications formed the backbone of dynamic usage by Mozart and Haydn. Audun Ravnan's study of dynamic indications reveals that in Mozart's sonatas *f* accounts for approximately 41 percent of all the dynamic marks and *p* for 44 percent of a total of 2,244.[15] In the twenty sonatas in which Haydn wrote a total of 991 dynamic indications, *f* and *p* each account for 26 percent, equaled in some movements by the frequency and importance of *fz.* In Beethoven's sonatas *forte* and *piano* have a still lesser role: *f* accounts for only 10 percent and *p* for 18 percent of the dynamics, while *sf* takes 30 percent and the term *crescendo* takes 11 percent. Because the intermediate indications *più forte, mf, mp,* and *più piano* were rarely used by Haydn, Mozart, and Beethoven, and because the more extreme *pp* and *ff* were used only occasionally by Haydn and Mozart—although more frequently by Clementi and Beethoven—*piano* and *forte* each represented a broader spectrum of sound in Classic music than they do in later repertoire. *Piano* might indicate anything from *pp* to *mp,* and *forte* might range from *mf* to *ff.* Correspondingly, *pianissimo*—especially Beethoven's more frequent and longer indications—may mean either soft or very soft, depending especially on the interpretation of a neighboring *piano.*

Support for the concept of "areas of sound" comes from many sources. In his landmark volume on violin playing, Leopold Mozart stressed that every *forte* should not be played at maximum strength:

> Wherever a *forte* is written down, the tone is to be used with moderation, without foolish scrapings, especially in the accompaniment of a solo part. Many either omit to do a thing altogether, or if they do it, are certain to exaggerate. The effect must be considered. Often a note demands a strong accent, at other times only a moderate one, and then again one which is hardly audible.[16]

Türk emphasized the desirability of matching tonal intensity with subtlety of affect:

> Compositions of a cheerful, joyous, lively, sublime, splendid, proud, bold, courageous, serious, fiery, wild, furious, and the like, character all require a certain degree of loudness. This degree must even be increased or decreased according to whether the feeling or passion is represented more intensely or more moderately. . . . in each composition itself different gradations are again necessary, all of which must be in a suitable relation to the whole. A *forte* in an *Allegro furioso* must therefore be considerably louder than in an *Allegro* in which only a moderate degree of joy prevails, etc.
>
> Compositions of a gentle, innocent, naive, pleading, tender, moving, sad, melancholy, and the like, character all require a softer execution. The degree of loudness [in 1802, "of softness"], however, must correspond accurately to the prevailing sentiment and therefore is different in most of the cases just named.[17]

Specific compositions also demonstrate the necessary variability of the basic *p* and *f* markings. Each of the three movements of Mozart's Sonata K. 280 begins with an implied dynamic of the *forte* range (see below, "Filling in the Missing Dynamics"). However, the strong differences in texture, style, and mood among the Allegro assai, the Adagio, and the Presto—an unusual tempo mark in Mozart's piano works—leave no doubt that the sound at the beginning of each has to have an individual quality that corresponds to the prevailing sentiment. Or within Mozart's Rondo K. 485, the dynamic in mm. 21–22 might be a gentle *forte,* in mm. 43–52 it would be more aggressive, while the level reached during the climactic passage starting in m. 125 might lean toward a *fortissimo* without being thick or ponderous (see p. 64).

Beethoven indicated a *piano* start for all four movements of his Sonata Op. 2/3, yet each has its individual mood, texture, meter, and tempo. Czerny's characterization of these movements in his valuable chapter "On the Performance of all Beethoven's Works for Piano Solo" makes it clear that Czerny would have played each with a different soft sound. The opening Allegro con brio "must be performed with fire and energy"; the Adagio with "great sentiment"; the Scherzo with a "light and short" staccato; the Allegro assai "quick and sprightly."[18] Czerny is more specific in discussing the theme and first three variations in the "Appassionata" Sonata, each marked *piano*. He had played this sonata "several times" for Beethoven[19] and may have known something of the composer's thoughts regarding it:

> The theme very *piano*. ... The 1st Variation ... with more tone. ... The 2nd Variation *pp* and with the shifting pedal [*una corda*]. ... The 3rd Variation without the pedal, animated and with constantly increasing power ... until it again falls into the theme.[20]

Concinnity of Dynamics and Form

Composers' frequent reliance on just *forte* and *piano* for characterization of themes and definition of structural sections reflects in part the sharp differentiation of melodic figures and the clearly articulated rhetoric and forms of Classic music. Thus, in the opening Allegro of Mozart's Sonata K. 457, the indicated *forte* and *piano* further define the "tutti" and "solo" segments of the initial phrase. (The reader may wish to follow a score as we trace the concinnous relationship of dynamics to form through this exposition.) Juxtaposition of those dynamics accompanies the alternation of bold and singing motives through the A section. Two *piano* transitional measures (17–18) lead to a *forte* restatement of mm. 1 and 2. They evolve into the brief transition, which I continue *forte* until the descending solo line in m. 22 diminishes to *piano* for the entry of a lyrical B theme. Increased activity starting in m. 27 is heightened by a *crescendo* to *forte;* however, the sound quickly falls away to *piano* with the entry of another transitional figure that introduces a second B theme (m. 36).

In m. 44 a new phrase enters; its two distinct members are once again delineated with contrasting *forte* and *piano*. Repetition of this *forte* motive is followed by a broad statement of cadential harmonies in which a change is forecast by the sudden appearance of a chromatically descending line marked *piano*. This dynamic continues into the closing theme (m. 59). A *forte* coincides with a restatement of the closing theme in a more brilliant form, followed by some cadential formulae. Unexpectedly the opening phrase reappears, its excitement heightened by a stretto-like entry of the initial *forte* motive in the bass. A quiet, sustained chord underlying the end of the phrase intimates a more settled effect to conclude the exposition. This momentous opening portion of K. 457/i illustrates well the Classic use of dynamics to clarify and enhance thematic structure and form, a concinnity that often includes harmonic design, texture, and rhythmic development as well.

Filling in the Missing Dynamics

The lack of dynamic indications in some compositions and their sparseness in others places the responsibility for their realization on the performer. Fortunately we are not without contemporary advice. Türk's comments on compositions that require "a certain degree of loudness" or "a softer execution" have been cited. Johann Rellstab stated succinctly, "Where none of these abbreviations [for dynamics] is found, one plays loudly, but the loudness is more moderate in slow tempo than in fast."[21] As late as 1802 Koch still wrote that in the absence of a "*piano* or another degree of reduced loudness of tone" a movement begins loudly; "strictly speaking, however, the degree of this loudness must be adjusted to the character of the movement." A fugue subject lacking a dynamic indication was also played in a "rather loud tone."[22]

In these remarks, *forte* or a "degree of loudness" is the basic point of reference; quiet sounds are reduced degrees of loudness. This approach may be a reflection of the early use of expression marks, when "*piano* (or occasionally *echo*) was used for dynamic contrast whereas *forte* denoted a return to normal dynamics: even in Corelli, *forte* does not appear except when preceded by *piano*."[23] Türk's "degree of softness" in the second edition of his tutor, noted on page 61 here, and his introduction to that same quotation in 1802, "Concerning the loudness or softness of tone required . . . ,"[24] evidence a departure from this attitude.

A fair try, then, in the absence of an initial dynamic sign, might be to start *allegro* and related movement types more or less loud. In first movements of sonatas by Haydn and Mozart this missing *forte* is often confirmed when the theme is marked *f* at a restatement (e.g., Haydn, Hob. 41/i/97), or sometimes much sooner when *p* occurs shortly after the opening (e.g., Haydn, Hob. 36/i/2). Contrast of *forte* and *piano* is common near the beginning of Classic movements in sonata-allegro form, as in K. 457 (reviewed earlier). At this time if an opening fast movement was to start *piano*, the composer frequently marked it so (e.g., Haydn, Hob. 50/i).

A *forte* start or a basic *forte* sound seems to have been less prevalent in final movements of sonatas. Of the seventeen fast finales in Mozart's sonatas[25] none carries a holographic *forte* at the start and only two can be assumed to begin *forte* based on customary practice: K. 280/iii by virture of a *p* in m. 2 (aut.); and K. 332/iii by virtue of its marked bravura quality, its contrast with the ensuing cantabile theme marked *p* and *dolce* (aut.), and *f* at the start of the recapitulation in the first edition (this part of the holograph, from iii/107, is missing). Of the movements remaining, six are marked *piano* in the autographs and four in first editions, of which two serve as primary sources and two as secondary sources. *Piano* also appears at the start of the Rondo K. 494 (finale to Sonata K. 533) in Mozart's holographic list of his works and in his hand at the recapitulation of K. 457/iii in a dedication copy for Therese von Trattner.[26] (In the first edition, not included in the count above, K. 457/iii has *piano* at the start of the movement as well.) The initial dynamic in the final movements of K. 283, 545, and 570 is more of an open issue, although the Rondo of K. 545 seems well served by a *mezzo-piano* start (see discussion of rondo dynamics below) and the Presto of K. 283 by *forte*. The latter does not necessarily remain unchanged until Mozart's *piano* in m. 18.

Of Haydn's sonatas from Hob. 35 on, five contain indications for the start of their closing movements, all *piano*. Two of these are holographic: the bumptious theme of the Presto of Hob. 52 is marked at the outset; the minuet theme of Hob. 49/iii is marked at its return. The finales of Hob. 37 and 50 are marked *p* in their first editions, both primary sources for those works.[27] The rondo theme of Hob. 35, also from a first edition primary source, is marked *p* when it returns in the A–B–A refrain (m. 18). *Forte* (from the first edition primary source) for the A theme at the beginning of the development section of Hob. 39 suggests a similar start for this movement, possibly a bright *mezzo-forte* at the opening and a *forte* where the octaves enter in m. 3. The opening dynamics for the remaining finales seem to me to vary from *forte* or *mezzo-forte* for Hob. 38/iii, a robust minuet of the "moderate" type (see "Fast and 'Moderate' Minuets" in chap. 9), and for Hob. 41/ii, with its quasi-polyphonic elements, to *mezzo-piano* for the swift, light Hob. 34/iii, and *piano* for the Rondo of Hob. 48/ii. In this movement Haydn twice indicated *p* just before the return of the A section (mm. 90, 169); he indicated *ff* (m. 193) and *f* (m. 221) for that theme when he wanted a louder sound.

This scan indicates that in respect to final movements and similar pieces, the advice of Türk and Koch was probably overgeneralized. In light of examples marked *piano* by Haydn and Mozart, there are bound to be other unmarked compositions of a "cheerful, joyous, lively" character that might well begin at some level of softer sound. Opening volume might be related to the role of a movement in a larger form, to the form of the movement itself, to the character of its initial theme and following material, and to a known inclination of the composer. For example, the pleasing tunefulness that prevails in the Classic rondo seems to have predisposed this genre to a light opening, and that is one reason many sonata-rondo finales do not begin *forte*. Mozart typically prescribed—or implied by later indications—*piano* or *dolce* for the first statement of a rondo theme, which he sometimes followed with a *forte* repetition, a design less used in the rondos of Haydn and Beethoven. Episodes tend to generate more varied, often fuller dynamics than those of the refrain. Mozart's characteristic treatment of rondo dynamics should be considered by anyone teaching the last movement of the Sonata in C major K. 545, for which no authentic dynamics exist. Beyond such aids, much is left to the discretion of the performer, who must decide when and when not to follow the textbook advice.

The opening dynamics of Beethoven's sonatas demonstrate that the advice of Türk and Koch for starting unmarked movements no longer applies, even in a general way, to first movements. Beethoven could not have regarded *forte* as an assumed point of reference, for in all movements of the sonatas from Op. 2 to Op. 57, only Op. 10/1/i begins *forte*. Op 13/i begins with a chord marked *fp;* the introduction to Op. 57/iii begins *fortissimo* but the first theme of the exposition proper starts *pianissimo*. With the exception of six movements that lack indications at the start, all the rest—fast and slow—are marked *piano* or *pianissimo,* affording new uses of dynamic growth in coordination with formal development.[28] Starting with Op. 78, composed in 1809, eight movements of varying positions in the sonatas and the introduction to another begin *forte*.

Predictably, Beethoven left clues in many of his unmarked movements. In the opening Allegro of the "Kurfürsten" Sonata No. 3, a youthful work composed in ?1783,[29] he still relied on the old custom, for the *piano* that enters after the two-beat opening motive suggests a *forte* start (Fig. 3.2). Twice more, in the beginning of the development, the unwritten dynamic level at an entry of the opening theme is *forte,* signified here as much by a previous (unchanged) *ff* or *f* as by the following *p*. At the recapitulation the first two motives of the theme in an altered form are marked *ff,* without the *piano* intervention. The Largo appassionato of Op. 2/2 contains several directives for a quiet start. First in importance is the indicated *piano* when the theme returns in m. 44. Second are the marks at two transitional measures. *Ffp* in m. 31 prepares the *piano* for the return of the A section in m. 32; *pianissimo* in m. 67 leads directly to a quiet final statement that provides a sharp contrast to the previous *fortissimo* presentation.

The Sonata Op. 49/2, composed in 1795–1796, contains only two dynamic marks in OE, both *pp*'s in the second movement. The opening chord of the first movement is a call for attention that wants a full sound, out of which the melody unfolds at a comfortably lower volume, usually *mf* or *mp*. In general this seems to me a light movement in which much of the sound is between *piano* and *mezzo-forte;* few passages reach a true *forte*. Yet there are many opportunities to highlight formal sections and repeated segments with dynamic change. The Tempo di Menuetto, like many of Beethoven's minuet types with prescribed dynamics, starts softly. Beethoven confirmed this with a notated *p* in the Tempo di Menuetto of his Septet Op. 20, composed just four years later, which shares the opening theme of the sonata movement (see Figs. 9.5 and 9.7). The two *pp*'s in Op. 49/2/ii—both near the ends of transitions to the A theme—are shrewdly placed, for they not only tell us to return to a quiet sound

Fig. 3.2. Beethoven, Sonata WoO 47/3/i (OE Bossler), mm. 1–2.

for the theme, but also imply activity at a higher volume for the preceding episodes of this Tempo di Menuetto in rondo form. Here again, in this early movement by Beethoven, the primary purpose of a simple dynamic plan is to outline the sections and to provide contrast between them.

The Allegretto in C minor WoO 53 was composed in 1796–1797 while Beethoven was working on the Sonatas Op. 10. A remark of his written at about the same time and the presence of the sketches for the Allegretto in conjunction with those of Op. 10 led Gustav Nottebohm to infer that the Allegretto might have been conceived as a scherzo for the C minor Sonata.[30] It bears similarities to three other movements, the Allegrettos of Opp. 10/2 and 14/1 and the Scherzo of Op. 26, all of which Beethoven marked *piano* at the start. The three *ff*'s in the autograph of WoO 53 (mm. 33, 129, and 144 in HE) locate important climaxes, after the third of which the markings *p, mancando,* and *pp* lead to the quiet coda.

The two movements with unmarked starts in Op. 14/2 provide straightforward clarification further on. The theme of the opening Allegro is marked *piano* at the beginning of both the development and the recapitulation. A surprising *piano* that cuts short the *forte* drive to the held dominant-seventh chord in m. 98 immediately precedes the false recapitulation. This *piano,* arriving before the theme, differentiates the dynamic contours of the approaches to the false and actual recapitulations. (A similar kind of rhythmic differentiation in Beethoven's Op. 51/1 is discussed on pp. 81–82.) The Schenker-Ratz and Tovey-Craxton editions place this *piano* directly under the first note of the theme,[31] but the *BNA* and other editions retain it under the chord, as it is in the first edition by Mollo (1799), in Simrock's reprint (1800), and in Haslinger's *Gesamtausgabe.* Unfortunately the holograph for this composition is lost. In the Scherzo of Op. 14/2, every entrance of the A theme but the first was designated *piano* in OE; the opening *p* was added in Simrock.

Similar clues can be read in other movements, including the first and third of Op. 101. They also start *piano,* contrasting with the second and fourth movements, which are marked *forte.* Finally, a look at the Minuetto and its Minore of Op. 22 will caution us not to let frequent patterns become unquestioned habits. Although the Minuetto opens with a typical *piano* period, it has as its contrasting middle section (mm. 9–16) two startling phrases that begin with assertive sixteenth notes and a *crescendo* to *fortissimo.* The quiet returns, but the stage has been set for a Minore in a brilliant style. Its energetic running figure and the syncopated *sforzando* chords suggest to me an opening dynamic that approximates a solid *mezzo-forte.*

Türk left additional suggestions for dynamics *within* a movement:

> One can generally assume that the livelier passages of a composition are played loudly, the gentle singing, etc. [passages] more softly, even if in the first case no *forte,* and in the second no *piano* is indicated. When an idea is repeated, then it is customary to play it softly the second time if it was played loudly the first. On the other hand, a repeated passage may also be played *louder,* especially

when the composer has made it livelier through elaborations. In general, even *single notes* of importance ought to be played more emphatically than the others.[32]

"Elaborations" include providing a more active accompaniment, as Mozart did in his Rondo K. 485/43, where he also placed the otherwise unchanged melody in a deeper register.

In early sonata movements by Haydn and in a few movements by Mozart, the entire dynamic scheme is left to the performer. The more elementary the structure, the simpler the basic plan, especially in those early movements of Haydn in which the melodic style and primitive development sections are reminders of the Baroque suite. Türk's advice to moderate the *forte* according to temper and speed suggests for the opening Andante of Hob. 12 a dynamic level that focuses around *mezzo-forte*. Nuances that seem appropriate to me include a *mezzo-piano* start for the B section in both the exposition and the recapitulation (mm. 11 and 46, beat 2) and a quiet ending for both sections, starting with either the first or second appearance of the closing motive (mm. 18 or 19). Alternatively the movement may end *mf,* from the second eighth note in m. 54.

The infrequent change of dynamics within this movement reflects a lack of marked contrast in material and texture but does not preclude sensitive inflections within the structural divisions when the instrument is the piano or the clavichord. *Crescendos* and *diminuendos* of varying degrees may be applied in such places as mm. 7–10 and 21–25. A *crescendo* from mm. 30–34 can generate enough energy to carry the full sound to the beginning of beat 2 in m. 36, where a *diminuendo* is appropriate; or that *crescendo* may give way to an echo in m. 35 (as suggested by Türk in the last quotation), followed by a return to *mf.*

For the simple, robust Finale of Hob. 12, I apply Türk's "certain degree of loudness" as a light *forte.* Echoes are attractive for the measures that return in the minor mode (mm. 17–18, 58–59). Measures 8–14 sound well in a less bright color than those that precede and follow.

Contemporary information also calls our attention to the small-scale, often unmarked dynamic changes related to dissonance and modulation. In his book *On Playing the Flute,* Quantz included a melody and figured bass with dynamics throughout that illustrate his accentuation of dissonances. They are all marked *mf* [!], *f,* or *ff,* according to his classification of the dissonant intervals involved.[33] Interestingly, after describing how one could bring about such dynamic change on the harpsichord by augmenting or diminishing the number of notes or parts, by arpeggiation of chords, or by the use of the "upper keyboard for the Pianissimo," Quantz lent early support to the piano: "But on a *piano-forte* everything required may be accomplished with the greatest convenience. . . ."[34]

Emanuel Bach and Türk also stressed the "rule" that "dissonances or dissonant chords must generally be struck with more intensity than consonant [ones]."[35] In addition to the accent, this technique produces a tapering effect

Fig. 3.3. Mozart, Adagio K. 540 (Aut.),[36] mm. 1–2.

or small *diminuendo* when the dissonance resolves. Mozart wrote out both *sf* and *p* for this effect in the opening motive of his Adagio K. 540 (Fig. 3.3). Whether there is a *crescendo* to the accented chord will vary with the interpreter and may change as the piece unfolds. Mozart also notated *sf* for the appoggiatura 6/4 chord at the start of m. 2. In "common practice" theory the sixth and fourth of this unstable chord act as appoggiaturas to their notes of resolution and are expected to be slurred to them (see Chart II, "Nonharmonic Tones and Ornaments"). Mozart failed to notate the slurs here but he did so in the left hand further on (Aut., *NMA*).

According to Türk, harmonies that effect a sudden modulation into a distant or unexpected key were also played "relatively loudly and emphatically" to increase the element of surprise.[37] His examples show *forte* indications under single chords or pairs that contain the telling chromatics. Unmarked dynamic change is also created by expressive accents in other contexts (p. 92) or by movement toward the expressive goal of a phrase (pp. 93–94).

Terraced and Graduated Dynamics

The Classic style embraces both terraced dynamics, in which the change from one sound level to another is immediate, and graduated dynamics, in which *crescendo* and *diminuendo* effect gradual change. Terraced dynamics may utilize the contrast of *forte* and *piano* to enhance an existing contrast of formal material (e.g., K. 457/i/1–4) or sections, or of registers, textures, or mood. Or the dynamics themselves may create contrast merely by a change of tonal intensity, as in an echo effect (K. 309/iii/46–47). In the context of terraced dynamics, change was not exploited for color but to enhance the articulated phrases and sections; therefore, the imposition of gradual change could well alter the listener's perception of the music.

Mozart's K. 540 contains notated dynamic contrasts within a theme (mm. 3–4, 11), between contrasting thematic material (mm. 2–3), and between sections of its form (e.g., mm. 10–11).[38] In this piece the contrasts originate to some degree in the notes themselves, through changes of register, texture, material, or various combinations of these; the prescribed dynamics support the inherent contrast. Mozart took a different tack with terraced dynamics in the first theme of his Sonata K. 284/iii. Here the first three melody notes of the antecedent and consequent phrases are the same, but he changed the dynamic from *piano* for the first phrase to *forte* (and staccato in the upbeat) for the second. Thus the dynamic change alone forecasts that what follows might be different, more energetic in some way, as indeed it is. (In relation to these beautifully shaped phrases it is appropriate to remark that a dynamic "terrace" or level need not be altogether flat.) As two examples of terraced (rather than gradual) change for written dynamics in Haydn's sonatas, I suggest Hob. 42/ i/4 and 8–9, and Hob. 50/i/42–44.

Although it can be assumed that unmarked graduated dynamics were used in various musical styles before the Baroque period,[39] and although they are known to have been used by the voice and by stringed and wind instruments from around 1600,[40] specific vocabulary to indicate gradual change in volume developed slowly. Through the Baroque period composers relied on series of familiar words or abbreviations, such as Giustini di Pistoia's *for., pia.; for., più for.*; and *for., pia., più pia.* (p. 5 above); or Handel's *f, p, pp*[41] for this purpose.[42] During the second half of the eighteenth century the words *crescendo* and *decrescendo* (or *diminuendo*) and their abbreviations appeared with gradually increasing frequency; however, hairpin signs for *crescendo* and *diminuendo*, $<$ $>$, which were found at least from Giovanni Antonio Piani's Sonatas for Violin and Continuo Op. 1, published in 1712,[43] did not come into customary use until the 1780s and 1790s. Very often in Classic music the performer still must determine from the context itself whether the change between adjacent indications is to be graduated or terraced.[44]

The Adagio of Mozart's Sonata K. 280—one of the more arresting movements in his first six sonatas—allows substantial variety of tonal level and manner of change in developing the composer's simple *piano* and *forte* signs. From a presumed *forte* in m. 1 (cf. m. 37), my suggestion is a graduated flow between each *forte* and *piano* until the end of m. 7, where I interpret *f* (Aut.) more as an emphasis than as a true *forte* (p. 87). Most of the tapering off to the first *piano* may take place in the second half of m. 2. Some swell in the rising thirds of m. 3 prepares for a fuller sound on the appoggiatura 6/4 chord; its resolution implies a *diminuendo*. From m. 9 a *crescendo* is appropriate to f^2 in m. 11, followed by a terraced drop to *piano*. From here to the repeat sign the clearly separated motives suggest terraced changes between the dynamics in mm. 12–16 and 21–24; a *crescendo* carries the line smoothly from *piano* in m. 17 to the following *forte*.

Although designations for *crescendo* and *decrescendo* are again conspicuously absent, the late Adagio K. 540 contains an unusually large number and variety of dynamic marks to convey the extent of nuance that Mozart considered appropriate for expressive slow movements. In addition to the notated accents and their resolutions, and the terraced dynamics (both already discussed), gradual dynamic change seems desirable between other indications. Among such places I include mm. 5 and 39, which seem to call for gradation between the initial *p*, the *mf*, and the following *p* as the melody rises, moves toward the dissonance (on beat 2), and tapers off; mm. 13 and 43, in which brief *crescendos* and *decrescendos* follow the increasing and decreasing harmonic tension; and mm. 14 and 44, which some performers build to a *forte* climax and others allow to trail off quietly. The repeated rise and fall of the melodic line between mm. 17–21 and 47–51 also suggests a related play in dynamics, with appropriate attention to the remarkable shift from the B-minor scale in m. 47 to its Neapolitan sixth chord, the C-major arpeggio, in m. 48. Mozart underlined this harmonic progression with the introduction of triplets against duplets.

According to holographs and first editions, Haydn introduced the hairpin signs sporadically (in addition to *cresc.* and *decresc.*) in his sonatas from Hob. 40 (pub. 1784) on, at first to indicate quite short effects within a beat (Hob. 40/i/96) or the tapering of a feminine cadence (Hob. 42/i/77). Gradually he used longer signs for both *crescendo* and *diminuendo,* but they never exceed one measure; abbreviations or the words themselves appear where the effect is longer. Clementi also used short hairpin signs in works written or revised after 1800. In his music, as in Beethoven's right from Op. 1, these signs may mark dynamic shading in considerable detail, sometimes for only two, three, or four notes. Mozart, on the other hand, seems not to have used the hairpin signs in his piano music,[45] although he did in some of his operas[46] and music for small ensemble (e.g., Serenade for Winds K. 361/iii/42–44; v/119, 121; String Quartet K. 387/i/57–58).

In the piano music of Haydn, Mozart, and Clementi, the effects of *crescendo* and *diminuendo,* however indicated, are of a relatively moderate scale. Even when a *crescendo* extends for three or four measures, the buildup does not embody the tremendous extension of power that typifies many of Beethoven's *crescendos.* Some tendency in that direction shows itself by the mid-1780s in Mozart's piano concertos and operas, two genres that reached new peaks of development in his hands. Obvious examples are the relentless climax (built in successive waves) in the Concerto in D minor K. 466/iii/14–63 and the *crescendo* at the end of the Overture to *The Marriage of Figaro.*

Mozart wrote *crescendo* much more often than *decrescendo* and *calando,* which he treated as synonyms (see "Evolution of *Calando . . .*" below[47]), perhaps relying to some extent on Koch's observation that a *forte* of full strength "usually moderates itself shortly."[48] However, he also relied on other signals. A *diminuendo* seems appropriate in Sonata K. 457/i/29–30, following a written *crescendo* to *forte.* Here the clues are the immediate melodic descent to a feminine cadence and a *piano* under the chord on beat 2 (m. 30). Thus the sequence *f, p* in conjunction with the notes themselves serves Mozart's purpose. I would also interpret the *f, p* sequence in m. 9 of this movement as a *diminuendo.*

Beyond such meager hints for the use of graduated change, we fall back on observing that designated *crescendos* are often associated with ascending passages, increasing tension, and climactic effects, as Mozart's directions in the Rondo K. 511 amply demonstrate. Conversely, *decrescendos* may be associated with descending passages, decreasing tension, and relaxation (e.g., Mozart, K. 284/iii/Var. 12/18–19; K. 310/ii/50),[49] although Mozart placed some of his few *decrescendo* indications exactly where it would otherwise be quite natural to build a *crescendo* or stay on a level (e.g., K. 281/ii/4–5, 62–63; K. 283/ii/7–8).

In addition to affording change between different dynamics, unmarked *crescendos* and *decrescendos* may also serve as nuances or dynamic inflections within long passages marked at a single dynamic level. However, in exercising this choice it is important to avoid superfluous dynamic variation that might displace a larger contrast or distract from the intended breadth of design. Such long passages appear frequently in Beethoven's works. In his Bagatelle Op. 119/2 there are two similar extended sections marked only *piano* at the start. The performer has three options: either maintain those sections at a relatively uniform tonal level until the succeeding *forte*, introduce more fluctuation of dynamics within a generally quiet framework while still providing a contrast at each *forte*, or build a gradual *crescendo* to the *forte*. The choice depends on the way the individual performer integrates the dynamics, form, and character of any piece among themselves and with a particular tempo. A faster tempo allows a leaner dynamic palette; a slower one may need more variation in color. In this Bagatelle the contrast among three registers seems to me to lessen the need for frequent fluctuation of dynamics.

This exploration of dynamic indications and usage brings us again to the opening topic of this chapter: the differences between dynamic levels on fortepiano and pianoforte. The far greater spread between soft and loud on today's instruments, along with the more ponderous quality of the *forte*, can easily overwhelm Classic music with change that seems to me too violent. Besides exaggerated *fortes* there is also the danger of *crescendos* that grow too quickly and too far. I believe that the degree of contrast and, in graduated dynamics, the rate of change, should be scaled to the character and degree of detail of any piece. Thus Mozart's passionate Adagio K. 540 would call for a greater spread of sound and stronger contrast than his more restrained Adagio from the Sonata K. 280. Yet even K. 540 can be turned from a masterpiece of Classic sensitivity to a caricature of Romantic indulgence if it is played with all the resources of a modern instrument.

Here, not halfway through this chapter and virtually at the outset of our study, it becomes apparent that suggestions or advice sometimes reduce to the use of good judgment and musicality within the framework of accepted Classic practices, as best they can be discerned and described. For many performance practice questions there is no single answer; a writer can do no more than suggest the possibilities. It is an inherent aspect of performance practices that in order to work successfully with the flexibility available, performers should strive to develop the "good taste" that is so often mentioned in eighteenth-century writing.

REPEATS

In certain circumstances repeats may suggest a change in dynamic intensity or a variation of a dynamic scheme. Repeats of the exposition and of the development and recapitulation in sonata-allegro form, and inner repeats in the minuet or scherzo *da capo* are of especial importance in Classic performance practices.

Repeats in Sonata-Allegro Form

In the main, writers of the early Classic and Classic periods offer no options in following notated repeat signs. According to Quantz, "If there are two dots on each side of a double bar. . . , they signify that the piece consists of two parts, and that each part must be played twice."[50] Türk, Koch, and Hummel all agreed with Quantz.[51] Clementi departed, with this observation: The DOTTED bars [repeat signs] denote the repeat of the foregoing, and following strain. N.B. The second part of a piece, if VERY LONG, is seldom repeated; notwithstanding the DOTS."[52]

André Grétry's objection to the repeats in sonata-allegro form, as stated in 1797, suggests that they were often played:

> I see almost all instrumental music chained to worn-out forms that are repeated for us without end. . . . Hüllmandel, one of the most perfect composers of this type [of music], was . . . the first to connect the two parts of his sonatas so that they do not repeat slavishly. . . . A sonata is a discourse. What would we think of a man who, cutting his discourse in two, repeated each half?[53]

Indeed, Nicolas Joseph Hüllmandel and Antonio Sacchini were among the early composers who omitted the internal repeat signs in a few such movements.[54] Nevertheless, Haydn and Mozart used the double repeat signs in all their opening sonata-allegro movements for keyboard except Hob. 52 and K. 576 respectively; in these two late works only the expositions are repeated. Clementi omitted the second repeat in Op. 9/3/iii, which he published in London ca. 1790–1795?.[55] In his autograph revision of Op. 13/6/iii, he put a repeat sign at the beginning of the development section (perhaps out of habit?) but none at the end of the movement, which is marked *Fine.*[56] The length and power of the second part of this movement convince me that Clementi's N.B. applies here. Of course, in reaching such a decision, a performer needs to consider its effect on the listener's perception of the entire form and of the relationships of the parts to each other.

Beethoven indicated repeats judiciously from the start. In his piano sonatas from Op. 2 on, only nine movements in sonata-allegro form contain repeat signs for the second part. The first movement without one is Op. 2/3/i. Here, presumably, Beethoven must have felt that the extensive coda, which is only about 20 percent shorter than the development section, would have made a repeat anticlimactic. From Op. 57 on, many of the movements have no repeats, although, interestingly, in Op. 57/iii only the development and recapitulation repeat (before the coda). Beethoven returned to repeats for the expositions of Opp. 106/i and 111/i.

An important letter from his brother, Carl, to Breitkopf & Härtel on 12 February 1805 contains Beethoven's request that the exposition of the first movement of the "Eroica" Symphony be repeated. "Before he had heard the music" Beethoven had believed that the symphony "would be too long if the first part were repeated; but after more frequent performance he found that it was actually detrimental" not to have that repeat.[57] Beethoven's thoughtfulness regarding repeats is observed as late as the String Quartet Op. 135, in which, surprisingly, his note at the end of the final movement, "Si ripete la seconda parte al suo piacere" (Repeat the second part if you wish), leaves the choice to the performer. In the face of this evidence, casual disregard of Beethoven's repeats would seem an affront to his formal designs. (See also p. 397.)

Inner Repeats in the Minuet or Scherzo *da Capo*

Recent research by Max Rudolf indicates that the omission of the repeats within the *da capo* of a Classic minuet or scherzo lacks any foundation in sources of the period and up to 1850.[58] Rather, the few relevant comments found suggest that it was the general custom to include the internal repeats the second time around unless otherwise specified. Johann Mattheson confirmed the custom in 1739.[59] Türk added an explicit direction in the second edition of his Klavierschule:

> A sort of repeat sign is also the *Da Capo*. . . . After the Trio of a Minuet we usually find the words *Minuetto da Capo,* or abbreviated, *Min. D.C.* . . . This indicates that the Minuet is to be played from the beginning, that is with the prescribed repeats, consequently like the first time, unless *ma senza replica* (but without repeat) is explicitly added.[60]

Koch, Hummel, and Czerny all supported this view.[61]

Composers made selective use of *senza replica* or similar instructions when they wished to avert an unwanted repetition. And again we see evidence of this from Beethoven's early years. In his Piano Trio Op. 1/1, the end of the Trio bears the marking "Scherzo d.C. Senza repetizione e poi la Coda." When Beethoven changed his mind about a repeat in the Scherzo of the String Quartet Op. 74 after the manuscript had gone to the publisher, he indicated the deletion of a repeat sign in two letters, and in another he wrote that he would send a special copy of the first violin part "so that there may be no misunderstanding."[62]

The most obvious intersection of inner repeats and dynamic schemes comes at this point. There is evidence that the inner repeats of a minuet or scherzo (and its trio) were sometimes played with dynamics that differed, at least in part, from those of the preceding statement, as was also true of Baroque practice. In the fifth movement of his Divertimento for String Trio K. 563, Mozart requested that for the first *da Capo* of the Menuetto each section was to be played with its written dynamics, then repeated softly ("Menuetto D.C. la replica piano").[63] However, the movement goes on to Trio II and a "da Capo senza replica," so that the Menuetto ends at its original *forte* (before the Coda).

Czerny left a general direction regarding dynamics in *da capo* repeats:

> On the repetition or Da Capo of a Scherzo after the Trio, the first part of it when played for the second time, and the following second part when played the first time, must be performed throughout *pp,* and almost without any emphasis.[64]

Few would want to use this formula with every *da capo,* to say the least; but the passage indicates observance of the internal repeats, a change of dynamics at least some of the time, and an inference that the movement does not end softly.

We do not know how often the dynamics were varied in the observance of *da capo* repeats during the Classic period; undoubtedly this matter was at the performer's discretion. But the evidence cited suggests that at least for some movements (Czerny mentioned scherzos; did he mean to include minuets?) a bright sound at the end was desirable. This little information is applicable to movements that have dynamic directions but is more important to those that do not, such as the minuets from Haydn's early sonatas. In Hob. 12, for example, one dynamic scheme for the *da capo* would be first section *forte* followed by a softer repeat; second section, mm. 11–16 *mezzo-piano,* followed by a *forte* return of A; a repeat of the same dynamics or with mm. 11–16 played *piano.*

Sources for the minuets in Haydn's keyboard sonatas often have varying bass lines in the last measure of each section. In some there may be a dotted half note; in others there may be the typical quarter note descent of 1–5–1. These differences are carried over into urtext editions. For example, compare the Menuet of Hob. 12 in *JHW* and HSU. It may be that the three-note bass was typically used for continuity but that at the end of the *da capo,* and perhaps after the repetition before the trio, the first bass note was held for the measure.[65] Such a hold was sometimes suggested by a *fermata* over the first of the three quarter notes.

EVOLUTION OF *CALANDO* AND RELATED TERMS

Origin; Use by Haydn and Mozart

Present-day understanding of the term *calando* in music of the Classic period is curiously uncertain. Many musicians would have it mean becoming both softer and slower; some would have it just becoming softer in some situations, softer and slower in others; a few would limit it to increasing softness only. These differences may exist because composers themselves used the term differently or because we have inherited a changed, nineteenth-century use of the term, or for both reasons. The following investigation of theoretical and musical sources will attempt to determine when and to what degree *calando* acquired a tempo connotation and will help to develop a rationale for making stylistically appropriate choices.[66]

Calando, along with other gerund forms such as *mancando, morendo, perdendo,* and *smorzando,* came into use during the latter part of the eighteenth century.[67] According to Türk and others, they were originally synonymous with *decrescendo* (*abnehmend*) and diminishing (*verringernd*),[68] although Türk added (and Koch agreed) that *diluendo, morendo, perdendo,* and *smorzando* in particular signified "a complete disappearance" of the tone.[69]

In Italian *calando* means diminishing or descending, from the verb *calare,* to diminish, decrease, decay, go down, descend. The many illustrative phrases in Italian-English and Italian-French dictionaries of 1787 and 1772 respectively show the linguistic association of *calare* primarily with decreasing amount (e.g., of price), descending direction or place, and weakening.[70] There is no allusion to speed. On the other hand, the definitions of *rallentare* and *ritardare* in the same dictionaries show unequivocally a primary relationship to speed and time. Milchmeyer's definitions of terms in his little-known but important *Die wahre Art das Pianoforte zu spielen* of 1797, include "A" after those concerned with expression (*Ausdruck*), "B" after those concerned with tempo (*Bewegung*), or both where appropriate. For *calando* he wrote, "with diminishing strength of the tone, A."[71]

On the basis of the musical contexts in which the word appears and on the additional contemporary evidence, my judgment is that Haydn and Mozart intended *calando* to indicate *decrescendo,* with no inherent connotation of tempo relaxation. Through his association with Italian musicians, Mozart became familiar with idiomatic Italian and would have known the vernacular meaning of the word. Secondly, Haydn and Mozart seldom indicated tempo flexibility in their keyboard music; on the whole, obvious flexibility seems to have been inimical to their styles. (See "Ritardando and Accelerando" in chap. 10.) Their few unequivocal indications for slowing down are often followed by *a tempo,* as in Mozart's Concerto K. 415/ii/51 and in Haydn's Sonatas Hob. 44/i/68–70 and Hob. 50/iii/68–71 (*JHW,* HE; 92–94 in HSU). *Calando,* on the other hand, is very rarely followed by an authentic *a tempo* in Classic music,[72] although as we shall see below, that fact in itself does not preclude tempo relaxation. Thirdly and most tellingly, once Mozart began to use *calando* in works with piano, an early example of which occurs in the Sonata for Piano and Violin K. 306 (comp. 1778; Fig. 3.4), *decrescendo* and *diminuendo* rarely appear in his holographs and first editions.[73] He must have considered *calando* a substitute for those terms. It was included as such on p. 70 above when the infrequency of their use was mentioned.

Türk's description of passages in which some discretionary tempo relaxation may be appropriate contains an early clue to the way *calando eventually* acquired the implication of tempo slackening:

> In the approach to certain fermatas . . . one takes the movement a bit slower, little by little. . . . The passages toward the end of a composition (or section [of

a composition]) that are marked *diminuendo, diluendo, smorzando,* and the like, may also be played with a little lingering [*verweilend*].[74]

The words "and the like" would have included *calando,* for Türk earlier grouped that term with the three just cited, plus *decrescendo, mancando, morendo,* and *perdendo,* as those that indicate a gradual decrease in the sound.[75] Since *calando* occurs most often near the ends of pieces or sections, and since some of those sections also end with a *fermata,* the connotation of tempo relaxation may have been acquired by association.[76] However, the "little lingering" was not an automatic assumption. Even a barely perceptible relaxation of the tempo in the works of Haydn and Mozart should be considered carefully because these composers indicated *ritardando* or *rallentando* so infrequently.

The *calando* in Figure 3.4 is near the end of a long written-out "Cadenza" for both instruments and is preceded by an extended chain of trills. The *crescendo* increases the tension even before the melody begins to move upward. Starting on the downside of the peak, *calando* provides a balancing *decrescendo* as the line relaxes into *unadorned* half notes that function as a written-out *ritard.* Any further perceptible delay would, in my opinion, cause the approach to the *fermata* to drag.

Haydn's *calando* in his Sonata Hob. 41/i/95–96 is used similarly. It appears immediately after the melodic peak of the retransition[77] and a measure and a half before a *fermata* at the end of the development. Harmonic movement

Fig. 3.4. Mozart, Sonata for Piano and Violin K. 306/iii (OE Sieber), mm. 221–230.

*This edition was published only in parts.

and textural activity are decelerated earlier. Coincidental with the peak of the melody and the *calando,* the melodic rhythm slows from eighth-note triplets to duplets and finally to quarter notes, and the line descends more than an octave from the top note of Haydn's keyboard. *Calando* directs the player to let the sound diminish to a notated *p* at the *fermata.* Because of Haydn's written-out *ritard,* the rhythmic stretching that may precede a *fermata* would—if applied—be completely independent of the *calando.* I might lengthen only the last two or three notes slightly.

Calando in the fourth measure from the end of Mozart's Rondo K. 485 also seems too early to signify the concluding gesture of "a little holding back." It stands as a *decrescendo* between *p* and *pp,* as it often does in Beethoven's early works. In the tempestuous first movement of Mozart's Sonata K. 310, *calando* occurs in the exposition (m. 14) and in the recapitulation during a brief feint toward a more lyrical mood. Realized as a *diminuendo* to the following *piano* (m. 15), *calando* heightens the momentary change, but any perceptible relaxation of tempo loses the tautness of the movement and seems to me an ill-placed indulgence.

Calando nel tempo in Mozart's Sonata for Piano and Violin K. 376 (comp. 1781) is in my opinion a singular exception in his usage (Fig. 3.5). Its translation is "decreasing in respect to the tempo." If Mozart had normally attributed this tempo meaning to *calando* he would not have had to specify it here. Certainly the tempo specification was not added in order to exclude a *decrescendo,* since that is the likely dynamic—written or not—between an assumed *crescendo* to the *fermata,* which caps a climactic dominant preparation for the return of the opening section, and a relatively quiet opening theme (based on our discussion pertaining to missing dynamics). Why didn't Mozart use *rallentando?* He seems to have reserved that term for somewhat longer stretches, very obviously so in another sonata of the same year, K. 379/i.[78] I submit that he decided to try *calando nel tempo* for this short, subtle slowing down in the simplest kind of "lead-in" (*Eingang*).[79]

In 1789, Mozart undertook a revision of Handel's *Messiah.* Eight times in the 56–measure aria "Er weidet seine Herde" (He shall feed his flock) he added the following sequence of indications: *cresc., f, calando, p,* which occupies only

Fig. 3.5. Mozart, Sonata for Piano and Violin K. 376/ii (Aut. and OE Artaria), mm. 53–55.

*"Tempo Primo" appears only in OE.

one and a half measures in the 12/8 meter (*NMA*).[80] In the context of this sicilienne-like aria there can be no question that *calando* is solely a synonym for *decrescendo*. Since each *calando* is either in mid-phrase or at the end of a short phrase segment that moves on immediately to the next, even a slight tempo relaxation at each or any of them would be out of character for a stylish eighteenth-century performance; it would disrupt its flow and disfigure the whole.

Clementi's Definition and Usage

Definitions of *calando* that embrace tempo appeared in London at the turn of the century. According to Clementi, *calando* (and *mancando*[81]) could mean "diminishing by degrees the sound, or slackening almost imperceptibly the time; or both."[82] Curiously, Thomas Busby omitted any reference to dynamics in his definition of about 1801: "a term signifying that the time of the passage ... is to be gradually diminished."[83] J. B. Cramer followed the lead of his teacher Clementi;[84] W. S. Stevens and an anonymous writer in the *Harmonicon* echoed Busby.[85] The publication in 1802 of Clementi's *Introduction to the Art of Playing on the Piano Forte* in German and in French brought his interpretation of *calando* to the Continent. Pleyel's French translation of Clementi's definition was exact.[86] Hoffmeister's German translation, from which most later German editions descended, omitted the significant words "almost imperceptibly" from "slackening ... the time."[87]

Clementi indicated *calando* primarily in his compositions of the late 1780s and 1790. Each of his interpretations finds appropriate application; although inevitably, with such a broad definition, there is room for ambiguity of intention and difference of interpretation. The suggestions for performance of Figures 3.6 to 3.8 represent my interpretations at the time of writing, based on available contemporary evidence.

The approach to the end of the section in Figure 3.6 carries thematic activity and rhythmic momentum to the very last notes. Although Türk favored slowing the movement before "certain fermatas" (which remained unclarified), the momentum here persuades me to interpret *calando* as just a *decrescendo,* allowing the ensuing pause to remain a surprise. (See chap. 10, p. 371.) In Figure 3.7 *calando* might be interpreted as just a tempo slackening if the preceding *decrescendo* has been carried out sufficiently. Yet some may see a reiteration of the *decrescendo* as well. *Calando* in Figure 3.8, approaching the recapitu-

Fig. 3.6. Clementi, Sonata Op. 23/1/ii (OE Longman and Broderip), mm. 129–132.

Fig. 3.7. Clementi, Sonata Op. 24/2/ii (*OC* Breitkopf & Härtel, Vol. VI), mm. 60–65.

Fig. 3.8. Clementi, Sonata Op. 25/4/i (OE Dale), mm. 81–83.

lation and with no lengthening of the note values, suggests both a *diminuendo* to *espressivo* and a subtle tempo slackening. The slight relaxation of tempo in Figures 3.7 and 3.8 is in keeping with Classic usage, for in addition to his comments already cited, Türk advised that some slowing of the tempo was appropriate in transitional approaches to important sections of a piece (p. 370 below).[88] Clementi's application of tempo slackening to *calando* about a decade before it was described in a written source exemplifies the familiar idea that theory or written descriptions often trailed practice by a decade or more.

When Clementi wanted both a *diminuendo* and a more obvious slowing down, he sometimes used *calando e rallentando,* as in his Sonata Op. 23/2/iii/38 (OE, Longman & Broderip). This usage points to an important difference in meaning between *ritard* and *rallentando* on the one hand and *calando*—when it has a tempo implication—on the other, for the three words were apparently not synonymous at this time. Türk's "a little lingering" at the end of a piece or section "marked diminuendo" and Clementi's "slackening almost imperceptibly the time" for *calando* indicate only slight nuances of tempo. But Clementi's definition of *rallentando* and *ritardando,* typical of the period, is simply "gradually slackening the time."[89] Thus, *calando* would have implied only a very subtle relaxation or stretching, whereas *ritard* and *rallentando* allowed more noticeable tempo modification. Since Clementi did not indicate *calando* in works composed after 1790, and since *rallentando* occurs frequently in his later dramatic sonatas, it would seem that in such works he chose the more pronounced effect.

According to this distinction, a *ritard* or *rallentando* might bend the flow of music in a way that a *calando* would not. Correspondingly, after *ritard* or *rallentando* Clementi wrote *a tempo* more than 60 percent of the time (according to some first editions and the *OC*); Haydn and Mozart wrote it some of the time, and Beethoven (after Op. 7) did so quite regularly. *Calando* is rarely followed by an authentic *a tempo,* although Dussek indicated just that in the Finale of his Sonata Op. 64, "Le Retour à Paris," published in 1807[90] (OE, Pleyel, mm. 38–39). Dussek included *calando* in his definition of *diminuendo,* which reads "gradual fall of the sound."[91] His entries for both *perdendosi* and *rallentando* read "see *calando,*"[92] for which, unfortunately, there is no separate listing (perhaps this was an engraver's lapse).

Use of *Calando* by Beethoven, Hummel, and Czerny

Beethoven's *calandos* are often interpreted as diminishing both the sound and the movement. However, a chronological appraisal rejects that assumption. There is some evidence that Beethoven may have changed his intention for the term during the approximately eight years in which he used it in his piano music. Yet, because *calando* so often appears where another factor could appropriately induce tempo slackening, it seems questionable to conclude absolutely that the term had a tempo connotation for Beethoven. In some instances evaluation requires sensitive consideration of many elements in the musical framework.

There is ample evidence in the Piano Trios Op. 1 and the Sonatas Op. 2/2 and 3 that at the time of their composition, 1794–1795, Beethoven's *calando* referred solely to dynamics. In Op. 1/3/iv/135, near the end of the exposition, *calando* only in the piano part cannot possibly indicate anything more than a *diminuendo* to the written *pp.* The simultaneous occurrences of *calando* and *rallentando,* reminiscent of Clementi, in Beethoven's Op. 1/2/iv/132–137 and Op. 10/1/iii/106–111 (comp. ?1795–1797), also demonstrate unambiguously the use of *calando* in reference to dynamics alone. But is it possible to make a five-measure (or in the second ending, a seven-measure) *diminuendo* in chordal writing when all the parts start at *pianissimo,* as they do there in the Trio? That *calando* directs the performer to become and to remain as soft as possible. This additional implication, which reappears later in Beethoven's music, is a further manifestation of his interest in soft sounds, discussed earlier. Similarly, *calando* near the end of the second movement of the Quintet for Piano and Woodwinds Op. 16 reinforces the preceding *decrescendo,* for *calando* and *rallentando* appear simultaneously (Fig. 3.9).

Readers looking at the last eight measures of the Finale of Op. 1/2 in *BGA,* in the Peters edition, or in some other editions currently used, would undoubtedly challenge the position that in these early works *calando* was just a dynamic indication. However, the misleading *a tempo* that follows *calando* in

Fig. 3.9. Beethoven, Quintet for Woodwinds and Piano Op. 16/ii (OE Mollo), mm. 108–112.

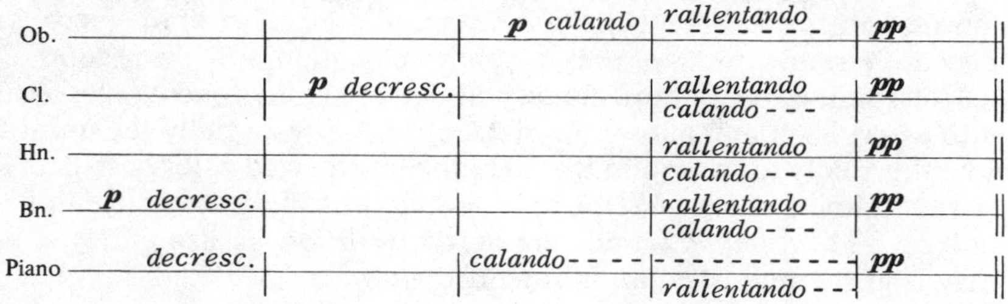

those editions was not in the primary source for this Trio, the first edition published by Artaria in 1795, or in numerous later editions to about the 1850s.[93] This *a tempo,* which surfaced—possibly for the first time—in the earliest issue of the *BGA,* is a spurious editorial accretion of the mid-nineteenth century that has created a false impression of Beethoven's intention.[94]

Beethoven placed *calando* after *pp* in other contexts where it also seems best realized as just a dynamic sign. These include its first occurrence in the sonatas, concluding the retransition of Op. 2/2/i. In part because of that *pp,* but also because this passage approaches a *fermata* and immediately precedes the recapitulation, some musicians attribute a tempo connotation to the *calando,* slowing the time between the *portato* eighth notes. Others observe that those downbeat eighth notes themselves constitute a written-out *ritard* after the preceding continuous motion and caution that the slur over the whole creates a single unit that should not be disturbed.[95] *Calando* here means as soft as possible. I prefer the passage with only an imperceptible stretching just to reach for the F-sharp in m. 223. The otherwise strict tempo places the pause for the *fermata* in sharper relief; the whole is enhanced by a firm (although unmarked) *a tempo* start for the impetuous A theme.

Beethoven's Rondo Op. 51/1, composed in ?1796–1797, contains a *calando* in a carefully prepared transition to a deceptive return of the main theme (Fig. 3.10). The Minore immediately preceding is impassioned, almost brusque, with sixteenth-note motion, full sound, and frequent syncopated accents. The staccato eighth notes in m. 72 slow the motion; the pairs of slurred notes that begin to appear in m. 73 smooth the surface. *Calando* suggests a *diminuendo* as the transition moves away from the insistent C's of the expected key toward the more lyrical *piano* refrain. But there is some oblique evidence in the other transitional sections of the Rondo that Beethoven might have intended the *calando* here to include a slight stretching of the beat, perhaps beginning in the second half of m. 74.

The less dramatic transitions to the two restatements of the theme in the tonic are both marked *decresc.* (mm. 42 and 91), which Beethoven could have used in mm. 73–75 if that was all he wanted. Further, the second deceptive return, in m. 106, is preceded by "ritar ⌢ dando ⌢," an indication for a spacious spreading out that is assumed to be over when the theme enters.

Clearly, Beethoven was focusing more attention on the two deceptive entries than on the tonic restatements. It fits the cumulative effect of the piece for the first deceptive return to have only a subtle relaxation and the second a purposeful retardation. A rhythmic nuance in mm. 74 and 75 encourages a calmer mood to assert itself and allows the sixteenth notes, especially the quintuplet, to lead unhurriedly to the rondo theme in the unexpected color of A-flat. Thus, Beethoven's choice of *calando* for m. 73 could hint of some change in his use of that term. (The *a tempo* found here in some editions is also purely editorial and may lead the pianist to an unintended *ritard*.)

Yet, another consideration reminds us of the complexities involved in the interpretation of *calando*. Beethoven seldom hyphenated the word *decrescendo*;[96] more often he put *calando* in that prominent role of emphasizing a longer, sustained softening, as in Opp. 1, 2, and 10. (From Op. 57 on he used *diminuendo*.) That alone could explain the *calando* in Figure 3.10; and, according to Türk (and others), the reentry of a main theme can, without any instruction, be preceded by some yielding of the tempo. Further, in several works whose composition overlaps Op. 51/1, the Sonata for Violoncello and Piano Op. 5/1/ii (comp. 1796), the String Trios Op. 9/1/iii and 9/2/iii (comp. 1797–1798), and Op. 10/1/iii (already mentioned), I judge *calando* to mean only *diminuendo*. (In Op. 9/1/iii, for example, any tempo nuance with the first two *calandos* lessens the surprise of the silence after the viola's question.)

The first *calando* in Op. 33/6 (Fig. 3.11), composed in 1801–1802, puts the question squarely on the line. Although *calando* has followed *pianissimo* or

Fig. 3.10. Beethoven, Rondo Op. 51/1 (OE Artaria), mm. 72–76.

*Artaria's turn signs, typically inverted (∽) in their Classic period publications, are corrected in this volume.

Fig. 3.11. Beethoven, Bagatelle Op. 33/6, (Aut.),[97] mm. 29–30.

decrescendo as reinforcement in several works, their simultaneous appearance is new. Is *calando* a second, perhaps anxious indication to diminish the tone to *pianissimo,* or does it represent a tempo nuance? Since the *fermata* itself can invite rhythmic stretching, we cannot prove either meaning for *calando* even here. A situation directly comparable to that in Figure 3.9 exists in the Piano Trio Op. 38/vi/132–135, an arrangement of the Septet Op. 20 that Beethoven made in ?1803.[98]

Significantly, in both the Piano Concerto No. 3, Op. 37/iii/23 (solo completed in 1804) and the "Kreutzer" Sonata Op. 47/iii/284 (comp. 1802–1803) *calando* appears with *ritardando,* as it had in Opp. 1 and 10 with *rallentando.* In the piano part of Op. 47, *decresc.* appears simultaneously, but dashes following the *calando* maintain its continuity for six measures. After these works Beethoven no longer used *calando.* Presumably he felt it was too ambiguous. A decade later, in 1813, he expressed his irritation at the confusion over the meaning of *andantino* (see "Diminutive Terms; *Andante,* and *Andantino*" in chap. 9).

In Hummel's works the tempo significance of *calando* is unequivocal. *Calando, in tempo* appears in both his Piano Sonata Op. 81 published in 1819 (e.g., i/21–22, 60–62) and his popular Piano Concerto Op. 85 published ca. 1821 (e.g., i/306–308—in my judgment just for tempo; iii/119–121). *Calando* also appears solely as a dynamic indication in those compositions. Surprisingly, in his extensive piano method of 1828, one of the most valued sources for the performance practices of late Viennese Classicism, Hummel mentioned *calando* only as a synonym for *diminuendo,* but attributed diminution in both sound and speed to *morendo.*[99] This is a classic example of a textbook description that lacks completeness.

According to Max Rudolf, nineteenth-century Italian composers retained the original linguistic meaning of *calando,* while the Germans used the dual meaning.[100] By 1839, when Czerny's great *Piano Forte School* appeared, the gerund forms that Türk and others had regarded as indications for *diminuendo* had all acquired tempo connotations. No doubt this trend was strengthened by the increasing role of tempo flexibility in the developing Romantic style. Czerny treated *calando* and *smorzando* together: "more and more composed. Refer chiefly to the gradual decrease of power or tone; but also imply a holding back in the time or movement."[101] Further on he suggested that that meant "a slight holding back,"[102] corroborating the distinction made earlier here. *Morendo* also meant that the passage should become gradually softer and slower,[103] while *perdendo* was a direction for "holding back in time"[104] and *mancando* was defined as "failing, losing oneself, &c, &c."[105]

QUALITATIVE (DYNAMIC) ACCENTS

Indications for Accents

The singling out of one note or chord for emphasis appeared increasingly, along with graduated dynamics, as the fortepiano became the preferred keyboard instrument. Indications for such qualitative or dynamic accents during the Classic period were mainly *sf, fz, fp, sfp,* and *ffp;* sometimes just *f* (Figs. 3.12, 3.13); occasionally *mfp,* the accent sign itself >, or the stroke ǀ or synonymous slender wedge ǀ (Figs. 3.14, 3.15), which were also staccato signs.[106]

That the *f*'s in Figure 3.13 were probably intended as *sf* accents is inferred from the *forte* established in m. 121 and reiterated in m. 125. Depending on the context, notes carrying accent wedges may also be detached to some degree,

Fig. 3.12. Haydn, Sonata Hob. 20/i (Aut. fragment), mm. 13–14.

*Natural from OE Artaria.

Fig. 3.13. Beethoven, Sonata Op. 13/i (OE Hoffmeister), mm. 129–132.

Fig. 3.14. Mozart, Duet Sonata K. 521/i (Aut.), mm. 19–22.

Fig. 3.15. Beethoven, Sonata Op. 2/3/i (OE Artaria), mm. 69–73.

as in Figure 3.15. Relative to that figure, I should mention that the original Artaria edition of 1796 used dots for all the staccatos in this movement and accent wedges only for mm. 69–72 and the analogous measures in the recapitulation. The *BNA* (ed. Hans Schmidt, 1971), which uses only dots for staccatos, preserves the same distinction; but *HE* (ed. Bertha A. Wallner, 1952), which also uses only dots for staccatos, has dots here too. In Beethoven's Sonata for Violin and Piano Op. 23/ii/110, the appearance of a wedge on the *first* note under each slur in the *BNA* is further unequivocal evidence of that sign as an accent. Accent strokes in a well-known sonata by Haydn occur at Hob. 35/i/34–35 (*HSU, JHW*).

The sign > was used only occasionally before 1800. Haydn may have become familiar with it in London. Relatively early occurrences are found in his Variations in F minor, Hob. XVII/6, composed in 1793, and in his late Sonatas Hob. 52 and 51 (e.g., ii/31–32, 67–68), composed in 1794 and ?ca. 1794–1795 respectively. In 1789 Türk had suggested the sign ∧ for accents, adding that he had already used it in his "easy and short sonatas."[107] Wolf quickly adopted Türk's sign in the third edition of his *Unterricht,* also published in 1789. He gave Türk credit for its invention but qualified its use for "a gentle accent."[108] Evidently the sign > was still not widely used in some parts of central Europe by 1804, when Johann Friedrich Schubert also adopted Türk's ∧ to fill that need.[109]

Classic accents function in all degrees of contrast, from a strong, brusque sound in a quiet context (e.g., Mozart's *f*'s in K. 332/i/6off. and Beethoven's *sf*'s in Op. 27/1/i/45ff.) or occasionally even an explosive effect (Beethoven's Op. 27/2/iii/2, 4, etc.) to a mild expressive stress. They are not necessarily very strong or loud, but depend for their interpretation on the known usage of each composer as well as on the dynamic level and mood of their surroundings. The recurring use of *fp* through the gentle middle movement of Mozart's Sonata K. 309 is an invitation merely to highlight the goal of that melodic segment (Fig. 3.16). The *fp* indications in K. 281/iii/55–59 ask for only slightly more expressive attention than the first note under those two-note slurs would normally receive; however, the absolute level of the *fp*'s increases with the natural *crescendo* in the passage.

The interpretation of *fp* as an absolute rather than a relative dynamic—*forte* followed immediately by *piano* on a single note or chord[110]—seems ap-

Fig. 3.16. Mozart, Sonata K. 309/ii (*NMA*), mm. 1–2.

propriate to me quite frequently in Beethoven's piano music, yet it is not indigenous to the modern piano, with its admirable sustaining power. The true home of this *fp* (along with *sfp* and *ffp*) is in music for stringed and wind instruments, for which Haydn requested that "the first attack of the *forte* be of the shortest duration, in such a way that the *forte* seems to disappear almost immediately."[111]

The incisive attack and rapid decay of sound on the fortepiano also produce an *fp*. On that instrument the opening chord of Beethoven's *Sonate Pathétique* Op. 13 collapses suddenly to a *piano,* creating a dramatic change. On a pianoforte that effect can merely be suggested by depressing the damper pedal as or after the chord is played, releasing the keys, and then fluttering (partially releasing and depressing) the pedal; this technique causes an unexpected decrease in dynamic level without losing the sound. *Sforzandos* and other strong accents also have a different expressive quality on a fortepiano than they do on a pianoforte, where in some contexts their effect may resemble a *forte* or a *fortissimo.* On a fortepiano the *sforzando* can produce more bite.

Composers' Uses of Accent Indications

Composers differed in their choice of accent indications, just as they did in their notation of dynamics generally. The more limited the variety of those indications, the greater the responsibility of the interpreter.

Haydn usually used *fz,* sometimes *f* (Fig. 3.12). He used the accent sign only in a few late works, including those mentioned above. Occasionally, as in Hob. 51/ii and the Piano Trio Hob. XV/29/iii, Haydn wrote a series of *fz* indications to shift the bar line or alter the meter temporarily.

An extreme example of the use of *f* as an accent indication appears in the sole source for Haydn's five Sonatas Hob. 35–39,[112] in which all accents are shown by *f* or, occasionally, *ff.* Where interpretation as an accent seems more appropriate than as a dynamic level, some editors, such as Georg Feder in the *JHW* and the Henle edition, use *f[z];* some, such as Christa Landon in the HSU, use *fz* where they are absolutely convinced and *f(z)* where there may be a choice; and others, such as Carl A. Martienssen in the Peters edition, use only *fz.* Further variability in modern editions occurs at places such as Hob. 35/i/43, where Artaria's first edition has *ff.* Feder retained that, but Landon interpreted it as *fz* and Martienssen as *ffz.* Since it is impossible to read a composer's mind, it is advisable for an editor to differentiate the interpretation of a source from the source itself by typographical means.

Clementi used *fz* or *sf* for most accents. They are abbreviations of *forzando* or *forzato* and *sforzando* or *sforzato* respectively, which mean forcing in the gerund form and forced in the past participle. Clementi considered *fz* and *sf* equivalent and interchangeable both in theory, as stated in his *Introduction to the Art of Playing on the Pianoforte,*[113] and in practice, as can be seen by comparing either the first edition of his Sonata Op. 7/3, published by Artaria, with his own edition published later in London, or his two versions of the

Sonata Op. 13/6 (see chap. 2, n. 11). In Clementi's very early works *f* sometimes serves as an accent; *fp* and, later, the accent sign appear occasionally. The sign occurs in Volume VI of the *Oeuvres complettes,* published in 1804 (e.g., Sonata Op. 9/2/iii/82–84, 86–88). This volume is the only one of that set whose text is considered authentic, since Clementi revised the contents specifically for its publication.[114] An accent sign also appears in the Sonata Op. 50/1/i/44 (OE, Clementi) under the first of a pair of slurred eighth notes that crosses a bar line. Probably to assure the subsequent tapering of the second note, which falls on the first beat of the measure, Clementi placed a *p* under it.

Mozart's more varied accent indications included *fp* and *sf,* followed by *sfp, f,* and sometimes the stroke or *mfp* (Duet Sonata K. 357/ii, Aut.), which suggests a weaker initial accent than *fp.* Beethoven used all the indications with the exception of *fz.* He also added *ffp* and *rinforzando,* the subtleties of which will be explored further on.

Sf is the most frequently used accent indication in the music of Beethoven. It appears in every dynamic context and is interpreted accordingly. He used the stroke and *f* as accents less frequently, the latter occasionally replacing *sf* in a *forte* setting (Fig. 3.13). Beethoven's *mfp* (in the sonatas only in Op. 49/ 1), *fp,* and *ffp* usually occur where an accent approximating the dynamic level of *mezzo-forte, forte,* or *fortissimo* followed immediately by *piano* is warranted. *Sfp* represents a relative accent followed by *piano.*

In Beethoven's music the accent sign has its own role: it occurs almost always in *piano* or *pianissimo* settings and often on syncopated notes. Op. 7/ i/166–167 and an analogous place in the coda illustrate this usage well, particularly since a similar figure that occurs in a *forte* context has *sf* accents (e.g., 127–131). *Sf* and > are also juxtaposed in Op. 2/1/iv/130–133, where the sign is on the thematic motive in the soprano and tenor, providing just enough emphasis to give the second beat prominence over the succeeding first beat, and *sf* is on longer, sustained bass notes. Clearly, for Beethoven *sf* was the stronger accent.

Another interesting juxtaposition of accents of differing strengths occurs between *ffp* and *sf* in Op. 2/2/i/203–215. The *ffp* functions as two absolute dynamic levels, an *ff* accent followed by a continuing *piano* sound. The *sf* is a relative accent, referring at first to the fairly quiet background set by *piano* in m. 199 and later to the louder background in m. 211.

Occasionally Beethoven used a short *diminuendo* hairpin to indicate an expressive emphasis followed by a return to the preceding dynamic level. In the opening measures of the Scherzo of the "Hammerklavier" Sonata Op. 106, pairs of small hairpin signs facing each other place the emphasis in the brief motive on the downbeat; in mm. 14–17 short *diminuendo* hairpins moved to the upbeat of the motive bring the emphasis with them. Contrasting downbeat and upbeat accentuations continue throughout the movement.

Not surprisingly, copyists and engravers could have confused the accent sign and the short hairpin in a composer's hand, or the engraved sign could

Fig. 3.17. Beethoven, Sonata Op. 31/3/iv, mm. 2–5. a. OE Nägeli, 1804. b. André, ca. 1809.

*_p_ from opening upbeat

be ambiguous. Paul Mies questions the nature of some signs in two important editions of Op. 31/3, for which the holograph is lost. In both the original edition by Nägeli and an edition "tres [*sic*] Correcte" published by Simrock at Beethoven's request, the signs between the staves at iii/9, 47, and 49, and at iv/3, 5, etc., are ambiguous (Fig. 3.17a). Both contexts are quiet but neither contains syncopation. It is possible that in both movements Beethoven intended small hairpin signs to call for accentuation that subsides back to the surrounding *piano*.[115] In André's reprint (pub. ca. 1809[116]) and in Haslinger's *Gesamtausgabe,* the signs are large enough and so positioned that the meaning understood by their engravers seems clear (Fig. 3.17b). *BNA* and HE have accent signs in those measures.

In rare instances Haydn may also have intended the small *diminuendo* hairpin under two notes to place an expressive accent. I believe this is the appropriate reading for Hob. 48/i/2, where the small hairpin suggests a weaker accent than *fz* or *f*. (Haydn had not yet begun to use the accent sign.) Whether his holographic sign in Hob. 51/ii/41–44 and 103–106 was a small accent (as in HSU) or a hairpin under two notes (as in *JHW*) is not clear, because "a rather unreliable manuscript copy served as the source for the first edition"[117] and the holograph is lost. In Breitkopf & Härtel's *Oeuvres complettes,* the second source for this sonata (the first edition is also by that firm), accent signs under single notes (e.g., ii/31–32) look exactly like small hairpins.

Schubert and, later, Brahms used the small hairpin as an accent-*diminuendo* sign fairly often (e.g., Schubert's Scherzo and Trio in A major D. 459, m. 2). Especially in Schubert's holographs it is sometimes difficult to distinguish that sign from an ordinary *diminuendo* hairpin.

Rinforzando

Rinforzando, rinforz, rinf, or *rf* represented two distinct expressive possibilities. One was a short, sometimes forceful *crescendo* over a few notes, usually two to four, as described by Clementi (Fig. 3.18);[118] the other was additional emphasis or accentuation on a single note or chord (Fig. 3.19) or on two or more notes (Fig. 3.20).[119] In Figure 3.19 the *rinforzando* occurs at the peak of a *crescendo* and wants a very full sound, while in Figure 3.20 it occurs in a *piano* setting and suggests a quiet emphasis on the first two legato octaves.

Curiously, most writers of the period described only one of the two meanings (as listed in nn. 118 and 119). A few, including Türk, used definitions brief and vague enough to encompass both: "*rf* or *rinf.—rinforzando, rinforzato, strengthened [verstärkt]*."[120]

In 1825 J. F. Danneley, a relatively unknown English writer, made a rather exacting distinction based on two different forms of the Italian word:

RINFORZANDO, strengthening of sound.
RINFORZATO, strengthened; it is thus abbreviated, R.F. and is placed over such notes as should be forcibly accented.[121]

Fig. 3.18. Clementi, Sonata Op. 13/6/ii (Aut. of composer's revised version, 1807 or 1808), mm. 17–18.

[Adagio patetico]

Fig. 3.19. Beethoven, Sonata Op. 14/1/i (OE Mollo), m. 74.

[Allegro]

Fig. 3.20. Beethoven, Sonata Op. 26/i (Aut.), Var. 2, mm. 18–19.

[Andante con variazioni]

Perhaps Danneley had *rinf.* in mind as an abbreviation for *rinforzando.* Yet there was unquestionably room for error in using these similar terms and abbreviations, whether or not composers made an effort to follow a distinction such as Danneley's. For example, in Beethoven's scores, and doubtless in those of other composers, engravers sometimes substituted *rf* or *rfz* for *rinf* or *rinforz* as well as for *sf,* hindering attempts at a fine distinction between these terms or their abbreviations.[122] (For a specific example, see Fig. 5.18 and chap. 5, n. 50.) In most situations the performer has to decide on the interpretation from the context rather than from the indication.

The two related uses of *rinforzando* existed side by side through the nineteenth century. Riemann's *Musik Lexikon* of 1882 gives definitions remarkably close to Danneley's but without the abbreviations. "*Rinforzando* (become stronger), designation for a strong crescendo; *rinforzato,* strengthened, is almost identical with *forte assai,* an energetic *forte.*"[123]

TYPES OF ACCENTUATION

The importance in Classic music of accentuation based on clearly understood principles is emphasized by the frequency with which it was discussed in contemporary books and other sources. Accentuation played a role in structural clarification—an inherent part of contemporary performance practice—as well as in expressivity. Significantly, in reporting on performances of works by Haydn, Mozart, and Beethoven in a letter from Vienna of 10 December 1808, J. F. Reichardt observed that Schuppanzigh "accents very correctly and meaningfully."[124] The weight of this remark can be appreciated by knowing Schuppanzigh's position. As a close musical friend of Beethoven and the first violinist most often associated with performance of the composer's quartets and symphonic music in Vienna, Schuppanzigh quite obviously represented a style of performance that was congenial to Beethoven's aural conception of his works. So important did Beethoven consider it to have Schuppanzigh lead the orchestra for the first performance of the Ninth Symphony, that he refused to have the concert in the Theater-an-der-Wien, where another violinist had that position.[125]

Accents were described and codified in various degrees of detail. Koch presented a clear introduction in his *Lexikon.* Just as certain syllables in speech are distinguished by special emphasis, particularly if the orator speaks with feeling, so must certain notes of a melody that embodies a well-defined feeling be executed in a telling way, he wrote. In music these accents arise "in part from an increased strength of the tone" (known variously as qualitative, dynamic, or stress accents) and "in part from a certain expressive lingering through which it appears that the accented note has been held an instant longer than its notation requires"[126] (known also as quantitative or agogic accents). ("Agogic Accentuation of Notes" is discussed in chap. 10.)

Koch recognized two basic categories of accents to which Reichardt's "correctly and meaningfully" relate closely: the "grammatical," and the "rhetorical" or "pathetic." Grammatical accents are those associated with expected metrical stress, from which they are more commonly called "metrical" accents. Koch compared them to the scansion of verse. They occur not only on the strong beat(s) of each meter but also on the first note of a group formed by division of the beat (Figs. 3.21a and b). Accents of the last kind were sometimes called group accents.

Tempo and note grouping could also affect the placement of grammatical accents, Koch continued. If the notes of Figure 3.21b appear in a slow tempo, and if they are "slurred together in pairs" (Koch did not mention the beaming), each pair receives a grammatical accent (Fig. 3.21c). In performance, grammatical accents are "scarcely noticeable," particularly "in passages of equal note values in lively movement."[127] Schulz showed *alla breve* meter subdivided into eighth notes with a hierarchy of stress on every other note, analogous to the accepted hierarchy of beats in 4/4 meter: strong, weak, secondary (less) strong, weak.[128] Türk also generalized, with no stipulations regarding context, that in "beat divisions" (*Taktglieder*) and smaller note values, the first, third, fifth, and seventh notes of duple figures and the first, fourth, seventh, and tenth of triple figures were regarded as "good" or strong (*gut*); the others were considered "bad" or weak (*schlecht*).[129]

Occasionally composers used beaming to indicate subtle aspects of grammatical accentuation. In Beethoven's Op. 22/iv, in 2/4 meter, the majority of 32d-note passages are beamed in half beats, calling for some degree of stress at the beginning of each beam, depending on its metrical placement. However, a few passages are beamed in groups of eight 32d notes, presumably indicating an even melisma throughout the beat with no interior emphasis. In m. 48 of the same movement Beethoven notated two triplets rather than a sextuplet, again presumably for accentual reasons. He made a similar distinction in beaming eighth-note triplets and sextuplets in Op. 31/1/iii. Other telling choices are the undivided beams that run through full measures of sixteenth notes in Op. 31/3/i/54–55 and 178–181 and the change in beaming—from 32d-note sextuplets to three 32d-note duplets (over a sixteenth-note triplet—that creates a hemiola at Op. 109/i/65. Examples of beaming across bar lines to alter the normal accentuation occur in Haydn's Hob. 50/i/26–27 and Beethoven's Op. 10/3/iv.

Fig. 3.21. Koch, *Lexikon.* a., b. cols. 49–50. c. cols. 51–52.

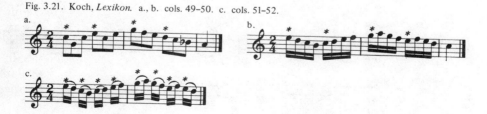

In contrast to the grammatical accents based on meter and note division are the rhetorical and pathetic accents (commonly termed "expressive") "through which the melody acquires its characteristic expression."[130] The two types are differentiated only by their strength, wrote Koch, the pathetic—seldom mentioned—being even more emphatic than the rhetorical. Expressive accents are more prominent than the grammatical, which are generally part of the background.

Expressive accents are very often not indicated, Koch continued. They can occur anywhere in the meter, depending on the composer's intended sense of the melody and the performer's taste. Notes that receive expressive accents in Classic music include those that are dissonant or that prepare dissonant intervals, those that are chromatic or syncopated, those distinguished by their length or by their high or low pitch,[131] and those that are first under a slur.[132] (See also "The Language of the Slur" in chap. 5.)

In addition to metrical and expressive accents, Schulz[133] and Türk recognized another group of accents that mark melodic segments of varying importance. Türk stated that the first strong beat of a section of melody between "every greater or lesser point of rest" should receive

an even more noticeable stress than an *ordinary* strong beat. Strictly speaking these beginning notes should themselves receive more or less emphasis depending on whether they start a larger or smaller part of the whole; that is, the first note after a full cadence must be more strongly marked than after a half cadence or merely after a phrase division [*Einschnitt*], and so on. Here is a short, concise example [Fig. 3.22].[134]

Türk explained that the number of plus signs represents the degree of emphasis of each strong beat. The *o* (for *ohne?*) over A in m. 6 indicates that when the first note of a phrase member is on an upbeat, it remains unstressed.

Further on Türk compared melodic sections that end with different degrees of finality to parts of sentences separated by different punctuation marks; he also stressed the importance of recognizing the ends of those sections of melody or "phrase members" (*Einschnitte*) that are not made obvious by rests.[135] The word *Einschnitt,* translated in dictionaries as cut, incision, or segment, was not clearly defined in its eighteenth-century usage; it could mean cut (*caesura*) or segment (of a phrase).[136] When it referred to a melodic segment, its length could vary from a single two- or three-note group (the equivalent of a poetic

Fig. 3.22. Türk, *Klavierschule*, p. 336.

or tone foot, p. 9 above) to a phrase member containing two or more such groups, comparable to a line of poetry or to a portion of a sentence separated by a comma (Fig. 3.23).[137] Türk's double slanted lines mark each phrase division (cut) at the end of a phrase member (segment). Examples of clearly separated phrase members are the two-measure groups in Figure 3.22. The *Einschnitt* of minimal length is sometimes referred to or translated as an *incise*, the word used for that purpose by several nineteenth-century French theorists.[138] Expressive shaping of incises and phrase members according to metrical placement (e.g., strong–weak) and dynamic direction (influenced by slurring and accentuation) is a significant interpretive function in Classic music. This repertoire gains enormously in dynamic variety and rhythmic interest from the flexibility of incises to reinforce or oppose the meter. (See "The Language of the Slur" in chap. 5.)

Since accents that mark the beginnings of phrase members, phrases, or periods (as in Fig. 3.22) delineate a level of rhythmic activity generated by phrase structure, they might be termed "phrase-rhythm" accents.[139] Like grammatical accents, their purpose is structural clarification. At this level of rhythmic activity there are strong and weak measures, just as there are accented and unaccented beats within a measure. In the typical eighteenth-century view of accentuation this larger scansion is often trochaic, with the emphasis at the start of a phrase or phrase member. (Some schools of nineteenth-century musical thought considered the first measure of a group an "upbeat," thereby generating iambic meter.[140])

Taken another step higher, Türk's mm. 1 and 2 form a strong phrase member or measure group, mm. 3 and 4 a weak group, mm. 5 and 6 a strong group, and so on, creating a still broader level of accentual structure or scansion. The first eight measures of Beethoven's Sonata Op. 90/i and of his Bagatelle Op. 126/5 (Plate V) display trochaic phrase-rhythm accentuation and phrase-member scansion. Beethoven supported those rhythmic arrangements in Op. 90/i/ 1–8 with his alternation of *f* and *p*. In the A section of Op. 126/5, ties often silence the melodic downbeat in weak measures (mm. 2, 4, 6) or those less strong (m. 8). The rising or falling melodic direction, which creates more or less drive respectively at the start of a phrase member (cf. mm. 1 and 3), also reinforces the larger trochaic groups (e.g., mm. 1–2 strong, 3–4 weak).

To summarize, phrase-rhythm accents take precedence over metrical accents. Analysis of measure groups and phrases provides the necessary information for appropriate hierarchical placement. Expressive accents, in turn, take precedence over phrase-rhythm accents.[141] A note that receives an expressive accent—indicated or not—may be the obvious goal or note of prom-

Fig. 3.23. Türk, *Klavierschule*, p. 345.

inence of its phrase. When no distinguishing melodic, harmonic, or rhythmic quality provides that expressive peak, the arch of a phrase may place the goal on the strong beat before the final note or, in a slow tempo, on the secondary strong beat before the final note.[142]

According to Schulz, appropriate observance of the types of accentuation provides "clarity, a great light and shade, . . . [and] the fine shading of strong and weak that the great virtuosos know how to bring to their execution."[143] For the sake of the music, Koch wished that composers would more often indicate the notes that were to receive expressive accents. He suggested the accent sign for gentle accents, *rinforzato*—abbreviated *rf*—for stronger accents, and *sforzato* or *sf* "when the note should be accented with vehemence."[144] The accent sign gradually gained wider use. By 1828 Hummel could write: "The *mark of emphasis* ($\wedge$ or $>$) is used both in *piano* and *forte* passages; it, in a slight degree, distinguishes from the rest, the note over which it stands."[145]

Notated expressive accents of varying intensity are shown in Figures 3.12–3.20 (in Fig. 3.18 only *fz*). Some of the accents fall with the expected metrical stress, others do not. The notes accented in Figures 3.14, 3.16, and 3.19 would have received some emphasis without the indication because of their greater length and higher pitch in relation to the surrounding notes. The chromatic notes in Mozart's K. 282/ii/49 and 51 would also have been accented without the *f*'s. Notes that can well support unmarked dynamic accents in accordance with historical custom include e^2 and d^2 in Figure 5.17; and in Beethoven's Op. 126/5, a^2 in m. 6, b^2 in m. 12, the opening third in m. 20, c-sharp^1 (barely perceptibly) in m. 20, the opening chord in m. 28, and e^3 (with agogic stress) in m. 41, to name those of importance. (See also p. 366 regarding m. 10.)

ACCENTUATION IN BEETHOVEN'S MUSIC; THE ANNOTATIONS TO CRAMER'S ETUDES

Descriptions of Beethoven's playing leave the impression that accentuation, including attention to metrical accents and strongly stressed expressive accents, helped create the characteristic energy and "fiery expression"[146] for which it was known. His varied use of accent indications has been noted above, as has the "very correctly and meaningfully" accented playing of his close colleague Schuppanzigh, this description presumably referring to metrical and expressive accents respectively. There is also information on this subject that has been thought to stem from Beethoven himself in the form of annotations to 21 of the Etudes of Johann Baptist Cramer, supposedly entered for the use of Beethoven's nephew, Karl.[147] Unfortunately, the copy of the Etudes with Beethoven's holographic annotations—if it ever existed—has been lost, leaving as the sole source a copy with annotations in the hand of Anton Schindler,[148] Beethoven's admirer and amanuensis for several years. Because Schindler's reputation has been tainted by inaccuracies in his *Biographie von Beethoven* and by his recently recognized forgeries in Beethoven's Conversation Books, other writing from his pen has become suspect as well.[149] Nevertheless, since Schindler had close contact with Beethoven in his late years, and since there is reliable contemporary evidence—including some in Beethoven's manuscripts, sketchbooks, and music (discussed below)—that acknowledges the importance of the concepts in these annotations, we shall consider two that bear on our present main topic and then consider the problem of their veracity.

The Annotations to Etudes IX and XII

The most sustained comments among the annotations are those concerned with the metrical aspects of rhythm in passage-work, thus underscoring the importance of metrical accentuation. A tendency toward prosodic diction surfaces in even the most unassuming passages. Additionally, the wording of some of the comments, including those to Etudes V and XXIV (pp. 155–156), emphasizes the relationship between prosody and musical performance that seems to have influenced the contemporary consciousness.

As we might expect from Koch's information, the metrical accents in passage-work almost always fall on the beginning of every beat, as in Etude V (Fig. 5.9a), or on the beat divisions, as in Etude IX. The opening measures of Etude IX:

Fig. 3.24. Cramer, Etude IX (OE By the Author),[150] mm. 1–2.

*In this old English fingering, + stands for the thumb, 1 for 2, etc.

are followed by this annotation:

> The triplets [function] as a melody-bearing figure in the bass. The accent falls throughout on the first note of each triplet, which almost always also supports the middle voices. At first this exercise must be practiced with a firm touch, as well as slowly. Since the character of the melody requires a certain breadth [in its interpretation], it should never be played quickly; even in moderate movement it is and remains difficult because the [player's] attention always remains intense.[151]

Generally triplets were played "quite lightly," more so than groups of three in 3/8 or 6/8 meter.[152] The strength of the accent on each triplet was adjusted according to its place in the metric scheme. The stress was greater when metrical and expressive accents coincided.

This regular accentuation at the start of each note group, whether on a beat or on a beat division, brings to mind those sections of passage-work in the piano sonatas in which Beethoven indicated metrical accents. The passage most like Figure 3.24 is that in Op. 14/1/iii/47–64; others with similar accentuation include Op. 13/i/93–98, Op. 53/i/280–281 and Rondo/51–54, Op. 109/iii/169–171, and Op. 110/i/12–16. Unfortunately these accents appear as dots rather than as accent strokes or wedges in many editions, for reasons that require some explanation.

In the holographs of Opp. 53, 109, and 110, Beethoven indicated the metrical accents cited with strokes, the handwritten equivalent of the printed wedge (Plate II, mm. 51–54). It is probable that he used strokes for similar indications in other works for which holographs are not extant. In the earliest sources for Opp. 13 and 14, first editions by Hoffmeister and Mollo respectively, the presence of wedges and strokes for metrical accents suggests the presence of strokes in the holographs. Unfortunately, however, an observable casualness in the use of wedges and dots throughout those editions makes us question how accurately the engravings represent Beethoven's hand in this respect. (We may also wonder whether Beethoven was consistent in indicating these accents.) Hoffmeister used wedges at Op. 13/i/93–98, in the exposition of the movement, but dots when that passage recurs in the recapitulation. Strokes predominate in Mollo's edition of Op. 14/1 at iii/47–64; but dots appear occasionally in a completely haphazard manner, for example, in m. 51. Yet, since Beethoven used dots only in somewhat limited situations, and since the frequent carelessness of contemporary engravers is well documented (see p. 185), it is likely

PLATE II. Beethoven, from the holograph of Sonata Op. 53, Rondo, Allegretto moderato, mm. 49–61. Courtesy of Beethoven-Haus Bonn, Sammlung H. C. Bodmer.

that at least some of these illogical differences arose during the engraving process.

Because of a layer of misinterpretation that may already exist in engraved primary sources for which there are no holographs, and because of frequent difficulties that editors encounter in trying to determine whether some of the holographic indications should be interpreted as dots or strokes, many modern editions use only dots for both, even where the intention of metrical accentuation rather than just staccato playing seems clear. (See "Dot, Stroke and Wedge" in chap. 5.) Knowing this, the performer should be alert to the possiblity that dots distributed regularly on beats or half beats in passage-work may be a substitute for strokes intended as accents. This happens in the *BNA* in the five sonata passages cited, although in a comparable passage in the Quintet for Piano and Winds Op. 16/i/54–57, a different editor for *BNA* retained the wedges in the first edition by Mollo.

Such basic metric accentuation lends drive to long lines of notes of equal value and helps to define their shape. This kind of accentuation should be considered wherever appropriate in similar passages. The annotation to Etude IX, for example, bears on the performance of the triplets in the Bagatelle Op. 119/2.

The annotations to Cramer's Etudes also pay special attention to places within a single line of figuration where part or all of a motive or melodic outline is in opposition to the metrical accents. The concept is clear in Etude XII, the opening measures of which are shown in Figure 3.25. This comment follows:

> The melody lies throughout in the second note of each group, the rhythmic accent on each first [note] of the group. *In the beginning* this is to be given [practised] in very moderate tempo and with quite strong, though not short [finger] strokes. Later, as the tempo is accelerated, the sharp accents diminish and both the melody and the character of the Etude emerge clearly.
>
> —Beethoven[153]

Interweaving metrical accentuation and melodic strands produces a polyphony of contrasting elements within the figuration. In Beethoven's Op. 57/ii/49–50 and 57–59, the important motive of a rising and falling whole step, emphasized with accented quarter notes in one hand, resides in the other in

Fig. 3.25. Cramer, Etude XII (OE By the Author), mm. 1–2.

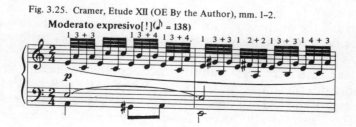

the second note of alternate groups of 32ds. Also analogous in the opposition of melodic and metrical elements within passage-work are Beethoven's Op. 26/i/Var.5/1–7 and his Bagatelle Op. 126/5/17–24 (Plate V). In such instances the off-beat melody is a counterweight to the metrical accentuation, creating another dimension of sound from the ostensible single line.

Schindler and Beethoven

Schindler met Beethoven as courier of a message in 1814.[154] Schindler was only nineteen; Beethoven was 44 and a year into what is considered his late period. Although Schindler was primarily a violinist, he learned to play the piano in Vienna, where he had come to study law. In his *Biographie von Beethoven* as well as in the Conversation Books, he reported that between 1818 and 1821 he had played a number of Beethoven's sonatas for the composer, who—he claimed—had sometimes tutored him in the performance of various movements.[155]

Considerable scrutiny of Beethoven's Conversation Books during the last two decades has led to the conclusion that Schindler forged over 200 entries after the composer's death, many of them devised specifically to prove that he had received the benefit of Beethoven's instruction.[156] Thus, he belatedly entered in mid-summer 1820:

> Next time I'll come with the *Sonata Op. 10 C-minor*. The *Largo* of the *D-major Sonata* is very difficult to understand. You will still be very dissatisfied with me. — I think just once more, and then I will remember it forever. So please [your] patience.[157]

Since all the entries by Schindler in the volumes of 1819 and 1820 are forgeries, it is apparent that he had no access to Beethoven until at least the fall of 1820 and possibly even much later,[158] leaving him without Beethoven's supposed instruction during that period. By August 1822 Schindler did figure regularly in Beethoven's life as amanuensis. In the fall of that year he also gave up his position as a clerk in a law office to become leader of the violins in the Josephstadt Theatre. Nevertheless, because of continuing forgeries related to performance of the symphonies and the sonatas,[159] it is difficult to determine to what extent Schindler had actually played any of the sonatas for the "master" and whether, in fact, Beethoven had offered any advice on their performance.

Presumably the main reason for Schindler's forgeries was to strengthen his position as Beethoven's disciple and chief exponent of his performance tradition, thus to lend greater importance to his biography of the composer as well as to his countless articles, many of which appeared in the *Niederrheinische Musik-Zeitung* during the 1850s.[160] (Schindler lived to 1864.) Schindler regarded the "perceptions" he had acquired from his claimed as well as his real musical contacts with Beethoven as "an intellectual property, which I have ever since regarded as the dearest and most inestimable legacy of my immortal friend and instructor."[161]

Some contemporaries of Schindler sensed trouble early. Ferdinand Ries wrote in 1836, "concerning Beethoven's life and letters . . . Schindler speaks and writes so much rubbish to make himself important. . . . Once he even presented himself as a student of Beethoven: in what?"[162] Adolph Bernhard Marx ridiculed Schindler for alleging in the *Biographie* Beethoven's intention of presenting "two principles, . . . a dialogue between husband and wife," in Op. 14/2/i.[163] Schindler acknowledged this criticism and withdrew some of his comments in the edition of 1860.[164] Alexander Thayer and Otto Jahn considered Schindler "afflicted with a treacherous memory . . . a proneness to accept impressions . . . as facts . . ." and to publish them as such.[165] Nevertheless, Peter Stadlen, Karl-Heinz Köhler, and others suggest that "some of these forgeries may be founded in fact" and are the belated recording of actual events, in an effort "to prove what he knew to be true."[166] From this point of view their general content cannot be dismissed out of hand, but might rather be considered in relationship to documented evidence.

AN ASSESSMENT OF THE ANNOTATIONS TO CRAMER'S ETUDES

Faced with the questionable authenticity of the uniquely instructive annotations to Cramer's Etudes, William S. Newman has proposed a solution not antithetical to the suggestions of Stadlen and Köhler. Newman's cleverly reasoned case, based on circumstantial evidence, holds that the annotations *"could very well be forgeries, yet still be largely true to and derived from Beethoven's own performance practices and intentions."*[167] Analogies between the annotations to the Etudes and evidence in Beethoven's hand, both verbal notations and internal evidence in his music, constitute Newman's evidence.[168] The main topics in the Etude annotations—all of which refer only to passage-work rather than to an obvious melodic line—are metrical accentuation, prosody and poetic feet, motivic and melodic elements in the passage-work, legato playing, and keyboard technique. According to Newman, evidence of Beethoven's attitude toward these topics is necessary if the annotations are to prove germane. (The reader may find it helpful to read the three other annotations, discussed on pp. 155–156 and 200, before proceeding to a brief presentation of analogies in the order of the topics listed.)

Beethoven's indication of regular metrical accentuation, often by means of the stroke, speaks to his concept of its importance. Beethoven was also a master at supporting, manipulating, and moving accentuation with short slurs (see "The Language of the Slur" in chap. 5) and occasionally with beaming (p. 91), not to speak of his use of *sf* and other accent indications, which make up fully one-third of the dynamic signs in his piano sonatas.

Contemporary interest and Beethoven's own interest in the relationship between prosody and music were sketched in chapter 1. Around 1801 to 1803 problems of text setting for theatrical music became particularly important to Beethoven; Salieri's corrections in the scene "No, non turbati" are largely concerned with prosody and accent.[169] In Beethoven's diary of 1812–1818, in the sketchbooks—even as late as 1824 on a sketch for the "Opferlied" Op. 121b and in the Conversation Books, indication of long and short syllables and occasional identification of the verse meter of a text demonstrate his working knowledge of poetic feet.[170] Among the terms found in his hand are trochee, dactyl, paeon, anapest, and hexameter. Further, a reference to *Metrik des Deutschen* by the contemporary authority on prosody, Johann Heinrich Voss, appears on leaf 52r of Sketchbook S.30, which dates from about 1826.

There is only a little inferred evidence suggesting conscious concern with poetic feet in Beethoven's instrumental music. Yet his direction "One must imagine that the time signature is 6/8" for each pair of 3/4 measures in the "quasi prestissimo" Trio of the Quartet Op. 74 is surely a sign of interest in small rhythmic groupings (see also pp. 324–325), as is his indication "ritmo di tre battute" in occasional instrumental works. So is his microscopic attention to the shaping of short groups of two to four notes by means of beaming, dynamics, and slurs.

The rhythmic character of certain of Beethoven's instrumental themes and motives has led some commentators to remark on relationships to poetic feet. Harry Goldschmidt points out the prevalence of spondaic *adagio* themes with an obvious syllabic quality and strophe-like form, including those in the "Emperor" Concerto Op. 73, the Sonata for Violin and Piano Op. 96, and the Sonata for Violoncello and Piano Op. 102/2, to name just three.[171] A decided strophic quality inhabits the themes and forms of the Adagio of the Piano Concerto Op. 19 and the Larghetto of the Violin Concerto Op. 61.[172] Czerny identified the importance of spondaic and dactylic patterns in three movements of the Seventh Symphony.[173] Listeners attuned to prosody might respond similarly to the contrast of the sharply etched spondees (e.g., mm. 11–12) and the reiterated amphibrachs (mm. 19–24) in the episodes of Op. 2/3/ii. Of course, the existence of these reactions does not prove conscious concern with poetic feet, but they do illustrate some themes that seem to point listener response in that direction.* Interesting recent research by Owen Jander has focused on the remarkable rhetorical quality of the Andante con moto of the Fourth Piano Concerto and on the close prosodic relationship of certain of its musical phrases to lines in a contemporary opera libretto based on the Orpheus legend, which was very popular in Vienna when Beethoven wrote that concerto.[174]

The presence of motives or melodies embedded on or off the beat in passage-work occurs often in Beethoven's piano music, as does its mention in the

---

*Found too late to include in the text is at least some support of concern on Beethoven's part with poetic feet in instrumental music. The little-known "Rolland" Sketchbook of late summer or fall 1823 contains "two melodies in C major with the inscription 'auf Sylbenmasse Instrumental Melodien (schaffen) machen' " (to create instrumental melodies according to syllabic meter). Douglas Johnson, Alan Tyson, and Robert Winter, *The Beethoven Sketchbooks: History, Reconstruction, Inventory* (Berkeley: University of California Press, 1985), 401, 403. The description of this sketchbook is by Sieghard Brandenburg.

annotations (e.g., on the beat, Etudes V, XXIV; off the beat, Etudes III, XII; sporadically on and off the beat, Etude XV). Czerny believed that Beethoven sometimes based "the structure of his pieces on single and apparently unimportant notes [that he] was accustomed" to bringing out in performance.[175] Occasionally Beethoven identified such melodic interest by double-stemming, as in Op. 7/iv/1–2L, and 8–9L, although in the same movement he left the discovery of the inverted half-step motive in mm. 2–3 and 6–7—here echoing the altered soprano line—to the pianist. In other contexts, as in Op. 26/i/Var.5/ 1–7 (the melody off the beat), and Op. 57/ii/33–40 (the melody on and off the beat), he offered the pianist no signal. (See also "The Prolonged Touch" in chap. 5.)

There is no need here to anticipate the comprehensive discussions of Beethoven's early interest in and extension of legato playing—only Clementi's was comparable—of his legato fingerings, and of his comments on technique. The verbal and musical evidence presented in chapters 5 and 6 is overwhelming.

Nor is it surprising that Cramer's Etudes were chosen as the vehicle for instructive annotations. Beethoven knew the Etudes at least from around "1815 on," when Czerny, who was then teaching Karl, claimed to have introduced Beethoven to them.[176] Schindler claimed (perhaps to bolster the importance of the annotations?) that according to Beethoven these Etudes "contained all the fundamentals of good piano playing." They "would have constituted most of the practical examples" had Beethoven written his intended "textbook of piano playing," since their polyphonic content made them "the best preparation for the playing of his own works."[177] In fact, Cramer was highly praised as a composer-performer in Vienna in 1799–1800, during which season he performed his three Sonatas Op. 23.[178] Along with many musicians, Beethoven considered Cramer an "outstanding player," especially for his legato touch (see chap. 5, n. 27). Czerny traced the "uniform, perpetually moving style" of Beethoven's Op. 26/iv to the influence of Cramer's stay in Vienna, mentioning specifically his Sonata Op. 23/1, "also in A-flat."[179] The Allegretto of Beethoven's Op. 54 is similar in style.

With this much by way of background on Schindler, of introduction to the annotations, and of evidence for their coincidence with Beethoven's known interests, readers may determine to what degree they will relate these annotations to Beethoven interpretation, whether or not they are ultimately proven to be apocryphal.

CHAPTER

4

Use of the Pedals

The Damper Pedal: Introduction

> The undamped register of the fortepiano is the most pleasing and, once the
> performer learns to observe the necessary precautions in the face of its rever-
> berations, the most delightful for improvisation.[1]

Thus in 1762 did Emanuel Bach express his pleasure in the extra resonance
and special color gained for the relatively weak sound of the fortepiano by
raising its dampers. Bach's reference to the "undamped register" reminds us
that the damper stop was originally conceived not as an aid for legato playing
but as a way of changing sound on a scale analogous to registration on the
harpsichord (see "Mutations: . . ." in chap. 2). His enthusiasm for and reservation about the use of the damper stop were reiterated in 1797 by Milchmeyer,
who wrote that according to the way in which they are used, the raised dampers
"make the most beautiful or the most detestable" effects. When they are used
badly they cause "such an unbearably dissonant sound that a person would
like to block his ears."[2]

Clementi's use of "open Pedal" (dampers raised) in Figure 4.1, published
in February 1798, represents the "undamped register," for it colors the entire
closing theme in both the exposition and the recapitulation of that sonata
movement. The length of the indication, which is undoubtedly meant to ter-
minate at the repeat sign, may appear startling at first, with nonharmonic tones
and changing harmonies over an unyielding drone. However, the absorbency
of the drone, with continuous repetition of the tonic note in a bass octave rich
in overtones; the *dolce* direction; and the lightness of the dissonant notes spaced
among the consonant melodic tones produce a combination that sounds very
pleasing to me on the fortepiano. Bach's "necessary precautions" presumably
included considerations of tempo, harmonic rhythm, dynamic level, and texture, all planned to avoid too much mixing of harmonic dissonance, for the
hand stop on his available instruments at the time of writing would have
precluded frequent dampening. Even on a modern instrument, Figure 4.1 works
well when it is played *dolce* with the pedal depressed only part way or thinned
(these techniques are discussed below).

Fig. 4.1. Clementi, Sonata Op. 37/1/i (OE Longman & Broderip), mm. 77–87.

In addition to the musical factors noted, the qualities of the fortepiano that contribute to the success of Figure 4.1 and other unusual pedalings* are its lighter sound, the characteristic differences of its registers, its clear sharp attack, and its relatively short tone duration. The quick decay leaves less sound from previous notes, and the bright attack obliterates a certain amount of what is in the background. The tonal decay is most striking in quiet pedaled passages with mixed harmonies or noticeable melodic dissonance, such as Figures 4.1, 4.16, 4.18, 4.25, and 4.26. Whenever the harmonic movement settles down even briefly, the listener can actually hear the notes played earlier fading out and the sound clearing itself while the dampers are still raised. In quiet passages the sound may become a gentle haze of harmonies, not unlike the effect of a carillon.[3] In *forte* passages with quickly moving lines or scales, such as Figure 4.23b, or mm. 501–504 in the first movement of Beethoven's Piano Concerto Op. 37, the effect becomes a rush of sound, a gesture as it were. The evidence offered by fortepianos themselves is of intrinsic importance in any assessment of the pedaling effects composers may have intended and of how we can interpret their notated pedalings on our modern instruments.

Some readers may find the sound of Clementi's pedal direction in Figure 4.1 unpleasant on any instrument, largely because today we are unaccustomed to any but "clean" pedaling in the repertoire of the Classic era. Yet careful sifting through primary sources such as holographs and first editions of music, fortepiano tutors, and articles in early music magazines reveals that while clean pedaling was "the rule" and apparently usual, some composers utilized the knee lever or pedal to create unusual sounds. As we shall see later, these effects reflected the contemporary taste for a capability unique to the new instrument.

*In this chapter the terms *pedal* and *pedaling* are sometimes used generically, without necessarily differentiating between the knee lever and the pedal unless that distinction seems important. However, since "partial" pedaling (introduced on p. 112) is somewhat unpredictable and rather treacherous with most knee levers, my suggestions for that practice appear only where actual pedals are involved.

Such passages may present a gulf between what the performance practice was and what some current taste, or prejudice, prefers. Is our aesthetic sense—to which an artistic performance must appeal if it is to fulfill the creator's basic intention—capable of broadening enough to embrace these sounds, as it has recently accepted, or even learned to prefer, the sound of Baroque keyboard music on the harpsichord? I believe it is, aided by an open mind and an informed ear. Implicit, of course, is the use of editions that present composers' pedal indications accurately.

Introducing the damper pedal with this special use demonstrates a link with the past in the exploration of the new instrument. Actually, in the Classic period even clean pedaled sound was considered something special—an effect employed to a limited extent. This will become clear as we attempt to trace the "conventional" uses of pedaling before returning to other special applications.

Only two pedal indications appear in Haydn's music. Both are in the first movement of his late Sonata in C major Hob. 50, and both indicate a mixing of harmonies, which undoubtedly explains why they were notated. (See "Indications That Highlight Form.") Mozart left no indications for a damper-raising mechanism. However, his description of Stein's pianos tells how much better the knee lever worked on them than on instruments of other makers (p. 22); he had obviously used the device before and was interested in it. Nevertheless, he must have used it judiciously and unobtrusively, for it is scarcely noted in the countless reports of his playing. He seems not to have raised the dampers for unusual effect. Mozart's use of the pedal board on his Walter piano would also have restricted simultaneous use of the knee lever to some degree. Still, Czerny's opinion that in Mozart's music "The Pedal [is] seldom used, and never obligato [required],"[4] would seem to be at least a little overstated. Hummel, a student of Mozart for several years until some time in 1788,[5] vigorously protested what he considered overuse of the pedal, writing that "Neither Mozart, nor Clementi [!], required these helps to obtain the highly deserved reputation of the greatest, and most expressive performers of their day."[6] His skeptical discussion of the pedals in his tutor and Czerny's report that "Hummel's followers reproached Beethoven with maltreating the forte-piano, said . . . that his employ of the pedal produced only a confused noise, . . ."[7] merely emphasizes Hummel's conservative attitude.

TYPES OF PEDALING

Rhythmic Pedaling

The type of pedaling described in tutors of the Classic period is now called "rhythmic" pedaling. The dampers are raised as a chord is played, simultaneously with the attack. When the pedal is to be changed, "the last notes of the chord must be damped, but the first notes of the following chord must be begun immediately without the dampers."[8] In Figure 4.2, which illustrates this early pedaling, P (*pedale*) and S (*senza* [without]) are the indications to depress and release the pedal respectively.

Lowering the dampers at or near the end of a harmony allowed time for the increased resonance to die away before a new chord was played and the dampers were raised again. That must have seemed the natural way to obtain a clean sound, since some early fortepianos did not damp well and the technique of using a damper-raising mechanism was new. Although improved damping was one of the attractions of Stein's instruments for Mozart in 1777, and "much improved . . . very well adjusted" dampers elicited praise from Petri in 1782,[9] the knee lever and early pedal mechanisms still required slightly more time to raise and lower the dampers than a modern pedal does.

Beyond the mechanical reasons for the use of rhythmic pedaling, the interstices of unpedaled sound often support two basic tenets of Classic performance, the fundamental significance of metrical structure (discussed in chap. 3) and the style of articulation, which results in part from the role of metrical structure (discussed in chap. 5). (For consideration of such pedaling in Beethoven's Op. 53, see p. 109 below.) Of course, releasing the dampers before sounding a new chord would discontinue the legato if it were not maintained by the fingers; however, the legato needed in Classic music seldom exceeded the grasp of the hands. (Figs. 4.7 and 4.8. are two exceptions.)

The pedaling in Figure 4.2 coincides with the meter, but rhythmic pedaling might have been used anywhere in a measure according to the musical needs. Thus, in Beethoven's Sonata Op. 10/1/iii/41, I depress the pedal with the *fortissimo* chord on beat 4 and raise it as my hands leave that chord at the end of the following downbeat. Many pianists today use rhythmic pedaling mainly to enhance the characteristic rhythms of marches, waltzes, and other dance types; to emphasize accented and syncopated notes or chords; and to enrich the tone of certain notes that are articulated individually. Because in all probability rhythmic pedaling was the predominant, if not the sole, style of pedaling in use during the Classic period, pianists concerned with stylistically appropriate performance will want to listen again to the effect of their pedaling, with special reference to clarification of the metrical structure and articulation. For example, if we pedal *with* Mozart's short slurs shown in Figure 5.45a, we are bound to use rhythmic pedaling.

Fig. 4.2. Pollini, *Metodo*, p. 62.

P   S   P   S

Syncopated or Legato Pedaling

The type of pedaling most frequently used today is termed "syncopated" or "legato" pedaling: the pedal is depressed immediately after the attack, released as a new harmony is played, then redepressed. This use of the pedal, which is slightly syncopated in relation to the chord changes, makes a perfect legato but requires a responsive damper mechanism and split-second damping.

We are uncertain as to when this style of pedaling was first used. It is not described clearly until the 1860s and 70s.[10] However, successive pedal indications without intervening release signs, usually considered evidence of syncopated pedaling, occur in some Romantic music of the 1830s—sporadically in Chopin's scores, a little more often in Liszt's.[11] Less-reliable evidence, if only because of the vagaries of engravers, would be the placement of release and *Ped.* signs as close as possible under the same note or chord. Throughout the Classic period both signs were used in succession, but with rare exceptions, they were placed as if to indicate rhythmic pedaling.

Czerny's well-illustrated discussion of the uses of the damper pedal in his *Complete Theoretical and Practical Piano Forte School* of 1839 includes what is probably the first attempt to describe syncopated pedaling. In Figure 4.3 he notated only a succession of ⊕ (pedal) signs. Although the ✳ (release) signs in Figure 4.4 would seem to indicate rhythmic pedaling, Czerny's directions before and after make it clear that that is not what was intended.

> In the *Tremolando,* the damper pedal is almost always necessary; but the pedal must always be relinquished and resumed at every change of chord [Fig. 4.3].
> The quitting and resuming the pedal must be managed with the utmost rapidity, *not to leave any perceptible chasm or interstice between the chords; and must take place strictly with the first note of each chord.* . . [Fig. 4.4]. The rapidly leaving and resuming the pedal must be practised, till we can manage it almost without thinking of it; and till such passages as the last 8 bars . . . *sound as if the pedal was held down without interruption* [italics added].[12]

If "the quitting and resuming . . . take place strictly with the first note of each chord," the pedal is raised as the note is played, and a seamless legato results.

Fig. 4.3. Czerny, *Piano Forte School,* III, p. 61.

*⊕ instead of ✳ must be engraver's error.

Fig. 4.4. Czerny, *Piano Forte School*, III, p. 62.

Fig. 4.5. Clementi, Sonata Op. 50/1/iii (OE Clementi), mm. 207–210.

Did any fortepiano players of the Classic period use syncopated pedaling? The placement of the successive signs in Figures 4.5 and 4.6, in *allegro* and *adagio* styles, suggest that mode of playing. (In OE the two measures of Fig. 4.6 are on one line. The signs are spaced as shown here, with the broken line representing the bar line.) Unfortunately, the dating of Figure 4.5 is uncertain. Clementi's last three Sonatas, Op. 50, were not published until 1821, relatively late in the Classic period. Plantinga has made a strong case for dating their composition in 1804–1805,[13] but it is conceivable that all the details—perhaps including pedal marks—were not completed until close to the time of publication. For Figure 4.6 the date of publication in England was April 1819.[14] In the same volume of Clementi's *Gradus* there is at least one other similar example, and in Opp. 50/2 and 3 there are several, confirming that the indications in Figures 4.5 and 4.6 are not accidental.[15] As far as is known, Clementi had given up his career as a public pianist by around 1790.[16] The question of whether and when he might have stumbled onto syncopated pedaling is valid but unanswerable. The technique is not as easy on the earlier fortepianos as it became with the pedal mechanisms of the Broadwood of 1804 and the Clementi of ca. 1805 that I have played. In any case, it seems fair to say that such pedaling must have been tried and used in performance before it was notated.

Fig. 4.6. Clementi, *Gradus ad Parnassum*, Ex. 39, "Scena patetica" (OE Clementi, Banger, Collard, Davis & Collard), mm. 116–117.

*Alternate arpeggio sign.

One further element of pedal notation may represent an intermediate step between rhythmic and syncopated pedalings: that is, the placement of the pedal release sign under a new harmony (rather than before it) when another pedaling is not immediately indicated (Figs. 4.15 and 4.20). The continued advice in tutors that the pedal should be let go before the change of chord, to allow prior damping, seems to have borne with it either the statement or the implication that the dampers would be raised again quickly for the beginning of the next note or chord.[17] I am unaware of any advice that the dampers could be lowered as the next chord is played if they are not going to be raised immediately; yet examples in the volumes of Adam and Pollini show such notation,[18] as do a number of figures in this chapter, the earliest of which is Dussek's "Adieu" (Fig. 4.10b). From what reliable evidence I have seen, it would appear that Dussek was inconsistent in this aspect of notation, often placing the pedal release before the change of chord in places where there does not seem to be any particular reason for doing so. Clementi took advantage of carrying the pedal to the changed chord in a higher percentage of instances. And Beethoven was fairly consistent in doing so: through his holographs and first editions, when a damper release sign is followed quickly by a sign to raise the dampers, the two are almost always placed in the customary manner of those in Figure 4.2 (e.g., Op. 57/i/218–223; Aut., *BNA, HE*). But when there is no immediately following pedal sign and no special circumstances cause an early release, the damper-lowering sign is under the changed harmony, as in Figure 4.15 and Figure 4.17, m. 4.

What, if any, relationship might the latter placement bear to improved speed and completeness of damping? We can speculate that since Dussek and Clementi wrote in the main for English fortepianos, whose inefficient dampers left a hovering reverberation (p. 46), this slightly later placement of the release sign may have had less advantage for them than for Beethoven, whose Viennese instruments damped instantly. Thus, in addition to their sense of the potential of the pedal itself, the instruments for which composers wrote may also have influenced their placement of the signs. In m. 4 of Figure 4.17 I would time the pedal release to connect the sound to the G-sharp major chord, but to let that chord sound "clean." When editors convert Beethoven's *con sordino* directions under changed harmonies to the modern pedal release, some place the signs directly under the marked chords, as Beethoven had them, while others place the signs slightly earlier.

When Beethoven changed his indications from the words *senza* and *con sordino* (p. 117 and Fig. 4.17) to *Ped.* and O, it would have been possible for him always to put both signs very close together under the same chord, as Clementi did occasionally. Had the earlier placement of the signs become merely a matter of habit, or did Beethoven have another reason for his notation? In the holograph of Op. 53, during the succession of pedalings in the Rondo at 278–283, Beethoven crossed out his first release signs, which were under the penultimate sixteenth note of each measure. He placed the new ones against each bar line (between the staves), after the last note; *Ped.* is written immediately under the ensuing notes. Many modern pianists apply syncopated pedaling here, but I follow Beethoven's carefully corrected notation exactly. The change of tone color as the dampers settle momentarily not only enhances the distinctness of the downbeat but also creates an effect similar to breathing, a kind of articulation, as it were.

Trying to follow this obscure trail, we come to the relationship between Beethoven and Czerny, whose discussion of pedaling in his *Piano Forte School* demonstrates astute observation of Beethoven's practices.[19] Although his pedal marks never specifically indicate syncopated pedaling, is it not possible that Beethoven had used it occasionally and that Czerny—who attempted to describe it—might have learned it from his association with Beethoven? (See "The 'Moonlight' Sonata.")

According to Adam (1804), the fortepiano could only sustain a note "for one measure," but the damper pedal would keep the sound from decaying so quickly, prolonging it "for several measures."[20] In an effort to prolong or enrich the sound of a series of chords, might not some especially skilled players have slipped into the rhythm of syncopated pedaling intuitively? Yet, if it was used, it must not have been widely cultivated or commonly taught, at least until the second half of the nineteenth century, to judge from available tutors and from the account by Amy Fay. She was first taught syncopated pedaling by Ludwig Deppe in December 1873, after having studied with such pianists as Liszt, Tausig, and Kullak.[21]

STYLISTIC USE OF THE DAMPER PEDAL

Contemporary Descriptions and Uses

"In *fortissimo*, through the raising of the dampers," Streicher wrote, we believe "that we hear an organ, the fullness of an entire orchestra . . . in *pia-*

nissimo ... the most tender tone of the glass harmonica."[22] Descriptions in tutors of the turn of the nineteenth century indicate that the damper pedal was most commonly considered a means for collecting, enriching, and prolonging a body of sound (which may account for its frequently being called the *forte,* or "loud," pedal[23]) or for holding a single bass note for several measures under the same harmony. Through amassing sound and reinforcing overtones, this pedal could enhance both *forte* and *piano* passages. It was to be used chiefly in slow movements with a leisurely harmonic rhythm and a simple melodic line, one without too many nonharmonic tones. It was also generally expected to be changed for each change of harmony.[24]

Adam's is not only the best early discussion but also important for its influence on later writers, particularly Pollini and Starke:

> Many people believe that the damper [*grande*] pedal should only be used to play *forte,* but that is mistaken. ...
> The damper pedal should only be used with consonant chords of which the melody is very slow and which do not change harmony at all; if these chords are followed by another that is no longer in agreement or that changes harmony, it is necessary to *damp* the preceding chord and to take the pedal again on the following chord, always being careful to raise it before each chord of which the harmony will not be the same as in the preceding.
> In general, one ought never use this pedal to play *forte* except in slow movements and when it is necessary to sustain the same bass or melody note for several measures without interruption or change of chord. One easily senses that if one were to apply pedal to a melody in fast tempo or to a mixture of scales, the sounds would become confused in a way that one would no longer be able to distinguish the melody. ...
> This pedal is most pleasing when one uses it to express gentleness [*le doux*].
> ...
> This pedal ... should be used only for pure, harmonious pieces, in which the sounds can be sustained for a long time, as, for example, in pastorales and musettes, in tender and melancholy airs, romances, religious pieces, and generally in all expressive passages in which the melodies are very slow and only change chord very rarely.[25]

In 1812 Pollini remarked on additional effects of the damper pedal that reflect the conventional usage. It "sweetens the sound" and in the *pianissimo* makes "an excellent effect" when the keys are played with "the greatest delicacy."[26] It also enhanced accentuation. The pedal could produce a larger and more noticeable *forte* or *sforzato,* he wrote, and with it, chords (arpeggiated or simple), long notes, or notes marked with the accent sign acquired more vigor.[27] This usage occurs in the last movement of Beethoven's "Moonlight" Sonata, composed in 1801 and published in 1802. There the repeated arpeggio figure, marked *p,* is capped with two *sforzando,* staccato, pedaled chords. The time span between 1801/1802 and 1812 demonstrates the general rule-of-thumb mentioned in relation to *calando,* that a theory often trails practice by a decade or more.

J. B. Cramer and Joseph Czerny later observed that the damper pedal "serves to make the tones smoother and to blend them one with another."[28] This pedal's ability to sustain a bass note opened the door to exploration of new piano sounds and textures discussed further on. Although until a much later date tutors invariably described the harmony over a prolonged bass note as unchanged, in 1804 Adam included in his *Méthode* a "Pastorale" with detailed pedal indications in which there is a limited mixing of predominantly tonic and dominant harmonies over held bass octaves. However, he cautiously indicated the moderator to mitigate any resulting dissonance.[29] Pollini's few examples mix I_4^6 and V.[30] By 1828 even the conservative Hummel showed two (of only three) pedaled passages with mixed harmonies and only some measures over held bass notes.[31]

Indications that point to the use of the damper pedal solely to create a legato line or to connect changing chords are rare. According to Classic treatises, legato touch was generally sustained with the fingers.[32] Early published damper indications from the 1790s on are concerned primarily with the timbre of sounds rather than with pedaled legato; yet to be sure, when the pedal helps to maintain a long note in a cantabile melody, as Adam described, it assists the legato as well. Nevertheless, in Figure 4.7, part of an eight-measure legato phrase, pedal is needed to connect the F and A-flat octaves. For those whose hands cannot span a major tenth, Mozart's Adagio K. 540 has a similar need in m. 19.

How would early pianists have applied pedal in such situations? Probably they would have depressed the pedal (or raised the knee lever) at the first note of the interval (or earlier if appropriate within the same harmony) and raised it some time after playing the second note if the harmony remained the same. In the case of a harmonic change, they would have raised the pedal as they played the second note. This suggestion is borne out by evidence in an unpublished autograph of Clementi, his revision of the Sonata Op. 13/4, which dates from 1807 or 1808. Figure 4.8 shows a pedal indication from the second sixteenth note of beat 2 to the beginning of beat 3. This pedaling eases the legato between the octaves F and B-flat, which is otherwise obtainable only by drawing the hand over a bent fifth finger; it also simulates a legato otherwise impossible between the octaves B-flat and F and improves the sustaining to the following chord.

Fig. 4.7. Clementi, Sonata Op. 7/3/i (OE Artaria), mm. 104–106.

[Allegro con spirito]

Fig. 4.8. Clementi, Sonata Op. 13/4/ii (Aut. of composer's revised version, 1807 or 1808),[33] m. 12.

Planning Appropriate Pedaling

In planning pedaling for Classic music on any piano, the performer will want to consider first the contemporary practice. In addition to the preceding descriptions, Chart I summarizes our present inferred knowledge of early pedaling. Beyond that, some additional suggestions may help develop stylistically appropriate pedaling—as best we can discern it from this distance—that sounds well in Classic music played on the modern piano.

In my judgment, where pedaling is appropriate, partial pedaling of one type or another is frequently preferable on the pianoforte. It keeps the resonance lighter, providing the advantages of undamped sound without accumulating the full tonal weight of the modern instrument. In many passages depressing the pedal to just one-half or one-quarter of its full depth (raising the dampers only part way) works best.[34] By retaining some contact with the strings, the dampers reduce but do not fully damp the vibrations. In other passages it may be better to start with the pedal fully depressed and then release it part way, or use a series of quick half changes—known as flutter or vibrato pedal—that partially damp the upper sounds, the lower ones much less.

Contemporary evidence and present-day experience have shown that it is preferable to be frugal rather than overgenerous with pedaling. Successful pedalings tend to be short and precise. Care must be taken not to cover the articulative detail provided by frequent short slurs (rhythmic pedaling is often necessary in such places), staccatos, nonlegato, and rests; not to thicken a finely wrought texture or a slender sound; and not to obscure any counterpoint or blend the notes of a chordal melody, making it sound more harmonic than linear. A descending melody built on chord tones might need a pedal change with each note. Should pedaling seem necessary on a 1–5–1 cadential bass line, as in a minuet, it should allow a separation between each note.

Arpeggios and other passage-work also require thoughtful treatment, for they may be partially melodic or motivic rather than merely harmonic or scalar in character. Any pedal deemed necessary for single staccato or nonlegato notes must be added discreetly; according to available evidence it might only be appropriate to support strong accents or to enrich the tone color of important notes with short dabs. Yet, in some thin-textured writing the unpedaled tone of the pianoforte sounds dry in comparison with that of the fortepiano, in part

CHART I. Apparent Uses of the Damper Pedal or Knee Lever in the Classic Period*

Influencing Factors

Harmony	Harmonies remained separate except where a composer indicated otherwise or, after ca. 1800, occasionally where a bass note might be maintained through harmonic change (often involving the primary triads) in a quiet context. Rapid harmonic rhythm required more frequent pedal change.
Rhythm	Pedal was considered most appropriate in slow pieces with a slow harmonic rhythm and a slow-moving melody. It reduced the tonal decay of the longer melody and bass notes, thus improving the sound and the legato. It could accentuate important notes.
Texture	Pedal was used primarily in homophonic textures, often blending the sounds of different registers but without obscuring the characteristic clarity. It could hold bass notes, increase the resonance of chords, and support arpeggiated accompanying textures.
Articulation	Almost all legato was sustained with the fingers. Occasionally pedal may have maintained the legato where fingers could not, *or might have helped reduce a gap between nonlegato chords while the hands moved. Pedal breathed with the phrasing, *never covering articulative detail provided by frequent short slurs and single nonlegato notes unless indicated by the composer. Rests were observed literally unless pedal was indicated through them, as it is in some of Beethoven's music. In staccato and nonlegato passages, occasional touches of pedal enriched the sound of accented or important notes, but not to the detriment of textural clarity.
Dynamics	Pedal increased *forte* sounds and accents, but was considered by some more agreeable in soft passages. It enhanced contrast between *forte* (with pedal) and *piano* (without pedal).
Melody	Pedal increased the resonance of long or important notes. *It should not create chordal effects from melodic lines built with chord tones, or obscure the melodic qualities of arpeggios.
Range	Pedal could reinforce high notes or passages that would otherwise sound thin. The lighter tones of higher registers could accept more pedal than could the lower registers, especially in stepwise melodic passages, trills, and other ornaments.

---

*Most entries are derived from sources identified in the main text; asterisks indicate my suggestions based on stylistic implications and playing experience.

because the tone of the modern instrument is less clear and less rich in partials. To compensate for that, today's pianists sometimes make judicious use of surface or half pedal, either as dabs or with frequent changes, to warm certain light-textured cantabile passages, chordal passage-work, and other nonlegato areas.

The slow tempo and relatively slow harmonic rhythm of Mozart's Adagio K. 540 invite some use of partial pedaling in selected places. It must neither blur the throbbing repeated chords nor obscure the delicate articulation and the many rests essential to the effectiveness of the piece. How much of the piece is pedaled will depend on the resonance of the instrument played and the taste of the performer. If pedal is used to enrich the three opening notes, it must be changed with each one so that the melodic motive does not become a chord. Any pedaling with the chords in m. 15 should be rhythmic, to retain the separations between them. Mozart's dynamic contrasts in mm. 24–25 and 28–30 can be heightened by pedaling the *forte* beats, whose high register benefits from the resulting increase in resonance, and not pedaling the *piano* beats, whose low register carries well on its own.

In Mozart's Rondo K. 485, touches of pedal on the dotted quarter and half notes in the refrain and related motives increase the resonance of those rela-tively long and often high tones (e.g., mm. 25, 54–57 [d^3 and e^3 on beat 1]). Selective pedaling can also help shape a phrase by highlighting its important notes; here the dotted quarter notes in mm. 2 and 4 are the goals of their phrase members (pp. 92–93). Where the Rondo refrain occurs in the left hand (mm. 43 and 125ff.), pianists usually forego pedaling, allowing the accompaniment to sound busy and brusque. The melody notes in that low range sing sufficiently without reinforcement.

The application of partial pedaling and other pedal refinements depends, in addition to the musical context, on the performer's tempo, on the acoustics of the room, and on the actual instrument being played. Some instruments respond more successfully than others to partial pedaling, depending on the characteristics of their sound and the adjustment of their pedal mechanism and dampers. However, the most important role in any type of pedaling belongs to the ear. The art of pedaling can only be developed by the kind of critical listening and experimentation that enables the pianist to achieve continuous feedback from the ear to the foot. The link then functions almost automatically, as if pedaling were a spontaneous reflex action. This reflexive connection is necessary for successful performance under the best of circumstances and will help control some of the uncertainty that might result when partial pedaling is used on an unfamiliar piano.

THE DEVELOPMENT OF PEDAL INDICATIONS AND THEIR AMBIGUITIES

England and France

"As of the present [1804], signs for the use of the pedals have not yet been fixed."[35] Because of the newness of independent damper action and the use of two different mechanisms—pedals on English and French pianos in the 1780s and 90s, knee levers on almost all German and Austrian instruments until the early nineteenth century—composers wrestled with various kinds of indications and explanations. What musicians wrote about their indications discloses something of their attitude toward undamped sound and will help us understand some of the unusual pedalings that exist in piano music of that time.

Milchmeyer credited Daniel Steibelt with being instrumental in developing the use of and popularizing the damper pedal.[36] Steibelt's earliest published indications, verbal directions such as "prenez la pédale qui ôte les étouffoirs" (take the pedal that removes the dampers), appeared in his 6me Pot-Pourri, published in 1792 or 1793 in Paris.[37] Steibelt was still not using signs in his first serious works published with pedal instructions, such as the Sonata Op. 27/1, which appeared in 1797 in Paris. To indicate pedaling for an episode (mm. 257ff.) in the Rondo of that Sonata, he took an eminently practical route:

> Use the pedal that raises the dampers, but when you hear that the harmony is mingling too much, release the pedal for the value of an eighth note and resume it again immediately.[38]

Seventeen measures later, where the episode ends, Steibelt added "sans pédale" (without pedal). At the return of the same quiet episode, "avec la pédale" and "sans pédale" reappear, giving the section a "characteristic" undamped sound, with the necessary intermittent damping—minimized by the nature of the writing—at the discretion of the performer.

By the time of the publication of his Concerto Op. 33, which contains the popular "Storm" Rondo, in 1798, and his Three Sonatas Op. 35, in 1799, Steibelt was using systematic signs that allowed an increase in number and specificity of directions. Both works were published in London and carried the same introduction:

> The Author wishing to make more Variety on the PianoForte, finds it necessary to make use of the Pedals, by which alone the tones can be united, but it requires to use them with Care; without which, in going from one Chord to another, Discord & Confusion would result. Hereafter the Author in all his Compositions will make use of the following signs to denote the Pedals.
> ⊕   The Pedal that raises the Dampers.
> ♣   The Piano Pedal.[39]
> ✳   To take the foot off the Pedal that was us'd before.[40]

Steibelt's concern about clarity of the harmonies has an air of ambiguity. How much "mingling" is "too much"? In 1799 Steibelt would have the pianist avoid "Discord & Confusion" in going from chord to chord, yet his pedal indications belie any intention of "clean" pedaling in our modern sense. The majority of his pedalings in Op. 35 mix at least two harmonies, most often tonic and dominant. The subdominant is frequently added, melodies and inner parts contain nonharmonic tones, and single pedalings for complete four-measure phrases are common. Some of Steibelt's pedalings work very well, but many sound poorly conceived. His standard of "Discord," his sense of what would work, or his attention to the pianistic textures where he placed long pedal indications must have been highly variable. (See Fig. 4.24 and its discussion.)

Dussek published his "Military" Concerto Op. 40 in 1798, and "Adieu," about 1799, with his own pedal signs explained: "N.B. the sign Ped: Signifies to rise [*sic*] the Pedal with the right foot and this ⊗ to leave it off."[41] Clementi adopted Dussek's "Ped." in his Sonatas Op. 40 (pub. 1802), stating that "Ped: is for pressing down the Open Pedal, and ✳ for letting it go again."[42] Clementi's student Cramer was more informative:

> Some authors prefer writing Ped: [rather than ⊕] when the open Pedal is to be used, and when it is to be dropt, they use this mark ✳. As the left hand Pedal is only used, in soft passages, it does not require any particular mark.
>
> The open Pedal is chiefly used in slow Movements, when the same harmony is to be prolonged. N.B. When a change takes place in the Harmony, the Pedal must be dropt.[43]

Germany and Austria

In Germany and Austria indications to raise and lower the dampers were developing differently and more slowly, probably for several interrelated reasons. Partly because of the differing nature of the instruments themselves (as described in chap. 2), until around 1800 the best music composed for Viennese pianos did not encourage or benefit from undamped sound to the extent that the music conceived for English instruments did. In turn, there was some resistance to the use of mutations in the German-speaking countries.[44] The mechanism on the pianos manufactured there was still generally the knee lever.

The chapter by Milchmeyer on the "mutations" (pub. 1797) reflects some difficulties associated with the terminology for and appropriate use of the damper pedal.[45] Although he wrote about the need to damp the notes with "every change" of chord,[46] he indicated only "Ohne Dämpfer" (without dampers) at the beginning of certain examples in which the changing harmonies would seem to require damping in order to avoid his "unbearably dissonant sound." In Figure 4.9, meant to imitate "the playing of small bells," he did add "(loss gelassen) genommen" ([let go] taken) to indicate a pedal change; however, this

Fig. 4.9. Milchmeyer, *Pianoforte zu spielen*, p. 59.

instruction is placed after m. 3, in which the sound was not bearable on any of the fortepianos I have played without at least one additional pedal (or knee lever) change. Was the tone of some square pianos—Milchmeyer preferred them to grands—such that his examples sounded acceptable when played according to his instructions, or were pianists to damp the sound on their own in addition to the indications? If so, then why the late indications?

In another example in which Milchmeyer wanted some beats pedaled and others not, he used o for *ohne Dämpfer* and m for *mit Dämpfer* (with dampers); still later he used *ohne Pedale* (with dampers) and *mit Pedale*.[47] Then, after explaining how "very well" the piano with raised dampers can imitate the [glass] harmonica, he urged caution:

> All the notes of the melody and the accompaniment must belong in the same chord, and if one changes the chord then the notes of the [chord] preceding gradually die away if the expression allows it, or are damped, and the notes of the new chord begin immediately without dampers; for without this care the resonance of the previous chord and the sound of the present notes would produce a horribly bad sound.[48]

Apparently harmonies might be blurred "if the expression allows it," otherwise the sounds should be damped before a change of chord. This is the dichotomy that existed regarding undamped sound. Much later Czerny referred to the mixing of soft "dissonant" chords as the "effect of the Eolian Harp."[49]

Interest in coloristic experiments was fostered not only by the novelty of the undamped sound of the fortepiano in contrast to the accustomed precision of the harpsichord, but also by the vogue of the glass harmonica. This instrument, invented by Benjamin Franklin in 1761, consists of graduated circles of glass that are made to revolve by a treadle.[50] The player's moistened fingers held against the moving glass produce clear, sustained sounds whose lingering and mixing occasionally approach a quasi-Impressionistic effect. Dussek, a virtuoso on the glass harmonica, often played it in addition to the fortepiano in his public concerts.

Another attempt to make explicit reference to the damper mechanism appeared in a letter of 24 January 1799 from Leopold Koželuh in Vienna to the British publisher John Bland. Koželuh referred to the raised dampers as "mutation open" (ouverte). "In German this mutation is called the damper [*Dämpfung*] and in French ordinarily the Forte."[51]

With the exception of the Sonata Op. 31/2, Beethoven used the Italian *senza sordino* or *senza sord.* (without damper [apparatus]) and *con sordino* (with damper) in his works through Op. 37 (see Fig. 4.17).[52] The indications closest to these in another language are Milchmeyer's *ohne* and *mit Dämpfer*. Although Beethoven did not use it in any published works, he had written the similar "ohne Dämfung" (*sic*) in a sketch dating from the fall of 1795.[53] During 1802 and 1803 he gradually adopted *Ped.* and O, which had been used earlier by Dussek and Clementi.[54]

The circumstances surrounding Beethoven's adoption of those terms and their use in Op. 31/2 remain unclear. An isolated, early use of "pedal," probably from the summer of 1802, occurs in an important sketch for Op. 35, Var. 8, on page 84r of the "Kessler" Sketchbook[55] (see p. 134 below). Op. 31/2, brought out by the Swiss firm of Nägeli in April 1803, is the first published work of Beethoven that shows *Ped.* and O. Because the holograph is lost, and because Beethoven continued to use *senza* and *con sordino* at least sporadically through the completion of Op. 37, it is not absolutely certain that he actually wrote the new signs in the sonata. A sketch for its first movement on page 65v of the "Kessler" Sketchbook shows *senza sordino*.

Beethoven completed Op. 31/1 and 2 during his stay in Heiligenstadt from late spring through part of October 1802.[56] Exactly when the scores were dispatched to Nägeli is not known. Clementi was in Vienna for some time in October or early November 1802,[57] and his Sonatas Op. 40, containing the indications *Ped.* and ⊕, were announced there on 17 November 1802.[58] Beethoven admired Clementi's works and owned a copy of the volume.[59] It is possible that, having heard about a growing use of the new signs in England and France, or having seen them in Clementi's Op. 40, Beethoven decided to try them or suggested their use to Nägeli. By this time Beethoven knew about Haydn's pianos by Longman and Broderip and by Érard, both of which had pedals (above, p. 50 and n. 106), and may well have heard (or played) those instruments or others (see n. 60). A remote possibility is that the publisher decided for his own reasons to substitute the newer signs for Beethoven's words. In any case, Beethoven's turn to the new terminology was probably not as closely related to the arrival of his own Érard, with its four pedals, as has previously been suggested; that instrument was not shipped from Paris until 8 August 1803.[60]

Beethoven retained his Italian terminology in the Bagatelles Op. 33, the "Eroica" Variations Op. 35, and the Concerto Op. 37, even though he did not complete the solo part of the Concerto until probably June or July 1804 (p. 35). The first work in which the new indications are known to be from Beethoven's hand is the "Kreutzer" Sonata for Violin and Piano Op. 47, which was ready for the publisher by 11 December 1803.[61] Beethoven entered the signs himself in the Finale of the engraver's copy.

SPECIAL EFFECTS BY BEETHOVEN, DUSSEK, CLEMENTI, AND OTHERS

In contrast to the Classic composers who did not notate indications for a damper control, Beethoven, members of the so-called London pianoforte school (including Clementi, Cramer, Dussek, and Field), Steibelt, and Koželuh, among others, left sporadic indications through their work. Not surprisingly, observers reported that these pianists performed with considerably more pedal than their notation shows. Dussek is supposed to have "kept the dampers almost constantly raised when he played in public,"[62] and Czerny wrote that Beethoven "used a lot of pedal, much more than is indicated in his works."[63] The difference may be accounted for with the observation that a high percentage of the notated pedalings may have been put down specifically because they indicate exceptional effects; the more conventional uses discussed earlier were left largely to the discretion of the performer.

The special effects fall into two groups: one serves primarily to alter the quality of sound or the tone color in a distinctive way; the other serves primarily to highlight–occasionally even to substantiate or complete—the formal structure. Often the undamped sound serves both purposes. Occasionally it creates an exceptional expressive mood.

Indications That Create Distinctive Timbres

The preceding comment about Dussek's pedaling is of particular interest in light of evidence from his "Adieu" (ca. 1799), which contains frequent pedal indications. In a not uncommon practice, the pedal was reserved for occasions where it could lend a distinguishing sound to the recurring main theme. "Adieu" demonstrates Dussek's well-practiced pedaling, which was more refined than many of Steibelt's wide swaths (e.g., Fig. 4.24), and his leaning toward a fuller keyboard texture than those of Haydn and Mozart. Dussek understood that cooperation between a widespread accompaniment and the damper pedal would materially enhance the vibrating characteristics of the piano and produce a more luxuriant sound. In "Adieu" he did not indicate pedal where the texture falls within easy grasp of the hands (Fig. 4.10a) but utilized the undamped sound only where it is essential for holding the fundamental bass notes while the left hand adds notes in a higher octave, often in the high treble above the right hand (Fig. 4.10b) but sometimes in the tenor range. Twice the notes held by the pedal extend from the lowest to the highest F, the full five-octave range of most instruments when the piece was published.

Slightly more than half the pedal marks in "Adieu" contain only one harmony, but the rest mix tonic and dominant (or another chord) with both roots usually in the bass, thus bringing changed bass notes into the same pedal. The mixed harmonies are always *piano* or *pianissimo*. In similar passages that are either louder or have a closely spaced texture, Dussek marked a pedal change

Fig. 4.10. Dussek, "Adieu," Craw 175 (OE Corri, Dussek). a. mm. 1–2. b. mm. 5–7.

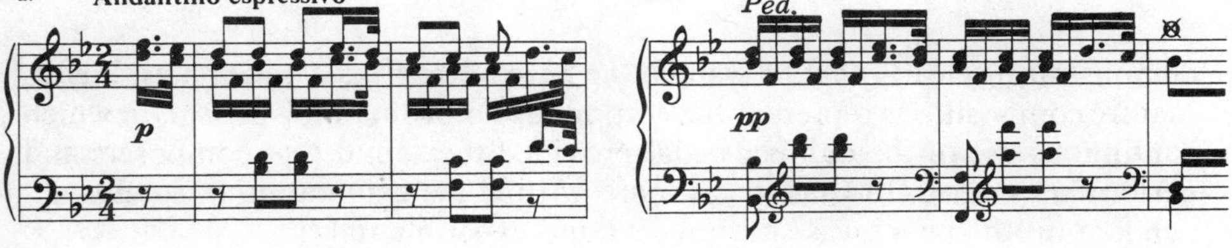

with each chord, demonstrating his sensitivity to the practicalities as well as
to the beauties of the instrument.[64] At the end of this piece the pedal collects
the sound of the tonic chord over four measures spanning four and one-half
octaves.

In 1800 Dussek used the damper pedal in his Sonata Op. 44 to collect and
warm high *piano* sounds in brief passages juxtaposed with lower unpedaled
forte sounds (Fig. 4.11), another effect not unrelated to the concept of harpsichord registration. Figure 4.11 brings to mind a similar passage in Beethoven's
Sonata Op. 101/iii/87–90. In these and many other pieces Dussek successfully
explored various kinds of contrast between pedaled and unpedaled sounds,
the extension of accompanying textures beyond the grasp of the hands, the
mixing of harmonies with changed bass notes, and other consonant and dissonant textures that depend on the damper pedal for their fruition.

John Field, an Irish-born pianist and composer, was influenced by Clementi
and Dussek. Although Dussek had sometimes arpeggiated his left-hand chordal
accompaniments and stretched them to a tenth,[65] it was Field who synthesized
the nocturne style, in which the flowing structure of the accompaniment depends on continuous use of the damper pedal. He also enjoyed and used very
well the coloristic capabilities of the fortepiano. In the holograph of an early
version of his popular Fifth Nocturne, probably written between 1810 and 1815,
Field originally had a pedal release above the sixth eighth note in m. 3 (Fig.
4.12); however, he crossed out that sign and moved it to the end of the measure,

Fig. 4.11. Dussek, Sonata Op. 44/i, Craw 178 (OE Longman, Clementi), mm. 23–26.

*f is preceding dynamic.
**fz may have been intended for the third eighth note.

Fig. 4.12. Field, Serenade (early version of Nocturne No. 5; Aut.),[66] m. 1–4.

demonstrating clearly that he wanted the haze of the mixed harmonies. Field's
mature compositions represent the cutting edge of Romantic pianism, in which
continuous use of the damper pedal provided the sound that composers and
performers shaped. In Classic keyboard writing the exploration of sounds dependent on the pedal was still unusual and experimental.[67]

Beethoven's earliest published indications for a damper control appeared in three works in 1801: the Piano Concertos Opp. 15 and 19 and the Quintet for Piano and Woodwinds Op. 16. Over all, a large majority of his pedal directions created unsuspected or unusual effects that were probably beyond the "conventional" practice. Effects that appear to be related primarily to altered tone color include pedaling through staccatos (as in Op. 27/2/iii, already mentioned) or rests, homogenizing particular kinds of sounds—often soft ones—into a mass of unusual timbre, blending sounds only from the extreme ranges of the keyboard, letting unterminated pedalings dissolve into the air at the ends of works or movements, sustaining bass notes through considerable length, and combining more than one harmony in a single pedal.

Insofar as Beethoven's pedal indications sustain a melody note that might otherwise disappear (e.g., the high A in Fig. 4.16), the pedal enhances the legato. However, as in Figure 4.16, the increased legato was more often a by-product of the pedal's main function. A late piece in which Beethoven's pedal signs have an important effect on the indicated legato as well as on the mass of sound is the Trio of the second movement of the "Hammerklavier" Sonata Op. 106 (comp. 1817–1818). Its pedaling makes possible the legato of the octave melody as well as the gathering of sound of an often widespread accompaniment. Such pedaling, designed to connect notes that the hands cannot manage, is again more typical of the Romantic than of the Classic period.

The care with which Beethoven heard and wrote his pedal directions must be appreciated if their importance is to be understood. He had notated many such special effects by the time he sensed some deterioration of his hearing, around 1800, and he wrote many more while he could still hear well. As his deafness worsened, his inner ear seems to have taken over, for I believe that his pedalings succeed consistently, while those of less-skilled composers do not.

Beethoven's moving and careful placement of pedal release signs was discussed on p. 109 above. In Figure 4.13, instead of a single eighth rest, he notated two sixteenth rests to indicate more specifically that the reverberation of each

Fig. 4.13. Beethoven, Piano Concerto No. 4 Op. 58/ii (OE Kunst u. Industrie Comptoirs), mm. 61–65.
[Andante con moto]

harplike broken chord should hang in the air until the end of the measure. Changes in placement of *Ped.* and release signs are frequent in his holographs, as in the Rondo of Op. 53 at mm. 8–9, where he gave up his first idea of having the left-hand sixteenth note G caught in the pedal; at mm. 57 and 174, where originally he had started new pedals for the continuation of the descending scale; and at m. 504, where he crossed out a release sign at the start of the measure and placed it at the second beat of the next measure.

Where Beethoven used pedal to collect and enrich a mass of sound with just one harmony, the passage often has an unusual pianistic color that needs the pedal to succeed. In Op. 31/2/i/219–225 the pedaling homogenizes the arpeggiated left-hand notes into an atmospheric *pianissimo* mass dominated by the bottom octave of Beethoven's keyboard. The pedalings in mm. 185–191 of the "Andante favori" WoO 57 are also in a very soft passage near the end of the piece, but here the two hands are at the extreme ends of the keyboard. The sympathetic vibrations caused by raising the dampers add sound to the void between the hands and alter the timbre of these measures. Other examples of pedalings that combine sounds from widely separated registers include Op. 109/iii/184 and Op. 110/ii/40–42 and 48–50.

Beethoven left unterminated pedal indications at the ends of movements or sections throughout his *oeuvre*. Some, such as those in Op. 26/iii and iv and Op. 27/1/i, allow the very soft, collected sound of a single harmony to linger and gradually slip away. (The termination signs at the ends of Op. 26/i and iii in the Henle edition do not appear in the holograph, in the original edition published by Cappi of Vienna in 1802, or in the reprint published by the Bureau de Musique of Leipzig in the same year.) At the end of Op. 26/i, a *crescendo* from *pianissimo* followed by a final *piano* chord carries more-active sound into the unterminated *senza sordino*. The great "Diabelli" Variations conclude with a held pedal under a single *forte* chord and a rest, providing a strong contrast with the preceding unpedaled *pianissimo*.

For Beethoven and his contemporaries, the ability to prolong a bass note in the damper pedal opened the door to innumerable effects, ranging from simple to structurally significant. Dussek explored color and texture over held bass notes in "Adieu." Clementi's pedal in Figure 4.14 (pub. 1802) not only prolongs the bass D "for several measures," as Adam described it two years later, but also allows the Rondo theme to emerge almost surreptitiously in m.

Fig. 4.14. Clementi, Sonata Op. 40/1/iv (OE Clementi, Banger, Hyde, Collard & Davis), mm. 83–86.

85 from a light mist of pedaled sound. This pedal indication and another immediately preceding it provide a change in tone quality before the only unvaried return of the Rondo theme.

Among his first published indications Beethoven used pedal to hold the bass underpinning of an arpeggio flourish—a favorite effect—in the first movement of the Quintet Op. 16 (m. 334). Later, in Op. 53 (Fig. 4.15), he contrasted *fortissimo* pedaled sound over sustained bass notes with *piano* unpedaled sound. Certainly the power of the continuously *fortissimo* passages in Beethoven's Op. 57/i/218–223 and 227–232 is greatly increased by having each note of the rising bass line sustained under its broken-chord pattern. From mm. 233–237 a single pedal not only maintains the low C and continues through rests but also incurs the dissonance of the D-flat and C in the left hand, which adds to the suspense at this important formal juncture before the Più Allegro. Lest the pianist doubt that indication, Beethoven twice added *sempre Ped.* Looking back to the end of the retransition, we see that here Beethoven stopped the similar long pedal just short of mixing the D-flat and C, perhaps saving that menacing sound for the more-climactic spot in the coda.

Beethoven sustained a much longer bass pedal point—this time under changing harmonies—in the pastoral second theme of the Rondo of his Fourth Piano Concerto Op. 58 (Fig. 4.16). Over the low D, played *forte,* which releases a rich collection of overtones, the two quiet upper parts mingle, introduce disparate harmonies, and fade gently away. In the sources for this concerto, the engraver's copy with Beethoven's corrections and the first edition by the Verlag des Kunst und Industrie of Vienna,[68] the pedal release is missing, apparently overlooked. (Such problematic unterminated pedalings are not rare in Beethoven's works.) It is my experience that on contemporary fortepianos the pedal can (and should) be carried through to the beginning of m. 92 if the passage is played as carefully as it is written.[69] Indeed, the exquisite success of this pedaling testifies to Beethoven's keen awareness of the striking differences among the fortepiano's three registers.[70] The *forte* note in the sonorous, long-lived bass is cleverly renewed by the quiet roving voice, which spends most of its time in the middle register. The dynamic level of those middle notes needs careful control to avoid too much dissonance. The melody rings out from the high register, which sounds clear and bell-like on the Viennese instruments.

Fig. 4.15. Beethoven, Sonata Op. 53, Rondo (Aut. facs.), mm. 441–447.

Fig. 4.16. Beethoven, Piano Concerto No. 4 Op. 58/iii (copy for engraver of OE [*Stichvorlage*], proofread by Beethoven), mm. 80–92.

Did Beethoven want both the long pedal and the dissonance that reverberated through it? Long pedals maintained through a theme were one of the special pedal effects cultivated by certain composers. In this example, had Beethoven considered the blurred harmonies undesirable he could have dispensed with the pedal point in the piano, letting the cellos carry the D. That he did not make such a choice reveals his positive response to this special capability of the piano and carries a message pertinent to many of his other pedalings.

Although less frequently, Beethoven also indicated pedalings in which functional harmonies change and mix with no underlying bass note to help alleviate the dissonance, for example in the Largo of his Concerto Op. 37 (pub. 1804).

The damper-control indications in Figure 4.17 are from the original edition by the Bureau des Arts et d'Industrie of Vienna.[71] Beethoven's juxtaposition of undamped and damped sound changes the timbre, hence the feeling, of successive chords and measures. Despite the relatively low setting of the first four measures and the full chords throughout, the pedalings are quite lovely at an appropriately slow tempo on fortepianos of the turn of the century. At the more rapid chord changes there is a colored haze that disappears gracefully with the decay of the tones played earlier.

As the fortepianos that I have played acquired a fuller and longer-lived sound, the pedaling in Figure 4.17 began to need adjustments. On the Stein of 1819 these measures were just acceptable with the pedaling as indicated, except for the chords in m. 6, for which I thinned the pedal. The entire example sounded better with half pedal[72] but best with full pedal and the *una corda,* as Czerny mentioned.[73] Using full pedal on the Graf of 1830, the pedal had to be thinned or lifted *before* the changed harmony in m. 4 rather than with it, as well as thinned in m. 6. However, with half pedal the original indications worked very well, better than with full pedal and either the *una corda* or the moderator. The effects Beethoven intended in this passage are among the most treacherous to simulate on the modern piano. Skillful performers manage it with very careful balancing of the voices, masterful use of partial pedaling, and sometimes an extra change in m. 6.[74] (For a more complete discussion see "Adjusting Early Pedal Indications to the Pianoforte.")

Little new had been written about the use of the damper pedal from the tutors of Milchmeyer and Adam until Czerny's *Piano Forte School,* in which there are several artful examples—not unlike Beethoven's—of mixing "different chords" in the damper pedal, with Czerny's explanations of each.[75] Finally,

Fig. 4.17. Beethoven, Piano Concerto No. 3 Op. 37/ii (OE Bureau des Arts et d'Industrie), mm. 1–11.

*Sixteenth note in OE.
**First two notes are a 32d and a sixteenth note in OE.

Fig. 4.18. Czerny, *Piano Forte School,* III, p. 61.

what had been done since the turn of the century was properly acknowledged. In two of Czerny's examples the pedal sustains a bass octave under a quiet treble passage, one with a scale over the progression I_4^6-V_7, the other with a series of changing treble chords. The crucial ingredients, Czerny wrote, are the sustained bass octaves, either loud or soft, and the *pianissimo* dynamic level of the rest.

Czerny's third example, with no held bass note, is Figure 4.18, in which the "dissonant chords," played "with extreme softness and delicacy" in one pedal, produce "the soft undulating effect of the Eolian Harp, or of very distant music. . . . In such cases the shifting-pedal may be added with advantage."[76] Measures 2–4 of this figure are reminiscent of the *pianissimo* undamped chords in Beethoven's Concerto Op. 15/i/335–339, a work Czerny had studied with the composer.[77] Beethoven's *senza sordino* in m. 335 is unterminated. The passage winds through two pair of chromatically descending diminished-seventh chords (each pair separated by rests); comes to rest on the diminished-, then the dominant-seventh chord of the tonic key; and finally descends with a *fortissimo* scale that ends at the recapitulation (m. 346). In its use of quiet diminished- and dominant-seventh chords and a *fortissimo* scale, this passage is similar to the pedaled measures that lead into the recapitulation at Op. 19/i/281–285 (the first composed of the two concertos). The question is whether Beethoven intended his pedal in Op. 15 to hold through the dissonant chords to m. 339, after which it can certainly continue to the recapitulation. What can we learn from contemporary pianos? On the Walter of ca. 1795, using the moderator, the passage sounds fine with no damping; it sounds equally well on the Stein with its *una corda* pedal. Thus, Czerny's advice for Figure 4.18 is well taken. Nevertheless, on a modern instrument some skillful flutter pedal is absolutely necessary to play Beethoven's passage successfully.

Indications That Highlight Form

Haydn's Sonata Hob. 50, given to Theresa Jansen Bartolozzi by the composer, was first published around 1800, when its owner released it to Caulfield of London. It contains two pedalings (one in Fig. 4.19) that have been questioned, in part because the usual dating of ca. 1794–1795 for composition of the Sonata may seem early for the terminology "open Pedal," and in part because, if interpreted as damper pedal, then the only pedal marks in Haydn's

Fig. 4.19. Haydn, Sonata Hob. 50/i (OE Caulfield), mm. 73–75.

Fig. 4.20. Beethoven, "Andante favori" WoO 57 (OE Bureau des Arts et d'Industrie), mm. 160–164.

music produce mixed harmonies.[78] On the former count, Richard Kramer has found historical evidence suggesting a later date of composition, "perhaps as late as 1799";[79] on the latter, musical evidence speaks strongly for the damper pedal and the blur.

Both indications occupy measures that have a subtle importance in the form of the movement. Figure 4.19, exactly midway in the development, is the point of farthest remove in Haydn's harmonic plan. Here the A theme is played legato and *pianissimo* for the first time, and it is clothed in the special color of the raised dampers and harmonic blur. The second indication occurs at the opening of the B section in the recapitulation (mm. 120–123), where, instead of the bright *forte* presentation in the bass that it had in the exposition (m. 20), the theme and its inversion appear in the treble, played legato, *pianissimo,* and pedaled. During his visits to London in the 1790s, Haydn had presumably heard some of the pianists there experimenting with coloristic pedaling. The indications in Hob. 50/i are among the subtlest touches in one of his most imaginative movements. Both pedalings are successful on Broadwood and Clementi grand pianos. The second and longer one sounds much like a carillon.

Beethoven used pedal to highlight or relate to form in more ways than did his contemporaries. His effects include enhancing a pivotal point, bridging sections within a form or between movements, coloring an important section or theme (as in Fig. 4.16), signaling the return of a theme or a section, and incorporating pedaling as an element of structure.

In Figure 4.20 Beethoven indicated that both pedal signs should be held across the end of the slur until the seventh chords are resolved. These pedalings, the first in that piece, are situated at an important formal juncture. The measures shown immediately precede the final climactic section. The seventh chord of the initial motive, an eighth note elsewhere, is here prolonged to four times that length, producing the effect of a fermata. The pedaled sounds form bridges between the suspended seventh chords—at the end of a slur—and their resolutions, at the same time providing a special tone color at this pivotal point in the piece.

This use of pedaled sound as a bridge leads naturally to speculation about the pedaling at the end of the "Andante favori," where the last three chords, separated by rests, are united under an unterminated pedal. Beethoven wrote this piece to be the second movement of the "Waldstein" Sonata but set it aside when he became convinced that the sonata would be too long.[80] Might he originally have intended the pedaling at the end of the Andante to bridge the second and third movements of the sonata, carrying this use of pedaling to a larger dimension? In the first movement of the "Appassionata" Sonata, composed about a year after the "Waldstein," Beethoven used pedaled sound as a bridge between the single *adagio* measure (m. 238) and the final burst of energy. In Op. 109 he linked the first two movements with pedal, although unfortunately some editions do not show Beethoven's release sign under the opening chord of the Prestissimo.

Particularly beautiful is Beethoven's use of pedal to gain color at a crux in the form of the Vivace alla Marcia in F major from his Sonata Op. 101. Here, at the arrival of the key of D-flat major, the Neapolitan of the dominant C (m. 30), the composer created a unique sound by sustaining a bass pedal point for four measures under the stepwise chord changes of the delicate, imitative upper voices. From this precipice we are led back to a long dominant preparation for the return of the tonic key and the final section of the alla Marcia.

These pedalings of Haydn and Beethoven have been subtly placed at formal junctures, some of whose importance may not be immediately apparent. One of the more obvious ways that pedaled sound is related to form is its use to highlight the return of important thematic material or recognizable structural sections. Often such pedaling is near the end of a transition to the reentry of a main theme, as in Figure 4.14. Clementi's most engaging combination of texture, range, and pedal to sustain a dominant note and to herald a recapitulation occurs later in his great Sonata Op. 50/3, "Didone Abbandonata" (Fig. 4.21). In spite of its chromatics, this section sounds splendid on many English and Viennese fortepianos (on the Graf the additional resonance required thinning the last two measures) and can be adjusted relatively easily for today's grand piano.

Clementi often added pedal marks when he revised works published earlier without them. The only such indication in the revision of his Sonata in F minor Op. 13/6 is shown in Figure 4.22 as it is in the holograph, lacking a release.[81] Since the sign occurs on V of V during a feint toward a recapitulation, pianists can go along with the hoax, maintaining the pedal into m. 70 and letting the motive (in the dominant minor) unfold as the sound gently clears. The two measures before the pedal are also part of the dominant prep-

Fig. 4.21. Clementi, Sonata Op. 50/3/i (OE Clementi), mm. 312–333.

Fig. 4.22. Clementi, Sonata Op. 13/6/i (Aut. of composer's revised version, 1807 or 1808), mm. 66–70.

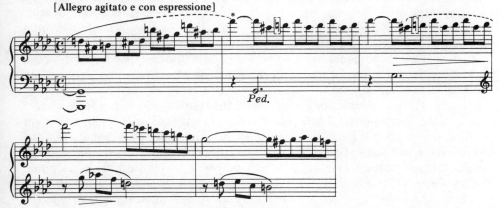

*The slurs completed with broken lines run off the top of the damaged autograph page.

aration. They can be played either without pedal or with touches of partial pedal, so that the pedaling indicated by Clementi provides the special lustre he desired. Not one to neglect his didactic and more salable works, Clementi added pedal indications—including some that illuminate form—to the Sonatinas Op. 36 for their fifth edition, published around 1815 by his own firm (e.g., Op. 36/3/iii/42–45; 36/5/i/42–44).[82]

For Beethoven the relationship of undamped sound to obvious formal events was fundamental from his first published indications. All the "pedalings" in Opp. 15, 16 and 19 (at the time of composition still carried out with a knee lever on Beethoven's pianos) mark either the return of a main theme (e.g., Op. 15/iii/148–152; Aut.) or some other aspect of the structure. Some of these indications involve only chordal figures; others include dissonant color. Most interesting are the indications in the first movement of the Quintet for Piano and Woodwinds Op. 16, which create the impression of framing certain sections of the sonata-allegro form (Fig. 4.23a).[83]

One of the scale passages in Figure 4.23b occurs in the right hand only, unpedaled (damped), at the ends of both the exposition and the recapitulation (shown as - - - in Fig. 4.23a). But the scales are pedaled at the start of the development (Fig. 4.23b) and at the start of the coda, although here again there is just a single scale in the right hand (shown as === in Fig. 4.23a). Since the exposition and the recapitulation contain no notated pedaling, the *fortissimo* undamped scales set the development off dramatically, the coda less so since the scale is not doubled. Near the end of the coda, just before the elongated closing tonic chord, Beethoven indicated pedaling once more (shown as ::: in Fig. 4.23a and marked *senza sordino* in Fig. 4.23c). The quiet coloristic sound created by this final piece of the frame provides a lovely contrast at the end of the movement, not only with the boldness of the earlier pedaled passages but also with the *fortissimo* unpedaled passages that immediately precede and follow it.

Throughout his works, a great many of Beethoven's pedalings that involve dissonance fall into the two types represented here: the ascending or descending scale passage, with few exceptions either *forte* or *fortissimo* throughout, or with a *crescendo;* and the passage with a succession of harmonies, often over a constant bass note and almost always *piano* or *pianissimo* throughout. How practical were these pedalings on the fortepiano? Both types succeed, some better on the Viennese instruments for which they were created than on the English instruments.

In the ascending scales of Figure 4.23b, the residual resonance from a solid start on the fundamental tone helps absorb some of the later dissonance. Each higher tone sings out over the existing sound with more ease. What is left of the played notes before their relatively rapid decay becomes one mass of sound under the new notes. In view of the frequency with which Beethoven used this forceful gesture, it probably achieved his aim.

Still, the damper directions in Figure 4.23b are unclear in two regards: precisely where the indicated *con sordino* should take effect, and whether Beethoven intended *con* and *senza sordino* directions in mm. 158 and 160. (The pedaling for the scale passage that opens the coda is also unterminated, as are several pedaled passages in Op. 15, published at the same time.) Did Beethoven expect the dampers to be lowered on beat 2 of m. 162, thus connecting the first and second staccato octaves, or before beat 2, allowing the suggested space between the staccato quarter notes to be heard? Did he expect similar articulation of the earlier octaves, followed by resumption of the *senza sordino* in m. 160, or did he mean the damper action as it appears?

Not to second-guess a composer, I tried the passage on several instruments, including the Walter of ca. 1795 in the Kunsthistorisches Museum (Plate Ia). In all likelihood, it is similar to the Walter—no longer extant—that Beethoven had in his apartment around 1800, before Op. 16 was published. On that instrument if the dampers are not lowered, the residual "G-major sound" does not disappear until the third or fourth group of triplets in the A-flat major scale. For this reason, and because I choose to believe that Beethoven would have preferred that the two sets of octaves be treated similarly, I insert the change, lowering the dampers sometimes as I strike the staccato octave on beat 1, sometimes midway between beats 1 and 2, depending on the tone quality of the fortepiano at hand. No additions to the damper signs in Mollo's original edition (1801) appear in either Simrock's *Nachdruck* of 1802 (these reprints provided an opportunity for occasional refinements [see chap. 5, n. 50]), or in Mollo's *Titelauflage,* published before 1804.[84] (A *Titelauflage* is a reissue of an edition with a new title page.)

The *pianissimo* passage of Figure 4.23c, with its changes of harmony over a tonic pedal and under two short scales, sounds wonderful on the Walter, the replica in the style of Graf ca. 1810, and the Stein. The amount of dissonance produced with full pedal on the Graf of 1830 was more than I could comfortably absorb, but the passage sounds very nice on that piano with full pedal and the moderator, or with just half pedal. (The sound of this instrument with its *una corda* is much brighter than the sound with its moderator, hence the *una corda* had little positive effect in these measures.) This passage also needs half pedal on the Broadwood of 1804 and the Clementi of ca. 1805 because of the fuller tone and greater resonance of the English instruments.

Identifying an element of form by coloring an entire theme or section with the pedal was discussed at the opening of this chapter, in connection with Figure 4.1, and again at Figure 4.16. While this practice was not used as often as less-risky pedal effects, numerous interesting examples exist. Another by Clementi is a sixteen-measure section built on three motives from the Rondo theme in Op. 40/1/iv (mm. 210–226, *OC*). The light, broken-octave writing stays above middle C; played *pianissimo,* as directed, the unchanged pedal creates a lovely Impressionistic quality that sounds particularly fine on the Clementi grand. This special effect is strategically placed at a surprise return from G minor to G major that leads quickly to the end of the movement.

The coda (the final eighteen measures) of the Adagio of Beethoven's Op. 19 is an unusually emotional concluding section. The recitative-like piano part

Fig. 4.23. Beethoven, Quintet for Piano and Woodwinds, Op. 16/i (OE Mollo). a. Diagram of pedaling. b. mm. 155–163. c. mm. 398–405.

is marked *con gran espressione,* simultaneously and for ten measures also *senza sordino.* The undamped sound of the piano's sighs, with a light haze from the nonharmonic tones, helps create an exceptional denouement for this move-

Fig. 4.24. Steibelt, Sonata Op. 63/2/iii (OE J. Dale), mm. 1–9.

ment, which Czerny compared to a "dramatic vocal scene"[85] and Owen Jander likened to the poetic *Romance*.[86]

Steibelt frequently indicated a single pedal for a complete theme or section. One of several that I could not play as marked is the rondo theme in Figure 4.24, which is characterized by the same pedaling at each return. On the Broadwood piano of 1804—an ideal instrument, considering that the piece was originally published in London in 1805 and that Steibelt had a strong predilection for English instruments[87]—I had to change the pedal at least in m. 4, and I found a change every two measures preferable, even with partial pedaling.

Comparison of Figures 4.24 and 4.1 shows that both textures have about the same number of notes per beat and are arranged in three tiers: bass note, filler, and melody. But Steibelt's filler changes chords regularly with the melody, thereby creating more dissonance; and his bass and filler are not as well disposed as Clementi's, in which a constantly reiterated fundamental tone in a lower octave is able to absorb more dissonance. Both figures are meant to be played *dolce,* but Steibelt's is not so marked until its first return.

Occasionally in Beethoven's music the pedaling not only clarifies the form but becomes an integral part of the structure. When the pedal is necessary to sustain a motivic note or to define and unite a theme or a part of a form, that pedaling must itself be considered structural. The theme in Figure 4.25 depends entirely for its interest on the color and unity created by sustaining the *fortissimo* bass note under the *pianissimo* blend of lighter timbres and changing harmonies.[88] Two such phrases form the B sections of this Bagatelle. The large contrasting A sections, built with related two- and three-note motives that emphasize the upbeat over a detached repeated note accompaniment, are precise and propulsive, almost brusque. They are best played without pedal. Thus the contrasting sound and texture fundamental to this piece rest on the capability of the damper control.

The Bagatelles Op. 33 were completed in 1802 and published in 1803, when Beethoven's hearing was still relatively good. Also composed and published in the same years was the "Eroica" Variations Op. 35, the theme of which reappears in the Finale of the Symphony No. 3 Op. 55.[89] The similarity in pianistic layout, texture, and pedaling of Var. 8 (Fig. 4.26) to the Rondo theme of Op. 53 illustrates how purposeful was Beethoven's exploration of this structural use of pedaling. A sketch for the variation reveals that the core of Beethoven's initial concept was undamped sound with a three-tiered texture: bass E-flat, sixteenth-note middle ground, and treble melody. Below the bass is the word *pedal;* between the staves is his usual *senza s:[ordino].* The final shape of the sixteenth-note accompaniment and of the melody, whose initial note remained the bass E-flat, emerged later. If the texture is carefully balanced, so that the theme is not overpowered by the mixing of the harmonies, this variation is beautifully effective on the contemporary Viennese pianos. It needs half pedal to make it just viable on the Clementi grand of ca. 1805 (Plate Ib).

Beethoven's fascination with the pedal as a structural device reached its zenith in the Rondo of Op. 53, composed in 1803–1804 (soon after Opp. 33

Fig. 4.25. Beethoven, Bagatelle Op. 33/7 (Aut.), mm. 21–28.

Fig. 4.26. Beethoven, 15 Variations Op. 35 (Aut.), Var. 8, mm. 1–8.

and 35) and published in 1805. The Rondo theme, like that of Op. 35, Var. 8, is complete only when the opening bass note is preserved by the pedal and when the entire theme has its identifying pedaled color. Beethoven exploited as many kinds of pedaled sound as possible with the varied textures in which this theme or its opening three-note motive appears: the opening *pianissimo* effect, the roaring *fortissimo* scales with the high treble trill and melody at mm. 55–56, the naked theme at mm. 98–113; and the two sections built on the opening motive, mm. 251–300 and 441–460 (Fig. 4.15).

In a marginal note on the holograph of Op. 53, we find Beethoven's only mention of the "split" damper mechanism with which some fortepianos were built until the 1830s: "N.B. Where [the designation] Ped[al] occurs the entire damper [apparatus] should be raised[,] from bass as well as treble. [The symbol] O means to let it fall again."[90]

When the damper control—whether stop, lever, or pedal—was divided, the right side operated the treble dampers from a little below c^1, and the left side operated the bass dampers from a little above c^1, allowing individual use of each half. The division was not necessarily precise or uniform among instruments. Very little is known about the extent of use of the split mechanism; I have not seen or heard of any signs indicating the use of either of its halves. Beethoven did not own a piano with a divided damper mechanism until 1818, but he was aware of the device and did not want it used in Op. 53. His note must reflect on similar coloristic pedalings in his other works. Significantly, none of the other composers who notated coloristic pedalings left any comments about or indications for using the divided dampers.

Now, with the multifarious uses of the damper pedal in mind, the reader may recall the observation that during the Classic period its use in any way was still somewhat special. Thus I agree with Grundmann and Mies, who have urged caution in adding pedal adjacent to a composer's own signs.[91] This point was made in relation to Figure 4.22 and would apply as well to Figures 4.15,

4.19, and others. If discretionary pedal seems advisable adjoining notated indications, the performer should avoid detracting from the composer's intended effect. Only in the Romantic period, with the music of Chopin and Schumann, did pedaled sound become the basic keyboard sonority from which pedaling was *removed* to create special effects.

The "Moonlight" Sonata

Above the first system of the "Moonlight" Sonata Beethoven wrote "Si deve suonare tutto questo pezzo delicatissimamente e senza sordino" (This whole piece ought to be played with the utmost delicacy and without damper[s]). Between the staves he added "Semper *pianissimo* e senza sordino."[92] This double instruction to play the entire Adagio sostenuto without dampers is often considered the most puzzling of Beethoven's unusual damper indications. Was it meant to be observed literally or only to indicate that the dampers should be in operation throughout, with deft articulation of the mechanism wherever too much blurring of the harmonies occurred? In 1801, when Op. 27/2 was composed, the damper-raising mechanism on Beethoven's piano was still the knee lever, and his terms for its use were the Italian words whose bulk may have discouraged frequent repetition. We also know that certain kinds of mixed harmonies were sought-after pianistic effects.

A striking predecessor to Beethoven's directions, but without ambiguity, appeared in the instruction Koželuh sent for the London edition of his Three Caprices for Piano Op. 44.

> N. B. These three Caprices ought to be played from beginning to end with the mutation open [*ouverte*]. In German this mutation is called the damper [*Dämpfung*] and in French ordinarily the forte. This mechanism is found on every Piano Forte; it is raised with the knee and produces the effect of a [glass] harmonica for the sound is not extinguished but remains sustained.[93]

Koželuh wanted to imitate the reverberant sounds of the glass harmonica with the "undamped register" of the fortepiano. Milchmeyer had suggested caution; Koželuh did not. His instruction, which would have seemed archaic to owners of English instruments, was not printed in the London edition—a shorter one appeared in the original Viennese edition[94]—nor are there any damper indications in the score itself.[95] Yet, measured against the kinds of blurred sounds already discussed, his Caprices are surprisingly successful in exploring the ebb and flow of numerous quasi-Impressionist sonorities with no damping of the strings. Koželuh was known as an excellent pianist, and the Caprices testify that he understood his instrument well. These pieces, in slow or moderate tempo, with generally slow harmonic rhythm; careful spacing of the texture; cleverly calculated use of bass notes, pedal points, dynamics, and rests; and chordal activity in sixteenth and 32d notes, move like improvisations through many kinds of chord progressions. By far the most important interpretive elements are the balancing of the indicated *forte* and *piano* sounds and the occasional adding of discretionary quiet dynamics.

Should the success of Koželuh's infatuation with the glass harmonica reflect on the interpretation of Beethoven's movement? Was Beethoven as captivated as some of his contemporaries by that instrument (or by the harp[96]), or was his exploration of novel undamped sonorities more purposefully related to other compositional goals? Considerable evidence to support the latter view has appeared in the preceding pages. Does the evanescent tone of the Viennese fortepiano allow Op. 27/2/i to be heard enjoyably without any damping of the dissonance, as some musicians suggest?

The answer to the last question is, of course, subjective; but I have not yet been convinced by any performance of this movement (including my own attempts) on contemporary fortepianos or replicas with the dampers continuously raised. Even on the Walter of ca. 1795 and on some small square pianos certain measures seemed to me unacceptably dissonant or muddy. Primarily these are places in which chords (sometimes without common tones) change on successive quarter notes, in which there are nonharmonic and/or chromatic tones, in which the bass octaves move in part by step, or in which any combination of these circumstances exists. Using the moderator or, on later instruments, the *una corda* pedal did not alleviate the problem, nor did a split damper mechanism that I tried. With divided knee levers I still had to lower and raise the bass and treble dampers separately. This created problems with the sound of the texture because the triplets extend over both ranges; moreover, it was impossible to use the moderator when necessary. Similarly, on Beethoven's Broadwood, use of the split damper pedal would have virtually precluded the *una corda,* which Beethoven "was accustomed to employ throughout the whole piece" except for a *forte* around mm. 35 and 36.[97] The improvisatory quality and the texture of Koželuh's Caprices allowed the composer to avoid these situations by interspersing more beats or rests between chord changes, by repeating fundamental bass tones that absorb the dissonance, and by other means. Beethoven's ideas for his movement presumably led him in other directions.

Malcolm Binns's attempt to play this Adagio sostenuto on a fortepiano with the dampers raised throughout resulted in a tempo of $\bbox = $ ca. 44 for an *alla breve.*[98] This performance is the slowest I have heard, far slower than any of the suggestions of Czerny or Moscheles, which range from $\bbox = $ 54 to $\bbox = $ 63 (see p. 357 and the discussion of "The Metronomizations of Beethoven's Sonatas . . ."). Among the more difficult passages, even at Binns's tempo, are m. 12 to the first quarter note of m. 13, m. 26 to the first quarter note of m. 28, the third quarter note of m. 48 to m. 50, and mm. 57–59. The last two each contain a one-measure *crescendo* followed immediately by a *piano.* A few performers interpret the *crescendo* as one from a *pianissimo* to the following *piano;*[99] however, more often pianists make a fuller *crescendo* followed by a "Beethoven *piano,*" which is certainly in keeping with the score. Quite apart from the dissonance in these measures, a *subito piano*—if that is what Beethoven intended—is lost unless the preceding sound is damped. In contrast, keeping the dampers up continuously from m. 28 to the second beat of m. 41 supports the G-sharp pedal point that underlines the transition to the A theme and is reminiscent of Beethoven's own pedalings that mark formal events.

We cannot know whether the sounds that we find objectionable would have been more tolerable to Beethoven or whether, in fact, he wanted the sound damped according to the performer's judgment, as Steibelt stated in his Sonata Op. 27/1 and as Milchmeyer may sometimes have intended. Nevertheless, this movement may be the first of Beethoven's works that would have allowed active use of the damper mechanism throughout, without any "unpedaled" notes. It maintains the same texture and character from beginning to end; slow tempos and generally quiet dynamic levels were considered the most advantageous for displaying undamped sound. Because of his cumbersome terminology at the time, is it not plausible that Beethoven decided simply to give a general direction at the beginning of the movement rather than trying to indicate each movement of the dampers throughout?

The number of pieces in the piano repertoire in which composers have written pedal marks continuously from beginning to end is remarkably small. Where that has been done—for example, occasionally by Chopin—the prescribed pedaling generally produces special effects in relation to the harmony or the phrasing. On the other hand, it is not at all unusual in nineteenth- and twentieth-century music to find *Ped.* at the beginning of a piece with no further related instructions. Indeed, in Schumann's works the practice is common. The appropriate interpretation is to "pedal throughout at your own discretion." Reluctance to supply complete pedal indications no doubt stems in part from the realization that pedaling may change to some extent any time a piece is played, for beyond the perception of the pianist, pedaling is inextricably bound to the acoustics of the room, the instrument available, and the dynamics and tempo of each performance. Bearing all this in mind, we should not be surprised that Czerny reported no unusual pedaling by Beethoven for the "Moonlight" Sonata[100] as he did for the Largo of the Concerto Op. 37 (above, pp. 124–125 and n. 73) and for the recitative in Op. 31/2/i.[101] He merely stated in what may be an oversimplification, "The prescribed pedal must be re-employed at each note in the bass; and all must be played *legatissimo.*"[102] Might Beethoven have intuitively fallen into a syncopated use of the damping mechanism in this movement, whose interpretive problem is unique in his *oeuvre?*

ADJUSTING EARLY PEDAL INDICATIONS TO THE PIANOFORTE

The study of early pedal indications is valuable for its contribution to our understanding of the Classical aesthetic but is more important for encouraging the performance of the notated pedalings. Pianists who have tried to understand the function of these markings, and to imagine the "sound idea" of the composer have a measure against which to test their playing. When the effect on an available instrument is unacceptable to an educated sympathetic ear, various adjustments can be made.

The best rendition of a difficult pedaling will be achieved if the performer tries to determine what the composer wanted to achieve. Was it to change the timbre purely for the sake of color or for another purpose? Is a blurring of harmonies a primary goal or a by-product of an attempt to sustain an important note in one voice? Does the pedal effect have a structural or formal function? Does the unity of a theme or section depend on it? The answers to these and other questions may lead to an effective adjustment for the pedaling.

The most critical factors in adapting early indications to a modern grand piano are the dynamic balancing of individual parts and notes, the choice of pedal strategy, a well-disciplined foot, and the skill with which the feedback from the ear is used by the foot and the hands. Two basic suggestions relative to the balancing or voicing of the texture emerge from my experience. First, the degree of dissonance or muddiness created by the mixing of harmonies can sometimes be lessened by lightening nonharmonic tones and even the inner parts if the arrangement of the texture permits, and conversely, by letting the consonant melodic notes (usually structural rather than ornamental) and the bass line dominate the sound. Experimentation will usually reveal the best balance. Second, if a bass note is being sustained, it should usually be played with as rich a sound as the dynamics and the texture allow, particularly if it is the root of the chord.

Pedal strategy varies with the degree of dissonance of the passage; its texture, tempo, and dynamics; the particular instrument being played; and how much mixing of sounds the pianist finds desirable or tolerable. Some of the techniques available are the same as those mentioned briefly in the section "Planning Appropriate Pedaling." The first step is to decide whether to begin with full or half pedal.

If one starts with full pedal, at a time determined by experimentation one can effect a partial release or half change by raising the pedal enough to reduce the vibrations without losing too much of the sound. Then the pedal may either be depressed completely again, kept at half depth, or "fluttered," for which the foot vibrates partway up and down but without a complete release. Starting with partial pedal is often just as effective and easier than starting with full pedal; in some cases partial pedal may eliminate the need for further thinning or flutter pedal. On most well-adjusted pianos, partial pedal works well for me in many of these problematic pedalings (e.g., Fig. 4.25 and Beethoven's Op. 57/i/233–237). At any time, if the sound becomes too muddy the pedal can be lightened or thinned, preferably without losing the desired blending of the tones.

Careful flutter pedaling after releasing the keys can also simulate the more-rapid decay of fortepiano sound, as discussed in chapter 3 relative to Beethoven's *fp* at the opening of Op. 13. That technique is equally appropriate in some places where Beethoven indicated pedaling through rests, such as Op.

53/iii/98–113, which also contains a rapid descent from a very loud accent to a *piano*.

Occasionally in *pianissimo* passages the addition of the *una corda* pedal is helpful in cutting down the degree of dissonance, as Czerny suggested for Figure 4.18. In any piece, use of the *una corda* pedal depends in part on whether its tone color on a given instrument is appropriate for the passage, on whether it can be added and deleted without creating an unwelcome change in timbre (see "The *Una Corda* Pedal" below), and on whether a satisfactory sound can be achieved without it. Figures 4.10b, 4.12, 4.16, and 4.23c are subdued passages for which a successful performance on a modern piano depends on a combination of playing the bass notes with a rich (not loud) sound, of adjusting the pedaling, and, where it does not interfere with the shaping of a line, of lightening the most obviously dissonant notes. According to the instrument, I sometimes add the *una corda* pedal in Figures 4.10b and 4.23c (both *pianissimo*)[103] but usually prefer Figures 4.12 and 4.16 without it.

Figures 4.1, 4.17, 4.19, 4.21, 4.23b, 4.25, and 4.26 are also easily susceptible to pedal adjustments if one has the requisite control of the foot and the ability to respond continuously with hands and foot to feedback from the ear. Partial pedaling may be subject to uncertainties on unfamiliar or—in some cases—even on familiar instruments, yet it is much subtler and far more satisfactory in effect than outright pedal changes. Complete change does not fulfil the composer's intention of mixing diverse elements or sustaining a tone through changing sounds. Adjusted pedaling is a solution compatible with the original concept.

Performance of the recitative-like passages in Beethoven's Op. 31/2/i, each with a single pedal, has its own special considerations and solutions. The passages are poetically evocative on contemporary fortepianos. Each opening arpeggiated chord, in mm. 143 and 153, decays enough, even with the damper pedal down, so that it is faint by the end of the following measure and gone completely by sometime in mm. 145 and 156 respectively. (The second chord lasts a few beats longer because it is followed by fewer notes.) Within the melodic voice a few dissonances, played quietly, produce momentary piquant effects that disappear as the tones fade. Thus there is an ebb and flow of consonant and dissonant sound. Czerny wrote that "the pedal is held down during the recitative, which must sound like one complaining at a distance."[104]

On a modern piano the performer can simulate Beethoven's intended effect in the following way. Let the left hand hold down its part of the chord beyond the written value until the sound disappears (on a modern instrument sometime in mm. 146 and 157); at the same time depress the damper pedal partially and thin it in response to the needs of the quasi-recitative, retaining an appropriate amount of gently produced dissonance. Occasionally a pianist uses the *sostenuto* pedal, which was not available until 1874,[105] for the initial chord; but this technique sustains the notes for considerably longer than is possible on a fortepiano or desirable on a pianoforte.[106]

Fig. 4.27. Clementi, Sonata Op. 50/3/ii (OE Clementi), mm. 1–10.

To conclude this discussion I have reserved a passage from Clementi's "Didone Abbandonato" that is stunning on the fortepiano but that needs exquisitely sensitive handling on the pianoforte. Clementi's intention in Figure 4.27 was presumably to sustain a backdrop of dominant sound from the opening through the stepwise thirds in mm. 6–10 and to create some expressive dissonance with the changing harmonies, all of which would provide a moving setting for the emotional content of the movement. My experience with many grand pianos ranging from 5′10″ to concert size provides the following suggestions, with further adjustments made according to each instrument and the flux of sound in each performance. A fully depressed pedal for the first four measures retains the important D's at maximum intensity. Raising the pedal a little in m. 5 or 6 and playing softly allows all the notes to be heard while the low D still dominates the sound. In m. 8 the repeated D should be well brought out and held with the finger to the end of m. 9. The thirds from the middle of m. 8 on require either thinning or flutter pedal, depending on the instrument and the management of sounds in the measures preceding.

THE *UNA CORDA* PEDAL

The *una corda* pedal, described in chapter 2, is mentioned in most tutors of the Classic period. All noted that it was used chiefly in *pianissimo* passages. Milchmeyer called it "a music from afar."[107] Some recommended it also for echo effects and for contrast with *fortissimo*—both reminiscent at times of harpsichord registration—and in *diminuendo* passages[108] (probably longer ones).

The performer will want to consider carefully where in a *diminuendo* the *una corda* pedal is most appropriately depressed because of the marked change in dynamic level and tone color it effects. On a well-regulated modern grand piano, when the *una corda* is engaged the hammers strike the strings on a less-worn part of the felt. A change in timbre results from this as well as from striking fewer strings and acquiring the sympathetic vibrations of the unstruck strings. If the regulation of an instrument is such that complete depression of the *una corda* pedal causes the hammer to strike strings two and three in the grooves of strings one and two, partial depression of the pedal will allow striking on fresher felt.[109]

The *una corda* is often best engaged at the beginning of a phrase or motive rather than in the middle, in order to avoid a noticeable change at an inappropriate place, as Milchmeyer observed.[110] However, this depends on the context and the degree to which the pedal changes the sound on any given instrument. Sometimes it seems appropriate to add the *una corda* in Mozart's K. 540 for the first half of m. 26 and the second half of m. 30, as well as for the two final chords. Adam added that the *una corda* pedal could also be used in *crescendo* passages.[111] Presumably he intended that the pedal be depressed at the start and released further on.

Interestingly, by the 1820s pianists were being warned that the availability of a device to soften the sound should not deter them from trying to develop a full palette of quiet tones produced with the fingers. In 1823 the *Harmonicon* printed "an almost literal translation" of an article from a "recently-published French bibliographical work on music," which cautioned that

> the soft pedal should very rarely be brought into action. Skilful [*sic*] masters wish, if I may be allowed the expression, that that pedal may be found only at the ends of their fingers.[112]

The reviewer of the *Sequel to Latour's Instruction for the Piano Forte* expressed a similar opinion:

> We wish that he had not mentioned the soft [*una corda*] pedal; this should only be employed by adepts. . . . In fact, the command of loud and soft should be in the finger of the performer.[113]

This point of view may reflect the increasingly substantial fortepiano actions that would allow pianists better control of the soft sounds.[114]

The *una corda* pedal was used alone or in combination with the damper pedal. The two together yield a less-muffled, richer color than the *una corda* alone because of the additional resonance created when the dampers are off the strings. According to Kalkbrenner, "The union of the soft and loud pedals produces an excellent effect in *dolce* passages."[115] Starke wrote that this combination produced a sound of "heavenly beauty" and could be used "with very good effect in unusually delicate, sentimental [or] melancholy passages."[116]

Beethoven called for the *una corda* pedal through most of the slow movement of the Fourth Piano Concerto and in less-extended areas of some of his late works, often specifying *una corda* or *due corde* (pp. 40–41 above). Although he left no pedal indications for his Bagatelle Op. 119/2, I find the second part of the *pianissimo* coda, set between c^2 and g^3 (mm. 36–39), irresistible for some

Beethovenian color. Unchanged damper (half) pedal and the *una corda* leave a bell-like wash of tonic and dominant sounds over the tonic drone as the piece ends.

Beethoven was surely aware that the *una corda* pedal changed the timbre as well as the dynamic level of the sound, for at the end of Op. 106/iii, after six measures played *pp* and *una corda,* the final arpeggiated chord is played *ppp* but *tutte le corde!* Other Classic composers rarely indicated this "species of tone,"[117] leaving it to the discretion of the performer.

Common indications for the *una corda* pedal in the Classic era and later were *u.c., due corde,* or *mit Verschiebung* (with shifting). Its release was signaled by *tutte le corde, tre corde,* or *ohne* (without) *Verschiebung.*

CHAPTER

5

ARTICULATION AND
TOUCH

INTRODUCTION

Articulation in performance is the delineation of motives or musical ideas by the grouping, separating, and related accenting of notes. Whether indicated by the composer or determined by the performer, it is a principal element in the internal shaping of phrases and—in alliance with harmonic and rhythmic activity—in the clarification of melodic segments and phrase lengths. Through this clarification music gains shape and meaning analogous to that provided for language by punctuation and accentuation.[1]

Articulation underwent conspicuous refinement in Classic keyboard music. Slurs and signs for staccato and *portato* appeared in scores with increasing frequency, until the degree of articulative detail expressed in some pieces was as complete as possible within the notational system and the customs of the time. Indeed, in the piano music of Mozart, in which dynamic indications are sometimes sparse or nonexistent, the wealth of articulation marks underscores the prime importance he placed on precise note groupings. His refined articulation may, in fact, be considered the single most significant interpretative element in his music; observing it exactly provides a finesse that the style would otherwise lack. Grace, nuance, diversity, sometimes brilliance, occasionally surprise, and countless other effects are created by the notated articulation, in which the contrast of touches also has an important role.

The Classic style of articulation developed gradually from, and is in some ways similar to, its Baroque and early Classic heritage. In these periods the understood contrast between the cantabile *adagio* and the crisp *allegro* styles formed the basis for certain contemporary conventions of articulation and touch. For early Classic and some Classic pieces in which articulation signs are either lacking or incomplete, the performer can supply the articulation by examining the general customs of the eighteenth century (described in Chart II) and the style of a composer's articulation in similar works. The newly refined elements important to successful performance as the Classic style ma-

CHART II. Likely Choice of Touch for Harpsichord, Clavichord, and Fortepiano Music until about 1790*

Influencing Factors	Staccato	Nonlegato	Legato
Ordinary Keyboard Playing		The basic touch for secular keyboard music was nonlegato. There was no sign to indicate it (Bach, 157; Türk, 356).	
Tempo	Merry or fast pieces (*allegro, presto*) had a preponderance of detached notes (staccato or nonlegato). (Quantz, 125; Bach, 149, 154–155; Türk, 359–360; Koch, 131, 43–44, 1299. These references also pertain to slow pieces discussed under Legato.)		Cantabile or slower pieces (*adagio*) were more legato, but with short slurred groups; generally from half a beat (♩ 𝅘𝅥𝅯𝅘𝅥𝅯𝅘𝅥𝅯𝅘𝅥𝅯) to one measure. Slurs did not often go over the bar line, especially when the notes before the bar line formed a short upbeat.
Rhythmic Construction	In pieces with three rhythmic values, notes of the middle value (♪ ♪ ♪) were likely to be staccato, depending also on tempo and melodic construction (Quantz, 133; E. Bach, 414). In pieces with two rhythmic values (♪ and ♪, or ♪ and ♪), the longer notes were more likely to the shorter ones were likely to be legato. Pieces in small meters (2/4, 3/4, 3/8) and short note values were often quite nonlegato (Türk, 360–361).	The shortest note values were likely to be legato or slightly nonlegato.	Large meters (2/2, 3/2) and long note values (𝅝, 𝅗𝅥) called for a more sustained performance. When notes in the rhythm ♩♫ were to be legato, the slurring was generally ♩♫ rather than ♩♫ (Quantz, 167; Bach, 157).

*Page references are to Carl Philipp Emanuel Bach, *Essay on the True Art of Playing Keyboard Instruments*; Heinrich Christoph Koch, *Musikalisches Lexikon*; Johann Joachim Quantz, *On Playing the Flute*; and Daniel Gottlob Türk, *Klavierschule*. Entries for which no source is identified have been generalized from practice observed in authentic sources of the period.

CHART II. Continued

Influencing Factors	Staccato	Nonlegato	Legato
Melodic Construction (All slurs and staccato signs are authentic.) (In addition to Figs. 5.1–5.5, see Bach, 154–155; Türk, 355; Koch, 43–44.)	In any tempo, large melodic skips were often detached. They were analogous to large dance gestures. See Figure 5.1.	Stepwise melodic movement and skips of thirds were often legato, sometimes nonlegato. See Figure 5.3. Stepwise runs were nonlegato or legato, depending on tempo and character. See Figure 5.4. Intervallic passages were usually nonlegato, but notes of an arpeggiated harmony in either fast or slow tempos were sometimes legato. See Figure 5.5. An interval following stepwise movement was generally not legato.	In slow tempos large melodic skips were sometimes legato, especially if they were particularly expressive or if they occurred in a "rocking" pattern or in short note values. See Figure 5.2.
Consistency of Articulation	Recurring motives seem generally to have had the same articulation unless the composer indicated otherwise. (See also Bach, 154–155; Türk, 354–355; Koch, 43–45.)		
Form and Texture	Contrasting motives, whether in the same or in different melodic lines, had contrasting articulation. This organization of articulation, which enhanced the thematic identity of motives in separate strands of texture, was especially important when two or more parts were played at the same dynamic level (or on the same manual), as in Figure 5.3.		

Influencing Factors	Staccato	Nonlegato	Legato
Accentuation		A note could be emphasized by detaching or shortening the one before it. Notes that were usually accented include first beats of measures, syncopated notes, long appoggiaturas, first notes under slurs (Bach, 163, 154; Türk, 335, 337, 355; Koch, 49–52). See also "Types of Accentuation" in chapter 3. Short upbeats were rarely slurred over the bar line.	
Nonharmonic Tones and Ornaments			Appoggiaturas and suspensions were slurred to their notes of resolution except where a break in articulation was suggested by a descending leap in an ornamental resolution. Turns and trills with turned endings were generally slurred to the note following (Bach, 155, 84; Türk, 218; Koch, 1300).
Influence of Vocal Style on Instrumental Playing (based on my own experience)	When in doubt, sing the line, perhaps adding scat syllables. The voice will help find the groups of notes that feel indivisible (legato), the natural separations between groups, and the notes that require individual articulation (nonlegato and staccato) (Bach, 151–152).		

147

Fig. 5.1. Gottlieb Theophil Muffat, *Componimenti Musicali*, Suite II, Fantasie (OE Leopold), mm. 6–7.

Fig. 5.2. J. S. Bach, Sonata for Flute and Cembalo BWV 1030/i (Aut. facs., *Neue Bach-Ausgabe*), m. 1.

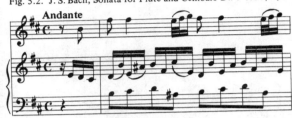

Fig. 5.3. J. S. Bach, Invention No. 9 BWV 780 (Aut.), m. 1.

Fig. 5.4. G. F. Handel, Partita in G major, Preludio *(Hallische Händel-Ausgabe)*, mm. 1–2.

Fig. 5.5. G. T. Muffat, *Componimenti Musicali,* Suite VI, Gigue (OE Leopold), m. 7.

tured were a gradual increase in the use of legato, a growing subtlety in the uses of the slur, and a developing distinction between the dot and the stroke or wedge.

NONLEGATO, LEGATO, AND THE PROLONGED TOUCH

Nonlegato, *Tenuto*, and Heavy and Light Execution

As suggested in Chart II, eighteenth-century keyboard touch divides into the basic groups of nonlegato, legato, and staccato. *Tenuto, portato, legatissimo,* and the prolonged touch were variants of the basic three. The most widely used touch through much of the century was the nonlegato, which is reflected in the contemporary term for it: the "usual" (*gewöhnliche*) way of playing. Türk's description is typical of the many that appeared before and after:

> For notes that are to be played in the usual way, that is, neither detached nor slurred, the finger is raised from the key a little earlier than the duration of the note requires. . . . If there are some notes intermingled that should be held for their full value, then *ten.* or *tenuto* is written over them.[2]

Türk specified that nonlegato reduced a note by one-eighth to one-quarter of its value. Marpurg's earlier description[3] agrees with Türk's, while Emanuel Bach would have nonlegato notes shortened by half their value,[4] for which advice he was faulted by Türk. As mentioned in chapter 1, Beethoven's impression of Mozart's pianism was colored by the prevalence of nonlegato touch. Haydn's keyboard writing and directions for performance imply a generally similar application of nonlegato. Chart II describes the contexts in which that touch was likely to be used. In addition, Figure 6.21, with typical nonlegato fingering, and Haydn's Hob. 28/i/1, as well as the many similar passages in that movement, illustrate standard nonlegato fare. In the Finale of Hob. 28, nonlegato playing of the arpeggiation in the first variation (m. 23) contrasts with the prominent two-note slurs in the theme itself, many of which span the bar line, as Haydn was wont to do. However, in the fourth variation (m. 107) of that movement and, for example, in the unmarked passage-work in Mozart's K. 540/17–18 and 47–48, a kaleidoscopic mix of nonlegato and legato works best under my hands.

Although Türk did not record a change of touch in the 1802 edition of his *Klavierschule,* legato was gradually gaining ground in practice. In the same year Beethoven indicated *leggieramente* [*sic*] in the Sonata Op. 31/1/ii to secure a light nonlegato, and thereafter he occasionally invoked that term or *non ligato,* e.g., Op. 79/i/12, 134, 191; Op. 111/ii/72 and 89 (in Plate III). With the *leggieramente* in Op. 31/1/ii he also supplied specifically nonlegato fingering, a string of 1, 3, 1, 3 (see p. 211 below). Presumably these scalar and arpeggiated passages may serve as models for other unmarked passages in his music.

The distinctions between notes played *tenuto,* that is, "held for their full value," and those played nonlegato or legato were significant in a performance style in which clarity and subtlety of declamation were prized. Since a *tenuto* note was not slurred, the following note retained its initial articulation. Clementi, Beethoven, and other composers wrote the term to ensure that a note

Fig. 5.6. Beethoven, Sonata Op. 2/2/ii (OE Artaria), mm. 1–2.

would be held its "full length,"[5] sometimes specifically in contrast to either preceding or simultaneous staccato (Fig. 5.6). *Tenuto* also occurs frequently, as here, over repeated notes, probably as a reminder that they should be held as long as possible before the key is released for replaying.

Legato groups in Baroque, early Classic, and some Classic music typically encompassed two to four notes and rarely extended uninterrupted over a bar line. Slurs in the original sources, along with the examples in Türk's *Klavier-schule* and other tutors support this observation, which relates directly to much of the music of Haydn and Mozart.

In addition to considering the individual touches, writers often described "heavy" and "light" execution by way of relating touch to other aspects of a composition. Türk's comprehensive explanation points out that there are many degrees of heavy and light:

> In a *heavy* execution each note must be played firmly (emphatically) and held out right to the end of its prescribed duration. *Light* refers to an execution in which each note is played with less firmness (emphasis) and the finger lifted from the key somewhat earlier than the duration of the note prescribes. In order to avoid a misunderstanding I must also remark here that the terms *heavy* and *light* generally refer more to the sustaining and separating of the notes than to their loudness and softness. For in certain cases, for example in an *Allegro vivo, scherzando, Vivace con allegrezza,* etc., the execution must be rather light (short), but at the same time still more or less loud; whereas a piece with a melancholy character, for example an *Adagio mesto, con afflizione,* etc., certainly slurred and therefore somewhat heavy, should nevertheless not be played too loudly. Still, to be sure, in most cases *heavy* and *loud* go together.
>
> Whether the execution is to be heavy or light can be determined 1) from the character and intended purpose of a piece . . . , 2) from the designated tempo, 3) from the meter, 4) from the note values, 5) from the way in which the notes progress, etc. In addition, even national taste, the style of the composer and the instrument for which a piece is intended, must be considered.

§. 44

> Pieces of a stately, serious, solemn, pathetic, etc. character must be delivered [in a] *heavy* [style, that is,] full and vigorous, strongly accented, and so on. To those kinds of pieces belong, among others, those that are headed *grave, pomposo, patetico, maestoso, sostenuto,* and the like. Pieces of an agreeable, gentle,

pleasant etc. character, therefore those that are usually marked *compiacevole, con dolcezza, glissicato, lusingando, Pastorale, piacevole,* and so on, require a *somewhat lighter* and noticeably more quiet execution. Pieces in which lively, playful, joyous feelings prevail, for example [those headed] *Allegro scherzando, burlesco, giocoso, con allegrezza, risvegliato,* and the like, must be played *quite lightly;* whereas melancholy and similar affects especially require *slurring* and *portato*[6] [*Tragen der Töne*]. Pieces of the latter type are designated by the words *con afflizzione, con amarezza, doloroso, lagrimoso, languido, mesto,* etc.

It is understood that in all the situations described, *varying* degrees of heavy or light execution must be used.

§. 45

Pieces that are written for a serious purpose, for example, fugues, well worked-out sonatas, religious odes and songs, etc. require a far heavier execution than, shall we say, certain playful divertimentos, humorous songs, lively dances, and so on.

§. 46

It can also be determined from the tempo whether one should choose a heavy or light execution. A *Presto* must be played more lightly than an *Allegro;* the latter more lightly than an *Andante,* and so on. Thus pieces of slower tempo require, on the whole, the heaviest execution.[7]

A Shift toward More Legato

The development of the Classic style, particularly in respect to increased breadth of cantabile lines, led gradually to greater use of legato touch during the end of the eighteenth century and the early decades of the nineteenth. Clementi's description of his change from a "brilliant execution" to "the more cantabile and refined style of performance" (see p. 25 above) suggests related developments in compositional and performance styles. Of the many improvements in English fortepiano construction during that period, those that would have effectively enhanced the sound of the legato include the addition of iron braces, the consequent increase in tension on the strings, equalization of string tension, precise location of the striking point, use of larger hammers, and a gradual deepening of the key dip. But most important was the development of a musical style appropriately expressed through cantabile performance, which included melodic lines and formal sections with less fragmentation and greater continuous sweep.

The first two movements of the Sonata Op. 7/3 show Clementi moving in these directions (see Figs. 5.27 and 9.19). The superficial brilliance has given way to more sensitive expressivity. Many of the melodic lines intimate a growing "cantabile and refined" performance; a few of the slurs embrace full four- or eight-measure phrases. Although a two-movement plan prevailed in most of Clementi's previously published works, all the Sonatas of Opp. 7, 8, and 9 are in three movements, and all but one contain a true slow movement that is conducive to a singing legato.

Beethoven's legato was considered remarkable by all who heard his playing. His remark on the piano part of the song "Klage" WoO 113, of which the probable date of composition was 1790, establishes his early interest in legato touch: "Throughout, the notes must be smooth, sustained as much as possible, and slurred together."[8] Junker's testimony in 1791 to the "altogether characteristic style of expression, . . . so different from that usually adopted," must have referred at least in part to the legato aspect of Beethoven's "great" *adagio* playing (p. 27 above). Beethoven's youthful study of both violin and organ undoubtedly contributed to his preoccupation with legato playing on the new fortepiano.[9] An autograph inscription on an undated sketch of a keyboard composition lends credence to the influence of the violin: "The difficulty here is to slur this entire passage so that the putting down [attack] of the fingers cannot be heard at all; it must sound as if it were stroked with a bow."[10]

Whether Beethoven might also have been influenced by Clementi's broad lines and long slurs is an interesting question, although hardly answerable. Some of Clementi's sonatas were available in Bonn; the music dealer Simrock advertised "3 Sonaten (mit Violin, Op. 13) by Clementi" in 1786.[11] After Beethoven moved to Vienna in 1792, before the composition of Opp. 1 and 2, he would have had access to more of Clementi's published works, including Opp. 7 and 9—originally published there—and perhaps the remaining three Sonatas of Op. 13 if Simrock had not carried them. It is well known that Beethoven admired Clementi's sonatas and, according to Schindler, had "almost all" of them in his library.[12]

Beethoven's disdain for the pervasive nonlegato at the expense of legato in contemporary piano playing was expressed picturesquely to Streicher in a letter of 19 November 1796:

> There is no doubt that so far as the manner of playing it is concerned, the *pianoforte* is still the least studied and developed of all the instruments; often one thinks that one is merely listening to a harp. And I am delighted, my dear fellow, that you are one of the few who realize and perceive that, provided one can feel the music, one can also make the pianoforte sing.[13]

And Czerny wrote of his studies with Beethoven, probably begun four years later, that he

> made me especially aware of the legato, of which he himself had control to such an incomparable degree, and which all other pianists at that time considered impossible on the fortepiano; the chopped and smartly detached playing (of Mozart's time) was still fashionable.[14]

Legato and Legatissimo Touches Described in Tutors

Nicolo Pasquali, an Italian composer, violinist, and theorist living in Edinburgh, anticipated the trend toward increased legato playing. In his Preface to *The Art of Fingering the Harpsichord,* probably written close to 1757, he compared keyboard playing to singing and string playing. The following comments are typical of others throughout the volume:

> The *Legato* is the Touch that this Treatise endeavours to teach, being a general Touch fit for almost all Kinds of Passages, and by which the Vibration of the Strings are made perfect in every Note.
> ... The holding the Fingers upon the Keys the exact length of the Notes, produces the good Tone; and the taking them off frequently before the Time, occasions the contrary.
> ... All those Passages that have none of these Marks [for other touches] must be played *Legato,* i.e., in the usual Way.[15]

Pasquali's contribution appears the more remarkable since Emanuel Bach's and Marpurg's affirmations of nonlegato as the "ordinary onward movement"[16] had just been published.

In 1775, Vincenzo Manfredini, a compatriot of Pasquali, wrote of the difficulty of playing "the *Cantabile*" on the harpsichord: "One must be careful not to raise the finger from the key before having played the next note. This rule is not only followed in this instance [for the cantabile], *but on almost any occasion*" (italics added).[17] The fourteen Preludes in Manfredini's volume contain relatively few short slurs over two to four notes. It is impossible to assess what impact either Pasquali's or Manfredini's volumes might have had; however, it would not be surprising if Clementi saw Pasquali's little book in the extensive library of Peter Beckford, in whose home he lived from 1766 to 1774,[18] or later in London.

Hüllmandel published his *Principles of Music . . . for the PianoForte or Harpsichord* early in 1796.[19] That he placed pianoforte ahead of harpsichord in the title is indicative of the changing times. For him, with the exception of notes to be played staccato, "holding a Key on 'till the next is struck" was "one of the most essential Rules."[20]

Between 1797 and 1804, six new methods written specifically for the fortepiano, rather than for harpsichord, clavichord, or keyboard instruments in general, were published in Germany, England, and France. In three of them, Milchmeyer, Clementi, and Adam described the use and growing importance of legato playing.[21] For Milchmeyer's "usual" or "natural" way of playing, each finger remains on the key "until the note has completed its allotted value" in order to avoid a "dry and tasteless playing"[22] (i.e., nonlegato).

> The finger is lifted from the first key when the second has been played, from the second when the third has been played, and so on. In this usual way of playing, two fingers should never lie [on two keys] simultaneously in a simple melody. Concerning passages with double notes, ... it is completely clear ... that here, also, the fingers may not be lifted from the pair of notes until the following two have been played.[23]

Milchmeyer described a "slurred" way of playing that might be termed *legatissimo.* It required that "the fingers remain somewhat longer, and on several notes." This overlapping was suggested for broken-chord figures in the left hand; runs and chromatic passages were specifically excluded. In addition, "all possible passages from C above the third line of the G clef to the highest notes of the piano" could be played in the "slurred" way "without offending the ear," but the player was permitted that only where the composer indicated it. Through this touch the upper tones of the instrument, "which are inclined to a certain hardness and dryness," could be "sweetened and made more gentle."[24] Milchmeyer's suggestions for touch produce excellent results on the Broadwood of 1804, which has a dry top octave and a half. From f^2 to c^4 some overlapping of notes is essential to a satisfactory legato sound on that instrument; from c^2 down, Milchmeyer's "usual" way of playing produces a fine legato.

By the time Clementi wrote his tutor in 1801, his attitude foreshadowed that widely held later in the nineteenth century, when legato became the prevailing keyboard touch:

> N.B. When the composer leaves the LEGATO and STACCATO to the performer's taste; the best rule is, to adhere chiefly to the LEGATO; reserving the STACCATO to give SPIRIT occasionally to certain passages and to set off the HIGHER BEAUTIES of the LEGATO.[25]

Other authors wrote similarly, some, like Adam, virtually quoting Clementi;[26] and many of the best-known virtuosos of the early nineteenth century, including Dussek, Clementi, and Clementi's students Cramer and Field, were admired particularly for their exquisite cantabile legato style.[27] After Milchmeyer, German writers added little to the information on touch until Hummel, but the tutors of Clementi and Adam, along with others published in England and France, were promptly translated into German.

The increase in legato playing, which was closely related to the changing musical style, was common to all music making. For example, changes in the shape and balance of the violin bow during the second half of the eighteenth century also allowed a more effective legato.[28] Thus it is not surprising that changes in the revised fourth edition of Leopold Mozart's *Violinschule*, published in 1804, included purging of the earlier assumption that nonlegato was the usual way of playing. Instead, "everything cantabile needs slurred, bound and sustained notes; this is even more imperative in an Adagio than in an Allegro."[29]

Nevertheless, as in almost all aspects of change in performance style, the shift to more extensive use of legato came about slowly enough so that Schubert could write to his parents in 1825, after giving a concert:

> What pleased especially were the variations in my new Sonata for two hands, ——, since several people assured me that the keys become singing voices under my hands, which, if true, pleases me greatly, since I cannot endure the accursed chopping in which even distinguished pianoforte players indulge and which delights neither the ear nor the mind.[30]

The Prolonged Touch

The prolonged touch[31] consisted of holding notes for considerably longer than their written values. Composers sometimes embedded a melodic strand or motivic element among other notes in passage-work or an accompaniment. If all (or most of) the notes are written in similar rhythmic values, melodic elements may be concealed in what looks to the eye like a single line. Applying the prolonged touch, or "overholding," to such melodic notes creates a second dimension of sound that illuminates the polyphony. Such "hidden" two-part texture occurs frequently in Baroque music, especially in that of Johann Sebastian Bach. Two written-out examples that illustrate this practice are mm. 17–18 of the Allemande of Bach's Partita No. 1, the notation of which provides the clue for performance of mm. 37–38; and the opening four beats of François Couperin's Rondeau "Les Bergeries," which Anna Magdalena Bach copied into her *Notebook,* presumably as Bach would have written the passage. Couperin's left-hand part was carefully notated in two lines (Fig. 5.8a), one quasi-melodic and one harmonic filler, which Anna Magdalena compressed into one line (Fig. 5.8b).

Some of the annotations to Cramer's Etudes describe the use of the prolonged touch. (For an introduction to these annotations see chap. 3.) Figures 5.9a and 5.10a show the beginnings of Etudes V and XXIV as Cramer notated and fingered them; Figures 5.9b and 5.10b are in the annotations. The annotation for Etude V reads:

> The piece is in four parts throughout. The melody lies in the top voice, as the notation shows [Fig. 5.9a]. However, even if the notation were as [in Fig. 5.9b], the first note of each group would still have to be similarly accented and sus-

Fig. 5.8. a. F. Couperin, *Pièces de clavecin,* Sixième Ordre, Rondeau "Les Bergeries" (OE Chés l'Auteur), mm. 1–3.
b. From the *Notebook of Anna Magdalena Bach,* Couperin's Rondeau BWV Anh. 183 *(Neue Bach-Ausgabe),* mm. 1–3.

a.

*These brackets are Couperin's slurs.

b.

Fig. 5.9. a. Cramer, Etude V (OE By the Author), mm. 1-2. b. From the annotation to Cramer's Etude V.

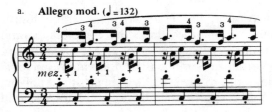

Fig. 5.10. a. Cramer, Etude XXIV (OE By the Author), mm. 1-2. b. From the annotation to Cramer's Etude XXIV.

tained. The middle voice, e c, f c, g c, etc., must not be struck as strongly as the top voice. The poetic foot turns out to be trochaic.

—Beethoven[32]

· Etude XXIV is introduced with this comment:

In the first five measures the first note of the first triplet should be connected as well as possible with the third [note] of the second triplet, so that the melody stands out like this [Fig. 5.10b]. Therefore the finger may not be lifted from the long [note]. In other respects the rule for the performance of the triplet is valid, but here the second triplet should be less strongly accented.

—Beethoven[33]

The mentioned "rule" is probably that "the first note [of each triplet] must receive a gentle accent"; but especially in fast passages the accent should not be so noticeable that the performance resembles "the gait of a lame person."[34]

Hummel also described the overholding of notes for realizing a melody: "There are certain groups of notes which include a melody, and which must not be played detached like other passages; the delivery of them must be connected, and the melody brought out."[35] His examples include those in Figure 5.11. In Beethoven's works the prolonged touch illuminates the hidden motivic half-steps in Op. 7/iv/2–3L, 6–7L, and 14–15L; the melodic sixteenth notes in Op. 57/i/51–52 and ii/33–48; and the melodic eighth notes (those on the beat) in the Bagatelle Op. 119/2, to name just a few. Overholding a single note for emphasis can also be effective.

The prolonging of chord tones in certain purely accompanimental patterns was also part of Classic practice, as Milchmeyer's description of touch suggests. When applied uniformly to the notes of a broken chord, this overholding, or "finger pedaling," was the continuation of a well-documented Baroque usage frequently signaled by the slur.[36] Emanuel Bach, Türk, and Franz Paul Rigler described the concept. "The slur over broken chords means that the first, second, and third notes must remain down until the fourth has been played."[37] To illustrate this literally, Rigler wrote out a chord whose four tones enter on successive beats of a measure in decreasing note values (whole, dotted half, half, and quarter notes). Interestingly, Brahms used slurs to indicate prolonging of chord tones in his song "Alte Liebe," Op. 72/1.[38]

Two versions of the opening of Clementi's Sonata Op. 41 demonstrate applicability of the prolonged touch in his works. His careful notation of the accompaniment in the completed version, Figure 5.12b, suggests the way Clementi might have expected a pianist to realize the implied parts of his early version, Figure 5.12a.[39] Thus, according to context, but usually in conjunction with a lyrical theme, many kinds of broken-chord accompaniments in two or more implied parts, including the Alberti bass, may invite overholding with or without the addition of the damper pedal. This touch may be implemented to varying degrees; the number of notes held and their duration will depend on the sound desired. By this means the dynamics and the resonance of the accompaniment are subtly altered, more noticeably when the pedal is not used.

Fig. 5.11. Hummel, *Pianoforte*, Pt. III, p. 60. a. No. 14, mm. 1–2. b. No. 16, m. 1.

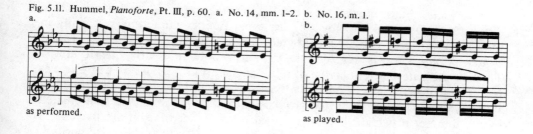

as performed.

as played.

Fig. 5.12. Clementi, Sonata Op. 41/i, mm. 1–4. a. First edition (Artaria, probably without Clementi's permission). b. Revised edition (*OC* Breitkopf & Härtel, Vol. VI[40]).

In Mozart's Rondo K. 485 pianists may decide to overhold just the bass line or all the notes of the accompaniment in mm. 21–24—where dabs of damper pedal may also warm the high notes—and in mm. 27–33. In mm. 53–57 and 148–152 the moving voice may be prolonged without necessarily overholding the bass. The livelier settings in mm. 43–48 and 125–132 preclude overholding in favor of a sparkling nonlegato accompaniment. In other pieces Mozart's articulation signs may shed light by implication on unmarked passages. Since in K. 457/i Mozart slurred the broken-chord accompaniments of the first (m. 23) and second B themes (the latter at its second appearance, m. 131 [*NMA*]), we may infer that he probably intended the unslurred Alberti bass of the closing theme (m. 59) to be played somewhat nonlegato. (See the additional comments in *NMA, Klaviersonaten*, I, xvii.) Overholding does not exclude simultaneous use of the damper pedal, but this touch is often appropriate where the presence of dissonance in a moving part or the lightness of the texture might make pedaling hazardous and the results questionable.

THE LANGUAGE OF THE SLUR

The Expressivity of Short Slurs

The increasing importance of refined articulation in Classic music led to diverse and subtle uses of the slur. Its most frequent function, especially in the earlier works of Haydn and Mozart and as described in the tutor of their contemporary Türk, is related to its use in Baroque and early Classic music. The slur indicates legato playing of relatively short groups of notes or motives within musical phrases. Concurrently, it provides these incises—short, individually accented and separated groups—with an expressive direction created by the manner in which the first and last notes under the slur are played.

According to virtually all writers of the early Classic and Classic periods, including Emanuel Bach, Türk, Starke, and Hummel, "the note over which the slur begins is very gently (almost imperceptibly) accented."[41] Türk's examples include slurs that begin just after the start of a beat (Fig. 5.13g), which, Türk points out, cause the accent to fall in an unexpected place (shown by +). (Remember that in the Classic period metrical stress was expected on strong beats and, to a lesser extent, at the start of other beats or half beats that are subdivided into short notes [p. 91].) Here the metrical accent yields to the expressive accent; in some circumstances (e.g., Fig. 5.18) that creates an effective aesthetic tension. Türk's upbeat slurring also causes the slur to continue over the bar line, a somewhat exceptional circumstance in 1789 that occurs

Fig. 5.13. Türk, *Klavierschule*, p. 355.

only four times in his 408-page volume. (See below, "Do All Slurs Indicate Attack and Release?") Türk concludes with an example of double slurring (Fig. 5.13k), explaining that "of course all the notes must be slurred, yet the first, third, fifth, and seventh tones should be very weakly marked." This slight emphasis would have been applicable on the clavichord or fortepiano but not on the harpsichord or organ.

Leopold Mozart was more emphatic about the effect of the slur on accentuation. His musical example consists of three measures of eighth notes in 3/4 meter that are slurred in 33 different ways, and differently once again as sixteenth notes in 3/8 meter. The first note of a group of "two, three, four and even more [slurred notes] must be somewhat more strongly stressed, but the remainder slurred on to it quite smoothly and more and more quietly." As the slurs are moved in Mozart's examples,

it will be seen that the stress falls now on the first, now on the second, or third crotchet, yea frequently even on the second half of the first, second, or third crotchet. *Now this changes indisputably the whole style of performance* . . . [italics added].[42]

The notes under a slur were played without "the slightest separation"[43] and with a single impulse, which Adam described as "without making any movement of the hand" between the first and last notes.[44] After the last slurred note, which was rhythmically weak, there was generally a separation to clarify the grouping and sometimes to let the music breathe. The rapidity with which the last note was released and the length of the silence between that note and the next varied considerably. The tempo and mood of the piece, the surrounding articulation, the kind of motive, the length of the slur, and even its place within the phrase and the period might affect the way in which the slur was ended.[45]

The last slurred note might be held for virtually its full value, so that the degree of articulation between it and the next note is all but imperceptible, an effect as subtle as that provided by a consonant or a glottal stop in speech or in a vocal line. Figure 5.22 and slurs at the ends of mm. 5, 6, 7, 61, and within m. 15 of Mozart's Sonata K. 333/ii provide examples. In such places the effect after each slur wants to be perceived as merely a new impulse after a fleeting lightness, rather than as a distinct separation. At the other end of the spectrum, the last slurred note might be shortened by as much as half its value to allow a light and complete separation. This interpretation often applied to the second of two equally long slurred notes either within a phrase or at a feminine cadence.[46] Accordingly, in Figure 5.14 the eighth-note G in m. 160 would be played as a sixteenth note followed by a rest of the same value.

Short slurs, with their initial accented attack, legato grouping, and variable release, provide a clear strong-to-weak linear direction in the shaping of a musical line, highlighting its speechlike or communicative quality. This expressive capability, for which their initial accent takes precedence over metrical or phrase-rhythm accents in case of conflict (p. 93 above), led composers to use short slurs for a diversity of melodic/rhythmic effects. The importance of these slurs and their proper performance continued to be discussed by nineteenth-century writers as diverse as August Leopold Crelle and Mathis Lussy.[47] I have adopted the term "incise" slur, which seems to me a more precise description of that slur function than the more familiar term "articulation" slur.

The initial stress of an incise slur often supports the meter and may also define the contour or quality of a motive or rhythmic pattern destined for subsequent development (Figs. 5.14–5.16). Thus the slur in Figure 5.16 informs us that the sixteenth-note F originates gently from the C rather than being a detached and more emphatic anticipation of the longer F. Here the articulative and dynamic effects of that slur further strengthen the first beat in relation to the second.

On the other hand, as Leopold Mozart and Türk pointed out, slurs can alter the expected metric accentuation. For example, a short slur that begins on an upbeat and goes over a bar line momentarily opposes the meter and mitigates its effect. Haydn was fond of this use of the two-note slur from his early years as a composer (e.g., Hob. 10/iii; 18/ii, HSU, *JHW*). In Figure 5.17, from his last composed sonata, the strong–weak direction of the first four slurs

Fig. 5.14. Haydn, Sonata Hob. 49/i (Aut.), mm. 158–160.

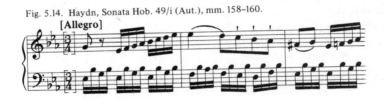

Fig. 5.15. Haydn, Sonata Hob. 40/i (OE Bossler[48]), mm. 1–6.

Fig. 5.16. Beethoven, Sonata Op. 31/3/i (Simrock[49]), m. 1.

Fig. 5.17. Haydn, Sonata Hob. 50/i (OE Caulfield), mm. 1–5.

Fig. 5.18. Beethoven, Sonata Op. 14/2/iii (Simrock[50]), mm. 1–8.

overrides the otherwise weak–strong metrical position of the incises. The contrast in touch and the dynamic direction created by these slurs highlight the sevenths in the right hand, which, along with the contrametric slurs, become important developmental features of this imaginative and humorous movement. By m. 4 the right-hand incises have shifted to reinforce the meter; the left-hand groups remain contrametric.

Beethoven used incise slurs for rhythmic and linear shaping with greater forcefulness and variety than did his predecessors, often upsetting the expected metric stress, sometimes creating illusory effects. In Figure 5.18 the unsuspecting listener might suppose a duple meter until mm. 3–4. Immediately the meter is upset again, but it is restored more emphatically in m. 7 with the help of the *sf*. Throughout there is a tension between the short–short–long (weak-to-strong) anapests and the expressive direction of the slurs. Performers resolve this problem variously, either by stressing the first sixteenth note (e.g., Claudio Arrau, Friedrich Gulda[51]) or the eighth note (Artur Schnabel[52]) or by maintaining a balanced tension with more stress occasionally noticeable on one or the other of those notes (Walter Gieseking, Wilhelm Kempff[53]). In some performances many measures of the movement sound almost without meter. This Scherzo concludes the Sonata Op. 14/2, whose first movement is also partially shaped by a slur that defies the meter. Other examples of contrametric incise slurs include those in Figures 5.28c (mm. 55–58) and 7.60.

Observing short slurs in rapid succession can affect the tempo at which a piece is played; the down–up motion required may take extra time, and the listener must also be able to perceive the effect created by the presence of the slurs. In the Finale of the Sonata Hob. 23, Haydn articulated the opening four-note motive in five different ways (Fig. 5.19). The need for these subtle distinctions to be heard limits somewhat the player's degree of Presto, as the

Fig. 5.19. Haydn, Sonata Hob. 23/iii (Aut. and OE Kurzböck).

Fig. 5.20. Haydn, Sonata Hob. 22/i (Aut. and OE Kurzböck), mm. 12–13.

Fig. 5.21. Beethoven, Sonata for Violin and Piano Op. 47/iii (engraver's copy with Beethoven's corrections), mm. 205–208.

movement is headed. Or consider the difference between ♪♩, as the theme of the Scherzo in Beethoven's Op. 28 is articulated in both holograph and first edition,[54] and ♪♩, as it is sometimes played and even printed. Interestingly, Czerny wrote about this motive that "The two eighth notes (in the 4th [!] measure &c.) [should be] broken off abruptly, without being connected to the following quarter note."[55] This articulation, involving two quick slurred notes followed by a staccato note, is common in Classic music. Other examples in Beethoven's works occur in the Rondo theme of his Concerto Op. 15 and the B theme (mm. 123 ff.) of his Concerto Op. 58/i.

Extremely subtle changes in rhythmic effect can be wrought by deliberate use of slurs over repeated notes. The slurs in Figure 5.20 appear in both the holograph (1773) and Kurzböck's first edition (1774) of Haydn's Sonata Hob. 22. Since a true legato between repeated notes is not possible on a keyboard instrument, Haydn presumably meant the four-note slurs to avoid an obvious two-note grouping with its attendant accent on the third note, as found on beats 2 and 4. Beethoven placed similar slurs over repeated notes in his Sonata for Violin and Piano Op. 96/ii/1–2, 39–40, 47–48 (Aut., *BNA*). The effect of his slurs in Figure 5.21 is to move some emphasis to a normally weak part of the meter and to diminish the importance of the quarter note on beat 2.

As a group among the slurs found in Classic music, incise slurs are the most reliable indication of attack and release; the resulting musical and physical gestures are also among the most important in this repertoire. Our information on how they were played appears in chapter 6. No doubt the projection of frequent short slurs and nonlegato touch requires more energy and finger effort on today's piano than on the fortepiano because of the deeper key dip, the heavier touch, and the longer tone duration of the modern instrument. Nonetheless it is altogether possible and absolutely necessary that the short slurs and the nonlegato be heard. It is precisely here that the impact of experience with the instrument for which the music was written has its greatest effect. Once the pianist is convinced of the efficacy of these slurs, he or she will produce them on the pianoforte as well.

Longer Legato Groups and Slurs

Longer legato groups and slurs began to appear between 1775 and 1780 (e.g., Mozart, K. 280/iii/29–31 and K. 281/ii/1–3, both composed early in 1775[56]). Haydn used them less frequently than did Mozart, in whose works slurs over one to two measures are not uncommon. Slurs that include these longer portions of a phrase are often complemented by shorter slurs, as in Figure 5.22 and the melody in Figure 5.23. It is of the utmost importance that such nuances as the barely perceptible separations (or lightnesses) at the ends of the slurs in Figure 5.22 not be overlooked. There is a very noticeable difference between the subtle sound of Mozart's slurring in those measures and the sound of the often heard delivery with one slur over the entire phrase. (The slurs over the sixteenth-note lines in Figure 5.23 will be discussed below.)

Slurs unite what belongs together but may also separate—in order to demarcate—specific motives or sections. In the opening of the "Appassionata" Sonata, Beethoven followed a long slur with two short ones carefully placed to call attention to the motive C, D-natural, C (Fig. 5.24). This motive is exploited throughout the first movement (in whole and half steps), forms the basis of the theme of the second (A-flat, B-flat, A-flat), and is imbedded in the main theme of the third movement (mm. 20–21). To ignore the short slurs that reveal such motives is to miss a major element in the architecture of a work.

Some slurs of moderate length—often one or two measures—may delineate phrase members, those sections of a phrase that end with a partial or transient "point of rest" or phrase division (see above p. 92). Classic theorists stressed

Fig. 5.22. Mozart, Sonata K. 545/ii (first German ed., André), mm. 1-2.

Fig. 5.23. Mozart, Rondo K. 511 (Aut. facs.[57]), mm. 163–171.

Fig. 5.24. Beethoven, Sonata Op. 57/i (Aut. facs.), mm. 1–4.

the importance of recognizing, shaping, and separating each phrase member.[58] Their inconclusive points of rest vary in clarity, often depending on the degree to which rhythm and harmony are involved in their articulation. Two examples of phrase members from Beethoven's sonatas illustrate differences in the clarity of phrase divisions. The four-measure phrase that introduces the second episode in Op. 13/iii/79–82 has two slurs, each over two measures. The end of the first slur marks a phrase division that might otherwise be overlooked, for it lacks clear melodic or harmonic definition; in performance it needs subtle clarification. On the other hand, the first right-hand slur in Figure 5.25 embraces a phrase member that is unmistakably identified by the rhythmic, melodic, and harmonic shaping of its point of rest. Although the strong-to-weak direction of the incise slur becomes less noticeable as slurs grow longer, the implication of attack and release is still generally valid for slurs over longer incises or phrase members.

Fig. 5.25. Beethoven, Sonata for Violin and Piano Op. 96/ii (Aut.), mm. 1–8.

Fig. 5.26. Clementi, Sonata *Oeuvre* 1/2/iii (OE Bailleux), mm. 32–39.

Schulz and Türk report that when a phrase division falls between notes that might otherwise be beamed together, composers sometimes indicate the division by separating the beams.[59] Thus, beaming itself may serve as a clue to articulative groupings (e.g., Haydn, Hob. 38/ii/7 [*JHW,* HSU]; Mozart, Rondo K. 485/123 [*NMA,* HE]).[60]

Clementi used a surprising variety of slurs in the early 1780s, near the start of his career as a composer. Incise slurs and slurs of moderate length are the most frequent, but he sometimes placed slurs over a complete phrase or even beyond. Indeed, as early as his *Oeuvre* 1/2, published in 1780 or 1781, Clementi wrote a single slur over the bass of the first half of a sixteen-measure variation (Fig. 5.26).[61] The resulting legato helps to unify this formal section, whose melody is highly fragmented—a slur usage frequent in his works. In his Sonata Op. 7/3 (pub. 1782), a number of slurs extend over four or more measures, some covering complete phrases, others covering large phrase members. The slur over the inner voice in Figure 5.27 coincides with the phrase and with the length of the bass pedal point, which underlies a play of tonic and subdominant harmonies (I, IV$_4^6$, I, V$_7$ of IV, IV$_4^6$, I). Thus in Clementi's conception the slur might have had a connection with the harmonic elements as well as with the phrase length.[62] By 1785, the date of the original publication of Op. 13/6, Cle-

Fig. 5.27. Clementi, Sonata Op. 7/3/ii (OE Artaria), mm. 21–24.

menti had placed a slur over two extended phrases that constitute the complete closing section in sonata-allegro form (Fig. 5.31).

Another noteworthy aspect of Clementi's slurring is his early use of slur elision: that is, the meeting of the end of one slur and the start of the next over a single note, making it at once the end of the preceding and the start of the following motive or phrase (as in Fig. 5.33, m. 26). A slur elision preserves a continuous legato while indicating the structural groups and the necessity of expressive nuance in playing the pivotal note.

Yet, in spite of Clementi's interest and skill in using slurs, compositions written before the maturing of his famed cantabile style display only partial and sometimes inconsistent directions for articulation. At times his intentions for unmarked passages seem clear; at others such passages seem open to more than one interpretation. Inconsistencies in the slurring of comparable lines within the same original or revised edition also appear. Since neither holographs nor engravers' copies exist for any of his published works, it is impossible to determine whether these differences stem from Clementi—deliberately or accidentally—or from engravers' indifference.

Beethoven, like Clementi, also used slurs over several measures or more; but Beethoven went further, eventually giving some slurs a function related to formal development. Slurs of many kinds, from those over two-note incises to a few over complete four- or eight-measure phrases—even an occasional one over almost all of a twelve-measure phrase—appear in Beethoven's music right from the Piano Trios of Op. 1.[63] By sidestepping expected cadences and symmetries through melodic, harmonic, and rhythmic means, Beethoven often drew out his lines to unpredictable lengths. The longer slurs are, in part, external evidence of this increased breadth. Interestingly, slurs over several measures or a complete phrase are least likely to occur in Beethoven's slow movements, perhaps because the expansiveness within each measure creates the need for internal breathing in the long, slow-moving phrases.

Two examples will demonstrate Beethoven's skill in utilizing slurs of varying lengths and legato structure as part of the development of a movement. Figure 5.28a shows his delineation of the melodic motives at the beginning of Op. 7/iii, with the inversion of the primary motive in the left hand. The opening slur spans a phrase member heard as one down–up rhythmic group. At the gentle release of the first soprano and bass slurs, the thread of sound is carried on by ties in the inner voices. The melodic line gains impetus as it rises to two fresh attacks. The first coincides with a secondary phrase-rhythm accent and an appoggiatura 6/4 chord; the second coincides with the goal of the phrase, which frequently—as here—associates with the last strong beat before the final note.

Further on in the movement (Fig. 5.28b) the texture is reduced to two parts, each playing the same expansion of the opening motive. In the left hand the slurs follow the original motivic grouping; in the right hand a five-measure slur creates an effect of greater space and continuity. Here Beethoven provided an almost gratuitous *crescendo* sign as the line reaches for each of its higher chromatic half notes. The first *crescendo* in Figure 5.28c places the climax of that phrase in the tonic minor earlier than in Figure 5.28a, but again on the last strong beat before the final note and coincident with a fresh slur. The denouement of the section immediately following, in C-flat major, is delayed by a chromatic movement of the bass in m. 65 that diverts the harmony from an expected cadence. The single seven-measure slur at this important place—

Fig. 5.28. Beethoven, Sonata Op. 7/iii (OE Artaria). a. mm. 1-4. b. mm. 25–30. c. mm. 51–68.

*A page break here may account for the partially omitted tie.

in eighteenth-century orthography combined with ties—is the longest in the movement.

In the Allegretto of the Sonata Op. 14/1 Beethoven used slurs of different lengths for one of his favorite purposes: to help create the contrasting moods of an ABA form. The 3/4 meter and the emphatic long–short–long (amphimacer) tone foot of the main motive, slurred individually within each measure, form the predominating interpretive elements of the A section. Many one-measure slurs as well as *sf* accents maintain the rhythmic drive. By contrast, in the more lyrical Maggiore there are only two slurs (excluding the *portato* indications) that do not cross a bar line (mm. 66 and 80). Most cover two measures, with one over four measures at the start to set the new mood, another in Figure 5.29, and a slur over four and a third measures (Fig. 5.29, mm. 73–77) that is, in effect, lengthened by an overlapping slur on the middle voice. In this context the meter is de-emphasized.

Although complementary phrases and periodicity were of primary importance in Classic music, and although longer slurs were used, slurs seem not to have acquired the specific purpose of designating phrase lengths. Their primary function remained that of signifying legato touch. Thus, the existence of phrase-length slurs remains more exceptional than expected and may be coincidental with other purposes. Some phrase-length slurs probably arose as an expression of the developing cantabile melodic style that naturally led to more extensive legato playing (e.g., Clementi, Op. 7/3/i/102–109). Indeed, occasional phrases that are completely slurred may have been conceived with that sound, just as Var. 8 of Op. 35 seems to have been conceived as an expression of pedaled sound (p. 134 above). Other phrase-length or longer slurs arose from the use of contrasting articulation for developmental purposes (Fig. 5.46c) or to secure a connective or unifying element where concurrent parts are fragmentary (Figs. 5.26, 5.30). Still others seem to be related to harmonic activity (Fig. 5.27).[64]

Fig. 5.29. Beethoven, Sonata Op. 14/1/ii (OE Mollo), mm. 71–78.

Fig. 5.30. Beethoven, Sonata Op. 28/i (Aut.), mm. 11–20.

Beethoven's phrase-length slur in Figure 5.30 is over the tenor line of uniformly moving harmonic notes. In the bass the reiterated pedal point on D, itself a "thematic" element in the movement, stretches unbroken from m. 1 to m. 25. In mm. 2–10 and again in mm. 12–20 the right hand has the A theme, which is slurred in the customary manner, highlighting the important melodic, rhythmic, and sometimes harmonic groups. The last six notes of the tenor line in Figure 5.30 are present in the first statement of the theme but are not slurred. Accompanying the second statement of the theme, the contrapuntal tenor appears full grown under a single slur. This line creates a third dimension and serves as a connective layer between the throbbing bass and the theme slurred in motivic groups. Not surprisingly, an identical arrangement of texture and slurs had occurred twenty years earlier in Clementi's Op. 7/3/ii/21–24 (Fig. 5.27).

As Clementi and Beethoven widened the circumstances in which they found meaningful use of slurs, they occasionally stretched those uses to what might be called illusory slurs or aural images. In its smallest dimension this concept appears in the opening theme of Beethoven's Op. 2/2/iv, where the compound interval of an octave and a sixth cannot be played as a literal legato. The slur suggests the ideally smooth linkage and the dynamic relationship of those notes in Beethoven's aural image. Could Mozart's hand span the slurred major tenth in K. 540/19 on his fortepiano, whose keys were very slightly narrower than those on modern instruments? Slurs in which a literal legato yields temporarily to an effective illusion also occur in conjunction with melodic phrases in octaves (e.g., Clementi's Op. 6/2/ii/94–96 [OC] and Op. 7/3/i/102–109 [about which the use of the pedal in mm. 105–106 was discussed in chap. 4] and Beethoven's Op. 106/ii/66–71, 74–79); with repeated notes (as in mm. 73–75R of Beethoven's Op. 26/ii); and with rests (as in Clementi's Op. 13/6/i/58–61, in the revised version only, and Beethoven's Opp. 10/2/i/41–43 and 101/i/19–20).

Occasionally slurs occur that include more than a single phrase: perhaps two phrases, such as those in Figures 5.31, 5.32, and 5.33, or large sections of two extended phrases, such as the single left-hand slur from the end of m. 159 to the end of m. 172 in the holograph of Beethoven's Sonata Op. 78/ii. Figure 5.31 is the conclusion of Clementi's passionate sonata Op. 13/6. Both the right-hand melody and the left-hand motives are new transformations of the opening theme of this sonata-allegro finale. The legato slurring of these twenty measures stands in strong contrast to the short motives preceding them and has a calming effect as the movement draws to a close. The long slurs in both hands of Figure 5.32 (with Beethoven's slur elision preserved in the left) embrace the first two phrases of this variation. Does Beethoven's verbal reinforcement, *sempre ligato*, reflect the rarity of such long slurs, or is it merely his way of pointing out the intended contrast with the detached articulation of the first variation? The double slurring of the bass in m. 36 is also unusual. I interpret the start of that short slur—which in practice occurs on the first of the tied A-flats, although custom at this time separated ties and slurs—as one way of capping

Fig. 5.31. Clementi, Sonata Op. 13/6/iii (first English edition, Printed for the Author, 1785), mm. 301–322.

Fig. 5.32. Beethoven, Sonata Op. 57/ii (Aut. facs.), mm. 33–40.

the pull of the octave with a gentle emphasis, perhaps somewhat more than one might otherwise place in the middle of a longer slur.

Some slurs in Clementi's revision of Op. 13/6/i, dated 1807 or 1808, and in Beethoven's Op. 78, composed in 1809, embrace sections that produce considerable thrust. In Figure 5.33 the two slurs joined by elision create a single unit whose impressive drive is generated by rhythmic momentum and motivic intensification in the right hand and by the tension of the initial legato octaves (mm. 25–26) followed by the rising bass in the left. In Beethoven's Op. 78/ii the generating force through the slurred section of mm. 159–172—during which the coda drives on toward its conclusion—is a development of the motive

Fig. 5.33. Clementi, Sonata Op. 13/6/i (Aut. of composer's revised version, 1807 or 1808), mm. 24–30.

originally heard in m. 3. The right hand has three slurs in these fourteen measures. The first begins in mid-phrase, after three initial chords, and continues to its conclusion (upbeat to m. 159 to m. 163); the second stands over a single presentation of the motive, whose secondary dominant thrusts the passage into its last section; and the third embraces a phrase extension built with repeated one-measure motivic units. All the while the left hand, which plays an inversion of the motive, has a single slur that unites the passage—except for the short beginning and end of the phrases—as it must have sounded in Beethoven's "inner ear."[65]

These last four examples of unusually long slurs still produce a literal legato in performance. One very long slur that twice has to ride over repeated—hence nonlegato—melody notes occurs in Beethoven's Op. 109/i/21–35. What these five long slurs have in common is that Clementi and Beethoven were using them not for an expressive purpose within a phrase but for an aesthetic effect over a section longer than a phrase. In every case the slur also emphasizes the essential unity of the passage rather than its individual parts. The *sempre legato* immediately following the slur in Op. 109/i/21–35 would continue the legato into the recapitulation, although it is at best an illusion in mm. 42–48, supported by the rolling sound of the parts under the repeated B's. This long, continuous legato, which creates a tremendous sweep with the continuously reiterated *vivace* motive, is actually one of the events of this development, in which several aspects of the musical structure change little. The length of this legato passage may remind us of some in the works of Chopin, in which single slurs with conspicuous structural breadth convey unity and sweep.[66]

Our investigation of "The Language of the Slur" has considered the effects on musical rhetoric of the multifarious slurs used in Classic music. It has also revealed the more extensive use of legato and long slurs by Clementi and Beethoven in comparison with that by Haydn and Mozart. This difference in performance style helps to explain the negative ring of Beethoven's comments about Mozart's playing quoted in chapter 1. Mozart played with more non-legato, shorter slurs, and more-regular metric accentuation. Although metric accentuation was important to Beethoven, he often mitigated its effect with both short and long slurs, further heightening the impression of a broad legato style. From today's vantage point, Beethoven's comments confirm a change in musical style and performance more than they criticize Mozart's legato.

Do All Slurs Indicate Attack and Release?

A casual look at a random sample of slurs in music of the Classic period often makes today's pianists wonder why some slurs end where they do. Since we are accustomed to the long line and perpetual legato of late nineteenth-century interpretation and to editions in which many slurs have been extended or joined to cover complete phrases, it is natural that we ask why authentic slurs so often end at a bar line, at the end of a beat, or before the final note of a phrase. Readers may already have noticed such slur endings in Figures 3.16 (beats 2–3), 3.17, 3.22, and 5.22 and in the bass line of 5.23, to name just a few. The reasons for these slurrings are both musical and historical.

The metrical accentuation discussed in chapter 3 as well as the prevalence of nonlegato and of short articulative groups played an important role in the development of other aspects of interpretation in seventeenth- and eighteenth-century performance. As the disciplines of bowing stringed instruments (viols and violins) and tonguing wind instruments started to become formalized during the sixteenth and seventeenth centuries, performers responded to the desire for stress on strong beats with appropriate techniques. In string playing the "Rule of the Down-Bow" evolved.[67] This phrase is best suited to the violin family, in which the down-bow has more strength than the up-bow and was naturally preferred for accentuation. (In viol playing the term *down-bow* is used for what is really an out-bow, the less strong stroke on this instrument; *up-bow* is used for the in-bow, which, in terms of musical effect, is roughly equivalent to a violin down-bow.) Slurs generally stopped at the bar line to allow for a fresh down-bow on the downbeat. Within measures slurs often extended only over the notes of one (or even half of a subdivided) beat, to allow for the subdivisions of metric accentuation and for the highly articulate style congenial to both the contemporary instruments and the music.

Since the development of expressive bowing and tonguing took place considerably ahead of any similar development in keyboard playing,[68] it was natural for keyboard composers to adopt a sign already in use. In his *Tabulatura Nova* of 1624, an important collection of music for organ and other keyboard instruments, Samuel Scheidt introduced slurs over groups of two or four sixteenth notes, sometimes accompanied by the words "Imitatio Violistica" (Fig. 5.34). He also provided an explanation (Fig. 5.35):

> Wherever the notes are drawn together, as here, it is a special way [of playing], just as violists [*Violisten*] are accustomed to do in sliding [*schleiffen*] with the

Fig. 5.34. Scheidt, *Tabulatura Nova*, Pt. I, "Wir gläuben all'an einen Gott," *Denkmäler Deutscher Tonkunst*, m. 53.

Fig. 5.35. Scheidt, *Tabulatura Nova.*
N.B.

bow. As such a style is not unknown among the more celebrated violists of the German nation, and also results in a very lovely and agreeable effect on the gentle-sounding organs, regals, harpsichords and instruments [perhaps clavichords], I have become fond of this manner of playing and have adopted it.[69]

In adopting the "special way, just as violists are accustomed to do in sliding with the bow," Scheidt was using the curved line to indicate groups of legato notes at the beginning and end of which there would be an articulation at least comparable to that at the change of bow direction on the contemporary stringed instruments. The early violin bow had a different curve and a different balance from the Tourte bow used in the nineteenth and twentieth centuries; like the convex viol bow, it also had less tension on the hair. These factors conspired to make a bow change on either instrument audible to some extent. With the fresh impulse of a change in bow stroke, the looser hair yielded enough as it was pressed against the string to produce some slack or inertia before the anticipated sound. Leopold Mozart described this effect as a small "softness":

> Every tone [or bow stroke], even the strongest attack, has a small, even if barely audible, softness at the beginning of the stroke; for it would otherwise be no tone but only an unpleasant and unintelligible noise. This same softness must be heard also at the end of each stroke.[70]

Under these circumstances, a series of bow strokes on single notes or a change of bow before or after a slur gave the effect of a nonlegato or fresh articulation even if the player kept the bow on the string. (This effect might be compared to the stoppage of sound before a hard consonant.)

The original relationship between the bowing slur and the keyboard slur remained alive and influenced the use of the keyboard slur into the nineteenth century, although to a gradually decreasing extent. Two quotations from George Simon Löhlein's *Clavier-Schule* speak for the mid-eighteenth century:

> If the same sort of arc [*Bogen*] is over different notes [as distinguished from the same notes under a tie], they should be played gently one after another, and

at the same time strung together. On the violin they would be played in one bow stroke. . . . They are called slurred notes [see Fig. 5.36].[71]

In respect to expression the keyboard is not as complete as the stringed and wind instruments. Nevertheless the same notes can be performed in different ways, and one can imitate several kinds of bowing [see Fig. 5.37].[72]

And in 1839 Carl Gollmick wrote that "The slur . . . originally stems from the violin, and . . . only later was used by keyboard players."[73]

The same desire for metric accentuation that supported the Rule of the Down-Bow and governed the length of the slur in string music also directed the early use of slurs in keyboard music to a considerable degree. Thus during the Baroque and early Classic periods the keyboard slur was typically short and only gradually came into use over bar lines. On the clavichord and later on the fortepiano, the first note after (in addition to the first note under) a slur was noticeable not only because of the preceding separation of sound but also because of the slight emphasis that came with the fresh impulse in playing. On the harpsichord and the organ the separation of sound itself drew attention to the first notes under and after a slur, creating an illusion of emphasis.

These considerations help to explain the placement of some of the apparently perplexing slur endings in the keyboard music of the Baroque and Classic periods. Figure 5.38 contains slurs that end before the second beat and slurs that end before the bar line, always to preserve the effect of the meter. I believe that there should be just the right amount of articulation at the beginning and end of each slur to provide a fresh impulse or just an appropriate distinctness (for a following unslurred note) without impeding the flow of the line. (In some editions produced under the spell of the "long legato," the right-hand slurs in mm. 75 and 76 include the final note of the motive, and there is only a single

Fig. 5.36. Löhlein, *Clavier-Schule,* p. 13.

Fig. 5.37. Löhlein, *Clavier-Schule,* p. 69.

Fig. 5.38. Mozart, Sonata K. 330/i (Aut.), mm. 75–79.

[Allegro moderato]

slur from beat 1 of m. 78 to the first g² in m. 79, thus diminishing the expected effects of the ornamental d² and the downbeat of m. 79).

In Figure 5.39 the final note of the phrase sounds just a little more distinct and deliberate coming after the slur; the projection of the theme is more interesting than it would be under a continuing slur with the final note simply tapered off in an unbroken legato. Of course the end of the slur must be all but imperceptible, sometimes heard more as a lightness than as a separation. Similar slurring exists in the opening phrase of Mozart's Rondo K. 485. The Scherzo of Beethoven's Sonata Op. 2/3 presents an analogous situation (Fig. 5.40). Some pianists find it "convenient" to continue each upbeat slur over the bar line, making the first separation on the staccato note; however, Beethoven's indicated effect produces a Scherzo of a more sprightly, rhythmic quality.

Does this mean that the legato should end every time a slur ends at a bar line? The answer is yes much of the time, because of the finesse imparted to the line by appropriate accentuation and articulation. However, there are some situations in which individual slurs may not always indicate an attack and release and where the legato may properly continue over the bar line even though the slur ends before it. This idiosyncratic Classic slurring occurs most commonly in four categories: a short motive slurred as one unit within a measure, but not when it crosses a bar line; a trill with written-out termination whose slur ends before the note that follows; successive measure-length slurs; and successive slurs that stop and start over a cantabile melody in unexpected places.

In Figure 5.41, Mozart's slur embraces the four-note motive each time it falls within the measure. When the motive crosses the bar line his slur stops at that psychological barrier. This two-measure pattern, whose rhythm is identical with that in Figure 5.13g, in which Türk's slur clearly crosses the bar line, appears four times in Mozart's movement with identical slurring in both holograph and first edition; yet it is difficult to imagine interpreting the shortened slur literally. Interestingly, in Mozart's Sonata for Piano and Violin K. 378/i/

Fig. 5.39. Mozart, Sonata K. 280/i (Aut.), mm. 1–4.

Fig. 5.40. Beethoven, Sonata Op. 2/3/iii (OE Artaria), mm. 1–3.

Fig. 5.41. Mozart, Sonata K. 310/ii (Aut.), mm. 22–23.

Fig. 5.42. Mozart, Sonata K. 333/i (Aut.), m. 26.

189–190 (*NMA*) and in Clementi's Sonata Op. 8/1/i/149–151 (OE) motives similar to that in Figure 5.41 are slurred consistently, bar lines notwithstanding.

A trill with a written-out turned ending is sometimes visually separated from the note that follows, which is its natural conclusion, by the termination of a short slur (Fig. 5.42). This notation may reflect the influence of metrical accentuation, especially on bowing. (Here I would expect as smooth a bow change as possible.) In such situations it most often seems preferable to follow Emanuel Bach's advice that "the last note of the embellishment must not be released until the following note arrives, for the primary aim of all embellishments is to connect notes."[74] Additionally, the tempo of the movement and an appropriate speed for the trill termination, which is usually played at the speed of the trill itself (p. 241 below), may make it technically unfeasible to observe the end of the slur literally. Emanuel Bach also gave examples of slurs over configurations in which a dotted note is followed by two notes that look like a trill termination. These slurs were to serve specifically as an injunction against adding trills[75] and may be regarded as a related situation in which the slur does not necessarily indicate actual articulation.

Support for slurring trills with turned endings to the note following, even over a bar line, was also suggested by Türk when he wrote that "the trill is joined . . . even more to the following note by the turned ending. . . ."[76] However, a trill at a *fermata* may have a "somewhat slower" turned ending followed immediately by the note an octave below the trilled note.[77] Here Türk's slur stops at the termination, implying that this more affective ending with a decorative melodic leap may be enhanced by a slight articulation.

Successive slurs over complete measures occur in widely varying circumstances; their rationale and performance remain problematic to varying degrees. In some contexts a series of measure-length slurs seems merely to indicate a prevailing legato; in other contexts the slurs may also have been intended to highlight rhythmic grouping or harmonic rhythm. The choices of interpretation offered in the ensuing discussion represent my judgments, founded on the scant authentic information available.

The custom of notating a prevailing legato with successive measure-length slurs was described as late as 1839 by Czerny.

> When, however, slurs are drawn over several notes, although the slurs are not continuous, but are broken into several lines, they are considered as forming but one, and no perceptible separation must take place [Fig. 5.43].
>
> Here the last note of each bar must not be played short or detached; but it must, on the contrary, be connected with the following one. Should the Composer desire to make it detached, he must place a dot or dash over it.[78]

This custom, like the others just observed, would seem to relate to the overriding importance of metrical structure in an earlier time and to the subsequent customs of bowing stringed instruments. Such slurring is easiest to interpret when it occurs over a straightforward accompaniment pattern, as in Mozart's Rondo K. 485, m. 156 to the end. Here the performer may continue the legato throughout, or perhaps provide a breath at the end of m. 160. Similar series of slurs are not infrequent in the works of Mozart, and still occurred in those of Beethoven, Schubert, and other composers of the early Romantic period.

Figures 5.44a and b illustrate the development in notating slurs between the original version of Clementi's Sonata Op. 13/6, published in 1785, and the revised version of 1807 or 1808. The slurring of the bass in Figure 5.44a seems to represent a mixture of notational custom and performable legato. The slur in mm. 38–41 designates a viable legato segment. On the other hand, the successive slurs in mm. 29–35 and 41–44 surely derive from the custom that suggests a prevailing legato between at least some, if not all, of them. I believe that Clementi would have played some of these individually slurred measures with a continuous legato when he wrote this sonata, for these slurs appear primitive in comparison with others in this work and with his earlier long slurs. Interestingly, at mm. 41 and 44 the slurs cross the bar lines to include each final note. Perhaps this notation can be taken to indicate that when successive measure-length slurs represent a prevailing legato, the last slur may be extended to the final note, as it is in m. 44.

That Clementi modernized the notation of the slurring when he revised this sonata is not surprising. The twenty-odd years that had elapsed between the publication of Op. 13 and its revision were crucial ones in which the developing cantabile melodic style led gradually to greater use of legato playing

Fig. 5.43. Czerny, *Piano Forte School,* Vol. I, p. 187.

Fig. 5.44. Clementi, Sonata Op. 13/6/i. a. First English edition, Printed for the Author (1785), mm. 29–44.
b. Aut. of composer's revised version (1807 or 1808), mm. 30–45.

and then to its more accurate notation. It is interesting, though, that when Clementi expanded the slurs, beginning and ending them with actual legato segments rather than mechanically at the bar lines, he left separations in mm. 32 and 33. From this I infer that today's performer, when faced with successive measure-length slurs indicating a prevailing legato, may determine which of the slurs to join and where—if at all—a breath is necessary or attractive. As Clementi showed in Figure 5.44b, there may be more than one possible interpretation.

The discussion of Figure 5.44 will prove helpful as we look back now at the sixteenth-note lines of Figure 5.23. Their melodic and harmonic richness is quite different from the simple accompaniment of K. 485/156–165, discussed earlier. Where should the legato be continued across the bar lines? How should the two isolated notes in the bass (mm. 166 and 168) be treated? My preference is to continue the legato between the first two slurs but to preserve an almost imperceptible separation between mm. 164 and 165 to emphasize the unexpected sound of F major. Extending the slur in m. 165 over the bar line to the low E-natural (as Clementi did at mm. 43–44 of Fig. 5.44a) seems musically

b. [Allegro agitato e con espressivo]

attractive. A breath at the octave skip renews the line on an upbeat, parallel to its beginning in m. 163. This fresh impetus carries through m. 167, connecting the two slurs. A subtle articulation for the final A (m. 168) provides a neat conclusion for the phrase and the authentic cadence. In the right hand I continue the legato between the first two and the next two successive slurs. The new slur on the second sixteenth note of m. 170 marks the start of a fresh sequence.

In Figure 5.45a we meet a potentially more thorny problem: measure-length slurs over the opening theme of a sonata-allegro movement.[79] Here a violinist would use a down-bow in m. 1, an up-bow—with its different psychological effect—in m. 2, and so on, following the slurred metric groupings. A change of direction with an eighteenth-century bow would not have been completely inaudible; neither do I believe that the pianist should glue these waves of melody together into one unbroken surge. A lightness or barely perceptible separation between the slurs, equivalent to the "softness at the beginning of the stroke" on an early bow and made by sliding the finger gently off each quarter note as the hand dips into the next key, preserves the rhythmically sequential aspect of the theme. Although these successive slurs remind us of

Fig. 5.45. Mozart, Sonata K. 570/i. a. OE Artaria, mm. 1–4. b. Comparative readings of slurs. Vertical lines represent bar lines at the start of each measure.; the fourth measure of each group is not closed.

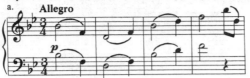

a. Allegro

b.

	Exposition			Development				Recapitulation		
	A	**B**						**A**	**B**	
Mm.	1–4	41–44	45–48	101–104	105–108	109–112	113–116	133–136	171–174	175–178
Aut.										
OE										
Bro										
SU										
HE										
NMA										

Czerny's illustration, a continuing legato here would iron out the wavelike motivic quality that defines the theme. In the development and in the B section of the recapitulation, when the theme appears only in a single voice, Mozart connected the slurs, possibly to gain the longer expanse of unbroken legato and less-accentuated rhythm as a foil for a more highly articulated counter-subject.

Mozart's connection of the slurs over selected recurrences of the A theme, the loss of mm. 1–64 of his autograph, and his use of "Da Capo" for mm. 133–160 of the recapitulation (instead of writing it out), raise vexing questions of slur transcription that confront editors and performers frequently in the Classic repertory. The most important problems are the lack of certainty about where a slur begins and ends in an autograph or a first edition, inconsistency of slurring within a movement, and inconsistency between primary sources. Individual editors may reach different solutions; consequently, performers sometimes find divergent readings among well-executed scholarly editions (see n. 48) or information for more than one reading in a single edition. These situations place related decisions in the performers' hands.

A synopsis of incongruencies related to the slurring of Figure 5.45a in later occurrences will illuminate some of the problems of slur transcription. Figure 5.45b can serve as a visual guide. The parts of the autograph (hereafter Aut.) extant show the A theme only in the development and as it recurs in the B section of the recapitulation.[80] In most of these occurrences Mozart connected the three short slurs but stopped before the fourth measure; in mm. 175–178 he slurred the measures by twos. The Artaria edition (hereafter OE) follows Mozart's autographic slurs in those sections except for mm. 175–178, where OE has a two-measure and a single-measure slur. But each of OE's slurs on this theme in the B section of the exposition embraces only one measure. Short of locating this part of the autograph, we may never know whether Mozart had slurred each measure there separately (and connected the slurs only later in the movement) or whether his slurring in the exposition was parallel to that of the extant part of the recapitulation but was incorrectly engraved. It is also unclear whether the longer slurs in OE are intended to end on the last note of the phrase or at the end of the previous measure. I interpret them in the latter fashion, but not all editors do (see Fig. 5.45b).

Readers will come to understand the connection of these problems to their own performances by considering the readings based on those sources in four superior editions of Mozart's Piano Sonatas.[81] Nathan Broder (Bro) has interpreted the lengthened slurs in the development as going to the end of the phrase. He followed Aut. in the B section of the recapitulation and applied those readings to the exposition. Karl Heinz Füssl and Heinz Scholz (SU) retained the three measure-length slurs over this theme throughout the movement, although at m. 101 they reported the lengthening of the slurs in Aut. and OE (inaccurately for OE) in a footnote. Ernst Herttrich (HE) read the lengthened slurs uniformly as stopping before the last measure and also applied those in the recapitulation to the exposition. He did not split the slur in mm. 175–178, perhaps considering the two clearly drawn slurs a slip of the pen, since m. 176 in Aut. is at the end of a system. Wolfgang Plath and Wolfgang Rehm (NMA) followed the slurring of Aut. (except in mm. 175–178, where they, like Herttrich, placed a single three-measure slur) and of OE where that is the only source; however, they placed single long slurs in broken lines over all the groups of short slurs and stated in the Vorwort their belief that Mozart meant long slurs throughout!

There are also other inconsistencies of slurring in the primary sources for this movement. The least complicated is that between mm. 74 and 204; OE shows one slur over the three broken octaves in m. 74 and both Aut. and OE show three individual slurs in m. 204. Broder placed individual slurs in both measures, giving preference to the holographic reading in the recapitulation as he had done with the main theme. Füssl and Scholz followed OE and Aut., giving the two different readings; Herttrich put a single slur in both measures, giving preference to OE's reading in the exposition. Plath and Rehm gave the two different readings but in each place included the other possible reading in broken lines. With just this much information it is not difficult to understand why each performer needs to know as much as possible about the rationale of a composer's use of slurs and why additional information related to the editor's reading may be helpful in making any necessary choices.

The successive slurs over primary motivic material in Beethoven's Sonata Op. 27/1/ii (Fig. 5.46a) ultimately assume a role in the shaping of the movement. Since three-quarters of this scherzo is based solely on these metric-melodic groups, their interpretation is of fundamental importance. The jocose character of the material, arranged in a "dance of the hands," and the nature of its development after the completely staccato middle section—particularly in the separation of the legato groups by rests (Fig. 5.46b), in the increasing struggle between the staccato and the syncopated legato groups, and finally in

Fig. 5.46. Beethoven, Sonata Op. 27/1/ii (OE Cappi). a. mm. 1–4. b. mm. 89–92. c. mm. 136–140.

attacca subito l'Adagio

the five-measure slur at the end (Fig. 5.46c)—suggest strongly that Beethoven intended discreet separations between the individual slurs throughout. What the music alone discloses, Czerny confirmed with his comment: "The three quarter notes in each measure are *legato* [and] are to be set apart in such a manner that the third quarter always appears disconnected, somewhat *staccato*."[82] It is not an exaggeration to state that through its major role in the rhythmic and expressive development of the form Beethoven here made the slur a structural element, just as he did elsewhere with the damper pedal.

With some hesitation I approach what may be the least understandable, most ambiguous type of slurring found in Classic piano music: consecutive slurs that seem to separate sections of a cantabile melody in the most unexpected places. The opening theme of the Adagio cantabile in Beethoven's "Pathétique" Sonata is one of the most frequently discussed examples. Unfortunately its holograph is lost, allowing a small measure of uncertainty; but the slurring in Hoffmeister's original edition is substantially the same in every recurrence of the theme and was presumably intended throughout as shown in Figure 5.47. Given this passage unslurred, most musicians would probably play the melody with more nearly symmetrical slurs and fewer interruptions in the legato. Beethoven, on the other hand, slurred over the expected phrase ending on E-flat in m. 4 and over a possible breath in m. 6; at the same time he inexplicably divided the slurs at the ends of mm. 3 and 5. All of these articulations affect the accenting and shaping of the line.

The first slur might have been intended to clarify the opening phrase member. It also predisposes the listener to a symmetrical response in m. 4 that is aborted. Perhaps the brevity of both slurs in m. 3 is related to the doubling of the harmonic rhythm, which propels the music more quickly; the bass slur there is the only one in this example that does not embrace two measures of more leisurely harmonic movement.[83] The separations between the melodic

Fig. 5.47. Beethoven, Sonata Op. 13/ii (OE Hoffmeister), mm. 1–8.

slurs over mm. 3 and 4 and mm. 5 and 6 are probably signals to project the E-flats—approached from different directions—with particular expressivity. Both pairs of slurs could conceivably indicate a prevailing legato as well. Many performers interpret the first three and then two melodic slurs as continuous legato sections with variations in degree of stress on the first note under each slur. They treat the slur endings within mm. 5 and 7 as separations. But some performers place a barely perceptible separation at the end of the slur over m. 3, and even a lightness at the end of the first slur. Surely the slurs in these exquisitely wrought eight measures create a message that calls for unusually sensitive rhetorical expression.[84]

By way of summary, it is fair to say that when successive measure-length or other unusual slurs occur in melodic or contrapuntal lines, the manner of performance may be more critical than when they occur in relatively straightforward accompaniment patterns. It should also have become clear that no editor may assume the prerogative of altering a composer's slurs. Such changes obscure the composer's perception of the music and remove the performer's opportunities for understanding and for choice where that may exist.

DOT, STROKE AND WEDGE

In the Baroque period the usual staccato signs were the equivalent stroke ǀ and wedge ǀ, the latter found more often in engraved music. The dot was sometimes used, primarily by non-French composers. (The French reserved the dot as one way to designate equal playing of pairs of notes in situations where inequality would otherwise have prevailed.[85]) By around 1750 dots, strokes, and wedges were being used. Many Germans who wrote about keyboard playing, including C. P. E. Bach, Marpurg, and Löhlein, considered the signs synonymous, with no distinction in type of staccato indicated. But Quantz described the staccato indicated by a dot as more sustained and gentle, that indicated by a stroke as crisp, shorter, and more emphatic—actually somewhat accented when the stroke appears over a single note.[86] Since Quantz here referred to orchestral bowing, this early differentiation may reflect the more-advanced state of stringed-instrument articulation and its notation.

Vogler's early (1778) attempt to distinguish between dot and stroke for keyboard playing has staccatos indicated by dots played "very quickly," those indicated by strokes held "longer."[87] This reversal may have been caused by the relative newness of carefully notated articulation in keyboard music, or perhaps by confusion with the use of the stroke as an accent sign, in which case the note may be held to some degree (p. 84 and Fig. 3.14). In 1789 Türk still believed that the stroke (or wedge) and the dot had

> one and the same meaning; yet some would designate a shorter staccato by the stroke than by the dot. . . .
>
> For notes that should be detached [*gestossen*], one raises the finger from the key when close to half the value of the written note is past. . . .
>
> . . . In performance of detached notes one must take into consideration particularly the prevailing character of the composition, the tempo, the prescribed loudness and softness, etc. If the character of a composition is serious, tender, sad, etc., the detached notes should not be played as short as [they would be] in pieces of a lively, playful, etc., character. Occasional detached notes in a songful *Adagio* should not be as short as [they would be] in an *Allegro*. For *forte* one can usually play [detached notes] somewhat shorter than for *piano*. Notes that skip are, in general, more detached than [those] in intervals progressing stepwise, etc.[88]

By 1795 and 1796, trailing the change, as theory usually does, Johann Adam Hiller and Hüllmandel differentiated clearly between stroke and dot,[89] and Clementi did so in 1801:

> The best general rule, is to keep down the keys of the instrument, the FULL LENGTH of every note; for which the contrary is required, the notes are marked either thus: ♯ ♩♩♩ called in ITALIAN, STACCATO; denoting DISTINCTNESS, and SHORTNESS of sound; which is produced by lifting the finger up, as soon as it has struck the key: or they are marked thus ♯ ♩♩♩ which, when composers are EXACT in their writing, means LESS staccato than the preceding mark; the finger, therefore, is kept down somewhat longer: or thus ♯ ♩♩♩ which means STILL LESS staccato: the nice degrees of MORE and LESS, however, depend on the CHARACTER, and PASSION of the piece; the STYLE of which must be WELL OBSERVED by the performer.[90]

In 1802 Koch still regretted the lack of agreement on which of the two signs indicated a "sharper" staccato,[91] but in 1804 Louis Adam made his distinctions even more precise than Clementi's. He stated that notes with a stroke lose three-fourths of their value, those with a dot lose one-half, and those with dots under a slur lose only one-fourth of their value.[92] Now properly called *portato*, this last touch was characterized by the gentleness with which the notes were played and detached, often losing less than one-fourth of their value in the manner of a nonlegato. Some writers indicated that each *portato* note also received a slight emphasis.[93] By this time the differentiation between the dot and the stroke seems to have achieved some degree of recognition, which was reported also by Pollini, Steibelt, Starke, Crelle, and Czerny, among others.[94] (Unfortunately, J. A. Hamilton, the English translator of Czerny's *Vollständige . . . Pianoforte-Schule,* obliterated the careful distinction between the dot and the stroke in Part III of the original German by substituting the word "dashes" for *Pünktchen* [little dots].[95]) Yet, while the dot represented a mild staccato that lightened a note, and the stroke represented a shorter, taut staccato that might emphasize a note, the stroke did not routinely indicate the accented staccatissimo with which it became associated later in the century (see below p. 198).

Unfortunately, in spite of all the good intentions of writers who described the meanings of dots and strokes, serious problems remain in interpreting the signs in holographs. When composers wrote hastily or used a softened quill, dots became elongated and strokes were shortened. The two signs appear in every possible variation; at times they are virtually indistinguishable. But even when the difference is clear, the fact remains that dots and strokes were sometimes used without much consistency. The signs may even appear differently when a motive returns: in the few extant holographs of Clementi's works there are chords and motives played simultaneously in both hands that are marked with apparent dots in one and strokes in the other! (Only the dot, however, was used in combination with the slur to indicate *portato* playing.)

To compound the difficulty, engravers of early editions were frequently casual—if not downright heedless—in reproducing staccato signs as well as slurs and other directions from holographs or authorized copies. This might well account for the simultaneous strokes and dots in the same motive at the end of Figure 3.4. Since chamber works were published only in single parts—the piano part did not contain the others—the engraver may not have noticed that he had used different indications. Unfortunately the holograph of that sonata is unavailable for examination.

The *sforzando* chords in the opening theme of Beethoven's Sonata Op. 27/ 2/iii always carry very clear strokes wherever Beethoven indicated those staccatos in the holograph; yet in the original edition by Cappi (Vienna, 1802), the engraver used dots in nine occurrences of that motive and strokes in the other nine, with no apparent logic of any sort. The lack of a known basis for this change and the seeming capriciousness involved lead to the suspicion that for this sonata, as often for other works, the extant holograph would take precedence over the first edition as a trustworthy source, at least for certain information. Of course, such a conclusion can only be drawn if a thorough comparison of both sources (and sometimes more) shows one to be consistently more reliable. The possibility that some changes in a first or following edition might stem directly from the composer via proofreading, letter, or another manuscript always needs to be considered in such a study. Interestingly, Simrock, a firm whose early reprint editions sometimes contain refinements probably supplied by Beethoven (see n. 50), used wedges consistently over those chords in Op. 27/2/iii.

A few conclusions regarding the use of strokes and dots by Haydn, Mozart, and Beethoven[96] may prove helpful to pianists in interpreting these signs in particular contexts, in understanding the choices made by editors, and in using the wide variety of editions available. Holographic evidence from my research, coupled with the conclusions of other scholars,[97] indicates that all three composers used strokes much of the time to indicate staccatos over single notes as well as series of notes. The gamut of interpretation may run from a distinct, short, and sometimes heavy or accented staccato to a gentle, less short one. Often—although inconsistently—Haydn and Mozart seem to have reserved the dot for certain groups of notes, usually repeated-note figures or passages in short note values, including upbeats and ascending or descending stepwise runs. Dots in such passages abound, for example, in the holograph of Mozart's Concerto K. 453, which disappeared during World War II but has recently come to light in the Biblioteka Jagiellońska in Kraków (e.g., i/116–117, 267, on ascending stepwise runs; i/284–288 on the triadic ascending anacruses). In this volume see Figures 3.5 and 7.57. Motives or passages with staccato dots often occur in contexts in which a light touch with a mild separation, sometimes akin to a nonlegato, seems appropriate.[98] To notate the *portato,* dots were always used under the slurs.

In spite of evidence that supports Beethoven's intention to differentiate his staccato signs[99]—starting by about 1800, according to Nottebohm[100]—the stroke and the dot took every conceivable variation of shape in his hand. Surprising fluctuations sometimes occur with no discernible rationale beyond haste in the act of creativity, as in mm. 89–90 of the holograph of Op. 111/ii (Plate III). From the context of those measures, which continue *sempre ppmo* in the same mood, it seems doubtful that any distinct differentiation or change in the sound of the staccatos was intended. In such situations editors are forced to make arbitrary decisions; performers must make the artistic decisions.

When Beethoven's strokes appear over groups of notes they are occasionally followed by *sempre staccato,* as in the bass of Op. 28/ii and in the Concerto Op. 15/i/414–415. In performance these signs may vary from a gentle sound to a real *marcato,* which Beethoven wrote several times concurrently with strokes in Op. 15.

Like Haydn and Mozart, Beethoven consistently notated dots under the slurs for *portato* touch. These dots are generally small and round, as in Plate II, m. 50. Relatively clear dots for staccatos are often heavier. The first staccato sign in Plate IV might suggest that Beethoven began to make a stroke but pulled back and followed it with dots, but some would say that it is a stroke followed by dots.

Beethoven's holographic staccato dots seem to appear by design in a few types of passages, some similar to those in the music of Haydn and Mozart.

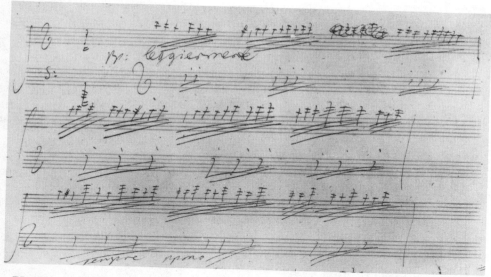

PLATE III. Beethoven, from the holograph of Sonata Op. 111/ii, Arietta, Adagio molto semplice e cantabile, mm. 89–92. Courtesy of Deutsche Staatsbibliothek, Berlin/DDR, Musikabteilung.

Examples are scale passages, as in Op. 19/i/100 (for which the final version of the solo part was written out only in April 1801, just before publication[101]), and—although again inconsistently—repeated notes of short value, often in *piano* settings, as in mm. 9 (six of eight staccatos) and 27 of the theme of Op. 26/i, in m. 11 of Var. 1, and in mm. 1 and 9–10 of Var. 2 (Plate IV). The remainder of the holographic staccatos in Var. 2 change from dots to vigorous strokes as the melodic bass line moves by progressively larger skips rather than by repeated notes or steps. This orthographic change suggests Beethoven's psychological response as his "inner ear" perceived an intensification produced by the skips, as well as his response to the greater physical effort needed to play them even in this relatively quiet setting. In the first edition, published by Cappi (Vienna, 1802), and in a reprint by the Bureau de Musique (also 1802), the staccatos mentioned above in the theme and in Var. 1, and all the staccatos in Var. 2 are dots, although many of the remaining staccatos in the movement are wedges.[102] Additional examples of holographic dots in stepwise runs occur in the Sonata for Violin and Piano Op. 30/3/ii/78 and 189, and iii/ 181, 183, 185, and 187. Dots on repeated notes occur in Op. 96/i/20 and on a pattern that alternates between two adjacent tones in a quiet setting in Op. 30/3/i/61–62 and 81–84 in the violin part. Interestingly, when this pattern occurs in octaves in the piano part it carries strokes.

Because some theorists, including Hummel,[103] did not acknowledge a difference between the stroke and the dot, because composers sometimes used

PLATE IV. Beethoven, from the holograph of Sonata Op. 26/i, Andante con Variazioni, Var. 2, mm. 1–16. Courtesy of Biblioteka Jagiellońska, Kraków.

them inconsistently, and because the signs are often unclear, a number of scholars have rejected the attempt to differentiate between them in printed editions.[104] This issue remains controversial. Similarly, the complexity of transcribing the holographic staccato signs and the more severe problems of information when holographs are not available have caused editorial policies to differ among editions—and even among works of different genres in the same edition—in reproducing the signs.[105] Editorial policy for *JHW* and *NMA* includes the dual signs where possible. The *BNA* represents all staccatos as dots, using the wedge rarely and only where it is absolutely clear that strokes indicate accents rather than staccatos (chap. 3, p. 85). But in most cases in that edition, Beethoven's strokes that represent metrical accents are still reproduced as dots (cf. chap. 3, pp. 96–97). When editors use two signs, strokes are more numerous, for they occur more frequently in the holographs. Performers should routinely consult the statement of editorial policy in any volume for relevant information.

Since Classic composers relied on the stroke so much of the time, it would seem appropriate to use that sign except where the dot is relatively clear; albeit the performer must remember that a printed stroke or wedge in Classic music does not necessarily indicate a staccatissimo. At the very least, where composers seem to have intended an accent or a metrically accented note, the printed sign should be a stroke or a wedge. The shape and size of the actual printed signs materially affect their impression on the performer and his or her response. Thus, a slender wedge (ꞌ), similar to those used in the eighteenth century, is preferable to the heavy triangles in some twentieth-century editions.

While every bit of reliable information from the composer's pen is desirable for the pianist, inevitably the messages of printed staccato signs will remain limited. Nevertheless, although staccato notation may still have been developing in the Classic era, and although we may not yet fully understand its intended meanings, at the present time I believe that whatever differentiation is clear may carry clues that are worth retaining, particularly when the information stems from extant holographs. The performer's sensitivity must bridge the gap between the understandably limited printed symbols and the wealth of available sounds.

In conclusion we might profit from Löhlein's comment, quoted earlier, that "in respect to expression the keyboard is not as complete as the stringed and wind instruments."[106] Perhaps the most serious lack of the piano is the possibility of controlling a tone once it has been struck. That is precisely why the numerous details related to touch, articulation, attack and release of slurs, and types of staccatos are worthy of the best attention a pianist can give them.

CHAPTER

6

HISTORICAL TECHNIQUE AND FINGERING

POINT OF VIEW

Early players of the fortepiano came to the instrument with techniques originally developed for the clavichord and the harpsichord. With an action different from that of the clavichord, the fortepiano made new demands on technique and touch for controlling its variable dynamics. Yet, because the actions of the three instruments have certain similarities, among them a relative lightness, fragility, and shallow key dip, it is not surprising that several basic characteristics of fortepiano technique evolved naturally from the techniques developed for the earlier instruments, just as certain characteristics of dynamics and articulation evolved from the earlier styles of performance.

A quiet hand and arm, primacy of finger technique with precise finger action, and an even touch with the fingers close to the keys were cultivated by clavichordists, harpsichordists, and fortepianists alike. Emanuel Bach wrote of caressing (*schmeichlen*) the keys of the clavichord, adding that the performer who "understands the correct principles of fingering . . . will play . . . in such a manner that the motion of his hands will be barely noticeable. . . ."[1] Türk and others recommended the clavichord as the best "for learning," for no other keyboard instrument allowed as much "finesse in playing."[2]

Rameau's unusually complete analysis of harpsichord technique is founded on the premise that "perfection of touch . . . consists mainly in well-controlled movement of the fingers."[3]

> The wrist must always be supple . . . the hand . . . serves merely as a support for the fingers . . . and as a means of conveying them to those parts of the keyboard which they cannot reach by their own particular movement alone.
> The movement of the fingers begins at their root. . . .
> Every finger must have its own movement, independent of the others. . . .
> . . . the hands have . . . to be held as if glued to the keyboard, affording the player's touch the maximum degree of contact.[4]

Now compare Rameau's remarks with Streicher's comments on playing the fortepiano:

The hand should lie naturally, just as it is attached to the arm. One should bend the wrist neither upwards nor downwards.

In moving the fingers, the hand must lie in the calmest possible position without, however, becoming stiff. . . .

The arm must support the hand; the hand its fingers. The calmer the arm and hand, the surer the motion of the fingers, the greater the dexterity, and the more beautiful the tone. . . .

When single notes are connected together, . . . you should move *only the fingers,* without raising the hand for the attack. . . . Only in the case of staccato notes or full chords may the hands be raised.[5]

The degree of finger strength and exertion necessary on a fortepiano is closer to what is needed on a harpsichord than on a modern pianoforte. Agility and finesse are more valuable than power. In my experience, unwarranted use of hand or arm in playing any of the early keyboard instruments produces a heaviness that contradicts the natural articulative style of the music. A very strong attack often proves a disadvantage with the light construction, for a sharp blow produces both a hard tone[6] and disturbing sounds in the action. We should also recall Hummel's remark that in spite of the heavier touch of the English pianos, "we gain no louder sound by a heavy blow, than may be produced by the natural strength and elasticity of the fingers" (p. 47 above). There was, of course, unprecedented development both in fortepiano construction and in playing technique during the Classic era. As composers and performers desired an increasing range of expressivity, and as public concerts became part of the fabric of musical life, fortepiano makers developed instruments with sturdier actions and greater resonance. Technical demands and participation of the hand and arm in playing increased concurrently.

This chapter will focus on the technical information relevant to performance practices that is gleaned from the Classic musicians themselves. They were sparing with precise descriptions of some aspects of technique, perhaps considering them in the domain of the teacher. For example, relatively little is found about the manner of movement from place to place on the keyboard and about the use of the hand, wrist, and forearm in playing incise slurs. To gain an adequate description of even the basic playing positions and movements we must frequently combine remarks from more than one source, and then we are often left with some conspicuous ambiguity. As in pianoforte playing and teaching today, different masters suggested different ways of doing the same thing. Nevertheless, there is much that is interesting and useful.

Adam's statement of aesthetic expectations serves as an appropriate point of departure:

In pressing the keys, [the student] should hear only pure sounds. It is in imitating the manner of singing of the great masters of all instruments, it is in imitating as much as possible the diverse inflections of the voice—the richest and most touching [instrument] of all—that the student will succeed in expressing the melodic lines, which alone create the charm of music, and without which one never produces anything but a noise that is as insipid as [it is] insignificant. Finally, in the different ways of striking the keys let him work at finding that [one] which he believes the most appropriate for rendering the expression of the sentiment indicated. . . .[7]

A discussion of touch by Crelle that points to some of the difficulties keyboard players had in handling the new instrument will complete the framework for this chapter:

> One frequently speaks of the touch of this instrument. . . . At times it is only understood as a definite and strong touching of the keys, necessarily linked with a mobility pleasant to the eye and a graceful use of the fingers. The usual consequence[s] of a touch that has only these attributes, however, [are] that the differentiation of *piano* and *forte* more or less disappears, that the strength is exaggerated, that all keys are played *staccato,* and that the *portamento* [sustaining][8] and the connecting of the notes . . . are more or less lost. Certainly it is better if one means by good touch the correct entrance of the notes, the correct relationship between their strength and weakness, and the independence of the fingers from one another and from [each specific] function, so that, for example, one does not hear whether a note is played by this or that finger, but that all fingers of both hands are equally capable of performing that which the composer presents them. . . . It is also necessary that the correct duration of the notes as well as the prescribed legato be heard, and that therefore nowhere a space, . . . nowhere a filling in [of sound] should appear where none should be. To be sure, when two hands are supposed to perform a four-voiced contrapuntal piece, all this together is difficult, and much more difficult than the riskiest leaps and movements of the fingers and arms; but it is truly necessary to a good touch, and even more so with an instrument that does not sustain the tone.[9]

SPECIFIC FUNCTIONS OF TECHNIQUE

Role and Position of the Arm and Hand

Mozart's entertaining description of Nannette Stein's pianistic gymnastics (p. 23 above) allows us to infer that good fortepianists, like good harpsichordists and clavichordists, played with a quiet demeanor, using noticeable arm and hand movements for relatively few tasks. According to Czerny, Beethoven's posture when playing "was ideally calm, noble and good to look at, without the slightest grimace. . . . His fingers were very powerful, not long, and flattened at the tips by much playing."[10] Of Clementi, who had written that "All unnecessary motion must be avoided,"[11] Czerny reported "tranquility of the hands, solidity of touch, . . . and grace of execution. . . ."[12] John Field, Clementi's student, is supposed to have practiced with coins on the back of his hands, a way of teaching alluded to by Starke.[13]

Adam stated his opinion succinctly:

All movement of the arms that is not absolutely necessary is prejudicial to the execution. One can allow only two kinds: the first, when one must leave the keyboard to observe pauses; the other when one must move the hand from right to left or left to right to take another position. . . . Only the forearm should move; the upper arm should remain immobile.[14]

More than twenty years later Hummel noted that, "Even in skips, the hand should scarcely be lifted up from the keys. . . ."[15] This restraint of arm motion provides economy of time and energy in the technique.

According to Milchmeyer the upper arm falls vertically from the shoulder, which should never be raised. The arm leads the hand to the high and low registers and to the "narrow" (black) keys. The elbow moves away from the body only when necessary, but especially when the right and left hands play in the high and low registers respectively, in order to allow free, unconstrained movement. The hands should be far enough in on the keyboard for the root of the thumbnail to be over the white keys.[16]

Milchmeyer's illustrations (Fig. 6.1) show the position most widely described in fortepiano manuals. The wrist and the hand are in a straight line with the forearm, which is sloped slightly toward the keyboard.[17] The hand is gently rounded, and in the detail, labeled "good," the finger plays on the fleshy pad just behind the nail. Hummel's description of a "somewhat rounded" hand and fingers striking the keys "with the middle of the tips" is similar.[18]

Hüllmandel explained that if the wrist is

kept below [the hand it] weakens and stiffens the Fingers, if too high it weakens them likewise, and raises the Thumb too much from the keys. . . .
    The least stiffness should never be felt in the arm, in the wrist, nor in the . . . Fingers, their motion must always be free.[19]

Concern over the amount of movement required for the short fingers to reach the black keys was also expressed. Steibelt suggested that the fifth finger should not be as curved as the others since it must always be ready to play a black key without requiring any movement of the hand.[20] By 1828 Hummel wrote that in melodies and passage-work in which both the thumb and the

Fig. 6.1. Milchmeyer, *Pianoforte zu spielen*, pp. 1–2.

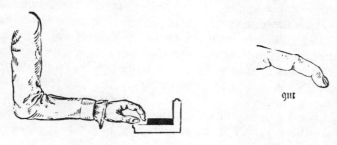

gut

fifth finger are used frequently on black keys, the entire hand should play further in on the keyboard: "The white keys are to be struck with the fingers, not in front of, but *between* the black keys."[21] Use of the thumb on black keys where advantageous was the last important development in the modernization of keyboard fingering[22] (cf. p. 212 below). Its acknowledgment came well after the fact.

Finger Technique

Endorsement of a clearly articulated finger technique based on free action of the fingers from the hand-knuckle was virtually unanimous in Classic sources. Once again Adam's writing provides a good starting point.

> It is only by means of touch that one can draw out beautiful sounds; therefore it is necessary to become accustomed to using only the strength of the fingers to bring out the *forte* sounds as well as the *piano*.[23]

Beethoven taught that

> the hands always lie on the keyboard in such a way that the fingers cannot be raised more than necessary, for only in this way is it possible to *create tone* and to learn to [make the instrument] *sing*. He detested the *staccato style* . . . called it "finger-dancing" or "manual air-sawing."[24]

Hummel supplied a natural continuation

> [Good finger touch] can be effected only by the finest internal sensibility in the fingers themselves, extending to their very tips, by which they are rendered capable of increasing their pressure on the keys, from the most delicate contact to the utmost degree of power. Consequently, the fingers must obey the player in the gentlest touch, and in the most natural and easy position of the hand, equally as in the firmest stroke, and in the most extended state of the muscles.[25]

Steibelt called it "an essential rule—the first for a good execution," that the fingers move alone without involving the hand.[26] Like Rameau, Adam stressed that finger movement was independent of the other fingers as well as of the hand: "When one finger is raised, the others should not be moved."[27]

Finger independence applied to the thumb as well, for that part of modern fingering by which the thumb serves as the pivot in moving the hand along the keyboard had gradually been adopted. The thumb was expected to pass under the other fingers smoothly, involving neither the arm nor the hand in the motion. The other fingers were not to change position until the thumb had played its note. "This is the only way to play with equal touch and to avoid interrupting the sound by the replacement of the fingers."[28]

As many fingers as possible should be prepared for the coming notes by lying lightly on the keys.[29] The movement of a finger as it plays is "flexible and spring-like," yet "innately firm," a quality that is communicated to the hammers and to the sounds they produce.[30]

> It is essential never to strike the key with the force of the arm, but only with the strength provided by the muscles of the fingers. These muscles must never be tense and must be allowed free movement. . . . The fingers must be curved and the muscles relaxed and supple, for all muscular tension blocks freedom of movement and makes it impossible for the hands to extend and contract the fingers promptly, which one needs to be able to do at all times.[31]

Surprisingly, Adam states that just before playing "one raises the fingers a little above the keyboard, but without straightening them, and lets them fall . . . on the notes indicated."[32] This unusual advice, presented with the basic information on finger position and movement near the beginning of Adam's volume, and long before the discussion of legato and staccato playing, must have been intended (although not necessary) for the nonlegato touch, in which each note receives a fresh and distinct impulse, rather than for the legato. My experience with the fortepiano indicates that a legato is best obtained by playing directly from contact with the key, as described in a little-known but remarkable document published in London in 1829:

> The legato style . . . is produced by . . . pressing [the fingers] down more firmly on the instrument, from whence they must never be lifted more than is absolutely necessary to let each key rise into its place after pressure; the fingers seem all *strung upon one wire,* and one is not taken up till the other is fairly set down, so that instead of each note telling separately upon the ear, they seem rather to flow into one another, each note being dependent on, and mingled with, the one next to it; yet not so much as to render it confused or indistinct.[33]

The anonymous author contrasted the legato style with "the distinct, round, brilliant style," in which

> each finger should move quite independently of the rest, as though they were all *hung upon separate wires,* and be not merely taken off, but slightly lifted up from every note the instant the following note is ready to sound.[34]

How to Practice

Emphasis on the role of the finger in early piano playing brought with it some basic information on ways of acquiring the desired finger technique. There was no lack of exercises in the instruction books. What is of interest here is the manner in which the exercises were to be practiced and, in particular, the early development of exercises in which the fingers not playing sustain other notes.

Some ways of practicing that have remained standard to this day were added by Pleyel to the text—originally by Dussek—of the Pleyel-Dussek *Mé-*

thode published in 1797.[35] Pleyel advised that each group of basic five-finger exercises should be repeated "according to the difficulty one finds in doing it":

> One must work at playing them as slowly and as quickly as possible, at first very lightly and with a great deal of gentleness; and to arrive by a *crescendo* to a *fortissimo* that one sustains for a few moments, to return by a *diminuendo* to a *pianissimo,* just as one began. The longer it takes to build this gradation, the more the player shows his intelligence and his skill.[36]

Pleyel included a set of exercises in which all the fingers either sustain or play notes (Fig. 6.2). Because of their particular effectiveness in building finger independence and strength, Clementi used patterns of this type in some of the

Fig. 6.2. Pleyel-Dussek, *Méthode pour le pianoforte,* p. 17.[37]

pieces in his *Gradus ad Parnassum.* [38] Similar patterns reappear in many later volumes on piano technique, including those by Fétis and Moscheles,[39] Liszt,[40] and Dohnányi.[41]

Pleyel suggested that scales as well as exercises be practiced at varying speeds and with *crescendos* and *decrescendos*. Adam included some cautionary advice for scale practice: One should give the same "degree of force" to all the fingers; one should never hold notes that have been played; one should not "jiggle the hand" or be able to hear any "separation of sounds."[42] In other words, scales were to be played with evenly graded dynamics and a continuous (but clean) legato.

Steibelt advised exercises on parallel thirds for making the fingers independent. Series of parallel thirds were to be practiced very slowly at first, then with increasing speed until one could play them at the highest possible speed. "If the right hand becomes tired one exercises the left, and when that becomes tired one returns to the right, and so on."[43]

Another still-current suggestion came from a relatively unknown source. William Seamen Stevens, who lived in London, wrote that

> to play all *allegro* passages with a strong finger or *pressure,* is good practice; it serves to strengthen the former, and gives a certitude of touch, the *forte* and precision acquired by it being easily relinquished, but not so readily gained.[44]

Perhaps the advice that *forte* practicing would produce a stronger finger technique stems from the heavier actions of the instruments built in London.

Staccato Touches

Several staccato touches, all used today, are described in primary sources. Here the hand itself is engaged to a greater or lesser degree, apparently depending on the individual pianism of the writer, sometimes on the speed of the notes being played, but not necessarily—judging from available evidence—on the type of piano action to which the writer was accustomed. According to Hüllmandel and Milchmeyer, all staccato notes, single and double, were made from the wrist with a "small movement of the hand, without moving the arm."[45] Stevens described this "hand" staccato for successive staccato octaves as "the finger and thumb by a spring leaving the keys that have been struck, and advancing to those succeeding by the motion of the wrist entirely."[46]

For other staccato notes Stevens spoke of "the lifting up of the finger only." When the velocity of a passage limits the degrees of staccato, some type of staccato "may be successfully imitated by giving more or less force to the finger, that is to play the passage . . . more or less *for.* or *pia.* . . ."[47] Adam and Starke, referring to French and Viennese instruments respectively, also believed that ordinarily the staccato ought to be played only with the fingers, with no movement of the wrist or hand. But in rapid passages, "where each note should be very detached and very dry," Adam suggested that

the wrist, which should be very flexible, must make a movement for each note, in order to provide the necessary movement to the fingers so that each note sounds separately, especially if the notes are located far from each other. . . .[48]

Starke agreed that "only [staccatos in] fast movement must result in a slight movement of the hand."[49]

Hummel, whose playing remained very much in the clear, delicate style of Mozart, and Czerny, who had been trained in part by Beethoven, both espoused techniques that incorporated a limited degree of hand movement for ordinary staccatos but used only a refined finger movement for fast staccato notes. According to Hummel, in playing staccato "the fingers touch the keys only briefly and push [away] without raising the hand very much."[50] However, when staccato indications appear over a series of short notes (sixteenths in Hummel's figure),

the hands are not raised at all, but the fingers are hurried away from the keys, very lightly and *in an inward direction* [italics added]. The greater the lightness with which these detached notes are played, the more pleasing the effect that they will produce.[51]

Removing the fingers "in an inward direction" is economical of both time and energy. Czerny recommended it for what he termed a "half staccato" over fast notes (e.g., *portato* sixteenths in an Allegro vivace) and compared it to the movement used in changing fingers (4, 3, 2, 1) on fast repeated notes.[52] In addition, "all passages designated with the words *Leggierm:* or *Leggieriss:* must be executed in this way. . . ."[53] This touch is widely applicable on the easy action of the fortepiano and is essential in limited circumstances—including fast finger staccato and the subtlest articulations—on the pianoforte. As a method of withdrawing fingers from the keys, this movement is another direct link between fortepiano, harpsichord, and clavichord techniques, for which Forkel's description of J. S. Bach's playing will serve as testimony: "The finger is not raised straight up from the key, but glides off the front of it by a gradual drawing back of the finger tip toward the palm of the hand."[54]

Hummel limited his description of staccato touches to what might have been appropriate on the light actions of the late eighteenth- and early nineteenth-century Viennese pianos. Czerny, bred in a later style of pianism, placed considerable emphasis on more forcefully accented staccatos. The "*marcato* or *staccatissimo*" was "the shortest manner of detaching notes" and could "be heightened to the *martellato* (or hammer-like attack)." This general kind of staccato was indicated by

> small perpendicular dashes or strokes over the notes, which [in playing] must be carefully differentiated from the little dots.
>
> A greater elevation of the hand and even of the arm (particularly in skips) is allowed here, since the *marcato* is generally employed only in *octaves, chords,* and passages in which the notes do not follow one another very quickly; and since, to enhance the effect, the player is often obliged to exert a good deal of strength.[55]

However, when "the extremely short staccato" occurs in soft contexts, "the arm must be kept far more quiet and the detaching [of the notes] is effected only by the fingers."[56]

By the 1830s the Viennese pianos were more robust and produced enough tone to sustain Czerny's vigorous *staccatissimo* attack.[57] Indeed, more than once in his chapters on the performance of Beethoven's piano works Czerny indicated that the piano had gained significantly in sonority since Beethoven's time.[58] On the earlier fortepianos I have played, such an attack produced more sound of mechanism than of music; or, as Adam said, when the instrument is attacked by the force of the arms "one hears the tiring noise of the hammers and the beating of the keys."[59] Yet there are places in the works of Clementi and Beethoven in which the drama invites forcefully attacked, detached chords, such as those in Clementi's Op. 7/3/i/16 and 56–58 and Beethoven's Op. 31/3/ii/34–35. In 1801 Streicher suggested for loud chords a "quick, sharp grabbing" (*nervöses Anprellen*) of the keys without hitting them, along with emphasis on the bass notes to maximize the sound.[60] On each fortepiano the performer can find the distance from the keyboard and the degree of attack that provide the right total volume—occasionally a combination of music and action sound calculated to shock—without violating the music or tiring the ear.

Stevens's *A Treatise on Piano-Forte Expression* of 1811 contains additional technical information related to staccato playing.[61] His analyses are of special interest for two reasons. First, he was a contemporary of Clementi in London during a period when the fine piano building, the rich concert life, and the warm hospitality of that city attracted outstanding musicians from all over Europe. This activity made London a center of artistic piano playing. Second, Stevens's approach, starting from "expression" rather than from basic elementary instruction, was specifically for the experienced pianist. Consequently it offers more sophisticated information in some areas than that found in the contemporary tutors of Hüllmandel, Dussek, Clementi, and Cramer, also published in London.

After a close look at those situations that require rapid departure from a note even without a staccato sign, Stevens wrote a description of the "staccato for time," so named because of the speed required to relocate the hand (Fig. 6.3). He explained why the wrist and the forearm are important in its execution:

> Here it is plain that from the last note of the fourth bar to the first of the fifth, is a distance beyond the *legato* reach of the finger . . . ; therefore, to execute this properly, the whole is played *legato* till the thumb, arriving at the last note of the fourth bar, strikes the key a little more *forte* than the others, and leaves it with a spring of the wrist and measured skip, and a velocity sufficient to carry it to the key required in due time to commence the succeeding bar.
> . . . [For a series of such leaps, the hand should move] with the thumb and little finger at full extent, which with the palm of the hand should describe an arch or curve [*sic*] line over the keys in making the necessary motion from key to key.[62]

Fig. 6.3. Stevens, *Piano-Forte Expression*, Plate 4.

Playing the Incise Slur

In view of the importance of the incise slur in the performance of Classic music, it is surprising that so little was written or made clear about the technique of playing it. Although the available information will raise as many questions as it answers, it is worth surveying nevertheless.

Steibelt mentioned only the removal of the hand from the keyboard. When the second of two slurred notes has been played, "raise the hand quite gently, in a manner so that it appears drawn away by a light movement of the arm."[63] Since there is no mention of the wrist, Steibelt may have intended the kind of arm movement in which the hand, wrist, and forearm work as one unit from the elbow, moving in a straight line. But that is not certain, and he left no musical examples on which to base further judgment.

The incise occurs in conjunction with Stevens's staccatos "for time" and "for expression." Whether the staccato is actually indicated on the last note under the slur is immaterial. His directions for playing the "staccato for expression" in Figure 6.4 (only those at the start of mm. 3 and 5; those on repeated notes are "forced" staccatos) specifically mention an "elevation of the wrist" that should follow the staccato attack:

> The fingers leave the last notes of the second and fourth bars *legato,* at the instant the impulse is made by two other fingers, on the succeeding keys . . . ; and this, with a smart blow and quick elevation of the wrist sufficient to sustain the fingers at a distance of a quarter, or at most half an inch, over the keys ready for the next application.[64]

In relation to a similar example, Stevens stated that "the lift [is] given by the two fingers that give the *staccato* blow . . . , which blow itself is the energy of the skip that follows."[65] Further on he allowed that since the staccato "must conform to the intended character of the phrase,"[66] the touch may at times have "less" rather than "additional force" in order to attain a desired degree of *piano* sound. Even so, a "spring" or "lift" of the hand and a raised wrist follow. These upward movements, in which the fingers bounce from the keys, give the playing a lightness, an up as well as a down direction. The incise slurs in Figure 6.4 are similar to those in Haydn's Sonata Hob. 50/i/2–3 (Fig. 5.17).

The annotations to Cramer's Etudes include one on the playing of two-note slurs. Figure 6.5 shows the opening of Etude XXIX; this comment follows:

> The purpose is to learn to withdraw the hand lightly. This will be achieved if it is always placed firmly on the first of the two slurred notes and is lifted almost vertically [*senkrechten*] as the second note is touched.
>
> —Beethoven[67]

Unfortunately the wording does not clarify *how* the hand was "placed firmly" and "lifted almost vertically": whether it was both placed and lifted in its playing position by a movement from the elbow in which the forearm, wrist, and hand remain one working unit in a straight line, i.e., vertically from the keyboard; or whether it was placed by dropping the wrist and then pulled into

Fig. 6.4. Stevens, *Piano-Forte Expression,* Plate 4.

Fig. 6.5. Cramer, Etude XXIX (OE By the Author), mm. 1–2.

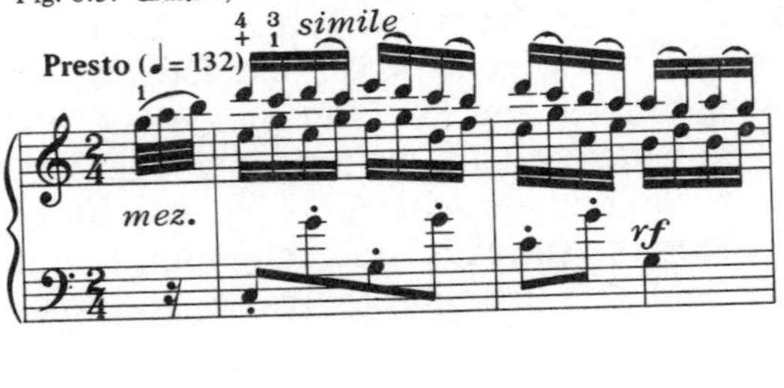

an almost vertical position and lifted from the keyboard by raising the wrist, as Stevens described. Since examples of this quick, two-note slurring occur in works by Beethoven (e.g., the Allegro motive in the opening of Op. 31/2/i, the Allegro vivace [mm. 12ff.] of Op. 78, and the Allegro molto [mm. 185ff.] of the Fantasy for Piano, Chorus, and Orchestra Op. 80), the way in which he might have played them is of interest regardless of whether he actually wrote the annotation (see pp. 94–95 and 98–101 above). Even if Beethoven was not familiar with Cramer's metronomization of $\jmath$ = 132 for this Etude,[68] the Presto heading, his reported bravura facility, and his proclivity to rapid tempos (p. 28 above)[69] would have assured a very fast pace. At such a speed I find it much easier on both the fortepiano and the pianoforte to let the forearm drop and be pushed up (by the fingering $\frac{3}{1}$ [$\frac{4}{2}$]) as an unbroken unit, via a small motion at the elbow, than to add wrist movement.

Although it is also incomplete and was written in the 1870s, Lussy's description of how to play an incise slur adds an intimation of wrist movement at the start and corroborates the essential stillness of the hand mentioned by Adam (p. 159 above).

> All the notes under a slur ——, no matter how many, should be played on the piano with a single articulation of the wrist dropping on the initial note. For all the notes that follow, the wrist makes no movement at all; [the hand merely] glides to the right or to the left and the fingers alone articulate [the notes]. When a passage requires several articulations of the wrist, it contains as many incises. All these notes require only one movement of the bow on the violin, only one prolonged exhaling of breath on the flute, the clarinet, the horn, etc.[70]

Lussy's "articulation of the wrist dropping on the initial note" could mean that the wrist dropped a little below the hand and arm. We cannot be sure how often Classic pianists may have dropped the wrist to place the hand "firmly" on the first slurred note; whether the arm, wrist, and hand customarily moved down in a straight line as one unit from the elbow; or whether both techniques were used, depending on tempo, note or interval pattern, dynamics, and fingering. Yet certainly those fortepianists who raised the wrist to withdraw the hand at the end of a slur would have dropped it back at least to its usual position, level with the hand and arm.

Repeated Notes, Octaves, and Glissandos

Suggestions for more difficult technical challenges drew limited attention in most of the early fortepiano manuals. Milchmeyer wrote about changing fingers on rapid repeated notes. It is done best

> if one separates the fingers a little and turns the hand outwards so that the fingers are almost in a perpendicular line [to their usual position on the keyboard]. These passages . . . are played faster and better the less deep the keys of a pianoforte fall and the more life the keys have under the fingers.[71]

Steibelt, whose bravura technique led him to describe trilling with the fourth and fifth fingers, also wrote about trills in general. He cautioned that a pianist would not be successful if the fingers were raised above the keys or if the wrist were rigid.[72]

As might be expected, there were at least two schools of thought about playing octaves. Milchmeyer advised playing them "merely with the joint of the hand, without the slightest constraint [but] without [any] movement of the arm."[73] Hummel played staccato octaves similarly.[74] Adam, on the other hand, claimed that the playing of nonlegato octaves "is the only circumstance where one may stiffen the forearm, the wrist, and the fingers, in order to preserve the necessary extension."[75] He played octaves with a movement of the forearm from the elbow. According to his description, Czerny played short, full-sounding staccato octaves in that manner, but short, soft octaves only with the fingers.[76] Then as now, in the actual playing a pianist might have varied the technique according to the demands of a given passage. It is also possible that the light action and shallow key dip of the early Viennese fortepianos encouraged playing octaves from the wrist, whereas the heavier action of the French pianos, which were influenced by English building practices at this time,[77] may have fostered octaves played from the elbow.

Other interesting material for advanced technique is Milchmeyer's advice for playing double-note glissandos, such as the one in sixths that Mozart wrote as early as 1778 in the cadenza of his Variations on "Lison dormait" K.264, or those in octaves, fingered $\frac{5}{1}$, that Beethoven wrote near the end of the "Waldstein" Sonata. Music, along with all the other arts, has its forms of showmanship, Milchmeyer began.

> As part of showmanship in the playing of the pianoforte I include glissando passages in thirds, sixths, and octaves, which can only be played in C major and on a keyboard without a deep key dip. If one wants to participate in this foolishness, which, however, some might consider an admirable skill, then one must turn the right hand quite far outwards in going up, so that the fingers that slide over the thirds, sixths, or octaves come virtually to lie on the keys; at the same time the thumb must be kept stiff and straight. Further, it is necessary that one give the two fingers playing a certain strength or elasticity so that they do not open and close with the thrust that one gives to the hand with the arm while playing. If the right hand has to play such a passage descending, then one must turn it so far inwards that the nail of the thumb lies almost completely on the key. What I have said of the right hand applies in reverse to the left.[78]

Of course it is much easier to play any glissando on a fortepiano than on a modern instrument.

Summary

From these descriptions, the participation of the various anatomical members in playing the fortepiano may be summarized briefly as follows: Finger activity carried the major share of the work, including legato, nonlegato, and for many pianists some form of staccato touch, although here there seems to have been a decided difference of opinion. Adam and Starke preferred playing ordinary staccatos with the fingers only and rapid staccatos with some hand movement from the wrist. But Hummel and Czerny recommended playing rapid staccatos with the fingers only and ordinary staccatos with some degree of hand movement, techniques that many pianists today find appropriate for playing Classic music on the pianoforte. Movement of the hand from the wrist was also used by some for playing octaves.

The forearm was used for moving the hand sideways to new locations, for playing incise slurs (with or without a wrist movement), and for some octave playing. The full arm, working from the shoulder, was the basic tool for shifting the hand into or back from the black notes when it could not remain positioned there, and for large shifts in keyboard location. By 1839 Czerny described use of the arm for *marcato* or *staccatissimo* octaves and chords.

In modern practice, when a larger physical unit is substituted for a smaller one used earlier, the reason is generally related to the handling of our much larger instrument. Yet, in spite of the increase in key dip and weight of the touch, many pianists today find that numerous subtleties of the Classic style are still expressed most effectively by means of finger activity and control. Sol Babitz, who studies Classic performance practices as they relate to the violin, has written similarly: "The arm-shoulder impulse needed for the modern ['big'] tone renders impossible many of the subtleties which are needed for the presentation of the old accents, etc."[79]

INCREASING TECHNICAL DEMANDS

Technical demands increased considerably in the larger works of Clementi and Beethoven. Greater strength and independence of the fingers became necessary to negotiate new keyboard patterns, more difficult passage-work, and the subtler musical requirements of articulation, accentuation, and gradation of dynamics, often within the context of increasingly fast tempos. Rapid octaves, double-note passages, and double trills also reached new levels of difficulty.

Clementi's *Introduction* and *Gradus*

In keeping with these developments, the fingered exercises in Clementi's *Introduction to the Art of Playing on the Piano Forte* emphasize passage-work, double notes, and legato octaves. For "opening the hand" Clementi introduced the arpeggiated diminished-seventh chord, which has since played an important role in many schools of technique that stress independence and equality of the fingers.[80] Clementi's final exposition of pianoforte technique, the *Gradus ad Parnassum,* published in three volumes in 1817, 1819, and 1826, maintains a balance between technical and artistic values, yet contains everything of

technical significance demanded of the pianist until the advent of Chopin's
Études. Unfortunately, only Carl Tausig's selection of 29 of the more mechanical pieces is what most twentieth-century pianists know of Clementi's
very varied collection of 100. The recent facsimile publication of the entire set
should be a boon to musicians and will ultimately influence reassessments of
Clementi as pianist and composer.[81]

Beethoven's Exercises and Other Fragments

Although Beethoven left few comments on technique and never wrote the
piano method he had mentioned to his good friend Gerhard von Breuning,[82]
his interest in digital facility and strength, in new pianistic patterns and sounds,
in virtuosic challenges, and in innovative fingering to help achieve those ends
is displayed in fragments of piano writing and actual exercises found in his
sketchbooks. Figures 6.6–6.20 represent some of his areas of experimentation.
(The captions for these figures give the sketchbook folio, the transcription page,
and the date.[83] Translations of Beethoven's German instructions are in the
text.)

Fig. 6.6. Kafka 88r, p. 228, October 1790.

Fig. 6.7. Kafka 88v, p. 229, October 1790.

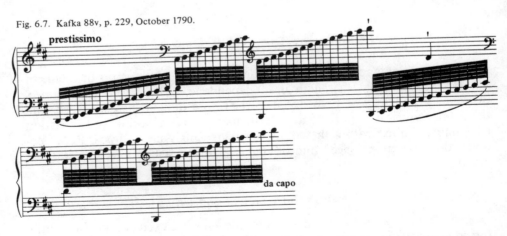

Fig. 6.8. Landsberg 6, p. 107, Nottebohm, *Two Beethoven Sketchbooks*,[84] p. 102, October–December 1803.

Fig. 6.9. Fischhof 4r, Nottebohm, *Beethoveniana* II, 362, probably 1793.

Die Hand so sehr als möglich zusammen gehalten.

pp auf das strengste ligato

Figure 6.6, which could be practiced "many times" with several different fingerings, would aid in developing finger strength, equality, and speed, all necessary for brilliant cadenza-like passages such as Figure 6.7, which is similarly marked *prestissimo*. The two were written on the front and back of the same sheet on which Beethoven completed the Cantata "Fliesse, Wonnezähre" in October 1790. Figure 6.14[85] also dates from the years in Bonn when the young Beethoven must have been developing the "great execution" that evoked Junker's effusive comment (p. 27 above). Figure 6.8, another of the many experimental scale patterns, is from a group in C major written shortly before Beethoven began sketching the "Waldstein" Sonata.

Beethoven's unusual direction with Figure 6.9, "The hand held together as much as possible," is indicative of other aspects of his playing beyond a generally compact hand. Contracting the hand after each melodic skip provides more technical solidity and security than a continuously extended hand and allows a better choice of fingering. Breuning's observation of 1826 also suggests a compact hand position. When Beethoven played a run, "he held his fingers very curved . . . ; he appeared really to have the so-called older hand position rather than that presently used, with more flattened [less curved] fingers."[86]

The essence of 6.9, a very soft melody "[played] strictly legato" and accompanied by repeated chords (to smooth their surface they should be replayed when the keys have risen only partially), reappears, refined and reclothed, in the Sonatas right from Op. 2/1/iv (mm. 59ff.). Indeed the opening measures of Op. 14/1/i are strikingly similar to Figure 6.9, which, like Figures 6.7, 6.12, and other sketches, might have served as more than an exercise; it could have been an experiment in piano sound and a springboard for improvisation or composition.[87]

Figure 6.10, which bears the instruction "Here the third finger must lie across the fourth until the latter withdraws and then the third takes its place," has been reproduced several times with but little commentary. What did Beethoven see as the advantage of playing the first D with the fourth finger, changing silently to the third (following his verbal direction would also minimize the separation when playing repeated notes with 4 and 3), and then repeating D with 3? I suggest that the fingering is related to dynamics and articulation. Perhaps he reasoned that the fourth finger would play a quiet D

Fig. 6.10. Kafka 39v, p.186, 1793.

Hie[r]bei muss der 3te Finger über dem 4ten solange kreuzweiss liegen, bis dieser wegzieht und alsdann der 3te an seine Stelle kömmt.

*Beethoven crossed out the sharps.

Fig. 6.11. Kafka 132v, p. 252, possibly second half of 1794 to early 1795.

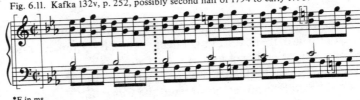

*F in ms.

more naturally than would the stronger middle finger; further, that transferring to 3 silently would allow the player to restrike D with the same finger, assuring a clear separation and with it a more pronounced *sforzando* attack than might result from playing the two D's with 4 and 3. The reiterated C's in the next measures are played with successive fingers. The unfingered quarter-note D allows us to wonder whether Beethoven intended legato or nonlegato movement to get to the phrase repetition at E. Since there is no direction for legato, which could only be achieved by playing D with 5 and crossing 4 over to E (a technique discussed in the next section), he might have assumed that both D and E would be played with 4, producing a gentle lift between the phrases. Thus, in this short passage Beethoven apparently experimented with three types of fingering that induce different qualities of sound and degrees of separation between repeated and adjacent notes.

The lack of fingering or articulation in Figure 6.11, a modulatory double-note exercise, is curious. Beethoven may have written it hastily during a lesson. The two outer parts can be played with a strict legato; the right thumb does heavy duty playing most of the inner notes for small hands, perhaps fewer for average or large hands. Depending on the right-hand fingering chosen, the third finger may cross over the fourth at the beginning of the second and third measures.

Beethoven's experiment, in the bass of the first section of Figure 6.12, of playing "all notes throughout with the third finger," allows the very strong middle finger to focus the energy of the arm and hand squarely and equally on each key, producing sounds of consistently solid strength throughout, not to speak of the psychological effect on the player of producing consecutive notes in this way. In the second section "all these notes [are] struck with the third and fourth fingers together." The coupling of 4 and 3 on each left-hand note helps the pianist attain the maximum possible *fortissimo* along with a

Fig. 6.12. Kafka 139v, p. 256, 1793 to early 1794, mm. 1-9, 25-31.

*Note unclear in ms.

Fig. 6.13. Kafka 51v, p. 205, 1793 to early 1794.

dollop of action noise on any instrument of the 1790s. Czerny's much later, amusing suggestion for this manner of fingering reminds us of the growth of pianos and piano technique:

> Cases occur in which a particular key must be struck with such unusual force, that a single finger would run the risk of not being sufficiently strong for the purpose, or of hurting itself in the attempt.
> In such cases we must strike the key with two fingers at once, almost pressed upon and held over each other.[88]

The link between fingering and musical result is unequivocal here.

At the other end of the sound spectrum, but also conceived in the early years during which Beethoven produced so many of these experimental sketches, is the quiet disappearance of tones in Figure 6.13. Robert Schumann chose this Romantic effect to conclude his *Papillons* Op. 2 (comp. 1829–1831). He also included it among the exercises in his Foreword to the *Studien nach Capricen von Paganini* Op. 3 (comp. 1832).[89]

Figures 6.14–6.20 provide a sampling of exercises in which Beethoven concentrated on the challenges of rapid octave passages (Figs. 6.14, played "up and down through all major and minor keys in as fast a tempo as possible," and 6.15, "octave leaps," to be transposed "from A-flat to A," then presumably continued); of patterns that utilize alternately the fingers on each side of the hand (Figs. 6.16–6.19); and of increasing and decreasing skips with the hands

Fig. 6.14. Miscellaneous leaf, Nottebohm, *Beethoveniana*, II, 360, 1790–1792.

staccato sempre

durch alle Tonarten moll und dur sowohl herauf als herunter in so geschwindem Zeitmasse als möglich.

Fig. 6.15. Kafka 68v, p. 224, late 1794 to early 1795.

presto   *aus as*
          ins a

8ven Sprünge

Fig. 6.16. Kafka 39v, p. 186, 1793.

Fig. 6.17. Kafka 89v, p. 230, 1793.

mit der Hand geworfen

Fig. 6.18. Kafka 40r, p. 188, 1793.

rechte H.

usw

in contrary motion (Fig. 6.20). The audacious fingering in Figure 6.17 creates a distillation of the athletic oscillation needed for octaves and larger intervals in these exercises and in Beethoven's pieces. There can scarcely be better testimony to his interest in the physical activity of playing. When octaves are "thrown with the hand," the notes are detached quickly with a bounce and a liveliness that would not exist were they marked staccato and played with the conventional 1, 5 fingering. It is logical to suppose that Beethoven designed the unusual octave fingering at Op. 2/2/i/84–85 and 88–89, which requires similar hand motion, with a related articulation and sound in mind.

A degree of thought in the writing of these exercises is shown by the progressive change in Figure 6.19: only after the pattern has been practiced in two

Fig. 6.19. Kafka 40v, p. 189, 1793.

Fig. 6.20. Kessler 23v, p. 70, winter 1801–1802.

increasingly difficult forms, using just the fifth finger for the outward thrusts (mm. 1, 3–4), is the exercise made more demanding with the addition of thirds in the outward thrust to the short, weaker fingers (mm. 7–8). Beethoven also wrote exercises for both hands using the patterns of mm. 7–8 in contrary motion. Interestingly, the Finale of the Piano Trio Op. 1/1 opens with three solo leaps of a tenth for the right hand—slurred across the bar lines—that become increasingly important as the movement progresses.

FINGERINGS BY CLEMENTI AND BEETHOVEN

To produce the BEST EFFECT, by the EASIEST MEANS, is the great basis of the art of fingering. The EFFECT, being of the highest importance, is FIRST consulted; the WAY to accomplish it is then devised; and THAT MODE of fingering is PRE-FERRED which gives the BEST EFFECT, tho' not always the easiest to the performer.[90]

Clementi was perhaps the most eloquent of the Classic writers in stating that fingering is inseparable from interpretation. Some of his and Beethoven's fingerings may seem to relate chiefly to technical problems, but in the context of a piece it is often difficult to separate the technical from the interpretive. The fingerings chosen are likely to affect the sounds produced, if not in a concrete manner—such as enhancing some particular articulation or accentuation—then on the more intangible level of the way the player feels about and projects the notes. Indeed, a significant number of fingerings relate more to musical than to technical considerations, and of these, the preferred fingering is not always the easiest. Figures 6.10, 6.12, and 6.17, all from around 1793, demonstrate both Beethoven's early interest in the relationship of fingering to interpretation and sound quality and his experimentation with novel fingerings that would put the player in a new psychological as well as physical relationship to tone production. These relationships are more fully developed in Figure 6.25, the fingerings of which are as innovative and as often ignored as any.

We know from chapter 5 that one area of common concern for Clementi and Beethoven was the adoption of a true legato touch. In his tutor, Clementi emphasized the importance of silent finger changing on a held note, "which mode of fingering should be much practiced in various ways, the LEGATO-STYLE requiring it very frequently."[91] He indicated this fingering frequently in his collections of teaching pieces; it was also one way in which he taught the playing of legato octaves and sixths.[92]

We have seen instructions by Beethoven for the silent transfer of fingers in an early sketch (Fig. 6.10). Later, in such pieces as the Sonata for Violoncello and Piano Op. 69/ii/1–6, and Op. 110/iii/5 and 125, he indicated the fingering 4, 3 for successive notes on the same pitch that are connected by a curved line: ♪ Is that line a tie or a slur? Opinions are divided. Heinrich Schenker thought it was a tie, with the finger change functioning as a psychological effect to help the performer feel the expressiveness of the passage.[93] Donald Tovey, on the other hand, claimed it was a slur, based in part on evidence in an edition of Op. 28 by Cipriani Potter, who had known Beethoven. At Op. 28/i/135–137, on motives similar to those in Opp. 69 and 110 but not fingered, Potter placed a dot under a dash (-̣-) over the middle of each slur, presumably to signal repetition of the second note.[94]

Czerny wrote of Op. 69:

> The ties in the right hand and the fingering placed over them, here signify something wholly peculiar. Thus, the second note is repeated in an audible manner . . . : that is, the first note . . . very *tenuto*, and the other . . . smartly detached and less marked. . . . The 4th finger must therefore glide aside and make way for the third.[95]

For Schnabel, the key "touched by the third finger should produce a tone hovering between reality and imagination—but must be heard. . . ."[96] Going a step further, Newman reasons that the finger change allows

> technical implementation of initiation and release *in one continuous motion,* whereas the use of the same finger to repeat the note would not be possible without two separate motions of the same body mechanisms.[97]

The gliding off of the fourth finger, allowing the key to rise only enough to be replayed gently by the third, requires essentially the same positioning and movement of the fingers that interested Beethoven in Figure 6.10. The only difference is that when the note is not repeated the third finger descends without letting the key rise at all.

Beethoven reflected on appropriate fingering for legato passage-work in a letter to Czerny about the instruction of his nephew, Karl. The probable date is 1817.

In certain passages such as  etc. I wish that all the fingers were used now and then, also in such things as etc. so that one might be able to slur them; of course such [passages] sound, as the saying goes, "pearled" or "like a pearl" [when] played with few fingers; but sometimes one wishes for another [kind of] jewel.[98]

Fig. 6.21. Clementi, Sonatina Op. 36/6/i (OE Longman and Broderip),[99] mm. 30 and 43.

[Allegro con spirito]

Passages identical to those in Beethoven's letter occur in the first movement of Clementi's Sonatina Op. 36/6 (Fig. 6.21). Although Clementi fingered most of the movement for legato playing, these passages show the two-finger patterns that were typical of the nonlegato playing to which Beethoven referred. Beethoven himself used repeated 1, 3 fingering for a similar passage marked *leggieramente* [sic] (lightly detached)[100] at Op. 31/1/ii/10. On the other hand, Figure 6.22, parts of which resemble Figure 6.21 and Op. 31/1/ii/10, is fingered explicitly to produce a legato sound. Beethoven may have felt that in a teaching context it would take more than the slurs to overcome what appears to have been common practice. These measures are from a shortened version of Beethoven's Op. 28/ii that appeared with this fingering in Friedrich Starke's *Pianoforte-Schule* of 1819. At the top of the page is a statement that the fingering was "marked by him [Beethoven] himself."[101] We may assume that Starke, a serious and modest man,[102] would not have issued such a statement falsely because of his continuous friendship with Beethoven over a number of years.[103] In fact, after the publication of Op. 28/ii and iii in Volume II of Starke's method, Beethoven contributed the then unpublished Bagatelles Nos. 7–11 of Op. 119 and a Concert-Finale in C major for Volume III, which appeared in 1821.

Fig. 6.22. Beethoven, Sonata Op. 28/ii (Starke, *Pianoforte-Schule*, II, 57), mm. 31–34 in Starke's shortened version, mm. 77–80 in the complete text.

It is apparent in Figure 6.22 that aside from necessary adjustments for black keys and for changes in note patterns (elsewhere for more abstract technical or musical reasons), Beethoven assumed that the same fingering would be repeated for a returning melodic passage. Earlier, by a sketch of a diminished-seventh arpeggio that rises and falls two and a half octaves, he had written: "N.B.: in long, wide ranging or extended passages [keep] the same fingering as much as possible."[104]

One puzzling fingering relevant to this point may be Haydn's own. In Hob. 42/i/23 a repeated three-note motive fingered 3, 2, 1 demonstrates a desire for consistent fingering to the degree that in both the first and the last patterns the thumb is on a black key in a position not especially convenient on a fortepiano or a piano. At least one other fingering—4, 3, 2—would have allowed the same consistency, coordination of the strong third finger with the *fz* indications—Haydn used 2 for that—and greater convenience. Unfortunately, the only source for this sonata is the first edition by Bossler. If Haydn actually preferred and wrote out the 3, 2, 1, perhaps he did so because at the time of composition of the sonata, "by 1784,"[105] performers were still avoiding the thumb on black keys in passage-work.[106] Mozart's avoidance of the thumb on black keys in his fingered exercises causes some awkward stretches and hand positions even with a nonlegato touch.[107] Clementi was also conservative in this regard; Beethoven sometimes indicated the thumb on black keys.

Beethoven's adroitness at fitting comfortable, secure fingering to a repeated, modulating passage shows in the Trio Op. 1/3/i/301–308 (*BGA*, HE). In a two-measure pattern that winds around stepwise within a range of seven scale tones, the fingering changes frequently to accommodate the changing location of the black keys and the eventual compression of the pattern. Beethoven's heavy reliance on the first three fingers, with frequent rapid turning of 1 under 2 and 2 over 1, means that smooth execution requires a compact hand and curved fingers, observed earlier as characteristics of his technique. (The thumb is not used on black keys in these measures.)

Fig. 6.23. Beethoven, Concert-Finale (Starke, *Pianoforte-Schule*, III, 62),[108] mm. 16–17 and 22–24.

His interest in metric accentuation, discussed in chapter 3 ("Accentuation in Beethoven's Music"), often led Beethoven to fingerings that support metric divisions (Fig. 6.22, m. 31) or subdivisions. In Figure 6.23 most of the shifts of fingering and generally the strong fingers fall on the first of each pair of sixteenth notes, the natural grouping at that subdivision in 6/8 meter. Additionally, his fingering at times reflects the same concern for such details as the relation between melodic outline and metrical accents that appears in the annotation to Cramer's Etude XII (p. 97). As both Jeanne Bamberger and William Newman have pointed out,[109] the paired fingerings $\frac{5}{2}$, $\frac{4}{1}$ within 6/8 meter at Op. 2/3/iv/269 call attention to the melodic sequence of pairs of eighth notes that oppose the metric subdivision of three eighth notes. In this staccato passage the fingerings clarify the contrametric groupings as slurs do elsewhere (e.g., Concerto Op. 73/iii/1–2). Four measures later (m. 273), with a change to a sequential motive that fits the normal 6/8 subdivision, Beethoven indicated $\frac{4}{2}$, $\frac{5}{1}$, $\frac{5}{1}$. This fingering alerts the pianist to the return of congruent melodic-metric groupings and at the same time provides the physical means for bouncing the rapid staccatos, especially as they approach the *fortissimo*. In Op. 78/ii/116–117, on the other hand, Beethoven's fingering of the arpeggiated line with three groups of 1 2, 2 4 aligns with the metric groups of two sixteenth-note pairs within each beat in the 2/4 meter but opposes the quasi-melodic motive of three sixteenth-note pairs within each octave.[110]

The music of Clementi and Beethoven occasionally requires two special kinds of fingering that are also needed in the Romantic repertoire, particularly in the works of Chopin and Schumann. The first is the passing of a longer finger over a shorter one (such as 3 over 4, or 4 over 5, variously termed *überschlagen* or vaulting) or a shorter finger under a longer one (such as 5 under 4, or 4 under 3, called *unterschlagen*), which had been the routine ways of moving the hand stepwise along the keyboard in the first half of the eighteenth century, when use of the thumb was still limited. As the thumb became the accepted pivot finger, these more difficult maneuvers were retained only where they still offered some advantage, usually in the form of a long finger over a short one.[111] This fingering sometimes provided the best way to keep a line or series of double notes going without interruption. In his didactic works Clementi often indicated long over short and short under long as a means of extending series of parallel thirds;[112] but in single lines he avoided those fingerings whenever possible by changing fingers silently on a single note of sufficient length. I find both techniques invaluable in his sonatas. The long over short fingering appears occasionally in Adam's *Méthode du doigté*, also usually in passages of double thirds.[113]

Beethoven specified the use of a longer finger over a shorter one in Op. 28/ii/31 (Fig. 6.22). The third finger crosses the fourth on an accented note, as Türk suggested;[114] the finger grouping and hand shift reinforce the metrical division. In Op. 2/1/iii/61–62 (Fig. 6.25) Beethoven indicated the less-used passing of a shorter finger (here 4) under a longer one (3) in order to continue the legato and to repeat the fingering pattern that aligns with the melodic pattern. Although not fingered by the composer, the passing of a longer finger over a shorter one is also needed to complete the legato thirds in m. 19 of his Bagatelle Op. 126/5 (Plate V).

The second special procedure is that of sliding a finger to an adjacent key in a legato manner, sometimes from white key to white key or white to black rather than from black to white (the last maneuver is much easier and may have been the predominant usage earlier in the eighteenth century). Clementi indicated finger sliding frequently, occasionally even between white notes, from the first edition of his *Introduction*.[115] It is indispensable for performance of his major works, including the Sonatas Opp. 7/3 and 13/6.

Finger sliding is needed for appropriate performance of Beethoven's piano music as well. For example, the composer's slur over both right-hand parts in Op. 126/5/18–19 removes any possible doubt about the requirement of sliding the thumb between C and B. One of Beethoven's indications for sliding between two white keys has a subtle implication for the articulation that follows. In Op. 28/ii/24 (Fig. 6.24), the 5, 4, 4, 3 fingering from Starke's volume is followed by an assumed $\frac{2}{1}$ at the start of the next measure. Rather than letting the conventional fingering of 5, 4, 3, 2 place 2, 2 on D and C-sharp at the break between slurs across the bar line, which—as Türk recommended[116]—would guarantee a separation, Beethoven's earlier finger sliding places 3, 2 there. This fingering allows a more easily controlled and subtler articulation.

In m. 59 of Figure 6.25 Beethoven's fingering requires that the right thumb "slide" from a black key to a nonadjacent white key. In the last beat of m. 60, fingers 5 and 1 are drawn from one pair of white keys to another, an action that can only be carried out by pulling the arm from the shoulder. This movement, related to a glissando (on the fortepiano it feels like one), contributes to the *crescendo* and to the performer's physical feel of approaching climax. The following $\frac{3}{2}$ fingering provides an articulation between the slurs so that the notes at the peak of the climax arrive with a fresh attack. In this example the

Fig. 6.24. Beethoven, Sonata Op. 28/ii (Starke, *Pianoforte-Schule*, II, 56), mm. 24–25 in Starke's shortened version, mm. 70–71 in the complete text.

Fig. 6.25. Beethoven, Sonata Op. 2/1/iii (OE Artaria), mm. 59–62.

composer's primary concern was certainly not the legato between the fourths fingered $\frac{5}{1}$, for which a far simpler fingering is available; rather, as Jeanne Bamberger has pointed out, his concern was the creation of a forceful approach to the climax of the Trio, for which he employed special fingering along with a *crescendo* to *ff*,[117] a high-pitched texture that adds to the intensity, and slurs that provide appropriate groupings and accents. Both finger sliding and passing a long finger over a short one were easier to execute on a fortepiano with its light action and shallow key dip. Nevertheless, the advantages they offer more than offset the effort of mastering their use on a modern piano.

Beethoven's trill fingerings, which carry significant information for performance, are discussed in chapter 7; many other fingerings are considered in the important articles on this topic by Jeanne Bamberger, William S. Newman, and Elfrieda Hiebert.[118] The few examples analyzed here may encourage pianists to use editions that provide Beethoven's fingerings and to approach those indications with positive curiosity rather than skepticism. Most important, though, is the realization that Beethoven's fingerings often have musical significance, "functioning as either an expressive device or an explication of structure, or both,"[119] and were sometimes specifically intended to avoid a conventional effect. We have already seen in chapters 4 and 5 that many of Beethoven's pedal indications and slurs were designed to create unusual expressive effects or to highlight structure, or both, in ways that were beyond the common practice. His use of fingerings for the same underlying purposes is indicative of his success in focusing many aspects of performance on an expressive or a structural goal when it served his musical ends.

CHAPTER

7

ORNAMENTS

INTRODUCTION

The development of the Classic style brought change in the role and the use of ornaments. A quick glance reveals that the vocabulary of ornaments became smaller; further, those that remained current were used considerably less often than they had been in the recent past. A historical overview discloses the Classic period as a time of gradual transition from late Baroque and early Classic ornament usage to that of the dawning Romantic period; from indicating the conventional, prescribed ornaments (*Manieren, agréments*) largely by sign to absorbing most of them into the notation of the melody; from a combined harmonic and melodic orientation to a predominantly melodic or motivic role. Charles Rosen has observed that

> The musical ornamentation of the first half of the 18th century was an essential element in the achievement of continuity: the decoration not only covered the underlying musical structure but kept it always flowing. . . . the *agréments* fill what empty space there was.
> The decoration of the classical style, on the other hand, articulates structure. The chief ornament retained from the Baroque is, significantly, the final cadential trill. Other ornaments are used more rarely, and they are almost always fully written out—necessarily so, as they have become *thematic*. This development was carried by Beethoven as far as it could go. In his later music the trill lost its decorative status: It is no longer an ornament but either an essential motif . . . or a suspension of rhythm. . . .[1]

Neither Haydn, Mozart, nor Beethoven left any systematic instructions for the performance of ornaments. From the next rank of composers, Clementi, Cramer, and Dussek left introductory tutors that contain some basic information, of which Clementi's is the most significant. This small number stands in marked contrast to the many major composers who left ornament tables in the late Baroque and early Classic periods and underscores the changes in ornament usage at this time. Applicable principles and examples included in this chapter stem from a wide variety of sources, generally those for keyboard but also some especially influential books for other instruments or voice. Of

the tutors used from earlier periods, Emanuel Bach's *Essay* is the most frequently quoted. It exercised a powerful influence on many later books, from
Löhlein's *Clavier-Schule* and Türk's *Klavierschule* to Starke's *Pianoforte-Schule;*
it was also an important part of Haydn's learning at a formative stage in his
career—Somfai suggests around 1762,[2] and it served Beethoven similarly under
his teacher Neefe.

The other, even more important, primary source for the study of ornamentation is the music itself. It can be mined for the obvious and the subtle.
Precious nuggets are occasionally wrested from authentic fingerings or from
those fortunate accidents of notation that reveal something in a new, clarifying
light.

Although many treatises discussed ornaments and gave instructions for
their performance, there was not—and is not now—complete agreement regarding either notation or performance. Since the second half of the eighteenth
century was a time of transition, some aspects of practice can only be deduced
from the musical settings of individual ornaments. Indeed, the very function
of being ornamental precludes adherence to a rigorous, unambiguous system.
The aesthetic basis of ornamentation requires of the performer a degree of
spontaneity and nuance whose subtleties would be at best difficult, if not impossible, to notate and whose expressiveness in performance might well be
lost if the notes were frozen into a rigid rhythmization. The signs used by
composers to indicate ornaments were an incomplete form of shorthand, and
most written-out realizations are at best only schematic. Neither signs nor
realizations necessarily indicate the number or speed of the oscillations in trills,
the trill termination, the precise rhythmic placement of ornaments shown in
small notes, the internal rhythmic arrangement of turns, and countless other
details. For all these reasons, textbook examples of ornament realization are
necessarily incomplete and abstract.

This chapter provides the player with the basic principles of ornament
realization for the Classic period. The player, in turn, must flesh out a realization in a way that discharges the performer's responsibility to the composer
yet fits the tempo and manner of his or her own interpretation. Within the
boundaries of stylistic integrity more than one musicianly choice is often possible. The final result will in some instances be influenced by the action of the
performance instrument—be it fortepiano or pianoforte.

Of some necessary general remarks, the first is that Classic composers often
notated ornaments with varying combinations of small notes, large notes, and
signs (e.g., compare Haydn's Sonata Hob. 12/ii/4 and 20, *JHW, HSU*), some
of which represented stages in the evolution from the earlier signs to the later,
more fully written-out notations. Second, ornaments were usually meant to be
played within the key of their immediate context. Thus, if a piece that begins
in A minor modulates to E minor, a trill on E would be played with an F-
sharp. Accidentals necessary for such upper or lower auxiliaries were expected
to be added by the performer when not indicated.

Third, although the majority of ornaments in the Classic style were illustrated in tutors as beginning on the beat, those indicated with small notes were sometimes played before or after the beat, more so as the eighteenth century drew to a close (explanations of this practice are given at appropriate places in the text). Finally, eighteenth-century composers often notated sixteenth and 32d notes with one less flag and a diagonal line across the stem. This notation did not determine whether small notes served as grace notes or as long or short appoggiaturas. That decision was based on the musical context.

Two important areas in which ornament realization differed in the Classic period and the preceding periods are the uses of one-note ornaments and the starting note of the trill.

APPOGGIATURAS AND OTHER ONE-NOTE ORNAMENTS

The several kinds of one-note ornaments used in the Classic period were all represented by similar looking small notes. Sometimes composers slurred a small note to the main note preceding or following it; this notation helped to determine the type and rhythmic position of the ornament. Generally, however, the small notes were left unslurred, giving the performer the freedom and the responsibility of making a choice according to the immediate context in which the ornament is found. Unfortunately, in many modern editions small notes left unslurred by the composer have automatically been slurred to the main note following, a practice that may give the performer an erroneous impression. It is important to notice whether ornament slurs are mentioned in an editorial statement at the beginning of a volume and whether the slurs added by the editor are differentiated typographically from those of the composer.

One-note ornaments can be divided into three categories according to their rhythmic position and slurring in performance. The terminology for these groups of ornaments has varied considerably in both contemporary and later writings, and it has often been confusing. I have tried to use names that are consistent with the basic relationships of the small notes to their main notes and to the beat.

Identification

A small note played on the beat, taking its time from the main note following, is called an appoggiatura (German: *Accent, Vorschlag;* French: *coulé* [descending], *port-de-voix* [ascending]). In performance it is always slurred to the following note (Fig. 7.1b, 1 and 4), and, with the exception of those short and unaccented, it usually provides accented dissonance. Additionally it serves as the basis for other harmonically oriented ornaments, such as the double appoggiatura and trills and turns that begin with their upper auxiliary. There are two types, long and short.

Fig. 7.1. Türk, *Klavierschule*, p. 230. a. As written. b. Performed "as appogiaturas." c. Performed "as afternotes."

A small note played before the beat, taking its time from the preceding note but slurred to the following note in performance, is called a grace note (German: *Vorschlag;* French: *coulé, port-de-voix*). This name is also the nineteenth- and twentieth-century term for a small note that anticipates the beat (e.g., Fig. 7.13). "Anticipatory" performance is intended here to be synonymous with realization as a grace note. Observe too that the German *Vorschlag* means only a note that "falls before" its main note, without specifying its relation to the beat or implying the idea of leaning, which is inherent in the Italian *appoggiatura.* The French *coulé* and *port-de-voix* are also free of implication regarding the beat. Because of this generic quality, these German and French terms serve for both appoggiatura and grace note in their respective languages.

A small note that belongs completely to the preceding note, being slurred from it and taking time from the end of its beat, is called an afternote (German: *Nachschlag;* French: *accent,*[3] *chûte;* Fig. 7.1c, 1–4). The German term, meaning a note that "falls after," has achieved fairly wide currency in English. Some afternotes, or *Nachschläge,* are also known by specific names that describe their melodic shapes. They include the passing tone (Fig. 7.1c, 4), the note of anticipation, ♪♩ , and the auxiliary, ♪♩ , all familiar nonharmonic tones encountered in any study of elementary harmony.

With Figure 7.1 Türk pointed out that because there was no difference in the usual way of writing the small notes, afternotes and appoggiaturas could easily become confused. (Of the two ornaments that take their time from the note preceding—grace notes and afternotes—he described only the latter.) He also included ornaments of two notes, which, if played on the beat are slides, but if executed at the end of the preceding beat are simply afternotes (Fig. 7.1b, 2, 3; Fig. 7.1c, 2 and 3). He suggested that single afternotes might be written with their flags turned back toward the main note (as in Fig. 7.15); but it would be preferable that all afternotes be slurred to the preceding main note or, better yet, be written as large notes.[4]

The Short Appoggiatura

It was customary to classify appoggiaturas in two categories: short and long. The short, or "invariable," appoggiatura took only a "very small, scarcely noticeable" part of the value of the note following,[5] to which it was always slurred in performance. Since its exact length was not measured, it was generally represented by a sixteenth (written either with two flags or with one flag and a diagonal stroke) or a 32d note, although it sometimes appeared as an eighth note—a holdover from the first half of the century, before the crystallization of "short" and "long," when appoggiaturas of many lengths were represented only by small eighth notes.

Once recognized in its surroundings as short, the ornament was generally played quickly on the beat, sometimes as quickly as possible (Fig. 7.2). Türk stated that "at the most," a sixteenth note played in very fast tempo, a 32d note in moderate, or a 64th note in slow tempo could be considered short appoggiaturas.[6] Their function was largely one of rhythmic accentuation, although the quick dissonant "twang" added harmonic color as well.

In the early Classic period short appoggiaturas had been used before quick notes (e.g., ♪♫♫ , ♪♫♩), repeated notes, long (half or whole) notes, triplets, syncopated notes, in caesurae before a relatively rapid note, and when the appoggiatura formed an octave with the bass (which meant that the main note itself was dissonant). An appoggiatura before the upper note where the melody rises a second and returns, was also short.[7] These are contexts in which a longer appoggiatura might obscure some facet of the melodic, harmonic, or rhythmic structure.

In the Classic period the short appoggiatura was retained in most of those contexts,[8] and its use was extended to additional situations. Once more these situations reflect the need to keep the melodic, harmonic, and rhythmic character of the structural notes clearly distinguishable. Thus, appoggiaturas were also short before melody notes that leap (Fig. 7.3, these are syncopated in addition); when the appoggiatura leaps to its main note (Fig. 7.4, here it is also after a rest); at the start of a piece (Fig. 7.5), a section of a piece, or a motive

Fig. 7.2. "The value of short appoggiaturas." Türk, *Klavierschule*, pp. 209, 223, 224.

*Discrepancy in the slurring occurs in both editions.

Fig. 7.3. Mozart, Sonata K. 310/ii (Aut.), m. 13.

[Andante cantabile con espressione]

Fig. 7.4. Haydn, Sonata Hob. 49/ii (Aut.), mm. 37–38.

Fig. 7.5. Haydn, Sonata Hob. 37/i (OE Artaria), m. 1.

Fig. 7.6. Haydn, Sonata Hob. 49/iii (Aut.), m. 38.

Fig. 7.7. Haydn, Sonata Hob. 49/iii (Aut.), m. 20.

after a rest (although Türk and others considered appoggiaturas in these lo-cations "misused"[9]); when the main note is staccato (but see discussion of Fig. 7.26 for very short or fast staccato notes); when the main note itself is dissonant (Fig. 7.6, i.e., the open fourth between soprano and bass); before a rhythmic group consisting of two, three, or four members, usually of equal value (Figs. 7.2b, 7.7); when chromatic small notes indicate intervals outside the key of the surrounding context (Fig. 7.3, C-sharp, F-sharp); where mistakes in the harmony (e.g., parallel octaves or fifths) would appear if the appoggiatura were long.[10] In an effort to be brief, Rellstab stated the obvious: "Harmony, affect, everything influences the length of the appoggiatura."[11]

Türk also included as short appoggiaturas those before breaks in phrases (*Einschnitte*) and before the upper note where the melody rises and falls a second (Fig. 7.8); yet in a footnote he conceded that "Both these rules already admit frequent exceptions, for example, in a slow tempo or when an ornament (on a main note) follows an appoggiatura, etc."[12] This comment and related ones in the second edition of Türk's book reflect changes from the practice of Emanuel Bach and suggest the possibility of varying realizations; they state that longer appoggiaturas are more suitable or usual at a cadence or a phrase division in slower movement, or directly before a cadence in which the melody rises and falls a step.[13]

There was some difference of opinion as to whether a short appoggiatura or its main note received the accent. Türk stated that Johann Friedrich Agricola (writing primarily for singers), Emanuel Bach, and Marpurg wanted the short small note to be stronger than the main note, but that Leopold Mozart (in a violin tutor) held the opposite point of view. Agreeing with Mozart, Türk preferred that the short small note be played "caressingly" (*schmeichelnd*), with the emphasis on the following note, although he added that in a variety of situations exceptions would be necessary.[14] Clementi placed the emphasis on the main note after "little notes" that leap or that precede main notes approached by leap.[15] According to August Eberhard Müller, the short appoggiatura takes "only very little" time from its main note but "throws a sharper accent" onto it.[16]

Whether a short, unaccented small note followed by an accented main note is perceived on or before the beat depends on its context and performance. When the small note occurs with other parts that mark the beat, it will sound on the beat if the accompaniment has sufficient weight and continues exactly in tempo, and if the accented main note does not overbalance the preceding notes. This unaccented, on-beat effect is more natural in moderate and slow tempos. The delayed emphasis on the main note may create an effect akin to contrametric *rubato* (see chap. 10). In other contexts, including fast tempos, a quick, forceful resolution of an unaccented small note can usurp the beat, making the ornament and its accompaniment sound anticipatory. Short, unaccented small notes will also be perceived before the beat when they lack accompaniment and should usually be played as grace notes (see "Afternotes and Grace Notes" below). On the keyboard there is the additional possibility of playing the short ornament and its main note so close together that both are heard as if on the beat; or even of playing them simultaneously, with the immediate release of the nonharmonic tone. Accordingly, Clementi's student

Fig. 7.8. Mozart, Sonata K. 331/ii (OE Artaria), mm. 17–18.

Cramer advised that an appoggiatura before a group of four sixteenth notes (as in Fig. 7.7) "is passed quick *with* the first note, so as not to break the regularity of the group" (italics added).[17] This often effective realization is similar to the simultaneous acciaccatura, in which the main note and its accessory a step or half-step below are struck at the same time and the accessory is released as soon as possible.[18]

Practice was undoubtedly mixed in regard to accenting short appoggiaturas. Criteria may have varied with time, geographic location, and, above all, musical context. From our distance it is at times difficult to decide whether some short appoggiaturas should be accented or not. In certain circumstances those that retain a more dissonant function might have been played with more emphasis, particularly in slower pieces. A dissonant small note preceding the upper note where the melody rises and falls a second (Fig. 7.8) and an appoggiatura that is shortened in order to avoid a mistake in the harmony might at times have been candidates for emphasis. On the other hand, small notes that precede accented or dissonant main notes presumably remain unaccented, sometimes becoming grace notes (see below). A short appoggiatura that leaps to its main note usually has little if any harmonic significance; after "short notes in fast tempo" and "in fiery, lively ideas" it may be passed over lightly.[19] Might this imply before the beat, as in Figure 7.23 or in Mozart's K. 330/i/7? Milchmeyer realized such leaping small notes as grace notes (Fig. 7.30), another step in the evolution of ornament performance during the Classic period.

The descriptions of short appoggiaturas imply that they also varied to some extent in the quickness with which they were played, a factor related in part to the tempo and the mood of a piece. Indeed, use of an ornament rather than a written-out note invites dynamic and rhythmic nuance. Thus, in moderate or slow tempos they might take slightly more time. My preference is to play the appoggiaturas in Figures 7.5 and 7.7 as quickly as possible—really as acciaccaturas, which leaves the accent to the main note (this avoids hobbling the opening of the movement in Fig. 7.5); to give the appoggiaturas in Figure 7.6 just a little more time and those in Figure 7.3 noticeably more, accenting the main notes in Figure 7.6 and at least the first two appoggiaturas in Figure 7.3. Here the "on-beat" nonharmonic tones, whose dynamic and rhythmic relationships to the main notes may vary as the line builds, underscore the syncopation. I play the appoggiatura in m. 37 of Figure 7.4 graciously, with still more time (perhaps slightly less than a sixteenth note) and with a gentle emphasis on the main note. Apropos Figure 7.4, Türk reported that before notes longer than a quarter note in value (in his examples a dotted quarter or a quarter tied to a sixteenth note), appoggiaturas that leap were sometimes played as eighth notes, which he claimed were "too short" to be classed "as long" and "too long" to be considered short. "Nevertheless, in tender, songful passages this division . . . can be of good effect."[20] Actually, Türk had prepared for these unclassifiable realizations by grouping them with other types of appoggiaturas (including those between descending thirds) whose realizations might be "uncertain"; "in some circumstances they must receive a somewhat longer value than the true short [appoggiatura]."[21]

My realization of Figure 7.8 takes into account Türk's allowed exception for this configuration, cited earlier. I emphasize it gently, varying its length from a sixteenth note, the value in which Mozart notated it, to a triplet eighth note. Again, it is "somewhat longer" than a "true" short appoggiatura. However, Türk recommended the 1:3 division in Figure 7.1b, 1 and 4; and Mozart, who, from approximately 1780, tended to represent appoggiaturas of one-quarter the value of the main note or longer in their real values, sometimes suggested this 1:3 division (see K. 310/i/2 and K. 332/iii/84), although not necessarily for small notes between descending thirds (see pp. 232–234). Thus, irrespective of classification, appoggiatura realizations that fall between short and long had a role in actual practice. In discussing the potential expressivity of short appoggiaturas, Heinrich Schenker wisely observed that "the ultimate limit of the short appoggiatura ends only where the long appoggiatura begins."[22]

The Long Appoggiatura

Appoggiaturas whose contextual settings did not classify them as short were long or "variable"; their function was both melodic and harmonic. A long appoggiatura always took the accent and a measurable portion of the value of its main note, to which it was slurred in resolution.[23] The appoggiatura generally received one-half of a duple note or two-thirds of a note divisible by three. However, the ornament might take three-quarters of a duple note (Fig. 7.9a) or, more commonly, one-third of a ternary note if such distribution provided a better musical effect (e.g., better rhythmic movement or harmonic progression).[24] Additionally there might be room for expressive nuance in filling out these approximate divisions.

A long appoggiatura before a tied note sometimes received the entire value of its main note and was resolved in the value of the second note (Fig. 7.9b).[25] Türk mentioned that "some music teachers" would give a long appoggiatura to a note before a rest the entire value of the note and would resolve it in the time of the rest (Fig. 7.9c). "However, in so doing they restrict themselves only to gentle passages."[26] Here Türk may have identified another changing practice. North Germans Marpurg, Emanuel Bach, and, later, Bach's follower Rellstab—even the Austrian Leopold Mozart—had written about such absorption of a

Fig. 7.9. Türk, *Klavierschule*, pp. 212–213.

rest as if it were common practice.[27] Presumably Türk would not partake of the practice, and those who still did may have used it only in a limited way. In his study of Mozart's ornamentation, Frederick Neumann writes that appropriate use of this "overlong" appoggiatura—even though taught by his father—is rare in Mozart's music, and so is observance of the two-thirds division of a ternary note.[28]

A small note in the value of a sixteenth, whether written as ♪ or ♪, could still represent either a long or a short appoggiatura, depending on the musical configuration. Thus the realization of the appoggiatura in the second measure of Figure 7.4 is long, taking half of the eighth note; that in Figure 7.7 is short. Another preference, much in vogue in the early Classic, north German school and elsewhere, for playing a short appoggiatura with the common pattern ♪♫ [29] was gradually given up during the Classic period for a long appoggiatura of sixteenth-note value. Türk observed that when the pattern follows other sixteenth notes the short appoggiatura "may be more customary," but musicians "of refined taste" play the long one.[30] Shortly thereafter, writers showed only the long realization.[31] Haydn demonstrated a preference for the four even notes in many situations by using both the shorthand and the written-out notation of the same motive in the same context within one movement (compare mm. 38 and 116 in his Sonata Hob. 18/i, comp. ca. 1771–1773[32]). The even realization also suits Mozart's keyboard music.

In Part I of his *Essay,* Emanuel Bach had discussed the importance of notating long appoggiaturas with small notes that represented their true values in performance[33] rather than uniformly with eighth notes or other irrelevant values. Other writers seconded this proposal,[34] and during the second half of the century it gradually began to take root. By 1789 Türk called for the notation of all long appoggiaturas in the "usual [large] notes" and mentioned that "it is already being done by some composers."[35] From the 1780s on, and in some works composed earlier, Haydn and Mozart gradually notated more long appoggiaturas in large notes and wrote the great majority of small notes representing long or one-quarter length appoggiaturas in the rhythmic values in which they wanted them played[36] (although Haydn was less consistent than Mozart in regard to the latter). This more accurate notation offers considerable help when the performer has access to a carefully prepared urtext or to reliable source material.

To a certain extent the primary decision—whether an appoggiatura is long or short—still remains, particularly when the small note is a sixteenth, which could stand for either. For example, the value of a small sixteenth before a quarter note would depend on the musical context. Haydn frequently used the configuration ♪♫ , which nearly always meant four 32d notes. Theoretically the "long" appoggiatura (taking half the value of its main note) should have been notated with a 32d note. His consistent use of the sixteenth-note appoggiatura in this pattern is part of his orthography. Occasionally Haydn wrote an eighth note instead of a sixteenth or a 32d in configurations that generally take a short appoggiatura, such as an appoggiatura before a group of four 32d

Fig. 7.10. Beethoven, Allegretto WoO 53 (Aut.), mm. 151–154.

Fig. 7.11. Beethoven, Sonata for Violin and Piano Op. 30/3/ii (Aut.), mm. 33–34.

notes (Hob. 49/ii/25 [Aut.; *JHW*]), an appoggiatura that leaps to its main note (Fig. 7.4, m. 37), or an appoggiatura to a main note that leaps (Hob. 40/ii/10).

Beethoven wrote most of his long appoggiaturas in large notes, leaving small notes primarily to indicate short appoggiaturas. Generally the exceptions are in his early works, such as the Allegretto WoO 53, composed between 1796 and 1798 (Fig. 7.10), and the Sonata for Violoncello and Piano Op. 5/1/i/237, dated 1796. One specific type of exception, the long appoggiatura in the familiar pattern in Figure 7.11, occurs from time to time throughout Beethoven's works.

In the revised edition of his *Klavierschule* (1802), Türk noted that "for some time, [and] with good reason," the small note with a diagonal stroke across the customary flag(s) had been used to indicate the short appoggiatura; "but this sign has not yet come into general use."[37] This is actually an early description of what was to become common practice later in the nineteenth century, but none of the Classic composers reserved that sign specifically for the short appoggiatura.

Afternotes and Grace Notes

In many sources afternotes and grace notes were treated as a single body of ornaments played between rather than on beats. Sometimes writers merely mentioned that the small notes took their value from the note preceding, without specifying either afternote or anticipatory rendition. In addition, writers and composers often did not slur the small notes, leaving that delicacy to the performer. Although in many situations there would have been little or no difference between afternotes and grace notes as far as rhythmic placement was concerned, slurring and other interpretive nuances would have differed.

Therefore, in this brief survey I shall retain each author's terminology and—as always—include only authentic slurs.

It is precisely in relation to ornaments indicated with small notes that Emanuel Bach tried to proclaim a universal rule of on-beat performance.

> All embellishments notated in small notes pertain to the following tone. Therefore, while the preceding tone is never shortened, the following tone loses as much of its length as the small notes take from it. This observation grows in importance the more it is neglected. . . .[38]

Yet the last sentence points to the fact that around 1753, when the *Essay* was written, there was not a unified practice. Although the trend during the first half of the eighteenth century had been strongly in the direction of placing ornaments on the beat, particularly in keyboard music, evidence shows that afternote performance had remained in limited use.[39] A review of Bach's *Essay* in the *Bibliothek der schönen Wissenschaften* of 1763 criticized his attitude toward the *Nachschlag* and recommended Marpurg's coverage of that topic,[40] which includes afternotes and grace notes, all carefully slurred.[41] During the 1750s, other musicians, such as Giuseppe Tartini, Leopold Mozart, and Quantz, who were writing primarily about violin and flute playing, described grace-note performance of one-note ornaments in certain contexts, including those before written-out appoggiaturas (as in Fig. 7.16) and those between descending thirds.[42] Mozart and Quantz called these ornaments *durchgehende Vorschläge,* which is appropriately translated as passing or grace notes. The common English translation of "passing appoggiaturas" is, of course, contradictory. In Tartini's Italian string-playing practice, grace notes were used "in any other place, even in descending runs," but only in pieces marked *andante cantabile* or faster.

Most German theorists of the second half of the eighteenth century were influenced to some extent by Emanuel Bach's *Essay*. Therefore, in the ensuing decades evidence for afternote and anticipatory performance was neither plentiful nor necessarily clear. A particularly interesting example of small notes realized as grace notes appears in Löhlein's *Anweisung zum Violinspielen* of 1774. After explaining long appoggiaturas Löhlein wrote:

> There is also a *fast kind of note before the main note [geschwinde Art Vorschläge]* that is not accounted for in the measure. They take either the upper neighbor note [Fig. 7.12d], or they repeat the preceding note [Fig. 7.12e], or they fill the empty space between two notes [Fig. 7.12f]. They are slurred very quickly to the following note. Sometimes they also fill in leaps of a third [Fig. 7.13g]; also just stepwise progressions [Fig. 7.13h].[43]

Fig. 7.12. Löhlein, *Anweisung zum Violinspielen*, p. 44.

Since all his "fast *Vorschläge*" except those in Figure 7.12f might otherwise belong to the category of short appoggiaturas, it seems reasonable to assume that Löhlein intended grace-note performance for all these examples although he did not realize d., e., and f. This brings us to a pivotal question: How frequently in keyboard music might small notes that could qualify as short appoggiaturas have been played as grace notes rather than on the beat?

In Abbé Vogler's *Kuhrpfälzische Tonschule* of 1778 we learn that "The small notes [*Vorschläge*] do not diminish the value of the note following, and are therefore always shown [as] smaller than half [its] value."[44] Vogler did not realize his example, but if we accept his statement literally we would play either acciaccaturas or grace-notes. Mozart and Vogler met in Mannheim during the winter of 1777–1778, when Mozart had ample time to hear Vogler's music and his keyboard playing.[45] Beethoven was acquainted with Vogler's *Tonschule*.[46]

Löhlein may also have provided some evidence in the third edition of his widely used *Clavier-Schule,* published in 1779. To the stave with his illustrations of the long appoggiatura Löhlein added Figure 7.14, about which he wrote: "The small notes that stand before eighths and sixteenths in a fast tempo are played short, so that the main note loses little or nothing."[47] If the main note loses little, the ornament would be a short appoggiatura; if nothing, either the two notes would have to be played simultaneously and the ornament released, or the ornament would be a grace note. Löhlein's acceptance of grace-note performance is beyond question. "Here the main note loses little or nothing" implies a choice between short appoggiatura or grace-note realization for those small notes meant to be played quickly.

Türk's examples (Fig. 7.1) and comments were noted earlier, including his statement that it would be better to have all afternotes written out in normal size. In the same year (1789), G. F. Wolf wrote that these ornaments were "very seldom indicated through small notes [but] much more in usual notes"; however, he, like Türk, urged that when small notes were used, their flags should be reversed to prevent misinterpretation, as in Figure 7.15.[48]

Fig. 7.13. Löhlein, *Anweisung zum Violinspielen,* p. 44.

*Slurs lacking.

Fig. 7.14. Löhlein, *Clavier-Schule,* 3d ed., p. 14.

Fig. 7.15. Wolf, *Unterricht*, p. 70.

By 1790 there is indisputable evidence that small notes in several kinds of configurations were being played before the beat even where that removed some dissonance, as in Figure 7.29. J. C. F. Rellstab, author of the small volume for keyboard players in which this figure appears, stated unabashedly that he was a follower of Emanuel Bach,[49] so it is not surprising that he considered the current grace-note performance improper. On the other hand, in their tutor of ca. 1786, Johann Christian Bach and Francesco Pasquale Ricci stated that "small notes, otherwise called *port-de-voix,* or *notes-de-goût,*" take their value "from the preceding or the following note";[50] and in 1797 Milchmeyer presented grace-note performance as the norm for a variety of small notes played quickly, as in Figure 7.30. Interestingly, his single grace notes (not all shown in this figure) are all of the types earlier categorized as short appoggiaturas.

Koch's writing in 1802 may still be difficult to calibrate. On the one hand Koch seems to describe grace-note performance when he states that the main note receives the accent and the note before [*Vorschlag*] "is slurred so quickly to the main note that it seems as if nothing at all [*nicht das Geringste*] would be taken from its value."[51] On the other hand he illustrates the small notes as 32d or 64th notes on the beat. But since those small notes occur "mainly in lively pieces," they might—as we have observed before—have slipped into a pre-beat position if the main note was noticeably accented. In another article Koch wrote that the difference between a short *Vorschlag* and an acciaccatura is "merely that the small note is played more closely [*mehr gleichzeitig*] with the main note when it is an acciaccatura than when it is a short *Vorschlag.*"[52] Koch's writing may, in fact, be evidence of transitional practice.

A few examples will illustrate some situations for which anticipatory performance might have been considered appropriate. These suggestions are editorial; nonetheless, they are based on historical evidence and on the criteria of preserving the musical integrity of harmony, melody, rhythm, or texture. In a very general way we can view this moving of some small single notes to a pre-beat position as another step in the progression from the largely on-beat (and some afternote) performance in late Baroque keyboard music to some very short on-beat ornaments, to anticipation in limited circumstances, and finally to the anticipation of all small single notes during the Romantic period. Some of the examples below are similar to Löhlein's Figure 7.12d.

In Mozart's K. 540/4 (Fig. 7.16) the E on beat 4 is part of the familiar "sigh motive" and is itself an appoggiatura. Anticipation of the ornament, as recommended by Quantz and Tromlitz (n. 42), avoids weakening this characteristic figure. The pronounced appoggiatura quality of the 6/4 chord in Figure 7.17 (m. 75) likewise suggests grace-note (or quasi-acciaccatura) performance of the A. At an appropriate tempo for Figure 7.18 the grace notes will be close

Fig. 7.16. Mozart, Adagio K. 540 (Aut.), m. 4.

Fig. 7.17. Mozart, Sonata for Piano and Violin K. 379/i (Aut.), mm. 74–75.

*As indicated in aut.

Fig. 7.18. Haydn, Sonata Hob. 49/i (Aut.), mm. 179–183.

Fig. 7.19. Haydn, Sonata Hob. 27/ii (OE Hummel), mm. 55–57.

* ∞ probably intended.

enough to their main notes to produce some of the "twang" of crushed acciaccaturas.

Anticipatory performance seems best in Figures 7.19 and 7.20, not only to
maintain written-out dissonance and the integrity of the melodic lines but also,
in Figure 7.20, to preserve an important rhythmic motive. The unaccompanied
small notes in Figure 7.21, if played appropriately without accent (the *fp*'s
emphasize the main note at the peak of each phrase member), become anticipatory and should be placed as such. Any attempt to avoid this will result in

Fig. 7.20. Mozart, Sonata K. 311/ii (Aut.), m. 1.

Fig. 7.21. Mozart, Sonata K. 309/ii (*NMA* and OE Heina), mm. 17–20.

* Compare Fig. 3.16.
**c² and e² respectively in *NMA*.

Fig. 7.22. Beethoven, Sonata Op. 2/1/i (OE Artaria), mm. 41–42.

Fig. 7.23. Beethoven, Sonata Op. 2/2/i (OE Artaria), mm. 181–183.

rhythmic and melodic chaos. Similarly, in Figure 7.22 the unaccompanied short D-natural, followed by a higher, much longer, and unexpected C-flat, is going to be heard as anticipatory regardless of when it is played. Some performers play the C-flat exactly in tempo, adding time for the *con espressione* after it; others stretch the first beat slightly, playing the C-flat on a delayed second beat.[53] In the Allegro vivace tempo of Figure 7.23 the strongly rhythmic character of the motive would be seriously disrupted if the small notes were given the beat and the soprano notes were delayed. Anticipation of the F in m. 35

of Figure 7.24 allows Mozart's written-out appoggiatura, rather than an open fifth, to sound on the downbeat. Finally, in Figure 7.25, where Haydn clarified the pre-beat position of the small note but not its slurring, grace-note performance seems infinitely more appropriate to me than afternote performance.

Some might wonder about playing grace notes rather than short appoggiaturas in Figures 7.5–7.7. I sometimes play grace notes in Figure 7.6 but I prefer the clash of an acciaccatura in Figure 7.7. This is an area in which the oft-invoked *bon goût* must prevail. For Figure 7.5 anticipation is another good alternative to an acciaccatura. At the start of the recapitulation Haydn wrote the C-sharp as a regular note at the end of a scale just before the bar line.

The interpretation of unslurred small notes between descending thirds (*tierces coulées*) varied considerably; musicians frequently found these ornaments ambiguous. Türk pointed out that they could be either appoggiaturas or afternotes (Fig. 7.1); other writers preferred them as grace notes. Tromlitz asked "Who is correct? The melody is good in both [ways]," with appoggiaturas or grace notes.[54] Presumably each decision was based on the style of the piece, the inclinations of the composer, if known ("the same taste does not prevail in the works of a [C. P. E.] Bach, Haydn, Mozart, etc."[55]), and the taste of the performer. In fast, light movements there may have been more of a tendency toward grace-note realization, particularly if that works well in the context. In the French style it was generally expected. Where the melody or texture seems to call for more participation or pull from the ornaments, and often in slower, expressive movements, the small notes may have been realized as appoggiaturas. In this role Türk considered them short "most of the time," although he generally preferred them played "caressingly," because they "should not make the melody very lively, but rather more gracious."[56] He realized such

Fig. 7.24. Mozart, Sonata K. 282/i (Aut.), mm. 34–35.

Fig. 7.25. Haydn, Sonata Hob. 50/ii (OE Caulfield), mm. 17–18.

appoggiaturas before quarter notes as sixteenth notes, but for *adagios* he approved Emanuel Bach's suggested rhythmization as the first third of the main note.[57] In the Andante cantabile con espressione of Mozart's K. 310, m. 9, I begin with appoggiaturas of one-third value but vary them toward one-half of the main note.

The contrast in performance between Figures 7.26 and 7.27 is important: the melodic configurations of ornament and structural notes are identical, but the *tierces coulées* are realized differently because of the contexts in which they exist. In the lively Allegro of Figure 7.26 grace notes are appropriate before the staccato notes, although on their return acciaccaturas might add spice. In the lyrical Adagio e cantabile of Figure 7.27, gentle appoggiaturas ranging from about one-third to one-half of the value exert a continuing tension in the melodic line. The Rondeau of Mozart's Sonata for Piano and Violin K. 296 contains small notes between descending thirds in two different melodic contexts, both times notated as sixteenth notes. In m. 4 of the theme I play them as grace notes; in the first episode (m. 33) I play them on the beat, gently and short.

Small notes between descending thirds are prominent in the theme of Mozart's popular Rondo in D Major K. 485. Here the ambiguity of their role has once again caused knowledgeable musicians to suggest different resolutions. Eva and Paul Badura-Skoda favor on-beat sixteenth notes on the basis of Mozart's fondness for the "Scotch snap," or Lombard rhythm. They also hypothesize that had Mozart wanted grace notes, he would have added another small note after the quarter-note D to provide continuity to the following G.[58] The majority of recorded performers play appoggiaturas. Neumann makes a case for grace-notes being more appropriate to the charm and gaiety of the piece, and Peter Serkin plays it this way; Neumann also documents how often Mozart wrote out the Lombard rhythm when he wanted its firmness.[59] At this

Fig. 7.26. Haydn, Sonata Hob. 50/i (OE Caulfield), m. 47.

Fig. 7.27. Haydn, Sonata Hob. 49/ii (Aut.), mm. 9–10.

writing I lean toward appoggiaturas of approximately sixteenth-note value, tripped over with insouciance to aid the melodic flow. They can be varied somewhat when the setting of the theme changes. Mozart may have used small notes to avoid the rigidity of written sixteenth and dotted-eighth notes. His written-out eighth notes in mm. 54 and 56, where the main theme is transformed into a closing theme in this rondo-sonata form, and his eighth-note appoggiaturas in mm. 155, 159, and 163 provide contrast to both of the above solutions without favoring either.

AFTERNOTE AND ANTICIPATORY PERFORMANCE
OF OTHER SHORT ORNAMENTS

Afternote and anticipatory performance of short ornaments indicated by two or more small notes was also discussed and debated. Some of these ornaments were slurred by their authors, others were not. In 1767 and 1782 Johann Samuel Petri wrote that the slide was used sometimes on and sometimes after the beat.[60] His Figure 7.28 shows afternotes—including the slide—and appoggiaturas in close proximity. J. C. Bach and Ricci showed their only two-note slide unslurred in a pre-beat position.[61]

Löhlein and Türk had also shown ornaments of two notes played before or after the beat (Figs. 7.12f; 7.1c, 2 and 3). Nevertheless, Türk was conservative, writing as if in echo of Bach. "All ornaments indicated by small notes (excepting only those *Nachschläge* mentioned . . .) receive their durations . . . from the following note."[62]

Türk's opinion notwithstanding, the tutors of Rellstab and Milchmeyer make it clear that anticipatory performance of a variety of ornaments was not uncommon. Rellstab still felt that this practice was inappropriate. He restated Bach's credo, followed by these revealing comments and examples:

> [The on-beat principle] is extremely important because there are so many keyboard players who play such an ornament not with the bass and other voices, but make all this [the bass and other parts] enter only with the main note.[63]

Nevertheless, in Figure 7.29, in addition to the single small note there is a double appoggiatura and a three-note slide, each realized first "as one tends to play" and then, "as one should play." Rellstab claimed that performers "often play many of the small notes in this distribution [before the beat] without being aware of it." Because players "slur the small notes to the main note [following], the poor performance is overlooked."[64]

Fig. 7.28. Petri, *Anleitung*, 2d ed., p. 151.

Fig. 7.29. Rellstab, *Anleitung*, p. vii.

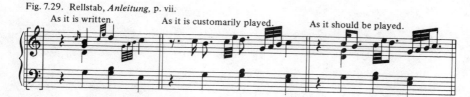

Milchmeyer's evidence is important because of his positive attitude. His introductory statement is also interesting for other reasons:

> Previously the embellishment of a melody was shown through small notes, considered a side issue in early instruction and left out in performance because it was believed that beginners did not possess sufficient musical feeling to perform them well. However, as our taste in very many things has improved during the last twenty years, many of the best composers now generally write all the ornaments of their pieces with the usual large notes, according to the true value that each should receive. Personally I find that very good. Beginners will not make mistakes and pieces will less frequently be disfigured by the player.... One inopportunely placed or badly performed ornament destroys the most beautiful passage and shows the player's bad taste. [Nevertheless, small notes as well as ornaments indicated by signs will be discussed in this chapter.] The value of these small notes is adjusted to the expression of the notes or of the passage where they appear, and they are therefore played quite slowly where it is required by the character of the piece or the emotion expressed, or quickly, as if they still belonged to the preceding beat.[65]

As examples of the small notes played "quite slowly," Milchmeyer illustrated the standard realizations of long appoggiaturas; but his examples of small notes played quickly, some of which are shown in Figure 7.30, include single notes, arpeggios, inverted turns, and the written-out *Schneller*,[66] all unmistakably realized before the beat. It is significant that Milchmeyer indicated pre-beat performance without explaining why it was valid. Evidently not captured by the previous pervasive, but now diminishing, influence of Bach's *Essay* and its followers, or perhaps his mind changed by more than ten years in Lyon and Paris, he simply described what he considered appropriate practice.[67]

Nevertheless, the change in manner of musical performance was gradual, and until well into the nineteenth century most writers still showed these ornaments only on the beat. In the second edition of his *Klavierschule* Türk reaffirmed his earlier stance in favor of on-beat realization and attacked Milchmeyer's position, fearing that "a crudeness, or—if one prefers—a kind of incorrect harmony would result."[68] With examples from unidentified passages by Mozart and Haydn, Türk illustrated potential parallel octaves, lack of time at the end of a beat to add more notes—no matter how quickly played, and the possible clash of harmonies that could arise if one hand played an anticipatory arpeggio while the other was still completing the previous chord.

Fig. 7.30. Milchmeyer, *Pianoforte zu spielen*, p. 38.

*4 in original must be engraver's error.
**2 in original must be engraver's error.

Indeed, common sense dictates awareness of such concerns when considering the possibility of afternote or anticipatory performance. Türk himself remarked that appoggiaturas "are largely a matter of taste" and that there are many "debatable cases,"[69] a comment that applies in some measure to the interpretation of many ornaments. Nor did Milchmeyer expect universal anticipatory performance; it was an option to be used according to "the expression of the notes or of the passage." Such controversy actually acknowledges the coexistence of the two styles of ornament realization. Preservation of the basic structural elements of harmony (including written-out dissonance and proper voice leading), melody, and rhythm was the primary factor in suggesting anticipatory performance for Figures 7.5, 7.6, and 7.16–7.24. Other specifics would include the composer's dynamics and our consideration of simultaneous melodic, rhythmic, or harmonic activity.

Beyond single notes, slides, inverted turns, and broken chords were the ornaments most often mentioned in tutors for off-beat performance. The following are a few examples from Beethoven's sonatas—with no intention of excluding the works of other composers—for which anticipation may be appropriate, although opinion is frequently divided. The *sf* on the main note in Figure 7.31 is an obvious clue. In Figure 7.32 the rapid tempo and the need for rhythmic clarity of the four-note group seem important; in Figure 7.33 the preservation of the written-out appoggiatura and motivic integrity hold sway. (The inverted turns in Beethoven's Op. 19/ii/15 and 39 also precede appoggiaturas.) In Figure 7.34 the need for a precise and strong entrance of the accented B on beat 2 suggests anticipation of the broken chord.

Opinion is strongly divided for Figure 7.35. Some writers and performers prefer pre-beat placement of the slides; Beyschlag pointed out the obvious

Fig. 7.31. Beethoven, Sonata Op. 49/1/ii (Simrock), m. 3.

Fig. 7.32. Beethoven, Sonata Op. 14/1/i (OE Mollo), mm. 25–26.

Fig. 7.33. Beethoven, Sonata Op. 7/iv (OE Artaria), mm. 4–5.

Fig. 7.34. Beethoven, Sonata Op. 2/2/iv (OE Artaria), m. 30.

Fig. 7.35. Beethoven, Sonata Op. 13/iii (OE Hoffmeister), mm. 4–6.

parallel octaves incurred between mm. 4 and 5 when the slides are played on the beat.[70] Yet others place them on the beat, either to avoid rushing the preceding eighth notes and the slides or perhaps because they prefer the slightly late main notes and the ensuing contrast with that same motive in mm. 9 and

10, where the same A-flat and G in octaves enter squarely on the downbeat with no ornamentation.

Finally, there are some ornaments for which neither on-beat nor pre-beat rendition seems to provide the necessary time or space. Even though the heading for Figure 7.36 is Adagio cantabile, the two beats surrounding the inverted turn are quite full, and only a rushed performance of the small notes allows them to be fully anticipated. What is needed here is "extra time" between the beats to allow the turn to breathe. Such a solution seems appropriate at this most elaborate place in the movement, which is also the climax of the ornate B section.

Czerny endorsed extra or added time for arpeggio performance in his *Piano Forte School*. The notes in an "arpeggioed" chord could be played extremely fast, but also in all gradations down to very slow. Then he provided some detail for Figure 7.37, modeled on the opening of Beethoven's Op. 31/2: "Here the single notes of the arpeggioed chords must follow one another extremely slow, *and we only begin to count the time prescribed from the last and highest note*."[71]

The last part of this description would also fit Figure 7.38. The first beat of m. 113 arrives only with f-sharp[1]. The Tempo I and *ff* at the beginning of the second arpeggio suggest an attempt to give the effect of a first beat, yet it seems impossible to me not to feel a beat again with the staccato g[1]. The space for both arpeggios is added time, and the counting does in fact begin "from the last and highest note," as Czerny suggested. Other kinds of ornaments that may need added time include decorative scale passages written in small notes, such as those in Haydn's Sonata Hob. 52/ii, and the small-note turn on the appoggiatura f-sharp[2] in Haydn's Hob. 42/i/73 (Fig. 7.39). This ornamental phrase ending occurs in several of Haydn's sonatas, in some of which a sig-

Fig. 7.36. Beethoven, Sonata Op. 13/ii (OE Hoffmeister), mm. 21–23.

Fig. 7.37. Czerny, *Piano Forte School*, Vol. III, p. 56.

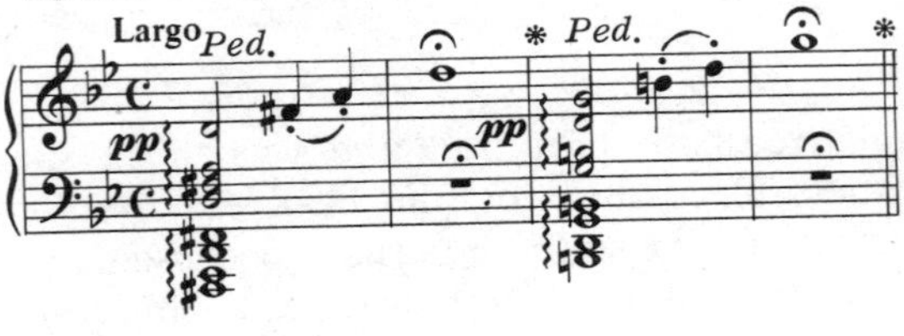

Fig. 7.38. Beethoven, Sonata Op. 10/1/iii (OE Eder), mm. 112–114.

Fig. 7.39. Haydn, Sonata Hob. 42/i (OE Bossler), m. 73.

* C-sharp ♪ here in OE and *for.* under the second note in the measure must be engraver's errors.

nificantly slower tempo for the movement allows both ornament and main note to be played gracefully without extra time (e.g., Hob. 29/ii/1).

THE TRILL

Overview

The full trill (*Triller, tremblement*) of the Classic period existed in three basic forms: the plain trill, the trill with termination (or suffix), and the trill with prefix. Examples from the tutors of Adam and Clementi illustrate some of the ways in which they were indicated, played, and varied (Figs. 7.40, 7.41).[72]

By this time there was some tendency to use *tr* for the full or long trill and to reserve the sign ～ for short trills or the *Schneller*. Yet the distinction was

Fig. 7.40. Adam and Lachnith, *Méthode...du doigté*, p. 142. a. Trill. b. Trill with prefix. c. Trill with prefix and suffix.

Fig. 7.41. Clementi/Rosenblum, *Introduction,* p. 11: "The shake legato with the preceding note, explained."

not reliable, causing Clementi to write: "N. B. the GENERAL mark for the shake is this *tr* and composers trust CHIEFLY to the taste and judgement of the performer, whether it shall be long, short, . . . or turned."[73]

Occasionally composers of this period indicated the trill start with a small note before the note to be trilled. In the early music of the period and in Haydn's music in general, such an initial upper auxiliary usually behaved in the manner of a long appoggiatura, creating the "prepared" trill so common in the late Baroque and early Classic periods.[74] Türk commented that "should an appoggiatura [in conjunction with a trill] actually receive half the value of the main note, then it should be notated exactly. . . ."[75] Haydn did so in Figure 7.42 (comp. by 1784), although the oscillations might begin just before the left-hand G to avoid the simultaneous sounding of two G's. Nevertheless, the notation of the small note was not always exact, particularly in Haydn's sonatas composed before 1762 (see n. 2; e.g., Sonata Hob. 12/ii/4, HSU, *JHW*). In these instances the guidelines for the length of long appoggiaturas generally apply.

Sometimes Haydn indicated prepared trills by writing out the initial upper auxiliary, slurred or unslurred (Fig. 7.124b, m. 52), rather than by indicating it as a small note. When the line is played legato, which is important if the main note is the resolution of an appoggiatura (including a cadential or appoggiatura 6/4 chord) or suspension, the oscillations may begin directly on the main note (Fig. 7.41b). But occasionally when there is time, tying over the upper auxiliary (as in Fig. 7.41a) proves attractive if the beat is marked in another part and if the tied note provides audible dissonance (Fig. 7.43).

In the keyboard music of Mozart (excepting some from the early years) and Beethoven, a small note before a trill indicates only the starting note (not its length), in Beethoven's case most often because it needs an accidental. Those composers seem to have written their lengthened preparations in regular notes, followed by the main note on the beat, as in Figure 7.41b, or the half beat.

Fig. 7.42. Haydn, Sonata Hob. 34/iii *(JHW)*, m. 4.

Fig. 7.43. Haydn, Sonata Hob. 46/ii (Contemporary ms. copy S. m. 9822), m. 5.

The duration and speed of the trill oscillations varied with the character of the piece, the particular context of the trill, and its function. Generally trills lasted for the full value of the main note, but Clementi and Pleyel-Dussek included realizations in which the beating stops slightly earlier at the discretion of the performer.[76] Perhaps this execution was considered more appropriate when the trilled note did not have a legato connection with the note following. The speed of the oscillations was adjusted to the tempo and expression of the passage.[77] In a long trill the performer also had the option of starting the oscillations somewhat slowly and accelerating them when this kind of ex-pressiveness seemed appropriate.[78] Beethoven wrote out such an acceleration in his elaborate development of the trill in Sonata Op. 109/iii/158–168.

A suffix to the trill in the form of a turned ending was frequently written out, as seen in Figures 7.47, 7.48, 7.59, and others. If such a termination was not indicated, the performer was expected to add one where it would fit and be advantageous, particularly in effecting a smoother transition from the trill back to the melodic line.[79] For example, when the trill is followed by a melody note a step or half-step above or below, a suffix adds considerably to the grace of reentry when that extra curve suits the context and when time allows. I would add terminations in Figures 7.46 and 7.62, but not in Figures 7.42, 7.50, or 7.54. These final notes were considered part of the trill and were generally played at the speed of the trill oscillations, although J. F. Schubert allowed the suffixes to be slower in slow tempos.[80] A widely recognized exception to main-taining the suffix at the speed of its trill was at the end of a cadenza. There, in order that the accompanying instruments be prepared to enter on time, the suffix was sometimes not only slower but might also have a few additional, decorative notes.[81]

There is very little information on when to conclude a trill tied over a bar line. Emanuel Bach gave an unrealized example of such a trill; his addition of a turned ending to the second note implies that the trill should continue without interruption to its termination.[82] Some modern writers have suggested that trills tied into the following measure should stop just short of the bar line so that the effect of the tie is felt.[83] I am unaware of any contemporary docu-mentation for this realization.

Evolution of the Trill Start

During the sixteenth century, when the art of improvising divisions flour-ished, and until the middle of the seventeenth century, the primary purpose of ornaments—including the trill—was to provide melodic decoration within a more horizontally oriented musical style. Trills, often written out, began either on the main note, which was most common, or on the upper (or lower) auxiliary if that form joined the melodic line more smoothly.[84] As the vertical structure of music became more strongly organized within the tonal system, the trill acquired the function of providing dissonance or a change in harmony, adding another dimension of interest to the sound. Hence, during the late

Baroque period, trills that began with the upper auxiliary on the beat (Fig. 7.40a) gradually evolved as the dominant form for keyboard music.[85] Later, Emanuel Bach's arbitrary stand acknowledging only the upper-note trill start may have strengthened their hold.[86] Bach's concept of ornaments was strongly harmonic, with appropriately used dissonance one of its goals. In 1755 Marpurg described the trill as "nothing more than a series of repeated falling appoggiaturas. . . ."[87]

Nevertheless, trills beginning on the main note or with the upper auxiliary played rapidly just before the beat as a grace note (hereafter termed grace-note trills)[88] were also used to a limited extent. Briefly, they were considered applicable for extended trills in noncadential settings whose function was to enliven long notes;[89] for places where an upper auxiliary on the beat would create unacceptable fifths or octaves; for situations in which the trilled note itself was dissonant with the bass; for trills serving predominantly as melodic decoration (rather than in a cadential or other structural function) where a musical aspect of the context, such as melody, polyphonic contour, or harmony, was best served by a main-note or grace-note start; and, finally, where an upper-note start might prove technically or musically awkward.[90]

Around 1775 evidence began to indicate a reversal of the pendulum that had swung so far toward the upper-auxiliary start; during the last quarter of the century more and more tutors and ornament tables included trills starting on the main note. In a volume of 1775, later praised by Galeazzi as "the best among the recent books for information on keyboard playing,"[91] Vincenzo Manfredini's only trill example begins its oscillations on the main note (Fig. 7.44a). The trill is preceded by the note above but lacks the connecting slur often associated with a written-out trill preparation. Theoretically it is possible to perceive this trill as beginning either on a prolonged upper auxiliary (without a slur) or on the main note; but Manfredini's description of the trill and the mordent (Fig. 7.44b) relates the two ornaments as mirror images, implying a trill with a main-note start:

> the trill, which is executed by playing alternately and as fast as possible two notes, a half or a whole tone apart, going upward; the mordent, which is executed by playing two notes in the same way, but only [those] a half tone from each other and going downward.[92]

The view that the trill and the mordent had a mirror relationship had been held by some musicians of the Iberian peninsula and Germany since the six-

Fig. 7.44. Manfredini, *Regole Armoniche*, p. 27. a. Trillo. b. Mordente.

teenth century, and to some extent it helped keep the main-note trill alive through the late Baroque era.[93] Manfredini left no fingering in the fourteen preludes in his book; nevertheless, the occasional upper auxiliary indicated before a trill (in Prelude II, two dissonant and two consonant) demonstrates that at least to some extent his practice was mixed.

Manfredini's trill was openly challenged two years later by Giambattista Mancini, a compatriot living in Vienna. He interpreted Manfredini's trill as starting on its main note, for his criticism—made public in his popular voice tutor—was that only the upper-note start was proper.[94] Controversy notwithstanding, the move toward a main-note start was soon joined by others. In his slim *Principi di Musica, Teorico-Pratici,* the earliest edition of which has been newly dated as from the late 1770s to the 1780s, Vincenzio Panerai included a trill example identical to Manfredini's second trill and added a trill with a main-note start approached from the note below.[95] There is also an undated manuscript by Johann Georg Albrechtsberger, acclaimed organist, contrapuntist, and a teacher of Beethoven, in which the only trills in the ornament table begin exactly like Manfredini's.[96] Fortunately, Albrechtsberger's fingering for numerous trills in the exercises that follow makes clear that all the trills are to begin on the main note, whether approached by step or by leap.[97] Other examples of main-note trill starts—both German and both from around 1778—include those in the table in J. A. P. Schulz's *Sonata per il clavicembalo* (Fig. 7.45) and Vogler's *Schnelzer,* a trill beginning on a consonant main note and ending with a termination, illustrated on a quarter note.[98] Both are without any specific approach.

An unusual contemporary source containing many pieces known to be by Haydn adds "live" evidence to the information about ornament realization in the 1790s. This source consists of three working mechanical or musical clocks (*Flötenuhren*), two built in 1792 and 1793 by Haydn's friend and composition student P. Primitivus Niemecz, and one, undated, that may have been built by Joseph Gurck, an apprentice to Niemecz, possibly as late as 1796 or 1797.[99] In a recording of the clocks of 1792 and 1793, and in the trill realizations from the three clocks written out in *Stücke für das Laufwerk* (*Pieces for Mechanical Clock*), JHW, XXI, all the extended, noncadential trills that merely color a tone begin on the main note. Among other trills main-note starts predominate (sometimes preceded by the same note [*JHW,* XXI, No. I.5, m. 4]), but there are also upper-auxiliary starts in no discernible pattern.[100]

Milchmeyer, a leader in recognizing anticipatory playing of short ornaments, showed both main- and upper-note trill starts in 1797. Interestingly, in his numerous examples he almost always maintained the dissonant upper-auxiliary start in a long cadential trill.[101]

Fig. 7.45. J. A. P. Schulz, Sonata per il clavicembalo Op. 2 (Berlin, ca. 1778), p. 15.

In 1796 Hüllmandel took the bold step of writing that "the Shake begins indiscriminately with either of the two Shaken Notes, or sometimes by a Note under those of the Shake. . . . "[102] Viguerie[103] and Baillot, Rode, and Kreutzer[104] wrote similarly in 1797 and probably 1803 respectively, adding that the manner of starting was determined by the taste of the performer unless, as Viguerie pointed out, the composer had indicated it with a small note. However, their compatriot Adam hewed more to the middle of the road in his *Méthode de piano du Conservatoire* of 1804, adopted for use by the Paris Conservatoire. Several of his models of full and short trills are strikingly similar to Clementi's;[105] but in more than 100 pages of fingered excerpts and pieces from Bach to Beethoven, Adam indicated the main-note (most often consonant) start for the great majority of full trills regardless of style and composer. The main-note start is almost always indicated when the trill begins a phrase and when the approach to the trill is stepwise, unless Adam wanted the dissonance provided by the initial upper auxiliary; it is sometimes indicated when the trilled note is approached by ascending leap, but only occasionally when approached by descending leap. Often a main-note start in conjunction with a melodic leap helps to preserve the clarity of an interval or motive. On the other hand, Adam showed a preference for the upper-auxiliary start—even against a bare octave—when the trill is approached by descending leap; is on a repeated note or on one equal to or longer than a whole note (none occur in the bass); or, more surprisingly, is part of a chain of trills.

Koch tried to give some perspective in his *Lexikon* of 1802:

> Music teachers do not agree in regard to the beginning of this ornament; the majority maintain with C. Ph. E. Bach, that the beginning of the trill must be made with the upper auxiliary; others, on the contrary, assert that one should always begin it with the main note.[106]

Koch maintained that as long as the ornament is performed only by a soloist, the way in which it is begun is of no special significance; the alternation of the notes is executed without giving either one any special importance, so that the difference in the way the trill is begun is not noticeable once the first note is passed.

Türk remained as adamant about the upper-auxiliary start in the second edition of his *Klavierschule* (1802)[107] as he had been in the first, going so far as to invoke Marpurg's description (quoted above) of the relationship between the trill and the descending appoggiatura. Clementi also remained rather conservative, endorsing only the upper-note start except in a stepwise legato approach and for short trills (discussed below). Even Starke's *Pianoforte-Schule* of 1819 merely restated Emanuel Bach's belief in the superiority of the upper-note start.[108] Thus the evolution to the exclusively main-note trill start must be viewed as a gradual one that reached completion only in the Romantic period.

The Trill Start in Works of Haydn, Mozart, and Their Contemporaries

Until about 1800 the trill beginning with the upper auxiliary may still have been used more frequently, although possibly less for Mozart than for Haydn and Clementi. Nevertheless, trills in any of the following contexts (and probably some others as well) might have been played with their oscillations beginning on the main note:

1. Trills approached by descending stepwise motion, with or sometimes without a written slur, but particularly if a legato line or clarity of the line is desired (Figs. 7.46, 7.47; supported also by evidence from *JHW*, XXI, No. I.5, m. 10 [Schmid, *Flute Clock*, No. 12]). This execution would have been considered especially important when the trilled tone is the resolution of a preceding appoggiatura or suspension, which—according to contemporary custom—was slurred to the note on which it resolves (Fig. 7.48). Therefore, the oscillations of a trill on the fifth or third of the dominant chord in a I$^6_4$, V progression usually begin with the main note (Fig. 7.49), for the sixth and fourth of the tonic 6/4 chord are appoggiaturas to the fifth and third respectively of the dominant chord. (For an exception to the main-note start in Beethoven's Trio WoO 39, see p. 251.) Nevertheless, descending conjunct motion to a trill does not always imply a main-note start on the beat, particularly if other

Fig. 7.46. Mozart, Sonata K. 533/ii (OE Hoffmeister), mm. 3–4.

Fig. 7.47. Variations for Piano transcribed from Mozart's Clarinet Quintet, K. Anh. 137* (OE Artaria), Var. 1, mm. 9–10.

*Author of the transcription is uncertain.

Fig. 7.48. Haydn, Sonata Hob. 49/i (Aut.), mm. 34–36.

* Flat from OE Artaria.

Fig. 7.49. Haydn, Sonata Hob. 35/i (OE Artaria), mm. 59–60.

Fig. 7.50. Haydn, Menuet for Flute Clock Hob. XIX/9 (Aut.), mm. 3–6.

Fig. 7.51. Mozart, Sonata K. 330/i (Aut.), mm. 36–38.

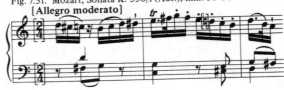

musical elements seem more important than a legato line. In the clock of 1792, each trill in Figure 7.50 begins on its upper note, which here enhances the fresh articulation and the downbeat of the dance. On the other hand, in the clock probably built by Niemecz's apprentice, these very trills start on their main notes, testimony to the flexibility in certain trill starts at this time.[109]

    2. Some trills approached by ascending stepwise motion, with or without a slur, particularly where it is important to maintain clarity of the line (including trills at the ends of rising scales). There seems to be no question among performers about the desirability of starting the trill in Figure 5.23 on its main note. The slurred chromatic line of even sixteenth notes presents a silky surface that would be noticeably roughened by the skip to an upper-note start. However, there is a decided difference of opinion regarding the trill start in Figure 7.51. Some favor the importance of the line and start the trill on E; others favor the dissonance provided by an upper-note start, particularly since the preceding staccato, the fresh articulation on the downbeat, and the dotted rhythm all add to a momentary prickly effect.[110] (Both of these trills may be played either as full trills or as short trills.)

    In the Classic style the decision between a main- and an upper-note trill start may involve the balancing of factors or the relative importance given to harmonic, melodic, and sometimes rhythmic elements. The interpreter's deliberations should be guided, insofar as possible, by the style of the piece and by any known proclivities of the composer. Figures 7.50 and 7.51, each of which has more than a single "correct" performance, are two among numerous situations in performance practices for which the answer depends on the performer's informed opinion and taste.

3. Some extended trills in noncadential settings where the purpose is melodic coloration of a note. These trill starts are open to choice, as they are also in music of the late Baroque period. In Figure 7.52 the insistent repeated notes (as well as those in mm. 282–286) create an impetus that reaches its climax as the A-flat (dissonant main note) bursts into a trill. Thus repeated notes that assume importance may predispose toward main-note trill starts. I also begin the trill in Figure 7.53 on the main note with unhurried oscillations that gradually become faster. Interestingly, the extended noncadential trills in Adam's *Méthode* of 1804 are fingered to begin just as often on the upper auxiliary as on the main note, while those in the three flute clocks invariably begin on the main note.

4. Trills on dissonant notes, in order to retain the significance and color of the dissonance. A trill beginning on A-flat in m. 19 of Figure 7.54 would sound bland indeed and would destroy the effect of appoggiatura and resolution that propels the phrase forward at this point. (See also Figures 7.47 and 7.52.)

5. Trills in the bass, expecially extended ones, if the harmonic function of the bass note would be weakened by an upper-note start (Fig. 7.55; supported

Fig. 7.52. Haydn, Sonata Hob. 52/iii (Aut.), mm. 289–294.

Fig. 7.53. Haydn, Sonata Hob. 12/i (Contemporary mss.), m. 1.

*Tie from secondary ms. source.

Fig. 7.54. Haydn, Sonata Hob. 38/iii (OE Artaria), mm. 18–20.

Fig. 7.55. Mozart, Variations on "Dieu d'amour" from Grétry's opera *Les Mariages Samnites*, K.352 *(NMA)*, Var. 4, mm. 9–12.

Fig. 7.56. Scarlatti, Sonata K. 463, mm. 1–2. a. Parma ms. b. Clementi's realization in *Scarlatti's Chefs-d'oeuvre*.

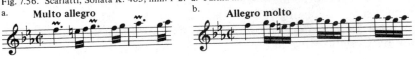

Fig. 7.57. Mozart, Rondo K. 511 (Aut.facs.), mm. 133–135.

also by the pinning of *JHW,* XXI, Nos. I.4, III.1 [Schmid, *Flute Clock,* Nos. 11 and 27]).

6. Sometimes in chains of trills. Here again practice was mixed. In two of the musical clocks each trill in a rising chain starts with its upper auxiliary (*JHW,* XXI, No. II.4). Clementi would no doubt have approached such trills by legato stepwise motion and begun them on the main note (as in Fig. 7.41b and c). Corroboration is found in the volume of sonatas by Domenico Scarlatti that Clementi published in 1791.[111] He transcribed Scarlatti's opening trill chain in Sonata K. 463 (Longo 471; Fig. 7.56a) in a way calculated to strengthen the impression of the melodic line (Fig. 7.56b). Yet Clementi's student John Field wrote an extended rising chain of trills, with an upper-auxiliary start notated for each, in his Third Concerto, published in 1816! The trills in Figure 7.57 must be played with main-note starts because of the importance of the ascending chromatic line in the rondo theme.

7. Where an upper-note start might prove less appropriate for other musical reasons (e.g., that it produces objectionable fifths or octaves; perhaps at the start of a piece [Fig. 7.53; or Mozart's K. 280/ii] or after a rest, where theorists considered appoggiaturas inappropriate [pp. 221, 244]) or might prove technically awkward. It seems to me that the trills in Figure 7.58 should begin on their main notes not only for harmonic reasons but also to preserve the identity of the motive, which Mozart carefully maintained throughout the set of variations. The trill in *JHW,* XXI, No. I.2, m. 14 (Schmid, *Flute Clock,* No. 2, m.

Fig. 7.58. Mozart, Variations on "Ein Weib ist das herrlichste Ding" K. 613 *(NMA)*, Var. 2, mm. 8–11.

14) was pinned with a main-note start, possibly to emphasize the note in a melodic leap of tonal importance. The main-note trill starts in the motive of the Fuga, *JHW,* XXI, No. II.7 (Schmid, *Flute Clock,* No. 24) surely help to preserve its jagged shape.

Tromlitz provides some evidence for the occasional use of the grace-note trill mentioned on p. 242. According to him, a trill at the beginning of a melody or a phrase could start directly on its main note or with a "very short note before [*Vorschlag*]." Since Tromlitz held that in all trills the oscillations should emphasize the main note, a "very short note before" would frequently have slipped into a grace-note position.[112] (His examples of trills begun with longer auxiliaries always give the main note a rhythmically strong position.) When there is no small note in the text, I find the most convincing use of an upper-auxiliary grace note to be that which occurs when the trill is on the same pitch as the preceding note and the trilled tone is an appoggiatura. The grace-note start is an attractive alternative to a main-note start in Figure 7.54 (m. 19) and in Mozart's Sonata K. 284/i/94, beat 1.

When making decisions about a trill start, the pianist should always evaluate carefully the situation and role of the ornament within its context. For the music of Haydn, Mozart, and their contemporaries, a checklist of possible clues would include the melodic approach to the trill (stepwise or by leap); the desired articulation (legato or detached); the harmonic and melodic roles of the trilled note (consonant, dissonant, or the resolution of a dissonance; whether its melodic or harmonic role outweighs other factors); the overall harmonic-rhythmic implications of starting on the main note versus the upper note (more or less dissonance; harmonic and/or rhythmic importance of the dissonance in relation to the meter; effect on harmonic functioning of a bass note, etc); and, finally, any other musical clues, such as preserving the identity of a motive.

In addition to contextual evidence, whatever may be known about the preferences of the composer should be considered. As remarked earlier, Clementi apparently favored the upper-auxiliary start with the exception of ascending and descending stepwise legato lines. On the other hand, if Niemecz's pinning of the 1792 flute clock is representative of Haydn's practice in the 1790s, Haydn might have expected main-note trill starts in many of the circumstances described above.

The Trill Start in Works of Beethoven

It is well known that under his teacher Neefe, Beethoven had studied Emanuel Bach's *Essay* thoroughly. However, during his Bonn years he had also studied Vogler's *Tonschule* of 1778,[113] in which the ornaments were treated quite differently from Bach's rigid approach. Vogler included the *Schnelzer* (p. 243 above) and many kinds of small notes played before or after the beat. With all the accumulated evidence for increasing use of main-note trill starts in the 1790s and later, Beethoven could scarcely have been unaware of the crosscurrents of change. Since he was also known for his independence of thought, we will explore what specific information he left regarding his own intentions during this period of transition. The regrettably few definitive indicators for trill starts occur in the form of a small number of fingered trills, of lower- or upper-auxiliary prefixes, and of the rare written-out trills.

On a manuscript leaf from before 1792, Beethoven experimented with a new fingering for right-hand double trills in sixths (mixing black and white keys). They begin on their upper auxiliaries, and the second finger crosses the thumb.[114] Although this fingering proved impractical in sixths, he continued to use it for smaller intervals (as in Fig. 7.59a).

Valuable information has come to light in the *BNA* edition of the Twelve Variations for Violin and Piano on Mozart's "Se vuol ballare" WoO 40, published in July 1793 by Artaria.[115] In the coda to the set there are three fingered trills; two begin on dissonant upper auxiliaries (Fig. 7.59a), and the third, a "Beethoven trill," begins on a consonant main note (Fig. 7.59b). In the double trill the thumb plays the upper auxiliary G of the lower voice and the second finger crosses over to the F, producing thirds with the top voice. The same crossed fingering reappears in a piece in Adam's *Méthode;* to avoid any possible misunderstanding the first trill oscillations are written in small notes with the fingering under each.[116] The consonant start of the trill in Figure 7.59b, just a few measures from the gentle final cadence, seems designed to allow the tension to dissipate; at the same time the melody, previously played by the right hand in conjunction with an unfingered "Beethoven trill" (mm. 53ff.),[117] is reduced

Fig. 7.59. Beethoven, Variations on "Se vuol ballare" from Mozart's *The Marriage of Figaro*, WoO 40, Coda *(BNA)*. a. mm. 59–60. b. mm. 74–75.

* Trill begins in m. 49.

to the recurring fragment e³, f³, played staccato with the fifth finger. Another example of Beethoven's early trill experiments is a melodic fragment for the left hand in which 4, 3 fingering under single notes would seem to indicate implied main-note starts (the *tr* signs are lacking), perhaps for their melodic advantage.[118] Douglas Johnson has dated this manuscript page from the second half of 1794 or early 1795,[119] when Beethoven was working on the Piano Trios Op. 1, the Sonatas Op. 2, and the Concerto Op. 19.

There are four later examples of fingered trills: one (subsequently repeated) in the Trio WoO 39, m. 8 (comp. 1812); one in Op. 111/ii/112 (the two right-hand parts of the triple trill); and two in Op. 119/7/1–2. Although in the Trio Beethoven slurred the soprano notes "mi, re, do" in a strong I_4^6, V_7, I cadence, he placed the thumb on "mi" and 4, 3 on "re"; this notation indicates—in spite of the slur and the progression—reiteration of the dissonant upper-auxiliary to begin the oscillations, but minimizes the resulting break in the legato descent by changing fingers (from 1 to 4) on the repeated note. Interestingly, of the several unfingered trills in this Trio, all but the extended trill in the coda create dissonance with a main-note start. Both trills in Op. 119/7 begin on their main notes with dissonant starts. The upper voice of the fingered double trill in Op. 111 begins on its upper auxiliary, but the meaning of the 1, 2 fingering for the lower voice has caused disagreement. William Newman has argued for the literal interpretation of the fingering, which gives a main-note start and greater dissonance to the trill.[120] Robert Winter and others believe in using a crossed fingering (as in Fig. 7.59a), which gives an upper-note start and a cadential I_4^6, V_7 progression.[121]

Small-note prefixes on the upper or lower auxiliaries sometimes occur in unaccompanied lines where their purpose is to indicate a chromatic alteration or the specific connection of the trill to the line. When these prefixes occur in a harmonic context they also generally create dissonant trill starts. Representative examples include those at Op. 10/2/i/58, the Variations Op. 34/6/45, Op. 53/iii/51, and the Sonata for Violoncello and Piano Op. 102/1/ii/15. Of three written-out trills in relatively early works, one begins on its upper auxiliary (Op. 5/1/i/31) and two begin on main notes (Op. 19/ii/67, Op. 27/1/iii/25); all three start with percussed dissonance.

Although the aggregate of information provided by these meagre clues leaves many unanswered questions, a few observations may provide some direction for making choices. First, Beethoven seems to have used both upper- (and lower-) auxiliary and main-note starts throughout his creative years. Second, the small number of fingered trills does not show a marked preference for upper or main-note starts *per se,* but of the seven such trills that have harmonic backgrounds, six start with some degree of dissonance. Third, in Beethoven's music many main-note trill starts that provide advantageous melodic flow also create dissonance; in addition to those already mentioned in WoO 39 and Op. 119, there are others in the examples below.

How does this information help the performer, who must make a decision wherever there is no specific indicator? The guidelines suggested for the music of Haydn and Mozart—linear approach, desired articulation, harmonic and melodic roles of the trilled note and the trill (including the consideration of dissonance), possible rhythmic implications, and other musical clues—bear on the music of Beethoven as well. The total integration of elements in Beethoven's style increases the likelihood that the trill start may also be influenced by a melodic or motivic relationship, or by the desire to preserve the outline of an interval or motive (e.g., Op. 27/2/iii/29–34). A main-note trill start generally favors melodic clarity even when it provides dissonance. Such clarity seemed the apparent reason for some of the main-note starts in Adam's *Méthode*. It was also one of Hummel's reasons for stating his "rule" that "in general, *every shake* should begin *with the note itself*, over which it stands, and not with the *subsidiary note* above, unless the contrary be expressly indicated."[122]

By 1828, when this statement was published, it was in fact a summary of the direction in which trill performance had already gone, for gradually, from about 1800, the main-note start seems to have become the more frequent form. Yet our observations based on evidence from Beethoven's music suggest that dissonance—an important factor in his compositional style—might properly be a consideration in determining trill starts when there is no other overriding element. For those who wish definitive answers, these few available hints may be of little comfort; on the other hand, they offer opportunity for more choice and more debate.[123]

A few examples from the sonatas of Beethoven will illustrate my application of the foregoing ideas. In Figure 7.60, from a sonata composed in 1793–1795, the trills should probably begin in the traditional way on the upper auxiliary to maximize their harmonic effect. The undecorated intervals have just been heard. In Figure 7.61 from the same sonata, Beethoven's instruction via the slur to begin the trill on the main note serves the same harmonic purpose. Other trills from sonatas composed before 1800 that I would begin on the upper auxiliary include those at Op. 7/iii/33 and iv/36–38, Op. 10/3/i/52, and Op.

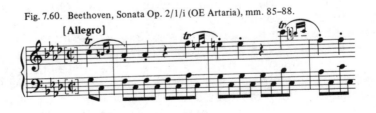

Fig. 7.60. Beethoven, Sonata Op. 2/1/i (OE Artaria), mm. 85–88.

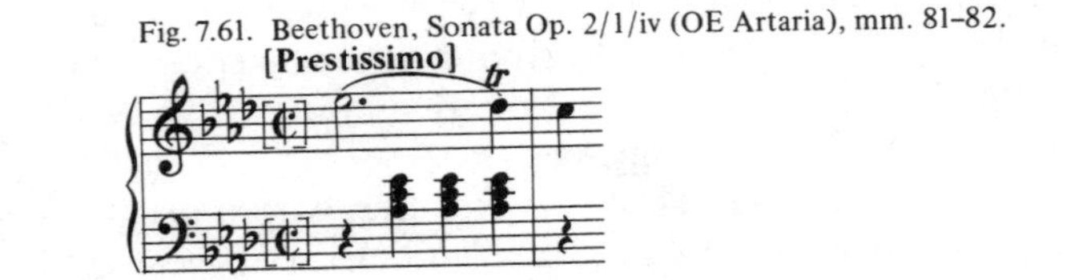

Fig. 7.61. Beethoven, Sonata Op. 2/1/iv (OE Artaria), mm. 81–82.

14/2/i/61 and 133. The trills at Op. 2/2/ii/9 and Op. 13/i/174 are among those that require the pianist to declare a leaning toward dissonance or line, perhaps influenced one way or another in the first by Beethoven's indicated dissonant start of the answering trill in the following measure. Main-note starts provide dissonance at Op. 2/3/i/21 and Op. 10/2/ii/15. The trill in Figure 7.62 (comp. 1800–1801) should begin on the main note to emphasize the effect of the unexpected G-flat and its attendant diminished-seventh chord.

Both trills in Figure 7.63a, from Op. 31/1 (comp. 1802), begin on the main note because of their obvious melodic coloristic (rather than harmonic) function, as well as to keep the outline of the triadic motive clear. The rising chromatic approach to the trill in m. 3 also suggests a main-note start. The motive that approaches the major cadential area in Figure 7.63b, from the same movement, begins to take shape in m. 23 and has an appoggiatura A at the beginning of m. 24. The trill in this measure might be begun either way.

Fig. 7.62. Beethoven, Sonata Op. 27/1/ii (OE Cappi), mm. 44–52.

Fig. 7.63. Beethoven, Sonata Op. 31/1/ii (Simrock).[124] a. mm. 1–4. b. mm. 23–26.

I prefer the main-note start, which lets both soprano and alto lines and the augmented fourth be heard clearly; stronger dissonance arrives immediately on the next beat. In m. 25 the opening appoggiatura is omitted, and the motive is rhythmically compressed and repeated three times. Some might argue that it is a matter of taste whether the trill at the beginning of m. 26 should begin on the main note, to preserve the final motivic shape, or on the upper auxiliary, to recall the appoggiatura in m. 24 and also to provide harmonic color on this suspenseful cadence preceding the written-out cadenza. For me, Beethoven's leaning toward dissonant trill starts and my own desire to vary the motive slightly are the determining factors.

A main-note start is mandatory in Figure 7.64 to retain the carefully prepared culmination of the harmonic progression. The accented D of an upper-note start would also weaken the effect of Beethoven's extended trill termination. In Figure 7.65a (a development of Figure 5.16), thematic clarity as well as the dissonance already present in m. 23 suggest main-note starts, as does preservation of the descending stepwise line and harmonic sequence in Figure 7.65b, along with the dissonance in m. 67.

The next two examples are from late works. A main-note start seems most appropriate in Figure 7.66 to establish and maintain both the identity of the interval of the fourth, which is so important in the first and last movements of this sonata, and the identity of the brief initial thematic motive that emerges from the trill. The function of the trill in relation to the motive may be heard as one of balance. The trill's presence on the opening B balances to some extent the forces that would emphasize the E—its higher pitch, its metrical placement, and the dissonance created with the harmony against which it is later set. The motive stretches out of the trill, which is more thematic than ornamental, and

Fig. 7.64. Beethoven, Sonata Op. 31/2/ii (Simrock), mm. 7–8.

Fig. 7.65. Beethoven, Sonata Op. 31/3/i (Simrock). a. mm. 22–23. b. mm. 67–70.

Fig. 7.66. Beethoven, Sonata for Violin and Piano Op. 96/i (Aut.), mm. 1-3.

Fig. 7.67. Beethoven, Sonata Op. 106/iv (OE Artaria), mm. 16–17.

falls back to the opening B, flowing in the beginning almost without reference to the meter. The frequently observed directness of both motive and movement persuades me to play the trill in its simplest form, without a suffix. Nothing would be gained by the addition of a suffix, and one aesthetic basis of the movement would be subtly undermined.[125]

Figure 7.67 is from a movement in which the trill itself becomes a structural thematic element. For that reason, and to keep the important half step from leading tone to tonic completely clear, a main-note start is imperative. In contrast to Figure 7.66, Beethoven here notated the trill suffix. The evidence offered by these two examples suggests that adding a suffix to a trill with thematic significance—an occurrence of Beethoven's later works—should be undertaken only with caution.

The Short Trill and the *Schneller*

The basic forms of the short trill as used in the Classic period are shown in Figures 7.68, 7.69, and 7.71. The short trill proper began on its upper auxiliary and had four or six notes. It was used on short notes (Fig. 7.68) or occasionally on longer notes where the rhythmic effect of stopping the oscillations and holding the main note seemed more desirable than that of a full trill (Fig. 7.73).

The "half or *Pralltriller*," another form of short trill, was used originally on the lower note of a slurred descending second. It was played very quickly with its initial upper auxiliary tied over from the preceding note (Fig. 7.69). This trill had been described and named by Emanuel Bach in 1753;[126] a "textbook" example occurs in Haydn's Hob. 46/i/2–3. It was a favorite of Bach and his followers, all of whom described it, including even Starke as late as 1819.[127]

Fig. 7.68. Pleyel-Dussek, *Méthode*, p. 7.

[Written]   Played

Fig. 7.69. Türk, *Klavierschule*, p. 272.

Fig. 7.70. E. Bach, *Essay*, p. 142.

Fig. 7.71. Marpurg, *Anleitung zum Clavierspielen*, Table V. a. From Fig. 1. b. From Fig. 2. c. Fig. 3.

Bach's *Schneller* was an ornament shaped like a three-note trill but indicated with two small notes; it was restricted to quick, detached notes before a descent (Fig. 7.70).[128]

Marpurg's *Anleitung zum Clavierspielen* of 1755 provides evidence that "in rapidly moving passages descending stepwise [Fig. 7.71a], when a long[er] appoggiatura precedes a short note [7.71b]," or when a note with a *Pralltriller* is considerably shortened by an appoggiatura (7.71c), the tied upper auxiliary of the *Pralltriller* was dropped and the trill oscillations began directly on the main note.[129] Ignoring some of the specific differences in performance required by Bach for the slurred *Pralltriller* and his *Schneller,* Marpurg equated these two ornaments.[130] This undoubtedly contributed to the confusion between *Pralltriller* and *Schneller* that existed during the second half of the century and to the breakdown of the distinction between them in sign, placement, and manner of performance. By 1774 Löhlein showed his "half" trill—realized with three notes—on the first note of slurred, descending pairs of sixteenth notes, introduced both with and without a preceding upper auxiliary.[131]

The three-note trill is now variously called a short trill, a *Schneller,* or an inverted mordent.[132] I shall use the terms *Schneller* or three-note trill, reserving short trill for the independent four- (or six-) note trill (Fig. 7.68) and *Pralltriller* for that ornament as described by Bach and Türk. The *Schneller* must also have been used to a limited extent as an exceptional short trill in the late

Baroque and early Classic periods under some of the same circumstances listed earlier that suggested the main-note start for full trills. Those contexts that might have seemed most appropriate for the *Schneller* would have included places where an upper-note start would create ugly-sounding fifths or octaves, where the shape of the *Schneller* is needed for aesthetic reasons—such as exact inversion of a passage with a mordent, and where the trilled note itself is dissonant with the bass.[133]

By around 1780 the *Schneller* was undoubtedly used with increasing freedom. Türk objected to the loss of the tied-over auxiliary in the *Pralltriller* (as in Fig. 7.71). He further observed that "at times even the best composers" placed the sign for the *Pralltriller* where a *Schneller* "properly" belonged. In 1789 he attributed these "exceptions" to composers' confusion of the ornaments; by 1802 he merely called attention to the usage.[134]

Where speed is not a primary consideration, the choice between a short trill and a *Schneller* might well have been determined by the same considerations that were applied to the full trill. (A good example is the discussion of Figures 7.51 and 5.23, both of which can be played as full trills or as some type of short trill.) Probably almost every trill on rapid, descending stepwise notes should be realized as a *Schneller* (Fig. 7.72). In other contexts, if there is no contraindication, short trills might be used where the increased brilliance of four notes seems advantageous. As always, the approximate date of composition and any known proclivity of the composer should be taken into account. For example, J. A. P. Schulz (ca. 1778, Fig. 7.45), Adam (in 1798 and 1804), and Clementi were among the earlier authors to include only three-note realizations for all uses of the short trill (Fig. 7.73), but J. B. Cramer offered both in 1812.[135]

As in the late Baroque and early Classic periods, if a tempo was too rapid or a passage too difficult for the performer to play the four oscillations of a short trill, and if it seemed desirable to retain the initial impact of dissonance,

Fig. 7.72. Haydn, Sonata Hob. 52/i (Aut.), m. 19.

Fig. 7.73. Adam and Lachnith, *Méthode . . . du doigté*, p. 142.

a turn or an appoggiatura could be substituted, whichever sounded better within the melodic context.[136] Evidence for this practice exists in the first movement of Mozart's Piano Concerto K. 453, where *tr* and an appoggiatura appear as synonymous notations in conjunction with an eighth note and a turned ending of two sixteenth notes. In the orchestral exposition (mm. 17, 20) the ornament is *tr;* in the solo exposition and recapitulation the ornament is variously notated as a sixteenth-note appoggiatura (e.g., m. 95), which makes the figure look like a turn, or as *tr*, with the two occurring simultaneously in different parts in m. 98 (*NMA*). In the eighteenth century the four-note turn was regarded as the skeleton of a trill with turned ending, providing the same harmonic effect and melodic link. A turn would sound well in Figure 7.74; a short appoggiatura would fit in figure 7.75, where the addition of a turn would make the following two notes redundant.

In the foregoing figures, those from tutors show ⁓ as the sign for the short trill and the *Schneller* (except when it is in small notes), presumably leaving *tr* for the full trill. However, most composers did not adhere to a consistent differentiation, as can be seen by Haydn's use of *tr* for the *Schneller* in Figure 7.72. On the other hand, Beethoven appears to have used ⁓ in an unexpectedly specialized way.

According to recent research by William Newman, Beethoven reserved that sign solely to indicate the *Schneller*, using *tr* for both full trill and short trill.[137] In Figure 7.76 the two different signs in the same melodic pattern would seem to be a certain demonstration of an intended difference, with the four-note trill closer to the climactic point. In the event that a performer finds the four notes difficult to negotiate, it would be appropriate to substitute a turn, but not a *Schneller*. Not surprisingly, in Figure 7.77, as in many places where Beethoven used the *Schneller*, the main-note start brings with it dissonance. Because considerable speed is required wherever Beethoven used this orna-

Fig. 7.74. Mozart, Sonata K. 282/iii (Aut.), mm. 9–10.

Fig. 7.75. Mozart, Sonata K. 570/iii (OE Artaria), m. 8.

Fig. 7.76. Beethoven, Sonata Op. 2/3/i (OE Artaria),[138] mm. 59–60.

Fig. 7.77. Beethoven, Sonata Op. 7/iv (OE Artaria), m. 43.

ment, Newman also concludes that in his works the *Schneller* was intended to be played as a triplet rather than with two short notes followed by a longer one, as in Figure 7.71.

A fascinating endorsement of Newman's conclusions came to light unexpectedly in the second edition of the *Méthode du doigté* by Adam and Lachnith, published in 1814. In a newly appended section the authors showed clearly that a short trill indicated by ᗡ was to be played as a *Schneller* in triplet rhythm, while a short trill indicated by *tr* was to begin with the upper auxiliary.[139]

THE MORDENT

As Clementi pointed out in 1801, the mordent (*Mordent, pincé*) was used much less frequently in music of the Classic period than it had been earlier.[140] Its realization remained similar to that of the early Classic style; Türk's presentation of the ornament is in many respects very close to Emanuel Bach's. Türk's examples in Figure 7.78 include the single (one set of oscillations), double, and longer mordents.

More than many writers, Türk stressed that mordents must be played "extremely quickly,"[141] and thus he supplied realizations adjusted according to tempo. To give the ornament more sharpness or bite the half step was often used without any written indication. He also remarked on the need for a substantial pause on the main note after a long mordent, as seen in Figure 7.78c.[142]

Figure 7.79 shows Türk's realization of a mordent following an appoggiatura. His dynamic signs indicate that the appoggiatura, which is allotted half

Fig. 7.78. Türk, *Klavierschule*. a. p. 275. b. p. 278. c. p. 278.

Fig. 7.79. Türk, *Klavierschule*, p. 276.

the value of the main note, receives the expressive emphasis and that the mordent follows it more gently. After the turn of the century many tutors no longer described the mordent.

THE TURN AND THE "QUICK" TURN

The turn (*Doppelschlag, doublé*), as its name implies, turns around its main note starting from the upper auxiliary. Türk identified the turn as

> one of the most beautiful and useful ornaments, by means of which the melody is made singularly charming and animated. For this reason the turn can be used in pieces of a tender as well as of a lively character, on slurred and detached notes.[143]

The placement of the turn sign, ∾, either directly over one note or between two notes, generally shows the intended position of the ornament, for it was used both on the beat and between beats or notes. The turn was also indicated with small notes, and sometimes with a special sign, ᴧ, by Haydn. According to evidence from the contemporary tutors that demonstrate both ∾ and small notes, this additional form of notation did not necessarily change the realization of the turn: three small notes were generally played on the beat and four were played between beats, as shown in Figures 7.80a and d.[144]

Once again the musical clocks provide valuable information, at least for practice in Haydn's circle, even though the rhythmic placement of some turns

Fig. 7.80. Common Realizations of Turns. The categories show usages suggested in contemporary sources. Many of these rhythmizations can be applied appropriately in adjacent tempo types.

Fig. 7.81. Haydn, Piece for Flute Clock Hob. XIX/15 (Ms. copy by Johann Elssler), mm. 8–11.

remains unclear on both the cylinders and the tape recordings.[148] In many pieces the same turns notated first with the usual turn sign and then with the three small notes are performed exactly alike. The clocks of 1793 and 1796 or 1797 play those in Figure 7.81 with four equal notes starting on the beat (compare *Flötenuhrstücke, JHW*, XXI, No. II.6). Turns notated by Haydn with three small notes and then with his special sign, ⌣, are also played alike. The clock of 1792 plays those in Figure 7.82 quickly, starting on the beat, and with a pause on the main note. The difference in internal rhythm between the turns in Figures 7.81 and 7.82[149] is related to musical factors explained below, not to the difference in the signs.

The interval between the outer notes of a turn was almost always meant to be a minor third.[150] When an adjustment is necessary it is usually made by raising the lower note a half step if that alteration fits the harmonic style. For example, in a major key the lower auxiliary of a turn on the dominant note

Fig. 7.82. Haydn, Piece for Flute Clock Hob. XIX/17 (Aut.), mm. 5, 7.

is generally raised; in a minor key the lower auxiliary of a turn on the tonic is raised, and that of a turn on the subdominant or dominant is usually raised. Occasionally the upper note is lowered if that seems preferable. In present editorial practice an accidental for the lower note may be placed below the turn sign, one for the upper note above the sign. However, in eighteenth- and nineteenth-century scores either such accidentals were not shown or an accidental for either note was placed above the sign and its proper application was left to the performer (see Fig. 9.18, or Fig. 7.126 for an accidental with a mordent).

The internal rhythmic arrangement of the turn was remarkably variable. It could assume a configuration congenial to the tempo and character of the piece, to the flow and articulation of the melodic line, or to a rhythmic pattern for which the composer may have left a clue. Milchmeyer stressed this aspect of turn interpretation;

> Since a great deal depends on appropriate performance of these turns, namely, whether they are played with taste and feeling, composers should not be satisfied with merely placing a sign over the note. . . . The question then is what value one should give these four notes. . . . Composers could prevent many a confusion . . . if . . . , in pieces that require much expression, they would give the turn in notes rather than with a sign.[151]

A sampling of the realizations commonly found in tutors and widely applicable in the Classic repertoire is shown in Figure 7.80. Many situations offer the performer more than one appropriate option; final selection may even vary according to the action of the instrument being played.

Turns over notes of sufficient length were generally played promptly and quickly on the beat, allowing a pause on the main note in all but the fastest tempos (Fig. 7.80a). (Exceptions, such as the "delayed" turn in Figure 7.80a, 7, are discussed below.) Turns over shorter notes, including eighth notes, and quarter notes in rapid tempos sometimes incorporated the main note into a group of four equal tones. This may have occurred more often (but not only) in places that are metrically weak, particularly if the rhythm of the line or the articulation benefits from an even flow (Figs. 5.15, 7.81, 7.83–7.86).

In respect to the rhythmization of turns over notes we can observe differing styles. Emanuel Bach and his followers, in this instance including Türk, limited turns performed evenly to those in which there was no time to include a pause at the end, such as a turn on a quarter note in a *presto* context (Fig. 7.80a, 5).

Fig. 7.83. Haydn, Piece for Flute Clock Hob. XIX/10 (Aut.), m. 9.

Fig. 7.84. Haydn, Sonata Hob. 49/i (Aut.), m. 59.

Fig. 7.85. Mozart, Sonata K. 457/ii (OE Artaria), m. 49.

Fig. 7.86. Beethoven, Sonata Op. 2/1/ii (OE Artaria), m. 44.

Other musicians of widely varying backgrounds realized turns evenly wherever it seemed appropriate, with no tempo qualifications. Milchmeyer and Clementi show even turns only on the second (i.e., rhythmically weak) half of a beat, while Löhlein and Adam also show them on the beat, including downbeats.[152] One of Löhlein's even examples, a downbeat eighth note in an *adagio*, comes with the explanation that "in slow and emotional pieces this ornament is also played slowly."[153] Emanuel Bach and Türk allowed a broader execution (in which the main note loses more of its value) occasionally in a slow expressive passage or with a *fermata*, but the first two notes had to be faster than the third, as in Figure 7.80a, 1.[154] The musical clocks contain many even turns, of which Figures 7.81 and 7.83 are but two illustrations. The chameleon-like turn was apparently played evenly (including its main note) when time was short or when that rhythm with its more legato sound and gentle effect better suited the line.

According to Emanuel Bach and Türk, turns appeared frequently after appoggiaturas. Figure 7.80c shows Türk's rhythmization of the combined ornaments.[155]

Turns between notes or over a dot are delayed until "shortly before the following note (or dot)"[156] (Figs. 7.80d–h). Again, the exact placement and speed are adaptable to the tempo and mood of the piece. Gustav Nottebohm, the eminent nineteenth-century Beethoven scholar, illustrated the rhythmization of a turn between notes with an intermediate step. Above the opening measure of Beethoven's Op. 2/1/ii, he penciled in the exact notation that Beethoven had used for the same theme in his Piano Quartet WoO 36/3/ii, composed in 1785 (Fig. 7.87b). At the bottom of the page Nottebohm wrote a full realization of both ornaments in the measure, placing the notes of the turn in the time of Beethoven's sixteenth note and the small note on the beat (Fig. 7.87c).[157] Milchmeyer had a bias toward pre-beat performance (Fig. 7.30), and that led him to the realization in Figure 7.87d, which—perhaps without knowledge of Beethoven's earlier notation of this theme—placed the turn earlier in order to anticipate the C. This arrangement lets the 6/4 chord on beat 2 stand out. Nottebohm's realization, especially if played with some rhythmic nuance, lets the flow of the ornaments straddle the two beats, producing a more graceful line.

Most tutors that demonstrate turns in dotted patterns show some in which the note after the dot is shortened (Figs. 7.80f, 1–3). Unless the composer wrote double dots, the length of the last note is left to the discretion of the performer. Lively or majestic pieces almost always benefit from shortening the last note (e.g., Figs. 7.91 and 8.18); many slow pieces do too, as Mozart demonstrated in the Adagio of the Sonata K. 457 (e.g., m. 4). (See also "Double Dotting and Overdotting" in chap. 8.) In a jaunty or majestic style the performer may also detach the final note of the turn from the note following, especially when the latter is shortened (e.g., Figs. 7.80f, 1 and 2).[158]

Türk emphasized that "especially for dotted notes," and even when four equal small notes symbolized the turn, "the last (fourth) note of the turn should fall just in the time of the dot. . . ."[159] Emanuel Bach specified that turns between tied notes be treated similarly: "the tying note acquires a dot and the tied note becomes the last tone of the turn"[160] (Fig. 7.80h). In view of its frequent occurrence in tutors, this rhythmization (or one concluding with two

Fig. 7.87. Beethoven, Sonata Op. 2/1/ii. a. OE Artaria, m. 1. b., c. From Nottebohm's copy, p. 5. d. Milchmeyer, *Pianoforte zu spielen*, p. 40.

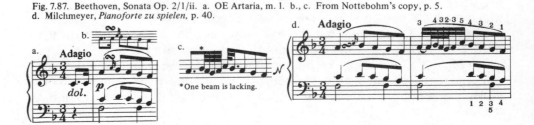

*One beam is lacking.

written-out short notes) was probably very widely used. Mozart wrote it out in large notes sufficiently often to make it seem quite appropriate, if not the generally preferred realization for a turn over a dot in his music (e.g., Sonata for Piano and Violin K. 376/iii/60–61; Rondo K. 494/17, 38, 49, etc.).

Sometimes Mozart signified the same melodic shape as a turn after a dotted note with the combination of small note and written-out mordent (Fig. 7.88). Türk suggested two realizations for such a figure: either a short appoggiatura before the two fast notes, which preserves the mordent, or a triplet of the first three notes, which forms a turn (Fig. 7.80a).[161] Eva and Paul Badura-Skoda prefer the turn solution for Mozart whenever the sixteenth notes are unaccented; but Frederick Neumann points out that Mozart usually slurred the small note-cum-mordent as a discrete unit that is often preceded and followed by staccato notes, whereas he generally slurred his written-out turns to the preceding note and sometimes to the note(s) following.[162] Presumably the message in Mozart's notation should warn us against straying too frequently from the more emphatic mordent—which may be preceded by an acciaccatura, a grace note, or a short appoggiatura—especially in the proximity of other written-out or symbolized turns after dotted notes, as in the Sonata for Piano and Violin K. 296/i or the Minore of K. 494. In 1804 Johann Friedrich Schubert actually offered 𝅘𝅥𝅮𝅘𝅥𝅯 as a possible realization of 𝆷 (Fig. 7.80a, 6).[163]

In another type of rhythmization for turns after dotted notes the turn was played in the time of the dot. Examples of this type, with small variations, appear in all the editions of the piano and violin tutors of Löhlein from 1765 to 1797.[164] They are represented here in Figures 7.80f, 3 and 5, and 7.80g, 1. Hüllmandel (in a "New Edition" of his tutor) and Starke represent this type of rhythmization without a pause on the final main note (Fig. 7.80f, 7).[165] Koch also espoused this rhythmization,[166] which may have been more widely used than was heretofore recognized. Its possible relevance to some of Haydn's turns is discussed below in "Haydn's Interpretation of the Turn over a Dot."

A turn between a dotted note and two notes in a further reduced value was also common. Löhlein's rhythmization (Fig. 7.80g, 1) places the ornament in the time of the dot; Figure 7.80g, 2, like Mozart's written-out version in the Rondo K. 494 (Fig. 7.89), places the fourth note of the turn on the dot. This rhythmization typifies the written-out turns in that Rondo, which contains a rich store of information on turn realization, thematic variation, and *tempo rubato*. In selecting a realization for a turn between a dotted note and two

Fig. 7.88. Mozart, Rondo K. 485 (Aut.), m. 5.

[Allegro]

Fig. 7.89. Mozart, Rondo K. 494 (as Sonata K. 533/iii; OE Hoffmeister), m. 101.

*Whether the slur starts on C or on the first B-flat is ambiguous in OE.

Fig. 7.90. Haydn, Sonata Hob. 26/i (OE Kurzböck), m. 9.

following notes, the performer should consider which of these rhythms seems more advantageous for a particular context, or whether another variant might be even better. My preferred rhythmization for Figure 7.90 is based on Figure 7.80g, 1, with the turn delayed, as in Figure 7.80f, 3. It allows the A-sharp to be heard prominently before the turn.

When a note with a turn sign is preceded by a small note on its own pitch, the turn begins on the beat with its main note (Fig. 7.80i). Türk and other Germans called this a "quick" turn[167] (*geschnellte Doppelschlag*) or *Rolle*. Haydn's Sonata Hob. 24 opens with a quick turn indicated by the composer. Where the same motive returns with only the sign of a simple turn, particularly at the beginning of the development and the recapitulation, Haydn undoubtedly expected the performer to play a quick turn.

Emanuel Bach noted that the "quick" turn was often indicated in keyboard pieces by "the simple sign of the turn."[168] Thus, at the performer's discretion, the turn could begin on its main note in stylistically appropriate places. According to Bach, the quick turn, which was usually introduced on detached notes and played briskly (as in 7.80i, 1), might be applied "at the beginning of a passage, in the middle, before stepwise motion or a leap," and "over the second of a pair of slurred notes in stepwise ascent."[169] Türk stated that the quick turn was generally used at the beginning of an idea or a phrase member, after a rest, or on detached notes, but did not specifically invite its use without the appropriate sign.[170] However, by 1796 Hüllmandel gave the turn starting on its main note—which, if a longer note, was sometimes held for part of its value (e.g., 7.80a, 7)—as one of two realizations for the normal sign, with no differentiation of name and no suggestions for use of either form.[171]

J. B. Lasser's ideas of two years later are not dissimilar. Showing the vertical turn sign for the usual turn, he realized the horizontal signs as quick turns in "lively, playful" passages and as slightly delayed turns (after holding the main note for about one-quarter of its value) in "expressive" or "flattering" passages.[172] In the "third" German edition of the Pleyel-Dussek *Méthode,* prepared in 1804 by "Music Director" Schicht of Leipzig, the instructions for discretionary use of the quick turn serve the same desire for melodic clarity inherent in Türk's suggestions. The turn should start on its main note at the beginning of any fresh melodic segment, from the rank of phrase member up.[173] And in that same year J. F. Schubert—in many respects a follower of Türk—suggested delayed turns for the realization of turn signs over quarter notes (Fig. 7.80a, 7) and dotted eighth notes in slow tempos.[174]

It is difficult to discern from these scattered sources how often a turn sign over a note might have been realized as a quick turn. There are a number of situations in which quick turns seem appropriate. The turns at the return of the main theme and at the start of sequential phrases in Haydn's Hob. 34/iii (e.g., mm. 33, 61, 65) sound best to me as quick turns if the editor and performer treat them as turns on, rather than after, the dotted eighth notes.[175] I play a quick turn at the suspenseful last entry of the theme in Haydn's Trio Hob. XV/29/ii/37, and again in the Sonata Hob. 39/ii/8, because the main note here signals the departure from an embellished repetition of the first phrase.

In Mozart's Sonata K. 310/ii/66 the turn sign is over the second slurred note in a stepwise ascent, one of Emanuel Bach's suggested locations for a quick turn. (Compare Fig. 5.15.) Neumann recommends quick turns for m. 25 of that movement (which is the same as m. 22, Fig. 5.41, but with turn signs over the first note of each group) because the accent is intended for the main note.[176] However, some may feel that following the undecorated motive in m. 22, an upper-note start might be fine. A quick turn in Mozart's Fantasy K. 475/112 avoids repeating the preceding B-flat and preserves the interval of a third, thus providing a more effective melodic line. (For possible use of a delayed turn, see the discussion of Fig. 7.110a.)

The turn in Figure 7.91 could reasonably have been played with its upper auxiliary starting on the beat, preceded by the E-flat sixteenth note. Similar situations in the pieces for musical clock (*JHW,* XXI, II.2/2, III.3 [Fig. 7.92]) were pinned precisely as they are notated.[177] Yet, because of the dotted patterns in Figure 7.91, the sixteenth notes after the dotted eighth notes as well as those immediately before will be delayed and shortened in performance (see "Double-dotting and Overdotting" in chap. 8). In an appropriately fast tempo the listener may perceive the configuration as a quick turn on the beat, particularly

Fig. 7.91. Haydn, Sonata Hob. 28/ii *(JHW),*[178] mm. 1-2.

Fig. 7.92. Haydn, Piece for Flute Clock Hob. XIX/29 (Aut.), m. 1.

where there is no accompaniment to mark the beat; where there is, the ornament may sound like a quick turn that straddles the beat. Might intentional quick turns have been an acceptable response in this context or in Figure 8.15? Unhappily, we may never be certain of the way Haydn would have played these movements.

Haydn's Notation of Turns and Mordents

Haydn's use of signs to indicate turns and mordents was unique. Many Italian and south German musicians of the eighteenth century, including Giuseppe Tartini and Leopold Mozart, regarded the three-note turn (the turn over a note) as "another type of mordent."[179] Following this tradition, Haydn also considered the turn and the mordent very closely related, as demonstrated by the manner in which he notated them:

1. While Haydn sometimes used the standard ∞ to indicate a turn over a note, and occasionally ✦ for a mordent—which he termed a "half mordent," more often he wrote ᷁, known as the "Haydn ornament," as an indication for either a turn over a note or a mordent. (A rare written reference to the use of ᷁ for ✦ occurs in *Knechts allgemeiner musikalischer Katechismus* of 1803. "The shorter [standard] mordent is shown by these signs, ✦ or ᷁ . . . ."[180])

2. Occasionally Haydn used ∞ and ᷁ interchangeably in parallel passages, but between notes in dotted figures he preferred the standard turn sign. Perhaps this was a signal that at least for some years, like Leopold Mozart, he considered this four-note ornament the true turn, or *Doppelschlag*.[181]

3. In his late piano sonatas, which seem not to contain any mordents indicated by sign, Haydn virtually gave up the ambiguous ᷁ for the standard turn sign.

Perhaps because of the ambiguity of his signs, and occasionally to ensure that an ornament would be played as he desired, Haydn frequently wrote the ornament in small notes at its first occurrence to indicate the shape of its realization and only later relied on a sign. Figure 7.82, for which we have a contemporary realization, demonstrates this practice. Other examples occur in the Sonata Hob. 32/i/1–2 (a mordent in small notes followed by what could be a hastily drawn mordent sign, or "Haydn ornament," in contemporary manuscript copies S.m. 9820 and S.m. 9819[182]) and in the Piano Trio Hob. XV/5/iii/6 (a turn in small notes in the piano part simultaneously with a Haydn ornament in the violin part in *JHW*). In the Trio Hob. XV/29/ii/1, one written-out appoggiatura instructs performers in a context in which they might well have played these recurring ornaments differently. Occasionally a mordent sign in an analogous passage may suggest an appropriate mordent interpretation for the Haydn ornament elsewhere. For example, the mordent sign at Figure 7.124b, m. 55 (in an important manuscript copy[183]) and the context persuade me to realize the Haydn ornament at the end of the exposition (m. 20) as a mordent. (Because of the problematic nature of the sources for this sonata, editions vary in their ornament signs at m. 20 and elsewhere.)

When Haydn left no clues as to whether the realization of the Haydn ornament should be a turn or a mordent, the performer must decide which to play. The choice should take into account the harmonic, melodic, and rhythmic aspects of the context, including the rules of voice leading, the harmonic effects produced by the different starting notes, and the direction, articulation, and feel of the line. Both the mordent and the turn were used on detached notes, but when circumstances warrant, a turn can sound more gracious and more legato, as in the opening of Hob. 12/i if the player chooses to realize the optional Haydn ornament instead of the trill in HSU. (*JHW* has only the Haydn ornament; some editions have only the trill.) Turns were used on ascending and descending notes.[184] Mordents were most frequently used on ascending notes or on a note at the beginning of a phrase; they were seldom used on notes that descend by leap and never on notes that descend by step. Of all the ornaments, mordents were the most freely introduced into the bass.[185] The comparative frequency of turns and mordents in small notes suggests that Haydn intended his ornament sign as a turn far more often than as a mordent.[186] Nevertheless, I believe that in such movements as Hob. 23/ii, in which many of the ornament signs printed as Haydn ornaments in *JHW* and HSU appear to me to be quite clear mordent signs in the holograph, and perhaps also at Hob. 34/i/22–24, the mordent finds its natural home.

The ornament indication at Hob. 34/i/22–24 is problematic, in large part because of the poor quality of the sources for this sonata, a number of which are manuscript copies.[187] Further explanation of the differences between the ornament signs offered in HSU and *JHW* may be helpful to the performer. In HSU there is a *tr*, directly above which, at the first occurrence, there is a mordent sign (with a question mark) in parentheses. Parentheses in HSU indicate that in lieu of an authoritative source, "the sign that may be presumed to be correct has been added."[188] The *Kritische Anmerkungen* (*Critical Annotations*) for HSU state that in one of the three sources that contain ornaments in mm. 22–24, and in two sources in the corresponding mm. 87–89, the ornament is a "turn instead of *tr*."[189] Thus the mordent may be Christa Landon's suggestion based on context and on the possibility that a mordent sign may have been mistranscribed as a trill or a turn sign; or it may be her interpretation and application of the turn sign mentioned. Feder gave priority to the turn sign, using it alone in all six measures—albeit in parentheses, which indicate (only for this sonata in HE) that something "is from a minority of sources."[190] He makes no mention of *tr*. At an appropriate *presto*, pianists of necessity play a mordent or substitute a turn for the trill.

The frequent close resemblance in Haydn's calligraphy of ᴕ, ✦, *tr*, and *t* (for *tr*), as well as ∞ and ᴖ , encouraged mistranscriptions in the past and allows a considerable degree of uncertainty at present. Haydn's squiggle in the holograph of Hob. 49/ii/71 (Fig. 7.93a) resulted in quite different interpretations by two highly respected Haydn scholars (Figs. 7.93b and c). In addition to, or perhaps because of, the problem of reading Haydn's hand, early copyists and engravers often transcribed his signs carelessly, converting those they may not have understood (e.g., the Haydn ornament) or those that may have looked similar from one to another without heed.[191] As a result, the signs ᴖ and ✦ might sometimes be misreadings of ∞ and ᴕ respectively (I suggest this for the mordent sign in Fig. 5.15, m. 5), or vice versa, and ornament signs may be different in two or more copies or early editions of the same piece. According to Päsler, in Artaria's early editions of Haydn's works, the holographic ᴕ was sometimes engraved as ∞, sometimes as *t*. for *tr*; and ✦ was occasionally substituted "where Haydn had written (or only could have written) ✦, ᴖ, *tr* (also ∞)."[192]

Indeed, Artaria heard about incorrect ornaments more than once from an unhappy Haydn. On 20 July 1781 the composer wrote:

> Above all I ask you to engrave the musical signs as I have written them: for instance, you will find the following: ᴖ, ∞, *tr*, ᴕ . . . .[193]

A letter of 10 December 1785 was blunter:

> On pages 6 and 8 most of the following signs are wrongly placed, for they ought not to be put directly over the note but over the neighbouring dot, in this way:  . . . All the way through, the dots ought to be further away from the notes, so that the sign ∞ comes directly over the dot. And on this very page, in the second stave, you should put instead of the sign *tr:* the following: ✦, for the first one, as the engraver has done it, means a trill, whilst mine is a half mordent. If, therefore, the Herr Engraver doesn't know signs of this sort, he should inform himself by studying the masters, and not follow his own stupid ideas.[194]

In the holograph to which this refers, that of the Piano Trio Hob. XV/7, Haydn had carefully written the three main ornaments, *tr*, ∞, and ✦, apart from everything else "in the bottom right-hand corner of the first page."[195]

Fig. 7.93. Haydn, Sonata Hob. 49/ii, m. 71. a. Aut. b. C. Landon (HSU). c. Feder *(JHW).* *

*In OE of questionable value, the ornament is a turn.

Since it is often difficult for editors to reconstruct Haydn's ornament signs with certainty, more than one editorial solution or performer's interpretation may be justified. We have explored the performer's choices at Hob. 34/i/22–24. Anyone playing the first movement of the Trio Hob. XV/17 may legitimately ask whether Haydn really meant to have trills, indicated by *tr*, in the piano part and the Haydn ornament in the flute part in an otherwise exact imitation of the piano (mm. 52–61). Prefatory material in the best editions sometimes contains information that explains editorial judgment and that helps the performer in interpreting the printed signs. For instance, Georg Feder, editor of the *Klaviersonaten* for *JHW*, states that he substituted the "Haydn ornament" for the mordent sign throughout, on the grounds that Haydn did not differentiate between the two.[196] In some editions alternate ornaments from differing sources are shown in parentheses when a holograph is lacking.[197]

Interpretation of Haydn's Turn "over the Dot"

The interpretation of Haydn's turn over a dot, most often between a dotted eighth and a sixteenth note (Fig. 7.94c), may present some special subtleties and choices. In his innovative writing on performance practices in Haydn's sonatas, László Somfai suggests that around 1776 Haydn left Emanuel Bach's interpretation of this turn, in which the last (fourth) note falls on the dot, for a simpler rhythmization in which the first note of the turn falls on the dot (Fig. 7.94b).[198] Somfai bases this hypothesis on the precise notation of the figure with the turn in the exposition of the Sonata Hob. 28/i (Fig. 7.94a), and on its return in the usual notation in the recapitulation.[199]

In Hob. 36, probably composed in the mid-1770s, the turn following a dotted eighth note appears as a major thematic element with a further simplified rhythmization. Haydn's written-out pattern in Figure 7.95a, realized by Somfai in Figure 7.95b, serves as the model for Somfai's realization in Figure 7.95d of the sign in m. 12 (Fig. 7.95c). Somfai believes that Haydn might also have favored this execution in works after Hob. 36. (This turn also sounds well played with five equal notes or even an acciaccatura at the start.) In Figures 7.8of, 3 and 5, from Löhlein's piano and violin tutors, the turn begins on, or

Fig. 7.94. Haydn, Sonata Hob. 28/i. a. mm. 22–23 (exposition; *JHW*). b. m. 22 (Somfai, *Haydn*, pp. 62–63). c. mm. 118–119 (recapitulation; *JHW*).

Fig. 7.95. Haydn, Sonata Hob. 36/i. a. m. 1 (OE Artaria). b. m. 1 (Somfai, *Haydn*, pp. 62–63). c. m. 12 (OE Artaria). d. m. 12 (Somfai, *Haydn*, pp. 62–63).

even slightly after, the time of the dot. Since these volumes were well known, and since the turn in the time of the dot reappeared in later sources (p. 265), we can assume that such realizations were part of contemporary practice. Application of this turn in the opening of Hob. 27/i and other fast movements is most effective.

Hob. 42, published in 1784, contains what subsequently became Haydn's favorite notation of a turn within a dotted rhythm (Fig. 7.96), a notation that occurs extensively in his late works. The small notes or a turn sign over the dotted sixteenth note (as in Fig. 7.97a) are interchangeable. Could this notation represent another step in Haydn's effort to clarify his preference for placing the turn in the time of the dot and retaining the dotted effect when time allows? A telling notational change (slip of the pen?) exists in the Trio Hob. XV/17, composed in 1790. The usual configuration of notes and turn, shown in Figure 7.97b, is the single exception in that movement to the notation of Figure 7.97a, suggesting a close association of the two forms for Haydn. But we should observe, too, that in the standard configuration the first main note and the ornament are generally played legato, while in Haydn's new figure the first main note is often marked staccato (as in Hob. 42/i/17), and in the piano music slurs are either from the small notes to the dotted sixteenth or between the last two notes (Fig. 7.96). What role might this difference in articulation have had in shaping Haydn's orthography?

Fig. 7.96. Haydn, Sonata Hob. 42/i (OE Bossler), m. 5.

Fig. 7.97. Haydn, Trio for Piano, Flute or Violin, and Violoncello Hob. XV/17/ii *(JHW)*. a. mm. 1–2. b. mm. 44–45.

We must also wonder how strongly Haydn's apparent interest in having the turn played in the time of the dot influenced the performance of his new figure. Even in his late works Haydn occasionally wrote out the realization of the turn before the dot in regular notes. Do these occurrences signal his acceptance of that interpretation elsewhere, or were they only the written-out exceptions? Some of the contexts in which Haydn's new configuration appears do not accept its aggressiveness on the half beat comfortably or do not allow time for a turn on the dotted sixteenth. Both situations suggest anticipatory realizations. Thus it is possible that both pre-beat and on-beat interpretations were used, depending on the circumstances. Somfai has proposed that two ways in which Haydn slurred this figure in music for stringed instruments may suggest the two interpretations: a slur over the entire configuration (as in the Quartet Op. 64/1/ii/7) might indicate a pre-beat realization of the turn, while a slur from the three small notes to the notes following (as in the Symphony No. 99/ii/9) might indicate realization in the time of the dotted sixteenth note (i.e., in the time of the dot).[200] Unfortunately, there are few slurs to guide us in the piano repertoire.

The pattern in Figure 7.96 is present in two of Haydn's pieces for musical clock, Nos. I.2 (an Andante played by the undated clock and the clock of 1792) and III.1 (an Allegretto played by the clock of 1793) in *JHW*, XXI (in Schmid, *Flute Clock*, Nos. 2 and 27). Analysis of these performances at the Haydn-Institut indicates that all but one of the ten occurrences of this pattern start on the beat (as realized in *JWH*, I.2/15, p. 3). (Compare also Fig. 7.107.) Although there are some imperfections around III.1 on the cylinder of 1793, it appears that in m. 8 this same turn anticipates the beat, and that in m. 12 a turn that usually falls in the time of the last sixteenth of a quarter-note beat—comparable to Figure 7.86—also starts early.[201] These two examples represent some (apparently infrequent) departure from the general on-beat performance of ornaments in the three clocks.[202] If we believe that these performances bear a relationship to the practice in Haydn's circle, then they corroborate to some extent both on-beat and pre-beat realizations of the turns under consideration. For other timely evidence of pre-beat realization the reader might look ahead to Figure 7.99 from Hüllmandel's tutor of 1796.

In m. 18 of Hob. 42/i, which contains the same turns and melodic figures as Figure 7.96, *forzandos* under the dotted sixteenth notes suggest that anticipatory performance would be appropriate to keep the accent on the main note. Should that anticipation influence the other realizations of this figure where there are no accent indications, as in mm. 5 and 17? In fact, the lack of accompaniment notes to help mark the half beats under the dotted sixteenths, as well as the particular expressive mood, are additional factors that have led most recorded performers to anticipatory performance of the turns in that pattern throughout the movement.

Among Haydn's sonatas from 1784 on, the very few appearances of the common dotted-eighth and sixteenth-note pattern with a turn between the notes occur only over fast-moving accompaniments where the simpler melodic notation may conceivably have allowed more flexibility in combining the parts and, not incidentally, where a slurred interpretation is appropriate (e.g., Hob. 48/i/83). It was the engraving of the Piano Trios Hob. XV/6–8, composed in 1784 and 1785, that caused Haydn's complaints in the letter of 10 December 1785 (quoted above) and his specific direction that the turn be put "over the neighbouring dot in this way." After this, just as in the sonatas, the use of the older pattern declined significantly in the trios. It was supplanted to some extent from 1790 on by Haydn's more personal notation, for which evidence supports realization according to the musical surroundings and the taste of the performer.

Early and Anticipatory Turn Realization

Turns sometimes occur where the usual placement or rhythmization may obstruct another element of interpretation, may provide a less than optimal melodic line, or may prove technically unfeasible. In these situations it often seems advisable to adjust the rhythmic placement of the turn, usually making it earlier: that is, either nearer to the beginning of the beat or before the beat. Here we are in an area of some uncertainty; yet the variety of turn realizations that have been documented and some further wisps of information in tutors lead to the conclusion that there may have been even more flexibility in practice.

In the 1750s, the tutors for violin and flute by Tartini, L. Mozart, and Quantz, in which turns are designated only with small notes (not signs), suggest some anticipation of three-note turns. According to Tartini, the three notes were played very fast and softly, while the main note was played with more force, "to make [it] more lively, bold and fiery."[203] Our earlier discussion of unaccented short appoggiaturas, with their varied relationship to the beat, seems applicable here. But even if readers interpret Tartini's and Mozart's statements to preclude any on-beat turns, the application of these violin tutors of the 1750s to Classic period piano music might have some limitations. Yet they demonstrate a background of practice. It has also been suggested that there might be a link between the use of small notes in these tutors and anticipation of turns notated in small notes in some Classic music.[204] Here we should consider that in the 1750s Italians still had not begun to use a sign for turns and thus had to indicate them with small notes regardless of how they were to be played. As late as 1795 even the German Hiller used only small notes to indicate three-note turns, but stated that they took their time from the note following.[205]

Emanuel Bach's *Essay* contained a turn realized with its last (main) note under the sign (Fig. 7.98). It showed "that the turn may be placed over the second note as well as after the first. The accompanying written-out division of the tones demonstrates conclusively that this employment requires a slow tempo."[206] Was this notation a way of delaying the ornament until slightly after the half-beat, at the same time avoiding a more complicated syncopated

Fig. 7.98. E. Bach, *Essay*, p. 120.

Fig. 7.99. Hüllmandel, Andante from *Principles of Music*, p. 45, mm. 1–6.

notation? Whatever its *raison d'être,* it is, in fact, a turn realized in anticipation of the note over which its sign appears. Beethoven may have observed Bach's configuration, for it appears in the Adagio con espressione of his Piano Quartet WoO 36/3 (1785) with a dotted 32d note followed by a 64th note. Nevertheless, it is impossible to know how broadly Bach's singular model might have influenced individual composers;[207] it did not reappear in any other tutors.

Is there any additional contemporary evidence or tangential information for realizing turn signs earlier than their indicated position? Curiously, even the writers who favored the use of afternote or anticipatory performance for some ornaments written in small notes, including the inverted turn or slide, did not mention the turn over a note—whether represented by sign or by small notes. Milchmeyer specifically recommended in 1801 that the turns over repeated dotted notes in Haydn's Hob. 35/i/29ff. be played on the beat![208] Might he have played anticipatory turns elsewhere?

A piece for practice in Hüllmandel's *Principles of Music* of 1796 opens with the excerpt in Figure 7.99. From the examples in his discussion of ornaments it is clear that the written-out turn in m. 5 illustrates the realization of the turn sign in m. 6. By analogy, the small notes in m. 1 must illustrate the realization of the turn in m. 3, which was probably intended to end at the time of the first dot. Hüllmandel's tutor is relatively brief and its pieces are elementary, but his reporting of performance practices, including that of the trill start, was up-to-date. Hüllmandel was active in London's brilliant musical life of the 1790s, when Haydn was also present. Finally, Frederick Neumann calls our attention to the realization of Figure 7.80a, 6, which, with a grace note and the first main note on the beat, achieves partial anticipation.[209]

Now we shall look at a small collection of special situations. A potential technical problem exists in Haydn's Hob. 39/i (Fig. 7.100), where an appropriate Allegro con brio may prohibit playing the turn clearly and in the time of the dot—as Haydn might have preferred, particularly when the instrument is the modern piano. The solution lies in placing the turn closer to the main note, either by shortening that note to approximately a sixteenth, after which the

Fig. 7.100. Haydn, Sonata Hob. 39/i (OE Artaria), mm. 19–21.

Fig. 7.101. Haydn, Sonata Hob. 41/ii (OE Bossler),[210] mm. 22–24.

Fig. 7.102. Mozart, Piano Concerto K. 450/iii (Aut.), mm. 113–116.

Fig. 7.103. Haydn, Sonata Hob. 48/i (OE J. G. I. Breitkopf), mm. 3–5.

turn and the two final notes run together, or by playing a quick turn (shown above m.20), which retains the omnipresent dotted effect. Similar rhythmizations might be desirable in Hob. 30/186 and in the Trio for Piano, Flute, and Violoncello Hob. XV/16/i/9.

In Figure 7.101, placement of the turn influences perception of the rhythm and melody. Since realization in the time of the main note weakens the potential effect of the syncopation and the repeated melodic B-flat, many present-day musicians anticipate this turn. For other reasons the turn in Figure 7.102 is also played before the beat. In this Allegro, Mozart's effect of the short staccato repeated note on the second beat, which is characteristic of this theme throughout the movement, would be lost if the turn were begun on the beat.

Figure 7.103 demonstrates a related problem in a slower movement of strongly rhetorical temperament. Instead of anticipation, which is intimated by written-out turns in mm. 3 and 6, Somfai suggests added time—discussed earlier in this chapter—for the turn in m. 5.[211] The small notes are played when the time for the eighth note has elapsed, but the second half of the beat begins only with the staccato C. That exact motive recurs once, and a variant in which the repeated note is not staccato occurs twice. All four are in measures separated from those before and after by expressive rests. (See "Rhetorical Rests" in chap. 10.) The "espressione" mood of this Andante, its varied rhythmic figures, and the asymmetrical, open, yet flowing phrase patterns allow enough rhythmic freedom to absorb the added time well. Figure 7.96, with a similar turn, is also in an Andante con espressione first movement, but one that is much more regular in structure and less rhetorical in spirit than Hob. 48. In Hob. 42 frequent notated on-beat accents require a steady pulse in which added time would seem to me a foreign element.

In spite of the Andante cantabile and Adagio headings of Figures 7.104 and 7.105, realization of either turn in the time of its main note congests and confuses both the melody and the rhythm. Anticipation seems best for these turns and, for the same reasons, those in Beethoven's Op. 22/ii/20. There, in the B theme of a sonata-allegro form, an eighth note followed by four sixteenths (in 9/8 meter) repeats the opening rhythmic motive of the A theme, an important reason for maintaining its clarity when it returns. Opinion is divided about the turn at the opening of Mozart's Rondo in A minor K. 511. Beyschlag and Neumann prefer anticipation, contending that on-beat realization disturbs the characteristic sicilienne rhythm.[212] Others, including Rudolf Serkin in a live performance, feel that the tempo and rhythmic pattern easily absorb an on-beat rendition, which may, however, be varied through the piece.

At first glance the turn in Figure 7.106 looks as if it might be played in the time of its main note. Yet, trying this turn both on and before the beat has convinced many musicians that the melody sounds awkward with the turn on the weak beat and that there are rhythmic and melodic advantages to anticipatory performance. The line has been gaining rhythmic momentum slowly since its beginning in m. 26. The *sf,* which arrived on beat 2 in mm. 28 and 30, is moved ahead by half a beat in m. 32. Playing the turn as a 32d-note

Fig. 7.104. Mozart, Sonata K. 333/ii (Aut.), m. 12.
[Andante cantabile]

Fig. 7.105. Beethoven, Sonata Op. 2/1/ii (OE Artaria), m. 29.
[Adagio]

Fig. 7.106. Beethoven, Sonata Op. 2/2/iv (OE Artaria), mm. 32–33.

Fig. 7.107. Haydn, Piece for Flute Clock Hob. XIX/26 (Ms. copy by P. Primitivus Niemecz), m. 6.

triplet before beat 4 fills in what is otherwise a dead stop during beat 3; more-over, sounding the two C's squarely on beats 3 and 4 provides contrast with the syncopation of beats 1 and 2 and preserves the basic shape of the melodic outline. Beyond these specific reasons—or in this case perhaps because of them—an underlying element of perception may be operative here. When a repeated note is shorter than its preceding note, and when the two together form a part (but not the whole) of one or more beats or tempo units (i.e., the note value in which the rhythm moves [see chap. 9, n. 205]), the turn is sometimes per-ceived as coming between, or connecting, the notes: in other words, as a turn after a dotted or a tied note.[213] As in Figure 7.106, this "formula" may transform the turn from an emphasized ornament, ill placed on a weak beat, to a con-necting ornament between beats. This brings to mind Figure 7.80h, shown by both Emanuel Bach and Türk, and Bach's direction that "the tied note becomes the last tone of the turn."[214] Written-out examples appear in Haydn's Hob. 34/ii/1ff. and Mozart's K. 311/i/29.

Nottebohm and Beyschlag both include Figure 7.106 in a small group of turns in works up to about 1800 for which they believe that Beethoven placed the signs too late.[215] He wrote the sign under or over the note, "whereas he manifestly intended an anticipated realization."[216] Beyschlag's group is some-what more selective than Nottebohm's; both also include Figure 7.105, Op. 22/ii/20, and others about which I have reservations. Figure 7.107, with its realization from the musical clock of 1793, will speak to those who may still apply to the Classic repertoire the later custom of anticipating all turns between repeated notes.

Composers might have indicated desired anticipatory rhythmizations be-tween repeated notes by placing the turn sign to the left of the second note rather than over it. Perhaps some feared that the ornament would be begun too early, as Türk described.[217] Mozart must have felt some anxiety about using sign notation for the delicate anticipatory turn in Figure 7.108, or he would not have written out the 64th notes 66 times during the movement, as the autograph shows. An analogous example occurs in K. 498/iii/157.

Fig. 7.108. Mozart, Trio for Piano, Clarinet, and Viola K. 498/ii (Aut.), mm. 5–6.

Fig. 7.109. Beethoven, Trio for Piano, Violin, and Violoncello Op. 1/2/ii (OE Artaria). a. m. 14. b. m. 50. c. m. 54. d. m. 63.

* Artaria's typical (inverted) turn sign.

Beethoven did not like ambiguity in notation, as his use and subsequent abandonment of *calando* demonstrated. There are palpable signs of his struggle with the notation of turns in proximity to repeated notes right from the Piano Trios Op. 1 (comp. 1794–1795) to about 1800. Figure 7.109a, in which the repeated note carrying a turn completes a beat, lends itself well to realization of the ornament in the time of the note over which it appears. (An eighth note rather than a dotted quarter gets the beat in this Largo.) In Figure 7.109b the two B's form part of two beats, the situation identified earlier in which the turn may be perceived as connecting the notes. Perhaps Beethoven used the small notes specifically to signal anticipation. Most performers would certainly have played the small notes in Figure 7.109c between the main notes; the placement of the sign in Figure 7.109d is also clear. Did Beethoven write notes in Figures 109b and c because he feared that an uncommon anticipatory sign might be misplaced by engravers if it were not preceded by an example of written-out small notes? Since Opp. 1 and 2/2 were both composed in 1794–

1795, and since the puzzling turn in Figure 7.106 appears four times, why did Beethoven not leave more information about its performance?

In the Sonata for Violoncello and Piano Op. 5/2 (comp. 1796), Beethoven used Haydn's favorite pattern, with the turn in small notes (cf. Fig. 7.96) at ii/103. It is in a new theme that derives part of its drive from dotted rhythms. Playing this turn before the beat keeps the dotted rhythm clear. Remember also the publication of Hüllmandel's turn realizations in 1796. The gracious Rondo Op. 51/1 (comp. 1796–1797) is embellished with many turns. Some signs are over and some are between notes; only the turn in the opening motive, shown in Figure 7.110a, is ambiguous. Does the anticipatory placement of the sign in Figure 7.110b indicate that the opening turn should not anticipate the second C? Would Beethoven have written the turn first in small notes to indicate anticipation, or put the sign between the notes as he did in m. 48? Although the C's involved do form part of a beat, a dead stop on the dotted eighth note after an anticipated turn would hardly sound "grazioso." Rudolf and Beyschlag both suggest graceful realizations after the second C,[218] perhaps the delayed turn mentioned earlier.

In his Op. 22/iv/21, 132, and 134, Beethoven again used the pattern ♩♪. , but only with the sign (not with small notes). In the copy prepared for the engraver, in the first edition by Hoffmeister, and in an early reprint by the Bureau des Arts et d'Industrie, the turn sign is always over the dotted sixteenth note; but in the first state of the Haslinger edition, for which Czerny was probably the editor (see p. 329) and which was based on C. F. Peters' *Titelauflage* of the first edition, the turn is between the repeated eighth and dotted sixteenth notes. If Czerny was responsible for moving the sign, was he merely modernizing the notation or actually changing its meaning? Op. 22 and the "Spring" Sonata for Violin and Piano Op. 24 were both written in 1800. In the latter, Beethoven clarified his intention that the small notes in Figure 7.111b should anticipate the repeated A not only by the placement of the turn sign in Figure 7.111c, but also by the gentle character of the written-out turn in Figure 7.111a as well as of the movement itself. Considering all the evidence, I believe that Beethoven also intended anticipation of those turns in the Rondo, Allegretto of Op. 22.

The dotted pattern in Figure 7.111c with the turn sign between the notes reappeared in the "Andante Favori" (comp. 1803), after which it seems to have lost its importance in Beethoven's piano works. It had been used as early as

Fig. 7.110. Beethoven, Rondo Op. 51/1 (OE Artaria). a. m. 1. b. m. 48.*

a. Moderato e grazioso

*Turn signs inverted in OE.

Fig. 7.111. Beethoven, Sonata for Violin and Piano Op. 24/ii (Aut.). a. m. 2. b. m. 7. c. m. 35.

Fig. 7.112. Hummel, *Pianoforte School*, Pt. I, p. 64.

1785, in the Adagio introduction to the Piano Quartet WoO 36/1/i, with the turn sign over the repeated note. How might Beethoven have performed it in 1785, ten years before his Op. 1, and not long after Haydn had begun to use that figure?[219] Questions and uncertainty are a natural response to an insufficiently documented transition in turn notation and realization, during which some of the problematic turns were undoubtedly played differently in different musical contexts and by different performers.

The next information from tutors about anticipatory turn realization appears in Hummel's *Complete . . . Course of Instructions on . . . Playing the Pianoforte*. In Figure 7.112 the careful alignment of the dot and the counting presumably indicate his intention that the small notes sound before the half-beat. Further on, turns notated with both small notes and signs before the half-beat in the figure ♩♫ (although none with repeated notes) "must be finished before the entrance of the second note."[220] The excerpts from Hummel's Chopinesque Piano Concerto Op. 85 that are included in the tutor also contain many turns whose realizations would raise questions similar to those already discussed[221] were it not for the additional information in the volume. Throughout the concerto a turn in conjunction with a shorter repeated note is always shown the first time (and almost always thereafter) in small notes. This seems to have been a way of ensuring anticipation in that context. (Hummel indicated turns between different pitches with either small notes or the sign.) Perhaps this effort to achieve unequivocal notation tells us that in 1816, when Hummel wrote the concerto,[222] interpretation of turns between repeated notes was still ambiguous and mixed.

What Hummel implied, Czerny made explicit in *Die Schule der Verzierungen* (The school of embellishments), published circa 1835. The turn between two notes on the same pitch serves "as a means of connecting the melody notes."[223] He showed the familiar figure ♪♫, with the turn in small notes and in actual values, played quickly before the repeated note. In other pieces he showed both three small notes and the sign to indicate turns performed exactly alike, quickly, and before the beat, with a slight stress on the final main note.[224] Strangely, the turn sign is over rather than between repeated notes, as Beethoven had begun to write it and as Czerny might have placed it in editing Beethoven's Op. 22 for Haslinger. Could this have been an engraver's error, or might it have been intended by Czerny to carry a message about Beethoven's earlier notation? As long as questions about the placement of turns persist, musicians can do no better than to seek musical clues for each composer and in each piece, to make choices that relate to the character of the music, and to play with conviction. Above all the listener should hear the ornaments as ornamental.

Beethoven's Ambiguous Placement of the Turn Sign

In a few of Beethoven's early works his placement of the turn sign presents another type of ambiguity. Figure 7.113 illustrates the problem. If we recognize the latent structure of the first motive as a dotted quarter note D ornamented with a turn and followed by an eighth note E, it becomes clear that the sign is placed over the written-out bottom note of the turn. Rhythmically (in an Allegro con brio), melodically, and harmonically, the turn fits this context most comfortably when it embellishes the true main note of the motive. To do so, its three notes—E, D, and C-sharp—are realized in the time of the C-sharp.

Fig. 7.113. Beethoven, Sonata Op. 2/3/i (OE Artaria), mm. 45–46.

Analogous situations occur in Beethoven's Op. 1/2/ii/21, Op. 51/1/23, and Op. 2/2/ii/22, to name just three. In the last instance, however, both Artur Schnabel and Claudio Arrau suggest an alternate solution of playing a "quick" turn on the note designated by the sign, [225] which offers the possibility of an increase in the degree of ornamentation between mm. 21 and 22.

THE INVERTED TURN

The inverted turn (*verkehrte Doppelschlag*) was indicated by ∞, sometimes by ⸨ (e.g., by Mozart and Dussek), but most frequently with three small notes.

Fig. 7.114. Türk, *Klavierschule*, p. 246.

Many writers from Emanuel Bach on considered the inverted turn not a form of turn but a three-note slide.[226] (Schenker attributed this idea to Bach's assumption that the turn was derived from a suspension.[227]) Other writers considered the inverted turn to be a turn,[228] while some discussed it as both a slide and a turn.[229] In tutors it was almost always realized on the beat in a manner similar to the turn (Fig. 7.114). In the tutor of J. C. Bach and Ricci, the start of a *diminuendo* hairpin precisely under the first small note of an inverted turn clarifies its accentuation and placement.[230]

The tendency toward the end of the century to anticipate ornaments written in small notes (especially those played quickly) included the inverted turn. Milchmeyer, the foremost proponent of anticipation, wrote that "inverted turns must always be written with [small] notes"[231] and realized them before the beat (Fig. 7.30e). Figures 7.32, 7.33, and 7.36 contain examples from Beethoven's sonatas. Inverted turns were seldom used after dotted notes or in other between-beat positions.

THE TRILLED TURN

Occasionally the signs of the trill and the turn are found combined vertically, $\approx$, forming an ornament called a "trilled turn" (*prallende Doppelschlag*). Like the *Pralltriller,* the trilled turn had been formulated by Emanuel Bach for use in descending seconds with the upper note tied over into the trill, as in Figure 7.115. The first notes were played extremely quickly and with great precision.[232]

As a follower of Bach, Türk also preferred this "*Pralltriller* with a termination"[233] in a descending second (Fig. 7.115); but again, as with the simple *Pralltriller,* he recognized its use in other contexts as exceptions, still apparently expecting an upper-note start in such instances as Figures 7.116a and b.[234] Reluctantly Türk acknowledged that the ornament in Figure 7.116c, with the

Fig. 7.115. Türk, *Klavierschule*, p. 291

Fig. 7.116. Türk, *Klavierschule*, p. 293.

main note specified, should "probably" have the meaning shown in Figure 7.116d. By 1802 he showed both upper- and main-note starts when the ornament appeared on a repeated note.[235] In Koch's example, on an isolated quarter note, the oscillations begin only after a lengthened initial main note, reflecting his approach to the trill start.[236] All but one of Haydn's trilled turns in Hob. 20/ i and most of Beethoven's (including those in the early Piano Quartets WoO 36/1 and 2 [comp. 1785]) lack a preceding upper auxiliary. Presumably in such cases the performer may determine the ornament start in the same way as one would choose between a short trill and a *Schneller* (p. 257).

THE DOUBLE APPOGGIATURA

The double appoggiatura (*Anschlag* or *Doppelvorschlag, port-de-voix double*) is signified by two small notes surrounding the main note (Fig. 7.117). The interval between the notes may be a third or larger. Türk made two points of special interest regarding this ornament. The first is that the speed with which the double appoggiatura is played depends on the placement of the bottom note. If it is just a step below the main note, the ornament is played quickly; if it is farther from the main note the ornament is taken more slowly.[237] In practice, of course, the speed of performance is also affected by the tempo and the mood of the piece.

Türk's second point is that "double appoggiaturas are all played more softly than the following main note,"[238] as shown on his on-beat realization. In a footnote he cited this as "proof that the invariable short appoggiaturas [*Vorschläge*] can be played softly." Relative to those unaccented, short small notes I suggested that the perceived relationship of the ornament to the beat would depend on a combination of context—mainly accompaniment and tempo— and performance (see pp. 222–223). In a fast tempo, a quick unaccented double appoggiatura might naturally slip into the pre-beat position shown by Rellstab (Fig. 7.29).

The dotted double appoggiatura consists of a long and a short appoggiatura, according to Türk.[239] It appears only in slow or moderate tempos and is played on the beat (Fig. 7.118). Türk's carefully marked dynamics show the accent on the long appoggiatura.

Fig. 7.117. Türk, *Klavierschule*, p. 242.

Fig. 7.118. Türk, *Klavierschule*, p. 244.[240]

THE SLIDE

Two- and three-note slides (*Schleifer, coulé*) have already appeared in many figures supporting both on-beat (Fig. 7.1b, 2 and 3) and pre-beat performance (Figs. 7.28, 7.29, 7.31, 7.35). In his violin tutor, J. A. Hiller wrote that it was not clear whether two-note unslurred slides should be played on or after the beat.[241] He realized his examples after the beat with two of the four slurred to the note following. Although some writers, including Türk and Adam, still realized the slide proper only on the beat, it must have been one of the ornaments most frequently played in a pre-beat position. This was a continuation of the similarly mixed rhythmic treatment accorded that ornament in late Baroque music.[242] We can determine its placement by means of the same musical considerations that have been discussed in relation to other ornaments. Two-note slides were usually played quickly; the speed of three-note slides was adjusted to the context in which the ornament occurred.[243]

THE ARPEGGIO

The arpeggio (*Brechung, batterie*) was indicated by ⸦, (, small notes, and sometimes an oblique line through the stem or occasionally between the notes of a chord. This last notation was shown by Müller in 1804 and by Steibelt around 1809.[244] It appeared in Mozart's Sonata K. 310/ii/3 (Fig. 7.119), in his K. 540/15 (Aut.), and in the first edition of Beethoven's Op. 2/1/i/7.

Unless differentiated by note value, as in the "Alla Turca" (Coda, R, m. 97, etc.) of Mozart's Sonata K. 331, all the notes of an arpeggio indicated by sign were held. (Aut. of K. 331 lacks arpeggio signs.) When indicated

Fig. 7.119. Mozart, Sonata K. 310/ii (Aut.), mm. 2–3.

with small notes, only the final note was held unless the notes were tied (Fig. 7.30c). A single arpeggio sign through the bass and treble staves signified successive playing of the notes. Arpeggiation from top to bottom could be indicated by the signs ⸹ or ⸢, both of which had been used in Baroque music (see also Fig. 7.30f). The speed with which the chord was broken depended on the character and the speed of the piece.[245]

Most tutors realized arpeggios beginning on the beat, but Milchmeyer included them among the ornaments that could be anticipated if played quickly. Although he gave no details, the choice of rhythmic placement might have been determined by the relative melodic, rhythmic, or harmonic importance of the top or bottom notes of the chord, or by other factors in the musical context. Earlier in this chapter we saw examples from Beethoven's music of an arpeggio anticipated for dynamic and rhythmic reasons (Fig. 7.34) and others that required added time (Fig. 7.38). For rhythmic stability I believe that the rapid-fire arpeggios in the left-hand "rhythm section" of Mozart's "Alla Turca" should allow the main notes to sound exactly on the beat. In the Coda the right-hand melody notes also take the beat, thus the arpeggiated quarter notes in m. 97, etc., sound with the left-hand arpeggios. However, in the Menuetto of K. 331 the right-hand arpeggios can start on the beat, played *forte*. The long melody notes in mm. 1 and 11 absorb the delayed accents graciously. In m. 13, enlarging on the arpeggio and the delayed melody note of m. 11, Mozart wrote out the arpeggio in beat 1, putting b^2 on beat 2 (Fig. 7.120).

The performance of arpeggios in chamber music is often influenced by coordination of the instrumental parts. In Figure 3.4 the need for the violin and piano to sound the accented G's simultaneously mandates anticipation of the arpeggio, which the placement of *fp* alone would support.

In the very lyrical slow movement of his Sonata K. 310, Mozart took pains to write out an arpeggio, placing two of the three notes before the beat (Fig. 7.119, m. 2). This allows the appoggiatura D, played with an accent (*fp*), to fall squarely on the beat. Anticipation of the first two notes of the arpeggiated chord in m. 3 seems advisable too; the chord is in a syncopated position, the effect of which would be weakened or lost if the entrance of the melody note were delayed. Thus, in Figure 7.119 Mozart wrote out his preferred interpretation first and then used a symbol.

Although in the Adagio K. 540, Mozart placed diagonal strokes through the right-hand chords in m. 15 only, the performer might consider arpeggiating the chords that occur in the recapitulation at m. 45, and perhaps those in mm. 21 and 51. Starting the bottom right-hand note on the beat with the left-hand

Fig. 7.120. Mozart, Sonata K. 331/ii (OE Artaria), mm. 1, 11, 13.

Fig. 7.121. Türk, *Klavierschule*, p. 297.

Fig. 7.122. Haydn, Sonata Hob. 46/ii (contemporary ms. copy S. m. 9822), mm. 27–28.

octave and spreading the upper notes rapidly gives the illusion of greater tonal intensity (requested by the *forte*) than would anticipating the first two arpeggiated notes.

Occasionally an arpeggio is preceded by an appoggiatura. Haydn enjoyed this effect at the ends of movements. A long appoggiatura receives its usual duration to sound against the notes of the chord before being resolved,[246] as in Figure 7.121. Some special treatment of the resolution in Figure 7.122 seems necessary since the upper part of the arpeggiated chord does not sound effective alone. Christa Landon suggests playing the notes of the octave and the appoggiatura chord simultaneously, then arpeggiating the entire A-flat major chord on beat 2 with additional chord tones within the bass octave.[247] A leisurely pace with the notes in succession allows the resolution to be heard clearly.

Since discretionary breaking of chords to enhance their sonority was inherent in harpsichord style,[248] Haydn would have expected a degree of arpeggiation for some of the unmarked cadential chords in his early sonatas. Certainly the five-note chords in Hob. 2/i/60–61 and perhaps the chord of resolution at ii/38 would sound well on the piano with their notes slightly spread.

IMPROVISED ORNAMENTATION

All musicians recognize a *fermata* over a tonic 6/4 (or infrequently another inconclusive) chord near the end of an aria or concerto movement as the place at which eighteenth- and nineteenth-century performers improvised a cadenza that would display their virtuosic skills. But it is not so well known that in some early Classic and occasional Classic sonatas, including a number by Emanuel Bach and Haydn, there are also *fermatas* over 6/4 chords that require short cadenzas. These expectant pauses are present in Haydn's Hob. 19/ii/112 and Hob. 39/ii/58 and in Clementi's Op. 24/2/i/126. Mozart occasionally wrote out such cadenzas in the score of a work, as in the Quintet for Piano and

Winds K. 452/iii, the Concerto K. 488/i, and the Sonata K. 333/iii/171–198. (The first two measures of the last are sometimes mistakenly termed a lead-in to what appears to be just a return of the A theme.) Rather than playing an editor's cadenza, particularly an unstylistic one written later in the nineteenth century, some performers are now returning to the practice of preparing their own when the composer did not leave one.

It is difficult to give "rules" for the preparation of a cadenza, Koch wrote. Nevertheless, he advised that an "appropriate cadenza" must relate to the "character" of the movement and to the "sentiment" of the performance, and that its content must bear "the closest relationship to some of the main ideas contained in the movement."[249] Cadenzas that are "merely a sign of mechanical proficiency always cast a real shadow on the good taste of the performer."[250] Christa Landon and Rudolf Steglich have written appropriate cadenzas for some of Haydn's sonatas;[251] Eva and Paul Badura-Skoda and Frederick Neumann have analyzed the style and given suggestions for composing cadenzas for Mozart's concertos, and Paul Badura-Skoda has published a collection of his own cadenzas and lead-ins for them.[252]

Broadly speaking, the term *cadenza* can refer to any *fermata* embellishment;[253] but some musicians, including Mozart, referred to brief, nonthematic ornamental passages intended as transitions between sections of a work as "lead-ins" (*Eingänge*).[254] These are most frequently signaled by a *fermata* over or after a dominant-seventh chord preceding the return of a theme or a larger formal section, as in the Rondo of Mozart's Quartet for Piano and Strings K. 478, m. 135. Their figuration may involve only one or several harmonies, but usually no modulation.[255] In performance nowadays the opportunity for a lead-in, such as in K. 478 or the Duet Sonata K. 521/iii/69 and 203, sometimes passes unnoticed. Mozart wrote out many lead-ins that can serve as models, including one each before refrains in the Rondeaux of the Sonatas K. 309 (mm. 187–188) and K. 311, and a choice between two—one more difficult than the other—for the Piano Concerto K. 414/ii/73, preceding the return of the A theme.

For as late a work as the "Kreutzer" Sonata, Beethoven is said to have been pleased when the violinist Bridgetower supposedly improvised a lead-in at a *fermata* in the first-movement recapitulation.[256] Whether a lead-in to the final return of the main theme is appropriate at the *fermata* in Haydn's Hob. 40/i/91, itself a variation movement, has generated some interesting debate.[257] The evanescent nature of the issue makes consensus or even reasonably certain guidelines difficult to attain.[258] By 1828 Hummel advised that "in Sonatas or variations of the present day, the Composer generally supplies the player with the required embellishment."[259]

The Baroque tradition of embellishing the body of a movement was carried on through the early Classic period and to a limited but undetermined extent into the Classic period itself. In the Preface to *Sechs Sonaten* . . . Wq. 50 (pub. 1760), Emanuel Bach stated that "Variation in repetition is indispensable today."[260] In these sample sonatas he varied all the movements, including complete repetitions in sonata-allegro form. *Sechs Sonaten* . . . became available in Vienna "by 1767 if not earlier."[261] Türk's suggestions offer some parameters. Beyond *fermatas,* "rondos and similar pieces that are so popular now also provide opportunities for improvised embellishments."[262] However, only passages that become tedious upon repetition should be so treated. While "it is customary on occasion to vary a passage in the repeat of an Allegro . . . , longer embellishments are most frequently appropriate in compositions of a tender, pleasing, etc. character in slow tempo. . . ." Further limitations prohibit changes in works of sad, serious, noble, and similar character.[263]

The mature Haydn and Mozart, and Beethoven from his early works, completed the notation of their scores with the exception of cadenzas and lead-ins; and Mozart left incomplete a few places in his concertos. He is known to have ornamented some of the slow movements of his piano concertos in performance, although he probably preferred that others, including his sister, not add to his music. According to a letter of 9 June 1784,[264] he sent her the written-out embellishments for mm. 56–62 of the Andante of K. 451.[265] Nevertheless, a few remaining skeletal passages in the concertos require filling out, including mm. 75–76 of the same Andante, in which the right hand has only three long D's in three adjacent octaves. A similar passage occurs in K. 491/i/467–470, and there is a longer one in K. 482//iii/164–172, both movements Allegros. Eva and Paul Badura-Skoda and Frederick Neumann have provided discussions of and models for these passages and for a few others in the concertos involving literal thematic repetition.[266]

The slow movement of Mozart's Sonata K. 309 and the elegantly ornamented Rondo K. 511 are models for tasteful embellishment of repeated material in his style. The existence of unembellished autographs (from which Mozart probably performed) and ornamented first editions for the Adagio cantabile variation of K. 284/iii and for the repetition of the aria-like melody in K. 332/ii has led musicians to conclude that Mozart supplied all the desired embellishments for the slow movements in his solo works. Certainly none demands further ornamentation. Nevertheless, some believe that there remain rare opportunities for discreet embellishment in sectional repeats of slow or even fast movements, as in the Allegro assai K. 332/iii/62–63, or the Adagio K. 282/i, perhaps from m. 10, beat 2 or 3, to m. 11, beat 1, and in mm. 16 and 21.

Since Beethoven composed the cadenzas for his piano concertos (for the Concerto No. 2 not until some years after its publication and with material more technically demanding than the piece itself), he considered his scores complete except for an occasional lead-in or cadenza in a smaller work. There are numerous accounts of performances of his works in which he improvised at *fermatas,* sometimes quite extensively, as in a performance of the Quintet for Piano and Woodwinds Op. 16.[267] But when the youthful Czerny allowed himself "many changes, in the way of adding difficulties to the music, the use of the higher octave, etc." in a performance of the same composition, the composer took him "severely" to task.[268] Beethoven's composing of the cadenza in the "Emperor" Concerto as an integral part of its movement, with this warning at the 6/4 chord: "N. B. Do not improvise a cadenza, but begin the following [written-out cadenza] immediately," heralded the end of the pianist's opportunity to add notes to a composer's score.

On the other hand, the early sonatas of Haydn as well as works by other composers of the period contain movements in moderate and slow tempos that invite appropriate ornamentation of the repeats. The basic approach is to add some of the formalized "essential" (*wesentliche*) ornaments (appoggiaturas, mordents, etc.) where they fit and to fill in occasional large melodic intervals, often with stepwise motion. In 1795 Hiller compared the adding of graces to music with the salting of soup or the peppering of salad, which—he warned—would certainly spoil the food if overdone.[269] Figure 7.123, from Haydn's Hob. 12/i (composed no later than 1766, but possibly as early as the mid-1750s),[270] shows an added ascending appoggiatura above m. 4 and two possible embellishments of the melodic skip in m. 3. Other ornaments that are appropriate for this cantilena, in which Andante applies to the eighth note, include some type of trill on the first melody notes in mm. 27, 28, and 37; an ornamental resolution of the appoggiatura A in m. 46; and a turn or a trill in m. 49 (perhaps depending on the ornament played on beat 2 of m. 48).

A more improvisatory approach to ornamentation is shown in Figures 7.124 to 7.126 (compare also Figures 10.6 and 10.7). Such embellishments were meant to enhance the affect of the movement as well as the reputation of the performer. Those in Figure 7.124, from the recapitulation of Hob. 12/i, may be played as suggested or modified. But bear in mind that if the repetition of an exposition in sonata-allegro form has been ornamented, so, presumably, must the repetition of the development and recapitulation in a manner that preserves the expected cumulative effect. Figures 7.125 and 7.126 are from Emanuel Bach's *Sechs Sonaten*. . . . Figure 7.125b shows one of his variations on the opening theme of that movement (Fig. 7.125a). In Figure 7.126 the lower system shows the first published version of this sonata; the upper staves show the variants of those measures that Bach entered in his *Handexemplar* (a composer's copy with holographic annotations).[271]

Hiller's instructions for free or extempore ornamentation (*willkührliche Veränderungen*), put clearly in a brief chapter in his *Anweisung zum musikalischen-zierlichen Gesange*, stress that such ornamentation should sound easy and pleasant even when it is difficult. "Legato and rubato ornaments"

Fig. 7.123. Haydn, Sonata Hob. 12/i (contemporary mss.), mm. 3–4.

*Tie from secondary ms. source

Fig. 7.124. Haydn, Sonata Hob. 12/i (contemporary mss.). a. mm. 43–46. b. mm. 51–55. Possible embellishments shown above.

a.

b.

Fig. 7.125. E. Bach, *Sechs Sonaten... mit veränderten Reprisen* Wq. 50/4/iii (OE Winter). a. mm. 1–8. b. mm. 21–28.

a.

b.

are the most appropriate in "slow and pathetic arias"; "staccato" ornaments are more suited to the "allegro" style. The approach to, and resolution of, dissonant notes should adhere to the harmonic practice of the Classic period, he added.[272] Further information on extempore ornamentation, with examples,

Fig. 7.126. E. Bach, *Sechs Sonaten* . . . Wq. 50/5/ii (OE Winter and Bach's *Handexemplar*). a. mm. 1–4. b. mm. 39–42.

is available in the article "Improvisation" in *New Grove,* and in the books listed in the Selected Bibliography by E. Bach, Badura-Skoda, Ferand, Manfredini, L. Mozart, Quantz, Tartini, and Türk.

CHAPTER
8

"MIXED METERS" AND DOTTED RHYTHMS

Throughout the history of written music, rhythmic notation has suffered from imprecisions of various kinds. Two specific areas of difference between actual notation and expected performance in the Baroque and early Classic periods were also operative to some extent in the Classic period: the interpretation of "mixed meters"—that is, two eighth notes against three, or dotted rhythms against triplets—and the practice of double-dotting or overdotting. During the second half of the eighteenth century the notation and performance of these rhythms gradually moved in the direction of greater accuracy and literalism. Yet the slow, often unrecorded, process of change left ample room for uncertainty.

MIXED METERS

The Theory

With the advent of an increased use of triplets in common or 4/4 time, as well as in 2/4 and 3/4, many pieces have appeared which might be more conveniently written in 12/8, 9/8, or 6/8. The performance of other lengths against these notes is shown in [Figure 8.1].[1]

Emanuel Bach's example illustrates the two kinds of binary notation commonly used in the Baroque and early Classic periods to express a form of compound ternary notation that did not yet exist: the quarter- and eighth-note triplet, or 2:1 relationship. The resulting combination of duple and triple notation was

Fig. 8.1. E. Bach, *Essay*, p. 160.

sometimes called "mixed meters." In performance, the dotted patterns were compressed and softened, and equal notes were expanded and made unequal. Both adjustments assimilated to the ternary rhythm, creating the sound of a quarter- and eighth-note triplet.

In reference to Figure 8.1b, it should be noted that exact performance of "two against three," now taken for granted, was not normally used in Baroque music. Only rarely is there a context in which contrapuntal development of motivic lines leads naturally to the precise playing of this cross-rhythm. One very convincing example is the Andante from J. S. Bach's Sonata for Flute and Harpsichord in B minor BWV 1030 (e.g., mm. 42, 45, 47). In music of the early Classic style a literal two against three, and even three against four, came to be considered fashionable by certain composers, including Georg Philipp Telemann and Johann Schobert, who exploited those rhythms for their effects.[2]

Although the difficulty of playing two against three, especially for beginners, is mentioned in almost every keyboard tutor of the Classic period, after about 1775 to 1780 such patterns were probably expected to be played literally, perhaps depending to some extent on the musical style. In 1774, for example, Schulz wrote that two notes against three was an "inimical" pattern and "hard to carry out" but was still to be played "without the slightest difficulty."[3] Türk and Milchmeyer expressed similar points of view, but both emphasized that the combination was considerably easier to play in fast tempos than in slow ones.[4] This brings to mind the serene Adagio of Haydn's Hob. 23, composed in 1773, in which it is not inappropriate to assimilate the sixteenth-note duplets to the triplets after the short appoggiatura (mm. 18 and 37; cf. the discussion of Fig. 8.19). Türk confessed in the second edition of his Klavierschule that the correct playing of two against three and four against three, "especially in slower tempos, . . . still remains, according to my taste, a beauty to which one must first become accustomed in order to find it tolerable."[5]

The compression of dotted patterns to triplets, illustrated by Emanuel Bach in Figure 8.1a, shortens the value of the dot and is sometimes called "under-dotting." This realization was common when the basic value of the note followed by the dot was the same as the value of the notes in the triplet. Löhlein described the practice in his Clavier-Schule of 1765.[6] Four years later, in an article in the Allgemeine deutsche Bibliothek, Agricola took issue with Löhlein on that point, writing that except "in extremely fast tempo . . . the note after the dot must be played not with but after" the third note of the triplet.[7] Löhlein tacitly acknowledged this criticism and changing performance style in the second edition of his tutor, published in 1773, by taking a position similar to Agricola's. He suggested assimilation in "fast" tempos; otherwise the dotted pattern should be played "according to its value."[8] Schulz gave no exceptions to playing the short note after the triplet in 1774.[9] Convenient as that might seem, it does not reflect contemporary practice, for the simultaneous performance of dotted patterns and triplets is fraught with questions until well into the nineteenth century.

In 1789 Türk wrote that the short note following a dotted note, as in Figure 8.2a, should be played "only after the last note of the triplet." However, since beginners often could not do that correctly, it might be better to shorten the dot somewhat and let them play the rhythm

as in [Fig. 8.2c]. Various composers may even intend this last arrangement in such situations.

In pieces of a forceful, etc., character, in which many dotted notes occur, the latter arrangement would certainly not correspond with the whole; however, such pieces are also not suitable for beginners.[10]

Türk's comment reveals both the uncertainty caused by changing practice and the attendant pedagogical problems. Here, also, character becomes another criterion to consider in making a decision.

This notational practice and the uncertainty about its interpretation persisted. In his *Musical Grammar* of 1809, John Callcott quoted three bars from Paisiello's "La Rachelina Molinara"[11] as an example of "Mixed Measures" (Fig. 8.3). He added in a footnote: "There is some doubt whether this Melody should be played as written, or as if it were compound; that is, one dotted Crotchet, one Crotchet, and one Quaver, in the first Measure."[12]

Starke seemed very positive about assimilation in his tutor of 1819, surprisingly in an Adagio variation (Fig. 8.4):

Fig. 8.2. Türk, *Klavierschule*, p. 104.

Fig. 8.3. Callcott, *A Musical Grammar*, p. 258.

Fig. 8.4. Starke, *Pianoforte-Schule*, Vol. I, Pt. 2, p. 8, m. 10.

[Adagio]

At (K) dotted notes are set beneath sextolets and triplets. Here the counting is not quite exact in [the music of] the recent famous composers. The note that comes after the dotted note is counted on the last note of the sextolet or the triplet.[13]

Czerny's view echoed those of Agricola and Löhlein: "In very quick times, the note which follows the dot must be played with the third note of the triplet."[14]

Application of the Theory

With the possibility of occasional underdotting in the Classic repertoire, the pianist will ask where that procedure might be appropriate. Simultaneity of both patterns in the same hand, especially in a fast tempo, is often a clue. An appropriate tempo for Figure 8.5 requires assimilation, which Mozart's holograph supports with deliberate alignment of the sixteenth note and the third eighth note at each occurrence of the combined rhythms. That clue can also be seen in Figure 8.6. Although the tempo is slower and the potentially antagonistic rhythms occur frequently in separate hands, they sound best to me as they are aligned here and throughout. Without any question, triplets dominate the rhythmic movement; the assimilated dotted patterns have no prior identity or individual importance. Nothing is lost through assimilation. In Cramer's Etude XXXIX (Fig. 8.7) the two rhythms are played by separate hands, yet three factors make rhythmic compliance the appropriate solution: the dominance of the triplet movement, the composer's extremely rapid metronomization, and the secondary role of the dotted materials. I treat Cramer's Etude VI similarly.

Beyond any help from trustworthy primary sources or recent scholarly editions, the pianist faced with a decision on underdotting must rely on his

Fig. 8.5. Mozart, Piano Concerto K. 450/i (Aut. and OE Artaria), m. 76.

Fig. 8.6. Clementi, Sonata Oeuvre 1/4/i (OE Bailleux), mm. 12–13.

Fig. 8.7. Cramer, Etude XXXIX (OE By the author), mm. 5–6.

or her perception of a piece or section of a piece. Technical problems in fast tempo suggest consideration of assimilation. In general, tempo, character, and the roles of the rhythms involved all have bearing. The importance and previous use of thematic material associated with the dotted pattern or the use of other binary patterns in the same theme would certainly affect a performer's rhythmic interpretation.

In the cantabile melody of Figure 8.21, from the Adagio of Haydn's Hob. 49, assimilation sounds convincing for the ♫♩ in m. 68. (See discussion of this section below.) But it is often more appropriate to let these two patterns go their separate ways, particularly if the motive in duple notation has established prior importance. Two movements, both headed Allegro moderato in 2/4 meter, come to mind: Mozart's K. 330/i/28, in which the four G's of the dotted pattern are a development of the repeated-note motive that opens the movement, and Beethoven's "Archduke" Trio/iv/152, in which staccatos give the dotted pattern a strong rhythmic effect that should not be compromised. Contrast must also be retained in the third variation of Mozart's Concerto K. 491/iii, in which a dotted version of the theme appears against a triplet accompaniment when the pianist plays both parts (in separate hands) and against a sixteenth-note accompaniment when the orchestra plays both.

The Allegro moderato from Haydn's Hob. 26 (comp. 1773) has contrasting triplet and dotted patterns in separate hands in its development section (mm. 33–38). Here the dotted patterns can be played either way, although I tend toward retaining the dotted effect, which harks back to m. 2 (Fig. 8.18). Interestingly, after writing the dotted pattern in m. 33, Haydn notated the same melodic motive—albeit with a trill on the second note—in even sixteenth notes (mm. 34–35). Since the dotted pattern returns, these even notes may represent another throwback to the more casual notation of the Baroque era, when one presentation often served as a model for a continuing pattern; or they may suggest assimilation to the triplets. Did Haydn intend to indicate contrast here? Either a dotted or a triplet interpretation can sound stylish if the tempo, the rhythmic adjustments, and the ornaments throughout the passage produce a flowing melody that spontaneously becomes more climactic and then subsides.

Beethoven's construction of the Tempo di Minuetto from his Sonata for Violin and Piano Op. 30/3 clarifies his intentions for its performance. The opening theme is laid out in the first eight measures against simple quarter-note movement in two other lines (Fig. 9.10a). Against the second presentation of the theme, this time by the violin, the piano introduces a triplet accompaniment (Fig. 9.10b). The establishment of the rhythmic contours and identity of the theme before the introduction of the triplets, along with the presence of additional binary rhythms—the eighth and two sixteenth notes in m. 3 and the four sixteenths in m. 4—should allay any thought of softening the dotted figures to fit the triplets in this movement. In the Andante sostenuto of Mozart's Sonata for Piano and Violin K. 296, the presence of the obvious two against three and four against three in m. 3 (Fig. 8.8) and a very moderate tempo convince me that Mozart intended the dotted rhythms here to function as binary configurations against the triplets. Again from the solo literature, the popular Allegro con brio of Haydn's Hob. 35 in C major serves as an example of thematic dotted patterns that retain their independence in the presence of frequent triplet accompaniment. A few players persist in arguing the merits of assimilation for the Adagio sostenuto of Beethoven's "Moonlight" Sonata, despite Czerny's specific instructions to the contrary.[15]

The incomplete pattern ♩. ♬ appears frequently in Clementi's music. In spirited or quick movements it may mean ♩. ♬ ; but sometimes, especially in slow cantabile contexts such as Op. 7/3/ii (Fig. 5.27), the reading ♩♬ sounds more appealing. This interpretation, in which the dot has less value, was a common form of underdotting earlier in the century. It is also applicable to turns between notes.

Binary notation in place of ternary occurs in nineteenth-century repertoire as well. The pattern ♩. ♪♪ is found in Schubert's "Erstarrung," Schumann's Novellette Op. 21/1, and Chopin's Polonaise-Fantaisie Op. 61 and Prelude Op. 28/9. For numerous other works whose notation is not as precise or for which there may not be a holograph, the question of where and where not to assimilate the dotted patterns to triplets is cause for considerable thought. The second movement of Schubert's Sonata in C minor D. 958 and Chopin's Nocturne Op. 27/1 exemplify the problem.

Fig. 8.8. Mozart, Sonata for Piano and Violin K. 296/ii (Aut.), mm. 1–3.

*Sixteenth notes in the dotted patterns are placed erratically in Aut., often well before the end of the triplet.

DOUBLE-DOTTING AND OVERDOTTING

The Theory

The gradual acceptance of the double dot to notate some of the rhythms that performers had previously been expected to achieve through alteration was a step toward more precise notation. Marpurg, Leopold Mozart, and others recommended the use of double-dotting for greater accuracy because, as Mozart described it,

> There are certain passages in slow pieces where the dot must be held rather longer than the [usual] rule demands if performance is not to sound too sleepy. For example, if [in Fig. 8.9] the dot were held its usual length it would sound very languid and sleepy. In such cases dotted notes must be held somewhat longer, but the time taken up by the extended value must be, so to speak, stolen from the note standing after the dot.

Fig. 8.9. L. Mozart, *Violin*, p. 41.

> ... The dot should in fact be held at all times somewhat longer than its value. Not only is the performance thereby enlivened, but hurrying—that almost universal fault—is thereby checked. ... It would be a good thing if this long retention of the dot were insisted on and set down as a rule. I, at least ... have made clear my opinion of the right manner of performance by setting down two dots followed by a shortened note.[16]

Türk wrote more extensively on the performance of dotted notes, pointing out that their treatment varied according to their context, but that they were usually prolonged. His text offers valuable insights about the discretionary application of double-dotting and overdotting (lengthening a dot by less than half its value):

> Various note values call for a more or less heavy [sustained] execution, regardless of the meter. For example, if in a composition there are primarily longer notes, such as whole and half, or quarter notes, then the execution must generally be heavier than if many eighths, sixteenths, etc., are intermingled. Dotted notes in particular require—according to the circumstances—a very varied treatment, not only with respect to the distribution [of the note values] but also to a heavier or lighter performance. Namely, dotted notes are usually* held longer (and the

---

*It is not possible to define all cases [of dotted notes]; however, it can be taken as a rule that the value of the dot is not lengthened when the note following it has the full value of a beat or, in slower tempo, of a beat division [*Taktglied*]. ... How necessary, therefore, is a more precise notation for dotted notes. Since almost everyone now knows what double dots mean, through their use or by means of another accurate notation all doubt could be removed in most cases.

following short notes therefore played more quickly) than the notation indicates. For example [Fig. 8.10]:

The execution of the dotted notes shown in [Fig. 8.10b] is generally chosen when the character of the piece is serious, solemn, stately, etc., thus not only for an actual *Grave* itself, but also for Overtures or pieces marked *sostenuto* and the like. In this case the dotted notes are played emphatically, therefore [they are] held out. For the expression of livelier, more joyful, etc. feelings, the performance must be somewhat lighter, approximately as in [Fig. 8.10c]. The execution in [Fig. 8.10d] is used above all for pieces to be played vehemently, boldly, etc., or for those marked staccato. The keys are struck firmly, but the fingers are raised sooner than in such places that are to be performed with a certain solemn majesty. For pleasant singing passages, as below in [Fig. 8.11e], the dotted notes are also lengthened a little—though not so noticeably—; but they are also played more gently (less accented). Especially in such cases the short notes after the dots are played softly and slurred. If a second voice is added where there are dotted notes, as in [Fig. 8.11f], then the prescribed division is retained.

Now and then where there are several voices, the dotted notes in only one voice are lengthened and the short notes in both voices are played simultaneously so that the whole is more consistent [Fig. 8.12].

In addition, the short rests that take the place of the dots, are often lengthened in pieces of lively, etc. character, as [in Fig. 8.13b].[17]

Türk's "rule," slipped into the footnote, that dots were not lengthened if they were followed by a note equal to one beat or, in slow tempos, equal to a

Fig. 8.10. Türk, *Klavierschule*, p. 361.

Fig. 8.11. Türk, *Klavierschule*, p. 362.

Fig. 8.12. Türk, *Klavierschule*, p. 362.

Fig. 8.13. Türk, *Klavierschule*, p. 363.

Fig. 8.14. Hummel, *Pianoforte*, Exercise 27, Pt. I, p. 79, m. 1.

beat division (one-half or one-third of a beat), deserves attention. Türk may have intended it to avoid the shortening of structural notes; rhythmic alteration was normally reserved for ornamental notes. In his revised edition of 1802, the material on dotted notes remained unchanged. (For more on the relationship of note values and meter to tempo and touch, see "Tempo Words, Meter, and Contemporary Practice" in chap. 9.)

No additional information on the tradition of unwritten double-dotting has so far come to light in the many tutors in which this custom is mentioned. It is interesting, though, that Crelle still explained the tradition in 1823.[18] Hummel's only comment is a reminder appended to an exercise completely in dotted notes (Fig. 8.14): "A movement like this, consisting entirely of dotted notes, must be played with a good deal of point" (in the German edition, "etwas pikant").[19]

Application of the Theory

Composers of the Classic period often wrote double dots, but there are still contexts in which the performer should consider alteration. For those situations that are holdovers from the traditional, more casual, notation, double-dotting is mandatory. Figure 8.15 illustrates the familiar rest and upbeat note of equal value in a context in which the rest is meant to be dotted and the note shortened. Other examples occur at the opening of Haydn's Hob. 18/i and in the Primo of Mozart's Duet Sonata K. 497/ii/28 (*NMA*). In line with Türk's sug-

Fig. 8.15. Haydn, Sonata Hob. 20/i (Aut. fragment), m. 28.

gestion, the dotted eighth note on beat 4 in Figure 8.16 should be lengthened so that "the short notes in both voices are played simultaneously." An identical situation appears in the fourth variation of Mozart's Andante and Variations (for four hands) K. 501. In both cases the simultaneous playing of quick passing notes at the octave sounds better than hearing those tones in rapid succession. Some musicians—myself included—prefer double-dotting in the opening measure of Mozart's Sonata K. 282, in mm. 16–18 of his Fantasy in C minor K. 396, and in some of his marches. Here and elsewhere the performance of dotted notes becomes increasingly one of taste and choice.

Perhaps because Haydn was a generation older than Mozart and Clementi, he retained some inner relationship to Baroque style at an instinctive level, and his works offer the richest opportunities for discretionary application of this unwritten rhythmic practice. The opening of the Largo from Hob. 2 could easily serve as the illustration for Türk's double-dotting of a piece in solemn character (Fig. 8.17). For a stylish performance of Figure 8.18 it is also best to double-dot the F-sharp and shorten the G-sharp after the turn in m. 2.

Many of Haydn's minuets and minuet-like sonata movements demonstrate his exuberant use of dotted notes. Thus, movements such as Hob. 18/ii, 33/iii, 28/ii (Fig. 7.91), and 49/iii seem to benefit from some degree of overdotting.

Fig. 8.16. Mozart, Suite K. 399, (Aut. facs. *NMA*), mm. 9–10.

Fig. 8.17. Haydn, Sonata Hob. 2/ii *(JHW)*, mm. 1–2.

Fig. 8.18. Haydn, Sonata Hob. 26/i (OE Kurzböck), mm. 1–2.

According to Türk's description, these lively, light dotted patterns would be played with a rest before the shortened final note unless there is some contraindication. In Hob. 33/iii and 49/iii Haydn provided contrasting articulation by slurring some of the dotted groups.

The question arises whether to overdot in the presence of triplets. According to available evidence it seems appropriate to overdot the opening C in Figure 8.19, assimilating the D-flat to the triplet rhythm, which dominates the movement completely.[20] In fact, when the note that is dotted is larger by one value than the notes in the triplet, as here, overdotting bypasses a "two against three." (Double-dotting here would place the sixteenth note after the last note of the sextolet.) Similar overdotting produces a climactic intensity in the central D-minor episode of the Andante con espressione of Hob. 42, as it does to an even greater extent in the development of Mozart's Fantasy K. 396.

In Figure 8.20 the first dotted A-flat can be lengthened and the eighth note can be played so close to the end of its beat that the turn (begun *on* the beat) sounds like a quick turn. Straddling the beats in this way gives the ornamentation a flowing quality that is continued by the written-out pre-beat start of the trill in m. 26 (as well as by those in mm. 35–39). The final sixteenth in m. 25 slips in just before the bar line.

A rich study in rhythmic interpretation with which to conclude this survey is the beautiful *minore* (mm. 57–75) of the Adagio e cantabile from Haydn's Hob. 49. The primary objective is to create a supple, expressive melodic line over the steady sextolet accompaniment. The mixed meters offer an opportunity for a variety of resolutions. Some performers consistently lengthen the dotted eighth note and fit the following sixteenth with the last note of the sextolet (Fig. 8.21, beat I); I prefer a freer approach, varying the placement of the sixteenth in the manner of contrametric *rubato* (discussed in chap. 10). An

Fig. 8.19. Haydn, Sonata Hob. 23/ii (Aut.), m. 1.

Fig. 8.20. Haydn, Sonata Hob. 41/i (OE Bossler),[21] mm. 24–26.

Fig. 8.21. Haydn, Sonata Hob. 49/ii (Aut.), mm. 67–68.[22]

exact interpretation of the 3/4 meter in the following beats of m. 67 provides a rubato-like four against three.

Assimilation by underdotting the ♩♫ in m. 68 (discussed on p. 294) is usually followed, at the end of the measure, by a three against two between the 32d notes and the sextolet sixteenths—also a slight underdotting. On the other hand, Gilbert Kalish stretches the second dot, playing the triplet with the last sixteenth only,[23] in an interpretation that sounds more spontaneous than cantabile. From here, as the melody moves toward its climax against the unrelenting sextolets, the situation seems made to order for further contrametric *rubato* and variety in resolving the dotted patterns. Not surprisingly, the highly expressive writing of this *minore* has a direct forerunner by about a decade in Haydn's Hob. 39/ii, also an Adagio in 3/4, in which a melody containing some of these same dotted rhythms is spun out over sixteenth-note sextolets.

CHAPTER
9

CHOICE OF TEMPO

> Time makes melody, therefore time is the
> soul of music. It does not only animate the
> same, but retains all the component parts
> thereof in their proper order.
> —LEOPOLD MOZART[1]

There is little doubt that choice of tempo is a fundamental yet elusive
aspect of performance practice. Tempo affects virtually every other aspect of
interpretation: dynamics, touch, articulation, pedaling, realization of ornaments, and the relating of all these details to the whole. Tempo also affects
what the listener perceives, hence it bears directly on the effectiveness of the
interpretation. This chapter explores the kinds of information from which
musicians can best learn to select tempos appropriate to Classic period keyboard music; for "this it is by which the true worth of a musician can be
recognized without fail."[2]

ELEMENTS IN TEMPO CHOICE

Interaction of Meter, Note Values, and Tempo Headings

"Clementi is a *ciarlatano*, like all Italians. He writes *Presto* over a sonata
or even *Prestissimo* and *Alla breve,* and plays it himself *Allegro* in 4/4 time."[3]
This well-known remark of Mozart's from a letter of 7 June 1783 reveals—in
addition to a degree of professional jealousy—several aspects of contemporary
tempo usage. It points first to a difference in the interpretation of tempo between the two musicians, something that might occur in any period. Clementi,
of Italian and English background, probably preferred a slower *presto,* for his
vast technical resources placed him in the forefront of the development of
virtuoso technique and he undoubtedly could have played his own *presto alla
breve* as fast as he wished. On the other hand, Mozart's *presto* seemed so
surprisingly fast in Italy that the Neapolitans attributed it to some magic of a
ring that he wore.[4] Such national styles and preferences of individual composers, when known, should influence the choice of tempo.

One implication of Mozart's remark particularly relevant to eighteenth-century practice is the role of the time signature in combination with the tempo inscription in establishing an appropriate speed. Mozart mentions not just *presto* or *allegro,* but contrasts *presto* (or *prestissimo*) *alla breve* with *allegro* 4/4. The connotations of time signatures and their prevailing note values were a vestige of the proportional notation and "tactus," or pulse, used in Renaissance music. Within a pulse that may have had only limited variability,[5] different meters had speeds relative to one another. Since modern time signatures evolved from proportional notation, some feeling of proportion remained with them at least into the early nineteenth century. Proportion is important to Quantz's use of meter and note values along with Italian tempo words and the human pulse to define his system of tempo measurement;[6] it continued so in the writings of Kirnberger, Schulz, and Türk. (See Appendix A to this chapter.)

The interaction of time signature, note values, and tempo heading on tempo choice, as described in Sulzer's *Allgemeine Theorie* and Türk's *Klavierschule,* reduces to a few principal ideas.[7]

1. Large note values generally implied "heavier" (i.e., notes played more firmly and held out) execution and somewhat slower tempos than did smaller note values. (For heavy and light performance see above pp. 150–151.)

2. Each time signature, with its characteristic note values, had its own manner of execution and inherent movement.[8] The larger the note represented by the denominator, in general, the heavier the execution and the slower the tempo. Thus, pieces in 4/2, 3/2, and 2/2 were likely to move more heavily and somewhat more slowly than pieces in 4/4, 3/4, and 2/4, and those more heavily and slowly than pieces in 4/8, 3/8, and 2/8. Or, putting it the other way, the lightness of the execution and the liveliness of the tempo would increase as the value of the fraction decreased: that is, from 3/2 to 3/4, 3/8, or 3/16; or from 4/4 to 2/4. Alexander Malcolm's summary, although written earlier, is interesting and relevant:

> In the *triple* [time], there are some Species that are more ordinarily of one kind of Movement than another: Thus the triple 3/2 is ordinarily *adagio,* sometimes *vivace* [for Malcolm, *vivace* was a moderate tempo in place of *andante*[9]]; the 3/4 is of any Kind from *adagio* to *allegro;* the 3/8 is *allegro,* or *vivace;* the 6/4, 6/8, 9/8 are more frequently *allegro;* the 12/8 is sometimes *adagio* but oftner [*sic*] *allegro.* Yet after all, the *allegro* of one Species of *triple* is a quicker Movement than that of another, so very uncertain these Things are.[10]

J. A. P. Schulz explained another subtle point about "the natural movement" of time signatures:

> For example, the eighths in 3/8 meter are not as long as the quarters in 3/4, but also not as short as the eighths of the same [3/4]. Therefore, a piece marked *vivace* in 3/8 time would have a livelier tempo than it would in 3/4 time.[11]

3. An "uneven" [triple] meter had "a greater gaiety in its expression" and was considered "more appropriate for the representation of lively emotions than an even [duple] meter."[12]

4. Subdivision of structural note values into many smaller notes necessitated slower movement:

> If a piece in 2/4 is marked *allegro* and contains only a few or even no sixteenth notes, then the movement of the meter is faster than when it is full of sixteenths; the case is the same with the slower tempos.[13]

Some further comments by Schulz lend additional perspective to the meter–note value–tempo relationship:

> [A skilled performer] has through experience acquired a certain feeling of tempo from the natural length and shortness of the note values. Therefore, he will give a piece that has no indication of the tempo, or is marked *Tempo giusto*—which is one and the same,[14] a slower or faster, but correct tempo and at the same time the proper heaviness or lightness in the execution, according to whether it consists of longer or shorter note values. And he will know how much he has to give to or take away from the natural length or shortness of the notes for slowness or quickness if the piece is marked with *adagio, andante,* or *allegro,* etc. From this the advantages of dividing the even and uneven meters into various time signatures of longer or shorter note values . . . become understandable; for through that each meter receives its own movement, its own weight in performance, consequently also its own character. Now, if a piece should have a light execution but at the same time a slow tempo, then the composer will select, according to the nature of the light or lighter execution, a meter of short or shorter values for it; and [will] make use of the words *andante,* or *largo,* or *adagio,* etc., because the slowness of the piece should exceed the natural movement of the meter. And conversely, if a piece should have a heavy rendition and at the same time a fast tempo, then the composer will select a heavy meter according to the kind of rendition and will mark it with *vivace, allegro,* or *presto,* etc. If an experienced performer now looks over the note values of such a piece, he is in a position to determine the execution and the tempo itself corresponding exactly to the ideas of the composer. . . .[15]

The *alla breve* time signature, ₵, had the most obvious relationship to the proportions of the past, for it made the next higher note value the basis of the tempo. Theoretically, a half note in *alla breve* was played at the tempo of a quarter note in common time, so that a piece was "once again as fast as usual."[16] In 1802 Türk modified his wording to "approximately twice as fast,"[17] but even that does not describe actual practice. There is ample proof going back at least to the end of the seventeenth century that neither the distinction between the signs C and ₵ nor the intention of a double tempo was universally observed.[18]

We know from the caustic description of Clementi's playing cited above, as well as from a letter of 20 February 1784,[19] that for Mozart *alla breve* was quite clearly faster than common time. That it was not necessarily twice as fast is demonstrated by Max Rudolf's apt observation regarding the beginning of Mozart's *Don Giovanni*. The Overture, marked Molto allegro ¢ (after its Andante introduction), is followed by "Notte e giorno," marked Molto allegro C; yet it would be as senseless to take the aria only half as fast as it would be to take both pieces at the same speed.[20] In practice then, an *alla breve* could mean anything from somewhat faster to twice as fast as common time.

Often as important as the faster half note in *alla breve* was the changed character of the movement, for this is what truly differentiated it from C in performance. Prevalence of half notes would suggest a heavier (more emphatic and fully held) performance, even if an *alla breve* were played at the speed suggested by C. In addition, the metric performance would be in terms of half-note spans rather than quarter-note spans. Kirnberger wrote that the alternation of only two types of beats in *alla breve* "feet," a heavy one and a light one of equal length, produced a "more straightforward and earnest" character than that of the same piece notated in C with smaller values and a hierarchy of accents.[21] Schulz described the character of *alla breve* as "earnest and spirited," adding that its movement carried no notes faster than eighths.[22] It was probably the *alla breve* accentuation and character that induced Beethoven to alter the C to ¢ for the Gloria of the Mass in C major because of "a bad performance at which the tempo was too fast."[23] What Beethoven may have wanted was a settling down of the tempo and a broader sweep. With the same note values but the change in meter, the Gloria was changed from a piece with four beats, or pulses, and two accents of different weights in each measure to a piece with only two beats, one accent, and the *alla breve* character. Since degree of speed is perceived as the time between beats (that is, the time spanned by the unit or note value in which the rhythm of a piece moves), the *alla breve* would sound somewhat slower and broader even if it were played at the same metronomic speed per quarter note that it had been in C.

Practical Results of These Customs

A look at some combinations of meter and tempo headings in Haydn's keyboard sonatas will bear out the influence of proportional relationships on his concepts of notation and tempo determination. Since common time was considered somewhat slower than the smaller 2/4 measure in the system of proportions, it is not surprising that common time appears in twenty first movements—all but one with tempos between *moderato* and *allegro,* and only once in the traditionally faster finales, where it is coupled with Presto (Hob. 40/ii). However, 2/4 appears in nineteen first movements and in twenty finales. Of the perhaps surprising number of first movements in 2/4, twelve are in very early sonatas, probably written before 1766; three are in sonatas written between ca. 1771 and ca. 1773 or in 1773; two are in sonatas written by 1776; one is in a sonata written by 1778; and another occurs in a sonata written by 1780.[24] Thus the lighter 2/4 in a first movement is predominantly a trait of his earlier sonatas, when Haydn evidently wanted some first movements faster than his C meter—still a longer Baroque measure—would have provided.[25]

Like the first movements in C, all but two in 2/4 bear headings between
moderato and *allegro*, but the distribution of headings is noticeably different.
Among the movements in C only four are *allegro*, five are *allegro moderato*,
and ten are *moderato;* among the movements in 2/4, seven are *allegro*, four
are *allegro moderato*, and only five are *moderato* (the remaining one in C and
two in 2/4 are *allegro con brio*). This demonstrates a tendency by Haydn to
associate 2/4 with faster tempos than he did C. The twenty finales in 2/4 are
for the most part *prestos*, or *allegros* modified to the faster side.

Of the nineteen sonatas that have first movements in 2/4 time, seven (five
written before 1766) also have finales in 2/4. In such situations note values
may assume added importance as determinants of tempo. For example, in
Hob. 9 the opening Allegro in 2/4 contains 64th and 32d notes along with
sixteenth notes and triplets. These subdivisions mandate a slower tempo than
that chosen for the final Scherzo in 2/4 (with "Allegro" added by C. Landon
and Feder), in which the smallest notes are sixteenths. Hob. 24 has both an
opening Allegro and a closing Presto in 3/4; the smallest note value in the
Allegro is the sixteenth, while in the Presto it is the eighth note.

In his keyboard sonatas Haydn wrote only two *largos*, both in 3/4. He
apparently did not wish to use this very slow tempo heading with either the
slower C or the lighter 2/4 meter; perhaps he regarded *largo* as slower than
adagio.[26] Thirty-second notes and triplet 32ds are frequent in the Largo movements of both Hob. 2 (Fig. 8.17) and 37; 64th notes occur in the former.

Adagio is coupled with C, ¢, 3/4, and 6/8 meters. Thirty-second notes are
frequent in the C and 3/4 meters and also occur in 6/8. In the *alla breve* the
smallest note values are sixteenths and 32ds. Adagio C, a weighty movement
sometimes reminiscent of the Baroque, does not occur after 1774. Adagio 6/8
occurs last in Hob. 38, composed in the mid-1770s (according to Brown, *Haydn*);
the sole Adagio ¢ is in Hob. 35, composed in the late 1770s. Only Adagio 3/4
appears from the early to the very latest sonatas. The fluent 3/4 meter was a
favorite of Haydn's in all tempo groups from *largo* to *presto;* its mood varied
from solemn to comic. Twenty-four finales, not to speak of other movements,
are in 3/4. On the other hand, because 2/4 meter was associated with a certain
lightness, Haydn used it in the sonatas only with tempo headings from *moderato* to *presto*.

A much broader study of Mozart's music also concludes that his "use of
tempo words and meter adhered to the conventions of his time as described
in contemporaneous treatises."[27]

The meters 4/2, 3/2 and 2/2 were used by Mozart rarely and for one purpose
only—the slow movements of church music.... This corresponds to the position
of these meters in Quantz's scheme and to the remarks in many contemporary
treatises that church music was performed more slowly than theatre or chamber
music. Common time was used by Mozart for any tempo from extremely slow
to moderately fast. Extremely fast movements in duple meter, however, he wrote
in 2/4 or ¢.... Similarly, 3/4 was used for very slow to rather fast movements,
but 3/8 only for moderate to extremely fast movements.

This brings us to the interesting point that for Mozart a piece in 3/8 with sixteenth-note motion predominating would have been faster than a piece in 3/4 with eighth-note motion, *if both had the same tempo indication.*[28]

In spite of the different samples involved, a comparison of this short statement on Mozart's usage with the preceding information on Haydn's suggests basic similarities and some individual differences in the way the proportional relationships were applied. For example, Mozart used 3/4 only from "very slow to rather fast movements," whereas Haydn used 3/4 through the entire range of *largo* to *presto,* at least in his keyboard sonatas. (Further comparison would, of course, require similar samples and studies.)

Another way of exploring the interaction of meter, note values, and tempo headings is to compare some expected theoretical relationships and actual performance tempos, which I did with Mozart's sonatas. In theory, an Allegro in 2/4 with sixteenth-note motion should be faster than an Allegro in 4/4 with similar motion. Several recordings of the first (C) and third (2/4) movements of K. 279 illustrate this difference. Christoph Eschenbach recorded i at $\downarrow$ = 132 and iii at $\downarrow$ = 152; Walter Gieseking recorded i at $\downarrow$ = 120 and iii at $\downarrow$ = ca. 144–152.[29] Lili Kraus minimized the difference, playing i at $\downarrow$ = ca. 126–132 and iii at $\downarrow$ = 138.[30] Similarly, the Allegro ¢ of K. 281/iii, in which eighth-note motion predominates, should have a considerably faster metronomization per quarter note than the Allegro C of K. 279/i and the Allegro C of K. 284/i, both of which have sixteenth-note motion throughout. This relationship is also clear in the recordings of these pieces by Eschenbach, Gieseking, and Kraus.[31]

Only two of Mozart's piano sonatas have opening movements in 2/4: K. 281 and K. 330. Their pulse is the eighth note, 32d notes prevail, and the movements are similar in basic style. However, the Allegro moderato heading of K. 330/i suggests a slightly slower tempo than does the Allegro heading of K. 281/i. Eschenbach recorded K. 330/i at $\downarrow$ = 138 and K. 281/i at $\downarrow$ = 152. Kraus recorded K. 330/i at $\downarrow$ = 132 and K. 281/i at $\downarrow$ = 144.[32] Malcolm Bilson's recordings show less difference, with K. 330/i at $\downarrow$ = 126 and K. 281/i at $\downarrow$ = ca. 132.[33]

Or consider two movements in Allegro 2/4, similar in basic style, of which one, K. 279/iii, has prevailing sixteenth-note motion and the other, K. 281/i, has prevailing 32d note motion. There is a high probability that the latter will be played with a considerably slower metronomization for the quarter note, and even that the quarter note in the former and the eighth note in the latter may be similar in tempo. A comparison of recordings of K. 279/iii and K. 281/i shows the correspondence to be almost exact, for the pulse in K. 281/i is felt in eighth notes. Thus, Kraus plays K. 279/iii at $\downarrow$ = 138 and K. 281/i at $\downarrow$ = 144; Conrad Hansen plays at $\downarrow$ = 126 and $\downarrow$ = ca. 126–132 respectively; Gieseking recorded at $\downarrow$ = ca. 144–152 and $\downarrow$ = 138 respectively.[34] (I consider a difference of one or two intervals on a metronome an insignificant change of tempo; a difference of three or more intervals is significant. See n. 164 below.)

The old proportional system also influenced Beethoven, at least in his early years. On a draft for the *minore* of his song "Klage" WoO 113, probably composed in 1790, he pondered the relationship between absolute tempo, meter, and note values:

> That which now follows will be sung still more slowly, *adagio* or, at the most *andante quasi adagio. Andante* in 2/4 time must be taken much faster than the tempo of the song here. As it appears, the latter cannot remain in 2/4 time, for the music is too slow for it. It appears best to set them both in ¢ time.
> The first [part], in E major, must remain in 2/4 time, otherwise it would be sung too slowly.
> In the past, longer note values were always taken more slowly than shorter ones; for example, quarters slower than eighths.
> The smaller note values determine the tempo; for example, sixteenths and thirty-seconds in 2/4 time make the tempo very slow.
> Perhaps the contrary is also true.[35]

Additional Elements in Tempo Choice

Other elements require consideration before a true rhythmic character and a carefully refined tempo can emerge for a particular piece or movement. They include the mood and inner meaning of the music and numerous elements of structure beyond meter, note values, and tempo heading. Harmonic rhythm; construction of the texture; degree and types of articulation; intricacies of harmony, rhythmic movement, or dynamics; degree of ornamentation; and even the formal structure itself may be important. Such characteristics as a relatively slow harmonic rhythm, light texture, straightforward and not too detailed articulation, uncomplicated rhythmic movement, and little ornamentation lend themselves to faster movement than do more complex stylistic elements. On the other hand, rapid harmonic rhythm, full or contrapuntal texture, short slurs over notes of short rhythmic value, quick changes in articulation, syncopation, conflict between binary and ternary rhythmic patterns, unexpected changes of thematic material, or other stylistic intricacies slow the tempo of a piece to allow the details to be played and perceived. Ornamentation should sound comfortable in the tempo chosen, without much need for tempo modification. The effect of articulation on tempo has already been mentioned in relation to the unusually varied treatment of the opening motive in Haydn's Hob. 23/iii; the same effect would apply to many of the detailed slurrings discussed in chapter 5 (see "The Language of the Slur"). Exploration of these principles will continue in the section "Beethoven's 'Moderate' Minuets: His Metronomizations, Extrapolated Tempos, and Present Practice."

After a tempo choice has been made on the basis of musical characteristics, small adjustments may be needed to suit the circumstances of a specific performance. Some are personal concerns—the performer's facility or mood or the time of day; others have to do with the environment—the size and acoustics of the hall or the touch and tone quality of the piano used. A light, shallow touch and a spare, supple tone allow more malleability of sound and ease of movement than a heavy, deep touch and a thick tone. The sustaining power of the instrument may affect the tempo chosen for a singing melody in which long notes are prominent. Finally, we should be watchful that we do not apply to Classic music the slower tempos (for certain tempo types) of the late Romantic performance style, under the influence of which many of us learned to make music. These tempo developments of the nineteenth century are discussed below in "Metronomizations of Beethoven's Sonatas ..." and "Beethoven's 'Moderate' Minuets."

Everything taken into account, the end result should be a tempo that allows the piece to be fully played and heard with all its musical details, that allows the phrases to move and the connections and relationships to be perceived, all with a perspective that brings out the sense of the whole. "Who will contradict me if I count this among the chiefest perfections in the art of music?"[36]

THE BASIC TEMPO GROUPS

Contemporary Descriptions

Tempos were divided variously into three to six groups, depending on the writer. The three basic groups were fast, moderate, and slow. Türk described four:

> the very fast, ... *Presto, Allegro assai*, etc., ... the moderately fast, for example the *Allegro moderato, Allegretto*, etc., ... the moderately slow, such as *Un poco Adagio, Larghetto, Poco andante*, etc., ... the very slow, for example *Largo, Adagio molto*, etc.[37]

Andante was widely considered to be "a middle tempo that is neither really slow nor fast."[38] Thus, division of tempos into the five basic groups named by Rousseau[39] and followed by Sulzer and Koch seems a better representation of practice:

1) *Largo*, slow;
2) *Adagio*, moderately slow;
3) *Andante* (going), signifies a serene and measured pace, which observes the mean between fast and slow;
4) *Allegro*, quick, and
5) *Presto*, fast.[40]

Koch's descriptions of the five terms and categories reinforce the association of "sentiment" and performance style with tempo:[41]

> *Largo*, strictly speaking, means broad or extended; with this word one indicates the most usual slow tempo, which is suited only to those feelings that are expressed with solemn slowness. Everything pertaining to the performance of slow movements that was mentioned in the article on *Adagio* must be even more carefully observed in the *Largo*. ...[42]

Adagio, moderately slow; . . . Adagio requires an especially fine performance, in part because of the slow tempo, through which every trait that does not correspond to the prevailing sentiment becomes noticeable, in part because it [the piece] will become tedious and unpleasant if it is not performed in a sufficiently interesting and attractive way.

It is difficult to set down general rules for the performance of every kind of piece, because performance is more an affair of feeling than of description, more of talent than of instruction. Nevertheless, it is still certainly true that an Adagio must be performed with very fine nuances of loudness and softness, and generally with a very noticeable blending of the notes.[43]

Andante, going, or walking. This term indicates the tempo that observes the mean between fast and slow. When this heading is not used with especially characteristic pieces that determine the manner of performance, as, for example, processions, marches, etc., then the pieces that bear it generally maintain the character of deliberateness, calm, and contentment. Here the notes should be neither as drawn out and blended into one another as in the Adagio, nor as sharply accented and detached as in the *Allegro;* everything here is moderated, even the strength of the tones requires moderation until the composer expressly prescribes a greater degree of strength occasioned by a specific change in the prevailing sentiment.[44]

Allegro, quick: is a familiar heading for pieces that should be played in a moderately fast tempo. Because the speed of this movement can be quite varied . . . it is customary that one often defines the actual degree of speed more closely through additional adjectives, for example, *allegro non tanto* (not too fast), *allegro di molto* (very fast) etc. . . . the performer must still try to determine the exact degree of speed . . . in part from the meter, . . . in part and mainly, however, from the content itself. . . .

The performance of an Allegro calls for a manly [*männlichen*] tone and a direct and clear projection of the notes, which in this movement are only slurred either when it is expressly indicated or when an obviously cantabile section makes it necessary; the remaining notes are usually separated with a certain decisiveness that is unique to the performance of moderately fast pieces. . . .[45]

Presto, fast, rapid . . . the fastest tempo group. . . . In purely instrumental music Presto generally calls for a fleet and light, but very direct playing of the notes; on the other hand, in opera, in which those sentiments that make themselves felt with the greatest passion are usually cast in this tempo, the performance requires more forcefulness. However, this forcefulness must appear only in sharper accentuation of the notes and must not damage the clarity of the performance.[46]

Which Was the Slowest Tempo?

There was considerable difference of opinion throughout the eighteenth century as to whether *largo, adagio,* or even *grave* represented the slowest tempo. The *largo–adagio* order seems to have been a practice of the French, the Germans, and some Italians. Its followers included (in chronological order) Brossard, L. Mozart, J. J. Rousseau, Kirnberger, Lorenzoni, Türk, Galeazzi,

Dussek, Pleyel, F. P. Ricci, Milchmeyer, Koch, Hummel, and Czerny.[47] Of this group, Mozart, Hummel, and Czerny ranked *grave* slower than *largo* and *adagio*, while Galeazzi placed it between them.[48]

Based on Haydn's statement that each of the seven "Sonatas" of his *Seven Last Words* takes "7 or 8 minutes,"[49] Isidor Saslav's metronomizations for them confirm Haydn as a follower of the *largo–adagio* order (cf. p. 309). He seems to have used *largo, lento, grave,* and *adagio* as progressively faster headings.[50] The use of Andante un poco adagio in the Sonata K. 309 is among the indications that for Mozart, too, *adagio* was closer to *andante* and *largo* was slower. Beethoven also followed the *largo–adagio* order. Supporting evidence includes his comment on "Klage," his metronomizations for the Adagio sostenuto and the Largo of his Sonata Op. 106, and his heading for Var. IV of the Sonata Op. 109/iii: Un poco meno andante ciò è un poco più adagio come il tema (a little less andante, that is, a little more adagio than the theme). Not surprisingly, stylistic differences indicate that many of Beethoven's *adagios* need tempos substantially slower than most of Mozart's *adagios* would tolerate.

Those who considered *adagio* slower than *largo* were primarily British musicians and some Germans, although this order stemmed from seventeenth-century Italian custom. They included Purcell, Malcolm, Grassineau, Quantz, Emanuel Bach (speaking for practice in Berlin), J. Hoyle, Vogler, Busby, Clementi, Mason, Knecht, and Cramer.[51] Purcell considered "Adagio and Grave . . . very slow . . . ; Largo . . . a middle movement; Allegro . . . fast."[52] Most of the others who placed *grave* in a tempo order ranked it between *adagio* and *largo;* however, Malcolm and Mason—like L. Mozart, Hummel, and Czerny—held it to be the slowest tempo.

A comment by Schulz in 1774 indicates that *adagio* was played quite slowly in some parts of Germany:

> In some German cities it has become the fashion to play the *adagio* so slowly that one has difficulty recognizing the beat. Such performance makes the finest pieces tedious and wearisome, and resembles the delivery of a school master intoning a psalm.[53]

Such a statement leaves us wondering whether this exaggerated *adagio* might have stemmed from those Germans who considered *adagio* the slowest tempo, or whether it was a more widespread phenomenon.

There was also a group of French and Germans who considered *grave* more descriptive of a mood than of a specific tempo. Türk's definition of *grave* as "serious, therefore more or less slow,"[54] approximates the opinions of Rousseau, Quantz, Pleyel and Dussek, Milchmeyer, Koch, and Müller. When it is not possible to resolve questions of tempo with the help of contemporary information, we can turn to Koch's advice (in his description of *allegro* above) that "the performer must still try to determine the exact degree of speed . . . in part and mainly, however, from the content itself."[55]

Diminutive Terms; *Andante* and *Andantino*

Of three frequently used diminutive terms, two seem to have remained constant in meaning. *Larghetto*, "a little slow," was less slow than *largo* or *adagio*. According to Koch, *larghetto* indicated a smoothly flowing quality and "calm and agreeable sentiments," with a tempo "usually similar to that of *andante*."[56] Clementi placed only *andantino* between *larghetto* and *andante*.[57]

Allegretto, "a little fast, or cheerful," fell between *andante* and *allegro*. Pieces marked *allegretto* were played "noticeably slower," "with less spirited expression," and with notes less sharply detached than those marked *allegro* "because they generally have the character of an agreeable serenity."[58] The third diminutive, *andantino*, was the subject of considerable confusion and therefore needs to be treated in some detail.

As evident in the descriptions of tempo groups, *andante* was not a slow but a going or walking tempo, "the mean between fast and slow." The term was derived from the Italian *andare*, which means "to move," "to go," or "to walk." Mozart's message in a letter to his father of 9 June 1784, "Please tell my sister that there is no *adagio* in any of these concertos [K. 449, 450, 451, 453]—only *andantes*,"[59] voices concern that these middle movements might indeed be played too slowly. In that same year, C. F. D. Schubart described *andante* as a tempo "that kisses the borderline of the Allegro."[60]

The slow *andante*, which even now overshadows the "going" *andante*, was a nineteenth-century development, although Thomas Busby's description of 1800 indicates that at least in England it had some roots by the turn of the century:

> Andante seems to have had in the last age a signification different from that attached to it by musicians of the present day; and is frequently to be found at the beginning of old movements of a grand, and even chearful [*sic*] style. But now it is used to imply a time somewhat slow, and a performance distinct and exact, gentle, tender and soothing.[61]

For Hummel, *andante* was still "moving on, going";[62] but in 1839 Czerny defined it as "Moving onward slowly; less so however than Adagio."[63]

Two of Neal Zaslaw's conclusions about tempos in Mozart's music are of particular interest and importance:

> Modern performers of Mozart's music usually choose tempos which are reasonable from a historical point of view. The outstanding exceptions to this statement are the Minuets and Andantes, which are often played too slowly in modern performances.[64]

When *andante* was understood as "going," *molto andante* meant "strongly" or very much going, and *più andante*, "more going." Türk was definite about this in 1789.[65] By 1802, Koch was less sure:

Some composers also use it [*molto*] with the word *Andante*, which, however, makes the meaning uncertain; one cannot determine exactly whether the tempo of the *Andante* should be faster or slower.[66]

With a slow *andante, molto* or *più* made the movement slower. Metronomic indications in the piano reduction of Mozart's *Die Entführung aus dem Serail*, published by Schlesinger of Paris not long after 1822, provide an example of misinterpretation based on this changed meaning of *andante*. Mozart's Finale (No. 21) opens with "Nie werd ich," an Andante in *alla breve*, marked ♩ = 120 in Schlesinger's edition. At "Verbrennen sollte man," Mozart altered the tempo to più Andante (¢), which he intended as the first step in a gradual acceleration to Allegretto, stringendo il tempo and then Allegro assai, all within eleven measures. However, the unknowing (and unknown) editor reduced the speed at più Andante to 108.[67]

Andantino became the subject of disagreement toward the end of the eighteenth century. According to most eighteenth- and some nineteenth-century musicians, including Marpurg, Rousseau, Türk, Ricci, Hiller, Clementi, Adam, Knecht, Starke, Hummel, Kalkbrenner, Schilling, even Ernst Pauer,[68] *andantino* was slower than *andante*, taking its place between *andante* and *larghetto* or *lento*. However, from the 1780s on, others—including Galeazzi, Cartier, Koch, Müller, and, later, Czerny[69]—defined *andantino* as faster than *andante*, a principle that was widely adopted only well into the nineteenth century.

Türk recognized the second opinion with a rather sharp comment:

> In most textbooks ["various textbooks" in the 2d ed., 1802] *Andantino* is translated as somewhat faster than *Andante*. However, if one considers that for *molto Andante* (strongly [*stark*] going) a greater degree of speed or movement is necessary than for *Andante*, then perhaps my translation of the word *Andantino* given above, which indicates just a diminutive degree of going or of the tempo, will be found suitable. . . .[70]

Hiller called for a musical "parliament" to make decisions regarding this and "many other things."[71] Hummel also protested, "for it is evident that . . . the diminutive of the original word . . . implies a less [*sic*] degree of movement."[72] In 1840 Schilling again defended the slower interpretation by reason of its linguistic derivation, and then added,

> Nevertheless, the tempo of *andantino* is often exchanged by mistake with that of *allegretto* and taken much faster than that of the true *andante*. . . . As far as . . . general performance is concerned, *andantino* concurs for the most part with *andante*: lightness, repose, and a smaller amount of passion are also its most natural attributes.[73]

Haydn used *andantino* only twice in works for keyboard, too infrequently to allow meaningful generalization. The term is qualified in both instances, suggesting that ambiguity may have discouraged him from using it more often (this problem bothered Beethoven as well). It appears in two middle movements, both in 6/8, of piano trios from the 1790s.[74] Andantino più tosto Allegretto in the Trio for Piano, Flute, and Violoncello Hob. XV/16 means "Andantino, rather in the manner of Allegretto." In this movement there is extensive use of 32d and triplet sixteenth notes, which would normally slow the tempo somewhat. Haydn may have added the qualifier to counteract that slowing at least partially and to suggest a more cheerful quality. More common in Haydn's works is the heading Andante più tosto allegretto, which Türk explains as "going, [but] preferably a little faster."[75] Its use would imply that for Haydn *andantino* was in fact slower than *andante*. Andantino ed innocentemente in the Trio Hob. XV/29 indicates, according to Koch's discussion of *innocentemente,* a simple, unaffected performance, perhaps somewhat slower than otherwise.[76]

Clementi did not use either *andante* or *andantino* very much, probably because he tended toward better-defined moods and slower, more dramatic middle movements. When he did use these terms, like Haydn, he often added modifiers. *Andante* appears sporadically throughout his works, but *andantino* is last found in the Capriccio Op. 17, published in 1787. In his tutor, Clementi placed *andantino* on the slow side of *andante.*[77] In his Sonata Op. 25/6, the middle movement is Un poco andante, synonymous with *andantino*[78] but less ambiguous.

Andantino found more of a home in Mozart's piano repertoire, occurring approximately a dozen times among the concertos, the sonatas, the sonatas for piano and violin, and the smaller pieces. In these works, Mozart, who had known Italian since his boyhood travels, seems also to have followed the older tradition. In Concertos K. 271 and 449 and in the Sonata for Piano and Violin K. 306, the *andantino* movements carry beautifully expressive, substantially ornamented lines that need the time allowed by the "slower than *andante*" interpretation. Rapid (often ornamental) notes were mentioned frequently by eighteenth-century writers as an important element in tempo determination, always toward the slower side.[79] In K. 306/iii the juxtaposition of Andantino and Allegretto at mm. 230–234 would lose some of its contrast if the Andantino were interpreted as faster than Andante. Further, neither of the qualifiers that Mozart used with *andantino* in the piano works—*cantabile* and *sostenuto* (or, for that matter, any of those used with *andantino* in the rest of Mozart's *oeuvre*[80])—suggests a tempo faster than the contemporary flowing *andante,* nor do the contexts of those pieces in which the qualifiers occur. In his study of tempo choice in Mozart's music, Max Rudolf suggests that among approximately 60 pieces marked *andantino,* the interpretation as slower than *andante* is open to doubt in only a few. Use of the term in some concert arias (e.g., K. 294, 505) and in Nardo's aria "Con un vezzo all'Italiana" from *La finta giardiniera* shows unequivocally that in these cases *andantino* is the slower tempo.[81]

Beethoven noted the confusion about *andantino* in his correspondence with Thomson, for whom he was arranging British folk songs, then very much in vogue. In a letter of 19 February 1813 he wrote:

> If among the airs that you may send me to be arranged in the future there are
> Andantinos, please tell me whether Andantino is to be understood as meaning
> faster or slower than Andante, for this term, like so many in music, is of so
> indefinite a significance that Andantino sometimes approaches an Allegro and
> sometimes, on the other hand, is played like Adagio. . . .[82]

Aside from the numerous folk songs to which the heading had already been
affixed and a few unimportant themes and variations, some based on folk
songs, Beethoven very rarely used *andantino*. He probably considered it non-
descript as well as ambiguous. An early use of the term for the naïve little
"Romanze" in the *Musik zu einem Ritterballet* (comp. 1790–1791) seems to
indicate a tempo on the slower side to suit the pastoral mood of that highly
popular genre. The pianist need face the issue of Beethoven's *andantino* only
in accompanying the songs, which include three of his own in addition to the
folk songs. Here we are out of the realm of "pure music" and beyond the
purview of this study, for the tempo of the songs is influenced by conditions
of text setting as well as by Beethoven's varied qualifiers to the enigmatic
heading. Some—such as the pretentious con moto grazioso e semplice assai
for "Sally in Our Alley"—were undoubtedly added to lighten the boredom of
the task at hand. Beethoven may even have intended some *andantinos* slower
and some faster, according to the texts.[83] Further effort here to find a definitive
answer seems unwarranted.

The Changing *Allegro*

In colloquial Italian *allegro* means "cheerful," "good-humored," or "lively."
In its musical application the aspect of speed began to gain prominence as
early as the turn of the eighteenth century, when *geschwinde* (fast), *alacriter*
(briskly), and *hurtig* (quick) appeared as translations in treatises.[84] By 1789
Türk wrote that *allegro* meant "quick [*hurtig*], i.e., not quite as fast as *Presto*."[85]
However, a few pages further on he ruminated somewhat on its variability.
The passage emphasizes again the role of note values, texture, character, and
inner meaning in determining tempo:

> If one only knew . . . that an *Allegro* must be played more quickly than a
> *Largo*, etc., one would still have a very vague notion of the tempo. Therefore,
> the question is: how fast is the tempo of an *Allegro assai*, and then of other
> pieces [other headings] relatively? This question cannot be answered with ab-
> solute confidence, because certain accessory circumstances make many modi-
> fications necessary. For example, an *Allegro* with thirty-second notes intermixed
> must not be played as fast as one in which the fastest passages consist only of
> eighths. An *Allegro* for the church or in sacred cantatas, in a trio or quartet,
> etc. in strict style [*gearbeiteten*], must be taken in a far more moderate tempo
> than an *Allegro* for the theatre or in the so-called chamber style, for example,
> in symphonies, divertimentos, and so on. An *Allegro* containing lofty, solemn,
> and great ideas requires a slower and more emphatic pace than a piece with

the same heading in which the prevailing character is [one of] light-hearted joy, etc.[86]

The second edition of Türk's *Klavierschule,* in which numerous comments and revisions point to changes in performance practice, reported a change in the speed of *allegro* during the eighteenth century: "A far more moderate tempo is generally taken for granted for an Allegro composed fifty years or more ago than for a more recent composition with the same heading."[87]

Türk's comment was neither the first nor the last in the same vein. Half a century earlier Quantz had written similarly:

> What in former times was considered to be quite fast would have been played almost twice as slow as in the present day. An Allegro assai, Presto, Furioso, &c., was then written, and would have been played, only a little faster than an Allegretto is written and performed today. The large number of quick notes in the instrumental pieces of the earlier German composers thus looked much more difficult and hazardous than they sounded. Contemporary French musicians have retained this style of moderate speed in lively pieces to a large extent.[88]

In his study of tempos in Haydn's string quartets, Saslav concluded that Haydn preferred tempos on the faster side—especially fast tempos[89]—and that he was "a prime mover" in the speeding up of fast tempos and minuets that took place during his approximately 50 creative years.[90] Haydn requested having "the allegros taken a bit more quickly than usual" in his famous "Applausus" letter of 1768;[91] he encouraged the use of quick tempos again in letters of the 1790s.[92] Giuseppe Carpani considered Haydn "the inventor of the *prestissimo,* which before him not even timid orchestras feared."[93]

By 1811 the Paris correspondent for *AMZ* wrote that he remembered "exactly" how Mozart and Haydn had led their own symphonies in Vienna.

> They never took their *first* Allegros as fast as one hears them here, and also now no doubt in various German orchestras. Both let the Menuetts go by hurriedly. Haydn liked to take the Finales faster than Mozart—which certainly follows from the character and the manner in which these movements are written; however now [this] is sometimes forgotten by other conductors.[94]

Beethoven commented on the change in interpretation of *allegro,* as well as on the general problem of tempos, in a significant letter to the Viennese conductor Ignaz von Mosel, probably written in 1817.

> Sir:
> I am heartily delighted to know that you hold the same views as I do about our tempo indications which originated in the barbarous ages of music. For, to take one example, what can be more absurd than Allegro, which really signifies *merry,* and how very far removed we often are from the idea of that tempo. So much so that the piece itself means the *very opposite of the indication—* As for

those four chief movements, which, however, are far from embodying the truth
or the accuracy of the four chief winds, we would gladly *do without them*. But
the words describing the character of the composition are a different matter.
We cannot give these up. Indeed the tempo is more like the body, *but these
certainly refer to the spirit of the composition*— As for me, I have long been
thinking of abandoning those absurd descriptive terms, Allegro, Andante, Adagio, Presto [the "four chief movements"]; and Maelzel's metronome affords us
the best opportunity of doing so.[95]

Criticism from sources as diverse as Friedrich Rochlitz in *AMZ* (1799), Ludwig
Spohr while visiting Paris, and the *Harmonicon* of London (1825)—but all
contemporary with Beethoven—reveals frequent condemnation of the current
"unreasonably quick" *allegros*.[96]

The Meaning of *Assai*

There is accumulating documentation for the existence of a dual tradition
in the meaning of *assai*. In 1703 Brossard's *Dictionaire* [sic] *de musique* stated
that according to some this "adverb of quantity" meant "MUCH," but according
to others it meant that "the tempo ought not to be exaggerated" but should
remain a "judicious moderation of slowness and of speed."[97] David Fallows
reports that the anonymous *A Short Explication* (London, 1724) gave only
"moderately."[98] J. G. Walther's German translation of *allegro assai* in 1732
was *ziemlich geschwinde*,[99] "rather" or "moderately fast."

Ziemlich geschwind is also the translation of *assai allegro* that Beethoven
used for the second song of the cycle *An die ferne Geliebte* Op. 98, in which
he gave most of the verbal performance directions in both Italian and German.
Stewart Deas claims this as one of the more obvious clues in his persuasive
argument that Beethoven sometimes intended *assai* to mean "moderately" or
"rather," instead of the traditional "very."[100] Among other examples there is
the well-known instruction over the Kyrie of the Mass in C major, in which
the meaning of *assai* is clear once we really notice it: Andante con moto assai
vivace quasi Allegretto ma non troppo. The same meaning is intended in the
heading Allegro assai vivace ma serioso for the Scherzo of the String Quartet
Op. 95, composed three years after the Mass.

Nor would Beethoven have had to resort to early dictionaries or other
unique sources for this usage. In the *Nuovo Dizionario Italiano-Francese*, published in 1771–1772, both *beaucoup* (considerably, much) and *assez* (enough,
rather) are included in the definition of *assai* as an adverb.[101] "Assai, alcune
volte significa mediocremente" (Assai, sometimes means moderately) is followed by several sentences translated from Italian to French in which *assai* is
translated *assez*. Thus a dual meaning was part of the Italian of Beethoven's
time. Türk's explanation of *assai* would seem to allow some flexibility, for his
equivalents include *genug* (*sehr*) and *ziemlich*,[102] which translate respectively
as "enough" or "sufficiently"; "very"; and "moderately" or "rather." In the

second edition of his *Klavierschule* Türk strengthened the moderate tendency by adding *hinlänglich*,[103] "sufficiently" or "adequately."

The Allegro assai heading of Beethoven's Sonata Op. 57/i has to be played at a tempo that allows for the Più Allegro near the end. There are also two earlier sonata movements headed Allegro assai, the finale of Op. 2/3 and the Scherzo of Op. 14/2. Donald Tovey recommended "fast enough" for both, reminding his readers that *assai* originally had the same meaning as *assez*.[104] The Scherzo of Op. 14/2—discussed in chapter 5 for its playful slurring, which disguises the meter (p. 161)—needs a tempo that permits its subtleties to be heard.

On the other hand, Quantz and the Mozarts used *assai* as "much" or "very." Leopold Mozart wrote that "*Presto*, means quick, and *Allegro Assai* is but little different. *Molto Allegro* is slightly less than *Allegro Assai*. . . ."[105] Based on the contexts in which it occurs, Wolfgang's intention for *assai* would seem to follow suit.[106] Clementi, Hummel, and Czerny all defined *assai* with the single word "very."[107]

INCREASING INDIVIDUALIZATION OF TEMPO

> When a work by Beethoven had been performed, his first question was always, "How were the tempos?" Every other consideration seemed to be of secondary importance to him.
>
> —ANTON SCHINDLER[108]

The amount of latitude possible in choice of tempo for much Baroque and early Classic music was no longer appropriate for music of the Classic style. This music had gradually become increasingly tempo sensitive and suffered from distortion by an inappropriately chosen tempo or by divergence from a composer's carefully worded direction.

Tempo sensitivity is reflected in Kirnberger's article on "Tempo" ("Bewegung") in the first edition of Sulzer's *Allgemeine Theorie:*

> No one but he who has composed a piece is in the position to determine the most appropriate degree of movement for it. A small degree more or less can do much damage to the effect of the piece. Although many words have been devised for this purpose, they are still not sufficient. The tempo could be indicated precisely by actual establishment of the time in which the entire piece should be played.[109]

Türk quoted this passage and one from Johann Adolph Scheibe's *Über die musikalische Komposition* (1773) stating that the composer should write the proper duration in minutes and seconds over each piece.[110]

For Beethoven, tempo was an inherent part of the character of a composition. A letter of December 1826 to the publisher Schott demonstrates the degree to which the composer felt that successful performance depended on appropriate tempos:

> The metronome markings [of the *Missa Solemnis*] will be sent to you very soon. Do wait for them. In our century such indications are certainly necessary. Moreover I have received letters from Berlin informing me that the first performance of the [ninth] symphony was received with enthusiastic applause, which I ascribe largely to the metronome markings. We can scarcely have *tempi ordinari* any longer, since one must fall into line with the ideas of unfettered genius.[111]

That the performer "must fall into line with the ideas of unfettered genius" was Beethoven's call for greater sensitivity to the increasing singularity or individualization of tempo required by the new language and expression of his music. Rate of movement had become a more organic part of the tightly integrated formal and expressive structure. A poorly chosen tempo might well change the character of a composition.

Beethoven's expression *tempi ordinari* refers to the conventional standard tempos—as in the basic tempo groups or his "four chief movements" (p. 320)—that were determined by note value, meter, and character if there was no tempo heading, or by the same elements and a basic tempo word suggestive of a rather generalized movement.[112] Many indications of Haydn, Mozart, their contemporaries, and Beethoven in his early works consist of only such simple directions. However, as music became more tempo sensitive, *tempi ordinari* and the basic indications were no longer adequate. Composers increasingly added qualifiers to point out to interpreters refinements of movement and mood. In addition to the "first generation" of common qualifiers, such as *moderato, assai,* and *cantabile,* Mozart and Haydn occasionally used a phrase that expressed more nuance, such as Andante un poco adagio in Mozart's Sonata K. 309 or Andantino più tosto Allegretto in Haydn's Trio Hob. XV/16.

The attempt to define new tempos led Beethoven to more extensive use of qualifying clauses. As early as his Op. 7 (comp. 1796–1797), three of the four movements had expanded headings: Allegro molto e con brio; Largo, con gran expressione; and Poco Allegretto e grazioso. By 1807 the Kyrie of the Mass in C major had a heading (mentioned under *Assai*) in which Andante con moto is qualified by two complete phrases, each also used as independent tempo headings by Beethoven: Andante con moto assai vivace quasi Allegretto ma non troppo. For some of the late works Beethoven tried double headings, the descriptive German for "the spirit of the composition" and the Italian tempo indication for the "body," as he had written to Mosel. Thus for Op. 101/i, we find Allegretto ma non troppo, *Etwas lebhaft und mit der innigsten Empfindung* (somewhat lively and with the most intimate feeling).

Beyond searching for more explicit tempo headings, Beethoven often altered headings some time after composition, or—as we have seen in the discussion of *alla breve*—even changed time signatures, all in an effort to clarify his intentions for performers. In 1809, after the manuscript of the song "Andenken" was sent to Breitkopf & Härtel but before its publication, he directed the firm to change the Andante con moto heading. "In the song in D mark the tempo Allegretto—for if you don't people will sing it too slowly."[113] Presumably it was for the same reason that he later added molto semplice e cantabile to the original Adagio heading in the holograph of Op. 111/ii, for a movement that goes too slowly cannot sing. (The four new words appear as a group in larger letters and at a different slant.[114]) But Beethoven had already endorsed the newly invented metronome as a way of achieving more effective performances of his music.

THE METRONOME

Beethoven and the Metronome

The invention of the metronome offered Beethoven the opportunity to leave more precise information about tempos for his music. His enthusiasm for the device—known in its earlier form as the chronometer—was first made public in the *Wiener Vaterländische Blätter* of 13 October 1813. The article reports that

> Herr Beethoven looks upon this invention as a welcome means [with which] to secure the performance of his highly original compositions in all places in the tempos intended for them, which he regrets is so frequently lacking.[115]

On 6 February 1817 Beethoven's name appeared in the *Wiener Allgemeine Musikalische Zeitung* along with the names of other "celebrated masters" who "committed themselves to marking their future compositions according to the scale of Mälzel's metronome."[116] From this time to the end of Beethoven's life, letters, publication of metronomic indications for some of his most important compositions, and another public notice demonstrated his continued support for the instrument. These documents include the letters to Mosel and Schott, quoted earlier; the publication in 1817 and 1819 of two pamphlets by Steiner and Co., the first containing metronomizations for Symphonies Nos. 1 to 8 and the enormously popular Septet Op. 20, the second giving them for the String Quartets through Op. 95;[117] and an enthusiastic notice cosigned by Beethoven and Salieri in the *Wiener Allgemeine Musikalische Zeitung* of 14 February 1818, which reads in part:

> Maelzel's metronome has arrived! The usefulness of his invention will be proved more and more. Moreover, all the composers of Germany, England and France have adopted it. . . . [We] recommend the metronome as . . . an indispensable aid to all . . . pupils. . . . For since the pupil . . . must not in the [teacher's] absence arbitrarily sing or play out of time, by means of the metronome his feeling for time and rhythm will quickly be . . . guided and corrected. . . . We think that we should acclaim this invention of Maelzel's, which

indeed is so useful from this point of view also, for it seems that for this particular advantage it has not yet been sufficiently appreciated.[118]

Beethoven's well-known negative exclamation, "the deuce take everything mechanical," has gained too much importance by being quoted out of context. It is contained in a letter to Schott of 19 August 1826 immediately followed by, "I have had a great misfortune. But with God's help all will perhaps turn out well."[119] Undoubtedly the attempted suicide by his nephew, Karl, whom Beethoven treated as a son, was a severe blow. Nevertheless, he sent metronomizations for the Ninth Symphony to Schott in a letter of 13 October 1826, and a letter of December 1826 to Schott is one of several in which Beethoven wrote of providing metronomizations for the *Missa Solemnis*.[120] A letter of 18 March 1827 to Moscheles—dictated only eight days before Beethoven's death—contained the metronomizations of the Ninth Symphony for a performance in London.[121] Beethoven also left metronomic indications for the Sonata Op. 106 and for some miscellaneous works.[122]

Problems Related to Beethoven's Metronomizations

The unusually fast tempos produced by some of the metronomizations Beethoven prescribed have raised questions about the accuracy of his metronome and about how seriously he meant those indications. Although it is true, as Schindler reports, that metronomes of two different sizes existed during Beethoven's life,[123] both types were based on the division of the minute into seconds and gave the same tempo at the same setting.[124] These tempos correspond to those on our modern metronomes, although individual instruments of any period may be subject to insignificant variations in calibration. That Beethoven was sensitive to the adjustment of his metronome and aware of its need of repair from time to time is also evident in his correspondence.[125]

In relation to fast tempos we should recall that Beethoven's playing was known for its unusual bravura and speed (see p. 28 and chap. 6, n. 69).[126] At times his intention even for an ordinary tempo heading was faster than his contemporaries understood. His comment about the tempo of "Andenken," quoted above, is explicit in this regard. Hermann Beck reports that in each successive version of *Fidelio* (1804–1805, 1805–1806, and 1814) many of the tempo indications were made faster. "Probably, according to Beethoven's conception, the tempos were taken . . . too slowly in the performances."[127] Originally the finale, "Wer ein holdes Weib errungen," was marked Maestoso. At the edge of the first version Beethoven wrote "Lebhafteres Tempo" (More lively tempo) according to Beck. In the second version the finale was marked Maestoso Vivace, in the third, Allegro ma non troppo.

Beethoven was aware that he may have been breaking new ground with his tempo requirement for the trio of the Quartet Op. 74. In an attempt to help performers understand the directions, he sent the following instruction after the manuscript had gone to Breitkopf & Härtel:

There is something else to be observed in the case of the quartet, namely that in the third movement in C minor, where the Più presto quasi prestissimo begins, another NB. should be added, that is to say, NB. Si ha s'imaginer la battuta di 6/8 [One must imagine that the time signature is 6/8].[128]

Thus two measures in 3/4 become one in 6/8. Nine years later Beethoven expressed this direction precisely by metronomizing the Presto at $\bullet$. = 100 and the trio at $\bullet$· = 100.

Further, although the speed of some of Beethoven's metronomizations exceeds expectations, the indications by Hummel, Czerny, and Moscheles are generally not inconsistent with his. Hummel's brisk indications for his chamber arrangements of Mozart's last six symphonies, published in 1823, compare directly with some of Beethoven's for movements of similar rhythmic character in his String Quartets Op. 18 and his Septet Op. 20.[129] (The concept of "rhythmic character" and tempo comparisons is explored in "Beethoven's 'Moderate' Minuets" below.) Czerny's metronomizations for Beethoven's works with piano and for his own four-hand arrangements of symphonies and chamber works by Haydn and Mozart demonstrate that Czerny, too, shared a related tempo sensibility.[130]

The remaining questions revolve around the care with which Beethoven prepared his metronomizations and the possible effect of his deafness on their practicality. Although he could no longer conduct effectively by 1817, the year in which his indications for Symphonies Nos. 1 to 8 and the Septet were published, there is continuing evidence of his successful efforts to correct tempos in rehearsals. In 1822, during the dress rehearsal of *Die Weihe des Hauses* for the opening of the Josephstadt Theatre, Beethoven was able to perceive that the soprano soloist was dragging the tempo and successfully pointed out to her those places that needed correction.[131]

Even in 1825 the violinist Joseph Böhm reported rehearsing the Quartet Op. 127 "under Beethoven's own eyes." "With close attention his eyes followed the bows and therefore he was able to judge the smallest fluctuations in tempo or rhythm and correct them immediately."[132]

Sir George Smart witnessed a rehearsal of the Quartet Op. 132 supervised by Beethoven on 9 September 1825:

He directed the performers. . . . A staccato passage not being expressed to the satisfaction of his eye, for alas, he could not hear, he seized Holz's violin and played the passage a quarter of a tone too flat. . . . All paid him the greatest attention.[133]

Beethoven's nephew, Karl, helped with the metronomizations for the Ninth Symphony.[134] Beethoven also brought to that process the experience of having conducted, coached, and heard many performances of his symphonies and string quartets in earlier years. Just as the lighter action of the fortepiano assisted fast playing, so did the other instruments and ensembles of the period. The orchestras were smaller. The lighter, differently balanced bows of the stringed instruments and the softer tonguing of the wind instruments, as well as their leaner pliant sound, made rapid tempos less difficult to attain. Rudolf Kolisch goes so far as to write,

> I can conscientiously maintain, . . . on the basis of experience, that all the tempi required by Beethoven of stringed instruments, at least, are perfectly playable on the basis of the average technique of today.[135]

At a recent performance of the Ninth Symphony, Benjamin Zander conducted the Boston Philharmonic Orchestra, playing modern instruments, with tempos very close to Beethoven's indications. The clarification of the structural notes and the ornamentation (usually played far too slowly) in the Adagio molto e cantabile was arresting. At these tempos it was also possible to adhere closely to Beethoven's dynamics, especially the prolonged soft ones. The resulting increase in dynamic contrast added to the excitement of this convincing rendition.

Unfortunately for pianists, Beethoven's only metronomizations for his solo piano works are those for the virtuosic "Hammerklavier" Sonata Op. 106. These indications, considered impractically fast to varying degrees for the first, third, and fourth movements (exclusive of the Largo introduction) by most who play it, have been widely discussed. Brief consideration of a few of the problems surrounding any metronomization may prove helpful in reflecting on the true role of the metronome and in dealing with the markings by Beethoven and other composers that seem problematic.[136] Once convinced of the significance of Beethoven's indications, the pianist can use information appropriate to the piano pieces that has been extrapolated from Beethoven's markings for the symphonies, quartets, and miscellaneous works based on similarities of rhythmic movement and musical traits. Rudolf Kolisch's "Tempo and Character in Beethoven's Music," which relates Beethoven's metronomizations to almost all the sonata movements, is a valuable contribution for such cross-referencing.[137] The sections "Beethoven's 'Moderate' Minuets" and "Extrapolations of Other Tempos" in this chapter will demonstrate the approach.

Universal Problems of Metronomization

It is not known how Beethoven arrived at the indications for Op. 106 or for most of his other metronomizations. The Conversation Book record of the sessions on 17 September 1826, during which metronomizations for the Ninth Symphony were determined, suggests that Beethoven played each incipit on the piano and that nephew Karl read the metronome.[138] Of course, metronomizing orchestral music at the piano has the danger that some of that repertoire can be played faster on the one instrument than would be practical or effective with the orchestra itself. (The situation might be even worse if a composer hummed the themes.) Presumably Beethoven's experience as a conductor tempered this risk to some degree.

A composer may also set a metronome going and arrive at an indication by readjusting the setting until the ticking sounds like the piece as he hears it in his mind's ear or as he conducts it in his study. However, when actually played, the notes may not fit well into the time allowed, either because they cannot be clearly heard at the suggested speed or because they cannot even be well played. It is easy to hear a piece in one's imagination at a tempo that does not allow the physical activity necessary for playing with nuance or, in some cases, even for playing all the notes.

However it is chosen, ideally a metronomization should be tested and, if necessary, adjusted at several different times to ensure that it does not represent an extreme occasioned by particular circumstances and that the tempo wears well. Brahms discussed this problem in a letter to Clara Schumann in February 1878, when they were preparing the complete works of Robert Schumann for publication:

> To give metronome marks immediately for dozens of works, as you wish, seems to me not possible. In any case you must allow the work to lie for at least a year, and examine it periodically. You will then write in new numbers each time and finally have the best solution.[139]

In addition to the many musical characteristics that influence tempo choice, there are also the circumstances and environment peculiar to each performance. Given all the variables, belief in one metronomic indication as an absolute tempo is untenable. In the nineteenth century Moscheles considered a metronomic indication "a slight guide for performers and conductors. Its object is to show the general time of a movement, particularly at its commencement...."[140]

More recently Max Rudolf has applied this interpretation to the problems of Beethoven's metronomizations:

> In Beethoven's case, the critics of his metronome figures have failed to explain why, sometimes within the same work or movement, some of his markings are readily accepted, others flatly rejected. Perhaps they forget that the metronome was never intended to pinpoint the speed of music. It was meant to provide information regarding the character of the music and to prevent the performer from straying too far from the composer's intention. For the conductor, metronome indications are invaluable as a guide to define a tempo span that preserves the character of the music.[141]

This interpretation of a metronomic indication also applies to those suggested by qualified contemporaries of a composer and to those derived indirectly by extrapolation, as in the studies of Kolisch, Beck, and Newman, and in the section "Beethoven's 'Moderate' Minuets" below. Of course, a performance of the Allegro molto e con brio of Op. 10/1 with three beats in a measure instead of a single pulse—as Czerny and Moscheles suggest (in Appendix B to this chapter) and as Beethoven metronomized all his triple-meter fast *allegros (con brio, vivace,* etc.)—would alter its character beyond what could possibly be considered appropriate. What matters is that the chosen tempo not violate the spirit of a piece as best the performer can discern it, not only from the music itself but also from any related information left by the composer.[142]

The "Hammerklavier" Sonata

Czerny studied Op. 106 with Beethoven "several times."[143] It is, therefore, not without significance that although he cited as "the major difficulty" of the first movement the "unusually fast and fiery tempo" designated by the composer ($\lrcorner = 138$), and also remarked that the second movement must be "as fleet as possible" and the fourth "very lively, very strong," he did not suggest, or report having resorted to, slower tempos. On the contrary, he added that "comprehension of the whole first movement . . . develops with frequent playing after [the movement] has been correctly studied in the proper tempo."[144]

It is not possible to know how close Czerny's performances were to the metronomizations. Certainly the shallow, light action of the Viennese fortepiano during Beethoven's life would have made it less difficult to come within the spirit of the indicated tempos. However, Moscheles's comment of 1841 shows that at least one important contemporary of Czerny considered Beethoven's indication for the first movement problematic:

> I have, in my edition of this Sonata, marked the time of the first movement 138 . . . because Beethoven himself had fixed that number. He . . . gives it with a minim—I with a crotchet; but neither of these can, to my mind, be made to suit the character of the movement. The minim increases it to so fearful a prestissimo as Beethoven could never have intended, since he desired the *Assai,* originally prefixed to the *Allegro,* to be omitted. The crotchet slackens the movement all too much; and although I have, in my edition, allowed Beethoven's numbers to remain, in deference to the great man, yet I would advise the player to hold a middle course, according to the following mark: $\lrcorner = 116$.[145]

Was Moscheles's reaction to the speed of this movement influenced by the deeper, heavier action of the fortepianos built in London—his permanent residence from 1825 to 1846—or by his preference for "precise execution," especially a crisp touch and clarity of phrasing?[146] Probably both. Apparently Moscheles understood the *assai* here in its more usual meaning as "very," for he implied that Beethoven reduced the speed with its removal.

Perhaps the essence of Beethoven's message is to play the movement as fast as possible with an appropriate interpretation; that, in turn, introduces the variables related to the technical capacities and interpretation of each performer. Moscheles's suggested reduction to $\lrcorner = 116$ is just at the bottom of Paul Badura-Skoda's recommended "compromise" of a ten to fifteen percent reduction in the tempos of the first and third movements.[147] Schnabel's recording at $\lrcorner = 126-138$ loses clarity and finesse.[148] Paul Badura-Skoda recorded the movement on a piano at $\lrcorner = $ ca. 116 and later on a fortepiano by Graf at ca. 126.[149] Peter Serkin plays at that same tempo on another instrument by Graf, suggesting the influence of the fortepiano's tone and action; yet Friedrich Gulda matched ca. 126 very successfully on a modern instrument.[150] Several first-rank performers, including a fortepianist, have recorded the movement noticeably slower at ca. 96.[151]

SIX METRONOMIZATIONS OF BEETHOVEN'S SONATAS

The Haslinger *Gesamtausgabe;* Czerny and Moscheles as Metronomizers

In December 1828 the Viennese publisher Tobias Haslinger announced his *Sämtliche Werke von Ludw. van Beethoven.* The reader is immediately informed that editing for "tempo indications according to Maelzel's metronome" and for "performance nuances" was being carried out by Carl Czerny, Ignaz Schuppanzigh, and Karl Holz.[152] Since Schuppanzigh and Holz were violinists, we can assume that Czerny edited at least the first state of the piano music, although nowhere in the printed works does his name or that of any other editor appear.

The pianist seeking guidance is well advised to consider the metronomizations of almost all of Beethoven's piano music provided by Carl Czerny and of the sonatas by Ignaz Moscheles. (The general importance of Czerny's observations on Beethoven performance was set forth in chapter 1.) Czerny's comments and his last two sets of metronomic indications were recorded long enough after the composer's death to raise questions regarding their credibility. However, comparison of his suggestions with contemporary information—including metronomizations by Moscheles and Beethoven's own indications for other works—demonstrates that on the whole Czerny's annotations are a fair representation and, therefore, significant for the pianist today. Nottebohm considered Czerny one of the few dependable witnesses to Beethoven's style:

> Czerny had not only had instruction in piano playing with Beethoven for some time (1801 and later) and had often heard Beethoven play, but he also knew what piano playing was and he certainly knew the playing of his time from every angle.[153]

And of Czerny's metronomizations:

> Although not of authentic validity, still these indications can lay claim to a certain confidence, especially for those works of which we know that Czerny either heard them played by Beethoven or studied [them] under his instruction. ... Anyone who knew Czerny personally, who had the opportunity to observe his nature, which was above all directed toward the practical, will believe him capable of impressing firmly on his memory a tempo that he had heard, and will have noticed the certainty that he had in such outwardly tangible musical matters.[154]

There can be no doubt that Czerny understood the full importance of his metronomizations. Following Beethoven, he placed "the right time" first among the "important conditions which are indispensably necessary, and upon which everything else depends. . . . the whole character of the piece is disfigured by a wrong degree of movement."[155]

Also instructive is the similarity of comments made quite separately by Beethoven and Czerny about the tempo of the fourth movement of the Piano Trio Op. 70/2. In a letter to Breitkopf & Härtel dated 26 May 1809, Beethoven wrote "there should be no ritardando in that whole movement."[156] Czerny's comment of 1846 on that movement concludes, "The whole in a steady tempo, without lingering anywhere."[157]

Neither did Moscheles attempt such editorializing lightly. Because of Schindler's attack on all the metronomizations of Beethoven's works,[158] Moscheles sought to defend the background and care that he brought to the task:

> In superintending for Messrs. Cramer and Co. the new edition of [Beethoven's] works, and in metronomising the several compositions, I have not merely listened to my own musical feelings, but [have] been guided by my recollections of what I gathered from Beethoven's own playing, and that of the Baroness Ertman [sic], whom I have heard perform many of his works in his presence, and to his entire satisfaction. . . . In some of the quick movements I have purposely refrained from giving way to that rapidity of piano-forte execution, so largely developed at the present time. It is with satisfaction that I add, that the *tempi* I have ventured to give differ very slightly from those affixed to Haslinger's Vienna edition, by Carl Czerny, whom I consider to be a competent authority in the matter.[159]

Czerny prepared three, perhaps even four, sets of metronomizations for the sonatas, and Moscheles prepared three. Six of these sets form Appendix B to this chapter. The two sets widely known as Czerny's are those in his *Proper Performance* of 1846 and in Simrock's edition of the sonatas published between 1856 and 1868,[160] for which Czerny was the editor. Another of Czerny's sets is in the original state of the Haslinger *Gesamtausgabe*. This edition also included the three early "Kurfürsten" Sonatas but lacked Opp. 2, 7, and 106 since Haslinger could not get Artaria's permission for their publication.[161]

At some time, probably from the mid to late 1830s to 1842, 60 percent of the metronomizations in Haslinger's edition were altered, and additional dynamics and slurs were added, creating a second state, which I call Haslinger 2.[162] We do not know the origin of these changes. They might have been entered piecemeal, as additional copies of particular sonatas were reprinted, or as a group, only after completion of the entire first state, which has been dated variously as 1832? and 1837?[163] On sonatas from the second state, evidence of the original metronomizations is often present in the form of remnants of older numbers under the new ones or blacker engraving for the freshly cut numbers.

The metronomizations in the Haslinger edition raise some interesting questions. What are the important differences between the indications of Haslinger

1 and 2? Why were these changes made? How do these sets compare with Czerny's later sets? Might there be any clues to the editor of Haslinger 2? Do the successive changes in these four sets relate to other tempo trends in European performance practices? And finally, what can we learn from these quasi-contemporary metronomizations that may be appropriate for our current performance of Beethoven's piano sonatas?

The *Gesamtausgabe* and Czerny's Other Metronomizations Compared

Chart III contains some numeric and percentage information relevant to these questions. In order to consider the possible significance of the tempo changes we need to compare the overall speeds of the four sets of metronomizations, the percentage of change from one set to the next later one, how much of the change is significant, and what kinds of movements or tempos were the most changed.

The first two columns in Chart III show the number and percentage of movements or sections (of movements) whose fastest and slowest metronomizations occur in each set. Sixty-seven of the 85 movements in the study, or 79 percent, have their fastest tempo markings in Haslinger 1; while nine movements, or eleven percent (including six *adagios* and *largos*) have their slowest indications in this edition. (Of the 67 movements that have their fastest indications here, 43 have the same fast marking in another set.) Comparable figures for the other sets show that the metronomizations are, overall, the fastest in Haslinger 1 and the slowest in *Proper Performance,* in which 69 percent of the movements have their slowest indications. After Haslinger 1, the metronomizations are the second fastest in the Simrock edition.

The remaining sections of the chart address changes between the successive sets of metronomizations. Of these columns, the first shows percentage of change; the others show degree and direction of change. Here I consider a difference of one or two metronome steps insignificant; but a change of three or more is significant, since that degree of tempo change is obvious to the listener and may alter the character of a movement.[164] As a point of reference, through all the sets the metronomizations of approximately half the movements in this survey fluctuated only insignificantly or, in three cases, remained the same. The indications of 24 movements fluctuated three steps—the smallest significant change, and those of only nineteen fluctuated four steps or more.

The number of indications changed between Haslinger 1 and 2 is the smallest of that between any of the sets: 60 percent (compared with 66 percent and 80 percent between the successively later sets). But more important is the kind of change—significant, insignificant, faster, slower—and the tempo and movement types involved. Interestingly, two measures of the changes between these two editions are the greatest in their respective categories: the proportion of significant change (37 percent) and of change in one direction (88 percent), here to slower tempos. (Fifteen movements became significantly slower, and 30 more became insignificantly slower; in all, 45 of the 51 indications changed

CHART III. Comparison of Four Metronomizations of Beethoven's Piano Sonatas

Based on the 85 movements or sections (of movements) with markings in all sets for which Czerny may have been responsible. Op. 106 is not included in these statistics. Of the 85 movements/sections surveyed, 54 (63.5%) are marked Allegretto or faster.

Set	No. of movements with fastest MM	No. of movements with slowest MM	Movements whose MM have changed from previous set									
				Degree of change								
				Significant			Insignificant			Total		
			No.	+	–	Total	+	–	Total	+	–	
Haslinger 1, Czerny 1828–ca. 1833 or 1837?	67 (43 shared)	9										
	79%	11%										
Haslinger 2, possibly by Czerny 183?–1842?	29	29	51	4	15	19	2	30	32	6	45	
	34%	34%	60%	8%	29%	37%	4%	59%	63%	12%	88%	
Proper Performance, Czerny 1846	11	59 (26 shared)	56	1	9	10	8	38	46	9	47	
	13%	69%	66%	2%	16%	18%	14%	68%	82%	16%	84%	
Simrock, Czerny 1856–1868	44 (33 shared)	20	68	14	3	17	42	9	51	56	12	
	52%	24%	80%	20.5%	4.4%	25%	62%	13%	75%	82.5%	17.4%	

became slower.) All but six of these changes pertain to fast movements.[165] Of the 29 movements that have their slowest indications in Haslinger 2, 59 percent had their fastest indications in Haslinger 1, a clear sign of the wide swing toward slower tempos between these two sets.

The trend toward slower tempos continued in the metronomizations that Czerny prepared for *Proper Performance*. Eighty-four percent of the changes were to slower indications, making this set, as noted earlier, the slowest. These changes, as well as the movements that are slowest in this set, are spread among all tempo and movement types, whereas the changes made in Haslinger 2 affected mainly fast movements.

Might the nature of the changes between Haslinger 2 and *Proper Performance* offer any clues to the identity of the editor of Haslinger 2? The eighteen percent of significant change between these two sets is the lowest between any— only half of what it had been between Haslinger 1 and 2. Compared with the indications in Haslinger 2, the changes for *Proper Performance* were primarily insignificant adjustments, suggesting by and large Czerny's approval of the direction taken by the changes in Haslinger 2. Therefore, it is conceivable that Czerny might also have been responsible for the metronomizations in Haslinger 2; or, at the least, that he found them close to what he considered appropriate when he prepared his indications for *Proper Performance*. As far as I can ascertain, the only other pianist known to have metronomized Beethoven's sonatas in the 1830s was Moscheles, and he was preparing the edition that Cramer of London published between about 1834 and 1838–1839 (see below).

The Simrock indications show the highest percentage of change, of which 82.5 percent is a marked redress toward faster tempos. These metronomizations also show the highest percentage of change to significantly faster tempos, 20.5. Fifty-two percent of the movements have their fastest indications in this edition, making it second in speed to Haslinger 1.

Tempo Trends in Europe

Were there any tempo trends in Europe that might provide insight into the changes in these metronomizations? Our earlier discussion of Mozart's reaction to Clementi's playing suggested that the differing tempo interpretations of the two performers might have resulted in part from differences in national style. Curt Sachs's conclusions that by the mid-eighteenth century tempos were more moderate in Italy, England, and France than they were in Germany[166] is supported by Emanuel Bach's statement: "In certain other countries [i.e., outside of Germany] there is a marked tendency to play adagios too fast and allegros too slow."[167] The wider spread of tempos in Germany has also been cited on pp. 314 and 319.

The trend for fast movements to be played increasingly quickly seems to have continued during and after Beethoven's life, particularly in central Europe (as discussed in "The Changing Allegro" above). Both Joseph Fischhof, a Viennese pianist and music historian, and Edward Holmes, an important English music critic, reported that the orchestra of the "first-rate Prague Conservatory took the tempos of the allegro movements in Mozart's symphonies far faster ... than they were performed according to tradition and hitherto existing custom ..."[168] or than was customary in England.[169] In 1847 Fischhof, who claimed to have observed tempos from 1819, wrote that from the 1820s there had been a tendency for German orchestras to take Beethoven's compositions faster than they were played in Vienna.[170] Mendelssohn and his followers generally favored fluent movement for slow tempos and quite rapid movement for fast tempos.[171] Robert Schumann, Eduard Devrient, and others wrote admiringly of Mendelssohn's interpretations,[172] but Wagner derided his choice of tempos.

Indeed, the faster tempos that pervaded German playing were a common cause for compliant. In 1839 G. W. Fink, music critic and editor of *AMZ*, wrote of the frequent "bitter complaints against the bungling of Mozart's works by the choice of exaggerated tempos."[173] Accustomed to more moderate tempos in France, Berlioz was "astonished" at the fast tempos he heard throughout Germany in 1841 and declared that their use in the performance of French operas represented an "unfaithfulness of execution."[174] In 1844 Ferdinand Gassner "protested against the tearing pace of quick movements at the present time."[175]

Liszt and Wagner reversed this trend. In the early 1840s Liszt adopted "the slower tempos [that were] customary in Vienna itself,"[176] where fast tempos had not accelerated as much as elsewhere. His Weimar performances were highly praised in the *AMZ* of 6 March 1844 by an anonymous critic, who noted specifically that "Liszt has taken the Beethoven symphonies generally in slower tempos than we heard them earlier, with surprising advantage for their effect."[177] Did the critic ask whether Liszt's tempos were consonant with Beethoven's tempo ideas, which we know to have been faster than those of many of his contemporaries?

Wagner was inclined toward fast tempos at the start of his conducting career,[178] but two and a half years in Paris (1839–1842), where François Habeneck was the premier conductor, seem to have initiated a change in direction. Habeneck, whose Beethoven performances were considered unsurpassed in his lifetime,[179] applied "conspicuously moderate" tempos to the Beethoven symphonies.[180] Even Schindler found Habeneck's tempos "very thoughtful and deliberate." He stated that Habeneck "explored" these "immense works ... as thoroughly as if the great master had been his personal guide."[181] High praise indeed from Beethoven's self-appointed posthumous guardian! Under Habeneck's influence Wagner turned in the direction that led eventually to his exaggeratedly slow tempos, based in part on what he considered the expression of the melodic line. Wagner's conducting gradually became a dominant force throughout Europe, and the term "Wagnerian tempo" was coined. This slowing down affected slow movements ("the pure Adagio ... cannot be taken too slow") and allegro movements with "*emotional sentimental* significance," especially Beethoven's; but in the "*naive* species of Allegro," especially that of

final movements "grown out of the Rondeau, . . . the purely rhythmic movement . . . celebrates its orgies; and it is consequently impossible to take these
movements too quick."[182]

Moscheles's reminiscence from around 1861 reflects the pervasiveness of
Wagner's influence:

> I know many think me old-fashioned, but the more I consider the tendency
> of modern taste, . . . the more strenuously will I uphold that which I know to
> be sound art, and side with those who can appreciate a Haydn's playfulness, a
> Mozart's Cantilena, and a Beethoven's surpassing grandeur. What antidotes
> have we here for all these morbid moanings and overwrought effects! . . . Here
> as elsewhere I miss the right "Tempi," and look in vain for the traditions of
> my youth. That tearing speed which sweeps away many a little note; that spin-
> ning out of an Andante until it becomes an Adagio, an "Andante con moto,"
> in which there is no "moto" at all, an "Allegro comodo" which is anything but
> comfortable. . . .[183]

This tradition of Wagnerian tempos, especially in regard to slow movements
and "moderate" minuets is very much alive today.[184] It has been an important
element in the strong resistance of many contemporary musicians to adopting,
or at least experimenting with and trying to understand, Beethoven's own
metronomizations and the next best that we have, those of Czerny and Moscheles.

On the basis of Beethoven's personal inclination toward unusually fast
tempos, as well as from what appears to have been a trend in central Europe
during most of the first half of the nineteenth century (although less so in
Vienna), it is possible to speculate that the metronomizations of Haslinger 1
might represent the essence of Beethovenian tempos, or as close a contemporary suggestion as we have for his piano sonatas. But what accounts for the
slowing down of these tempos so dramatically in Haslinger 2? Was there, after
all, a different editor? Had Czerny been too caught up in the trend toward
faster tempos when he metronomized Haslinger 1? Was he insufficiently experienced in the subtleties of using the relatively new tool? I doubt it. Had he
chosen the indications in Haslinger 1 by listening to the metronome at his desk
but without actually playing the pieces? If the editor of Haslinger 2 was also
Czerny, did he conclude that many of his original metronomizations were too
fast for what he later considered Beethoven's intentions to have been? Was
the editor of Haslinger 2 adapting the tempos to the increasingly heavy actions,
deeper key dip, and changing tone quality of the developing piano? Was he
influenced by sheer practicality, by the inability of pianists to play the original
tempos, or by the results of pianists trying to achieve them?[185] It is often said
that as musicians age their perceptions deepen, and that change broadens their
sense of time and tempo. Is this part of what was happening to Czerny? For
the present, at least, there are no certain answers.

Czerny's Metronomizations of the 1840s and 1850s

By the time Czerny prepared the metronomizations for *Proper Performance,* the slowest set, he might have been influenced by the Liszt–Wagner tempos. In this set, for example, he slowed the Grave of Op. 13 from ♪ = 58 to ♪ = 92, the Andante of Op. 14/2 from ♩ = 66 to ♩ = 116, and the Allegro ma non troppo of Op. 78 from ♩ = 132 to 116. Only the Prestissimo of Op. 109 became significantly faster. Another interesting observation about the indications in *Proper Performance* is that of twelve *andantes* in this survey, nine became slower, two significantly. Ten of the twelve had remained unchanged in Haslinger 2, but the other two had been slowed there, one significantly. By the 1840s Czerny might have been bending toward the slow *andante* of the nineteenth century, whose roots actually antedated the development of the Liszt–Wagner tempos (cf. p. 315). It is the prevailing persistence of this slow *andante* today that leads many musicians to treat Baroque and Classic *andantes* as slow movements rather than as "the mean between fast and slow." Any reader can easily perceive the difference between the two *andantes* by playing the Theme of the Andante con variazioni of Op. 26 first at ♩ = 80, as Czerny (and later Moscheles) metronomized it in Haslinger 1 and Simrock, and then at ♩ = 63, as it is not uncommonly played today.

Czerny's metronomizations in the Simrock edition, all presumably prepared by 1857, moved back to a position between the tempos of Haslinger 1 and 2. Perhaps Czerny felt he had strayed too far from the Beethovenian spirit. The movements that became faster were spread through all tempo types, but they included eight of ten minuets and scherzos, and nine of twelve *andantes* (one changed significantly), perhaps countering any influence of the slow *andante*. Most of the slow movements in the Simrock edition have either the same metronomic indication that they had in Haslinger 1 or one somewhat faster. Thus to the end Czerny resisted the trend toward Wagnerian *adagios* for Beethoven's sonatas.

Unfortunately we may never know the rationale for the changes in the four sets of metronomizations. Curiously, the indications for sonatas that Czerny said he had studied with Beethoven were changed about as much as the others.[186] The only movements about which he seems not to have changed his mind at all are Op. 53/i (Allegro con brio), Op. 109/i (for the Adagio espressivo), and in sonatas metronomized in only three sets—Op. 49/2 (Allegro, ma non troppo and Tempo di Menuetto) and Op. 79/ii (Andante).

Nottebohm was attentive to the differences in metronomizations of at least three of these sets, as evidenced in his bound collection of Beethoven's sonatas in the Gesellschaft der Musikfreunde. His copy of Op. 13 is from the second state of the Haslinger edition, in which the Adagio cantabile became significantly faster and the final Allegro significantly slower. Nottebohm either put more trust in or preferred the earlier metronomizations, for he abraded off those of the second set that had been changed and entered those of the first. Even if he knew who had prepared the metronomizations for Haslinger 2, he did not mention it in his writing. Possibly Nottebohm preferred the earlier indications out of conviction that they were closer to Beethoven's time and practice, or because the greater spread of slow and fast tempos was more in keeping with his taste. However, he was interested enough in Czerny's indications of 1846 that he wrote those that differed from the printed indications into many of the sonatas, including Op. 13, with the label "Cz."

Moscheles's Metronomizations; Comparison with Czerny's

Moscheles prepared his first complete set of metronomizations for an edition by Cramer of London, probably published between about 1834 and 1838–1839.[187] His second set, in which only 26 (23 percent) of the 115 indications (excluding those of Op. 106) differ from those of the first set, was prepared for an edition by Hallberger of Stuttgart published between "1858? and 1867 at latest."[188] Moscheles's changes for the Hallberger edition were divided equally between movements made slower and faster, but only four movements were made significantly slower while eight were made significantly faster. Moscheles's two sets of indications are much closer to each other than are any two of Czerny's.

The closest relationship of the six sets of metronomizations is between those of the 1850s to the 1860s: Czerny's for Simrock and Moscheles's for Hallberger. Of 115 movements or sections of movements with indications by Czerny in the Simrock edition and by Moscheles in the Hallberger edition, 66 (57 percent) are the same. This remarkable correspondence is significantly higher than that between any two of Czerny's sets. From Op. 78 to Op. 111 all but three of Moscheles's metronomizations are the same as Czerny's.

Only twenty (17 percent) of all the indications in those two sets differ significantly. Twelve of Moscheles's set are significantly faster (two slow movements, two *andantes,* and eight faster movements); eight are significantly slower (two *andantes* and six faster movements). While fifteen (63 percent) of all the slow movements or sections have the same metronomizations in both sets, five of the remaining nine are faster in Moscheles's edition—two by four steps, the others insignificantly. Similar proportions prevail among the *andante* movements or sections: ten (63 percent) are the same in both sets, and four of the remaining six are faster in Moscheles's, two significantly so. Overall, Moscheles's indications in the Hallberger edition are slightly faster than Czerny's for Simrock.

Conclusion

We may still ponder the question of whether the tempos of Haslinger 1, those closest in time to Beethoven, or the tempos of the Simrock and Hallberger editions, which represent the considered opinion of two respected pianists from Beethoven's circle, better approximate the composer's intentions. Regardless, the differences found among performance tempos of many movements today are considerably greater than the differences for the same movements among all the metronomizations by Czerny and Moscheles. A habituated late nine-teenth-century tradition still influences our tempo sense. The metronome marks in Appendix B can help us close the gap between present practice and some-thing closer to Beethoven's, at least as two of his associates recorded it.

FAST AND "MODERATE" MINUETS

Two types of minuets existed during the eighteenth century and through the Classic era. The type more usual in Classic music, a fast piece although often headed Allegretto, moves with one pulse per measure; the more moderate minuet,[189] frequently headed Menuetto, Moderato or Tempo di Menuetto, moves with three beats per measure and sometimes contains subdivisions of eighth-note triplets and sixteenth notes. The ancestry of these types may derive from the original differences between the generally faster Italian minuet, often notated in 3/8 or 6/8,[190] and the stately French minuet, "more moderate than fast,"[191] in 3/4 time. The young Mozart was aware of these differences, for in a letter of 24 March 1770 from Italy, he described a minuet for the theater that was danced "slowly," with "many notes" (probably sixteenths).[192] A sampling of minuet tempos reported by eighteenth-century theorists provides some guid-ance for each tempo type.

L'Affilard	1705	MM $\downarrow.$ = 70 or $\downarrow.$ = 75
La Chapelle	1737	MM $\downarrow$ = 126
Quantz	1752	MM $\downarrow$ = 160
Choquel	1762	MM $\downarrow.$ = 80[193]

Hummel's metronomizations for the minuets in his quartet arrangements of Mozart's last six symphonies range from $\downarrow.$ = 66 to 88,[194] thus bracketing closely the indications of L'Affilard and Choquel.[195] Beethoven's own indica-tions for minuets with one pulse per measure extend these fast tempos con-siderably. They range from $\downarrow.$ = 69 for the Allegretto of the String Quartet Op. 59/2 to $\downarrow.$ = 108 for the Menuetto, Allegro molto e vivace of the First Sym-phony.

The majority of minuets by Haydn, Mozart, and Beethoven are of the fast type, but those composers wrote some of the slower type as well. An outstand-ing example of the moderate minuet occurs in the finale of the first act of Mozart's *Don Giovanni,* for which there exists a metronomization of $\downarrow$ = 96 suggested by Wenzel Tomášek. He "remembered" the tempo from hearing many performances by the musicians of the Prague Opera, who were trained by Mozart himself.[196] Max Rudolf suggests ca. 96 as a generally appropriate tempo for Mozart's moderate minuets.[197]

BEETHOVEN'S "MODERATE" MINUETS: HIS METRONOMIZATIONS, EXTRAPOLATED TEMPOS, AND PRESENT PRACTICE

Beethoven used both types of minuet in his String Trio Op. 3, composed before 1794. Their opening measures in Figures 9.1 and 9.2 show a clear difference in rhythmic construction between the predominantly unembellished quarter-note movement of the Menuetto, Allegretto, and the continuous eighth-note subdivision with articulative detail (and short trills added further on) of the Menuetto, Moderato. The metronomizations of $\bullet$. = 96 and $\bullet$ = 152 respectively from the Haslinger *Gesamtausgabe,* probably by Ignaz Schuppanzigh or Karl Holz, reflect the difference.[198]

Beethoven left metronomizations for three of his moderate minuets—those of the Eighth Symphony, the Septet Op. 20, and the String Quartet Op. 59/3 (Figs. 9.4–9.6). Although these works are not for piano, the possibility exists of a close tempo relationship between the Tempo di Menuetto of the Septet and the corresponding movement of Op. 49/2—known to all pianists—because they share the same main theme. Beyond this we will see what tempo information from Beethoven's indications may be applicable to others of his moderate minuets for piano. (This necessarily brief discussion will comment on the structure and tempo of each minuet proper but not its trio. Some trios adhere to the tempos of their minuets; others may vary to some degree if a change of character occurs.)

Fig. 9.1. Beethoven, Trio for Strings Op. 3/iii (*BNA*), mm. 1–8.

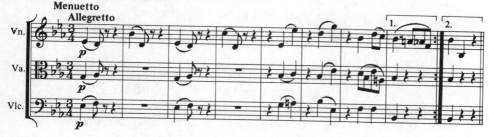

Fig. 9.2. Beethoven, Trio for Strings Op. 3/v (*BNA*), mm. 1–5.

If a metronomization assigned by a composer to one of his pieces is to be considered an approximate guide for another, preferably one of about the same period, the two must share three aspects of rhythm that together make up what William Newman terms their "rhythmic character": the same meter, the same prevailing note values and basic rhythmic patterns, and the same tempo heading.[199] Not surprisingly, these determinants are reminiscent of the elements influential in tempo choice described at the start of this chapter. As a group, moderate minuets share the 3/4 meter, a quarter-note pulse, and, for many, the heading Tempo di Menuetto. Qualifiers in the headings provide some clue to tempo differences among the movements, but differences in prevailing note values and rhythmic patterns are more intrinsic to the determination of appropriate tempos. Thus, the increasing subdivision in Figures 9.11–9.13 would slow the tempo accordingly. Consideration of the additional elements of structure that influence tempo choice (p. 311) will yield further tempo refinements for each piece.[200] We must bear in mind, though, that as time elapsed between dates of composition increases and the similarities of musical characteristics (including texture and articulation) decrease, tempo extrapolation from one piece to another becomes increasingly subjective and risky.

Figures 9.3–9.13 show incipits of the three moderate minuets that Beethoven metronomized as well as others from his piano repertoire. Of the group, the Menuett Moderato WoO 82 (Fig. 9.3) is the simplest in rhythmic structure, style, and performance detail. Eighth-note embellishment of the pulse is important only in the second half of the piece; the rhythm of its unadorned harmonic progressions is leisurely; and the melody itself is plain and predominantly stepwise. According to our premises, this Menuett might bear the fastest tempo of the group. The metronomization in Haslinger's *Gesamtausgabe*, probably by Czerny, is $\quarternote = 138$, but the Menuett also moves a little faster with ease.

Beethoven's fastest metronomization for a moderate minuet is $\quarternote = 126$[201]— the tempo suggested by La Chapelle—for the Tempo di Menuetto of the Eighth Symphony Op. 93 (Fig. 9.4). In this movement the pulse is embellished most of the time with melodic eighth-note motion. The rhythm of the simple harmonic plan is again leisurely (most often one harmony per measure, occasionally for two measures); the melodic skips are usually triadic; and the articulation is straightforward. On the other hand, the scoring for full orchestra with horns, trumpets, and tympani; the *sf* accents on five successive beats at

Fig. 9.3. Beethoven, Menuett WoO 82 (*BNA*), mm. 1–6.

Fig. 9.4. Beethoven, Symphony No. 8/iii Op. 93 (*BGA*), mm. 1–8.

the opening; and the generally full sound and continued frequent *sforzandos,* often with syncopated chords, are undoubtedly some of the factors that have led conductors, including Bruno Walter, Felix Weingartner, and Karl Böhm, to tempos around ♩ = 108–112. Furtwängler's 100 seems positively ponderous. Toscanini's 120–126 is an athletic rendition with no loss of detail.[202]

The antipodal spirit of those performances by Furtwängler and Toscanini is a reverberation of the two opposing views on tempo discussed briefly on pp. 334–335, but more specifically of the disagreement between Wagner and Mendelssohn regarding the speed of that particular minuet. In about 1843 they sat together at a performance of Beethoven's Eighth Symphony conducted by Capellmeister Reissiger in Dresden. Wagner thought he had convinced both Reissiger and Mendelssohn of the necessity of playing the third movement in his idea of a "true minuet tempo"—that is, much more slowly than in the usual Classic taste, which Wagner considered a "meaningless waltz time."

Mendelssohn's approval of Reissiger's performance in "customary waltz tempo" incensed Wagner, who never forgave the older musician.[203] In 1889 Hans von Bülow conducted this movement at $\rfloor$ = 92, believing that "The Menuetto is so to say the *vice-adagio* in that work . . . ,"[204] an idea ably refuted by Henry Edward Krehbiel, Nottebohm, and others.[205] Von Bülow and Furtwängler were staunch followers of Wagner; Toscanini represented the composer.

Beethoven indicated $\rfloor$ = 120 for the Tempo di Menuetto of the Septet Op. 20 (Fig. 9.5). In contrast to the symphonic minuet, this piece, with its lighter scoring and dynamics, more stepwise melody and homophonic texture, and the easily played articulation, moves readily at 120. The Boston Symphony Chamber Players perform at Beethoven's tempo; members of the Vienna Octet play only at 112.[206]

Beethoven's indication for the Menuetto, Grazioso of the Quartet Op. 59/3 (comp. 1805–1806), is slightly slower, at $\rfloor$ = 116 (Fig. 9.6). With the scoring for only four instruments using idiomatic articulation, this tempo accommodates an increase in passing chromaticism as well as in motivic and rhythmic development that includes hemiola and almost continuous sixteenth-note movement. The Amadeus Quartet plays at ca. 116, the Juilliard Quartet at 108.[207]

Now we must consider whether Beethoven's metronomization for the minuet of the Septet Op. 20 (comp. 1799–1800), whose main theme was borrowed from the Tempo di Menuetto of Op. 49/2 (comp. 1795–1796; Fig. 9.7), will suit the movement for piano. This piece is scored with basic keyboard patterns easily played in the prescribed legato and implied nonlegato articulation. The dynamics, discussed in chapter 3, are kept simple to fit the modest style and formal design. Indeed, the unpretentiousness of both movements and their similarities suggest that Beethoven's $\rfloor$ = 120 applies to Op. 49/2/ii as well. Only the sixteenth notes in the B section and the subtle right-hand articulation in mm. 28 and 29 might prove challenging for some student pianists at that brisk tempo. (A significantly slower tempo would create the need for increased dynamic fluctuation.) Schnabel played this movement at ca. 120, Paul Badura-Skoda at ca. 116–120.[208] Many performers settle at a tempo between 112 and 100, but one well-known pianist-conductor has recorded it at a lullaby-like 88. Czerny, whose tempos for the "moderate" minuet sometimes seem slow, suggested 112; Moscheles referred back to 126.

The Minuetto of Op. 22 (comp. 1800; Fig. 9.8) differs little in basic style from those already considered. Its prevailing rhythmic patterns include an eighth-note background, some dotted rhythms, and the short, easily played groups of sixteenth notes—some preceded by an appoggiatura—found in Op. 20. Yet, the section immediately following the first repeat introduces a startlingly forceful element in the key of the coming Minore; and in a change of mood near the end of the minuet (mm. 27–30), the melodic line is tucked into the tenor between two other voices. Czerny described this movement as "No scherzo, but a true *Menuet*, though a little more lively."[209] His marks of $\rfloor$ = 120 and 126 from different metronomizations, and Moscheles's of 132 and 126

Fig. 9.5. Beethoven, Septet Op. 20/iv (*BGA*), mm. 1–8.

indicate that both musicians related the general character and speed of this movement to those that Beethoven had metronomized and to the historical tempos.

Many modern performers view this minuet more subjectively, choosing tempos between 108 and 96, changing tempos for mm. 9–16, and placing more emphasis on individual details. On the other hand, Friedrich Gulda offers a performance at about 120 throughout that enhances the more dramatic sections

Fig. 9.6. Beethoven, String Quartet Op. 59/3/iii (Aut.), mm. 1–8.

Fig. 9.7. Beethoven, Sonata Op. 49/2/ii (OE Bureau des Arts et d'Industrie), mm. 1–4.

Fig. 9.8. Beethoven, Sonata Op. 22/iii (OE Hoffmeister), mm. 1–4.

Fig. 9.9. Beethoven, Sonata Op. 31/3/iii (OE Nägeli), mm. 1–4.

(mm. 8–16, 27–30) while allowing the rest to flow.[210] He plays the Minore at ♩ = 126, "just a little more lively than the *Menuet*," as Czerny also suggests. Murray Perahia plays the movement only insignificantly slower, at ca. 116, and the Minore at ca. 120.[211]

In addition to the similarity of their headings, the Menuetto, Moderato e grazioso of Op. 31/3 (Fig. 9.9) and the Tempo di Minuetto, ma molto moderato e grazioso of Op. 30/3 (Fig. 9.10) have in common the key of E-flat major (in Op. 30 juxtaposed between movements in G major) and composition within months of each other in 1801–1802. Beethoven's "moderato e grazioso" indicates that these movements may be slower than the minuets so far discussed.

The predominantly three-part texture of the minuet of Op. 31/3 and some increase in contrapuntal interest stand out in comparison with the minuets of Op. 49/2 and Op. 22. The melody and overall mood have become more reflective, abetted by the unexpected color of an extended C-flat appoggiatura—a minor ninth over the dominant—at the start of the second section, perhaps in lieu of a contrasting tonality. Other details that enhance the "affective" quality of the movement include the four-measure legato grouping at the end of the minuet (mm. 13–16) and a harmonic reflection of the earlier C-flat with the entrance of F-flat and then the Neapolitan sixth chord over a tonic pedal on the same motive in the Coda. I play this Menuetto, Moderato e grazioso at ♩ = ca. 108, a little slower than Beethoven's 116 for the Menuetto, Grazioso of Op. 59/3. Here Moscheles's 112 seems a better approximation than Czerny's 96 and 88 (1846), about which Czerny wrote "The time tranquil, as in the real dance minuet."[212] Friedrich Gulda plays it at 100; Glenn Gould presents a stodgy caricature at about 69.[213]

The inner movements of Op. 31/3 create an unusual relationship. Instead of a slow movement followed by a quick minuet or scherzo, Beethoven wrote a moderately paced but jocular Scherzo, Allegretto vivace in 2/4, with the quarter note as the tempo unit (see n. 205), followed by a moderate minuet (the only movement of the four not in sonata-allegro form). In the metronomizations of Czerny and Moscheles, the quarter note of the Scherzo (subdivided into staccato sixteenth notes throughout) is anywhere from two to five metronomic steps slower than that of the Menuetto. This sonata has no true slow movement; instead there are two strongly contrasting inner movements of which the Menuetto is the more lyrical. Is this Beethoven's joke in an overall humorous work? Not convinced, many modern performers have created a marked fast–slow relationship between the Scherzo and the Menuetto by playing the Scherzo with a faster quarter note and sometimes by slowing the Menuetto considerably. Badura-Skoda considers Op. 31/3 a sonata for which "certain internal evidence suggests that Czerny was aware of Beethoven's intentions" (n. 154).

The more complex rhythmic and contrapuntal construction of the extended Tempo di Minuetto from Op. 30/3, along with a certain tenderness, bears out its "ma molto moderato e grazioso" heading. Interestingly, the holograph conveys the impression that Beethoven added these qualifiers later, first "ma molto moderato," then "e grazioso." The contrapuntal texture, a variety of rhythmic patterns using sixteenth notes, and five ornaments are present in the opening eight measures, which have eight repetitions in the through-composed form. When the theme moves into the violin part for mm. 9–16, triplets in the accompaniment create rhythmic conflict with the binary patterns of the melody (Fig. 9.10b). Intermittent rhythmic conflict, episodes in the minor mode, and finely wrought articulation have a moderating effect on the tempo. The metronomization in the Haslinger *Gesamtausgabe* is ♩ = 92.[214] According to Czerny,

Fig. 9.10. Beethoven, Sonata for Violin and Piano Op. 30/3/ii (Aut.). a. mm. 1–5. b. mm. 8–10.

a.

Tempo di Minuetto ma molto moderato e grazioso

b.

Fig. 9.11. Beethoven, Sonata Op. 54/i (OE Bureau des Arts et d'Industrie), mm. 1–4.

In tempo d'un Menuetto

*Slur to F in OE must be engraver's error.

the Menuetto should be "played throughout with simple grace and gentle feeling, but without dragging."[215] Placed between an Allegro assai and an Allegro vivace, this Tempo di Minuetto is indeed the slow movement of its sonata. Yet the tempos of around 80 and 76, at which the movement is frequently played,[216] introduce an alien sentimentality.

The "minuet" (exclusive of its trio) from In Tempo d'un Menuetto of Op. 54 (comp. 1804) undergoes progressive ornamentation through diminution in its two variations and coda, thus diverging significantly in style and structure from the movements discussed so far. The rhythmic pattern of the opening measures (Fig. 9.11) continues throughout the theme with the addition of some trilled turns. Diminution to sixteenth notes, appoggiaturas, and some syncopation (mm. 88, 91) are incorporated in the first variation. Further diminution, contrapuntal rhythmic groups, and the conflict of binary against ternary patterns in the second variation and coda suggest that the tempo of this minuet may be still slower than some of the others, even without a further modified heading. Something of the difference can be sensed from the dark color of the opening and the dissonant B-flat left hanging in m. 1 and from the discontinuity of the melody.

Outer boundaries of speed may be determined by considering tempos in which the opening statement sounds like a Classic moderate minuet (i.e., not too slow), and in which the later variations are also playable. Here the touch of the instrument may not be a negligible factor. Surprisingly, the indication in Haslinger 2 is ♩ = 120; Moscheles's indications are 126, then 120; all are astonishingly fast for the piece. In 1846 Czerny wrote, "The tolerably earnest character of it must be expressed by a solid, determinately energetic performance," and reduced the tempo to 108.[217] Schnabel's performance at about 100 (but 96 for the second variation and 112 for the trios) is the fastest I have heard.[218] Badura-Skoda suggests 96–100 in his Commentary to Czerny's *Proper Performance,* but plays at ca. 96–92.[219]

In Czerny's metronomizations of this two-movement sonata, the *perpetuum mobile* Allegretto in two-part counterpoint is faster than the Menuetto. Moscheles reversed the tempo relationship by metronomizing the Allegretto at ♩ = 108. Modern performers generally keep the Allegretto significantly faster than the Menuetto; Schnabel recorded at 126, Badura-Skoda at 132–138, and Wilhelm Backhaus at Czerny's 144.[220]

In 1802, when Beethoven was at work on Opp. 30/3 and 31/3, he also wrote the Six Variations Op. 34, in which he used a Tempo di Minuetto for the fourth variation (Fig. 9.12). Details such as the slurring of some sixteenth-note passages by two's, other sixteenth notes in parallel thirds, *portato,* syncopated octaves, abrupt dynamic change (m. 14), and the florid ending speak for a rather moderate tempo. Yet, although Czerny's metronomization in the Haslinger *Gesamtausgabe* is ♩ = 96,[221] I have not heard a performance faster than Denis Matthews's 72.[222]

There remains finally the variation and coda, Tempo di Menuetto moderato (*ma non tirarsi dietro*) (*aber nicht schleppend*), of the monumental Variations on a Waltz by Diabelli Op. 120 (Fig. 9.13). The only moderate minuet from Beethoven's last period, this work is separated by time and concept from the others. In it Beethoven transformed the waltz, the more recent faster dance with which the set begins, into an abstract reminiscence of the stately minuet. Everything about its style, from note values, texture, articulation, and virtuosic

Fig. 9.12. Beethoven, Six Variations Op. 34. (Aut. and OE Breitkopf & Härtel), Var. 4, mm. 1–4. Indications in parentheses are from OE.

Fig. 9.13. Beethoven, Variations on a Waltz by A. Diabelli Op. 120 *(BNA)*, Var. 33, mm. 1–3.

writing to its contemplative character, removes its tempo from a close relationship with the group of tempos just discussed. The commonest tempos range around $\quarternote = 63$ or 66.[223] Charles Rosen plays it at ca. 58, Leonard Shure at ca. 72.[224]

EXTRAPOLATION OF OTHER TEMPOS

For Beethoven

My timings of performances and recordings demonstrate that pianists generally play Beethoven's fast sonata movements within the range of the metronomizations by Czerny and Moscheles. However, one that many treat significantly slower, for no apparent reason, is the Allegretto of the "Moonlight" Sonata (comp. 1801, Fig. 9.14). Its meter, tempo heading, and rhythmic design in quarter and half notes compare directly with those of the Menuetto, Allegretto of the Quartet Op. 18/4 (comp. 1798–1800, Fig. 9.15), which Beethoven metronomized at $\dottedquarternote = 84$. Both movements contain short articulative groupings and a prominent motive of suspension and resolution (Figs. 9.14b, 9.15b). The Trio of Op. 27/2/ii also incorporates the third beat *sforzandos* of the quartet Menuetto. Czerny's indication for the Allegretto of the sonata is also $\dottedquarternote = 84$ in Haslinger 1, but the only performance I have heard at this tempo is Malcolm Bilson's. Why do pianists alter this movement by presenting it at $\dottedquarternote = $ ca. 63 (or even slower)?[225]

Although movements with similar rhythmic character occur less frequently in moderate and slow tempos, there are some comparisons that provide un-

Fig. 9.14. Beethoven, Sonata Op. 27/2/ii (Aut.). a. mm. 1–4. b. mm. 8–12.

Fig. 9.15. Beethoven, String Quartet Op. 18/4/iii (*BGA*). a. mm. 1–4. b. mm. 27–31.

Fig. 9.16. Beethoven, String Quartet Op. 18/1/ii (*BGA*), mm. 1–7.

questionable tempo clues. Consider the Adagio movements of three early works: Op. 18/1 (comp. 1798–1800, Fig. 9.16), Op. 20 (comp. 1799–1800, Fig. 9.17), and Op. 22 (comp. 1800, Fig. 9.18). We might expect an Adagio cantabile to be more flowing than an Adagio affettuoso ed appassionata, but Beethoven metronomized the former at ♪ = 132 and the latter at ♪ = 138. Beyond the similar tempo headings, the three movements share a 9/8 meter, a steady eighth-note accompaniment, and melodic movement primarily in eighth and sixteenth

Fig. 9.17. Beethoven, Septet for Strings and Winds Op. 20/ii (*BGA*), mm. 1-4.*

*For instrumentation see Fig. 9.5.

Fig. 9.18. Beethoven, Sonata Op.22/ii (OE Hoffmeister), mm. 1–5.

notes, although the quartet and piano movements also have some significant 32d-note passages. Additionally those two movements share the melodic motive that opens Figure 9.18 and *portato* indications in the accompaniment, and they have more contrapuntal interest than does the Adagio of the Septet.

The performance closest to Beethoven's indication for the Adagio cantabile is one conducted by Toscanini at ♪ = 126 in an arrangement for small orchestra.[226] The Amadeus Quartet plays the Adagio affettuoso at ca. 120, the Juilliard Quartet at only 104.[227] These two recordings also demonstrate effectively the influence of tempo on other aspects of performance. The slower tempo naturally engenders a noticeable increase in vibrato, especially on the longer notes, and more fluctuation in the dynamics. The Juilliard performance seems too slow to me, as do Czerny's indications of $\flat$ = 104 and 100 for the Adagio of Op. 22 in Haslinger 2 and *Proper Performance* respectively. Moscheles's 132 for this movement intimates an awareness of Beethoven's indications for the other movements, but Moscheles later changed that to 116, the tempo at which Czerny finally arrived as well. It is significantly slower than Beethoven's indications, yet it is relatively close compared to most of the tempos at which this movement is played today. I prefer $\flat$ = 116–120; more usual is the range of 88–104, and even 76, which is ten steps slower than 116.[228] A slow movement stretched to such Wagnerian proportions may also sound oversentimentalized and overemphasized in proportion to the composition as a whole.

For Clementi

Clementi began to publish metronomizations with Volume I of his *Gradus ad Parnassum* in 1817, the same year that saw Beethoven's first published indications. Volume II of the *Gradus* (1819) and Clementi's three Sonatas Op. 50 (1821) also contain metronomizations. Tempos for certain movements from Clementi's other sonatas can be extrapolated from these indications.

Clementi's metronomization of $\quarternote$ = 80 for the 2/4 finales of Op. 50/2 (Allegro con fuoco, ma non troppo Presto) and Op. 50/3 (Allegro agitato, e con disperazione) feels too fast to me for the lyrical and dramatic qualities of the first movement, Allegro con spirito, in his much earlier Op. 7/3/i (Fig. 9.19). In the *Gradus* he marked No. 41, an Allegro vivace in 2/4 (also the Finale for a Suite of Five Pieces) at $\quarternote$ = 72 (Fig. 9.20). This piece has a contrasting theme in two- and three-part texture (mm. 54ff, Fig. 9.20b) that is surprisingly reminiscent of the opening of Op. 7/3/i; yet the demands for sudden changes of register, material, mood, and dynamics in the sonata movement and my preference for playing it with very little tempo flexibility have led me to the insignificantly slower $\quarternote$ = 66. Note also that in his English edition Clementi amended the heading of this movement to Allegro espressivo.

Two sonata movements that bear close rhythmic relationships to the Cantabile e lento of Op. 7/3 have contemporary metronomizations. The sections in 3/4 of the Adagio sostenuto e patetico of Op. 50/1 are built of rhythmic

Fig. 9.19. Clementi, Sonata Op. 7/3/i (OE Artaria and English ed. for the Author), mm. 1–4.

*The slur is from the English edition.

Fig. 9.20. Clementi, *Gradus ad Parnassum*, Exercise 41 (OE Clementi, Banger, Collard, Davis & Collard). a. mm. 1–4. b. mm. 62–66.

Fig. 9.21. Clementi, Sonata Op. 50/1/ii (OE Clementi), mm. 9–10.

patterns and texture similar to those of Op. 7/3/ii, including the dotted eighth followed by three 32d notes in Figure 9.21 (compare Fig. 5.27). Beyond the time of composition, only the headings are notably different, for at least in 1801 Clementi considered *adagio* the slowest tempo. His order of terms, becoming faster, is *adagio, grave, largo, lento, larghetto, andantino,* and *andante.*[229] His metronomization for Op. 50/1/ii is ♪ = 72. Since his *lento* is faster, and since he defined *cantabile* as "in a singing and graceful manner,"[230] Op. 7/3/ii will be somewhat faster, at ♪ = ca. 80 as I play it. The Larghetto con espressione of Clementi's Sonata Op. 11 relates both in approximate time of composition (1784) and in rhythmic construction to the Cantabile e lento of Op. 7/3. His friend William Crotch left tempo indications by means of pendulum lengths for four of Clementi's sonata movements, including this Larghetto. According to Leon Plantinga, the indication for Op. 11/ii converts to a metronomization of ♪ = 84.[231] This result, insignificantly faster than my 80, corroborates Clementi's *lento, larghetto* order.

No close analogy exists among Clementi's metronomizations for the Presto in 6/8 of Op. 7/3. Quantz's tempo for a *presto* in 3/8 with sixteenth notes works out to ♩. = 107 (Appendix A), quite fast for the demands of this movement. Türk considered some of Quantz's tempos too fast (which they may well be

Fig. 9.22. Clementi, Sonata Op. 7/3/iii (OE Artaria and English ed. for the Author), mm. 1-4.

for Clementi) and began the top of his scale at 136 instead of 160. (Unfortunately, Türk's scale does not include 3/8 or its multiples.) We also know from
Mozart's comment (at the start of this chapter) that Clementi's *presto* was not
always especially fast. Further, for his London edition of this sonata in the
early 1790s, Clementi altered the heading of this movement to Allegro agitato.
Quantz's metronomization for an *allegro* in 6/8 is ♩. = 80. Taking everything
into consideration, a tempo of ♩. = ca. 96 might not be inappropriate.

The theoretical and practical source materials introduced in this chapter
can guide musicians toward tempos appropriate to Classic period music. In
the course of considering this body of information, we have seen among present-day performances some pronounced deviations from historically based
practice. Changes in musical taste and differing aesthetic ideas resulting from
the intervention of time are the fundamental causes of such differences.

Significant tempo deviations today tend toward the slow side. Apparently
we can lay to rest the once-fashionable notion that our faster pace of life, our
"improved" instruments, and our superior technique incline us to faster tempos than those used in the eighteenth and nineteenth centuries.[232] If anything,
the changes in the piano have made it more difficult to attain appropriate
performance tempos while maintaining all the details of articulation and phrasing. An understanding of this role of the instrument and of other causes of
tempo change provides perspective that will help us approach tempos at once
consistent with the ideals of Classic composers and convincing to our audience.

Appendix A
Theoretical Tempos of Quantz and Türk

	Quantz* ♩	Türk* ♩
Common Time		
Allegro assai, allegro di molto, presto	160	136
Passage-work in sixteenth notes or eighth-note triplets.		
Allegro, vivace	120	102
Allegretto, allegro ma non tanto, moderato	80	68
Passage-work in 32d notes or sixteenth-note triplets.		
[Andante	60]	51
Adagio cantabile, arioso, larghetto, poco andante, maestoso,	40	34
alla Siciliana		
[Adagio	30]	25
Adagio assai, lento, largo assai, grave.	20	17

	♩.
3/8 and Its Multiples	
Presto without sixteenths (in 6/8)	160
Presto with sixteenths (in 3/8)	ca. 107
Allegro with sixteenths (in 3/8 and 6/8)	80
Alla Siciliana	53
[Adagio cantabile	ca. 27]

French Dance Music**

Bourrée	¢	♩ =	160
Canarie	6/8	♩. =	160
Chaconne	3/4	♩ =	160
Courante	3/4	♩ =	80
Entrée		♩ =	80
Furie	2/4 ♩ = 80 or 3/4	♩ =	160
Gavotte A little more moderate than a bourrée.			
Gigue	6/8	♩. =	160
Loure	6/4	♩ =	80
March	¢	♩ =	80
Menuet	3/4	♩ =	160
Musette	3/4 ♩ = 80 or 3/8	♪ =	80
Passecaille A little faster than a chaconne.			
Passepied Slightly faster than a menuet.			
Rigaudon	¢	♩ =	160
Rondeau	¢ ♩ = 80 or 3/4	♩ =	160
Sarabande	3/4	♩ =	80
Tambourin A little faster than a bourrée or rigaudon.			

---

*Quantz, *Flute,* 284-287; Türk, *Klavierschule,* 111-112, as calibrated by Saslav, *Tempo in the String Quartets of Joseph Haydn,* 50-51. When applied to specific works, some of Quantz's tempos may seem inordinately fast and will bear moderation.

**Quantz, *Flute,* 290-292.

Appendix B
Six Sets of Metronomizations for Beethoven's Piano Sonatas*

	Haslinger		Czerny		Moscheles	
	First state	Second state	Proper Performance	Simrock	Cramer	Hallberger
Op. 2/1						
Allegro			104	108	108	108
Adagio			80	84	100¹	100¹
Menuetto, Allegretto			69	72	72	72
Prestissimo			104	108	112	112
Op. 2/2						
Allegro vivace			132	138	144	144
Largo appassionato			80	88	88	88
Scherzo, Allegretto			63	66	60	60
Grazioso			132	144	144	144
Op. 2/3						
Allegro con brio			80	80	76	76
Adagio			50	56	56	56
Scherzo, Allegro			80	76	88	88
Allegro assai			116	116	116	116
Op. 7						
Allegro molto e con brio			116	126	116	126
Largo, con gran espressione			80	84	100²	100²
Allegro			72	80	80	80
Poco Allegretto e grazioso			120³	132	138	138

*Occasional movements or sonatas in these series are without metronomizations. Those for Haslinger 1 and 2 were compiled from extant copies of the sonatas in the Boston Public Library, the British Library, the New York Public Library, the Princeton University Library, and the Österreichische Nationalbibliothek in Vienna.

1. Given as ♪ = 50.
2. Given as ♩ = 50.
3. Given as ♪ = 60.

Appendix B. Continued

		Haslinger		Czerny		Moscheles	
		First state	Second state	*Proper Performance*	Simrock	Cramer	Hallberger
Op. 10/1							
Allegro molto e con brio	3/4 ♩=	80	69	72	76	76	76
Adagio molto	2/4 ♪=	63	72	69	72	72	72
Prestissimo	¢ 𝅗𝅥=	112	96	96	100	108	108
Op. 10/2							
Allegro	2/4 ♪=	108	100	104	108	96	112
Allegretto	3/4 ♩=	76	72	72	76	72	72
Presto	2/4 𝅗𝅥=	96	88	80	80[4]	80[4]	80[4]
Op. 10/3							
Presto	¢ 𝅗𝅥=	152	132	126	132	132	132
Largo e mesto	6/8 ♪=	66	76	72	76	72	72
Menuetto, Allegro	3/4 ♩=	84	80	76	84	84	84
Allegro	C ♩=	160	152	152	152	152	152
Op. 13							
Grave	C ♪=	58	58	46[5]	63	60	60
Allegro di molto e con brio	¢ 𝅗𝅥=	152	152	144	144	144	144
Adagio cantabile	2/4 ♪=	54	60	54	60	60	60
Allegro	¢ 𝅗𝅥=	112	100	96	104	104	104
Op. 14/1							
Allegro	C ♩=	144	132	132	144	152	152
Allegretto	3/4 ♩=	72	72	69	72	72	72
Allegro comodo	¢ 𝅗𝅥=	100	100		96	80[6]	80[6]
Op. 14/2							
Allegro	2/4 ♪=	88	80	80	80[7]	80[7]	80[7]
Andante	¢ ♩=	132[8]	132[8]	116	112	84	96
Scherzo, Allegro assai	3/8 ♪=	88	88	80	88	88	88

Op. 22								
Allegro con brio	C	♩ =	84	80	76	84	92	84
Adagio con molta espressione	9/8	♪ =	112	104	100	116	132	116
Minuetto	3/4	♩ =	126	120	120	126	132	126
Allegretto	2/4	♩ =	76	69	69	76	76	76
Op. 26								
Andante con Variazioni	3/8	♪ =	80	80	76	80	80	80
Var. 1	3/8	♪ =				88		88
Var. 2	3/8	♪ =	92	92	92	100	104	104
Var. 3	3/8	♪ =	84	84	76	92		92
Var. 4	3/8	♪ =	100	100	92	100		100
Var. 5	3/8	♪ =	80	80	76	80	92	80
Scherzo, Allegro molto	3/4	♩ =	104	92	92	88	88	88
Marcia funebre	C	♩ =	72	72	72	66	60	60
Allegro	2/4	♩ =	152[9]	132	132	120	120	108
Op. 27/1								
Andante	¢	♩ =	72	72	66	69	69	76
Allegro	6/8	♪. =	116	108	104	104	104	104
Allegro molto e vivace	3/4	♩ =	138	126	112	120	126	126
Adagio con espressione	3/4	♩ =	69	66	66	72	76	76
Allegro vivace	2/4	♩ =	160	138	132	132	132	120
Op. 27/2								
Adagio sostenuto	¢	♩ =	60	63	54	60	60	60
Allegretto	3/4	♩. =	84	80	76	80	76	76
Presto agitato	C	♩ =	92	84	80	92	92	92

4. Given as ♩ = 160.
5. Given as ♪ = 92, since the range of Czerny's metronome was only 50 to 160.
6. Given as ♪ = 160.
7. Given as ♪ = 160.
8. Given as ♩ = 66.
9. Given as ♪ = 76.

Appendix B. Continued

		Haslinger		Czerny		Moscheles	
		First state	Second state	Proper Performance	Simrock	Cramer	Hallberger
Op. 28							
Allegro	♩. = , 3/4	76	72	72	72	69	69
Andante	♪ = , 2/4	92	92	84	88	104	104
Scherzo, Allegro vivace	♩. = , 3/4	104	92	96	100	100	100
Allegro ma non troppo	♩. = , 6/8	96	84	88	88	92	92
Op. 31/1							
Allegro vivace	♩ = , 2/4	80	80	72	76[10]	80[11]	80[11]
Adagio grazioso	♪ = , 9/8	126	116	116	126	132	132
Allegretto	♩ = , C	108	100	96	100	76	84
Op. 31/2							
Largo	♪ = , C	44[12]	44[13]	104	50	50	50
Allegro	♩ = , ¢	112	104	84	108	126	126
Adagio	♪ = , 3/4	92	92	84	92	92	92
Allegretto	♩. = , 3/8	84	76	76	88	88	88
Op. 31/3							
Allegro	♩. = , 3/4	180[14]	152	144	152	160	160
Scherzo, Allegretto vivace	♩ = , 2/4	88	80	80	88	92	92
Menuetto, Moderato e grazioso	♩ = , 3/4	96[15]	96	88	96	112	112
Presto con fuoco	♩. = , 6/8	116	104	100	96	96	96
Op. 49/1							
Andante	♩ = , 2/4	92	88		60	60[16]	69
Allegro	♩. = , 6/8	108	100		60	60	100
Op. 49/2							
Allegro ma non troppo	♩ = , ¢	104	104		104	80[17]	80[17]
Tempo di Menuetto	♩ = , 3/4	112	112		112	126	126

Op. / Tempo	Note value						
Op. 53							
Allegro con brio	C 𝅗𝅥 =	88	88	88	88	88	88
Introduzione, Adagio molto	6/8 ♪ =	54[18]	54[18]	56	60	60	60
Allegretto moderato	2/4 ♩ =	100	92	88	100	112	112
Prestissimo	¢ 𝅝 =	88	80	88	84	84	80
Op. 54							
In Tempo d'un Menuetto	3/4 ♩ =		120	108	108[?][19]	126	120
Allegretto	2/4 ♩ =	152[20]	152[20]	144	120[?]	108	108
Op. 57							
Allegro assai	12/8 ♪ =	120	108	108	120	138	126
Andante con moto	2/4 ♪. =	120	108	108	112	92	92
Allegro ma non troppo	2/4 ♪ =	138	138	132	144	152	152
Presto	2/4 𝅗𝅥 =		92		96	100	100
Op. 78							
Adagio cantabile	2/4 ♪ =	76	76	72	76	76	76
Allegro ma non troppo	C ♩ =	132	132	116	138	138	138
Allegro vivace	2/4 ♪ =	144	138	132	132	132	132
Op. 79							
Presto alla tedesca	3/4 ♩. =	88	84	84	84	84	84
Andante	9/8 ♪. =	56	56		56	46[21]	46[21]
Vivace	2/4 ♪ =	152	138	138	138	160	138

10. Given as ♩ = 152.
11. Given as ♩ = 160.
12. Given as ♪ = 88; corrected to an eighth note in the second state.
13. Given as ♪ = 88.
14. Given as ♪. = 60.
15. Note value mistakenly engraved as a dotted quarter note.
16. Note value given as an eighth note; undoubtedly a typographical error.
17. Given as ♩ = 160.
18. Given as ♪ = 108.
19. See chapter 9, n. 217.
20. Given as 𝅗𝅥 = 76.
21. Given as ♪ = 138.

Appendix B. Continued

| | Haslinger | | Czerny | | Moscheles | |
	First state	Second state	Proper Performance	Simrock	Cramer	Hallberger
Op. 81a						
Adagio	72	66	63	72	76	72
Allegro	126	116	112	126	108	108
Andante espressivo	72	66	72	72	76	72
Vivacissimamente	116	108	108	108	108	108
Op. 90						
Mit Lebhaftigkeit und . . . mit Empfindung und Ausdruck	160	160	160	198[22]	180[23]	198[22]
Nicht zu geschwind und sehr singbar vorgetragen	92	92	88	96	96	96
Op. 101						
Allegretto, ma non troppo	80	80	72	72	66	72
Vivace alla Marcia	168[24]	144[25]	152[26]	132	132	132
Adagio, ma non troppo, con affetto	54	58	60	60	60	60
Allegro	132	120	132	132	132	132
Op. 106 (Beethoven's MM)						
Allegro		138	138	138	138	69[27]
Scherzo, Assai vivace		80	80	80	80	80
Presto			152[28]			
Adagio sostenuto		92	92	92	92	92
Largo		76			76	76
Allegro risoluto		144	144	144	144	144
Op. 109						
Vivace, ma non troppo	100	100	100	112	112	112
Adagio espressivo	66	66	66	66	72	72

Prestissimo	6/8 ♩. =	152	138	160[29]	160	160	160
Andante molto cantabile ed espressivo	3/4 ♪ =	72	72	63	66	66	66
Var. 1, Molto espressivo	3/4 ♪ =						
Var. 2, Leggiermente	3/4 ♪ =				84	84	84
Var. 3, Allegro vivace	2/4 ♪ =	152	152	132	138	120	138
Var. 4, Etwas langsamer als das Thema	9/8 ♪. =	66[30]	66[30]		56	56	56
Var. 5, Allegro, ma non troppo	¢ 𝅗𝅥 =	69	69	76	76	76	76
Op. 110							
Moderato cantabile molto espressivo	3/4 𝅗𝅥 =	80	80	76	63	63	63
Allegro molto	2/4 ♩ =	120	120	120	112	108	112
Adagio ma non troppo	C ♪ =	66	66	66	69	69	69
Arioso dolente	12/16 ♬ =	58	58		60	60	60
Allegro ma non troppo	6/8 ♪ =	100	100	100	92	76	92
Op. 111							
Maestoso	C ♩ =	54[31]	60[32]	54[31]	56	56	52
Allegro con brio ed appassionato	C ♪ =		132	132	126	125[!]	126
Adagio[,] molto semplice e cantabile[33]	9/16 ♬ =	63	63	63	60	52	60

22. Given as ♩ = 66.
23. Given as ♩. = 60.
24. Given as ♩ = 84.
25. Given as 𝅗𝅥 = 72.
26. Given as 𝅗𝅥 = 76.
27. Given as ♪ = 138; see Moscheles's explanation on p. 328.
28. This is Czerny's indication; Beethoven did not leave an indication for this tempo change.
29. Given as ♩. = 80.
30. The dot is missing from the quarter note in Haslinger 1 and 2.
31. Given as ♪ = 108.
32. Given as ♪ = 120.
33. Editorial comma separates Beethoven's original "Adagio" heading from his later addition (see p. 323).

10

FLEXIBILITY OF
RHYTHM AND TEMPO

INTRODUCTION

It is in the nature of Classicism that contrasting elements within a coordinated design are made compatible and balanced by unifying factors. What is known of performance in the Classic era suggests that aside from the obvious exceptions—fantasies, variations of a markedly different mood, trios that deviate strongly in character and structure from their minuets and scherzos, and pieces containing specified tempo changes—most movements or pieces were played in one underlying tempo. Noticeable alteration of that tempo where it was not indicated was considered disturbing to coherence of form and character; but subtle unspecified alteration under defined circumstances was accepted as a special means of expression, along with certain alterations of the rhythm within an (often) undisturbed tempo. The prevailing tempo at once pulled back the subtle internal fluctuations, kept the movement taut, and created a balanced relationship between the whole, its parts, and individual details.[1] Important theorists of the period provide background for the inquiry of this chapter.

Emanuel Bach addressed one aspect of a unified tempo in the 1787 revision of his *Essay:*

> In affettuoso playing the performer must avoid frequent and excessive retards, which tend to make the tempo drag. The affect itself readily leads to this fault. Hence every effort must be made despite the beauty of detail to keep the tempo at the end of a piece exactly the same as at the beginning, an extremely difficult assignment.[2]

In 1795 Koch complained that there were many performers whose tone, facility, and execution were masterful, but who neglected a steady tempo as a matter of fashion.[3]

Hummel wrote explicitly about tempo in relation to contrasting themes. Among "SOME LEADING OBSERVATIONS RESPECTING BEAUTY OF PERFORMANCE," he stated that "singing passages" in an *allegro* may be played with some little relaxation as to time, in order to give them the necessary effect; but we must not deviate, too strikingly, from the predominating movement, because, by so doing, *the unity of the whole will suffer, and the piece degenerate into a mere rhapsody* [italics added].[4]

Further on, Hummel reemphasized the delicacy necessary with tempo flexibility:

All relaxation of the time in single bars, and in short passages of melody, in pleasing and intermediate ideas, must take place almost imperceptibly, ... so that the difference between the remission in the time and the natural progress of the movement may never appear too striking with regard to the original measure. The graces must ... neither add to nor take from the strict time. ...[5]

In addition to underlining the essential unity of tempo, these statements lend credence to the accepted practice of subtle deviation for the sake of the effect. Schulz discussed the contribution of rhythm and tempo to the expressive aspect of performance, telling us that among

a thousand other nuances of expression ... [a soloist] will feel where he should hold a note beyond its length, [where he should] stop another before the same; he will even hasten or slow down where it serves to strengthen the expression. ...[6]

Türk used the words "extraordinary means" when he introduced the several kinds of rhythmic flexibility that might provide the final touch for the "most essential requisite for good performance"—expression of "the feelings and passions":[7]

Even when the composer has indicated the proper expression as best it can be done, for the whole piece and at specific places, and the player has suitably put to use all the means [of expression] discussed in the previous sections, there still remain special situations in which the expression can be heightened by *extraordinary* means. Here I consider especially 1) playing without strict time [in "free fantasies, cadenzas, fermatas ... and passages marked *Recitativo*"], 2) quickening and slowing, 3) the so-called *tempo rubato:* three means that, *used sparingly and at the proper time,* can be of great effect.[8]

Finally, Czerny's comments about the performance of Beethoven's music, especially regarding the sonatas through Op. 28, support a steady tempo with minimal deviation. Czerny agreed with Hummel that a noticeable change of tempo would disturb the perception of form and characterization. Of Beethoven's Sonata Op. 2/3 Czerny wrote:

The first movement must be performed with fire and energy.—The melodious passages from the 27th and 48th bars must be played with great expression; which is to be produced more by the touch, than by the employment of the *rallentando.* ...

The beginning of this *Adagio* must be played with great sentiment, but strictly in time, otherwise the hearer cannot comprehend the course of the melody at the rests.[9]

Interestingly, Türk did not include accentuation by "expressive lingering"—the slight lengthening of a note—among his "extraordinary means" for enhancing expression. Because rhythmic as well as dynamic accentuation was considered *necessary* for fine performance, he had discussed it earlier as part of "clarity of execution."[10] I shall consider this agogic accentuation first, as one of the subtlest yet most essential types of rhythmic flexibility. I should point out though that it is difficult if not sometimes impossible to separate one type of agogic nuance from another.

RHETORICAL ACCENTUATION BY AGOGIC MEANS

Emanuel Bach advised that

In order to avoid vagueness, rests as well as notes must be given their exact value except at *fermate* and cadences. Yet certain purposeful violations of the beat are often exceptionally beautiful.[11]

[Included are] various examples [Fig. 10.1] in which, for reasons of the affect, both notes and rests are occasionally held longer than their notation requires. In some cases I have written out this broadening clearly; in some it is shown by small crosses. . . . In general this expression is more appropriate in slow or moderate tempos than in very fast ones.[12]

Bach expanded on the rhythmic treatment of phrase divisions, *fermate*, and cadences in Part II of his *Essay:*

In slow or moderate tempos, caesurae [phrase divisions, *Einschnitte*] are usually extended beyond their normal length, especially when the [lengths of the] rests and notes in the bass are the same as those in the other parts, or in the principal part in the case of a solo. . . . This applies to *fermate*, cadences, etc., as well as caesurae. It is customary to drag a bit and depart somewhat from a strict observance of the bar, for the note before the rest as well as the rest itself

Fig. 10.1. E. Bach, *Versuch über die wahre Art . . .*, Table VI, Figure XIII.

Fig. 10.2. E. Bach, *Essay*, p. 375.

is extended beyond its notated length. Aside from the uniformity which this manner of execution achieves, the passage acquires an impressiveness which places it in relief [Fig. 10.2].[13]

Agogic Accentuation of Notes

Türk described "the lingering on certain notes" as

another means of accentuation [in addition to dynamic accents] that is used more seldom and with great care. . . . The speaker not only places more emphasis on the more important syllables and the like, but he also lingers somewhat on them.[14]

The term *agogic* was adapted from the Greek "*agōgē*," or "tempo," by Hugo Riemann, who introduced it into the musical vocabulary to designate deviations from strict tempo necessary for expressive musical performance.[15] Thus "agogic accent" describes the effect produced by Türk's "lingering."

Türk then raised two obvious questions: "What are the more important notes" to be so lengthened, and "how long can one hold them?"[16] Notes eligible for qualitative accents "are mainly those that, depending on the circumstances, can be lengthened," he continued. (See "Types of Accentuation," in chap. 3.) Thus, among the types of notes designated for occasional broadening in Figure 10.1 are accented dissonances and those distinguished by their high pitch.

Musical context and musicianly taste determined how often this unmarked agogic freedom was used and how long a note might be held.

This lingering cannot always be of the same duration. . . .

I would establish the rule that one could lengthen a note no more than about half [its value] at most. Usually the lingering should be scarcely noticeable if the note already—by and of itself—becomes sufficiently important, for example, because of an occasional accidental, distinguishing high pitch, and unexpected harmony, and the like. It is understood that the following note loses as much of its value as the accented note receives from it.

Whether the delay is longer or shorter depends also on the length of the note and on its relation to the others, for it is easy to understand that one can linger longer on a quarter note than on a sixteenth. If faster notes follow an accented note then the lingering is omitted completely, for in this case the longer note is automatically accented.[17]

Because the figures in this volume are from places of particular interest in relation to performance, there are a number in which agogic stress coupled with a dynamic accent would enhance the affect, and others in which one form of emphasis alone might be preferable. Agogic stress can appropriately be combined with the *fz* in Figure 3.18 and with some of the dynamic accents when the opening theme of Mozart's K. 309/ii, shown in Figure 3.16, returns later in the movement. Depending on the mood of the interpretation, a purely agogic accent might be more affective on the D-sharp in Beethoven's Bagatelle Op. 126/5/10. In m. 24 of Figure 7.63b, Beethoven himself used the peak of the crescendo, the trill (with a turned ending), and a rising melodic skip to focus attention on the D—the note that completes this motive and on which I linger subtly. However, any agogic nuance would weaken certain strongly rhythmic passages, such as that in Figure 3.15.

Some performers place a barely perceptible dynamic and agogic emphasis on the first note of the motive in Figure 5.16 at some of its appearances,[18] the more so when its harmonic underlay is dissonant. But another example associated with the start of a two-note slur, Figure 5.17, sounds best if, in addition to the ear-catching change of touch and range, any emphasis placed on the E and D in mm. 2 and 3 is limited to dynamic stress alone. (Haydn has already lengthened those notes by slurring them.) Finally, in Figure 7.119, the slightest agogic emphasis on the dissonant d^2 adorns a note that Mozart marked with a qualitative accent and that he approached with an unusual written-out arpeggio.[19]

Rhetorical Rests

In 1763 Marpurg wrote an extended description of the "rhetorical rest" based on the relationship—widely accepted in the eighteenth century—between the rhetoric of speech and that of music.[20] He divided the punctuation marks of speech into two groups: the "usual," which he renamed the "grammatical," and in which he included the period, comma, semicolon, and colon; and the "unusual," which he renamed the "rhetorical," and in which he included the question mark, exclamation sign, parentheses, and dash.[21] The parallel to the eighteenth-century division of musical accents is obvious. Grammatical punctuation (in music, slight pauses—sometimes incises and phrase divisions—or rests) clarifies the ideas and sections of speech and music; grammatical accents clarify the organization of meter; rhetorical punctuation (in music, rests) and accents heighten the expression of both speech and music. In music, rhetorical rests occur "in the midst of a conversation" or in the midst of a section to act as punctuation, or because of the affect, or for both reasons.[22] In vocal music rhetorical rests are generally found where the music "follows the declamation in the text most exactly."[23]

To help the musician further, Marpurg identified the places in which the various punctuation signs characteristically appear in language and the analogous places in which the pauses might have similar qualities in instrumental and vocal music. He recognized rhetorical rests in the following melodic situations: Melodies that cadence *"with ascending notes, by leap and stepwise,"* distinguish the question.[24] Exclamations may be carried by short phrases or by brief melodic interjections that usually end with an ascending or a descending leap.[25] For the most "correct" and "comfortable" way to describe the idea of parentheses around a musical phrase, Marpurg suggested places in dramatic recitative that have a brief melodic segment sung as an aside, after which the main line is resumed as if unbroken.[26] In language the dash may apply when a thought remains explicitly incomplete or when there is a sudden change of thought or subject; in music it is expressed through a dissonance whose resolution is either delayed or left to the bass or to the other person speaking in a recitative dialogue. Rhetorical rests in this sense may also occur in arioso style.[27]

With these suggestions, rests that partake of unmarked rhetorical affects are not difficult to find. They are most common when music has a poetic, conversational, or declamatory tone (Haydn's Hob. 34/ii), when it expresses quick changes of mood (Mozart's Fantasy K. 397), when it surprises (Fig. 5.28c), and when it leans toward the dramatic (Fig. 10.3). In Clementi's Sonata Op. 7/3/i the opening theme has an uneasy mood. Still, the crash of the *fortissimo* chord is unexpected and commands the complete attention of the performer and the audience. As the waves of sound die away, action and time cease, bound by the silent tension of the rest. Before this concentration dissipates, the movement continues—*pianissimo* and almost breathlessly—with the important repeated-note motive rhythmically diminished but exactly in tempo. The sense of timing is critical.

The amount of time added to that rest might be measurable, if anyone remembered to try. The time added for rhetorical rests varies just as the broadening of notes does, and both forms of agogic expression may also vary with repetition within a movement. Occasionally there may be a rhetorical rest without discernible added time. Here the drama of the notes preceding it and a special tension during the rest provide the rhetorical quality. The overtly emotional Adagio K. 540, in which Mozart repeatedly provided time and silence to prepare for thematic, dynamic, and emotional change, contains a number of places where more than the allotted time seems necessary before the music wants to proceed. It is appropriate to extend some of these rests to varying degrees, controlled by an alert sense of timing.

Fig. 10.3. Clementi, Sonata Op. 7/3/i (OE Artaria and English ed. for the Author), mm. 13–20.

*Allegro espressivo in the English edition. **p is the preceding dynamic.

Additional examples of rhetorical rests occur at Haydn's Hob. 26/i/31, Hob. 32/iii/18–20, and Hob. 52/ii/32; Mozart's K. 281/iii/89, K. 333/iii/89, and K. 570/i/80; and Beethoven's Op. 2/1/i/147, Op. 7/ii/1–2, Op. 10/3/iv/1–2, and Op. 31/1/iii/232–237. In general such rests are more at home in lines of sharply etched motivic groups and unusually expressive passages, or in music of declamatory recitative-like or arioso styles, than they are in smoothly flowing melodies and serene environments. Thus they are more common in the *empfindsamer Stil* of Emanuel Bach, in the music of Haydn—especially from the mid-1760s on, in Clementi's more dramatic works, and in Beethoven's music than they are in the music of Johann Christian Bach and Wolfgang Mozart.

The *Fermata*

Like Emanuel Bach, Koch also linked the use of the *fermata* to a rhetorical spirit. Here are the situations that "cause the composer to stop the movement in the midst of its flow":

> The expression of surprise or astonishment, a feeling whereby the movements of the spirit itself appear to come to a brief standstill, or such places where the actual feeling appears to have exhausted itself through its full effusion, are sufficient to favor the presence of . . . fermatas.[28]

Every musician can easily recall at least a few of the rests marked with *fermatas* by Haydn, Mozart, Clementi, and Beethoven (e.g., Haydn, Hob. 46/i/91 and Hob. 52/iii/8; Mozart, K. 283/ii/13, 36 and K. 545/iii/52; Clementi, Op. 7/3/iii/49; and Beethoven, Op. 2/1/i/8). These extended rhetorical rests are calculated to produce a larger effect than would unmarked rests.

Fermatas over notes—whether or not a brief "lead-in" or a cadenza is to be improvised—also arrest the momentum in a dramatic way. (Concerning obligatory embellishments at some *fermatas*, see "Improvised Ornamentation" in chap. 7.) For Haydn the *fermata* was a favorite device skillfully integrated into the structural plan where it could have the greatest effect, often as a surprise. Frequently the *fermata* immediately precedes a return or change of theme; in sonata-allegro form it may appear in any section (e.g., Hob. 46/i/17, 23 [exposition]; Hob. 22/i/36 [development]; Hob. 52/iii [in all sections]). Mozart also used *fermatas* over notes, but like those over rests, less freely, less frequently, and less surprisingly than did Haydn and Beethoven. The *fermatas* over notes in Mozart's sonatas are generally where we might expect them, associated with a written-out cadenza (K. 333/iii/171), a "lead-in" (e.g., K. 281/iii/43), or an occasional *a piacere* passage.

Some composers spun out brief *adagio* passages in conjunction with *fermatas*. Meant to be played slowly, in a rather free, declamatory style, these reflective moments, from two beats to two or three measures in length, use *adagio* in its literal sense of "at ease" (*ad agio*) or "leisurely"[29] and broaden the rhetorical effect of the *fermata*. Emanuel Bach interpolated *adagio* passages—before, after, or sometimes without a *fermata*—throughout his works (from the early "Württemberg" Sonatas, e.g., Nos. 1/ii and 2/i, to the late *Clavier-Sonaten ... Rondos ... für Kenner und Liebhaber,* e.g., Zweite Sammlung, Rondo I/132; Vierte Sammlung, Sonata II/ii/50). At Hob. 35/i/100, following a *fermata* on a dominant harmony capped by the minor ninth, Haydn inserted *adagio* over just the following partial resolution in order to relieve the tension built up in the development section of this twirling Allegro con brio. The *adagio* at Hob. 43/i/98–100 is longer, allowing the quasi-cadenza that actually begins in m. 94 to become more recitative-like as it concludes the retransition. Not surprisingly, the earliest interpolated *adagio* passages in Haydn's sonatas occur in the passionate Hob. 20/i, a landmark in his increasing range of emotional expressivity.

RITARDANDO AND ACCELERANDO

Haydn and Mozart seldom wrote *ritardando* or its synonyms into their piano music and—with one exception—seem not to have used *accelerando* at all in this repertoire. Directions for these gradual changes in Haydn's works include *sempre più adagio* in the Sonata Hob. 44/i/68; *sempre più largo* in Hob. 39/ii/58 and the Piano Trio Hob. XV/15/iii/125; *ritardando* in Hob. 50/iii/68 (*JHW, HE;* 92 in HSU); and the sequence *più presto, rallentando* spread over an extended embellishment written in small notes in the Piano Trio Hob. XV/27/ii/66. Haydn's intention for the *più presto* could be considered ambiguous; it might have meant an immediate change to a faster tempo. But since the context is a nine-note pattern that recurs four times—twice in eighth notes and twice in sixteenths—the gradual change of an *accelerando* contrasts with the terraced, written-out change and introduces some variety in the repetitive context. Unambiguous directions for *ritards* are fewer in Mozart's keyboard music: mainly *rallentando* in the Fantasy K. 397/86, the Concerto K. 415/ii from the end of the lead-in to m. 51 (*NMA*), the incomplete Duet Sonata K. 357/ii/110 (Aut.), and the Allegro of the Sonata for Piano and Violin K. 379 (several occurrences).[30] Here the prolonged and repeated *rallentandos* with *crescendos*—each followed by a *fermata* over a rest—intensify the threatening insistence and the fury of the movement.

Like *fermatas* and some rhetorical rests, but in contrast to the subtler agogic accentuation of notes, *ritards* and *accelerandos* are meant to heighten the drama in a noticeable way. Of the indications just listed, all but those in Mozart's K. 379 are at places significant to the overall form. Four are associated with written-out embellishments, cadenza-like passages, or the approach to a *fermata* near the end of a movement; those in Haydn's Hob. 50 and Hob. XV/15 and Mozart's K. 357 and K. 415 provide conspicuous gestures—an extended and humorsome one in the Trio—rather than subtle transitions between thematic sections. Mozart's extension of the A theme *a piacere* at K. 457/iii/228–243 would also involve at least some *rallentando* and is comparable in intent (but not mood) to Haydn's *sempre più largo* at Hob. XV/15/iii/125.

Clementi and Beethoven designated these tempo modifications with greater frequency, Beethoven especially in his later works. Clementi used *rallentando* (or a synonym) frequently in all genres, *accelerando* only in his capriccios and cadenzas (e.g., Capriccio Op. 34/1/9). Examples in Beethoven's works do not need illustration.

After *ritardando, accelerando,* or their equivalents, composers often indicated *a tempo*. When that direction is lacking, as in Haydn's Trio Hob. XV/27/ii/66 and in Mozart's Sonata for Piano and Violin K. 379/i/62, 74, etc. (Aut.), resumption of the basic tempo would have been understood following a *fermata* (if one is present) or at the return of a main theme.

Türk identified the situations in which discretionary addition of an *accelerando* or a *ritardando* by the performer was considered appropriate:

> In pieces whose character is vehemence, anger, wrath, fury, and the like, one can play the most forceful passages somewhat more quickly (*accelerando*). Similarly, individual ideas that are repeated more intensely (usually at a higher pitch) require that one also increase the speed to some extent. At times, when gentle feelings are interrupted by a lively passage, that passage can be played somewhat hurriedly. Hastening is also permitted in an idea in which, unexpectedly, a more passionate affect should be aroused.[31]

The unexpected, forceful phrase (mm. 85–88) interpolated near the start of the development section in Clementi's Op. 7/3/i seems to fuel an *accelerando* in the chromatic ascent of m. 87. In 1802 Türk added that it would be safer if the composer himself indicated the places to be performed with an *accelerando:*

> In exceptionally tender, languishing, [or] melancholy passages in which the emotion is as if brought to a peak, the effect can be greatly strengthened by an increasing hesitation [*ritardando*] (*Anhalten, tardando*). Likewise, in the approach to certain fermatas ... one takes the movement a bit slower, little by little, as if the energies were gradually becoming exhausted. The passages toward the end of a composition (or part [of a composition]) that are marked *diminuendo, diluendo, smorzando,* and the like, may also be played with a little lingering [*verweilend*].[32]

Further on Türk added that some slowing of the tempo was appropriate "in written-out ornamentation and transitions notated in small notes or [marked] *Senza tempo*" and in transitional approaches to important sections of a piece, even when written in the usual notation.[33] That would presumably include the return to a principal theme.

A *ritard* at places of unusually intense feeling would include some passages marked *espressivo*. Clementi's definition of *con espressione* is significant here, as is his reference to the usual "severity of time":

> CON ESPRESSIONE, or CON ANIMA, with expression; that is, with passionate feeling; where every note has its peculiar force and energy; and where even the severity of time may be relaxed for extraordinary effects.[34]

Czerny, who suggested a *ritard* "almost always where the Composer has indicated an *espressivo,*"[35] recommended an "increasing *ritardando*" at the *con espressione* in Beethoven's Sonata Op. 2/1/i/41–44.[36] In two of Beethoven's late works, the sonata-form Prestissimo of Op. 109 and the last movement of the Sonata for Violin and Piano Op. 96 (Aut., *BNA*), the succession of terms *espressivo, a tempo* appears, each time with several measures between the two words. Presumably the tempo modification at these places would be greater than that for a solitary *espressivo,* especially one in Beethoven's early works.

Türk clarified his reference to *ritards* "in the approach to certain fermatas" with the advice that "When the affect requires it, one customarily takes the tempo somewhat slower, little by little, already for the notes *before* the fermata. . . ."[37] Each performer must consider whether, according to his taste, the affect is best served by arriving at a given *fermata* as a total surprise, which requires an approach in strict tempo (cf. discussion of Fig. 3.6), or by preparing the *fermata* as the end of an event, which often suggests an approach with a *ritard.* The approach to the *fermata* in Haydn's Trio Hob. XV/27/i/48–51 is one about which two distinguished musicians, Georg Feder and Malcolm Bilson, had different opinions in 1975.[38]

Türk's *ritards* in "passages toward the end of a composition (or section [of a composition]) that are marked *diminuendo, . . . , smorzando,* and the like," and in transitional approaches to important sections of a piece, are *ritards* at structural joints. *Fermatas* also appear at similar places. This use of *ritards,* especially applicable to the multithematic forms of the Classic period, was described in greater detail in the first half of the nineteenth century, when tempo modification occurred with increasing frequency.[39] Significantly, the *ritards* suggested by Czerny in his comments on the performance of Beethoven's works are often closely related to formal structure.[40] Lastly, Türk's suggestion that *ritards* are also appropriate in written-out embellishments finds a welcome home in Haydn's Hob. 52/ii/e.g., 20 and 23, and in Mozart's Concerto K. 365/ii/46–47, to cite just two compositions.

From Türk's description, from the examples written in scores, and from what seems to succeed best in performance, it is not difficult to deduce that the dominant agogic tendency in Classic music was the *ritard.* Its use far exceeded the *accelerando.* Concerning the application of the *ritard,* Türk had two further suggestions:

> By and large, the slowing down can occur most appropriately in passages in slow tempo.[41]

> The slower passages must not be drawn out too broadly, however; rather, one plays only gradually a little—almost imperceptibly—slower, than the tempo requires.[42]

Türk also cautioned the performer to use the same care in making a discretionary *accelerando.*

Were discretionary *ritards* and *accelerandos* played more subtly than those specifically indicated? I would say yes in many instances, particularly in the music of Haydn and Mozart, whose rare written indications occur where they seem to have wanted a special intensity. Overall, Haydn wrote fewer performance directions than did Mozart, and those are often concerned with unusual effects. There are, of course, pieces that are best played throughout in strict tempo. They include many dance movements and works that depend for their effect on a steady rhythmic propulsion.

Sectional Change of Mood and Tempo

In Türk's opinion,

> A tenderly moving passage between two lively, fiery ideas . . . can be played somewhat hesitatingly; only in this case one does not take the tempo gradually slower, but *immediately* a little (however, only a *little*) slower [in 1802, "a little, (however, barely perceptibly) slower"]. In particular, an appropriate opportunity for such slackening of the tempo occurs in compositions in which two characters of contrasting types are represented.[43]

Although single movements or pieces in the Classic style were generally played in one underlying tempo, a subtle change of tempo was occasionally used, particularly in an *allegro,* to enhance the new mood of a strongly contrasting theme. After reminding the performer again that this tempo change, like the *ritard,* must be "well nigh unnoticeably slower," Türk observed that "many players . . . change from an Allegro almost to an Adagio, which often makes a very bad effect."[44]

Surely Türk intended his description to represent a very slight pulling out of the tempo, of which the listener is barely aware. This tempo alteration corresponds to a strict, nineteenth-century interpretation of the term *ritenuto,* which is an immediate rather than a gradual slowing down.[45] (When *ritenuto* is explicitly indicated in nineteenth-century music, the tempo change may be more obvious.) The lyricism of the theme in Mozart's Sonata K. 330/i/19–25 attracts some pianists to Türk's drawing out of the tempo—by just one metronome mark in the performances I have heard; others maintain their original tempos for this theme.[46] A similar adjustment is effective in Clementi's Op 7/3/i, from the last eighth note of m. 58, where the important motivic half step emerges in a tender melodic element marked *espressivo* in the London edition, to m. 69. Haydn's sonata-allegro movements seldom offer the opportunity for a sectional change of tempo because of their tendency toward monothematic or tightly unified motivic structure.

Czerny's description of a sectional change for Beethoven's Trio Op. 1/3/i stresses the essential subtlety more than those of Türk and Hummel (pp. 362–363 above):

The first movement is played with passionate excitement, noticeably quickly but not precipitously. The middle theme (from measure 58 [*sic*]) calm and with great melodic expression, but not slower.

(Here we must insert the special, generally pertinent remark, that there is a certain way of playing melodically beautiful passages more calmly and yet not perceptibly slower, so that everything appears to move in one and the same tempo, and that the difference would only be noticed at best if the metronome were going at the same time. An obvious change of tempo is only allowed where the composer has expressly indicated it with *più lento, ritardando,* etc.)[47]

Czerny would achieve his purpose by coordinating several elements of performance. His tranquillity is effected at least as much by a change of mood and manner (including articulation and tone quality) as by a barely discernible tempo change. Only where the composer himself specifically indicated a change should it be noticeable. A good example of such a written indication is Beethoven's *espressivo* at Op. 2/2/i/58, for a B theme that has a mood markedly different from that of the A section. In this movement Beethoven prepared for the slower tempo with a *rallentando* at a point in the transition where the material also takes on something of the shape and character of the coming theme.[48]

Eighteenth-Century *Tempo Rubato*

Tempo rubato, or "stolen time," was another facet of rhythmic interpretation. Because this term was applied to two strongly contrasting concepts of rhythmic flexibility in the eighteenth and nineteenth centuries, each usage will be traced separately.

Freely Shifting Contrametric *Rubato*

The underlying concept of *tempo rubato* held by eighteenth-century musicians was a redistribution of rhythmic values in a solo melody against an accompaniment that maintained *a steady beat in a constant tempo.* This expressive device was a time-honored part of music making with the new name of *rubato.*[49] I use the term "contrametric" *rubato,* which describes its characteristic shifting away from the meter (although sometimes around rather than against it) and differentiates it from the usual nineteenth-century *rubato.* Some contrametric *rubato* seems to have moved rather freely and subtly; another type was more uniform in its shifting of notes by anticipation or retardation. Their roles in the performance of Classic music can best be appreciated by meeting the two types as they were earlier in the eighteenth century.

In 1723 Pier Francesco Tosi held that "good Taste" included

going from one Note to another with singular and unexpected Surprises, and stealing the Time exactly on the true *Motion* of the Bass.[50]

The stealing of Time [*Il rubamento di Tempo*], in the *Pathetick,* is an honourable Theft in one that sings better than others, provided he makes a Restitution with Ingenuity.[51]

Tosi's English translator, Galliard, elaborated on these remarks in a footnote:

Speaking of stealing the Time, it regards particularly the Vocal, or the Performance on a single Instrument in the *Pathetick* and *Tender;* when the Bass goes an exactly regular Pace, the other Part retards or anticipates in a singular Manner, for the Sake of Expression, but after That returns to its Exactness, to be guided by the Bass.[52]

Unfortunately, neither Tosi nor Galliard left any musical examples.

In the following remarks Leopold Mozart emphasized the accompanist's role in *tempo rubato:*

To a sound virtuoso he ["a clever accompanist"] certainly must not yield, for he would then spoil his tempo rubato. What this "stolen tempo" is, *is more easily shown than described* [italics added].

Many, who have no idea of taste, never retain the evenness of tempo in the accompanying of a concerto part, but endeavour always to follow the solo-part. These are accompanists for dilettanti and not for masters. . . . when a true virtuoso who is worthy of the title is to be accompanied, then one must not allow oneself to be beguiled by the postponing or anticipating of the notes, which he knows how to shape so adroitly and touchingly, into hesitating or hurrying, but must continue to play throughout in the same manner; else the effect which the performer desired to build up would be demolished by the accompaniment.[53]

Like Tosi and Galliard, Mozart was disinclined to attempt any examples of this supple, improvisatory, and freely shifting "stolen tempo."

Emanuel Bach described *tempo rubato* in the 1787 edition of his *Essay.* For him the essentials included the presence of more or fewer notes than the division of the meter usually provided. Their performance "exactly equally" would give the impression of one hand playing against the meter and the other hand with it.

The tempo rubato also belongs here [in this discussion of rhythmic aspects of performance]. In its indication the [rhythmic] figures sometimes have more, sometimes fewer notes than the [usual] division of the measure allows. In this manner one can distort, so to speak, a part of the measure, a whole measure, or several measures. The most difficult and most essential thing is this: that all notes of the *same* value must be played exactly *equally.* When the execution *is such* that one hand appears to play against the meter while the other strikes all the beats precisely, then one has done everything that is necessary. Only very seldom are all parts struck simultaneously. . . . Slow notes, caressing and sad thoughts [melodies] are the best for this. Dissonant harmonies are better suited to it than consonant passages. Proper execution of this *tempo* requires a great sense of judgment and an especially great sensitivity. He who has both will not find it difficult to shape his performance with complete freedom and without the least constraint, and he would be able—if necessary—to reshape any passage. . . . Singers and instrumentalists, *when they are accompanied,* can introduce this *tempo* much more easily than the keyboard player, particularly if he must accompany himself. . . . In my keyboard pieces one finds many examples of this *tempo.* Their division and indication is expressed as well as it could be. Whoever has mastered the performance of this *tempo,* is not always bound by the indicated numbers, 5, 7, 11, and so on. He sometimes plays more, sometimes fewer notes, according to his mood, but always with the appropriate freedom [my translation].[54]

Bach's phrase "against the meter" (*wider den Tact*) is the equivalent of "contrametric" rubato. Figures 10.4 and 10.5 are from his important *Sechs Sonaten fürs Clavier mit veränderten Reprisen* (with varied reprises) Wq. 50, published in 1760. The necessary independence of the hands and equality of the notes are expressed in the original edition of Figure 10.4 by the precise alignment of the left-hand quarter note under the space between the central notes of the *rubato* figure, as shown here. Some years after the publication of Wq. 50, Bach notated additional *rubato* ornamentation in Sonatas 3, 4, and 5. Sketched in the margin without beams, the variant in Figure 10.5 is to be played relatively evenly over the two beats. Etienne Darbellay's hypothesis that the variants date from after 1786[55] would place their origin at the same time as Bach's description of *rubato* in his *Essay.*

Fig. 10.4. E. Bach, *Sechs Sonaten . . . mit veränderten Reprisen* Wq. 50/4/i (OE Winter), mm. 112–114.

Fig. 10.5. E. Bach, *Sechs Sonaten. . .* Wq. 50/5/i (OE Winter and Bach's *Handexemplar*), m. 88. a. First edition. b. Bach's variant.

*Bach's notation in the margin is difficult to decipher here; c^2 and d^2 are questionable.

Almost a century after Tosi, in 1808, Koch left a little more information about the Italianate *rubato,* but declared it obsolete along with the need for improvised ornamentation. He described it as

> that manner of performance of this or that cantabile passage of a solo part, in which the player intentionally digressed from the assumed movement of the tempo and from the usual distribution of note values, and executed the melodic line as if without any fixed division of time, while the accompaniment played on absolutely strictly in tempo. Among others, Franz Benda often made use of this manner of performance as a special means of expression in the Adagio movements of his concertos and sonatas. Although there are . . . virtuosos who . . . occasionally make use of a similar manner of performance . . . , still there is usually only a far less noticeable deviation from the tempo than previously, so that one can maintain that kind of execution . . . to be obsolete nowadays. The neglect . . . may well be far more advantageous than detrimental for the art . . . , in part because modern composers work out fully the melody of the Adagio movements of their concertos. . . .[56]

It is easy to see how melodic embellishment and *tempo rubato* often went hand in hand.

Copies exist of some of Franz Benda's sonata movements with the written-out improvisatory embellishments for which he was celebrated (Figs. 10.6 and 10.7). According to Burney, Benda was "so very affecting a player, so truly pathetic in an *Adagio,* that several able professors have assured me that he has frequently drawn tears from them in performing one."[57] Benda's style, Burney continued, was "formed from that model which should be ever studied by all instrumental performers, *good singing.*"[58] The effusive elaboration of the melody in Figure 10.6 was a perfect vehicle for that flexibility "inexpressible through notation,"[59] in which the melodic line is played "as if without any fixed division of time." Reichardt praised Benda's *rubato* as an "extremely meaningful laxity in the tempo of the notes."[60]

Fig. 10.6. Franz Benda, Sonata for Violin and Thoroughbass, i (Ferand, *Improvisation,* p. 137), mm. 55–56. Realization of thoroughbass by Ferand.

Fig. 10.7. Benda, Sonata for Violin and Thoroughbass, iii (Ferand, *Improvisation,* p. 142), m. 97. Realization of thoroughbass by Ferand.

Contrametric *Rubato* by Uniform Displacement

The German translator of Tosi's instructions for singers, Johann Friedrich Agricola, interpreted "stealing the time" with the examples in Figure 10.8. This illustration of *rubato* portrays not what Tosi described or what Emanuel Bach and Benda realized, but represents instead a rigidly formulated adaptation of rhythmic displacement.[61] The same concept was shared by other musicians, some but not all of them north Germans. Marpurg's *Anleitung,* published two years earlier, contains the identical melodic figures described as anticipation (*Vorausnehmen;* Fig. 10.8b) and retardation or suspension (*Aufhalten;* Fig. 10.8c) under the classification "figures of composition."[62] Marpurg included the term *tempo rubato* only in the index: "this is what the Italians call various ways of anticipating notes. See Anticipation."[63] Two further notes in Marpurg's *Principes de Clavecin* of 1756 (his own French translation of the *Anleitung*) associate *tempo rubato* with anticipation and retardation.[64] Johann Adam Hiller's *rubato* was based on the same principle, and even in 1805 Johann Baptist Lasser repeated Agricola's figure, though he furnished it with text and added an upbeat.[65]

Türk's explanation of this schematized *rubato* is the clearest:

Usually one understands it as a kind of shortening and lengthening of the notes, or a displacement (shifting) of them. That is to say, something is taken away (stolen) from the duration of one note and therefore that much more is given

Fig. 10.8. Agricola, *Anleitung zur Singkunst,* p. 219.

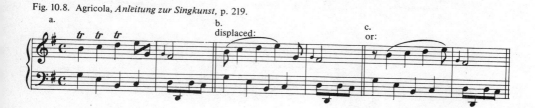

to another, as in [Figs. 10.9b and c]. . . . In [Fig. 10.9b] *Tempo rubato* is achieved by means of *anticipation* (*anticipatio*) and in [Fig. 10.9c] by means of *retardation* (*retardatio*). . . . With this manner of execution neither the tempo nor the meter as a whole is disturbed. . . .[66]

His *rubato* examples also include Figure 10.10, for which he specified that "both voices must coincide correctly again at the beginning of each measure."[67]

In 1802 Türk made the point that the *rubato* of Figure 10.9 is based on syncopation.[68] Compared to the flexibility of the vocally derived Italian style, this *rubato* is a simplification. Perhaps it was rendered more freely. Yet it was just this systematization that allowed, toward the end of the century, the inclusion under the rubric *tempo rubato* of two types of notated displaced accents. The first is the shifting of the accent by means of dynamic indications (Fig. 10.11).[69] I would guess that inclusion of this qualitative concept as a form of *rubato* was a degenerative offshoot of the practice of playing melody notes in uniform syncopation against the meter. The second type occurs in vocal music when composers set accented syllables on strong beats with short notes and unaccented syllables on weak beats with long notes. This writing qualified as *rubato* for some musicians but created a controversy because of the effect on the scansion of the text.[70]

Koch espoused the *rubato* of Figure 10.11 in the same article in which he declared the original *tempo rubato* obsolete. For him the shifting of accents from strong to weak beats represented the true meaning of *rubato* at that time (1808). It included as well the simple syncopation created by placing a long note on a weak beat and the effect produced by repeating in succession a melodic motive written in binary meter within a ternary meter, and vice-versa.[71]

Fig. 10.9. Türk, *Klavierschule*, p. 374.

Fig. 10.10. Türk, *Klavierschule*, p. 375.

Fig. 10.11. Türk, *Klavierschule*, p. 375.

Contrametric *Rubato* in the Piano Works of Mozart, Haydn, and Beethoven

Wolfgang Mozart described his use of *rubato* in a famous letter to his father from Augsburg on 24 October 1777:

> Everyone is amazed that I can always keep strict time. What these people cannot grasp is that in tempo rubato, in an Adagio, the left hand should go on playing in strict time. With them the left hand always follows suit.[72]

Fortunately Mozart left some written-out approximations of what he might have meant, although he could hardly have expressed in notation the rich rhythmic subtlety of his south German/Italian heritage. Figure 10.12 shows two versions of an excerpt from the Adagio of his Sonata K. 332. The autograph was presumably his playing copy, on which he improvised at will when the main theme returned. A desire to have the published score more complete, so that others would not be tempted to add to his works, probably compelled him to write out some of his "extemporaneous" ornamentation, including the stylized *rubato* in mm. 34 and 35. Figure 10.13b, a variation of Figure 10.13a further on in the Rondo, illustrates a more expressive version of the same uniform displacement.

Most contemporary composers wrote out that same kind of *rubato* in their keyboard works. No doubt the melody was frequently meant to be realized in a suppler, more improvisatory rhythm. In a movement such as the Adagio of Haydn's Sonata Hob. 39, the solo line could occasionally contain minute shifts within the beat. But notating such brief, possibly irregular and irrational shifting would have been too fussy, sometimes impossible in normal notation, and altogether contrary to the spirit of improvisatory freedom (directly comparable to writing out trills, for example). Yet, even as notated, the regularized con-

Fig. 10.12. Mozart, Sonata K. 332/ii, mm. 34–35. a. after Artaria. b. after Aut.

*In Artaria this slur was mistakenly placed as a tie to the preceding D.

Fig. 10.13. Mozart, Rondo K. 511 (Aut. facs.). a. mm. 5–7. b. mm. 85–87.

trametric *rubato* achieves a heightened expression and is similar to a form of syncopation used in twentieth-century jazz.

By 1802 Türk wrote that an appropriate opportunity for a player to add *rubato* may arise "only very seldom . . . since the composers indicate [it] most of the time."[73] But certainly Mozart and Haydn did not suggest it all on paper, especially not before their late works. Dare we admit a momentary inspiration in performance? A pianist might experiment with a touch of this *rubato* in the Adagio of Mozart's K. 282 at the repetition of the B theme in mm. 28–29, or in the Andante of K. 545. Here, for example, in m. 43 the four sixteenth notes from f-sharp[2] to b-flat[2] might anticipate the bass or even be subdivided as in Figure 10.10f. I would continue beat 3 as written. A few of Mozart's concerto movements provide more fertile territory for ornamentation-*cum-rubato* because of the occasional skeletal nature of the melody. In general the most natural home for this *rubato* is in slow movements with a relatively simple, homophonic accompaniment. (See "Improvised Ornamentation" in chap. 7.)

There seems not to be any evidence that Beethoven used the term *tempo rubato*,[74] but there is some that he would have been familiar with its meaning at least in the general contrametric sense. His teacher Neefe described it in a letter of 2 March 1783 to Cramer's *Magazin der Musik*. The Countess von Hatzfeld, niece of the Elector (of Bonn), to whom Beethoven dedicated his variations on "Venni amore,"

had been trained in singing and keyboard playing by the best masters of Vienna to whom, indeed, she brings much honor. She declaims recitatives admirably and it is a pleasure to hear her arias *di parlante*. She plays the fortepiano very brilliantly and in playing gives way completely to her emotions. For that reason one often hears her *tempo rubato*, which is not at all unsteady in its time.[75]

Examples of written-out *rubato* in Beethoven's works include Op. 27/1/iii/ 13–16, the fourth variation of the Andante of the "Archduke" Trio, and Op.

Fig. 10.14. Beethoven, Sonata Op. 106/iii (OE Artaria), mm. 27–33.

106/iii/117–124 along with its counterpart in Figure 10.14. Many performers intensify the *grand Espression* with additional contrametric and some agogic nuance.[76] (See "Agogic *Rubato* in the Piano Works of Beethoven" below.)

Descriptions of Contrametric *Rubato* in French Tutors

Less was written about *rubato* in French tutors, but two descriptions may imply use of both freer and more regulated rearrangement of melody notes. Adam's statement, with no examples, is unspecific, and could include both concepts:

> Without doubt, expression requires that one hold back or hurry certain notes of the melody . . . but only in those places where the expression of a languishing melody or the passion of an agitated melody requires a delay or a more animated movement. In this case it is the melody that should be altered and the bass ought to mark the time [*mesure*] strictly.[77]

Later Baillot, a leader of the turn-of-the-century French violin school, wrote that *temps dérobé*

> is similar to syncopation. . . . It expresses unrest . . . , and few composers have indicated it specifically; the character of the passage usually suffices to indicate to the player where he should use it according to the inspiration of the moment. . . . He must preserve the tempo. . . .[78]

His examples are uniformly displaced half a beat by retardation or anticipation.

There is ample evidence that Chopin carried on the practice of contrametric *rubato* in the styles described by Tosi and Emanuel Bach. The description by his student Carl Mikuli conveys the impression of a spontaneous and flexible manner:

> In his oft-decried *tempo rubato* one hand—that having the accompaniment—always played on in strict time, while the other, singing the melody, either hesitating as if undecided, or, with increased animation, anticipating with a kind of impatient vehemence as if in passionate utterances, maintained the freedom of musical expression from the fetters of strict regularity.[79]

Chopin notated some of this *rubato* in the opening and closing sections of his Nocturne Op. 48/1 (e.g., mm. 1–2, 4ff.).

TEMPO FLEXIBILITY AS *TEMPO RUBATO*

Early Evidence of Agogic *Rubato*

During the nineteenth century the term *rubato* became identified with tempo flexibility or elasticity. The practice of spontaneous, expressive flexibility is an old one that has varied in degree from style to style and time to time;[80] what is new is its inclusion as *rubato*. Yet, from Mozart's letter of October 1777 (quoted on p. 379), it would seem that at least some musicians may already have associated the term *rubato* with tempo flexibility, perhaps resulting from a weakening of the basic concept of contrametric *rubato*. When "the left hand always follows suit," the result is a form of flexibility related to the effect of *ritardando* and *accelerando* to a greater or lesser degree. This is now often called "agogic" *rubato* in contrast to the contrametric, although in the nineteenth century it was simply *tempo rubato*.[81] From here on, except in quotations, I shall use the terms "agogic *rubato*" and "tempo flexibility" interchangeably for the nineteenth-century style, reserving *tempo rubato* for its true meaning in the eighteenth-century sense.

At its subtlest, agogic *rubato* may be merely a suppleness in the movement within a small number of beats, induced, perhaps, by an especially expressive turn of phrase or harmony. It might even include the lingering on individual notes described earlier as agogic accentuation. In more openly expressive moments the tempo may be noticeably stretched or accelerated, in practice actually more often the former. Frequent and noticeable use of agogic *rubato* is characteristic of the Romantic or subjective part of the Classic-Romantic cycle of artistic styles. Hence this *rubato* is most used in music expressing the individualistic, the different, the seeking, the unending.

An early definition that recognizes the validity of agogic *rubato* appears in Busby's *Complete Dictionary of Music*, ca. 1801. Busby defined *tempo rubato* as "An expression applied to a time alternately accelerated and retarded for the purpose of enforcing the expression."[82] In 1802 Türk recognized this usage with an addition to his section on *rubato:* "The intentional hastening or slowing mentioned above [discussion of *accelerando* and *ritardando*] is also signified by some with the expression *Tempo rubato*. . . .[83]

The *Méthode de Violon* of 1803 by Baillot, Rode, and Kreutzer, which was adopted by the prestigious Conservatoire in Paris, contains a somewhat ambiguous description of tempo elasticity that might admit both agogic *rubato* and agogic accentuation:

> Expression sometimes allows an insensible deviation from the time, but either that deviation is gradual and almost imperceptible, or the time is merely disguised; that is to say, in pretending to lose an instant one finds oneself soon afterwards as exact in following it as before.[84]

Czerny did not deal with the concept of contrametric *rubato* in his *Piano Forte School;* in a section on "Musical Accent applied to Single Notes," those displaced uniformly were "syncopated notes," by then a typical point of view.[85] Nor did he use the term *rubato* when he described agogic *rubato* in Vol. III of his *Piano Forte School*[86] or in *Proper Performance.* Only in relation to "Advice on the Performance of the most recent Compositions by Thalberg, . . . Chopin, . . . Fr. Liszt . . . ," another chapter in Op. 500/IV, did Czerny use the term *tempo rubato* in defining its nineteenth-century usage—"namely, the arbitrary holding back or hastening of the tempo."[87] In addressing what he considered its widespread, flagrant abuse, Czerny also included a reflection on Hummel's playing:

> How often have we had to hear in recent time, for example, in the performance of a Hummel Concerto, already in the first movement (which is still only in one tempo), the first line played *allegro,* the middle melody *andante,* the passage following that *presto,* and then again individual places stretched out endlessly, and so on,—while Hummel himself played his compositions in such a constant tempo that one could almost always have let the metronome beat to it.[88]

Agogic *Rubato* in the Piano Works of Haydn, Mozart, and Clementi

In certain ways the degree to which composers indicate rhythmic and tempo flexibility in their music may properly be regarded as one reliable clue to the kind and degree of discretionary flexibility appropriate in performance of their works. For example, we have seen that Haydn's music contains more unexpected *fermatas* and *adagio* passages than does Mozart's, and that it is also susceptible to more unmarked rhetorical rests. A similar spirit informs both the written and the unwritten means of expression.

According to this thesis, it would seem that noticeable tempo flexibility is seldom appropriate in the piano works of Mozart and Haydn. Mozart's keyboard music contains remarkably few directions for *ritards.* In his letters Mozart often mentioned the importance of playing "in time" (see above, p. 23);[89] he also referred to the use of *tempo rubato* in which his left hand kept "strict time." Haydn left no comments about tempo modification and, again, indicated few *ritards* and only one *accelerando*. However, while his *fermatas* and short *adagio* sections have a more dramatic function, they exemplify the use of rhythmic devices for expressive ends. In the Adagio movements in Haydn's sonatas from Hob. 38 on, there are also frequent ornamental runs containing enough notes to force a yielding of the tempo (as occurs too in Mozart's Sonata K. 457/ii). Might Haydn have expected a little more discretionary use of agogic *rubato* than did Mozart, particularly in those movements that contain a strong element of fantasy, discourse, or drama?

The scarcity of indications by Haydn and Mozart for tempo modification is surely a sign that for the most part those composers preferred the *impression* of steadily ongoing tempos. Performers should respect that, perhaps even more so for Mozart's music than for Haydn's. (In speaking of strict or steady tempo, I always include the expectation that music is allowed to breathe, particularly at important transitions, and that the various kinds of rhythmic flexibility condoned by relevant theorists are applicable with the proper restraint.) Nevertheless, occasionally, particularly in slow movements, there is sufficient growth of tension or emotional expression to allow a modest hastening or broadening within what might be considered the bounds of Classic restraint. The Adagio of Mozart's K. 457 provides an example, in mm. 35–40, where the climb from the unexpected, sunny key of G-flat major to the dominant of C minor and then to E-flat major takes the listener through some tortuous dissonance and chromaticism. Improvisatory rhetoric, the dominating element of the Adagio of Haydn's Hob. 34, not only inspires but requires some agogic flexibility.

Clementi's music, with its more-frequent written indications for tempo modification and its predilection for the dramatic in many works (e.g., Opp. 13/6 and 25/5), would seem to offer a more natural home for agogic *rubato*. His definition of *con espressione* (cited above) and the "inimitable rapture" of his playing, with "*lentando* and *rubando*" that "would be impossible to express . . . on paper" (p. 26), support this view. Nevertheless, his pointed wording that "even the severity of time may be relaxed for extraordinary effects" would indicate that Clementi, also, generally respected the parameters of Classic performance style.

Agogic *Rubato* in the Piano Works of Beethoven

There is considerably more relevant information regarding tempo flexibility in the performance of Beethoven's piano music. It exists in three types of sources: the increasing variety and frequency of notated indications for flexibility in his piano music; contemporary observations on his own playing and conducting; contemporary observations on the playing of his music by his colleagues.

It is not without interest that even in his Opp. 1 and 2 Beethoven included more directions for tempo flexibility than exist in any of the sonatas and chamber works with piano of Haydn and Mozart. Nevertheless, his indications in the sonatas before Op. 31 are, in the main, unremarkable except for the rarity with which he specified tempo flexibility in slow movements before the late sonatas. Although there is a *fermata* near the end of Op. 2/3/ii, and there are occasional *fermatas* and lead-ins in slow sonata movements starting with Op. 27/1/iii, the first written *ritard* appears in Op. 81a/ii. This observation suggests that performers maintain a firm tempo structure in these slow movements, with some barely perceptible elasticity intimated by such headings as Largo, con gran espressione for Op. 7/ii. Czerny expressed a similar opinion in regard to many of the slow movements (see below, pp. 390–391).

A number of the early sonatas have no indications (in any movement) for flexibility in the sense of *ritardando* or *stringendo;* however, with one exception, all contain *fermatas* that arrest the tempo at structural joints. Only the Sonata Op. 26 and these individual movements in other sonatas have no tempo alteration of any kind. Yet Czerny's suggestions for the performance of the sonatas include enough tempo flexibility to imply that Beethoven wanted even his earlier works played with a little more flexibility than he notated.[90] The intensity of expressiveness attributed to his improvisatory playing by Junker as early as 1791 bespeaks a musician of unusually keen sensibility (p. 27). When such a pianist permits it, this sensibility often expresses itself at least partially through a degree of agogic variation. Might not Beethoven have expected the same of others playing his music?

From the sonatas of Op. 31, composed in 1802, Beethoven gradually wrote more tempo variation of all kinds into the musical structure by increased use of devices such as *fermatas,* recitative-like passages, strongly contrasted meter or tempo changes within a movement, lead-ins, and other elaborate embellishments, including broken chords. For example, the figuration in m. 53 of Op. 31/3/i may force a slight yielding that is brushed aside in m. 54.[91] Also starting from Op. 31, Beethoven's written directions for tempo modification not only became more numerous and more varied than in the earlier compositions, with *accelerandos* as well as the much more frequently used *rallentandos,* but also appeared more often in places other than the structural joints at which they had traditionally occurred. The *poco ritardando* in mm. 12–13 of the sixteen-measure period that opens the "Appassionata" Sonata is hardly expected. Nor is the sequence *poco ritenente, a tempo* in mm. 22–23 of Op. 111/i. Here the Allegro con brio ed appassionato has barely begun when it is interrupted abruptly by a *fermata,* then followed only two measures later by a slowing down of the tempo. These examples of tempo flexibility spring from and emphasize feeling rather than form.

Observations about Beethoven as a performer supply a little information about his own use of unmarked tempo flexibility. Ferdinand Ries studied piano with Beethoven from the fall of 1801 to 1805 and had the unique opportunity of playing his Concerto Op. 37 in public as the composer's pupil and under his baton. Ries's description of his teacher's playing during those years speaks of occasional agogic *rubato* as a means of expression:

> In general he played his own compositions very spiritedly, yet for the most part remained absolutely in time, and only occasionally, but not often, hurried the

tempo a little. Sometimes during a *crescendo* he held the tempo back with a *ritardando*, which created a very beautiful and highly striking effect.

In playing he sometimes gave a passage, whether in the right or the left hand, a lovely, but utterly inimitable expression. . . .[92]

Ignaz von Seyfried, a musician and friend, wrote of Beethoven's orchestral conducting, probably as it was during approximately the first decade of the nineteenth century:

He was very meticulous with regard to expression, the more delicate shadings, an equalized distribution of light and shade, and an effective *tempo rubato*, and without betraying the slightest impatience always took pleasure in discussing them individually with the various musicians.[93]

Seyfried did not clarify what type of *rubato* he meant or the extent of its use; neither did he mention any soloists. Since contrametric *rubato*, even in its more regulated form, was useful only in solo parts, it seems reasonable to assume that Seyfried's comment (actually written many years later) referred to agogic *rubato*. Busby and Türk had associated tempo flexibility with that term at the turn of the century.[94]

How those close to Beethoven performed his music is our third potential source of information for relevant performance practices. Schuppanzigh's importance in introducing Beethoven's music in Vienna was mentioned in chapter 3; his quartet had also played pieces by Haydn in that composer's presence (p. 90 and n. 125). Reichardt's description of the way Schuppanzigh's group performed the quartets of Haydn, Mozart, and Beethoven in 1808 suggests some use of agogic *rubato:*

Herr Schuppanzigh himself has an original, interesting [*pikante*] style that is very well suited to the imaginative [*humoristischen*] quartets of Haydn, Mozart, and Beethoven; or rather, perhaps, it has resulted from the spirited [*launigen*] manner of performance suited to these masterpieces. He plays the most difficult passages clearly, although not always absolutely in tune, about which the local virtuosos seem, on the whole, not to care. He also accents very correctly and meaningfully. His cantabile, too, is often quite singing and full of feeling. Likewise, he skillfully leads his well-chosen colleagues, who truly enter into the spirit of the composer. . . .[95]

Several entries in the diary of the professional violinist Michael Frey from the winter of 1815–1816 are more specific about the use of tempo flexibility by the Schuppanzigh Quartet at this time:

They played it [Op. 59/2] with great precision and skill, so that one need wish for nothing more. In menuetts in general, in the playful places they sometimes exaggerate the playful and casual [elements] in the performance. They usually do it twice in a row, which does not make a good effect since something like that can only be pleasing once in quick passing.[96]

Even more interesting is Frey's comment that in a performance of Op. 18/4 "in the last Allegro they introduced a Rittartando [*sic*] right at the beginning, which interrupted the fast pace of the whole too much."[97] Frey also mentioned the use of *rubato* to a surprising degree in the Menuetto, Presto, of Haydn's Op. 76/6. "They played the Menuett in a very mannered [way] with a varied, retarded tempo that disturbed the flow of the whole too much."[98]

The collective evidence, then, suggests progressive change in what Beethoven might have viewed as appropriate agogic *rubato* for the performance of his music. In the early years (to about 1802) he presumably favored a steady beat that was occasionally tempered by the performer—probably more often than in the music of Haydn and Mozart—to heighten the expression. A gradual increase in his notation of tempo flexibility from 1802 on is complemented by reports of its use in his performances from about that same time.[99] The Schuppanzigh Quartet, too, seems to have heightened its use of agogic *rubato* in the seven years between the reports of Reichardt and Frey. Finally, Beethoven's inscription on the song "Nord oder Süd" WoO 148, composed in 1817, testifies unequivocally to his view of tempo flexibility as an empathic response necessary for interpreting the music of his late period: "100 according to Maelzel; but this must be held applicable to only the first measures, for feeling also has its tempo and this cannot entirely be expressed in this figure (i.e., 100)."[100]

SCHINDLER AND CZERNY ON TEMPO FLEXIBILITY IN BEETHOVEN'S PIANO MUSIC

It remains now to consider more fully the evidence left by Anton Schindler and Carl Czerny apropos tempo flexibility in Beethoven's piano music. (The question of Schindler's relationship to Beethoven was introduced in chapter 3.) In his *Biographie* of 1840, Schindler stated his point of view:

> All the pieces which I have heard Beethoven himself play were, with few exceptions, given without any constraint as to the rate of the time. He adopted a *tempo-rubato* in the proper sense of the term, according as subject and situation might demand, without the slightest approach to caricature. Beethoven's playing was the most distinct and intelligible declamation, such, perhaps, as in the same high degree can only be studied in his works. His old friends, who attentively watched the development of his genius in every direction, declare that he adopted this mode of playing in the first years of the Third Period of his life, and that it was quite a departure from his earlier method, which was less marked by shading and coloring. . . .[101]

The scheming Schindler had actually forged an entry in a Conversation Book of July 1823 to create the impression that Beethoven himself had used the term *tempo rubato* for his alleged tempo flexibility. Notice also Beethoven's supposed "two principles" (*zwei Principe*):

Do you remember, how I was allowed to play you the *Sonatas* Op. 14 several
years ago?—now everything is clear.... —2 [opposing] principles also in the
middle movement of the *Pathetique*—Thousands don't understand that—confusion might well result from the many indications of *tempo rubato*, I, too,
believe that.[102]

In the revised *Biographie* (1860), Schindler backtracked:

We must note that the term "free performance" has falsely been equated with
the *tempo rubato* of the Italian singer.... Beethoven protested against the use
of the Italian term in regard to his music....[103]

In the first edition of his *Biographie* Schindler suggested numerous specific
changes of tempo for movements from the sonatas of Op. 14 as well as for
some symphonic movements.[104] Again, under pressure of criticism, when he
published the revised third edition he withdrew his advice on these works
because it was "regarded as something strange, incomprehensible, the inventions of the author...."[105] (For example, to carry out his idea of two opposing
principles in the Allegro of Op. 14/2 Schindler had suggested *andantino* and
andante tempos for certain passages.[106]) Yet he added new, equally exaggerated
suggestions for other movements, including some from the sonatas of Opp. 10
and 13.

The comments of Schindler and Czerny on two movements from these
works show the gulf between their points of view. The Sonata Op. 10/1 is one
that Schindler implied he had played for Beethoven (see the forged entry quoted
on p. 98).[107] There is no record of Czerny's having done so.

On Op. 10/1/i Czerny wrote:

In a quick and fiery time. An earnest spirit must here sway the feelings. The
tranquil passage (from the 32nd bar) very *legato,* the four parts *cantabile,* and
then the counter melody in the bass with much expression.—The character of
the whole decided and manly.[108]

Schindler's comment on the same movement:

The opposition that appears at the very beginning of the C minor sonata
between strength and gentleness or, more expressively, between passion and
tenderness, are the rhetorical principles expressed in the first and third movements, which move side by side with appropriate variations in the tempo. It is
one of the most precarious contests between emotion and intellect but, when
it succeeds, it is of indescribable aesthetic and soul-revealing effect.

From the thirteenth to the twenty-first measures we find the rhetorical pause....
The quarter-note rests in the upper voices are all to be extended to about double
length, and the disconnected phrases violently flung out. The objective is a
heightening of tension. With the twenty-second measure, the agitated statement
is resumed and continues in a regular rhythm until the measure rest in all voices,
measure thirty[-one]....

The cadence before the coda of the exposition and the first measures of the coda itself illustrate the application of Beethoven's instructions regarding rests where the composer has not specifically marked them [!]. These pauses also serve to set off the coda more distinctly. The passage in question is [Fig. 10.15]. The passage plunges downward impetuously and stops abruptly on B flat. The coda has a relaxing effect, and so continues calmly in the tempo of the Allegro....[109]

Schindler added the three *fermatas* and the indication for a caesura, by which he intended a "sudden break in the flow, ... akin in music to the rhetorical pause ... or the lengthening of a written note."[110] In order to create "space" for the caesura he also slurred the bass E-flat back to the B-flat, disconnecting it from the rest of the bass quarter-note motive under which Beethoven had a slur! Schindler's "rhetorical pauses" (i.e., lengthened rests), *fermatas,* and caesurae destroy the propulsion of the movement and create a caricature of those means of agogic expression.

Czerny did study Op. 13 with Beethoven. Through a series of forged references Schindler implied that he had both played it for Beethoven and discussed it on other occasions.[111] Czerny's comment on the opening Grave is brief:

The introduction is played so slowly and affectingly that we could only indicate the metronome mark in sixteenth notes. The chords all very massive-sounding, and the left-hand accompaniment in the 5th to the 8th measure very *legato*. The chromatic run at the end very fast and light until the hold.[112]

Schindler's comments are lengthy, but those for the first four measures are sufficient to illustrate his extravagance:

The opening chords in the first, second, and third measures should be struck firmly, then allowed to die away almost completely. The long and short notes that follow are played with a light touch and in a free rhythm. The dotted sixteenth-note rest in the bass in all these measures should be given somewhat more than its full value. The last three chords of the third measure are the first to be played in a firm, even tempo, which continues to the *fermata* [Schindler's] in the fourth measure.[113] The last three notes of this measure are to be played freely, in the way that an Italian singer treats every *fermata*. The composer's directions merely ensure a definite measure length without imposing on the

Fig. 10.15. Schindler/MacArdle, *Beethoven*, p. 419.

performer the duration of the notes any more than the poet will dictate to the orator or actor the metre of his lines. Both are determined only by the cultivated taste of the singer, musician, or orator.[114]

No corroboration for Schindler's excesses has come to light; yet, some of his suggestions demonstrate misguided use of *bona fide* aspects of interpretation. It would seem that the rhetorical rest, so exaggerated in Schindler's discussion of Op. 10/1/i, has an appropriate role in Beethoven performance. The "two principles," which Schindler attempted to establish in the Conversation Books so that he could discuss them authoritatively in the *Biographie,* reduce to the frequent contrasts of material and mood in Beethoven's music. Expression of these so-called opposites in a stylistically appropriate manner can be achieved far better without Schindler's hyperbolic "lover" and his "obdurate mistress" for Op. 14/2/i.[115] The crucial issues for the application of many concepts of performance practice, both notated and discretionary, are where and how they are applied; and in just these respects Schindler is often inept. Both Ries and Czerny wrote of the influence of specific subjects and poetic ideas on Beethoven's compositional process;[116] yet neither Ries's reports nor any of Czerny's advice suggests exaggerated or mannered performance.

The nature of many of Schindler's suggestions leaves them open to doubt on musical grounds alone. In addition, his lapses of memory, the casualness of his reporting, and the forgeries should put students of Beethoven on notice that Schindler's statements on performance—particularly those regarding tempo—must be treated with skepticism unless they are supported by other, more reliable evidence. Schindler's jealousy of certain of the pianists among Beethoven's friends, notably Czerny and Moscheles, is well known, and his efforts to discredit them as Beethoven disciples should be recognized.[117]

On the other hand, Czerny's suggestions regarding tempo flexibility in the performance of the sonatas—looked at collectively—show in some subtle ways his recognition of change in Beethoven's indications and expectations during the course of his creative years. Czerny discussed specific aspects of the treatment of tempo for 29 of the 54 movements in the fifteen sonatas of Opp. 2 to 28. Eight were to be played in steady or strict tempo. Of the Adagio in Op. 2/1 he wrote:

> The soft and tranquil Adagio ..., which is full of feeling and of beautiful melody, ... must be played *cantabile* throughout, in a slow, but not dragging time. Here, a refined touch, a perfect *legato,* and a strict preservation of the time, are especially effective.[118]

Sometimes, as for Op. 13/i, Czerny cautioned against tempo flexibility for a particular part of a movement. "The middle subject (in E-flat minor) lightly staccato and with mournful expression, but not *ritardando,* except in the last three bars before the commencement of the quaver movement."[119]

Of the eight movements for which he suggested a strict tempo, six are slow. (This underscores the importance of the observation made earlier, that Beethoven's first written *ritard* in a slow sonata movement appears as late as Op. 81a/ii.) Here Czerny may have been trying to keep sentiment from overcoming reason, which would be detrimental to form and character—certainly a Classicistic approach for these early works.

The tempo modifications suggested by Czerny for fourteen movements in the Sonatas Opp. 2 to 28 fall into those types that were most commonly used in the Classic period and that are often related to formal structure: short *ritards,* usually at structural joints (e.g., Op. 13/i); *ritards* before *fermatas* or where *espressivo* is written (Op. 2/1/i); sectional change of mood and imperceptibly slower tempo for a more tranquil theme (Op. 2/2/i, Op. 7/iv); short *accelerandos* placed according to Türk's advice (Op. 10/3/ii[120]). The comment for Op. 10/1/iii stands out:

> This Finale is written completely in that fanciful humor that was so peculiar to Beethoven. This mood finds expression particularly in the middle subject (from the 17th measure on) through a whimsical *retardation* of single notes, although there also, on the whole, one must remain true to the very fast tempo.[121]

Of the 41 movements in the fourteen Sonatas Opp. 31 to 111 on which Czerny commented,[122] he mentioned the treatment of tempo for 23. He suggested that fifteen movements be played in "strict time"; of these, six have many tempo changes in the score. Several comments are similar to the one for Op. 31/3/ii: "The lively time must be strictly preserved (except where the contrary is expressly indicated). . . ."[123] Perhaps Czerny was concerned that Beethoven's increased indications for tempo flexibility would lead to excesses by the performer.

Czerny suggested tempo modification for only eight movements in the Sonatas Opp. 31 to 111, possibly because Beethoven had notated it so much more frequently. Half of his recommendations, all of which occur in the Sonatas Opp. 53 to 109, are still of the kinds related to formal structure. However, with the long, gradual *accelerandos* suggested for Op. 57/ii and iii Czerny seems to reach beyond the usual, into the realm of freer, more obvious tempo change, just as Beethoven did in his scores and is reported to have done in performance. For the first movement of Op. 90, composed in 1814, Czerny's comment begins, "This remarkably beautiful Sonata obtains its full effect by the rapid, unrestrained time [*das rasche, freie Tempo*]. . . ."[124] But time without constraint is what Schindler recommended for properly interpreting the "poetic ideas"[125] of a number of Beethoven's early (as well as later) sonatas, including Op. 2/ 1, Op. 10/1, Op. 13, Op. 14/1 and 2, and Op. 27/2.[126] He protested "earnestly and indignantly . . . the suspicion that these hints and other observations did not emanate from Beethoven, but have been the offspring of my invention."[127]

The evidence of gradually increasing tempo flexibility from Beethoven's pen and from his reliable contemporaries is impressive. Think back also to the qualities of Beethoven's playing described by Junker, Ries, Reichardt, von Seyfried, and Czerny. In 1839 Czerny recalled it as "energetic, profound, noble, and particularly in the Adagio, highly feeling and romantic" (p. 28 above). Beethoven's fervid, fiery personality led to playing that Clementi heard in 1809 and recalled years later as "frequently impetuous, like himself, . . . always full of spirit."[128] The character of the composer and the character of his continuously developing musical style trod the same path.

Yet Beethoven repeatedly reminded performers that proportions must be preserved even with the sanctioned use of freedom. Part of the metronome's value lay in guiding the pupil, who "must not in the [teacher's] absence arbitrarily . . . play out of time . . ." (above p. 323). And in 1825, in the last movement of the Ninth Symphony at m. 8 he wrote: "In the manner of a recitative, but in tempo."

11

PERFORMING BEETHOVEN'S BAGATELLE OP. 126, NO. 5

This concluding chapter will demonstrate the application of historically founded performance practices to one piece, Beethoven's Bagatelle Op. 126/5. The first edition of this Bagatelle, shown in Plate V, is followed by a Critical Report on the sources and text. Style, form, and the place of a piece within the composer's *oeuvre* have been mentioned in this study whenever they related to the topic under discussion. Since this kind of information often contains clues to stylistically appropriate performance, it provides a good orientation for the start of this discussion.

Bagatelles are short pieces, often in a light vein and, as here, in ABA form. Those by Beethoven mark the beginning of the vast nineteenth-century repertoire of character pieces for the piano. Op. 126 is the last significant piano music that Beethoven wrote. In contrast to the Bagatelles of Op. 119, which were conceived separately, those of Op. 126 seem to have been planned as a series for consecutive performance with a cycle of major thirds (including one enharmonic spelling) connecting the keys. The words "Ciclus von Kleinigkeiten" (cycle of bagatelles) appear on a sketch for the second one.[1] Composition took place in 1823–1824; a sketch for Bagatelle No. 5 was entered into a Conversation Book shortly after the premiere of the Ninth Symphony on 7 May 1824.[2] In spite of their title, the pieces bear affinities with Beethoven's great piano works of the 1820s. According to Edward Cone, these Bagatelles also served Beethoven as experiments in compositional techniques.[3] When Beethoven offered the set to the publisher Schott, he wrote that several "are more fully worked out and probably the best of this kind which I have composed."[4]

USE OF THE INSTRUMENT

Use of the extreme registers of the keyboard is characteristic of Beethoven's treatment of the piano in some works of his middle period and all of his late works. Here, from m. 25 the two hands separate progressively as they move toward the climax of the piece. The right-hand parts are high and thin, with nothing between them and the gradually descending bass, whose fullness supports the texture. In mm. 39–40 the melody moves still higher, this time with only moderate tonal support from the left-hand thirds, which should not overpower it. Pianists try to play this delicate ending with a clear, bell-like tone.

DYNAMICS AND ACCENTUATION

No dynamic signs appear until the *cres.* in m. 25. From about 1806, Beethoven frequently placed dashes after that abbreviation to indicate how far it should extend. (Where he has not given any indication there may be a choice about the length of the *crescendo* [e.g., Op. 101/ii/60–64] and occasionally about its dynamic range.) Here, the *rf* in m. 29 confirms the peak of the *crescendo*. The climactic notes played with the *rinforzando* are also the most widely spaced and introduce a more settled rhythm in the right hand, demonstrating Beethoven's typical coordination of resources—this time range, dynamics, and rhythm—to support a structural landmark.

The somewhat reflective mood and comparatively thin texture of the A section, coupled with the *diminuendo* leading to its return, suggest that the piece should begin and end rather quietly, with the dynamics inflected gently as the longer phrases rise and fall. (Compare chap. 3, pp. 64–66.) Before the *crescendo* in the more extroverted B section, the melody wants to sing in a *dolce* manner above the murmuring bass. Not surprisingly, Beethoven provided dynamic and tempo contrast immediately preceding and following this Bagatelle, although No. 4 ends quietly, as if setting the mood for what follows.

Beethoven's annotation to Cramer's Etude XII (p. 97) is directly applicable to the playing of the left-hand passage in mm. 17–24. Here, as in the Etude, the rhythmic stress falls on the first note of each group (the recurring C's), the melodic element on the second. Try to give each its due without creating a rhythmic limp.

Edward Cone suggests a dual interpretation for m. 32. When the B section is to be repeated, the harmonies in that measure should be perceived as V of V, V (twice) with the G-major triad "prominent" enough, "even though in an unaccented position," to be heard as the dominant of C. At the end of the repetition, m. 32 should speak as the dominant of G, with the D chord (and the bass D's) sufficiently prominent to forestall the definitive arrival of G major until the reentry of the theme in m. 35.[5]

SLURS, ARTICULATION, AND FINGERING

The eye immediately grasps the successive slurs in the left hand in mm. 1–4, but the ear does not want to hear the flow of this contrapuntal motive broken as it moves from a weak to a strong beat over each bar line. The slurs, which coincide with the harmonic rhythm, are in part a vestige of the earlier influences of stringed-instrument bowing and the bar line on legato playing in keyboard music. (See "Do All Slurs Indicate Attack and Release?" in chap. 5.) Perhaps Beethoven would have expected or accepted either of the two following responses to those slurs. The first, and my preference, would be a lightness of sound—a suggestion of articulation comparable to that produced by a consonant in speech or by the "softness" at the start of a stroke with an early bow—rather than an obvious break between mm. 1 and 2, and 3 and 4, followed by a clearer articulation at the ends of mm. 2 and 4. The second response would be a legato between the measures of each pair, like that created by the slur-tie-slur in the melody,[6] with grammatical accents at the starts of mm. 2 and 4. (Performers might overlook or avoid this accent if there were a single slur in the left hand along with the tie in the right.) Between mm. 7 and 8 the same alternatives are available for the right-hand melody. A lightness of sound between slurs is possible on a pianoforte with carefully chosen fingering, exquisite coordination between the release of one key and the playing of the next, excellent dynamic control, and a fluent tempo. The effect is easier to produce on a fortepiano.

The slur over mm. 17–19 has purposefully run its course at the peak of the phrase, which immediately precedes the last strong beat, the goal of this phrase. A very delicate articulation at the end of the slur and a slurred playing of m. 20, which increases the emphasis on the first beat, give more focus and finesse to the shaping of the phrase than would a single slur from start to finish.

The performer's interpretation of the unslurred measures should be based on those slurred by Beethoven. Eighteenth-century sources agree that for unmarked passages, articulation of the same thematic material elsewhere (usually earlier) in the piece remained valid unless countermanded (see Chart II). Articulations for analogous material were also adopted when necessary. Here mm. 21–24 (until the last eighth note) are virtually the same as mm. 17–20; and m. 9 repeats m. 1. But m. 10 is not comparable to m. 2, for the lines change, carrying the legato further; in the right hand it continues to the first eighth note in m. 11, in the left possibly to the first beat of m. 12.

In several places, fingering that maintains the appropriate note grouping calls for the passing of a longer finger over a shorter one, as Beethoven himself indicated occasionally. (See "Fingerings in the Music of Clementi and Beethoven" in chap. 6.) From the end of m. 1 to the start of m. 2, the left-hand thirds might be fingered $\frac{2}{4}$, $\frac{1}{3}$, particularly on a fortepiano with its shallower key dip. The right-hand thirds in m. 19 and the preceding upbeat would probably be fingered $\frac{2}{1}$, $\frac{3}{1}$, $\frac{4}{2}$, $\frac{5}{1}$, $\frac{4}{2}$, with the fourth finger vaulting over the fifth at the end.

PEDALING

Any pedaling in the A section of this Bagatelle must avoid running afoul of the bass thirds that move in eighth notes. Quick dabs of partial pedal earlier in those measures will suffice. In mm. 5, 6, 12, and 13, where the scoring is thinnest and the bass parts move more slowly, judicious pedaling can add body to the sound, including the higher tied notes. The exact placement and the depth of the pedaling should be adjusted to the sound qualities of the instrument being played, the acoustics of the room, the rapidity of the stepwise notes, and the range of the right hand, which can sustain more pedal as it moves higher. Some pianists play the first section with remarkably little pedal; others use more.

Pedal seems essential to me for the completion of the B section. The pedal rhythm is the dotted-quarter note. Surface pedal often sounds best, especially where the right hand is more active (mm. 19, 23, 24). If the bass pedal point on C is played quietly but firmly and the moving tenor part is brought out slightly, the hazy dissonance will be similar to some of Beethoven's notated pedalings discussed in chapter 4. Further, the sympathetic vibration of all the strings, set free by the use of this pedal, will fill the void between the disparate registers, creating a whole that is greater than the sum of its parts. For this reason I also prefer mm. 39–41 with pedal, again coinciding with the dotted-quarter rhythm.

TEMPO CHOICE AND TEMPO FLEXIBILITY

Beethoven's direction "quasi [almost] Allegretto" tells us not to emphasize the reflective quality of this Bagatelle, but to play it in a somewhat lively or cheerful, hence faster, tempo. The tempo choice is also important in maintaining balance and variety with this cycle, in which the first, third, and sixth (after a brief Presto introduction) Bagatelles are all Andantes with a "con moto" or "cantabile" qualifier. An introverted performance of No. 5 that moves too slowly seems to me to anticipate and upstage the effect of No. 6, in spite of its Presto introduction.

Beethoven left no metronomization for any movement with a rhythmic character and texture directly analogous to Op. 126/5, but his indications on two movements are worth considering for the broad parameters they draw, even though they were composed much earlier than Op. 126. He metronomized the Andante con moto quasi allegretto in 6/8, from the Quartet Op. 59/3, at $\quarternote. = 56$. Although it is built primarily of eighth notes, its more complex rhythmic structure and polyphonic texture, series of sixteenth notes with some slurred in pairs, frequently changing dynamics, many offbeat accents, and stated connection to an *andante* spirit, along with the fact that it is the slow movement of the Quartet, all combine to produce a tempo that would be much too slow for this Bagatelle. Faster than the Bagatelle and divergent in meter and note values, is the Allegretto quasi allegro in 3/8, from the Quartet Op. 18/6, which Beethoven metronomized at $\quarternote. = 88$. This movement is related by rhythmic character, motive, and spirit to the Allegretto of Op. 31/2/iii, which Czerny twice marked at $\quarternote. = 76$, although both he and Moscheles finally decided on 88.

I suggest ♩. = ca. 76 as a tempo that presents the "agreeable serenity" (p. 315) of this quasi-Allegretto and supports its role in the cycle. Contemporary metronomizations for the Allegretto, ma non troppo, "Etwas lebhaft und mit der innigsten Empfindung" of Sonata Op. 101/i seem to support this tempo choice. The movement, in 6/8, is built of the same note values as Op. 126/5. Its heading suggests that it might sound somewhat faster than the Bagatelle, which would occur at the same metronomization or even one a little slower because of its more complex texture, form, and substance. The contemporary metronomizations are fastest in Haslinger (both states), at ♩. = 80; Moscheles tried 66 in the Cramer edition. Later both Czerny and Moscheles settled on 72. Present-day pianists whose tempos for Op. 101/i center around 72 inflect their performances with a wide agogic *rubato* in both directions.

The Bagatelle also accommodates some tempo flexibility within its easy flow. A degree of agogic *rubato* in mm. 10–12 or 13, the climax of the A section, appeals to some performers. A *ritard* coupled with the *crescendo* enhances mm. 27–29 and matches Ries's description of Beethoven's playing quoted on pp. 385–386. The last few measures may appropriately taper off in both tempo and sound.

REPEAT OF THE MIDDLE SECTION

It is noteworthy that Beethoven went to the trouble of writing out both the first and the second endings of the B section, even though they are exactly the same. (The second ending is usually omitted in modern editions.) Perhaps he wanted to emphasize the importance of the repeat,[7] or hint at its different relationship to what follows (mentioned above), or both. The final chord of the *Prima volta* serves as the resolution of the feminine cadence. Beethoven left no hint that this rhythmically weak G should be tied; presumably it is repeated at the beginning of m. 17.

CRITICAL REPORT

Primary Sources

Aut.   The set titled *Kleinigkeiten*. Beethoven-Haus, Bonn; Sammlung H. C. Bodmer, Mh 23.

OE   *Six Bagatelles pour le Piano-Forté*. B. Schott Fils, Mayence, [1825], p.n. 2281. Music Division, The New York Public Library at Lincoln Center, Astor, Lenox and Tilden Foundations.

Inaccuracies in OE may stem from the copy used for engraving.[8] Note the incorrect key signature of the last two braces and the omission of numerous ties and a slur. Broken lines added to Plate V in mm. 6–7, 7, 12–13, 16b–17,

PLATE V. Beethoven, Bagatelle in G major, Op. 126/5. First edition, Mayence: B. Schott Fils, [1825]. Courtesy of Music Division, The New York
Public Library at Lincoln Center, Astor, Lenox and Tilden Foundations.

18, 30, and 35–36 represent signs present in Aut., which is the authoritative primary source for this piece. Measure numbers have also been added.

Secondary Sources

Aside from a *Titelauflage* (reprint with new title page) published by Schott in Paris, [1827],[9] which I have not been able to locate, Kinsky-Halm lists only a *Nachdruck* (reprint) by Dunst, Frankfurt, [after 1830], p.n. 266,[10] of which the Beethoven-Haus, Bonn, has a copy. It is from Dunst's edition of Beethoven's *Oeuvres complets de Piano,* 1re Partie, No. 54, which is the same as OE in all details, including the incorrect key signature in the last brace (only).

Measure	Hand	
6–7	R	Tie lacking in OE. In Aut. these measures are the last and first on their systems. The tie on the B's is lacking in m. 6 (as it is in the same circumstances on the D in m. 35 and the G in m. 39). Beethoven's tie, written over the system brace at m. 7, was omitted in OE. It was entered in the original issue of *BGA* but removed in a revision for which there is additional evidence that the editor consulted only OE (see *Beethoven's Werke* . . . in the Selected Bibliography).
7	L	Tie is lacking in OE.
12–13	R	Tie on A is lacking in OE.
16a,b	L	Slurs are lacking in Aut.
16b-17	R	The tie on G in Aut. is lacking in OE and *BGA.* It is incorporated in recent editions of Beethoven's *Klavierstücke* by Henle (New improved ed., ed. Otto von Irmer, [1976]) and Schott/Universal (formerly Universal; ed. Alfred Brendel, 1968).

Measure	Hand	
18	R	Ties are lacking in OE.
19–25	L	Slurs are lacking in Aut.
29		*rf* written as *rinf.* in Aut.
30	R	Slur is lacking in OE.
34, 39	T	C-sharp in the key signature is a copyist's or an engraver's error.
35	R	Slur is lacking in Aut.; tie lacking on D in OE.
41	R	In Aut. slur is split by the tie. (In m. 40 both Aut. and OE have a single slur.)

NOTES

Abbreviated Citations

After the first citation, references to titles in the following list use the abbreviations or abbreviated titles shown. Complete citations for these works are given in the Selected Bibliography. For other sources the first citation in each chapter is complete; thereafter only the author, short title, and page are given. For sources not included in the Selected Bibliography, the note number of each complete citation is given in later abbreviated citations.

AMZ   *Allgemeine musikalische Zeitung.*
BGA   *L. van Beethoven's Werke: Vollständige kritisch durchgesehene überall berechtigte Ausgabe.*
BNA   Ludwig van Beethoven, *Werke, neue Ausgabe sämtlicher Werke.*
Bro   Wolfgang Amadeus Mozart, *Sonatas and Fantasies for the Piano,* ed. Nathan Broder.
Clementi/Rosenblum, *Introduction*   Muzio Clementi, *Introduction to the Art of Playing on the Pianoforte.* Facs., ed. Sandra P. Rosenblum.
Czerny, *Piano Forte*   Carl Czerny, *Complete Theoretical and Practical Piano Forte School,* Op. 500, 3 vols., 1839. Trans. from German, J. A. Hamilton.
Czerny, *Proper Performance*   Carl Czerny, *On the Proper Performance of all Beethoven's Works for the Piano,* 1846. Trans. from German anon. Facs., ed. Paul Badura-Skoda.
Czerny, *Richtigen Vortrag*   Carl Czerny, *Über den Richtigen Vortrag der Sämtlichen Beethoven'schen Klavierwerke.* Facs., ed. Paul Badura-Skoda.
Haydn Studies   *Haydn Studies. Proceedings of the International Haydn Conference, Washington, D.C., 1975.*
HE   Joseph Haydn, *Klaviersonaten, Auswahl (Selected Keyboard Sonatas),* ed. Georg Feder. (In other contexts HE indicates Henle Edition.)
HSU   Joseph Haydn, *Complete Piano Sonatas (Sämtliche Klaviersonaten),* ed. Christa Landon.
Hummel, *Pianoforte*   Johann Nepomuk Hummel, *A Complete Theoretical & Practical Course of Instruction on the Art of Playing the Pianoforte.* Trans. from German, anon.
JAMS   *Journal of the American Musicological Society.*
JHW   Joseph Haydn, *Werke.*
Kinsky-Halm, *Beethoven Verz.*   Georg Kinsky and Hans Halm, *Das Werk Beethovens Thematisch-Bibliographisches Verzeichnis.*
Landon, *Correspondence*   H. C. Robbins Landon, trans. and ed., *The Collected Correspondence and London Notebooks of Joseph Haydn.*
Manfredini, *Regole Armoniche*   Vincenzo Manfredini, *Regole Armoniche o sieno precetti . . . i principi della musica, il portamento della mano, . . . sopra . . . il cembalo, ...*
MGA   *W. A. Mozart's Werke: Kritisch durchgesehene Gesammtausgabe.*
MQ   *The Musical Quarterly.*

NG   *The New Grove Dictionary of Music and Musicians,* 6th ed., ed. Stanley J. Sadie.
NGMI   *The New Grove Dictionary of Musical Instruments,* ed. Stanley J. Sadie.
Newman, "Checklist"   William S. Newman, "A Chronological Checklist of Collected Editions of Beethoven's Solo Piano Sonatas Since His Own Day."
NMA   Wolfgang Amadeus Mozart, *Neue Ausgabe sämtlicher Werke.*
PQ   *The Piano Quarterly.*
Streicher, *Brief Remarks*   Andreas Streicher, *Brief Remarks on the Playing, Tuning, and Care of Fortepianos.* Trans. from German and ed. Preethi de Silva.
Sulzer, *Allgemeine Theorie*   Johann George Sulzer, ed., *Allgemeine Theorie der Schönen Kunste.* Unless otherwise noted, references are to the first edition.
Thayer/Dieters/Riemann, *Beethoven*   Alexander Wheelock Thayer, *Ludwig van Beethovens Leben,* trans. from English, Hermann Dieters, rev. Hugo Riemann. 5 vols.
Tyson, *Clementi Cat.*   Alan Tyson, *Thematic Catalogue of the Works of Muzio Clementi.*

1. Background for the Study

1. The newer term "early Classic" for this period, rather than "pre-Classic," seems to describe more accurately the emergence of the Classical style. (See Friedrich Blume, *Classic and Romantic Music,* trans. M. D. Herter Norton [New York: Norton, 1970], 30–31; also Bathia Churgin, "Music of the Classical Era," *The Musical Quarterly* LXVIII/ 2 [April 1982]:232–233.) However, a discussion of musical style beyond what may appear in conjunction with considerations of performance is not within the purview of this volume.

2. If less force is applied, the plectra will not pluck; but more force will not produce a louder sound because the plectra will already have gone by the strings at the force for which the action is regulated.

3. Dates from *The New Grove Dictionary of Music and Musicians,* 6th ed., ed. Stanley J. Sadie, 20 vols. (London: Macmillan, 1980), VIII, 231, 234. For a report from the *Europaeische Zeitung* of 6 August 1765 about such a harpsichord built by Tschudi, see Otto Erich Deutsch, *Mozart: A Documentary Biography,* trans. Eric Blom, Peter Branscombe, and Jeremy Noble (Stanford: Stanford University Press, 1965), 48.

4. Rosamund Harding, *The Pianoforte,* 2d ed. (Surrey, England: Gresham, 1978), 4.

5. Edwin M. Good, *Giraffes, Black Dragons, and Other Pianos* (Stanford: Stanford University Press, 1982), 30.

6. Edward Francis Rimbault, *The Pianoforte, its Origin, Progress and Construction* (London: Cooks, 1860), 95.

7. Ibid., 95–97. The remainder of the report describes the action. According to Rimbault, this report was published in the *Giornale de' Litterati d'Italia* V (Venice, 1711):144.

8. *The Bach Reader,* ed. Hans David and Arthur Mendel, rev. ed. (New York: Norton, 1966), 259. This widely quoted information stems originally from Johann Friedrich Agricola's report in Jacob Adlung, *Musica mechanica Organoedi,* 2 vols. (Berlin: Birnstiel, 1768), II, 116–117. For accounts of Bach's visit to Potsdam in 1747, see *The Bach Reader,* 176, 305–306.

9. Christoph Wolff, "New Research on Bach's *Musical Offering,*" *MQ* LVII/3 (July 1971):399–403. Wolff bases this suggestion of instrument on the importance of elements from the *empfindsamer Stil* in this Ricercar and on the fact that it represents the "worked-out version" of Bach's improvisation on one of the king's pianos. "In his last years Bach acted as sales agent for Silbermann pianofortes in Leipzig" (ibid., 403).

10. Carl Philipp Emanuel Bach, *Essay on the True Art of Playing Keyboard Instruments,* trans. and ed. William J. Mitchell (New York: Norton, 1949), 36.

From 1740 to 1767 Emanuel Bach was harpsichordist in the court of Frederick the Great, who—as an early fancier of the fortepiano—owned a number of grand pianos made by Silbermann.

11. Ibid., 172, 369.

12. Carl Hermann Bitter, *Carl Philipp Emanuel und Wilhelm Friedemann Bach und deren Brüder,* 2 vols. (Berlin: Müller, 1868), I, 336. Christian Ernst Friederici invented a square piano in 1758 (*NG,* VI, 849).

13. Lodovico Giustini di Pistoia, *Sonata da Cimbalo di piano e forte* (Florence, 1732; facs. Cambridge: Cambridge University Press, 1933), e.g., 35, 55, 31, 36.

14. Johann Gottfried Eckard, *Oeuvres complètes,* ed. Eduard Reeser (Amsterdam: Heuwekemeijer, [1956], v.

15. Eva Badura-Skoda, "Prolegomena to a History of the Viennese Fortepiano," *Israel Studies in Musicology* II (1980):82.

16. For greater detail, see ibid., 82–90.

17. *NG,* V, 824.

18. E. Badura-Skoda, "Viennese Fortepiano," 83.

19. Nathan Broder, "Mozart and the 'Clavier,' " in *The Creative World of Mozart,* ed. Paul Henry Lang (New York: Norton, 1963), 81; Horst Walter, "Haydns Klaviere," *Haydn-Studien* II/4 (December 1970):263–264; see also quotations from Haydn's letters on pp. 20 and 21, below. Other generic terms include *Clavierconzert* (keyboard concerts) and *Clavierspieler* (keyboard player).

20. E.g., Johann Philipp Kirnberger in Carl Friedrich Cramer's *Magazin der Musik* I (1783):512; and Heinrich Christoph Koch, *Musikalisches Lexikon* (Frankfurt: Hermann dem Jüngern, 1802; facs., Hildesheim: Olms, 1964), cols. 341–342.

21. Georg Kinsky and Hans Halm, *Das Werk Beethovens: Thematisch-Bibliographisches Verzeichnis* (Munich: Henle, 1955), 32, 63, 66, 67.

22. The details relating to this leaf, which is not included in the published facsimile of Op. 26 (ed. Erich Prieger [Bonn: Friedrich Cohen, 1895]), are in Kinsky-Halm, *Beethoven Verz.,* 63.

23. See chap. 7, n. 124, regarding publication of Op. 31.

24. Cf. also *Haydn Studies. Proceedings of the International Haydn Conference Washington, D.C., 1975,* ed. Jens Peter Larsen, Howard Serwer, and James Webster (New York: Norton, 1981), 290.

In his article "Per il Clavicembalo o Piano-Forte," Herbert Grundmann addressed the issues that relate to instrument indications in the titles of Beethoven's keyboard works published before 1803 (*Colloquium Amicorum—Joseph Schmidt-Görg zum 70. Geburtstag,* ed. Siegfried Kross and Hans Schmidt [Bonn: Beethoven-Haus, 1967], 100–117). Unfortunately, of the numerous works with questionable or double indications, holographs exist for only five, and four of those holographs carry no instrument indication. These include the *Variations pour le Clavecin Sur le Theme "Bey Männer* [sic] *welche Liebe fühlen,"* WoO 46, composed in 1801 and published by Mollo of Vienna in 1802. Not only is Mollo's choice of keyboard instrument in that title bizarre on the basis of the writing and the dynamics, but also the partner in the duo, the violoncello, is not even mentioned. By 1802 Mollo was not unfamiliar with Beethoven's works; the firm had already published Opp. 14, 15, 16, and 17, in which the keyboard instrument was specifically the piano. The publisher Artaria and Beethoven were on familiar terms, yet Artaria also showed a decided preference for including *Clavecin* in the titles of Beethoven's early works.

25. E. Badura-Skoda, "Viennese Fortepiano," 78.

26. Charles Burney, *A General History of Music,* 4 vols. (London: Printed for the author, 1789); ed. Frank Mercer (New York: Harcourt Brace, 1935; rep., New York: Dover, 1957), II, 874, fn. ∗. The term "benefit" concert belies its nature, for the proceeds generally went to the organizer and main performer.

27. Charles Sanford Terry, *Johann Christian Bach* (London: Oxford University Press, 1929), 113. Coincidentally, Bach's Op. 5 was his first set of solo keyboard sonatas (*NG*, I, 871) and was titled "pour le Clavecin ou le Piano Forte."

28. Michel Brenet (Marie Bobillier), *Les Concerts en France sous l'ancien régime* (Paris: Librairie Fischbacher, 1900), 292.

29. Virginia Pleasants, "The early piano in Britain (c. 1760–1800)," *Early Music* XIII/1 (February 1985):40.

30. Rimbault, *Pianoforte,* 139.

31. Michael Kelly, *Reminiscences,* 2 vols. (London: Colburn, 1826), I, 15–16, 18–20, 65, 185, 189, 198. The year 1779 for the use of the piano in operatic performances in Dublin is inferred from the apparent proximity of those performances to Kelly's departure for Italy on 1 May 1779. (See also S. M. Ellis, *The Life of Michael Kelly* [London: Gollancz, 1930], 21–24.)

32. Leon Plantinga, *Clementi: His Life and Music* (London: Oxford University Press, 1977), 37–38.

33. Max Unger, *Muzio Clementis Leben* (Langensalza: Beyer & Söhne, 1914; facs., New York: Da Capo Press, 1971), 16.

34. Plantinga, *Clementi,* 288.

35. Deutsch, *Mozart: A Documentary Biography,* 167–168 (for the original German see Otto Erich Deutsch, Mozart: *Die Dokumente seines Lebens* [Kassel: Bärenreiter, 1961], 149–150). Johann Andreas Stein, a leading piano builder responsible for some early improvements, was located in Augsburg. Mozart described Stein's instruments with great enthusiasm in a letter dated 17 October 1777, five days before this concert (see p. 22 below). Stein's daughter Nannette was married to Johann Andreas Streicher and established the important Streicher firm in Vienna (below, chap. 2, n. 34).

36. Robert Haas, *Mozart* (Potsdam: Akademische Verlagsgesellschaft Athenaion, ca. 1933), 26.

37. Emily Anderson, trans. and ed., *The Letters of Mozart and His Family,* 2d ed., ed. A. Hyatt King and Monica Carolan, 2 vols. (London: Macmillan, 1966), 888–889. The piano described was made by Anton Walter.

38. Cf. also Walter, "Haydns Klaviere," 264.

39. Ibid., 260; H. C. Robbins Landon, *Haydn: Chronicle and Works,* 5 vols. (Bloomington: Indiana University Press, 1976–1981), III, 151.

40. Ibid., III, 43–46.

41. Rosemary S. M. Hughes, "Dr. Burney's Championship of Haydn," *MQ* XXVII/1 (January 1941):93; also Walter, "Haydns Klaviere," 271–272. See Samuel Wesley's mention of the piano on p. 19 below.

42. Harding, *Pianoforte,* 69.

43. Good, *Pianos,* 68.

44. Daniel Gottlob Türk, *Klavierschule* (Leipzig and Halle: Schwickert; Hemmerde und Schwetschke, 1789); facs., ed. Erwin R. Jacobi (Kassel: Bärenreiter, 1962), 332.

45. "Leidenschaft, Affect," in Koch, *Lexikon,* col. 894.

46. Daniel Gottlob Türk (1750–1813) was a German musician, theorist, and composer whose musical education stemmed in part from the tradition of J. S. Bach. In Dresden his primary mentor was the Kantor G. A. Homilius, a former student of Bach and teacher of J. A. Hiller and J. F. Reichardt. In 1772 Türk enrolled in the University of Leipzig, where he studied keyboard with J. W. Hässler, whose teacher, J. C. Kittel, had also studied with Bach (*NG*, XIX, 266). Hässler used Emanuel Bach's *Essay* as his "instructional manual" (Daniel Gottlob Türk, *School of Clavier Playing,* trans. and ed. Raymond Haggh [Lincoln: University of Nebraska Press, 1982], xxiii).

From 1774 until his death, Türk's key musical positions in Halle's churches and educational institutions gradually led to his becoming the "leader in Halle's musical life" (*NG*, XIX, 266). Through performances of Handel's oratorios early in the nineteenth century, Türk is credited with starting the Halle Handel tradition. Although he composed a number of cantatas and lieder, Türk seems to have placed more value on his keyboard sonatas and pieces, which are primarily pedagogical. They were published in numerous editions during his lifetime.

Türk's book *Von den wichtigsten Pflichten eines Organisten* (1787) helped establish his reputation as "an outstandingly thorough and scholarly teacher" (*NG*, XIX, 267). His *Kurze Anweisung zum Generalbassspielen*, along with writings of E. Bach, J. J. Fux, and J. G. Albrechtsberger, was used by Beethoven in the instruction of Archduke Rudolf and was among the books in Beethoven's estate. (Albert Leitzmann, *Ludwig van Beethoven: Berichte der Zeitgenossen, Briefe und persönliche Aufzeichnungen* [Leipzig: Insel, 1921], II, 381. Pp. 379–383 list the volumes that Beethoven owned at the time of his death, so far as they are known.) Türk wrote anonymously for the *Allgemeine musikalische Zeitung* "and other journals" (*NG*, XIX, 267).

47. Türk, *Klavierschule*, e.g., 338, 340–343.

48. Ibid., 390. Cf. Schulz's description, which predates Türk's, on p. 11 below.

49. Kirnberger, "Instrumentalmusik," in Johann George Sulzer, *Allgemeine Theorie der Schönen Kunste*, 2 vols. (Leipzig: Weidmann, 1771, 1774), I, 559; see also "Ausdruck in der Musik," ibid., I, 109–111.

50. Koch, *Lexikon*, col. 941; original from Schulz, "Melodie," in Sulzer, *Allgemeine Theorie*, II, 748.

51. George J. Buelow, "Rhetoric and music," *NG*, XV, 793.

52. Johann Mattheson, *Der vollkommene Capellmeister* [The perfect chapel master] (Hamburg: Herold, 1739); trans. and ed. Ernest C. Harriss, retaining the German title (Ann Arbor: UMI Research Press, 1981). All references in this volume are to the English edition.

The topic of rhetoric and music is introduced in the Foreword (pp. 47, 57–58, 62–64); it is discussed further on pp. 133–134, 309–310, 317, and 321–322 and in chaps. 4, 6, 9, and 14 of Pt. II. Chap. 6 deals exclusively with *Klang-Füsse* (tone-feet) and their applications in specific types of compositions.

Johann Mattheson (1681–1764) was a north German composer, theorist, and performer who enjoyed success as a young singer and a virtuoso organist. From 1715 to 1728 he served as music director of the Hamburg Cathedral, and from 1719 also as Kapellmeister to the Duke of Holstein (*NG*, XI, 833–834). As a result of this broad practical experience, Mattheson's writings on late-Baroque German music form the most complete record that we have. His single most valuable treatise, *Der vollkommene Capellmeister*, contains—along with an encyclopedic wealth of information—his codification of two major aspects of Baroque style germane to our discussion: the theory of the affections and the relationship of the doctrines of rhetoric to composition.

53. Ibid., Pt. II, chap. 9. Mattheson's analysis of a minuet on pp. 452–453 is helpful in understanding chap. 9, since eighteenth-century theoretical terminology is far from uniform or clear. For brief descriptions of the smaller melodic segments (two types of *Einschnitte*) and terminology as they apply to Classic-period performance, see below, chap. 3, p. 92 and n. 136, and chap. 5, pp. 158–165.

54. E.g., Mattheson, *Der vollkommene Capellmeister*, 104–111, 290–291, 326, 426.

55. I use *galant* in the broad sense as contemporary musicians did, referring to the generally homophonic, *free* style of theater and chamber music in the Classic period as opposed to the *strict* and *learned* styles associated with church music (e.g., Koch, *Lexikon*, cols. 1451–1453). Many modern writers use *galant* in the more restrictive sense of the simple, "ear-tickling" periodic melodies with light accompaniment that were especially characteristic of the early Classic period (e.g., Blume, *Classic and Romantic Music* [n. 1 above], 30–31).

56. Buelow, "Rhetoric and music" [n. 51 above], 802.

57. Bellamy Hosler, *Changing Aesthetic Views of Instrumental Music in 18th-Century Germany* (Ann Arbor, MI: UMI Research Press, 1981), 223; see also pp. 177–180. Johann Nikolaus Forkel discussed these ideas in *Über die Theorie der Musik* (Göttingen:

Witwe Vanderhück, 1777), 25–27; and *Allgemeine Geschichte der Musik,* I (Leipzig: Schwickert, 1788), 8, 20, 36–37, 49–50.

    58. See n. 45. Heinrich Christoph Koch (1749–1816) was a German violinist, composer, and theorist. After studies in his native Rudolstadt (near Weimar), he pursued further training in violin and composition in Berlin, Dresden, Hamburg, and, according to Gerber, in Weimar (Ernst Ludwig Gerber, *Historisch-biographisches Lexicon der Tonkünstler,* 2 vols. [Leipzig: Breitkopf, 1790–1792], I, col. 741). Eventually Koch gave up his post as court musician in Rudolstadt to devote himself to writing (*NG,* X, 132).

    Koch's major achievements are *Versuch einer Anleitung zur Composition* and *Musikalisches Lexikon,* the most complete and informative works of their type from the Classic period. In three volumes published between 1782 and 1793, the *Versuch* discusses composition from its most basic elements, keys and chords, to the writing of large forms, including a detailed discussion of phrase and period structure. Koch was conversant with the music of Haydn and Mozart; his analyses show that he distinguished between the styles of early and mature Classicism (Leonard Ratner, "Eighteenth-Century Theories of Musical Period Structure," *MQ* XLII/4 [October 1956]:451–454).

    Koch's *Lexikon,* published in 1802, is the best dictionary source of its time. Many articles provide valuable information on aesthetics and theory as well as basic material. Interestingly, a musician as well informed as Koch still deemed it appropriate to draw on ideas and articles in Sulzer's *Allgemeine Theorie der schönen Künste.*

    59. Johann Joachim Quantz, *On Playing the Flute,* trans. and ed. Edward R. Reilly (London: Faber and Faber, 1966), 119, 124–125; *Versuch einer Anweisung die Flöte traversiere zu spielen* [Berlin: Voss, 1752], 100, 107). See also the translation of similar comments by Marpurg in E. Bach, *Essay,* 80–81, fns. 3, 4.

    Quantz (1697–1773) was a north German flutist, composer, and writer on music whose periods of study in Italy, England, and France were reflected both in his preference for a musical style containing French and Italian elements and in the breadth of his writings (*NG,* XV, 495–496). His compositions were mainly sonatas, trio sonatas, and concertos for flute, many written for Frederick the Great of Prussia, a devoted flutist in whose court Quantz served from 1741. Quantz's most important contribution is his *Versuch einer Anweisung die Flöte traversiere zu spielen,* in which, in addition to the material exclusively for flutists, he left information on performance practices for all musicians in discussions of "good execution in general," of the "duties" of the accompanying instrumentalists, of the main types of vocal and instrumental music, and of the characteristics of the Italian, French, and German styles.

    60. Friedrich Wilhelm Marpurg, *Kritische Briefe über die Tonkunst,* 3 vols. (Berlin: Birnstiel, 1763), II. For background on Marpurg, see below, chap. 7, n. 41.

    Johann Philipp Kirnberger, *Die Kunst des reinen Satzes in der Musik,* 2 vols. Vol. I (Berlin: Voss, 1771; rep. Berlin and Königsberg: Decker und Hartung, 1774). Vol. II (Berlin and Königsberg: Decker und Hartung, Pt. 1, 1776; Pt. 2, 1777; Pt. 3, 1779). Vol. I and Vol. II, Pt. 1, trans. David Beach and Jurgen Thym, ed. David Beach (New Haven: Yale University Press, 1982), see Vol. I, chap. 6; Vol. II, Pt. 1, chap. 4. See also "Abschnit," "Accent in der Musik," "Einschnitt," in Sulzer, *Allgemeine Theorie,* I, 5–7, 9–11, 306–309. For background on Kirnberger, see n. 100 below.

    Johann Abraham Peter Schulz, "Vortrag," in Sulzer, *Allgemeine Theorie,* II, 1247–1258. For background on Schulz, see n. 61 below.

    Johann Nikolaus Forkel, *Über die Theorie der Musik* [n. 57 above], 21–28.

    Koch, "Accent," *Lexikon,* col. 49.

    61. Schulz, "Sonate," in Sulzer, *Allgemeine Theorie,* II, 1094. Koch's quotation from this excerpt is in "Sonate," *Lexikon,* col. 1417.

    Johann Abraham Peter Schulz (1747–1800), German composer and conductor, was the author of the music articles from S to Z and the co-author of those from J to S, in collaboration with J. P. Kirnberger, in Sulzer's *Allgemeine Theorie.* (Raymond A. Barr, "Schulz," *NG,* XVI, 821–823; also *Vorrede* [Preface] to Vol. II, *Allgemeine Theorie,*

1774. Unless otherwise identified, the remaining material in this sketch is summarized from Barr's article.)

Schulz was educated in Lüneburg and Berlin. He studied with Kirnberger from 1765 to 1768 and was his "most important pupil" (*NG*, X, 81). At some time Schulz evidently studied with Emanuel Bach, too ("C. P. E. Bach," *NG*, I, 847). Then, as accompanist and teacher to a Polish princess, Schulz traveled widely in Europe for three years, gaining a broader musical background. After several positions in Prussia, Schulz was appointed Hofkapellmeister in the court of Copenhagen and director of the Royal Danish Theatre, positions he held until retirement. As a composer he was known primarily for his large stage works and his lieder, which—with their texts by leading poets—set a standard for later lied composers.

Apropos of Schulz's distinction between symphony and sonata, Charles Rosen writes, "To play a symphony of Mozart or Haydn as if it were a sonata, interpreted and molded in an individual way . . . , is to betray its nature. . . (*The Classical Style: Haydn, Mozart, Beethoven* [New York: Norton, 1972], 144).

62. Burney, *A General History of Music* [n. 26 above], II, 847–848.

63. Schulz, "Sonate," in Sulzer, *Allgemeine Theorie*, II, 1095.

64. Schulz, "Symphonie," ibid., 1122; cf. Türk, *Klavierschule*, 391–392. The articles "Sonate" and "Symphonie" remained unchanged in Sulzer's enl. 2d ed. For a recent discussion of the sonata and symphony styles and the manners in which they are mixed, see Michael Broyles, "The Two Instrumental Styles of Classicism," *Journal of the American Musicological Society* XXXVI (Summer 1983):210–242.

65. Arnold Schering, "Carl Philipp Emanuel Bach und das 'redende Prinzip' in der Musik," *Jahrbuch der Musikbibliothek Peters, 1938* XLV (1939):15.

66. Ibid.; see also pp. 16–17.

67. Carl Philipp Emanuel Bach, *Versuch über die wahre Art das Clavier zu spielen*, 2 Pts. (Berlin: In Verlegung des Auctoris, 1753, 1762), 121–122.

68. Vera Schwarz, "Missverständnisse in der Haydn-Interpretation," *Österreichische Musikzeitschrift* XXXI/I (January 1976):27.

69. Georg August Griesinger, *Biographische Notizen über Joseph Haydn* (Leipzig: Breitkopf & Härtel, 1810); Albert Christoph Dies, *Biographische Nachrichten von Joseph Haydn* (Vienna: Camesinaische, 1810). Both biographies have been translated and edited by Vernon Gotwals in *Joseph Haydn: Eighteenth-Century Gentleman and Genius* (Madison: University of Wisconsin Press, 1963). The accounts mentioned are on pp. 12 and 95.

70. Ibid., 95; A. Peter Brown, *Joseph Haydn's Keyboard Music: Sources and Style* (Bloomington: Indiana University Press, 1976), Essay VII, esp. 219–229. For specific evidence of 1762 as the year of purchase, based on Haydn's notation of appoggiaturas, see chap. 7, p. 217 and n. 2. Haydn's purchase of Bach's *Essay* has sometimes been rather casually ascribed to the 1750s, since Pt. I (concerned with performance, not theory) appeared in 1753.

71. Brown, *Haydn's Keyboard Music*, 210, 218.

72. Ibid., 119. Although certain characteristics of Hob. 2/ii "seem almost North German in their aesthetic stance," Brown denies that any work of Bach's "available in Vienna before 1760 could have served as its model" (ibid., 284).

73. Ibid., 207–208, 211. The sonatas in the unauthorized print are Wq. 62/8, 13 and Wq. 65/9, 10, 18, 22.

According to Dies, "The second textbook Haydn subsequently bought was Mattheson's *Der vollkommene Kapellmeister*" (Gotwals, *Haydn* [n. 69 above], 96). That volume and two others by Mattheson were among Haydn's effects at the time of his death. Also listed in the catalogue of his possessions are a number of compositions (but not the *Essay*) of Emanuel Bach and four volumes by Marpurg: *Anfangsgründe der theoretischen Musick, Anleitung zum Klavierspielen, Kritische Einleitung in die Geschichte und Lehr-*

sätze der alten und neuen Musick, and *Handbuch vom Generalbass und der Komposition* (Landon, *Chronicle,* V, 402).

74. Brown, *Haydn's Keyboard Music,* 209, 217. Nevertheless, Brown finds the strongest evidence of Bach's influence on Haydn to be from the *Essay,* bearing especially on Haydn's capriccios and fantasias (ibid., 220–229).

The obbligato recitative in Hasse's operas was itself a formative influence on the rhetorical aspect of the *empfindsamer Stil.*

75. Eva Badura-Skoda in a discussion of "'Rhetorical' Performance," in *Haydn Studies,* 271.

76. George J. Buelow, "Rhetoric and music," *NG,* XV, 802. The quotation is from Johann Friedrich Daube, *Der musikalische Dilettant: eine Abhandlung des Generalbasses* (Vienna: Kurzböck, 1770–1771), 10 (Buelow, personal communication).

77. George J. Buelow, "Johann Friedrich Daube," *NG,* V, 253.

78. Max Rudolf, "Storm and Stress in Music," *BACH: The Quarterly Journal of the Riemenschneider Bach Institute* III/2 (1972):3–13; III/3 (1972):3–11; III/4 (1972):8–16; source of quotation, III/3:6.

79. The beginning of *Sturm und Drang* in music actually preceded the German literary movement from which the name was subsequently taken. In his excellent article "Storm and Stress in Music," Rudolf also notes an implication of translation: "'Stress' indicates emphasis or pressure, often an unwelcome influence from outside, while 'Drang' is an inner impulse" (ibid., III/2:6).

80. E.g., Jens Peter Larsen, "Haydn," *NG,* VIII, 335, 351.

81. Koch, *Lexikon,* 1391.

82. Daniel Heartz, "Classical," *NG,* IV, 453; see also Landon, *Chronicle,* II, 271.

83. Rudolf, "Storm and Stress in Music" [n. 78 above], *BACH* III/2:12.

84. Daniel Heartz, "Sturm und Drang," *NG,* XVIII, 311. In Mannheim Mozart heard Georg Benda's duodramas *Ariadne* and *Medea,* both heightened by the use of very dramatic instrumental music in the obbligato recitatives. In a letter of 12 November 1778 Mozart wrote, "I like those two works of his so much that I carry them about with me" (Anderson, *Mozart,* 631).

85. Stanley Sadie, "Mozart," *NG,* XII, 697.

86. According to the worklist in *NG,* K. 397 was composed early in 1782 or in 1786–1787 (XII, 745). Mozart is supposed to have played regularly in the Sunday concerts of Baron van Swieten during the early part of 1782 (*NG,* XII, 701). Had he not known Emanuel Bach's music earlier, he would have become acquainted with it at those concerts, for the Baron was an enthusiastic champion of the music of J. S. Bach, Handel, and Emanuel Bach.

87. Lothar Hoffman-Erbrecht, "Christian Gottlob Neefe," *NG,* XIII, 91. Beethoven also used Bach's *Essay* when he taught Czerny (Carl Czerny, *On the Proper Performance of all Beethoven's Works for the Piano,* trans. anon., [1846]; facs., ed. Paul Badura-Skoda [Vienna: Universal, 1970], 5).

88. Richard Kramer, "Notes to Beethoven's Education," *JAMS* XXVIII/1 (Spring 1975):92–94.

89. Ibid., 73–92.

90. Ibid., 95–98. Matteson's *Der vollkommene Capellmeister* was in Beethoven's library at the time of his death (Leitzmann, *Beethoven: Berichte...* [n. 46 above], 383). Probably around 1802–1803 Beethoven also studied the examples of recitative in Sulzer's *Allgemeine Theorie,* thus acquainting himself with these influential volumes had he not known them previously (Richard Kramer, "Beethoven and Carl Heinrich Graun," *Beethoven Studies* I, ed. Alan Tyson [New York: Norton, 1973], 24, 37–38). (On Beethoven and Sulzer, see also chap. 10, n. 116.) For a comprehensive discussion of the influence of rhetoric in Beethoven's *Missa Solemnis,* see Warren Kirkendale, "New Roads to Old Ideas in Beethoven's *Missa Solemnis,*" *MQ* LVI/4 (October 1970):665–701.

NOTES FOR PAGES 14–16

91. Eve Bartlitz, *Die Beethoven-Sammlung in der Musikabteilung der Deutschen Staatsbibliothek* (Berlin: Staatsbibliothek, 1970), 214–215. P. 25 of *Betrachtungen* contains underlining in Beethoven's hand.

92. Schindler states that Beethoven knew Horace's *Epistle to the Pisos* [*On the art of poetry*] and could quote sections of it from memory (Anton F. Schindler, *Beethoven as I Knew Him*, trans. Constance Jolly, ed. Donald W. MacArdle [Chapel Hill: University of North Carolina Press, 1966], 366). Schindler "and others" have referred to Homer, Plato, Plutarch, Aristotle, Euripides, Pliny, Ovid, Horace, Quintilian, Tacitus, Lucian, and Xenophon as authors whose works Beethoven had read. He had underlined and marked many passages of special interest in his copy of Homer's *Odyssey* (Leitzmann, *Beethoven: Berichte*... [n. 46 above], 380). See also *Thayer's Life of Beethoven*, rev. and ed. Elliot Forbes (Princeton: Princeton University Press, 1967), 246; Theodor von Frimmel, *Beethoven Handbuch* (Leipzig: Breitkopf & Härtel, 1926), I, "Bibliothek" (40), "Lesestoff" (338–341); and Ludwig Nohl, *Beethovens Brevier* (Leipzig: Günther, 1870), especially ci–cvii, 17–32, 108–109.

93. Cramer's *Magazin der Musik*, I (30 March 1783):377; translation from Thayer/Forbes, *Beethoven*, 33–34.

94. Thayer/Forbes, *Beethoven*, 104.

95. Cramer's *Magazin der Musik*, I (30 March 1783):387–388; for the complete quotation from which this is excerpted, see below, chap. 10, p. 380.

96. For a concise exposition of the characteristic figures and "topics" of the Classic style, see Leonard G. Ratner, *Classic Music: Expression, Form, and Style* (New York: Schirmer Books, 1980), chap. 2.

97. From the memoirs of Wenzel J. Tomášek, "published in installments in the Prague periodical *Libussa* between 1845 and 1850" (*NG*, XIX, 33). Quotation from Howard Allen Craw, "A Biography and Thematic Catalog of the Works of J. L. Dussek (1760–1812)," Ph.D. diss., University of Southern California, 1964; University Microfilms: 64-9611, 127, 458. For the larger context of this quotation, see chap. 5, n. 27.

98. Anonymous review, *Harmonicon*, I/7 (July 1823):103. The keyboard music played on this occasion included Cramer's Sixth Piano Concerto in E-flat major, a "grand duet" by Hummel (performed by Cramer and Kalkbrenner), "a new quintett, MS., for pianoforte, violin, tenor, violoncello, and contra basso," and a "grand duett" by Moscheles (performed by the composer and Cramer).

99. In 1744 Emanuel Bach even included numerous alterations of tempo along with his other editing in the first movement of the "Württemberg" Sonata No. 2.

100. Kirnberger, "Ausdruck in der Musik," in Sulzer, *Allgemeine Theorie*, I, 109.

Johann Philipp Kirnberger (1721–1783) was a German musician whose importance lay in his theoretical works rather than in his compositions. He played violin and organ; he had studied the latter with Johann Peter Kellner and with Heinrich Nicolaus Gerber, a student of Bach's. According to Marpurg, Kirnberger also "studied composition and performance with Bach for two years" around 1739 (Howard Serwer, "Kirnberger," *NG*, X, 80). Kirnberger's significant writings are *Die Kunst des reinen Satzes, Anleitung zur Singcomposition, Die wahren Grundsätze zum Gebrauch der Harmonie* (with J. A. P. Schulz's help in writing), and the articles A through I in Sulzer's *Allgemeine Theorie*. Kirnberger also supervised Schulz's writing of the articles J through S in that encyclopedia.

101. Schulz, "Vortrag," in Sulzer, *Allgemeine Theorie*, II, 1252, 1255.

102. For an explanation of this term as it relates to musical style, see Jan LaRue, *Guidelines for Style Analysis* (New York: Norton, 1970), 16, 53, 61.

103. Schulz, "Symphonie," in Sulzer, *Allgemeine Theorie*, II, 1122. This quotation from Schulz was brought to my attention by Bathia Churgin's article, "The Symphony as Described by J. A. P. Schulz (1774)," *Current Musicology* 29 (1980):9.

104. Charles Burney, *Dr. Burney's Musical Tours in Europe*, 2 vols., 2d ed. (London: Becket, Robson, and Robinson, 1773, 1775); ed. Percy A. Scholes (London: Oxford University Press, 1959), II, 96.

105. Schulz, "Vortrag," in Sulzer, *Allgemeine Theorie,* II, 1255.

106. Abbé Georg Joseph Vogler, *Kuhrpfälzische Tonschule* (Mannheim: Auf Kosten des Verfassers, [1778]), 28.

107. Emily Anderson, trans. and ed., *The Letters of Beethoven,* 3 vols. (London: Macmillan, 1961), 1241–1242.

108. Good, *Pianos,* 65–66; Harding, *Pianoforte,* 54–55, 264–266.

109. Gustav Nottebohm, "Zur Reinigung der Werke Beethoven's von Fehlern und fremden Zuthaten," *Allgemeine Musikalische Zeitung* (3d series: *Leipziger AMZ,* 1866–1882) XI/21 (24 May 1876)–XI/33 (16 August 1876).

110. Bischoff's original publisher was Steingräber. During the 1940s the American firm of Kalmus reprinted a number of his editions, including those of Bach's works.

111. Occasionally an urtext edition may have a different focus. A recent edition of selected *Klaviersonaten* by Muzio Clementi (ed. Sonja Gerlach and Alan Tyson, 2 vols. [Munich: Henle, Vol. I, 1977; Vol. II, 1982]) contains only the readings of the first editions even though Clementi published revised editions of several of these works. The importance of Clementi's revisions varies considerably. Some take advantage of the expanding range of the keyboard, while others add more significantly to the music; some show a more developed use of performance directions; still others seem arbitrary, perhaps included to make the publication more interesting commercially.

112. E.g., Landon, *Chronicle,* III, 47 (in his cantata "Arianna a Naxos"), 171, 284.

113. Ibid., 139; reproduction of the music, 535–536.

114. Edwin Ripin, "Clavichord," *NG,* IV, 468; Brown, *Haydn's Keyboard Music,* Essay V, especially pp. 141, 147, 148–171. Compare also Horst Walter, "Haydn's Keyboard Instruments," in *Haydn Studies,* 213–216.

115. Four sections in *Haydn Studies* present information pertinent to these issues, with marked differences of opinion among the discussants: "Sonority: Keyboard Sonatas," 288–290; Edwin Ripin, "Haydn and the Keyboard Instruments of his Time," 302–308; A. Peter Brown, "Realization of an Idiomatic Keyboard Style in Sonatas of the 1770's," 394–400, and the open discussion on pp. 216–217. See also Walter, "Haydns Klaviere," 256, 260–264, and the most recent and thorough appraisal by Brown in *Haydn's Keyboard Music,* Essay V.

116. Landon, *Chronicle,* II, 343. Rotenstein was "writing in Johann Bernouilli's *Sammlung kurzer Reisebeschreibungen* (Jg. 1783, IX. Band, p. 282)" (ibid.).

117. E. Badura-Skoda, "Viennese Fortepiano," 87. Further hypothetical support for a date in the early 1770s appears in Brown, *Haydn's Keyboard Music,* 140.

118. Joseph Haydn, *Gesammelte Briefe und Aufzeichnungen,* ed. Dénes Bartha (Kassel: Bärenreiter, 1965), 195–196. Haydn's new piano was a Schanz (see his letters of 27 June and 4 July 1790, which follow).

119. Anthony van Hoboken, *Joseph Haydn: Thematisch-bibliographisches Werkverzeichnis,* 3 vols. (Mainz: Schott, 1957–78), I, 765.

120. Haydn, *Briefe,* 202.

121. Ibid., 242–243. For the translation of *Flügl* as a smaller, less expensive fortepiano rather than as a harpsichord, see E. Badura-Skoda, "Viennese fortepiano," 87–93.

122. H. C. Robbins Landon, trans. and ed., *The Collected Correspondence and London Notebooks of Joseph Haydn* (London: Barrie and Rockliff, 1959), 107. Anton Walter and Wenzel Schanz, the favorite makers for Mozart and Haydn respectively, produced some of the best instruments made in Vienna. See below, chap. 2, pp. 49–50.

123. Ibid., 107–108.

124. Anderson, *Mozart,* 328–329. Regarding Stein, see n. 35 above.

125. Broder, "Mozart," 80–84.

126. Anderson, *Mozart,* e.g., 748, 374, 448–449, 460, 875, 323, 339–340.

127. Ibid., 391. Abbé Sterkel, priest and musician in the court of the Elector of Mainz, was widely known for his piano playing. Beethoven was impressed with the refinement of his style in 1791 (Thayer/Forbes, *Beethoven,* 103).

128. Anderson, *Mozart,* 339–340. Cf. Streicher's similar description of "how not to do it" in Andreas Streicher, *Brief Remarks on the Playing, Tuning and Care of Fortepianos* (Vienna: Alberti, 1801); trans. Preethi de Silva (Ann Arbor: Early Music Facsimiles, 1983), 6–7.

129. Kelly, *Reminiscences,* I, 225. For other reports see Deutsch, *Mozart: A Documentary Biography* [n. 3 above], e.g., 69–70, 208, 290, 347, 504.

130. Gerber, *Historisch-biographisches Lexicon,* I, col. 979 (the second 9 is printed upside down).

131. Carl Czerny, *Über den richtigen Vortrag der sämtlichen Beethoven'schen Klavierwerke* (Vienna: Diabelli, 1846), 11.

An entry in the Conversation Book of about 25 December 1825 to 1 January 1826, presumably by Karl Holz, adds credence to Czerny's remark. "Was Mozart a good piano player?—At that time it [the piano] was still in its cradle" (Karl-Heinz Köhler, Dagmar Beck, Grita Herre, et al., eds., *Ludwig van Beethovens Konversationshefte,* 8 vols. [Leipzig: Deutscher Verlag für Musik, 1968–], VIII, 235). The dash between sentences indicates a space or paragraph, possibly implying a remark by Beethoven.

132. H. C. Robbins Landon and Donald Mitchell, eds., *The Mozart Companion* (London: Faber and Faber, 1965), 33, fn. 3. Legato playing had long been cultivated on the organ. Leopold Mozart himself refers to this practice in a letter of 25–26 January 1778 to his wife and son: "Reicha, . . . who is an excellent clavierist and who had previously been playing on our harpsichord very smoothly and in the style of the organ, . . ." (Anderson, *Mozart,* 453).

133. A. J. Hipkins, "Pianoforte," *Grove's Dictionary of Music and Musicians,* 1st ed. (London: Macmillan, 1879–1889), II, 717.

134. *NG,* II, 355. Since Beethoven told Ries that Mozart "never played for him," the lessons may have been in composition, and Beethoven may have heard Mozart perform on another occasion (Thayer/Forbes, *Beethoven,* 88).

135. Plantinga, *Clementi,* 36.

136. Alan Tyson, *Thematic Catalogue of the Works of Muzio Clementi* (Tutzing: Schneider, 1967), 310.

137. Plantinga, *Clementi,* 288–289. In a few respects, such as the two-part texture and the use of octaves and thirds, Clementi's early keyboard writing is an extension of Scarlatti's virtuosic style.

138. Ibid., 290.

139. Broder, "Mozart," 79. For a complete report see Otto Jahn, *Life of Mozart* [Leipzig: Breitkopf & Härtel, 1856–1859, as *W. A. Mozart*], 2d ed., 1867, trans. Pauline D. Townsend, 3 vols. (London: Novello, Ewer, 1882), I, 151.

140. Anderson, *Mozart,* 791–793.

141. Ludwig Berger, "Erläuterung eines Mozart'schen Urtheils über Muzio Clementi," *AMZ* XXXI/27 (July 1829): col. 468. Compare Plantinga's comments in *Clementi,* 66–67.

142. Berger, "Erläuterung eines Mozart'schen Urtheils. . ." [n. 141 above], col. 468.

143. See a report in Cramer's *Magazin der Musik* II (26 July 1787):1378–1379.

144. Presumably Clementi would have practiced organ legato, since he had passed the organist's examination in Italy at the age of nine. See also Muzio Clementi, *Introduction to the Art of Playing on the Pianoforte* (London: Clementi, Banger, Hyde, Collard & Davis, 1801); facs., ed. Sandra P. Rosenblum (New York: Da Capo, 1974), x, fn. 28.

145. Cramer's *Magazin der Musik* II (1784 [date/month lacking]:228, 229.

146. Ibid. (11 December 1784):369. Excerpts from this lengthy report (pp. 365–373), titled "News of the Keyboard player Clementi. Bern, October 1784," were translated by John S. Shedlock for *The Monthly Musical Record* XXIV/284 (1 August 1894):171–173.

147. Cramer's *Magazin der Musik* II (11 December 1784):369–370.

148. Plantinga, *Clementi,* 117.

149. Alexandre E. Choron and François J. M. Fayolle, *Dictionnaire historique des musiciens,* 2 vols. (Paris: Valade, 1810–1811), I, 144.

150. E.g., during his visit to Vienna in 1807, Clementi secured the English rights to a number of Beethoven's works. Some of Clementi's editions, including those of the "Emperor" Concerto, Op. 73, and the Piano Sonatas Opp. 78, 79, and 81a, actually preceded those of the Continental publishers (Alan Tyson, *The Authentic English Editions of Beethoven* [London: Faber and Faber, 1963], 79, 62, 82). See also p. 35 below.

151. Clementi was financially involved with Longman and Broderip before founding Longman, Clementi, and Co. in 1798. Around 1801 Longman left the firm, and Clementi took in new partners (Plantinga, *Clementi,* 155). Regarding Clementi's interest in the quality of his firm's instruments, see Clementi/Rosenblum, *Introduction,* viii.

152. An Introduction to the facsimile edition of Clementi's tutor discusses his contributions to performance practices and piano technique, provides a List of Editions that demonstrates the extensive use of the tutor, and identifies some of the more blatant cases of its plagiarism (e.g., ix, xi). See also Sandra P. Rosenblum, "Clementi's Pianoforte Tutor on the Continent," *Fontes Artis Musicae* 27/1 (January–March 1980):37–48.

153. E.g., Carl Czerny's "List of the best and most useful Works . . . for the Pianoforte from Mozart to the present Time" includes, after about 30 works by Mozart—solo, chamber, and concertos—and two sonatas of Haydn, the following Sonatas by Clementi: Opp. 2/2; 7/2, 3; 9/3; 12/1; 25/1, 4, 5; 33/3; 34/1, 2; and 40/2, 3. The three volumes of the *Gradus* are "absolutely necessary for better pianists" (*Die Kunst des Vortrags* [Vienna: Diabelli, 1846], 165–166).

154. Cramer's *Magazin der Musik* I (30 March 1783):387, 392, 395–396; see also Ludwig Schiedermair, *Der junge Beethoven* (Leipzig: Quelle & Meyer, 1925), 69.

155. Cramer's *Magazin der Musik* I (30 March 1783):394.

156. Influential books of the period still regarded the clavichord as the preferred instrument for beginning keyboard instruction (e.g., Türk, *Klavierschule,* 11); it was the favorite instrument for many north Germans, probably including Neefe (Carl Parrish, "Criticisms of the Piano When It Was New," *MQ* XXX/4 [October 1944]:437).

157. When Beethoven was eleven and a half he substituted for Neefe at the organ, and at twelve he was harpsichordist in the court orchestra (Theodor von Frimmel, *Beethoven-Studien,* 2 vols. [Munich: Müller, 1905, 1906], II, 215). The biography of Beethoven in *NG* refers frequently to the piano in his early years, including a translation of *clavier* as piano in the quotation from Neefe discussed above. Further, "at a very early age he received instruction from his father on the piano and the violin." One Tobias Pfeifer may also have given him "piano lessons" (Joseph Kerman and Alan Tyson, "Beethoven," *NG,* II:355). See also Thayer/Forbes, *Beethoven,* 61.

158. Date according to *NG,* II, 398.

159. Schiedermair, *Der junge Beethoven,* 187.

160. Cramer's *Magazin der Musik* II (26 July 1787):1386; Frimmel, *Beethoven-Studien,* II, 222. William Newman pointed out that the correct date is 1788 rather than 1787 ("Beethoven's Pianos Versus His Piano Ideals," *JAMS* XXIII/3 [Fall 1970]:486).

161. Thayer/Forbes, *Beethoven,* 105; original from Bossler's *Musikalische Korrespondenz,* No. 48 (30 November 1791), col. 380. Junker explains that Beethoven "did not perform in public" in Mergentheim; "probably the instrument here was not to his mind. It is one of Späth's make, and at Bonn he plays upon one by Stein" (ibid.).

Karl Ludwig Junker (1748–1797) was an amateur composer, critic of the arts, and author of a number of small works about music. Yet, according to Thayer/Forbes, at the time at which he wrote about Beethoven, "he was a man of no small mark in the musical world of Western Germany" (ibid., 104).

Abbé Vogler, an early enthusiast of the piano, was a widely known theorist, keyboard player, and teacher. For his significant contributions see below, chap. 7, n. 44.

162. Johann Ferdinand von Schönfeld, *Jahrbuch der Tonkunst von Wien und Prag* (Vienna: von Schönfeld, 1796); facs., ed. Otto Biba (Munich: Katzbichler, 1976), 7.

163. Johann Friedrich Reichardt, *Vertraute Briefe geschrieben auf eine Reise nach Wien, 1808–1809*, 2 vols. (Amsterdam: Im Kunst- und Industrie-Comtoir, 1810), I, 257. In the eighteenth and nineteenth centuries *adagio* was often used to denote a slower movement, regardless of its exact tempo heading, that contrasts with a fast movement (*NG*, I, 88–89). In this Concerto the middle movement is an Andante con moto. Writers frequently contrasted the "allegro" and "adagio" styles of performance.

164. Carl Czerny, *Complete Theoretical and Practical Piano Forte School*, Op. 500, 3 vols., trans. J. A. Hamilton [London: Cocks, 1839], III, 99. Czerny distinguished between types of legato when he reported to Nottebohm that Beethoven "understood exceptionally well how to connect full chords to each other without using the pedal. This legato playing is different from that required for playing fugues; the latter needs more finger action (Gustav Nottebohm, *Beethoveniana*, 2 vols. [Leipzig: Rieter-Biedermann, 1872, 1887], II, 356). See also below, chap. 5, p. 152.

165. Oscar G. T. Sonneck, ed., *Beethoven: Impressions of Contemporaries* (New York: G. Schirmer, 1926; facs. New York: Dover, 1967), 29.

166. Czerny, *Proper Performance*, 15.

167. Ludwig Nohl, *Beethoven nach den Schilderungen seiner Zeitgenossen* (Stuttgart: Cotta, 1877), 146. Interestingly, in his comments on Cramer's Etude LXXV, Anton Schindler encouraged the acquiring of that same "light floating of the hands over the keyboard [along] with the most strict legato. . ." (Hans Kann, ed., *Johann Baptist Cramer, 21 Etüden für Klavier: Nach dem Handexemplar Beethovens aus dem Besitz Anton Schindlers* [Vienna: Universal, 1974], v).

168. Schindler/MacArdle, *Beethoven*, 413.

169. Ibid.

170. Charlotte Moscheles, ed., *Aus Moscheles Leben: Nach Briefen und Tagebüchern* (Leipzig: Duncker & Humblot, 1872–73), I, 15–16.

171. Thayer/Forbes, *Beethoven*, 578, 610.

172. Alexander W. Thayer, *Ludwig van Beethovens Leben*, trans. Hermann Dieters, rev. Hugo Riemann, 5 vols., 2d ed. of Vol. II (Leipzig: Breitkopf & Härtel, 1910), 307.

173. Sonneck, *Impressions*, 52.

174. Czerny, *Richtigen Vortrag*, 10. Czerny's "Erinnerungen aus meinem Leben" ("Memoirs"), extracts of which form part of the introductory material to *Richtigen Vortrag*, was written in 1842 and first published by Georg Schünemann, with commentary, as "Czerny's Erinnerungen an Beethoven" in the *Neues Beethoven-Jahrbuch* IX (1939):47–74. Czerny's complete holograph is in the Gesellschaft der Musikfreunde in Vienna. It appeared in an English translation by Ernest Sanders as "Recollections from My Life," *MQ* XLII/3 (July 1956):302–317.

175. Although sometimes given as the previous year (Schünemann, "Czerny's Erinnerungen an Beethoven" [n. 174 above], 50, fn. 10; reprinted from this source by Paul Badura-Skoda in Czerny, *Proper Performance*, 17, n. 12), this date is based on Czerny's age and on his own statement that he had "in his early youth (from the year 1801) received instruction from Beethoven" (Czerny, *Proper Performance*, 20, fn.*).

176. Czerny, *Richtigen Vortrag*, 11.

177. Thayer/Forbes, *Beethoven*, 391.

178. Ibid., 526. The premiere of this concerto seems to have taken place in Leipzig in 1811, with a "little-known pianist named Friedrich Schneider" as soloist (Lewis Lockwood, "Beethoven's Unfinished Piano Concerto of 1815: Sources and Problems," in *The Creative World of Beethoven*, ed. Paul Henry Lang [New York: Norton, 1970], 123).

179. E.g., Schünemann, "Czerny's Erinnerungen an Beethoven" [n. 174 above], 74; William S. Newman, *Performance Practices in Beethoven's Piano Sonatas: An Introduction* (New York: Norton, 1971), 14, 29–30; Bathia Churgin and Joachim Braun, "A Report Concerning the Authentic Performance of Beethoven's Fourth Symphony, Op. 60," Research Project of the Beethoven Seminar at Bar-Ilan University, Ramat Gan,

Israel, 1977, 74–75; Alice L. Mitchell, "Carl Czerny," *NG,* V, 139; Paul Badura-Skoda, below, chap. 9, n. 154.

180. See Moscheles's defense of his own and Czerny's metronomizations of Beethoven's *Piano Sonatas,* below, chap. 9, p. 330.

181. Moscheles met Beethoven in 1809 and from then on heard the composer play whenever possible. Moscheles also attended many programs, such as those by the Schuppanzigh Quartet, at which Beethoven was likely to be present and for some of which he may have coached the performers. From 1814 Moscheles was included among the composer's personal friends (Alfred C. Kalischer, *Beethoven und seine Zeitgenossen,* 4 vols. [Berlin and Leipzig: Schuster & Loeffler, (1908–1910?)], IV, 46–47). When Hummel's duet arrangement of the Overture to *Fidelio* did not satisfy Beethoven, he "tore it up and gave the job of completing a piano score to Moscheles" (*NG,* VIII, 782).

In 1816 Michael Frey, who was not afraid to criticize what he deemed inappropriate, considered Moscheles "one of the first keyboard players in Vienna" (Joseph Schmidt-Görg, "Das Wiener Tagebuch des Mannheimer Hofkapellmeisters Michael Frey," *Beethoven-Jahrbuch* VI [1965–1968]:164). For Frey's importance, see below, chap. 10, n. 96.

182. Brahms wrote about Czerny to Clara Schumann in a letter of March 1878: "I certainly think Czerny's large pianoforte course [Op. 500] is worthy of study, particularly in regard to what he says about Beethoven and the performance of his works, for he was a diligent and attentive pupil. . . . Czerny's fingering is particularly worthy of attention. In fact I think that people today ought to have more respect for this excellent man" (*Letters of Clara Schumann and Johannes Brahms,* ed. Berthold Litzmann, 2 vols. [New York: Longmans, Green, 1927; rep., New York: Vienna House, 1973] II, 29). Brahms may never have met Czerny but formed his opinion from Czerny's *Piano Forte School* and some of his other valuable works, possibly from his fingering in Simrock's edition of Beethoven's *Piano Sonatas* (referred to below, chap. 9), and from what Nottebohm and others in Vienna had told him.

2. The Fortepiano circa 1780–1820

1. Abbé Georg Joseph Vogler, *Kuhrpfälzische Tonschule* (Mannheim: Auf Kosten des Verfassers, [1778]), 28.

2. Three inventions that are taken for granted today, but that are essential to the development of the pianoforte, were actually patented in the 1820s and adopted only gradually between the 1830s and 1850s: The double-escapement action was invented by Sébastien Érard in 1821 and patented later that year by his nephew Pierre in London; the felt hammer was patented by Jean-Henri Pape in France in 1826; and the cast-iron frame was patented for the square piano by Alpheus Babcock of Philadelphia in 1825 (*NG,* XIV, 698, 702). With some modifications, the double-escapement, or repetition, action may have been the first of these inventions to become widely used. It overcame in part a liability of the heavy English action by permitting rapid note repetition, a boon to the quickly developing virtuosity. (See also n. 108 below.) Interestingly, the large American square pianos were equipped with Érard's repetition action by 1830 (*NG,* XIV, 702). The felt hammer was not universally adopted until the 1850s (William Leslie Sumner, *The Pianoforte* [New York: St. Martin's Press, 1966], 85; Rosamund Harding, *The Pianoforte,* 2d ed. [Surrey, England: Gresham, 1978], 179); and some Viennese makers still retained a layer of leather over the felt until late in the century (*The New Grove Dictionary of Musical Instruments,* ed. Stanley J. Sadie, 3 vols. [London: Macmillan, 1984], III, 85). Metal bracing and framing underwent considerable experimentation from the 1820s to the 1850s (e.g., *NG,* XIV, 696–702). In 1855 Steinway of New York built a grand piano with a cast-iron frame and overstringing of the bass, after which the iron frame gradually became standard (Harding, 208).

3. This chapter has benefited from information very kindly provided by Owen Jander of Wellesley College, John Koster of New Bedford, Massachusetts, and Robert E. Smith, fortepiano maker of Somerville, Massachusetts.

4. *NG*, XIV, 686.

5. Harding, *Pianoforte*, 54.

6. Eva Badura-Skoda, "Prolegomena to a History of the Viennese Fortepiano," *Israel Studies in Musicology*, II (1980):80, 88. For Mozart's enthusiastic assessment of Stein's pianos, see above, chap. 1, p. 22.

7. Harding, *Pianoforte*, 42.

8. Malcolm Bilson, "Pianos in Mozart's Time," *PQ* 86 (Summer 1974):30.

9. For improvisation and concerto playing, Mozart extended the bass of his five-octave Walter by having it equipped with a pedal board similar to that of an organ. His pedal board has disappeared, but judging from others of the time, its lowest note would have been CC, a fourth lower than that of the keyboard, and its range close to two octaves (Eva and Paul Badura-Skoda, *Interpreting Mozart on the Piano*, trans. Leo Black [London: Barrie and Rockliff, 1962], 13–14). (In addition to pianos, clavichords and harpsichords were occasionally equipped with pedal boards, in most cases probably for simulated organ practice at home.) Presumably Mozart played, doubled, and extended bass passages *ad lib* on the pedal board, leaving his left hand free for adding fullness and variety to the texture. Although he refrained from including the additional notes in published works, perhaps in part so that the enriched passages would remain his own, there is one holographic passage in his Concerto in D minor K. 466/i/88–90 that probably stems from his intention to perform the piece with the pedal board. There Mozart placed chords in the middle register for the left hand and bass notes for the pedal (Wolfgang Amadeus Mozart, *Neue Ausgabe sämtlicher Werke* [Kassel: Bärenreiter, 1956–]; Konzerte für Klavier, VI, ed. Hans E. Engel and Horst Heussner, xiv–xv).

10. On the dating of this Sonata, see chap. 4, p. 126. Edwin Ripin speculates that because Haydn planned to give the exclusive rights of publication for Hob. 50 to Theresa Bartolozzi, he was less concerned with sales on the Continent, where the five-octave range was still more common ("Haydn and the Keyboard Instruments of His Time," in *Haydn Studies*, 308).

11. Cf. the original version of Sonata in F minor Op. 13/6, in Muzio Clementi, *Klaviersonaten, Auswahl* (ed. Sonja Gerlach and Alan Tyson, 2 vols. [Munich: Henle Verlag, 1978], I, 82–95), with the revised version (ed. Sandra P. Rosenblum as Op. 14/3 [Boston: E. C. Schirmer, 1968]).

The correct opus number of this Sonata in F minor is 13/6, as given here in the main text. Unfortunately, it was published on the Continent by Imbault of Paris as Op. 14/3 in November 1785, only six months after Clementi's edition appeared in London. Imbault's edition, which aside from the numbering appears to be based directly on Clementi's, was reprinted by a number of Continental publishers. Its erroneous opus number gained currency and was widely used until the publication of Tyson, *Clementi Cat.*

12. The first version of Op. 15 was completed and performed in 1795—the clue to the original ceiling of f^3; it was revised around 1800. Hans-Werner Küthen, editor of the Piano Concertos for *BNA*, has provided an exhaustive analysis of the problematic f^3 in Beethoven's final version of Op. 15 and of his reasons for retaining f-natural (Ludwig van Beethoven, *Werke: neue Ausgabe sämtlicher Werke* [Munich: Henle, 1961–], *Kritischer Bericht* for *Klavierkonzerte*, I, 15–16). I am grateful to Prof. Küthen for making available to me detailed information about the sources of Opp. 15 and 37 before the publication of this edition.

Mollo published a *Titelauflage* (reissue with new title page) of Op. 15 before 1804 (Kinsky-Halm, *Beethoven Verz.*, 35), in which there still is no sharp.

13. The g^3 often found in the Trio Op. 1/2/iv/315 is not authentic. It occurs only in those modern editions in which that entire measure has been transposed up an octave to match other appearances of the theme. In OE (Artaria, 1795) the notes in m. 315 are d^2 and b^2. Beethoven actually called attention to "the F at the top" of the piano in a sketch between those for this Finale and the Allegro con brio of Op. 1/3 (Beethoven's

Autograph Miscellany from circa 1786 to 1799, ed. Joseph Kerman, 2 vols. facs., transcription [London: Trustees of the British Museum, 1970], I, f. 86v; II, 227). His instrument at the time might have been the Stein he received in 1788 (see above, p. 27).

The Trio WoO 38 extends to g³ twice in both the first and the third movements, according to OE (Dunst). Since this Trio may have been composed as early as 1790–1791 in Bonn, since the holograph is missing, and since the Trio was not published until 1830 (Kinsky-Halm, *Beethoven Verz.,* 480–481), those notes appear somewhat problematic.

14. Czerny, *Richtigen Vortrag,* 10.

15. *BNA, Klavierkonzerte,* ed. Hans-Werner Küthen, I, xi. A number of Anton Walter's fortepianos of this period and earlier have both f-sharp³ and g³, including two in splendid condition in the Kunsthistorisches Museum in Vienna. One dates from ca. 1785, the other from ca. 1795. Other Viennese instruments in the museum's collection also have those notes, including one by Schanz of the 1790s and one by Michael Rosenberger from the beginning of the nineteenth century (*Katalog der Sammlung alter Musikinstrumente* [des Kunsthistorischen Museums], Vol. 1, *Saitenklaviere,* ed. Victor Luithlen [Vienna: Kunsthistorisches Museum, 1966], 29–30, 32–34). Yale University has a fortepiano by Johann Jacob Könicke dated "ca. 1790" that has those additional treble notes (*Checklist: Yale Collection of Musical Instruments,* ed. Richard Rephann [New Haven: Yale University, 1968], 33); the Smithsonian Institution houses an instrument of the 1790s by Johann Ludwig Dulcken with the same range (*A Checklist of Keyboard Instruments at the Smithsonian Institution,* ed. Cynthia A. Hoover and Scott Odell, 2d ed. [Washington, DC: Smithsonian Institution, 1975], 10).

16. S. V. Klima, "Dussek in London," *The Monthly Musical Record* XC (January–February 1960):18. Broadwood's innovative approach and high standards made his grand pianos among the best produced in London until the middle of the nineteenth century. See especially "Tone and Touch" below.

17. Philip James, *Early Keyboard Instruments from their Beginnings to the Year 1820* (London: Davies, 1930), 55, fn. 1. An upright piano of six octaves was patented by Southwell of Dublin, also in 1794 (ibid.).

18. Wilhelm Lütge, "Andreas and Nannette Streicher," *Der Bär* (Jahrbuch von Breitkopf & Härtel) IV (1927):63.

19. *Keyboard Instruments at the Smithsonian Institution* [n. 15 above], 2–3, 20–21, 36–37, 10–11. On the early use of five and a half octaves in England, see also n. 21 below.

20. *Katalog der Sammlung alter Musikinstrumente,* 33.

21. Anonymous review, *AMZ* II/45 (6 August 1800), col. 782. Derek Adlam's research supports this view: "From 1792 the compass of FF–c⁴ became standard in England, but these pianos ... were soon supplanted by those having six octaves...." ("Anatomy of the Piano," in *The Book of the Piano,* ed. Dominic Gill [Ithaca: Cornell University Press, 1981], 29).

22. Leon Plantinga, *Clementi: His Life and Music* (London: Oxford University Press, 1977), 53.

23. Harding, *Pianoforte,* 68.

24. Edwin M. Good, *Giraffes, Black Dragons, and Other Pianos* (Stanford: Stanford University Press, 1982), 60–61; Alec Cobbe, *A Century of Keyboard Instruments, 1760–1860: Catalogue of the Exhibition at the Fitzwilliam Museum Cambridge, 5 July–31 August 1983* (Yattendon, England: Cobbe, 1983), 26; also "Broadwood," *NG,* III, 324. Exceptions to this trichord construction occur in some pianos whose compass extends below FF. The Clementi piano of ca. 1810–1812 listed on p. 54 is double-strung from CC to FF and triple-strung from FF-sharp up. The Kunsthistorisches Museum has a Stodart of ca. 1830 that is double-strung from CC to EE (*Katalog der Sammlung alter Musikinstrumente,* 48). On the other hand, three six-octave Broadwood instruments with whose details I am familiar (including Beethoven's) are triple-strung right

down to CC. (Beethoven's Broadwood is described in several sources, including Kurt Wegerer, "Beethovens Hammerflügel und ihre Pedale," *Österreichische Musikzeitschrift* XX/4 [April 1965]:203–204.)

25. *NG*, XIV, 697–699; Harding, *Pianoforte*, 199–200. See also n. 108 below. These long braces were distinct from the short iron "gap spacers" used across the action gap between the wrest plank (often called the pin block) and the belly rail in late eighteenth-century English grands. Late eighteenth-century south German and Viennese grands usually had only one gap spacer (Adlam, "Anatomy of the Piano," 36); otherwise they were generally free of metal framing until around 1835.

26. *NG*, XIV, 695.

27. This piano, owned by Kenneth Drake of Baileyville, Illinois, is identical to Beethoven's Broadwood except in the decoration of the case.

28. Richard Kramer, "On the Dating of Two Aspects in Beethoven's Notation for Piano," *Beethoven Kolloquium, 1977: Documentation und Aufführungspraxis,* ed. Rudolf Klein (Kassel: Bärenreiter, 1978), 160–161.

29. Date according to *BNA, Klavierkonzerte,* ed. Hans-Werner Küthen, I, xii; also *Kritischer Bericht,* 42.

30. Küthen, *Kritischer Bericht* for *BNA, Klavierkonzerte,* I, 44–45.

31. Date according to *NG*, II, 395. The notes c-sharp^4, d^4, and e^4 were added to the transcription in *BGA* without further mention. For the contract between Clementi and Beethoven, see Emily Anderson, trans. and ed., *The Letters of Beethoven,* 3 vols. (London: Macmillan, 1961), 1419–1420.

32. Anderson, *Beethoven,* 271.

33. Ibid., 292, 300.

34. Nannette Streicher, daughter of Johann Andreas Stein (chap. 1, n. 35), and her brother Matthäus Andreas (known as André) moved their father's renowned workshop to Vienna (as Frère et Soeur Stein) in 1794, two years after his death (Good, *Pianos,* 77). By 1796 the firm had loaned Beethoven a new piano that he deemed "excellent" (Anderson, *Beethoven,* 24), and Nannette was judged "third great master" builder in the city (Johann Ferdinand von Schönfeld, *Jahrbuch der Tonkunst von Wien und Prag* [Vienna: von Schönfeld, 1796]; facs., ed. Otto Biba [Munich: Katzbichler, 1976], 7). When André opened his own shop in 1802, Nannette continued as Streicher née Stein. Her husband, a successful pianist and teacher, joined his wife's flourishing business around 1800. ("Streicher," *NG*, XVIII, 267. See also Streicher, *Brief Remarks,* xv.)

35. E.g., in 1815 Beethoven had a piano by Schanz (Anderson, *Beethoven,* 523) about which nothing is known but the name. Before that he had an instrument by S. A. Vogel from Pest, later probably one by Kirschbaum (William S. Newman, "Beethoven's Piano Versus His Piano Ideals," *JAMS* XXIII/3 [Fall 1970]:488).

36. Good, *Pianos,* 121.

37. Date based on recent research by Deborah Wythe, "The Pianos of Conrad Graf," *Early Music* XII/4 (November 1984):457; and on evidence in *Ludwig van Beethovens Konversationshefte,* 8 vols., ed. Karl-Heinz Köhler, Dagmar Beck, Grita Herre, et al. (Leipzig: Deutscher Verlag für Musik, 1968–), VIII, 288–289. In 1826 Beethoven's only work for piano was his transcription of the "Grosse Fuge" Op. 133 as a piano duet, Op. 134.

Conrad Graf was "the most eminent Viennese builder from the early 1820's until his retirement in 1840" (*NG*, XIV, 695–696). Convinced that iron affected the sound of a piano, he remained faithful to the tradition of wooden framing. The instrument that Graf presented to Clara and Robert Schumann, in honor of their marriage in 1840, still made with leather hammers (*Katalog der Sammlung alter Musikinstrumente,* 49), has a full, sweet, clear sound. After Robert Schumann's death this instrument was in the possession of Brahms; it is now in the Kunsthistorisches Museum in Vienna.

38. Otto Clemen, "Andreas Streicher in Wien," *Neues Beethoven-Jahrbuch* IV (1930):112.

39. Good, *Pianos*, 88.

40. During those years Mathias Swarz prepared copies of most of Beethoven's published works under Haslinger's direct supervision. These manuscripts, in 62 bound volumes, were to have served as engravers' copies for a collected edition of Beethoven's works published during his lifetime. They carry Beethoven's signed attest to an authoritative version (Otto Erich Deutsch, "Beethoven's gesammelte Werke: Des Meisters Plan und Haslingers Ausgabe," *Zeitschrift für Musikwissenschaft* XIII/2 [November 1930]:62–63). Haslinger dropped this project in 1821. When he started again to produce a *Gesamtausgabe* in 1828 he did not use these volumes, which are now in the archive of the Gesellschaft der Musikfreunde in Vienna.

41. Artur Schnabel, ed., Ludwig van Beethoven, *Sonatas for the Pianoforte*, 2 vols. (New York: Simon and Schuster, 1935), II, 648. Schnabel did not add the EE's in Op. 14/1/i/152–154, but considered the octave with EE in Op. 2/3/ii/26 "both permissible and convincing" (ibid., I, 68, fn. a).

42. Dates according to Kinsky-Halm, *Beethoven Verz.*, 272. Beethoven also borrowed his autograph of this Trio from Steiner in December 1815, before its publication (Anderson, *Beethoven*, 536).

Marian Zwiercan, Vice-Director of the Biblioteka Jagiellońska, very kindly examined the autograph for me; she believes that the 8 is in ink of the same color and the same hand as the rest of the score.

43. Tyson, *Clementi Cat.*, 43.

44. Schnabel, Seraphim IC 6063, released 1970; Claudio Arrau, Philips 6747 035 [1972?]. Curiously, in the new Peters edition of Beethoven's *Sonatas for Piano*, in which it appears that the interpretative editing was done by Arrau and the musical text was prepared by Lothar Hoffmann-Erbrecht, the EE's are printed with no sign that they are not in the primary source (2 vols. [New York: Peters, ca. 1973–ca. 1978], I, 169).

45. Czerny, *Proper Performance*, 22. For a similar opinion from the late nineteenth century, see Theodor Pfeiffer, *Studien bei Hans von Bülow*, 3d ed. (Berlin: Luckhardt, 1894), 35.

46. Anton F. Schindler, *Beethoven as I Knew Him*, trans. Constance Jolly, ed. Donald W. MacArdle (Chapel Hill: University of North Carolina Press, 1966), 444, 402.

47. Alexander Wheelock Thayer, *Ludwig van Beethovens Leben*, trans. Hermann Dieters, rev. Hugo Riemann, 5 vols. (Berlin: Schneider, Vol. I, 1866; Weber, Vol. II, 1872; Vol. III, 1879; Leipzig: Breitkopf & Härtel, Vol. IV, 1907; Vol. V, 1908), V, 119.

48. Personal communication from Owen Jander. A replica of a five-octave Walter of ca. 1785 weighs approximately 155 pounds; a replica of a six-octave Viennese piano in the style of Graf, of ca. 1810, weighs approximately 325 pounds (see list of pianos, pp. 52–53).

49. Streicher, *Brief Remarks*, 1.

50. Ibid., 4, 5.

51. Johann Peter Milchmeyer seems to have been the first, in 1797, to attempt some detailed description of touch appropriate to the fortepiano. The adjustment just mentioned is in his instructions in *Die wahre Art das Pianoforte zu Spielen* (Dresden: Meinhold, 1797), 5–7. See also chap. 5, pp. 153–154 below.

52. Derek Adlam and Cyril Ehrlich, "Broadwood," *NG*, III, 324.

53. *NG*, XIV, 692; Harding, *Pianoforte*, 183. According to Eva Badura-Skoda, the marked difference in tone quality between the pianos of J. A. Stein and Anton Walter was caused in part by different striking points as well as by different thicknesses of their sound boards ("Viennese Fortepiano," 96, 80).

54. *NG*, III, 324.

55. Like the hand stop, the knee lever had also been used earlier on the harpsichord (Edwin M. Ripin, "Expressive Devices Applied to the Eighteenth-Century Harpsichord," *The Organ Yearbook* I [1970]:69).

56. Good, *Pianos*, 62.

57. *NG,* XIV, 686.

58. However, cf. Harding, *Pianoforte,* 41–42, and the square piano of 1791 by Broadwood listed on p. 53 below.

59. *NG,* XIV, 695. Graf had opened his own workshop in 1804 (*Katalog der Sammlung alter Musikinstrumente,* 43).

60. Stewart Pollens, "The Pianos of Bartolomeo Cristofori," *Journal of the American Musical Instrument Society* X (1984):45, 47; also a private communication from the author.

61. This date from Kenneth Mobbs, "Stops and other special effects on the early piano," *Early Music* XII/4 (November 1984):472; also Good, *Pianos,* 152.

62. Harding, *Pianoforte,* 70.

63. Louis Adam, *Méthode de piano du Conservatoire* (Paris: Magasin de Musique du Conservatoire Royal, [1804]), 220.

64. Daniel Steibelt, *Méthode de piano/Pianoforte-Schule* (Leipzig: Breitkopf & Härtel, [ca. 1809]), 64.

65. Harding, *Pianoforte,* 44.

66. *Schubert Neue Ausgabe, Lieder: Quellen und Lesarten,* I, ed. Walter Dürr (Kassel: Bärenreiter, 1972), 12.

67. The only suggestive reference I have found is Dussek's unique definition of *Mezzo,* "to use the Pedal of the grand piano forte, taking off only one String" (Jan Ladislav Dussek, *Instructions on the Art of Playing the Piano Forte or Harpsichord* [London: Corri, Dussek, (1796)], 46).

68. Lütge, "Streicher," 62–64; *Beethovens Sämtliche Briefe,* ed. Alfred C. Kalischer, 5 vols. (Berlin: Schuster & Loeffler, 1906–1908), I, 105.

69. Harding, *Pianoforte,* 72.

70. Adam, *Méthode,* 218.

71. Steibelt, *Méthode,* 64–65.

72. Harding, *Pianoforte,* 72. An exception is the piano by André Stein that I played (p. 53 below).

73. Wegerer, "Beethovens Hammerflügel," 202–205.

74. Carl Parrish, "Criticisms of the Piano When It Was New," *MQ* XXX/4 (October 1944):437–438.

75. Lütge, "Streicher," 63–64.

76. Carl Czerny, *Die Kunst des Vortrags* (Vienna: Diabelli, 1846), 5.

77. *NGMI,* III, 76–77.

78. Clear descriptions and illustrations of fortepiano actions are provided in "Pianoforte," I, History (*NG,* XIV, 682–708); Harding, *Pianoforte,* 23–26, 58; and Adlam, "Anatomy of the Piano," 20–24, 30–31.

79. Franz Josef Hirt, *Meisterwerke des Klavierbaus: Geschichte der Saitenklaviere von 1440 bis 1880* (Olten, Switzerland: Urs Graf, 1955), 102–105; bilingual edition with English title *Stringed Keyboard Instruments,* trans. M. Boehme-Brown (Dietikon: Urs Graf, 1981), 72–74.

80. Harding, *Pianoforte,* 54; *NG,* XIV, 691.

81. Johann Nepomuk Hummel, *A Complete Theoretical & Practical Course of Instructions on the Art of Playing the Pianoforte,* trans. anon. (London: Boosey, 1829), Pt. III, 64–65. Hummel's two footnotes are omitted.

82. *Katalog der Sammlung alter Musikinstrumente,* 35.

83. Adlam, "Anatomy of the Piano," 25. Érard, a leading French firm, contributed a number of important technological improvements to piano building during the first half of the nineteenth century.

84. E.g., Lütge, "Streicher," 65; Anderson, *Beethoven,* 292. The difference in touch between contemporary Viennese pianos and Beethoven's Érard, which I was also able to examine in the Kunsthistorisches Museum, is noticeable immediately, particularly

in the additional weight needed to depress a key; yet by today's standards both types of action are very light.

85. Lütge, "Streicher," 66.

86. Ibid., 65.

87. Von Schönfeld, *Jahrbuch der Tonkunst von Wien und Prag,* 89–90. The other two "master" builders whose instruments were described are Walter and Schanz (see p. 50 below).

88. Lütge, "Streicher," 67.

89. Ibid., 62–64.

90. Ibid., 64.

91. Ibid., 66–67.

92. *AMZ* IX/34 (19 May 1807), cols. 544–545.

93. Johann Friedrich Reichardt, *Vertraute Briefe geschrieben auf einer Reise nach Wien, 1808–1809,* 2 vols. (Amsterdam: Im Kunst- und Industrie-Comtoir, 1810), I, 385–386.

94. For other comments on the effects of altering the Viennese action, see *NGMI,* III, 84–85.

95. *AMZ* XLII/19 (6 May 1840), cols. 407–408.

96. Good, *Pianos,* 51.

97. E.g., Anderson, *Beethoven,* 24–26, 271, 282, 292, 702.

98. E.g., ibid., 292, 300, 686. From a letter to J. A. Stumpff we learn that André Stein was also asked to repair Beethoven's Broadwood in 1824 (ibid., 1145).

99. Ibid., 271.

100. Ibid., 82.

101. Date according to Nathan Broder, "Mozart and the 'Clavier,' " in *The Creative World of Mozart,* ed. Paul Henry Lang (New York: Norton, 1963), 80.

102. Ulrich Rück, "Mozart's Hammerflügel Erbaute Anton Walter, Wien," *Mozart Jahrbuch* VI (1955):251.

103. Von Schönfeld, *Jahrbuch der Tonkunst von Wien und Prag,* 88–89.

104. Ibid., 91.

105. Horst Walter, "Haydns Klaviere," *Haydn-Studien* II/4 (December 1970):283–284, 280. I have not seen any further description of this instrument, which, like Haydn's other pianos, is lost.

106. Ibid., 282–283. In 1802 Beethoven was looking for a Viennese piano more modern than his Walter. A letter written in November to Zmeskall indicates that any new instrument had to have a *una corda* shift (*Zug mit einer Saite;* literally, register with one string) and that Beethoven would take a prospective maker to see Haydn's instrument (*Beethovens Sämtliche Briefe,* ed. Kalischer, I, 105). This suggests that Beethoven knew either Haydn's Longman and Broderip, which almost certainly had an *una corda* pedal, or his Érard, or both.

107. Clementi/Rosenblum, *Introduction,* viii, fn. 22.

108. Charlotte Moscheles, *Life of Moscheles,* trans. A. D. Coleridge, 2 vols. (London: Hurst and Blackett, 1873), I, 252. Moscheles recorded his reactions to various makes of pianos from about 1821 to 1852, providing invaluable information on their characteristics and development. In 1822 he described some differences between the instruments of Broadwood and Clementi: "The strong metal plates . . . used by Broadwood in building his instruments, give a heaviness to the touch, but a fulness and vocal resonance to the tone, which are well adapted to Cramer's legato. . . . I, however, use Clementi's more supple mechanism for my repeating notes, skips, and full chords" (ibid., I, 65). See also I, 50–51, 109, 111–112, 219; II, 29.

In 1825 Moscheles played an Érard with the new double escapement, which he found of "priceless value for the repetition of notes"; but only in 1830 was he satisfied that Érard had "attained great excellence," improving especially the touch and tone (ibid., I, 106–107, 245–247).

109. *AMZ* IV/40 (30 June 1802), col. 652.

110. While the piano was at Streicher's warehouse, before shipment to Beethoven at Mödling, Streicher expressed concern about its action, saying that "Moscheles and others could do nothing with it—the tone was beautiful but the action too heavy" (*Thayer's Life of Beethoven*, rev. and ed. Elliot Forbes [Princeton: Princeton University Press, 1967], 695).

111. As pointed out by Newman in "Beethoven's Pianos," 488–490.

112. Thayer/Dieters/Riemann, *Beethoven*, V, 127.

113. Wythe, "The Pianos of Conrad Graf" [n. 37 above], 458. Two other quadruple-strung instruments by Graf are known, both of which predate Beethoven's (ibid., 454).

114. Theodor von Frimmel, *Beethoven-Studien*, 2 vols. (Munich: Müller, 1905, 1906), II, 230–231.

115. Oscar G. T. Sonneck, ed., *Beethoven: Impressions by His Contemporaries* (facs., New York: Dover, 1967), 202.

116. Newman, "Beethoven's Pianos," 485, 487, 490, 500–501.

117. Thayer/Dieters/Riemann, *Beethoven*, V, 127.

118. Ibid., 326, fn. 1.

119. Czerny, *Piano Forte*, III, 100.

120. Removable resonance boards, often mistakenly considered dust covers, were fitted into some pianos above the strings and parallel to the soundboard. Little is known of their purpose or precise effect. Presumably they quieted the sound somewhat and may have altered its quality.

Clara Schumann used an instrument of this kind, built in 1827, for her first public appearance in the Leipzig Gewandhaus on 20 October 1828. This piano is in the Schumann-Haus in Zwickau (*Katalog der Sammlung alter Musikinstrumente*, 43).

121. Graf placed a piano of this kind at the disposal of Chopin for his first concert in Vienna, on 11 August 1829. Chopin called it a "wonderful, perhaps the best Viennese instrument" (ibid., 46).

3. Dynamics and Accentuation

1. Cf. Leonard G. Ratner, *Classic Music: Expression, Form, and Style* (New York: Schirmer Books, 1980), 200.

2. Robert Donington, *The Interpretation of Early Music*, New Version (New York: St. Martin's Press, 1974), 61.

3. Cf. Randall R. Dipert's "low, middle, and high-level intentions" in "The Composer's Intentions: An Examination of Their Relevance for Performance," *MQ* LXVI/2 (April 1980):205–218; or Erich Leinsdorf, *The Composer's Advocate* (New Haven: Yale University Press, 1981), 51–57, 59–60.

4. Daniel Gottlob Türk, *Klavierschule* (Leipzig and Halle: Schwickert; Hemmerde und Schwetschke, 1789); facs., ed. Erwin R. Jacobi (Kassel: Bärenreiter, 1962), 347–348.

5. Dates of publication for Hob. 35–39 and 40–42 according to Anthony van Hoboken, *Joseph Haydn: Thematisch-bibliographisches Werkverzeichnis*, 3 vols. (Mainz: Schott, 1957–1978), I, 761, 765. Throughout, dates of composition for Haydn's sonatas are from *NG*, only occasionally from Brown, *Haydn's Keyboard Music*, unless otherwise indicated.

6. I would remind readers using Christa Landon's edition of the Sonatas that the Sonata in F major Hob. 47 (No. 57 in HSU, as published by Artaria in 1788), which contains no dynamics, is chronologically misplaced and is excluded from consideration. Its problematic genesis is best described by A. Peter Brown in *Joseph Haydn's Keyboard Music: Sources and Style* (Bloomington: Indiana University Press, 1986), 71–73. László Somfai considers the first movement unauthentic (*Joseph Haydn zongoraszonátái* [Budapest: Zeneműkaidó, 1979], 298. The second and third are properly found, in E minor

and E major, as the first and second movements of Sonata No. 19 in HSU, written ca. 1765 (Brown, 123).

For the sources of information on Haydn's dynamics, see n. 27.

7. Dates according to Leon Plantinga, *Clementi: His Life and Music* (London: Oxford University Press, 1977), 60, 84.

8. These statistics and those cited further on have been compiled from the Summary of Audun Ravnan's unpublished paper, "A Statistical Study of Dynamic Indications in the Piano Sonatas by Haydn, Mozart, and Beethoven." All accent indications are classed as relative. I rounded the percentages to the nearest integer.

9. The Sonata K. 547a (in Wolfgang Amadeus Mozart, *Sonatas and Fantasies for the Piano*, ed. Nathan Broder [Bryn Mawr, PA: Presser, 1956; rev. ed., 1960]) was not included in Ravnan's study and is not considered in this volume. It is no longer believed that Mozart arranged its three movements (Wolfgang Amadeus Mozart, *Neue Ausgabe sämtlicher Werke, Klaviersonaten*, ed. Wolfgang Plath and Wolfgang Rehm, 2 vols. [Kassel: Bärenreiter, 1986], II, viii).

10. Türk's explanation that if a *crescendo* hairpin "refers only to a single note, then its form is quite small" (*Klavierschule*, 117, fn.∗) relates to the clavichord, on which the player can create an illusion of a small *crescendo* on one note by increasing the pressure on the key after it has been depressed. This technique is called *Tragen der Töne* (see chap. 5, n. 6).

11. Clementi/Rosenblum, *Introduction*, 9.

12. Türk, *Klavierschule*, 117. E.g., Mozart K. 457/ii/1.

13. Johann Adam Hiller, *Anweisung zum Violinspielen* (Grätz: Troetscher, 1795), 70; Johann Samuel Petri, *Anleitung zur Praktischen Musik* (Lauban: Wirthgen, 1767), 36; Heinrich Christoph Koch, *Musikalisches Lexikon* (Frankfurt: Hermann dem jüngern, 1802; facs., Hildesheim: Olms, 1964), col. 444.

14. Türk, *Klavierschule*, 116. Koch interpreted *pf* as either *poco forte* or *piano forte*, meaning that "the note sounded immediately after the soft note should again be played with full tone" (Koch, *Lexikon*, cols. 1131, 1155). But other writers before and after Koch specified that *pf* did *not* mean "*piano forte*, . . . as it is explained in some instruction books" (Türk, *Klavierschule*, 116, fn.∗). See also Carl Gollmick, *Kritische Terminologie für Musiker und Musikfreunde* (Frankfurt: Lauten, 1833), 2; Hugo Riemann, *Musik-Lexikon*, 1st ed. (Leipzig: Verlag des Bibliographischen Instituts, 1882), 662.

15. See n. 8. It has so far not been possible to study enough authentic Clementi sources to prepare a statistical study comparable to Ravnan's.

16. Leopold Mozart, *A Treatise on the Fundamental Principles of Violin Playing*, trans. Edith Knocker, 2d ed. (London: Oxford University Press, 1951), 222.

17. Türk, *Klavierschule*, 1st ed., 349; 2d ed., 389.

18. Czerny, *Proper Performance*, 26–27.

19. Ibid., 3.

20. Ibid., 49.

21. Johann K. F. Rellstab, *Anleitung für Clavierspieler* (Berlin: Rellstabschen . . . Musikdruckerey, 1790), xii.

22. Koch, *Lexikon*, 589–590.

23. David Fallows, "Tempo and expression marks," *NG*, XVIII, 682.

24. "Stärke oder Schwäche des Tones," in Türk, *Klavierschule*, 2d ed., 389; in the 1st ed., "Stärke des Tones," 349.

25. I excluded the Andante K. 284/iii.

26. *NMA, Klaviersonaten*, II, 166, xxix, xiv. The other information on Mozart's dynamics is drawn from films of holographs and first editions in the Toscanini Memorial Archive of the Music Division, The New York Public Library, Astor, Lenox & Tilden Foundations; from the volumes of *Klaviersonaten* in *NMA;* and from those in Wolfgang Amadeus Mozart, *Klaviersonaten*, ed. Ernst Herttrich, 2 vols. (Munich: Henle, 1977).

27. Information on Haydn's dynamics is from available primary sources; from Joseph Haydn, *Werke, Klaviersonaten,* ed. Georg Feder, 3 vols. (Munich: Henle, 1966–1970); and from Joseph Haydn, *Complete Piano Sonatas,* ed. Christa Landon, 3 vols. (Vienna: Schott/Universal [formerly Universal], [ca. 1964–1966]). Landon provided documentation of sources in the Preface to each volume and in the volume of *Kritische Anmerkungen.* The *Kritischer Bericht* for *JHW* is not yet available; however, Feder, editor of the *Klaviersonaten* for *JHW,* included some documentation in his edition of *Klaviersonaten, Auswahl* [Selected], 2 vols. (Munich: Henle, [ca. 1972]).

28. Paul Mies has questioned the *piano* indications at Op. 31/1/i/1 and 45. On the basis of the dynamics at all other presentations of the theme—especially the *forte* in m. 111, where the A theme begins for the repeat of the exposition—and of the dynamic design of its three motives, Mies speculates that the initial *p* may have been moved from the end of m. 3 to the opening upbeat by the engraver of OE, who presumably lacked the knowledge to infer the opening *forte* (*Textkritische Untersuchungen bei Beethoven* [Munich: Henle, 1957], 117–119).

29. Unless otherwise indicated, in this chapter dates of composition for works of Mozart, Hummel, and Beethoven, and dates of publication for works of Beethoven, are from *NG;* dates related to Clementi are from Plantinga, *Clementi,* or Tyson, *Clementi Cat.*

30. Gustav Nottebohm, *Beethoveniana,* 2 vols. (Leipzig: Rieter-Biedermann, 1882, 1887), II, 31–33. Nottebohm's careful study of Beethoven's sketches and manuscripts led to important revisions of chronology and texts. His work ranks as a significant predecessor of similar studies today.

31. Heinrich Schenker and Erwin Ratz, eds., Ludwig van Beethoven, *Piano Sonatas,* 4 vols., 2d ed. (Vienna: Universal, 1962), I, 98. Donald F. Tovey and Harold Craxton, eds., Ludwig van Beethoven, *Sonatas for Pianoforte,* 3 vols. (London: Associated Board of the Royal Schools of Music, [1931]), I, 212.

32. Türk, *Klavierschule,* 350.

33. Johann Joachim Quantz, *On Playing the Flute,* trans. and ed. Edward R. Reilly (London: Faber and Faber, 1966), 255–258.

34. Ibid., 259.

35. Türk, *Klavierschule,* 350–351; Carl Philipp Emanuel Bach, *Essay on the True Art of Playing Keyboard Instruments,* trans. and ed. William J. Mitchell (New York: Norton, 1949), 88, 128, 163.

36. Mozart often notated the dynamics separately for each hand, as here. Under his pen the letters of the signs *sf* and *sfp* may combine into a single graphic unit in which the "s" appears to be part of the "f": *sfp*. This way of writing has led to inaccurate interpretation of these indications in some editions.

37. Türk, *Klavierschule,* 351.

38. Cf. Eva and Paul Badura-Skoda, *Interpreting Mozart on the Piano,* trans. Leo Black (London: Barrie and Rockliff, 1962), 24.

39. According to David Fallows, the twelfth-century *Nibelungenlied* includes a description that he translates as "then his strings sounded so that all the house relaxed . . . and he began to fiddle more sweetly and more quietly" ("Diminuendo," *NG,* V, 480).

40. David D. Boyden, "Dynamics in Seventeenth- and Eighteenth-Century Music," in *Essays on Music in Honor of Archibald T. Davison* (Cambridge: Department of Music, Harvard University, 1957), 185–189. For more detail see Rosamond Harding, *Origins of Musical Time and Expression* (London: Oxford University Press, 1938), 85–107.

41. See mm. 42–46 of "Glory to God" from *Messiah (Hallesche Händel Ausgabe).*

42. Writing in 1685, Mylius described this interpretation of *piano, forte* in relation to the *messa di voce:* "Regarding both [*p* and *f*] it is to be noted that one does not go suddenly from *piano* to *forte,* but should gradually strengthen the voice and again let it decrease, so that *piano* [is heard] at the beginning, *forte* in the middle, and again

piano . . . at the close" (W[olfgang] M[ichael] M[ylius] [under the initials W. M. M. M. T. C. M. G.], *Rudimenta musices* [Gotha: der Autor, 1686], chap. 5, [n.p.]).

43. Boyden, "Dynamics" [n. 40 above], 187.

44. E.g., L. Mozart, *Violin,* 218.

45. Artaria's posthumous (1796) first edition of K. 570, "with the accompaniment of a violin," has *decrescendo* hairpins in the piano part at i/31 and 33. Their origin is uncertain since the holograph for mm. 1–64 is missing. Because hairpins are uncharacteristic of Mozart's piano works, Karl Heinz Füssl and Heinz Scholz, who edited Mozart's *Piano Sonatas* for Schott/Universal (formerly Universal; Vienna, 1973), suggest that those indications "have some sort of connection with the violin part," which they speculate may have been written by Johann Mederitsch (Gallus) (II, xxxv–xxxvi). They did not include the hairpins. (The violin part is missing from the copy of Artaria's edition that I examined.)

Of the SU, Bro, and HE editions of K. 576, only Broder's contains a number of hairpins and other dynamic signs, most in parentheses, from the 1805 edition by the Bureau de Musique in Leipzig, a secondary source. Since many of these signs appear atypical of Mozart's dynamic indications, I judge that they were added at the time of printing or shortly before.

46. In a personal communication Max Rudolf cites *Idomeneo* as one.

47. Also Boyden, "Dynamics" [n. 40 above], 190.

48. Koch, *Lexikon,* col. 590.

49. Johann Nepomuk Hummel referred to such occurrences of *crescendo* and *decrescendo* as a "rule" that could also be "inverted" or laid aside (*Pianoforte,* Pt. III, 42).

50. Quantz, *Flute,* 70.

51. Türk, *Klavierschule,* 118; Koch, *Lexikon,* col. 1742; Hummel, *Pianoforte,* Pt. I, 64.

52. Clementi/Rosenblum, *Introduction,* 8.

53. William S. Newman, *The Sonata in the Classic Era* (Chapel Hill: University of North Carolina Press, 1963), 654.

54. Ibid., 654, 734.

55. Muzio Clementi, *Klaviersonaten,* Auswahl, eds. Sonja Gerlach and Alan Tyson, 2 vols. (Munich: Henle, 1978), I, vii. In the original Viennese edition (1783), whether by design or as the result of an engraver's error, both repeats are missing from the first and third movements of Op. 9/3.

56. Sonata in F minor, published as Op. 14/3, ed. Sandra P. Rosenblum (Boston: E. C. Schirmer, 1968), xiii.

57. Thayer/Dieters/Riemann, *Beethoven,* Vol. II, 2d ed. (Leipzig: Breitkopf & Härtel, 1910), 625–626. See also Elfrieda Hiebert, "Beethoven's 'Pathétique' Sonata, Op. 13: Should the Grave Be Repeated?" *PQ* 133 (Spring 1986):33–37, on the question of including the opening Grave in the repeat of the exposition.

58. Max Rudolf, "Inner Repeats in the Da Capo of Classical Minuets and Scherzos," *Journal of the Conductors' Guild* 3/4 (Fall 1982):145–150.

59. Johann Mattheson, *Der vollkommene Capellmeister* (Hamburg: Herold, 1739); trans. and ed. Ernest C. Harriss (Ann Arbor: UMI Research Press, 1981), 452.

60. Türk, *Klavierschule,* 2d ed., 143; trans. according to Max Rudolf, "Inner Repeats," 145.

61. Heinrich Christoph Koch, *Kurzgefasstes Handwörterbuch der Musik für praktische Tonkünstler und für Dilettanten* (Leipzig: Hartknoch, 1807; facs., Hildesheim: Olms, 1981), 104; Hummel, *Pianoforte,* Pt. I, 71; Czerny, *Piano Forte,* III, 12.

62. Emily Anderson, trans. and ed., *The Letters of Beethoven,* 3 vols. (London: Macmillan, 1961), 285, 294–296.

63. This movement is discussed in Rudolf, "Inner Repeats," 146–147.

64. Czerny, *Piano Forte*, III, 12; German edition, *Vollständige theoretisch-praktische Pianoforte-Schule* (Vienna: Diabelli, 1839), III, 10. The direction is reiterated further on (*Piano Forte*, III, 85).

65. H. C. Robbins Landon, *The Symphonies of Joseph Haydn* (New York: Macmillan, 1956), 133.

66. I wish to thank Max Rudolf for his extensive and insightful correspondence pertaining to the interpretation of *calando*.

67. Hans Heinrich Eggebrecht, ed., *Handwörterbuch der Musikalischen Terminologie* (Wiesbaden: Steiner, 1972), "Retardatio, ritardando," 6.

68. E.g., Christian Friedrich Daniel Schubart, *Ideen zu einer Ästhetik der Tonkunst,* ed. Ludwig Schubart (Vienna: Degen, 1806), 365. This volume actually dates from 1784–1785 (*NG*, XVI, 750) but was published posthumously. Türk, *Klavierschule*, 117; Francesco Galeazzi, *Elementi di musica,* 2 vols. (Vol. I, Rome: Cracas, 1791; Vol. II, Rome: Puccinelli, 1796), I, 47; Joseph Nicolas Hüllmandel, *Principles of Music, Chiefly Calculated for the Piano Forte or Harpsichord* (London: By the Author [1796]), 15; Johann Peter Milchmeyer, *Die wahre Art das Pianoforte zu Spielen* (Dresden: Meinhold, 1797), 52–54; George Simon Löhlein, *Anweisung zum Violinspielen,* 3d ed., ed. Johann Friedrich Reichardt (Leipzig: F. Frommann, 1797), 97; Koch, *Lexikon,* cols. 282, 926; August Eberhard Müller, *Klavier und Fortepiano-schule* (Leipzig: F. Frommann, 1804), 30; Friedrich Starke, *Wiener Pianoforte-Schule,* 3 vols. (Vol. I, Vienna: Bey dem Verfasser, 1819; Vol. II, Vienna: Sprenger, 1819; Vol. III, Vienna: Berman, 1821), I, Pt. I, 19–20. The French seem not to have used this term.

69. Türk, *Klavierschule,* 117; Koch, *Lexikon,* cols. 431, 983, 1149, 1399.

70. Giuseppe Baretti, *Dizionario delle lingue italiana, ed inglese,* 2 vols. (Venice: Francesco di Niccolò Pezzana, 1787); Francesco de Alberti di Villanuova, *Nouveau dictionnaire françois-italien, Nuovo dizionario italiano-francese,* 2 vols. (Marseille: Mossy, 1771–1772).

71. Milchmeyer, *Pianoforte zu spielen,* 52.

72. Editors have often added *a tempo*—sometimes in parentheses or in small type— after *calando,* thereby imputing a tempo meaning to the term. Two examples are discussed below.

73. *Diminuendo* in the Rondo K. 511/127 is a notable exception.

74. Türk, *Klavierschule,* 371.

75. Ibid., 117.

76. The same can also be suggested for *mancando, morendo, perdendo,* and *smorzando,* although there seems to be less information for the first three terms than for *calando.*

77. "Retransition" designates the last part of the development section, which prepares for the recapitulation in sonata-allegro form.

78. In K. 378/i/113, published with K. 376 and K. 379, Mozart again used *calando* as a *diminuendo* from *forte* to *piano.*

79. Lead-in, or *Eingang,* is a term used in the late eighteenth and early nineteenth centuries for a brief, nonmodulatory transition between sections of a work. In its improvised form it was usually signaled by a fermata over a dominant-seventh chord (*NG*, VI, 85 and III, 592).

80. I am indebted to Max Rudolf for having called this aria to my attention.

81. Differing interpretations of *mancando* may have appeared earlier than those for *calando.* In 1789 Georg Friedrich Wolf defined *mancando* specifically as "decreasing in respect to tempo" (*Unterricht im Klavierspielen,* 3d ed. [Halle: Hendel, 1789], 85). Rellstab echoed Wolf in 1790 (*Anleitung,* xvi).

82. Clementi/Rosenblum, *Introduction,* 14. Like Türk, Clementi described *morendo, perdendosi,* and *smorzando* as "extinguishing gradually the sound, 'till it be almost lost" (ibid.).

83. Thomas Busby, *A Complete Dictionary of Music* (London: R. Phillips, [ca. 1801]), n.p. Busby defined *mancando* as a *diminuendo*.

84. Johann Baptist Cramer, *Instructions for the Piano Forte* (London: Chappell, 1812), 44.

85. W. S. Stevens, *A Treatise on Piano-Forte Expression* (London: Jones, 1811), "Vocabulary"; *Harmonicon* XI (November 1823): 162.

86. Muzio Clementi, *Méthode pour le pianoforte* (Paris: Pleyel, [1802]), 14.

87. *Clementi's Einleitung in die Kunst das Piano-Forte zu spielen* (Vienna: Hoffmeister; Leipzig: Hoffmeister und Kühnel, [1802]), 21. For the families of editions descended from this and Pleyel's translations, see Sandra P. Rosenblum, "Clementi's Pianoforte Tutor on the Continent," *Fontes Artis Musicae* 27/1 (January–March 1980):47.

88. I recommend interpreting *calando* with tempo nuance only when that seems consonant with Classic practice of tempo flexibility as presented in chap. 10.

89. Clementi/Rosenblum, *Introduction*, 14.

90. Date according to Howard Allen Craw, "A Biography and Thematic Catalog of the Works of J. L. Dussek (1760–1812)," Ph.D. diss., University of Southern California, 1964; University Microfilm 64-9611, 353.

91. Jan Ladislav Dussek, *Instructions on the Art of Playing the Piano Forte or Harpsichord* (London: Corri, Dussek, [1796]), 45.

92. Ibid., 46.

93. These publications include reprints by Simrock in 1797 and Kühnel in 1810, both dated by Kinsky-Halm (*Beethoven Verz.*, 5); Cappi's "Nouvelle édition" of 1825; an edition by André probably published in 1838 based on p.n. 6102 (in Otto Erich Deutsch, *Music Publishers' Numbers* [London: Association of Special Libraries and Information Bureaux, 1946], 6); one by Bote and Bock published between 1853 and 1856 based on p.n. 2908 (ibid., 8); and one by Cramer, Beale & Chappell published between 1844 and 1861 (based on the imprint). *A tempo* appears in an edition by Litolff [1867] and in one by Peters [ca. 1869] based on p.n. 4903 and 4904 in the violin and cello parts respectively (Deutsch, 13).

94. Coincidentally, the editor of the Piano Trios for both Peters and *BGA* (*Beethoven's Werke: Vollständige kritisch durchgesehene überall berechtigte Ausgabe* [Leipzig: Breitkopf & Härtel, 1862–1890]) was Ferdinand David.

95. Suggestion of Max Rudolf.

96. Infrequent examples occur in Opp. 7/iv; 9/3/iii, iv; 10/1/i, ii (*BNA*).

97. In OE, Bureau des Arts et d'Industrie, the tempo heading is given as "Allegretto quasi Andante."

98. The identical place in the Septet Op. 20 (comp. 1799–1800), approaching a *fermata* and a cadenza, has only *calando* (*BGA*).

99. Hummel, *Pianoforte*, Pt. I, 71. An insightful review of Hummel's volume appeared anonymously in the *Quarterly Musical Magazine and Review* X (1828):359–369.

100. Max Rudolf, personal communication.

101. Czerny, *Piano Forte*, I, 190.

102. Ibid., III, 31. This distinction was explained carefully one year later in the important *Encyclopädie der gesammten musikalischen Wissenschaften, oder Universal-Lexicon der Tonkunst,* ed. Gustav Schilling, 7 vols. (Stuttgart: Köhler, 1838–1842), "New" ed. of Vol. II (1840), 79–80.

103. Czerny, *Piano Forte*, I, 190.

104. Ibid., III, 32.

105. Ibid., I, 156.

106. The engraved wedge represents a written stroke. See also "Dot, Stroke and Wedge" in chap. 5.

In Fig. 3.14, m. 21, a dot over g² in Aut. was changed by analogy with mm. 20 and 22.

107. Türk, *Klavierschule,* 338.

108. Wolf, *Unterricht,* 38.

109. Johann Friedrich Schubert, *Neue Singe-Schule* (Leipzig: Breitkopf & Härtel, 1804), 101. This volume also shows other influences of Türk's *Klavierschule* and of Johann Adam Hiller's *Anweisung zum musikalisch-zierlichen Gesange* (Leipzig: Junius, 1780).

110. E.g., Müller, *Fortepiano-Schule,* 29; Hummel, *Pianoforte,* I, 67.

111. Karl Geiringer, *Joseph Haydn* (Potsdam: Akademische Verlagsgesellschaft Athenaion, 1932), plate facing p. 114.

112. The only source for these sonatas is the first edition published by Artaria in 1780 (Hoboken, *Werkverzeichnis,* 761). Unfortunately, the sources for Haydn's sonatas are often first editions in which the precise rendering of performance directions seems questionable or, worse yet, manuscript copies of unknown origin.

113. Clementi/Rosenblum, *Introduction,* 9.

114. Tyson, *Clementi Cat.,* 125. The texts of the other volumes are reprints, many surprisingly inaccurate, of various editions.

115. Cf. Mies, *Textkritische Untersuchungen,* 121. Mies refers to the small hairpin signs merely as *diminuendo* signs rather than as a combination of emphasis followed by *diminuendo.*

116. Date according to p.n. 2778 (Deutsch, *Music Publishers' Numbers,* 6). I do not know on which earlier edition André's reprint was based.

117. Haydn, *Sonatas,* HSU, III, xx.

118. Clementi/Rosenblum, *Introduction,* 9; also Dussek, *Instructions,* 45; Milchmeyer, *Pianoforte zu spielen,* 53.

119. E.g., Rellstab, *Anleitung,* XVI; Bernard Viguerie, *L'Art de toucher le piano-forte* (Paris: Chez l'auteur [1797]), 23; Koch, *Lexikon,* col. 1200; Stevens, *Piano-Forte Expression,* "Vocabulary."

120. Türk, *Klavierschule,* 116.

121. J. F. Danneley, ed., *Dictionary of Music* (London: Printed for the Editor, 1825), n.p.

122. See also Mies, *Textkritische Untersuchungen,* 124–129; and Gustav Nottebohm, "Zur Reinigung der Werke Beethoven's von Fehlern und fremden Zuthaten," *AMZ,* 3d series, XI/30 (26 July 1876): cols. 469 (bottom) to 470.

123. Riemann, *Musik-Lexikon,* 1st ed. [n. 14 above], 772.

124. Johann Friedrich Reichardt, *Vertraute Briefe geschrieben auf einer Reise nach Wien, 1808–1809,* 2 vols. (Amsterdam: Im Kunst- und Industrie-Comtoir, 1810), I, 206. For the larger context of this quotation, see chap. 10, p. 386.

125. *Thayer's Life of Beethoven,* rev. and ed. Elliot Forbes (Princeton: Princeton University Press, 1967), 901–907. The concert took place in the Court Theater. Thayer also commented on the importance of the Schuppanzigh Quartet in general and to Beethoven specifically: "From 1794 to 1799, the four [Schuppanzigh, first violin; Sina, second violin; Weiss, viola; Kraft, cello] appear to have practised much and very regularly together. They enjoyed an advantage known to no other quartet—that of playing the compositions of Haydn and Förster under the eyes of the composers, and being taught by them every effect that the music was intended to produce. Each of the performers, therefore, knowing precisely the intentions of the composer, acquired the difficult art of being independent and at the same time of being subordinate to the general effect. When Beethoven began to compose quartets he had, therefore, a set of performers schooled to perfection by his great predecessors, and who already had experience in his own music through his trios and sonatas" (ibid., 228).

126. Koch, *Lexikon,* cols. 49–50.

127. Ibid., col. 51.

128. Schulz, "Takt," in Sulzer, *Allgemeine Theorie,* II, 1136–1138.

129. E.g., Türk, *Klavierschule,* 92. By "beat division" (Max Rudolf's suggested translation for *Taktglied*) Türk referred specifically to the value of one-half or one-third of a beat in meters divisible by two and three respectively (ibid., 90).

130. Koch, *Lexikon,* cols. 51–52.

131. L. Mozart, *Violin,* 218–219, 221; Türk, *Klavierschule,* 337; Hummel, *Pianoforte,* Pt. III, 54.

132. Türk, *Klavierschule,* 354–355; Koch, *Lexikon,* cols. 51–52.

133. Schulz, "Vortrag," in Sulzer, *Allgemeine Theorie,* II, 1249.

134. Türk, *Klavierschule,* 336. This description is substantially the same in the 2d ed., 375–376. The term "phrase division" is Raymond Haggh's, as explained in n. 136.

135. Türk, *Klavierschule,* 342–347.

136. Haggh's helpful discussion of the *Einschnitt* in eighteenth-century theoretical writing clarifies certain concepts of melodic structure (Daniel Gottlob Türk, *School of Clavier Playing,* trans. and ed. Raymond Haggh [Lincoln: University of Nebraska Press, 1982], pp. 506–511, n. *19). Haggh points out that *Einschnitt* could mean either a melodic segment, which he translates as "phrase member," or a point of rest, or break, in a melodic line, which he translates as "phrase division." Other theoretical sources in addition to Türk include Kirnberger, "Einschnitt," in Sulzer, *Allgemeine Theorie,* enl. 2d ed., II, 35–37 (the article was clarified in this edition); and a better-developed discussion with musical examples by Jérôme-Joseph de Momigny, *Cours complet d'harmonie et de composition,* 3 vols. (Paris: Chez l'Auteur, 1808), II, 406–425; III, 157–160.

137. Mattheson/Harriss, *Der vollkommene Capellmeister,* Pt. II, chap. 9; Momigny, *Cours complet . . . ,* II, 406–425.

138. E.g., Mathis Lussy, *Le Rhythme musical,* 2d ed. (Paris: Huegel, 1884), 31–32, 53–54. These later writers had separate terms for the longer *Einschnitt,* or phrase member, thus keeping their distinctions clearer. Several, including Lussy, used *hémistiche.*

139. I chose not to use the term "phrase" accent here because it is sometimes used to designate an accent that is the expressive goal of a phrase.

140. E.g., Hugo Riemann, *System der Musikalischen Rhythmik und Metrik* (Leipzig: Breitkopf & Härtel, 1903), 196–213.

141. Schulz implied the relationship among the three kinds of accents in "Vortrag," Sulzer, *Allgemeine Theorie,* II, 1249–1250. Matthis Lussy stated the relationship unequivocally in *Traité de l'expression musicale,* 1873 (2d ed., Paris: Heugel, 1874), 11–12.

142. Badura-Skoda, *Mozart,* chap. 7, contains a related discussion of melodic accentuation.

143. Schulz, "Vortrag," in Sulzer, *Allgemeine Theorie,* II, 1250.

144. Koch, *Lexikon,* cols. 53–54.

145. Hummel, *Pianoforte,* Pt. I, 67; see also Pt. II, 2, 4ff.

146. Franz Kullak, *Beethoven's Piano Playing,* trans. Theodore Baker (facs., New York: Da Capo, 1973), 5.

147. Anton Schindler, *Beethoven as I Knew Him,* trans. Constance Jolly, ed. Donald W. MacArdle (Chapel Hill: University of North Carolina Press, 1966), 379. Beethoven might logically have made the annotations when he taught Karl for some time in 1818 (Thayer/Dieters/Riemann, *Beethoven,* 2d ed. of Vol. II, [n. 57 above], 82, fn. 1). Strangely though, their mention in the 3d ed. of Schindler's *Biographie* (1860) seems to be the earliest (William S. Newman, "Yet Another Major Beethoven Forgery by Schindler?" *The Journal of Musicology* III/4 [Fall 1984]:412).

148. Schindler's copy, Mus. ms. 35, 88 in the Deutsche Staatsbibliothek, is a Haslinger edition with p.n. 4138–4141 (Eve Bartlitz, *Die Beethoven Sammlung in der Musikabteilung der Deutschen Staatsbibliothek* [Berlin: Staatsbibliothek, 1970], 207). In it, annotations in pencil are covered by strips of paper on which they have been revised in ink. Both sets are in Schindler's hand. According to Harry Goldschmidt's study of this volume using X-rays, the changes between the apparent first version in pencil and

the second version in ink represent occasional supplements to the text or polishing of the language but do not appear to alter the original meaning. Goldschmidt theorizes that Schindler had probably transcribed Beethoven's comments into his own volume in pencil and that the ink wording was provided in anticipation of future publication. Probably toward that same end, Schindler added his own comments to other Etudes, identifying them with "A. S." (Harry Goldschmidt, "Beethovens Anweisungen zum Spiel der Cramer-Etüden," in *Die Erscheinung Beethoven* [Leipzig: Deutscher Verlag für Musik, 1974], esp. 115–118). Any known differences between the pencil and ink versions of the annotations discussed in this volume will be given in notes.

149. Alan Tyson may have been the first of those who expressed skepticism about the Etude annotations in his review of Johann Baptist Cramer, *21 Etüden für Klavier: Nach dem Handexemplar Beethovens aus dem Besitz Anton Schindlers*, ed. Hans Kann (Vienna: Universal, 1974) in *Music and Letters* LVIII/2 (April 1977):247–249.

150. Cramer published his 84 Etudes, titled *Studio per il pianoforte*, in 1804 and 1810, a few years before the invention of the metronome. On 10 September 1817 he published his indications "according to Mälzel's metronome" in *AMZ*, XIX/37: cols. 633–636. In this volume Cramer's metronomizations are given in parentheses at the heading of each example.

151. Kann, ed., *Cramer's Etüden*, 18.

152. Sulzer, *Allgemeine Theorie*, II, 1182.

153. Kann, ed., *Cramer's Etüden*, 20.

154. Donald W. MacArdle, "Anton Felix Schindler, Friend of Beethoven," *Music Review* XXIV/1 (February 1963):50.

155. E.g., Schindler/MacArdle, *Beethoven*, 45, 466, n. 319; Schindler, *Biographie von Ludwig van Beethoven*, 3d ed., 2 vols. (Münster: Aschendorff, 1860), I, 14.

156. Dagmar Beck and Grita Herre, "Einige Zweifel an der Überlieferung der Konversationshefte," in *Bericht über den Internationalen Beethoven-Kongress ... 1977 in Berlin*, ed. Harry Goldschmidt, Karl-Heinz Köhler, and Konrad Niemann (Leipzig: Deutscher Verlag für Musik, 1978), 257–274. A list of the forged entries in the volumes of the Conversation Books published before this discovery is provided in vol. VII of *Ludwig van Beethovens Konversationshefte*, 8 vols., ed. Karl-Heinz Köhler, Dagmar Beck, Grita Herre, et al. (Leipzig: Deutscher Verlag für Musik, 1968–).

157. Ibid., II, 200. See also pp. 387–388 below. Dashes in the entries indicate a space or a paragraph, possibly implying a remark by Beethoven.

158. Beck and Herre, "Einige Zweifel an der Überlieferung der Konversationshefte" [n. 156 above], 265. Also Peter Stadlen, "Schindler's Beethoven Forgeries," *The Musical Times* 118/1613 (July 1977):551. Unfortunately, there are no extant Conversation Books from the period of September 1820 to March–April 1822.

159. For an interesting collection of these forgeries, see Peter Stadlen, "Schindler and the Conversation Books," *Soundings* 7 (1978):2–18.

160. *Niederrheinische Musik-Zeitung für Kunstfreunde und Künstler* (1853–1867) was founded and edited by Ludwig Bischoff, who worshiped Haydn, Mozart, and Beethoven but "to the end regarded Schumann as too advanced" (*Grove's Dictionary of Music and Musicians*, 5th ed., ed. Eric Blom [New York: St. Martin's Press, 1954], I, 721).

161. Anton F. Schindler, *The Life of Beethoven*, trans. and ed. Ignaz Moscheles, 2 vols. (London: Colburn, 1841), II, 92; Schindler, *Biographie von Ludwig van Beethoven* (Münster: Aschendorff, 1840), 203.

162. *Ferdinand Ries: Briefe und Dokumente*, ed. Cecil Hill (Bonn: Röhrscheid, 1982), 730.

163. Adolph Bernhard Marx, *Ludwig van Beethoven: Leben und Schaffen* (Berlin: Janke, 1859), 176–179; also in Schindler/Moscheles, *Beethoven*, II, 123–127.

164. Schindler/MacArdle, *Beethoven*, 406–407; but see chap. 10, p. 388.

165. Alexander Wheelock Thayer, *The Life of Ludwig van Beethoven*, ed. Henry Edward Krehbiel, 3 vols. (New York: The Beethoven Association, 1921), II, 376; Thayer/Dieter/Riemann, *Beethoven*, IV, 50.

166. Peter Stadlen, "Schindler's Beethoven Forgeries" [n. 158 above], 552. Karl-Heinz Köhler also asks, "Who can say with absolute certainty that [the forged conversations] did not in fact take place?" ("The Conversation Books," in *Beethoven, Performers, and Critics,* ed. Robert Winter and Bruce Carr [Detroit: Wayne State University Press, 1980], 160–161). Beck and Herre express a similar idea in "Einige Zweifel ..." [n. 156 above], 263, 266.

167. Newman, "Yet Another Major Beethoven Forgery ... ?" 414. This provocative paper appraises Schindler and the contents of the annotations systematically against their "cultural context," the circumstantial evidence (ibid., 413–414).

168. Ibid., 414–415. Some of the analogies here are indebted to Newman's study.

169. Richard Kramer, "Beethoven and Carl Heinrich Graun," *Beethoven Studies* I, ed. Alan Tyson (New York: Norton, 1973), 22–24, 34.

170. Maynard Solomon, "Beethoven's *Tagebuch* of 1812–1818," *Beethoven Studies* III, ed. Alan Tyson (Cambridge: Cambridge University Press, 1982), e.g., 219, 232; Harry Goldschmidt, "Vers und Strophe in Beethovens Instrumentalmusik," in *Die Erscheinung Beethoven,* 25–29; Nottebohm, *Beethoveniana,* II, 328, 474, 542. For examples in the *Konversationshefte,* ed. Köhler et al., see Vol. VI, 19, 39.

171. Goldschmidt, "Vers und Stophe ... " [n. 170 above], 29–31. Of Op. 73/ii Czerny wrote, "When Beethoven wrote this *Adagio,* he had in mind the religious songs of devout pilgrims, ..." (*Richtigen Vortrag,* 107).

172. See Owen Jander, "Romantic Form and Content in the Slow Movement of Beethoven's Violin Concerto," *MQ* LXIX/2 (Spring 1983):159–179, for a convincing presentation of the direct influence of the poetic *Romanze* (as described in Sulzer, *Allgemeine Theorie;* Heinrich Christoph Koch, *Versuch einer Anleitung zur Composition,* 3 vols., 1782–1793 [facs., Hildesheim: Olms, 1969]; and Rousseau, *Dictionnaire de Musique*) on these movements.

173. Goldschmidt, "Vers und Strophe ... " [n. 170 above], 25–26; also Newman, "Yet Another Major Beethoven Forgery ... ?" 415, fn. 53.

174. Owen Jander, "Beethoven's 'Orpheus in Hades': The *Andante con moto* of the Fourth Piano Concerto," *19th-Century Music* VIII/3 (Spring 1985):195–212.

175. Czerny, *Proper Performance,* 38; also 25, 29, and 45.

176. Nottebohm, *Beethoveniana,* II, 356.

177. Schindler/MacArdle, *Beethoven,* 379. See also p. 204 below for Beethoven's contemplation of a piano method reported by another source.

178. Newman, *The Sonata in the Classic Era,* 516.

179. Czerny, *Proper Performance,* 38.

4. Use of the Pedals

1. Carl Philipp Emanuel Bach, *Essay on the True Art of Playing Keyboard Instruments,* trans. and ed. William J. Mitchell (New York: Norton, 1949), 431.

2. Johann Peter Milchmeyer, *Die wahre Art das Pianoforte zu spielen* (Dresden: Meinhold, 1797), 59.

3. In the first edition of J. B. Cramer's *Trois Grandes Sonates,* the third movement of Op. 25/1 (comp. 1801(?) [*NG,* V, 21]), containing many quiet pedaled passages with harmonies mingling gently over a sustained bass note, is titled "Rondo en Carillon."

4. Czerny, *Piano Forte,* III, 100.

5. *NG,* VIII, 781, 783–784; also Czerny, *Piano Forte,* III, 99. Hummel was born in November 1778, making him only between nine and ten years of age when he left Mozart's tutelage.

6. Hummel, *Pianoforte,* Pt. III, 62.

7. Oscar G. T. Sonneck, ed., *Beethoven: Impressions by His Contemporaries* (facs., New York: Dover, 1967), 29.

8. Milchmeyer, *Pianoforte zu spielen,* 61.

9. Petri, *Anleitung zur Praktischen Musik,* 2d ed. (Leipzig: Breitkopf, 1782), 371. Petri also referred to many "changes of register" that can be made with speed "in the midst of playing," by means of pedals [*Fusstritte*]. This is an early reference to pedals in Germany. However, from 1770 to 1808 Petri lived in Bautzen, not far from Dresden, where Johann Gottlob Wagner had begun building square pianos with pedals in 1774 (Franz Josef Hirt, *Stringed Keyboard Instruments,* trans. M. Boehme-Brown [Dietikon: Urs Graf, 1981], 89, 224).

10. E.g., Louis Kohler, *Der Clavierunterricht* (Leipzig: Weber, 1860), 172–177; also 3d enl. ed. of 1868. Hans Schmitt, *The Pedals of the Piano-Forte,* four lectures at the Conservatory of Music, Vienna, pub. 1875; trans. from German Frederick S. Law (Philadelphia: Presser, 1893), 4–9. Amy Fay, *Music-Study in Germany in the Nineteenth Century,* 1880 (rep., New York: Dover, 1965), 297–298.

11. According to the Henle and Schott/Universal (formerly Univeral) editions of Chopin's Nocturnes (ed. Ewald Zimmerman and Jan Ekier respectively), there are eight Nocturnes in which there are one or more instances of no release between *Ped.* signs in any of the sources. Many of these pedalings carry an elaborate embellishment into the measure following (e.g., Op. 9/2/32–33) or connect a transitional passage or notes to the next theme (Op. 15/1/47–49); some occur where any "breathing" allowed by even the slightest space between pedalings would dispel some of the musical intensity (e.g., Op. 48/2/98–101). There are fewer syncopated pedal changes in the Mazurkas, but a very telling single example appears in the autograph of the Preludes. In the "Raindrop" Prelude there are successive *Ped.* marks at the starts of mm. 81 and 84, which allow the uninterrupted sound to carry Chopin's subsiding outcry across the phrase articulation between mm. 83–84 to the final phrase of the piece.

12. Czerny, *Piano Forte,* III, 61–62. Czerny's discrepancy between notation and intention may help to explain those pedalings of Chopin and other Romantic composers at places where the hands cannot hold what may seem—after due consideration—to be necessary continuing sound between release and *Ped.* signs. The placement of signs as if for rhythmic pedaling may have become an idiosyncrasy of notation that was intended precisely in many contexts but not in all.

13. Leon Plantinga, *Clementi: His Life and Music* (London: Oxford, 1977), 216–217.

14. Tyson, *Clementi Cat.,* 87.

15. *Gradus ad Parnassum* (OE, Clementi, . . .), II, Exercise 31, m. 73; Sonatas Op. 50/2/i/122–125, ii/1–2, 22–28 and Op. 50/3/ii/36–37 (OE, Clementi, . . .).

16. Plantinga, *Clementi,* 117.

17. Louis Adam, *Méthode de piano du Conservatoire* (Paris: Magasin de Musique du Conservatoire Royal, [1804]), 219; Francesco Pollini, *Metodo per Clavicembalo* (Milan: Ricordi, [1812]), 61.

18. Adam, *Méthode,* 224–226; Pollini, *Metodo,* 62.

19. Czerny, *Piano Forte,* III, chap. 6, especially 59–61. Beethoven's special pedalings will be discussed further on in this chapter.

20. Adam, *Méthode,* 218.

21. "Among other refinements of his teaching, Deppe asked me if I had ever made any pedal studies. I said 'No—nobody had ever said anything to me about the pedal particularly, except to avoid the use of it in runs. . . .' He picked out that simple little study of Cramer in D major in the first book . . . and asked me to play it. I had played that study to Tausig, and he found no fault with my use of the pedal; so I sat down thinking I could do it right. But I soon found . . . that Deppe had very different ideas on the subject. He sat down and played it phrase by phrase, pausing between each measure, to let it 'sing.' I soon saw that it is possible to get as great a virtuosity with the pedal as with anything else, and that one must make as careful a study of it. You remember I wrote to you that one secret of Liszt's effects was his use of the pedal, and how he has a way of disembodying a piece from the piano and seeming to make it float

in the air? He makes a spiritual form of it so perfectly visible to your inward eye, that it seems as if you could almost hear it breathe! Deppe seems to have almost the same idea, though he has never heard Liszt play. 'The Pedal,' said he, 'is the *lungs* of the piano.' He played a few bars of a sonata, and in his whole method of binding the notes together and managing the pedal, I recognized Liszt. . . . Unless Deppe wishes the chord to be very brilliant, he takes the pedal *after* the chord instead of simultaneously with it. This gives it a very ideal sound." Amy Fay, *Music-Study in Germany* [n. 10 above], 297–298.

22. Streicher, *Brief Remarks,* 5. For a description of the glass harmonica, see p. 117 below.

23. As in Friedrich Starke, *Wiener Pianoforte-Schule,* 3 vols. (Vol. I, Vienna: Bey dem Verfasser, 1819; Vol. II, Vienna: Sprenger, 1819; Vol. III, Vienna: Bermann, 1821), I, Pt. 1, 16.

24. E.g., Milchmeyer, *Pianoforte zu spielen,* 59–62; W. S. Stevens, *A Treatise on Piano-Forte Expression* (London: Jones, 1811), 15; Pollini, *Metodo,* 61–63; Hummel, *Pianoforte,* Pt. III, 62.

25. Adam, *Méthode,* 219. For its similarity to Adam, compare Starke, *Pianoforte-Schule,* I, Pt. 1, 17.

Louis (or Jean-Louis) Adam (1758–1848) was a French composer, pianist, and highly influential teacher. He was born in Alsace but settled in Paris about 1775 to pursue his musical studies and career. In 1797 he was appointed "Professeur de piano" at the Conservatoire, where he taught until 1842. (See also Georges de Saint-Foix, "Les premiers pianistes parisiens [IV], Jean-Louis Adam," *La Revue musicale* VI/8 [1 June 1925]: 209–215.) Although not as detailed as some German volumes, Adam's two important methods (listed in the Selected Bibliography) offer a thorough grounding in the contemporary principles of fingering and additional information on the performance style and piano repertoire of the day.

An interesting reference to Adam appears in Ries's letter of 22 October 1803 to Simrock, after the firm had agreed to publish Beethoven's "Kreutzer" Sonata for Violin and Piano Op. 47: "[The Sonata] . . . is probably dedicated to Adam and Kreutzer as first violinist and pianist [*sic*] in Paris, because Beethoven has an obligation to Adam on account of the Parisian piano. . . ." Erich H. Müller, "Beethoven and Simrock," *Simrock Jahrbuch,* II, (Berlin, 1929), 27.

26. Pollini, *Metodo,* 63.

27. Ibid., 62.

28. Johann Baptist Cramer, *Praktische Pianoforte-Schule,* 1826; 2d ed. (Berlin: Lischke, 18— ?), 46; Joseph Czerny, *Der Wiener-Klavier-Lehrer,* 2d ed. (Vienna, [ca. 1826 or 1827]), 15.

29. Adam, *Méthode,* 224–226.

30. Pollini, *Metodo,* 63.

31. Hummel, *Pianoforte,* Pt. III, 63.

32. Milchmeyer, *Pianoforte zu spielen,* 59, 65–66; Adam, *Méthode,* 218–219; Pollini, *Metodo,* 63; Hummel, *Pianoforte,* Pt. III, 63.

33. Although the slur in Figure 4.8 trails off over the high B-flat for lack of space in a tightly squeezed manuscript (a manner of notation for which Clementi was notorious), in a later analogous context it is continued to the end of the measure. Unfortunately Clementi did not notate the pedal signs there.

34. Some pianists and writers apply the terms "half" or "quarter" pedal to mean a half or quarter release for partial clearing of the sound. For this I use the terms "half" or partial release or "thinning" the pedal.

35. Adam, *Méthode,* 220.

36. Milchmeyer, *Pianoforte zu spielen,* 58.

37. David Rowland, "Early pianoforte pedalling," *Early Music* XIII/1 (February 1985):5, 7.

38. Daniel Steibelt, *Six Sonates pour le PianoForte, Avec Accompagnement d'un Violon obligé,* Op. 27 (Paris: Imbault [1797]), 34. Steibelt's *Trois Grandes Sonates pour le Piano-Forte, Avec Accompagnement d'un Violon obligé,* Oeuvre 27, published by Preston of London in 1797, are those of the original *Six Sonates . . .* Op. 27 that had no pedaling. David Rowland suggests that because of the conservative English taste, Steibelt at first withheld those sonatas that had pedaling. Op. 27/1, with pedaling, appeared in London in 1798 (Rowland, "Early pianoforte pedalling," 10).

39. Since English grand pianos usually had just the damper and *una corda* pedals, the latter was sometimes called the "piano" pedal (Rosamund Harding, *The Pianoforte,* 2d ed. [Surrey, England: Gresham Books, 1978], 69). Steibelt's description of the pedal designated by ⑂ in his *Méthode* leaves no doubt that that sign refers to the *una corda* effect and not to a moderator (Leipzig: Breitkopf & Härtel, [ca. 1809], 65).

40. Daniel Steibelt, *Three Sonatas for the PianoForte with an Accompaniment for a Violin ad libitum,* Op. 35 (London: Longman, Clementi & Co., [1799, based on date of entry at Stationers' Hall]), [1].

41. "Adieu," 1. The description on the title page reads, "A favorite duett composed by Mr. Kelly as sung in Lionel and Clarissa . . . , arranged for the pianoforte by J. L. Dussek." The imprint is merely "Printed & sold at No. 28 Haymarket," the address of the firm Corri, Dussek from 1796 to 1801. According to information kindly supplied by J. A. Parkinson of The British Library, the vocal duet by Michael Kelly upon which Dussek's piece was based was published by Corri, Dussek on paper bearing a watermark of 1797. Thus the date ca. 1799, suggested by Howard Allen Craw for Dussek's "Adieu," seems appropriate ("A Biography and Thematic Catalog of the Works of J. L. Dussek (1760–1812)," Ph.D. diss., University of Southern California, 1964; University Microfilms 64-9611, 322).

42. In the authorized Continental editions of Op. 40, published in October 1802 by Pleyel and in November 1802 by Mollo (Tyson, *Clementi Cat.,* 80–81), as well as in Breitkopf & Härtel's *OC* (Vol. III, 1803), the full text (in French and German respectively) reads "N.B. *Ped.* means to raise the dampers, and this sign ⊕ to let them fall back."

43. Johann Baptist Cramer, *Instructions for the Piano Forte* (London: Chappel, 1812), 43.

44. See a review of Milchmeyer's volume in *AMZ* I/9 (28 November 1798), especially col. 136; also p. 44 above.

45. The reference to "pedals" for the four mutations that Milchmeyer described (damper, *una corda,* harp, and cover-raising) may reflect the presence in Dresden, his home when this volume was published, of a tradition of square pianos built with pedals (see n. 9 above). Unfortunately, his chapter is tainted by an overabundance of fanciful descriptive writing designed to popularize the mutations (e.g., referring to pedaled sounds that imitate the rising sun, human voices, and other phenomena of nature) and by his praise of Steibelt's "pots-pourris." In spite of his strong bias in favor of square pianos, I have not found any evidence that Milchmeyer himself was a piano builder.

46. Milchmeyer, *Pianoforte zu spielen,* 61.

47. Ibid., 62, 64.

48. Ibid., 62.

49. Czerny, *Piano Forte,* III, 61. See also p. 126 below.

50. The heyday of this quasi-Impressionist instrument in Europe lasted until around 1830. Mozart composed the Adagio and Rondo K. 617 for glass harmonica, flute, oboe, viola, and cello in 1791 (A. Hyatt King, "Musical glasses," *NG,* XII, 823–824).

51. Christa Flamm, "Ein Verlegerbriefwechsel zur Beethovenzeit," *Beethoven-Studien: Festgabe der Österreichischen Akademie der Wissenschaften zum 200. Geburtstag von Ludwig van Beethoven;* Veröffentlichung der Kommission für Musikforschung, 11, ed. Erich Schenk (Vienna: Böhlau, 1970), 75. The full quotation is discussed on p. 136 below. This source came to my attention in Richard Kramer, "The Sketches for Bee-

thoven's Violin Sonatas Op. 30," Ph.D. diss., Princeton University, 1973; University Microfilms 74-17,468, 174–175.

52. Modern editors have generally converted the verbal instructions to the later signs, a procedure that is not without hazards in determining exactly where Beethoven intended these bulky instructions to take effect. See pp. 109 and 130–131.

53. Douglas P. Johnson, *Beethoven's Early Sketches in the "Fischhof Miscellany,"* 2 vols. (Ann Arbor: UMI Research Press, 1980), I, 351–355, 467. Beethoven's earliest pedal indication, "mit dem knie," occurs on folio 96r of the "Kafka" Sketchbook, dated between 1790 and 1792 (*Beethoven, Autograph Miscellany from circa 1786 to 1799*, ed. Joseph Kerman, Vol. I Facsimile, Vol. II Transcription [London: Trustees of the British Museum, 1970], II, 293).

54. During the early nineteenth century, after the signs *Ped.* and ⊕ had become widely accepted for engaging the damper pedal, a few composers (other than Beethoven) occasionally used *con sordini* and *sordino* somewhat ambiguously for either the lute stop or the moderator. Opinion is divided, for example, regarding Schubert's intentions in "Der Tod und das Mädchen" and for the Andante of the Sonata in A minor D. 784. The song, composed in 1817, bears the inscription "sempre con pedale e sordino" in the manuscript copy of Albert Stadler, a good friend of Schubert. Stadler's copy "probably goes back to a holograph copy that has disappeared" (*Schubert Neue Ausgabe, Lieder: Quellen und Lesarten*, I, ed. Walter Dürr [Kassel: Bärenreiter, 1972], 20). Harding contends that *sordino* signals the lute pedal here (*Pianoforte*, 127); Virginia Pleasants finds 1817 late for that effect (personal communication). Kurt Wegerer feels that both *sordino* and *con sordini* in the "mysterious" recurring passages marked *ppp* in the Andante of D. 784, composed in 1823, are "unequivocal indications" for the moderator ("Beethovens Hammerflügel und ihre Pedale," *Österreichische Musikzeitschrift* XX/4 [April 1965]:209). Since the Sonata passages are slurred throughout, the effect of the lute stop would seem antithetical.

55. Date according to Sieghard Brandenburg, ed., Ludwig van Beethoven, *Kesslersches Skizzenbuch*, 2 vols. (Vol. I Transcription, Bonn: Beethoven-Haus, 1978; Vol. II Facsimile, Bonn: Beethoven-Haus, 1976), I, *Einleitung*, 13, 15–16.

56. Franz Gerhard Wegeler and Ferdinand Ries, *Biographische Notizen über Beethoven* (Koblenz: Bädeker, 1838), 87–88; *NG*, II, 362.

57. Plantinga, *Clementi*, 191.

58. Tyson, *Clementi Cat.*, 81. For the wording of the instruction in French and German, see n. 42 above.

59. This volume is now in the Deutsche Staatsbibliothek in East Berlin (Eve Bartlitz, *Die Beethoven-Sammlung in der Musikabteilung der Deutschen Staatsbibliothek* [Berlin: Staatsbibliothek, 1970], 216).

60. Kramer, "Sketches for Beethoven's Violin Sonatas Op. 30" [n. 51 above], 180. Still another hypothesis concerning the appearance of *Ped.* and O in Op. 31/2 was advanced by Owen Jander in a lecture at the Westfield Center for Early Keyboard Studies on 24 April 1987. Jander suggests that in 1800, when Steibelt was in Vienna, Beethoven heard him play the "Storm" Rondo and other pieces that depended heavily on the damper pedal, presumably on an English instrument. Steibelt is known to have preferred them and may well have left England with one in 1799. An anonymous report from Dresden, written in "mid-February" 1800, states that Steibelt "plays only on English fortepianos. . . . [He] played very much with, not only on this instrument." In that city it was the instrument of the English ambassador. (*AMZ* II/22 [26 February 1800]: cols. 399–400.) Thus Jander speculates that Beethoven may have written the "Tempest" Sonata with the pedals and sonority of the English pianos in mind. Cf. also *Thayer's Life of Beethoven*, rev. and ed. Elliot Forbes (Princeton: Princeton University Press, 1967), 257, for a report on at least two events at which both Steibelt and Beethoven performed.

61. Based on Ries's letter of that date to Simrock (Kinsky-Halm, *Beethoven Verz.*, 112). The sketches for the "Kreutzer" Sonata in the "Wielhorsky" volume (*A Sketchbook of 1802–1803*, ed. N. L. Fishmana [Moscow: Gos. muzykal'noe izd-vo, 1962]), dated April-May 1803 (Kramer, "Sketches for Beethoven's Violin Sonatas Op. 30" [n. 51 above], 187), show *senza sordino* on pp. 171 and 172. Late that year, when Beethoven was completing Op. 47, sketches made in "Landsberg 6" for an implied Adagio for piano (p. 116, November-December) and for the "Waldstein" Sonata (pp. 137 and 139, December 1803 to early 1804) show *Ped.* and O; but a sketch for an implied Andante still has a lone *senza sordino* (p. 121, December or early January 1804). Identification and dating in "Landsberg 6" are from Rachel W. Wade, "Beethoven's Eroica Sketchbook," *Fontes Artis Musicae* XXIV/4 (October-December 1977):254–289.

62. Friedrich Kalkbrenner, *A New Method of Studying the Piano-forte*, 3d ed. (London: D'Almaine, [1837]), 9.

63. Czerny, *Proper Performance*, 16; also Czerny, *Die Kunst des Vortrags* (Vienna: Diabelli, 1846), 4.

64. Dussek's coloristic pedaling had been replaced with "clean" pedalings in an edition of "Adieu" published between 1880 and 1889 by Brewer & Co. and probably in earlier editions as well. (Date based on the publisher's imprint in Charles Humphries and William Smith, *Music Publishing in the British Isles*, 2d ed. [Oxford: Blackwell, 1970], 85.)

65. E.g., Sonatas Opp. 44 and 45, both published in 1800. In his sonatas "Elégie harmonique" Op. 61 (Leipzig: Breitkopf & Härtel, 1807; e.g., i/32–33) and "Le Retour à Paris" Op. 64 (Paris: Pleyel, 1807; i/13, 15–16), Dussek occasionally included pedal indications that would catch the initial bass note of an arpeggiated accompaniment.

66. The early version has no dynamic signs; "*p*" is from the edition of Charles Lissner, St. Petersburg, p.n. 2606, a Breitkopf & Härtel first edition with a Breitkopf plate number (which would date publication in 1817) and the imprint altered on copies for the Russian publisher (Cecil Hopkinson, *A Bibliographical Thematic Catalogue of the Works of John Field* [London: Printed for the Author, 1961], 92). The dating of the early version is based on a watermark of 1810 and on the publication date of the Nocturne.

67. Charles Rosen discusses some of the abstract differences between Classic and Romantic pedaled sound in "The Romantic Pedal," *The Book of the Piano*, ed. Dominic Gill (Ithaca: Cornell University Press, 1981), 106–113.

68. Only the first and third movements of the engraver's copy (*Stichvorlage*) are extant, housed in the collection of the Gesellschaft der Musikfreunde.

69. Where this theme returns at m. 299, the engraver's copy lacks both *Ped.* and O. *Ped.* was entered in OE, but not O.

70. Beethoven left a relevant remark on a sketch of some bass notes held (without pedal) under rising right-hand scales. "The held notes in the bass produce a good effect because the bass sustains longer than such notes in the upper register" (Gustav Nottebohm, *Beethoveniana*, 2 vols. [Leipzig: Rieter-Biedermann, 1882, 1887], II, 361).

71. Unfortunately, the completed piano part used by the engraver of OE is lost. Although there is only one pedal indication in the incomplete holograph score (*con sord.* at ii/49), Hans-Werner Küthen is convinced that the pedal indications in OE are Beethoven's own (personal communication).

72. Since the Stein has pedals rather than knee levers it was quite possible to vary the depth of the pedaling.

73. According to Czerny, when the composer played this work in 1803 for its premiere, he "continued the pedal during the entire theme [*sic*], which on the weak-sounding pianofortes of that day, did very well, especially when the shifting pedal was also employed. But now [1846], as the instruments have acquired a much greater body of tone, we should advise the damper pedal to be employed anew, at each important change of harmony..." (*Proper Performance*, 97–98). Czerny's opening remark is not

in accord with the published pedal indications, nor would his suggested pedal changes have fulfilled Beethoven's intention. Czerny wisely advised retaining Beethoven's pedal indications for the Rondo of the "Waldstein" Sonata, which he had played for the composer (*Proper Performance*, 47, 3).

74. The difficulty of playing this passage on modern pianos led Hans-Werner Küthen to place the damper release sign in m. 6 before the two arpeggiated chords and the sign in m. 4 slightly before the chord (*BNA, Klavierkonzerte*, I, 201).

75. Czerny, *Piano Forte*, III, 60–61. A misunderstanding of the term *Grundharmonie* caused Robert K. Formsma to credit Starke with describing the concept of mixing harmonies over a bass note held by the pedal ("The Use of Pedal in Beethoven's Sonatas," *PQ* 93 [Spring 1976]:43). *Grundharmonie* properly refers only to the common harmony underlying the inversions of a chord. Starke merely restated much of Adam's material, including the necessity of damping the preceding harmony before a new one (*Pianoforte-Schule*, 16).

76. Czerny, *Piano Forte*, III, 61. Some pieces in Starke's *Pianoforte-Schule* also contain single pedal indications under changing harmonies without a sustained bass note. In my opinion, these pedalings of Starke and of other primarily instrumental composers represented in his tutor, such as Joseph Weigl and Adalbert Gyrowetz, are in general not as successful as the harmonically mixed pedalings of such keyboard masters as Beethoven, Clementi, and Dussek. Many in Starke's tutor either need significant adjustment or do not work at all, even on the Stein of 1819 and especially not on the Graf of 1830. They are not successful because the accompanying figures are in close position in the middle register or because of miscalculated harmonic rhythm or chromatics. In some instances an underlying bass note would have helped.

77. Czerny, *Proper Performance*, 3.

78. H. C. Robbins Landon and László Somfai have suggested that Haydn intended "open pedal" to refer to the *una corda* pedal as a reinforcement of the *pp* (Landon, *Haydn: Chronicle and Works*, 5 vols. [Bloomington: Indiana University Press, 1976–1980], III, 445; Somfai, *Joseph Haydn zongoraszonátái* [Budapest: Zeneműkaidó, 1979], 114). Unfortunately the holograph of this sonata is lost.

79. Kramer's revised dating is based on evidence from Georg August Griesinger, *Biographische Notizen über Joseph Haydn* (Leipzig: Breitkopf & Härtel, 1810) and Albert Christoph Dies, *Biographische Nachrichten von Joseph Haydn* (Vienna: Camesinaische, 1810). Richard Kramer, "On the Dating of Two Aspects in Beethoven's Notation for Piano," in *Beethoven Kolloquium, 1977*, ed. Rudolf Klein for *Österreichische Gesellschaft für Musik, Beiträge '76–'78* (Kassel: Bärenreiter, 1978), 168.

80. Thayer/Forbes, *Beethoven*, 351.

81. Clementi originally published this sonata in London in May 1785. He revised it, along with other works, in 1807 or 1808 for inclusion in Breitkopf & Härtel's *Oeuvres complettes*. Probably because of disturbances in communications caused by the Napoleonic Wars, these revisions never reached Leipzig and the sonata was published only recently (Muzio Clementi, Sonata in F minor [as] Op. 14/3, ed. Sandra P. Rosenblum [Boston: E. C. Schirmer, 1968]). Survival of these holographs is attributable to lack of prior publication, for Clementi seems to have discarded all his working materials and finished copies when publication was completed.

82. Publication ca. 1815 is based on a watermark of 1813 observed and kindly forwarded to me by J. A. Parkinson of The British Library.

83. According to the *BNA*, this quintet was performed in a concert on 6 April 1797 (*Klavierquintett und Klavierquartette*, p. vii); however, it is not possible to determine whether the pedal indications had been notated by then or whether they were added later, perhaps just before publication in 1801.

84. Date according to Kinsky-Halm, *Beethoven Verz.*, 37.

85. Czerny, *Proper Performance*, 105.

86. Owen Jander, "Romantic Form and Content in the Slow Movement of Beethoven's Violin Concerto," *MQ* LXIX/2 (Spring 1983): 161–163.

87. *NG,* XVIII, 102.

88. This is one of Beethoven's combinations of texture and pedaling that Czerny described in his *Piano Forte School* (III, 61).

89. Before writing Op. 35, Beethoven had used this theme in the Finale of the ballet *Prometheus* Op. 43 (performed March 1801) and in No. 7 of the Contretänze für Orchestre WoO 14 (comp. 1801–1802).

90. Translation from William S. Newman, "Beethoven's Pianos Versus His Piano Ideals," *JAMS* XXIII/3 (Fall 1970):495.

91. Herbert Grundmann and Paul Mies, *Studien zum Klavierspiel Beethovens und seiner Zeitgenossen* (Bonn: Bouvier, 1966), 27–28.

92. Since the first page of the holograph is missing, both inscriptions are from the original edition by Cappi (Vienna, 1802).

93. Flamm, "Ein Verlegerbriefwechsel zur Beethovenzeit" [n. 51 above], 75.

94. Kramer, "On the Dating of Two Aspects in Beethoven's Notation for Piano," 164.

95. The first British edition was "Printed for Rt. Birchall at his Musical Circulating Library[,] 133 N Bond Strt" in 1799. The Viennese edition, as Op. 45, was published by Koželuh's *Musikalisches Magazin* in 1798 (Alexander Weinmann, *Verzeichnis der Verlagswerke des Musikalischen Magazins* [Vienna: Österreichischer Bundesverlag, 1950], 25).

96. Beethoven may occasionally have intended the piano to imitate the harp, particularly in the concertos (e.g., Op. 19/ii/41–46; Op. 37/ii/39–50), but his pedalings in such passages work well.

97. Czerny, *Proper Performance,* 39. Although Beethoven did not have an instrument with an *una corda* shift in 1801, when he composed Op. 27/2, by 1802 he sought a new piano for which he specified the *una corda* (see chap. 2, n. 106).

98. Malcolm Binns, L'Oiseau-Lyre DSLO 603, pub. 1981.

99. E.g., Alfred Brendel, Murray Hill S-3456, [1968].

100. Paul Badura-Skoda includes Op. 27/2 among the works for which "a certain internal evidence suggests that Czerny was aware of Beethoven's intentions" (Czerny, *Proper Performance,* 3). For Badura-Skoda's complete list of such works see chap. 9, n. 154.

101. Czerny, *Proper Performance,* 43.

102. Ibid., 39.

Friedrich Rochlitz's review of this sonata quotes Beethoven's direction for performance of the Adagio approvingly but offers no clarification. Beethoven, Rochlitz wrote, has laid out the execution of the Sonata "as far as something can be expressed with conventional signs" (*AMZ* IV/40 [30 June 1802]: col. 652).

103. Relative to Fig. 4.23c, the reader may recall that on the Graf of 1830 the moderator was much more successful than the *una corda* (p. 131), which produced a different sound—much brighter for one thing—with the leather-covered hammers of the fortepiano than it does with our present-day felt hammers.

104. Czerny, *Proper Performance,* 43.

105. The American Steinway firm patented the *sostenuto* pedal for square pianos in 1874 and for uprights and grands in 1875 (Cyril Ehrlich, *The Piano: A History* [London: Dent, 1976], 54).

106. Additional suggestions for coping with Beethoven's blurred pedalings appear in Joseph Banowetz, *The Pianist's Guide to Pedaling* (Bloomington: Indiana University Press, 1985), chap. 8; Howard Ferguson, *Keyboard Interpretation* (London: Oxford, 1975), 163–164; and Gershon Jarecki, "Die Ausführung der Pedalvorschriften Beethovens auf dem Modernen Klavier," *Österreichische Musikzeitschrift* XX/4 (April 1965):197–200.

107. Milchmeyer, *Pianoforte zu spielen,* 65.

108. E.g., ibid.; Adam, *Méthode,* 220, 221; Starke, *Pianoforte-Schule,* I, Pt. 1, 16. Lack of an acknowledged nomenclature led Starke to call this the "guitar pedal"; others used no name, referring to the pedal by describing its effect on the keyboard.

109. On an upright piano the *una corda* pedal can only move the hammers closer to the strings. The shorter stroke produces a quieter sound with the same finger exertion but cannot change the timbre.

110. Milchmeyer, *Pianoforte zu spielen,* 65.

111. Adam, *Méthode,* 220.

112. Anonymous article, *Harmonicon* I/9 (September 1823):123.

113. Anonymous review, *Harmonicon* VI/10 (October 1828):228; see also Czerny, *Piano Forte,* III, 65.

114. See chapter 2, pp. 44 and 47–49.

115. Kalkbrenner, *New Method,* 9.

116. Starke, *Pianoforte-Schule,* I, Pt. 1, 16; see also Steibelt, *Méthode,* 65.

117. Czerny, *Piano Forte,* III, 65.

5. Articulation and Touch

1. Daniel Gottlob Türk is particularly lucid on these points (*Klavierschule* [Leipzig and Halle: Schwickert; Hemmerde und Schwetschke, 1789], facs., ed. Erwin R. Jacobi [Kassel: Bärenreiter, 1962], 340–347). For references to other eighteenth-century writers who discussed analogies between structural aspects of language and music see chap. 1, nn. 52 and 60.

2. Türk, *Klavierschule,* 356.

3. Friedrich Wilhelm Marpurg, *Anleitung zum Clavierspielen,* facs. of 2d ed. (New York: Broude, 1969), 29.

4. Carl Philipp Emanuel Bach, *Essay on the True Art of Playing Keyboard Instruments,* trans. and ed. William J. Mitchell (New York: Norton, 1949), 157.

5. Clementi/Rosenblum, *Introduction,* 14.

6. The term *portato* is used both as a translation for the clavichord's *Tragen der Töne,* an additional pressure that gives the tone a new impulse after the key has been played (cf. Bach, *Essay,* 36; Daniel Gottlob Türk, *School of Clavier Playing,* trans. and ed. Raymond Haggh [Lincoln: University of Nebraska Press, 1982], 348), as well as for another touch on the piano (see pp. 184–185 below), both of which are indicated with dots under a slur. For the *Tragen der Töne* the dot indicates the later pressure, and the slur indicates that the note is held until its written value has been completed (Türk, *Klavierschule,* 354). This touch is not possible on the fortepiano or the pianoforte.

Türk's additional remarks on the *Tragen der Töne* in 1802 recognize that the same sign was sometimes intended and executed differently, although he did not mention the fortepiano: "In some newer works one finds places marked with ⌢⋯ [Fig. 5.7] that perhaps should be only slurred (or detached)....

Fig. 5.7.
Andante cantabile

*Probably each of these notes should be delivered with a certain emphasis; however, their subsequent holding out may well have to be omitted with such short note values" (*Klavierschule,* 2d ed., 399–400).

7. Türk, *Klavierschule,* 358–360; see also Schulz, "Vortrag," in Sulzer, *Allgemeine Theorie,* II, 1254. The interaction of tempo heading, meter, and note values and their effect on tempo and touch is explored further in chap. 9, pp. 305–311.

8. *BGA,* Ser. 25 (Supplement), No. 283, p. 269; also Johann Baptist Cramer, *21 Etüden für Klavier: Nach dem Handexemplar Beethovens aus dem Besitz Anton Schindlers,* ed. Hans Kann (Vienna: Universal, 1974), iii.

9. See chap. 1, n. 157. Beethoven was appointed assistant court organist in his native Bonn in 1784 and became a violist in the court orchestra in 1788. It was during a visit of this orchestra to Mergentheim in 1791 that Junker heard Beethoven improvise on the fortepiano. Czerny mentioned the influence of the organ on Beethoven's piano playing to Otto Jahn (p. 24 above).

10. Theodor von Frimmel, *Beethoven-Studien,* 2 vols. (Munich: Müller, 1905, 1906), II, 214. This sketch was sold at the Liepmannssohn auction in May 1904.

11. Ludwig Schiedermair, *Der Junge Beethoven* (Leipzig: Quelle & Meyer, 1925), 70. Clementi's Op. 13 consisted of six sonatas, of which only the first three had the stylish "accompaniment for violin or flute." Since Simrock was selling a divided edition, it may have been the one published by Jean-Jérôme Imbault (pub. 1785 as Op. 13/1–3 with violin, Op. 14/1–3 for piano alone) rather than Clementi's.

12. Anton F. Schindler, *Beethoven as I Knew Him,* trans. Constance Jolly, ed. Donald W. MacArdle (Chapel Hill: University of North Carolina Press, 1966), 379. When Beethoven actually acquired Clementi's early sonatas is not known.

13. Emily Anderson, trans. and ed., *The Letters of Beethoven,* 3 vols. (London: Macmillan, 1961), 25–26. Andreas Streicher used the same comparison in his *Brief Remarks,* 1.

14. Czerny, *Richtigen Vortrag,* 11.

15. Nicolo Pasquali, *The Art of Fingering the Harpsichord* (Edinburgh: Bremner, [1758]), 26, Preface, 27. Bremner published this volume "without any Alteration" a year after Pasquali's death. He found the work "ready for the Press" among the "musical Effects of the Author" (publisher's note after the title page).

16. Marpurg, *Anleitung,* 29.

17. Vincenzo Manfredini, *Regole Armoniche . . . i principi della musica . . . sopra . . . il cembalo* (Venice: Zerletti, 1775), 28.

18. Clementi/Rosenblum, *Introduction,* vi.

19. Date according to entry at Stationers' Hall.

20. Hüllmandel, *Principles of Music . . .* (London: By the Author, [1796]), 20. For all its brevity this volume is progressive also in its differentiation of staccato stroke and dot as well as in its attitude toward the trill start and the realization of certain turns (see chap. 7).

21. Of the others, Bernard Viguerie, *L'Art de toucher le piano-forte* (Paris: Chez l'auteur, [1797]) is uninformative about touch; Ignaz Pleyel and Jan Ladislav Dussek, *Méthode pour le piano forte* (Paris: Pleyel, [1797]) merely reiterates that a finger leaves its key "at the same time that another finger plays the note following" (14); Louis Adam and Ludwig Lachnith, *Méthode ou principe général du doigté pour le forte-piano* (Paris: Sieber, [1798]) includes fingering techniques necessary for legato playing (cf. "Fingerings by Clementi and Beethoven" in chap. 6).

Jan Ladislav Dussek, *Instructions on the Art of Playing the Piano Forte or Harpsichord* (London: Corri, Dussek, [1796]), the predecessor of Pleyel and Dussek's *Méthode,* bears little specific relationship to the pianoforte except for the inclusion of some flexible dynamics and a cursory listing of the *una corda* pedal in the dictionary at the end.

22. Johann Peter Milchmeyer, *Die wahre Art das Pianoforte zu spielen* (Dresden: Meinhold, 1797), 3.

23. Ibid., 5. W. S. Stevens's description of legato playing is the same (*A Treatise on Piano-Forte Expression* [London: Jones, 1811], 2).

24. Milchmeyer, *Pianoforte zu spielen,* 6. Even on pianos with a more generous sound, a legato is often improved to some extent when the continuing sound of the preceding note softens the initial articulation of the next.

25. Clementi/Rosenblum, *Introduction,* 9; also x–xi.

26. Louis Adam, *Méthode de piano du conservatoire* (Paris: Magasin de Musique du Conservatoire Royal, [1804]), 151. Both Stevens (*Piano-Forte Expression,* 2) and Johann Baptist Cramer (*Instructions for the Piano Forte* [London: Chappell, 1812], 43) also agreed that legato was used unless there were indications to the contrary. Gottlieb Graupner, who asserted a strong musical influence in Boston between 1797 and 1836, plagiarized about one-third of Clementi's *Introduction,* including the material on touch, in his *Rudiments of the Art of Playing on the Piano-Forte* (Boston: G. Graupner, 1806).

27. Dussek's father was an organist. Jan Ladislav (1760–1812) began to study organ at the age of nine and held two posts as church organist before 1782 (*Grove's Dictionary of Music and Musicians,* 5th ed., ed. Eric Blom [New York: St. Martin's Press, 1954], II, 825). His early acquaintance with the organ, like Clementi's and Beethoven's, may have predisposed Dussek toward a legato style.

In his *Autobiography,* W. J. Tomášek, a compatriot of Dussek and a pianist, described Dussek's playing in Prague in 1802. "After the opening bars . . . the public uttered one general Ah! There was in fact something magical in the manner in which Dussek, . . . through his wonderful touch, drew from his instrument delicious and at the same time emphatic tones. His fingers were like a company of ten singers. . . . His truly declamatory style, especially in cantabile movements, remains the ideal for every artistic performance—something that no pianist after him has attained" (Howard Allen Craw, "A Biography and Thematic Catalog of the Works of J. L. Dussek (1760–1812)," Ph.D diss., University of Southern California, 1964; University Microfilms: 64-9611, 127, 458).

Beethoven singled out Cramer (1771–1858) "as an outstanding player" among pianists (Franz Gerhard Wegeler and Ferdinand Ries, *Biographische Notizen über Beethoven* [Koblenz: Bädeker, 1838], 99–100). "Beethoven assured him [Cramer] that he preferred his touch to that of any other player . . ." (*Thayer's Life of Beethoven,* rev. and ed. Elliot Forbes [Princeton: Princeton University Press, 1967], 209).

In 1821 Moscheles's reaction to Cramer's playing was that his "well shaped fingers are best suited for legato playing; they glide along imperceptibly from one key to the other. . . . [He] sings on the piano in such a manner that he almost transforms a Mozart andante into a vocal piece . . . " (Charlotte Moscheles, *Life of Moscheles,* trans. A. D. Coleridge, 2 vols. [London: Hurst and Blackett, 1873], I, 51). Later, an anonymous reviewer of Cramer's *25 New and Characteristic Diversions* wrote that this publication instructs "the far-advanced practitioner . . . in the legato manner" (*Harmonicon* III/39 [May 1825]:87).

Field (1782–1837) was described by Charles Salaman, the English pianist, as "a really great player. . . . in the singing quality of his touch . . . he was unrivalled in his day (Harold C. Schonberg, *The Great Pianists from Mozart to the Present* [New York: Simon and Schuster, 1963], 103). Alexander Dubuk, a Russian who knew Field at the height of his powers when he lived in St. Petersburg, claimed that "the chief beauty" of Field's compositions "lay in his playing [of them]—his touch on the keys—the way his melodies sang. . ." (Patrick Piggott, *The Life and Music of John Field, 1782–1837* [Berkeley: University of California Press, 1973], 102).

In a periodical of the 1830s Glinka wrote of Field: "He possesses some kind of magic ability to touch the keyboard in a special way: under his fingers it is no longer the usual piano with a limited sound—it reminds you rather of the singing voice with all its nuances" (ibid., 103).

28. *NG,* III, 129–131.

29. Eva Badura-Skoda, "Performance Conventions in Beethoven's Early Works," in *Beethoven, Performers, and Critics: The International Beethoven Congress, Detroit,*

1977, ed. Robert Winter and Bruce Carr (Detroit: Wayne State University Press, 1980), 70–71.

30. Otto Erich Deutsch, *Schubert: A Documentary Biography,* trans. Eric Blom (London: Dent, 1946), 436.

31. This term is adopted from Czerny, *Piano Forte,* I, 186.

32. Kann, ed., *Cramer's Etüden,* 10. The first and last sentences are present only in the ink copy, but the inscription "Trochee—the piece four voices," which contains the essence of those sentences, is found in pencil beside the first staff (Harry Gold-schmidt, "Beethovens Anweisungen zum Spiel der Cramer-Etüden," in *Die Erscheinung Beethoven* [Leipzig: Deutscher Verlag für Musik, 1974], 232, n. 118). For an explanation of the annotations in pencil and ink, see chap. 3, n. 148.

33. Kann, ed., *Cramer's Etüden,* 34. In the pencil copy the final sentence reads: "In other respects the rule for the performance of the triplet is valid; the first [note] always has the accent because the syllable is pronounced on it" (Goldschmidt, "Bee-thovens Anweisungen" [n. 32 above], 232, n. 119). The references to "syllable" here (also found in the ink annotation to Etude VII), as well as to trochaic verse feet in the note to Etude V, interject a reminder of the contemporary awareness of rhetoric.

34. Heinrich Christoph Koch, *Musikalisches Lexikon* (Frankfurt: Hermann dem jüngern, 1802; facs., Hildesheim: Olms, 1964), col. 1598.

35. Hummel, *Pianoforte,* Pt. III, 60; see also Pt. II, 2, 12.

36. E.g., Michel de Saint-Lambert, *Les Principes du clavecin* (Paris: Ballard, 1702; facs., Geneva: Minkoff, [1972]), 12–14; Jean-Philippe Rameau, *Pièces de clavecin . . .* (Paris, 1724; rev. 1731), in the Table of Ornaments; ed. Erwin R. Jacobi (Kassel: Bär-enreiter, 1960), 20–21.

37. Franz Paul Rigler, *Anleitung zum Gesänge, und dem Klaviere . . . zu spielen . . .* (Ofen, 1798), in Isolde Ahlgrimm, "Unter dem Zeichen des Bogens," *Österreichische Musikzeitschrift* XIX/4 (April 1964):156, 158. Ahlgrimm's article includes other uses of the slur in Baroque practice and some in Classic practice discussed in this chapter. Emanuel Bach's reference to the prolonging of chord tones is in his *Essay,* 155; see also Türk, *Klavierschule,* 355.

38. Johannes Brahms, *Sämtliche Werke,* ed. Hans Gál and Eusebius Mandyczewski (Leipzig: Breitkopf & Härtel, 1926–1927), XXV, 63–67. I am indebted to Ahlgrimm's article [n. 37 above] for this example.

39. Alan Tyson has pointed out that the first version, which appeared early in 1804, may not have been intended for publication ("Clementi's Viennese Compositions, 1781–82," *Music Review* XXVII/1 [February 1966]:22–24).

40. See comment regarding Vol. VI in the Selected Bibliography.

41. E.g., Türk, *Klavierschule,* 355; Hummel, *Pianoforte,* Pt. III, 55, 58.

42. Leopold Mozart, *A Treatise on the Fundamental Principles of Violin Playing,* trans. Edith Knocker, 2d ed. (London: Oxford, 1951), 123–124.

43. Türk, *Klavierschule,* 355. Friedrich Starke's discussion of the slur, although written 30 years later, seems to be derived in large measure from Türk's (Starke, *Wiener Pianoforte-Schule,* 3 vols. [Vol. I, Vienna: Bey dem Verfasser, 1819; Vol. II, Vienna: Sprenger, 1819; Vol. III, Vienna: Bermann, 1821], I, Pt. 1, 13).

44. Adam and Lachnith, *Méthode du doigté,* 2d ed., 155. See also Streicher's com-ments on pp. 190–191 below. For string players the single impulse was one bow stroke, which encompassed all the notes under a slur.

45. Türk, *Klavierschule,* 341–347. Johann Mattheson showed clearly that different degrees of articulation helped to make perceptible different levels of formal structure—such as motives, phrase divisions, and phrases (*Der vollkommene Capellmeister,* 1737; trans. and ed. Ernest Harriss [Ann Arbor: UMI Research Press, 1981], Pt. II, chap. 9, 380–404).

46. Adam, *Méthode,* 151, 153; also Türk, *Klavierschule,* 340, 342; August Leopold Crelle, *Einiges über Ausdruck und Vortrag: für Fortepiano-Spieler . . .* (Berlin: Mau-

rerschen Buchhandlung, 1823), 93; Hummel, *Pianoforte*, Pt. III, 55. Hugo Riemann described Crelle's little-known volume as a book "on keyboard aesthetics important for a knowledge of Beethoven's time" (*Musik-Lexikon*, 9th ed., ed. Alfred Einstein [Berlin: Hesse, 1919], 230).

47. E.g., Crelle, *Ausdruck und Vortrag*, 93–95; Mathis Lussy, *Le Rhythme musical*, 2d ed. (Paris: Heugel, 1884), 56–70, 89–90. See also p. 201 below. For another recent study see William S. Newman, "The Incise and Phrase as Guides to Rhythmic Grouping and Dynamic Direction," chap. 6 in *Beethoven on Beethoven—Playing His Music His Way* (New York: Norton, 1988).

48. Since the Bossler edition, the primary source for this sonata, is imprecise in regard to slur placement and dynamics, the readings in *JHW* and HSU differ in certain details that had to be resolved by editorial decision. As one example, Bossler used *for.* for both *forte* and *forzato*. Thus in Fig. 5.15, *for.* almost certainly should have read *fz* at the fourth eighth note in m. 3 and the sixth eighth in m. 4. (The intended dynamic placement is clear later in the movement.) *JHW* reads *f[z]* at those places; HSU reads *fz*, which does not show the editorial change.

49. Relative to the edition used for Op. 31, see chap. 7, n. 124.

50. Simrock's edition of 1800, which followed unusually quickly on the heels of Mollo's first edition (1799), serves as the source here because it contains corrections of a number of errors along with revisions of some minutiae that may stem from Beethoven. However, Simrock's change of the original *sf* in m. 7 to *rfz* has not been retained since that seems to have been substituted automatically throughout Op. 14 for Beethoven's (and Mollo's) *sf* indications. According to Mies, Beethoven used only *rinf.* and *rinforz.* as abbreviations for *rinforzando;* when *rfz* appears it is sometimes an engraver's substitution for *sf* (Paul Mies, *Textkritische Untersuchungen bei Beethoven* [Munich: Henle, 1957], 124–129). Interestingly, William Newman has concluded that the Simrock editions of Opp. 2 and 10, published in 1798 and 1801 respectively, also contain refinements requiring enough judgment to suggest that they were supplied by Beethoven, although Simrock's Op. 10 also contains some corruptions of the text, including the same change of *sf* to *rfz* ("And Yet Another New Edition of Beethoven's Piano Sonatas," *PQ* 87 [Fall 1974]:42; "On the Problem of Determining Beethoven's Most Authoritative Lifetime Editions," in *Beiträge zur Beethoven-Bibliographie*, ed. Kurt Dorfmüller [Munich: Henle, 1978], 136).

51. Claudio Arrau, Philips 6747 035, [1972?]; Friedrich Gulda, Amadeo 415 246–2, 1968.

52. Artur Schnabel, Seraphim ID6063, recorded in April 1934.

53. Walter Gieseking, Angel 35652, [1959]; Wilhelm Kempff, DGG SLPM 138938, [1966].

54. OE was published by the Bureau d'Arts et d'Industrie (Vienna, 1802).

55. Czerny, *Richtigen Vortrag*, 45.

56. Date according to *NG*, XII, 744.

57. The B-flat in m. 169 is from Breitkopf & Härtel's *OC* (1799); the F-natural in m. 170 is from Hoffmeister's OE (1787). Discrepancies of slur beginnings and endings among the best recent editions of K. 511 stem from ambiguity in the holograph.

58. See also Koch, *Lexikon*, cols. 521–527; and Nancy K. Baker, "Heinrich Koch and the Theory of Melody," *Journal of Music Theory* XX/1 (Spring 1976):1–48; especially 11–15. Koch's discussion comments on the harmonies appropriate at the cadence of a phrase and of a phrase member.

59. Schulz, "Vortrag," in Sulzer, *Allgemeine Theorie*, II, 1250–1251; Türk, *Klavierschule*, 344–345.

60. However, in Hob. 38/i/1–2 the pairs of eighth notes involved in the phrase divisions on both fourth beats are beamed together. Here the short slurs that bind the written-out appoggiaturas to their notes of resolution clarify the phrase divisions. Examples of beaming that indicate articulation for motives or short groups of notes rather

than for phrase divisions appear at Haydn's Hob. 19/i/16–17R, Mozart's K. 311/ii/74, and Beethoven's Op. 109/i/65R (Aut.).

In holographs, a reversal of stem direction with a continuous beam may also signal or coincide with an articulative grouping, as in Mozart's Rondo K. 511/166 (Fig. 5.23) and 175. Most modern editions either notate all the stems in one direction, regardless of the intervals between notes, or separate the beams (as *NMA* does at K. 511/175). The effects of beaming on grammatical accentuation are discussed in chap. 3, p. 91.

61. Clementi's *Oeuvre* 1, ostensibly a revised version of his Op. 1 (London, [1771]), "preserves little of the original material" (Tyson, *Clementi Cat.*, 34). Similar long slurs as well as others over short phrases or several measures of passage-work also occur in Clementi's Sonatas Op. 5, published by Bailleux at about the same time as *Oeuvre* 1. (Publisher and date from Tyson, *Clementi Cat.*, 40.)

62. Measures 21–24 are a restatement of the opening measures, in which, however, there are three separate slurs for mm. 1, 2, and 3–4. Since neither the holograph nor the engraver's copy is extant, it is not possible to determine whether Clementi actually wrote the two different slurrings or whether in the opening phrase on a crowded system at the bottom of the page the engraver casually produced slurring that was more customary and fit with less effort. (On the following page there is more room between the staves of each system.) My experience is that during the 1780s Artaria's engravers were none too careful in reproducing composers' slurs.

63. E.g. (all slurs in piano part), Op. 1/1/iii/42–52, 185–192; iv/180–191; Op. 1/2/iv/250–258, 358–362; Op. 1/3/i/206–213; ii/8–12, 48–53 (HE; *BNA* not yet published).

64. In Beethoven's Op. 2/2/i/324–332 the progression I, V is played four times over a tonic pedal. Each two-measure segment is clarified by a slur over the scalar inner voice, while a single slur unites the whole, as it must have been in Beethoven's aural image.

65. Mies has pointed out several ways in which Beethoven's notation reflects his aural conception of structure and sound (*Textkritische Untersuchungen*, 27–31, 86–87). See also below, pp. 186–187. Additional aspects of Beethoven's slurs are discussed in William S. Newman, "Some Articulation Puzzles in Beethoven's Autographs and Earliest Editions," in *Report of the Eleventh Congress of the International Musicological Society, 1972*, 2 vols. (Copenhagen: Hansen, 1974), II, 580–585.

66. Three works in which holographs confirm comparable slurs are the Prelude Op. 28/9 and the first of the *Trois Nouvelles Etudes*, in each of which one slur extends from before the middle of the piece to the end, and the Prelude Op. 28/5, in which one slur extends over all but the last two measures.

67. David D. Boyden, *The History of Violin Playing from its Origins to 1761* (London: Oxford University Press, 1965), 157–163; also *NG*, III, 131–133. The terms *out-bow* and *in-bow* used below for viol bowing are Boyden's suggestion (pp. 78–79).

68. Diego Ortiz first described slurred bowing in the Introduction to his *Trattado de glosas* (Rome: Dorico, 1553), f. 3r. Sylvestro di Ganassi discussed slurred tonguing in chapter 8 of his *La Fontegara* (Venice, 1535); trans. from Italian to German, Dahnk-Baroffio and Hildemarie Peter (Berlin: Lienau, 1956). Richardo Rogniono's discussion in his *Passaggi per potersi essercitare nel diminuire terminatamente con ogni sorte d'instromenti* of 1592 implies the use of slurred bowing on violins and viols (Boyden, *The History of Violin Playing* . . . [n. 67 above], 82–83). According to Imogene Horsley, by 1620, when Francesco Rogniono wrote about slurred bowing in the Introduction to the second book of *Selva de varii passaggi*, "it was already established as a common procedure in composed works" ("The Solo Ricercar in Diminution Manuals: New Light on Early Wind and String Techniques," *Acta Musicologica* XXXIII/1 [1961]:34).

69. Samuel Scheidt, *Tabulatura Nova für Orgel und Clavier* (Hamburg: Hering, 1624); *Denkmäler Deutscher Tonkunst*, Ser. I, new ed., ed. Hans Joachim Moser (Wiesbaden: Breitkopf & Härtel, 1958), Pt. I, [84].

70. L. Mozart, *Violin*, 97.

71. George Simon Löhlein, *Clavier-Schule* (Leipzig: Waisenhaus und Frommann, 1765), 12–13.

72. Ibid., 69.

73. Carl Gollmick, *Kritische Terminologie* (Frankfurt: Lauten, 1833), 23.

74. E. Bach, *Essay,* 84.

75. Ibid., 106.

76. Türk, *Klavierschule,* 259.

77. Ibid., 261.

78. Czerny, *Piano Forte,* I, 187.

79. Although the Sonata K. 570 was originally published by Artaria in 1796 as *Sonata per il Clavicembalo o Piano-Forte con l'accompagnamento d'un Violino,* Mozart entered it in his list of compositions as *Eine Sonate für Klavier allein* (*NMA, Klaviersonaten,* 2 vols., ed. Wolfgang Plath and Wolfgang Rehm, II, xviii). For speculation on who created the violin accompaniment, see chap. 3, n. 45.

80. All that exists of the holograph of this sonata are two consecutive pages of the first movement. They include mm. 65–132 (the last part of the exposition and the development), a note that reads "D.C.: 28 measures" (for the beginning of the recapitulation), and m. 161 to the end. These pages are reproduced in *NMA, Klaviersonaten,* II, xxx–xxxi.

81. Wolfgang Amadeus Mozart, *Sonatas and Fantasies for the Piano,* ed. Nathan Broder, rev. ed. (Bryn Mawr: Presser, 1960); Wolfgang Amadeus Mozart, *Piano Sonatas,* ed. Karl Heinz Füssl and Heinz Scholz, 2 vols., 3d ed. (Vienna: Schott/Universal [formerly Universal], 1973); Wolfgang Amadeus Mozart, *Klaviersonaten,* ed. Ernst Herttrich, 2 vols. (Munich: Henle, 1977); and *NMA, Klaviersonaten.*

82. Czerny, *Richtigen Vortrag,* 44.

83. The only divergent slur in OE that warrants consideration is one over the melody from the beginning of m. 31 to the first quarter note of m. 33, the equivalent of mm. 3–5 in Fig. 5.47. If Beethoven wrote that single slur, it would support the suggestion that the separate slurs over mm. 3 and 4 were intended to indicate a prevailing legato. On the other hand, the change could have been an engraver's error since the slurring in the third statement of A repeats that of the first. *BNA* ignores the changed slur. In m. 62 the engraver ended the slur prematurely on E-natural. Beyond this there is occasional lack of clarity as to where a slur begins or ends; I interpret them as those in Fig. 5.47.

84. Other discussions of this slurring in Beethoven's Op. 13 are found in Herbert Grundmann and Paul Mies, *Studien zum Klavierspiel Beethovens und seiner Zeitgenossen* (Bonn: Bouvier, 1966), 77–78; and Franz Kullak, *Beethoven's Piano Playing . . .* (1881), trans. Theodore Baker (New York: G. Schirmer, 1901; facs., New York: Da Capo, 1973), 37–41.

85. Robert Donington, *The Interpretation of Early Music,* New Version (New York: St. Martin's Press, 1974), 453; Johann Joachim Quantz, *On Playing the Flute,* trans. and ed. Edward R. Reilly (London: Faber and Faber, 1966), 123–124.

86. Quantz, *Flute,* 223, 232.

87. Abbé Georg Joseph Vogler, *Kuhrpfälzische Tonschule* (Mannheim: Auf Kosten des Verfassers, [1778]), 25; Table VI, fig. 12 in Vogler, *Gründe der Kuhrpfälzischen Tonschule in Beyspielen . . .* (Mannheim, 1778). [Justin Heinrich] Knecht, a disciple of Vogler, followed his attributions of length for each sign but retained the generally understood quality of each: a stroke meant to "hit the notes somewhat forcefully and a little longer [!]"; a dot indicated a quick, delicate staccato (*Knechts Allgemeiner musikalischer Katechismus* [Biberach: Gebrüder Knecht, 1803], 48).

88. Türk, *Klavierschule,* 353–354. Türk did not modify his view about the meaning of dot and stroke in his revised edition of 1802.

89. Johann Adam Hiller, *Anweisung zum Violinspielen* (Grätz: Trötscher, 1795), 41–42; Hüllmandel, *Principles of Music,* 14.

90. Clementi/Rosenblum, *Introduction,* 8.

91. Koch, *Lexikon,* cols. 45–46.

92. Adam, *Méthode,* 154–155.

93. Daniel Steibelt, *Méthode de Piano* (Leipzig: Breitkopf & Härtel, [ca. 1809]), 57; Starke, *Pianoforte-Schule,* I, Pt. 1, 13; Hummel, *Ausführliche theoretisch-praktische Anweisung zum Piano-forte-spiel,* 3 vols. (Vienna: Haslinger, 1828), I, 64; Czerny, *Piano Forte,* III, 24. The emphasis intended here coincides with the attack; in the clavichord *portato* (*Tragen der Töne,* n. 6) it is added after the key has been depressed.

94. Francesco Pollini, *Metodo per Clavicembalo* (Milan: Ricordi, [1812]), 58; Steibelt, *Méthode,* 56–57; Starke, *Pianoforte-Schule,* I, Pt. 1, 13; Crelle, *Ausdruck und Vortrag,* 92–93; Czerny, *Vollständige theoretisch-praktische Pianoforte-Schule* (Vienna: Diabelli, 1839), Pt. III, 21–23. W. S. Stevens reported that "some authors" follow these "simple and significant" distinctions and urged others to do so (*Piano-Forte Expression,* 4).

95. Cf. Czerny, *Vollständige . . . Pianoforte-Schule,* Pt. III, 21–23 with his *Piano Forte,* III, 27. In the first part of *Vollständige . . . Pianoforte-Schule,* which is a general introduction for the uninitiated, Czerny did not distinguish between the dot and the stroke. The third section of this tutor, for advanced players, is far more detailed in every area of interpretation.

96. It has not been possible to assess Clementi's usage from the few holographs available.

97. E.g., Feder, ed., *JHW, Klaviersonaten,* "Zur Gestaltung des Ausgabe," n.p.; H. C. Robbins Landon, *The Symphonies of Joseph Haydn* (New York: Macmillan, 1956), 86–87; Hans Albrecht, ed., *Die Bedeutung der Zeichen Keil, Strich und Punkt bei Mozart: Fünf Lösungen einer Preisfrage* (Kassel: Bärenreiter, 1957). The last consists of essays by Herman Keller, Hubert Unverricht, Oswald Jonas, and Alfred Kreutz.

98. Cf. Hummel's description of the playing technique on p. 197 below.

99. E.g., Beethoven insisted that his copyist Rampel observe a clear distinction in the manuscript of the String Quartet Op. 132 (Anderson, *Beethoven,* 1241–1242). See also Hubert Unverricht, *Die Eigenschriften und die Originalausgaben von Werken Beethovens in ihrer Bedeutung für die moderne Textkritik* (Kassel: Bärenreiter, 1960), 56–63; Bathia Churgin and Joachim Braun, "A Report Concerning the Authentic Performance of Beethoven's Fourth Symphony, Op. 60," Research Project of the Beethoven Seminar at Bar-Ilan University, Ramat Gan, Israel, 1977, 80–83.

100. Gustav Nottebohm, *Beethoveniana,* 2 vols. (Leipzig: Rieter-Biedermann, 1872, 1887), I, 107–125, especially p. 109.

101. Kinsky-Halm, *Beethoven Verz.,* 46.

102. The reprints of Op. 26 published by Simrock in 1802 and by the Bureau des Arts et d'Industrie in 1803 have wedges throughout Var. 2. My observation of staccato signs in numerous Classic period editions leads me to suspect that some publishers or engravers exercised their own inclination toward one staccato sign or the other most of the time, unless they were instructed otherwise. This topic, which certainly would have consequences for our interpretation of early sources, must await further investigation.

103. Hummel did not express any distinction between the dot and the stroke in his tutor. While this lack could have resulted from incomplete reporting, as has been observed in his treatment of *calando,* it is significant that throughout the volume all the staccatos in Haslinger's German edition are strokes and most (but not all) in Boosey's English edition are dots. In the few first editions of his compositions that I have seen, strokes and dots appear somewhat inconsistently; I have not seen any of the surviving autographs.

104. E.g., Robert Riggs, "Articulation in the Works of Mozart and Beethoven: Problems of Notation and Performance," paper read at the American Musicological Society

meeting in Louisville, Kentucky, 1983. Mozart, *Variationen für Klavier*, ed. Ewald Zimmermann (Munich: Henle, 1959), 4–5; also Zimmermann's essay in Albrecht, ed., *Die Bedeutung der Zeichen . . . bei Mozart* [n. 97 above], 97–110. *Editionsrichtlinien musikalischer Denkmäler und Gesamtausgaben*, ed. Georg von Dadelsen (Kassel: Bärenreiter, 1967), guidelines for the collaborators on the *BNA*, 141.

105. Cf. *Editionsrichtlinien* [n. 104 above], 91, 122–123, 141.

106. Löhlein, *Clavier-Schule*, 69.

6. Historical Technique and Fingering

1. Carl Philipp Emanuel Bach, *Essay on the True Art of Playing Keyboard Instruments*, trans. and ed. William J. Mitchell (New York: Norton, 1949), 38, 43.

2. Daniel Gottlob Türk, *Klavierschule* (Leipzig and Halle: Schwickert; Hemmerde und Schwetschke, 1789), facs., ed. Erwin R. Jacobi (Kassel: Bärenreiter, 1962), 11.

3. Jean-Philippe Rameau, *Pièces de clavecin, avec une méthode pour la mécanique des doigts* (Paris: Hochereau, 1724, rev. 1731); in Rameau, *Pièces de Clavecin*, ed. Erwin R. Jacobi (Kassel: Bärenreiter, 1960), 16.

4. Ibid., 17, 19. Cf. also Vincenzo Manfredini, *Regole Armoniche . . .* (Venice: Zerletti, 1775), 28.

5. Streicher, *Brief Remarks*, 2.

6. François Couperin, *The Art of Playing the Harpsichord*, 1717; trilingual ed., ed. and German trans. Anna Linde; English trans. Mevanwy Roberts (Leipzig: Breitkopf & Härtel, 1933), 12. Cf. the comments following Czerny's description of *staccatissimo* playing, p. 198 below.

7. Louis Adam, *Méthode de piano du Conservatoire* (Paris: Magasin de Musique du Conservatoire Royal, [1804]), 149.

8. Crelle later clarified his use of *portamento* as the sustaining of a note for its full value (August Leopold Crelle, *Einiges über musicalischen Ausdruck und Vortrag: für Fortepiano-Spieler . . .* [Berlin: Maurerschen Buchhandlung, 1823], 80–81).

9. Ibid., 78–80.

10. Czerny, *Proper Performance*, 15.

11. Clementi/Rosenblum, *Introduction*, 15.

12. Czerny, *Piano Forte*, III, 99.

13. Friedrich Starke, *Wiener Pianoforte-Schule*, 3 vols. (Vol. I, Vienna: Bey dem Verfasser, 1819; Vol. II, Vienna: Sprenger, 1819; Vol. III, Vienna: Bermann, 1821), I, Pt. 1, 4.

14. Adam, *Méthode*, 8.

15. Hummel, *Pianoforte*, 4; also 24.

16. Johann Peter Milchmeyer, *Die wahre Art das Pianoforte zu spielen* (Dresden: Meinhold, 1797), 1.

17. See also Adam, *Méthode*, 7; Daniel Steibelt, *Méthode de piano* (Leipzig: Breitkopf & Härtel, [ca. 1809]), 19.

18. Hummel, *Pianoforte*, Pt. I, 3.

19. Joseph Nicolas Hüllmandel, *Principles of Music* (London: By the Author, [1796]), 19–20. Hummel also cautioned against stiffness (*Pianoforte*, Pt. I, 3).

20. Steibelt, *Méthode*, 19.

21. Hummel, *Pianoforte*, Pt. II, 224; also 226.

22. Early systems of keyboard fingering differed among themselves, but they used the three longer fingers more, and the thumb and fifth finger substantially less than we do today. The thumb was rarely used as a pivot for changing hand positions on the keyboard (cf. p. 213 below). Clear descriptions of early fingerings and their effects on performance are found in Robert Donington, *The Interpretation of Early Music*, New Version (New York: St. Martin's Press, 1974), 580–581; Howard Ferguson, *Keyboard Interpretation* (London: Oxford University Press, 1975), chap. 5; Peter Le Huray and

Glyn Jenkins, "Fingering, Keyboard," *NGMI,* I, 744–751; and, most detailed and an-
alytical, Mark Lindley, "Keyboard Technique and Articulation: Evidence for the Performance Practices of Bach, Handel and Scarlatti," in *Bach, Handel, Scarlatti Tercen-
tenary Essays,* ed. Peter Williams (Cambridge: Cambridge University Press, 1985), 207–
243. Here I shall point out only that the early fingering patterns may not have had as
strong an effect on articulation as is often alleged, since on instruments with light,
shallow actions and keys somewhat narrower than those of the modern piano, the
middle fingers can easily be passed over and under each other to produce an even legato
with the hand held slightly sideways. Many of the basic principles of modern fingering
achieved wide dissemination through Emanuel Bach's *Essay.*

23. Adam, *Méthode,* 149.

24. Anton Schindler, *Biographie von Ludwig van Beethoven* (Münster: Aschendorff,
1840), II, 228. When all the fingers rest on the keys as described, there is a natural limit
to how high each can be raised.

25. Hummel, *Pianoforte,* Pt. III, 41.

26. Steibelt, *Méthode,* 19.

27. Adam, *Méthode,* 8.

28. Ibid.; cf. also Steibelt, *Méthode,* 19.

29. Milchmeyer, *Pianoforte zu spielen,* 3; Adam, *Méthode,* 8.

30. Steibelt, *Méthode,* 19. Others also wrote of an "elastic" attack (e.g., Streicher,
Brief Remarks, 3).

31. Louis Adam and Ludwig Mendel Lachnith, *Méthode ou principe général du
doigté pour le forté-piano* (Paris: Sieber, 1798), iv.

32. Adam, *Méthode,* 8.

33. Anonymous, *A Letter to a Young Piano Forte Player,* Printed for the Benefit
of the Spanish Refugees (London: Hailes, [1829]). The quotations are from an anonymous review of the *Letter* (*Harmonicon* VII [October 1829]:250), which—according to
the reviewer, contains "some of the most sensible remarks, and most useful advice"
on playing the pianoforte "that have ever fallen under our view."

34. Ibid.

35. Most of the text of Ignaz Pleyel and Jan Ladislav Dussek, *Méthode pour le
piano forte* (Paris: Pleyel, [1797]), is a translation of Dussek's *Instructions on the Art of
Playing the Pianoforte or Harpsichord,* published in 1796, to which Pleyel seems to have
added eighteen lessons of his own composition and some sections of text, including
pages 16–17 (Sandra P. Rosenblum, "Clementi's Pianoforte Tutor on the Continent,"
Fontes Artis Musicae 27/1 (January–March 1980):42). Their titles notwithstanding, the
contents of these tutors that relate specifically to the piano (in contrast to the harpsichord) or to contemporary advances in technique and performing style are limited to
the mention of flexible dynamics and to Dussek's linking of "mezzo" with use of the
una corda pedal (*Instructions,* 46). Some of Pleyel's additions, including pp. 16 and 17,
make the Pleyel-Dussek manual more pianistic than Dussek's version.

36. Pleyel-Dussek, *Méthode,* 16.

37. An A in the initial quarter-note chord only, undoubtedly an error, is here
corrected to G; C in the second chord is corrected to D. In line 2, D in the first chord
is corrected to C.

38. Muzio Clementi, *Gradus ad Parnassum,* 3 vols. (Leipzig: Breitkopf & Härtel,
1817, 1819, 1826), facs., ed. Leon Plantinga (New York: Da Capo Press, 1980), Pieces
Nos. 1, 3, 27. Above No. 27 Clementi wrote "To make the fingers independent of each
other."

39. François-Joseph Fétis and Ignaz Moscheles, *Méthode des méthodes de piano*
(Paris: M. Schlesinger, 1840; facs., Geneva: Minkoff, 1973), 10–11.

40. Franz Liszt, *Technical Exercises,* ed. Alexander Winterberger, 1886; ed. Julio
Esteban (Port Washington, N.Y.: Alfred Music, ca. 1971), Bk. I, Nos. 1–6, 10, 14, 18,
26, etc.

41. Ernő Dohnányi, *Essential Finger Exercises,* 1929 (Budapest: Editio Musica Budapest, 1950), Exx. 1, 7, 9, 20, etc.

42. Adam, *Méthode,* 20.

43. Steibelt, *Méthode,* 53.

44. W[illiam] S[eaman] Stevens, *A Treatise on Piano-Forte Expression* (London: Jones, 1811), 14. Stevens defined pressure as "the measure of the performer's sensations, as to the degree of *forte,* he intends or feels it necessary to give . . . to any passage . . . , in order to produce all the degrees of *pia* and *for,* either dictated by taste, or the intention of the composer . . ." (ibid., 13).

45. Hüllmandel, *Principles of Music,* 20; quotation from Milchmeyer, *Pianoforte zu spielen,* 7.

46. Stevens, *Piano-Forte Expression,* 4.

47. Ibid.

48. Adam, *Méthode,* 156.

49. Starke, *Pianoforte-Schule,* I, Pt. 1, 13.

50. Hummel, *Ausführliche theoretisch-praktische Anweisung zum Piano-forte-spiel* (Vienna: Haslinger, 1828), I, 64. (Hummel's *anstossen* requires a somewhat free translation.) Reminders against lifting the hand too much in ordinary staccato playing reappear in the fingered exercises (e.g., German ed., Pt. II, 322, 367; English ed., Pt. II, 239, 292). See also Czerny, *Vollständige theoretisch-praktische Pianoforte-Schule* (Vienna: Diabelli, 1839), Pt. III, 21.

51. Hummel, *Ausführliche . . . Anweisung zum Piano-forte-spiel,* I, 64.

52. Czerny, *Vollständige . . . Pianoforte-Schule,* Pt. III, 19–20.

53. Ibid., 21.

54. Johann Nikolaus Forkel, *Über Johann Sebastian Bachs Leben, Kunst und Kunstwerke* (Leipzig: Hoffmeister und Kühnel, 1802), 13. See also Johann Joachim Quantz, *On Playing the Flute,* trans. and ed. Edward R. Reilly (London: Faber and Faber, 1966), 259–260.

55. Czerny, *Vollständige . . . Pianoforte-Schule,* Pt. III, 21–22.

56. Ibid., 23.

57. E.g., Deborah Wythe, "The pianos of Conrad Graf," *Early Music* XII/4 (November 1984):454–455.

58. Czerny, *Proper Performance,* e.g., 93, 97.

59. Adam, *Méthode,* 149.

60. My translation from the German of Streicher's chapter "On Tone" in *Brief Remarks,* which appeared, along with another translation, in Richard A. Fuller, "Andreas Streicher's notes on the fortepiano," *Early Music* XII/4 (November 1984): 461–469; trans. from pp. 464–465.

61. Relatively little is known about William Seamen Stevens. Only François-Joseph Fétis gave his place and date of birth: London, 1778 (*Biographie universelle des musiciens* . . . [Brussels: Meline, Cans, 1837–1844], viii, 283). Sainsbury listed some of his teachers, including "Thomas Smart, a pupil of Drs. Pepusch, Nares, and Boyce, . . . R. J. S. Stevens of the Charterhouse, and lastly, . . . Dr. Cook of Westminster abbey" (John S. Sainsbury, ed., *A Dictionary of Musicians from the Earliest Ages* [London: Sainsbury, 1824; facs., New York: Da Capo Press, 1966], 457). Stevens was the pianist and master of the choristers at the Haymarket Theatre, "which situation he held until a new management expelled the piano-forte from the orchestra" (ibid.). No date is provided for that event or for any of Stevens's published songs, sonatas, and other pieces listed at the ends of both brief accounts.

62. Stevens, *Piano-Forte Expression,* 8.

63. Steibelt, *Méthode,* 55.

64. Stevens, *Piano-Forte Expression,* 9.

65. Ibid., 10.

66. Ibid., 11.

67. Johann Baptist Cramer, *21 Etüden für Klavier: Nach dem Handexemplar Beethovens aus dem Besitz Anton Schindlers,* ed. Hans Kann (Vienna: Universal, 1974), 38.

68. See chap 3, n. 150. Curiously, there are two errors in the *AMZ* entry for this Etude: *Simile,* over the right-hand notes in m. 1 to indicate repeated fingering, is entered as the tempo heading, and C is listed as the time signature (*AMZ* XIX/37 [10 September 1817]: col. 634).

69. Cf. also Thayer/Dieters/Riemann, *Beethoven,* III, 58; and Hermann Beck, "Studien über das Tempoproblem bei Beethoven," Ph.D. diss., Friedrich-Alexander Universität, 1954, 56–57.

70. Mathis Lussy, *Traité de l'expression musicale,* 1873; 2d ed. (Paris: Heugel, 1874), 31.

71. Milchmeyer, *Pianoforte zu spielen,* 18.

72. Steibelt, *Méthode,* 62.

73. Milchmeyer, *Pianoforte zu spielen,* 30.

74. Hummel, *Pianoforte,* II, 249. This is Hummel's only comment on playing octaves.

75. Adam, *Méthode,* 52.

76. Czerny, *Pianoforte,* III, 29–30; see also p. 198 above.

77. *NG,* XIV, 695.

78. Milchmeyer, *Pianoforte zu spielen,* 29.

79. Sol Babitz, "Modern Errors in Beethoven Performance," in *Bericht über den Internationalen Musikwissenschaftlichen Kongress, Bonn, 1970* (Kassel: Bärenreiter, 1971), 327.

80. Clementi/Rosenblum, *Introduction,* xv, 18–19.

81. See n. 38 above.

82. Franz Gerhard Wegeler, *Nachtrag zu den biographischen Notizen* (Coblenz: Bädeker, 1845), 22–23. According to Schindler, Beethoven first mentioned this project in 1818 (Anton F. Schindler, *Beethoven as I Knew Him,* trans. Constance Jolly from Schindler, *Biographie,* 3d ed., ed. Donald W. MacArdle [Chapel Hill: University of North Carolina Press, 1966], 379). Coincidentally, 1818 was the year that Beethoven himself gave his nephew, Karl, piano lessons (see chap. 3, n. 147).

83. Dates for Figs. 6.6–6.20 are from the following sources: Figs. 6.6 and 6.7, Ludwig van Beethoven, *Autograph Miscellany from circa 1786 to 1799* ["Kafka"], ed. Joseph Kerman, Vol. II, Transcription (London: Trustees of the British Museum, 1970), 293; Fig. 6.8, Rachel W. Wade, "Beethoven's Eroica Sketchbook," *Fontes Artis Musicae* XXIV/4 (October–December 1977):267; Figs. 6.9 and 6.14 (dates and sources), Douglas P. Johnson, personal communication; Fig. 6.20, Ludwig van Beethoven, *Kesslersches Skizzenbuch,* ed. Sieghard Brandenburg, Vol. II, Facsimile (Bonn: Beethoven-Haus, 1976), Nachwort, p. iv. Dates for the remaining figures are from Douglas P. Johnson, *Beethoven's Early Sketches in the "Fischhof" Miscellany,* Vol. I (Ann Arbor: UMI Research Press, 1980), as follows: Figs. 6.10, 6.18, and 6.19, 102; Fig. 6.11, 124–126; Figs. 6.12 and 6.13, 86–88; Fig. 6.15, 47, 131–133; Fig. 6.16, 102; Fig. 6.17, 367.

84. Gustav Nottebohm, *Two Beethoven Sketchbooks,* trans. Jonathan Katz, Foreword by Denis Matthews (London: Gollanz, 1979). This book contains Nottebohm's *A Sketchbook of 1802* (pub. 1865) and *A Sketchbook of 1803* [Landsberg 6] (originally published as *Ein Skizzenbuch von Beethoven aus dem Jahre 1803* [Leipzig: Breitkopf & Härtel, 1880]).

85. Fig. 6.14 appears on a bifolium in the Stadtbibliothek, Vienna; it is No. 392 in Hans Schmidt, "Verzeichnis der Skizzen Beethovens," *Beethoven-Jahrbuch* VI (1965–1968):117.

86. Albert Leitzmann, *Beethovens Personlichkeit: Urteile der Zeitgenossen* (Leipzig: Inselverlag, 1914), II, 368.

87. See also Joseph Kerman, "Beethoven's Early Sketches," in *The Creative World of Beethoven*, ed. Paul H. Lang (New York: Norton, 1970), 13–36. Perhaps the Bagatelle Op. 119/2, which was sketched as early as 1794–1795 (*NG*, II, 401), originated from some experimentation with the contrasting registers of the fortepiano during this period.

88. Czerny, *Pianoforte*, II, 169.

89. Robert Schumann, *Werke*, ed. Clara Schumann (Leipzig: Breitkopf & Härtel, 1879–1893), *Vorwort* to the *Studien*, Op. 3, Ser. VII, Vol. 1, 26.

90. Clementi/Rosenblum, *Introduction*, 14.

91. Ibid., 17.

92. Ibid., 19.

93. Heinrich Schenker, *Beethoven: die letzten Sonaten, Sonate AS dur Op. 110, Erläuterungsausgabe*, 1914; rev. Oswald Jonas (Vienna: Universal, 1972), 64–72, especially 70–71.

94. Donald F. Tovey and Harold Craxton, eds., Ludwig van Beethoven, *Sonatas for Pianoforte*, 3 vols. (London: Associated Board of the Royal Schools of Music, [1931]), II, 68–69; III, 216. Tovey's reference to Potter's edition was brought to my attention in William S. Newman, "Beethoven's Fingerings as Interpretive Clues," *The Journal of Musicology* I/2 (April 1982):187–188.

95. Czerny, *Proper Performance*, 78.

96. Artur Schnabel, ed., Ludwig van Beethoven, *Sonatas for the Pianoforte*, 2 vols. (New York: Simon and Schuster, 1935), II, 808.

97. Newman, "Beethoven's Fingerings," 188.

98. Ludwig van Beethoven, *Sämtliche Briefe*, ed. Alfred C. Kalischer, 5 vols. (Berlin: Schuster & Loeffler, 1906–1908), III, 214.

99. In the fifth and sixth editions, ca. 1815 and 1820 respectively, Clementi fingered m. 30 as +, 2, +, 2; 3, +; 1, 2, 1, 2 [!]; 1, 3, 1, 3; m. 43 remained the same.

100. Cf. "Leggero," *NG*, X, 612. Beethoven continued to use *leggiermente* for a light, detached style in fast passages, similar to nonlegato (e.g., Piano Concerto No. 5/i/151, 281; iii/194). His more unusual use of *leggeramente* [!] for the quiet *legato* bass in Op. 120, Var. 25, was echoed by Czerny: "LEGGIERMENTE. *free, light, agile;* is most properly employed in quick movements and in the somewhat staccato style or touch; though it may also be applied to the Legato as well as to the Staccato" (*Piano Forte*, I, 189).

101. Starke, *Pianoforte-Schule*, II, 56–57.

102. *Thayer's Life of Beethoven*, rev. and ed. Elliot Forbes (Princeton University Press, 1967), 762.

103. Starke was respected by Beethoven as a musician and teacher (*Die Musik in Geschichte und Gegenwart*, ed. Friedrich Blume, 16 vols. [Kassel: Bärenreiter, 1949–1979], XII, col. 1189). The two men were good friends from 1812 until Beethoven's death; Starke was often mentioned in the Conversation Books.

104. Herbert Grundmann and Paul Mies, *Studien zum Klavierspiel Beethovens und seiner Zeitgenossen* (Bonn: Bouvier, 1966), 117; listed as Sketch 699 (with the quotation cited) in Hans Schmidt, "Die Beethovenhandschriften des Beethovenhauses in Bonn," *Beethoven-Jahrbuch* VII (1969–1970):311.

105. Date according to *NG*, VIII, 390.

106. Haydn's only other fingering, in the autograph of Hob. 45/iii/20 (comp. 1766), shows the most logical choice—3, 2, 1—for three very rapid B-flats. It is probably also meant for the repeated D's and F's that follow. Haydn's fingerings appear in *JHW* and HSU.

107. "Fingerübungen," *NMA, Klavierstücke*, II, ed. Wolfgang Plath, 172, mm. 23, 28, 38. These 40 measures of easy, broken-chord exercises, which were probably written at the end of the 1780s (171), contain the only fingerings in Mozart's piano music that can be verified as his.

108. Engravers' errors in Starke's volume have 5 over the first f¹ in m. 22; a sharp preceding the first c² in m. 22; and in m. 24, the last 1 over the f-sharp rather than over g².

109. Jeanne Bamberger, "The Musical Significance of Beethoven's Fingerings in the Piano Sonatas," *The Music Forum,* IV (1976): 254–255; Newman, "Beethoven's Fingerings," 191.

110. For some early fingerings that variously support metric divisions and motives in a manuscript of Handel's Ciacona in G major, see Lindley, "Keyboard Technique and Articulation . . ." [n. 22 above], 240–242.

111. Türk, *Klavierschule,* 136–137, 147–148; Starke, *Pianoforte-Schule,* I, Pt. 1, 8–9; Hummel, *Pianoforte,* Pt. II, 237–251. Hummel's tutor also incorporates finger sliding between keys, the other special fingering technique.

112. E.g., Clementi/Rosenblum, *Introduction,* 19; Muzio Clementi, *Appendix to the Fifth Edition of Clementi's Introduction to the Art of Playing on the Piano Forte* (London: Clementi, Banger, Collard, Davis & Collard, 1811), 68.

113. Adam and Lachnith, *Méthode du doigté,* e.g., Pt. A, 74, 112; Pt. B, 5, 11.

114. Türk, *Klavierschule,* 148, fn. *.

115. Clementi/Rosenblum, *Introduction,* e.g., 19, 55. Curiously, Clementi did not discuss finger sliding until the eighth edition.

116. Türk, *Klavierschule,* 343.

117. Bamberger, "The Musical Significance of Beethoven's Fingerings . . . ," 252. Fig. 6.25 is also discussed in Grundmann and Mies, *Beethoven,* 116–117.

118. Elfrieda F. Hiebert, "Beethoven's Fingerings in the Piano Trio in B flat, WoO 39," *Early Keyboard Journal* IV (1985–1986):5–27.

119. Bamberger, "The Musical Significance of Beethoven's Fingerings . . . ," 238.

7. Ornaments

1. Charles Rosen, *The Classical Style* (New York: Norton, 1972), 107–108. See Fig. 7.67 and discussion on p. 255 below.

2. László Somfai, *Joseph Haydn zongoraszonátái* [The piano sonatas of Joseph Haydn] (Budapest: Zeneműkaidó, 1979), 46. Somfai's hypothesis is based on the observation of Georg Feder that during 1762 Haydn changed from indicating all long (i.e., variable) appoggiaturas as eighth notes to indicating each in the value of its appropriate realization (Feder, "Zur Datierung Haydnscher Werke," in *Anthony van Hoboken: Festschrift zum 75. Geburtstag* [Mainz: Schott, 1962], 50–52). Somfai relates this information to Emanuel Bach's statement of the importance of indicating these ornaments in their "real values" (see p. 225 below).

3. An *accent* (not to be confused with the German *Accent,* an appoggiatura) is an afternote that leaves its main note by step and moves by step or leap to the following note. A *chûte* moves down from its main note to anticipate the following note or to resolve to it by step after leaping from its main note. See Frederick Neumann, *Ornamentation in Baroque and Post-Baroque Music* (Princeton: Princeton University Press, 1978), 92, for more detail.

4. Daniel Gottlob Türk, *Klavierschule* (Leipzig and Halle: Schwickert; Hemmerde und Schwetschke, 1789), facs., ed. Erwin R. Jacobi (Kassel: Bärenreiter, 1962), 230–231.

5. Ibid., 208–209, 219.

6. Ibid., 209.

7. Carl Philipp Emanuel Bach, *Essay on the True Art of Playing Keyboard Instruments,* trans. and ed. William J. Mitchell (New York: Norton, 1949), 91–94. Relative to this last configuration, Bach gave one example (his Fig. 79, Ex. a) in which the second

and third notes were dotted half notes in 3/4 time (that is, quite long notes) and wrote that "a long appoggiatura may also be used here" (pp. 94, 92).

8. However, long notes were no longer listed as a separate category; they appear in the examples of other categories, such as long repeated notes or a long note at the start of a piece.

9. Türk, *Klavierschule,* 205, 220–221; Pierre Baillot, Pierre Rode, and Rodolphe Kreutzer, *Méthode de violon* (Brussels: Weissenbruch, [1803]), 139.

10. E.g., Türk, *Klavierschule,* 219–230; George Simon Löhlein, *Clavier-Schule,* 5th ed., ed. Johann Georg Witthauer (Leipzig: N. S. Fromanns Erben, 1791), 24–25; Friedrich Starke, *Wiener Pianoforte-Schule,* 3 vols. (Vol. I, Vienna: Bey dem Verfasser, 1819; Vol. II, Vienna: Sprenger, 1819; Vol. III, Vienna: Bermann, 1821), I, Pt. 1, 16. The most thorough discussion is Türk's.

11. Johann Karl Friedrich Rellstab, *Anleitung für Clavierspieler* (Berlin: Rellstabschen . . . Musikdruckerey, 1790), viii.

12. Türk, *Klavierschule,* 221–222.

13. Ibid., 2d ed. (Leipzig and Halle: Schwickert; Hemmerde und Schwetschke, 1802), 253–254.

14. Ibid., 1st ed., 218–219.

15. Clementi/Rosenblum, *Introduction,* 10.

16. August Eberhard Müller, *Klavier und Fortepiano-Schule* (Leipzig: F. Frommann, 1804), 34.

17. Johann Baptist Cramer, *Instructions for the Piano Forte* (London: Chappell, 1812), 35.

18. Türk calls the simultaneous acciaccatura a *Zusammenschlag* (literally, strike together) or *pincé étouffé,* a suppressed or smothered mordent (*Klavierschule,* 279).

19. Ibid., 227.

20. Ibid.

21. Ibid., 222.

22. Heinrich Schenker, *Ein Beitrag zur Ornamentik,* 2d ed. (Vienna: Universal, [1908]), 33; trans. Hedi Siegel, "A Contribution to the Study of Ornamentation," *The Music Forum* IV (1976):68.

23. E.g., Türk, *Klavierschule,* 217–218.

24. Johann Adam Hiller, *Anweisung zum Violinspielen* (Gratz: Troetscher, 1795), 49–50; Francesco Galeazzi, *Elementi di Musica,* 2 vols. (Vol. I, Rome: Cracas, 1791; Vol. II, Rome: Puccinelli, 1796), 191; Clementi/Rosenblum, *Introduction,* 10. Galeazzi also suggested that an appoggiatura to a note "of large value" should not be "stubbornly" held for half the value "since, being a note outside the harmony . . . , it would produce, if held too long, an ill effect rather than a good one" (*Elementi di Musica,* 191–192). Galeazzi's example (Table XI, no. 11) is an appoggiatura to a whole note realized as an eighth.

25. George Simon Löhlein, *Clavier-Schule* (Leipzig: Waisenhaus und Frommann, 1765), 14; Türk, *Klavierschule,* 210–212.

26. Türk, *Klavierschule,* 212–213.

27. E. Bach, *Essay,* 90–91; Friedrich Wilhelm Marpurg, *Anleitung zum Clavierspielen* (Berlin: Haude und Spener, 1755; facs. of 2d ed., New York: Broude, 1969), 47, Table III, Figs. 20, 21; Rellstab, *Anleitung,* viii; Leopold Mozart, *A Treatise on the Fundamental Principles of Violin Playing,* trans. Edith Knocker, 2d ed. (London: Oxford, 1951), 170.

28. Frederick Neumann, *Ornamentation and Improvisation in Mozart* (Princeton: Princeton University Press, 1986), 16, 21, 31.

29. E.g., E. Bach, *Essay,* 91; Johann Adam Hiller, *Anweisung zum musikalisch-richtigen Gesange* (Leipzig: Junius, 1774), 166. Quantz demonstrated a grace-note in-

terpretation (Johann Joachim Quantz, *On Playing the Flute*, trans. and ed. Edward R. Reilly [London: Faber and Faber, 1966], 227–228).

30. Türk, *Klavierschule*, 225–226.

31. E.g., Jan Ladislav Dussek, *Instructions on the Art of Playing the Piano Forte or Harpsichord* (London: Corri, Dussek, [1796]), 6; Johann Peter Milchmeyer, *Die wahre Art das Pianoforte zu spielen* (Dresden: Meinhold, 1797), 38; Bernard Viguerie, *L'Art de toucher le piano-forte* (Paris: Chez l'Auteur, [1797]), 29.

32. Date according to work list in *NG*.

33. E. Bach, *Essay*, 87.

34. E.g., Adolf Friedrich Petschke, *Versuch eines Unterrichts zum Klavierspielen* (Leipzig: Böhme, 1785), 31; Johann George Tromlitz, *Ausführlicher und gründlicher Unterricht die Flöte zu spielen* (Leipzig: Böhme, 1791), 240–241.

35. Türk, *Klavierschule*, 202.

36. Cf. Adolf Beyschlag, *Die Ornamentik der Musik*, 1908; 2d ed. (Leipzig: Breitkopf & Härtel, 1953), 204.

37. Türk, *Klavierschule*, 2d ed., 235.

38. E. Bach, *Essay*, 84.

39. Walter Emery's discussion of *Nachschläge* (with a few examples slurred as grace notes) in the music of J. S. Bach provides some of the background for this conclusion (*Bach's Ornaments* [London: Novello, 1953], 77–78, 93–100). For extensive and detailed documentation see Neumann, *Ornamentation in Baroque . . . Music* (an important innovative study), 47–199.

40. E. Bach, *Essay*, 98, fn. 13.

41. Marpurg, *Anleitung*, 50, Table IV, Figs. 1–6.

Friedrich Wilhelm Marpurg (1718–1795) was a north German composer, journalist, and theorist whose interest for later scholars lies solely in his writings. Significantly, in his *Anleitung zum Clavierspielen* the sections on ornaments (including *Nachschläge*) and other discussions show Marpurg's absorption of the French style during his stay in Paris around 1744–1746 (dates according to *NG*, XI, 697). In addition to Marpurg's own French translation of his *Anleitung* as *Principes de clavecin* (1756), this volume was translated into Dutch in 1760 (*NG*, XI, 698). For an English translation and commentary on the *Anleitung*, see Elizabeth L. Hays, "F. W. Marpurg's *Anleitung zum Clavierspielen* . . . ," Ph.D. diss., Stanford University, 1976; University Microfilm 77-12,641. Of Marpurg's periodicals, *Der critische Musicus an der Spree* (1749–1750) contains introductory essays on music theory and other subjects of interest to amateurs, such as the greater merits of engraved over hand-copied music and the performance of ornaments; while *Kritische Briefe über die Tonkunst* (1760–1764) includes material of interest to more serious musicians, such as reviews of books about music and discussions of theoretical topics, including music and rhetoric, and aspects of composition. (See "Rhetorical Rests" in chap. 10).

42. Giuseppe Tartini, *Traité des Agréments de la Musique*, [1752–1756]; trilingual ed., English trans. Cuthbert Girdlestone, ed. Erwin R. Jacobi (Celle: Moeck, 1961), 69–73; L. Mozart, *Violin*, 177–179; Quantz, *Flute*, 93–94, 97. Compare also in this respect the tutor of Quantz's follower J. G. Tromlitz, *Ausführlicher . . . Unterricht die Flöte zu spielen* [n. 34 above], 247–249.

43. George Simon Löhlein, *Anweisung zum Violinspielen* (Leipzig: Waysenhaus und Frommann, 1774), 44. Löhlein (1725–1781) was born in Neustadt, near Coburg. After studying in Jena, he spent the greater part of his professional life in Leipzig. Although Löhlein was also a performer and composer, his importance lay primarily in his teaching, which provided the impetus for some of his compositions and for his highly regarded tutors (*NG*, XI, 135).

44. Abbé Georg Joseph Vogler, *Kuhrpfälzische Tonschule* (Mannheim: Auf Kosten des Verfassers, [1778]), "Clavierschule," 21, Table VI, Fig. 7. Vogler also described and

realized *Zwischenklänge* (notes that fall "between consonant tones") and *Nachschläge* (ibid., 20–21, Table VI, Figs. 2, 4).

Abbé Vogler, German theorist, teacher, keyboard player, and composer, was born near Würzburg in 1749 and died in Darmstadt in 1814. He had "one of the most original minds of the century" (Paul Henry Lang, *Music in Western Civilization* [New York: Norton, 1941], 589). Both the strong spirit of French culture at the court in Mannheim and an extended trip to Italy influenced his musical development in the 1770s. In addition to his other musical activities, Vogler wrote books and articles on music theory, history, and performance. His theoretical writings emphasized the importance of the triad and its root as the basis of harmonic functions in a system that allowed chromatic modulation into distant keys (*NG,* XX, 59–60). The wide dissemination of Vogler's books is apparent in Leopold Mozart's letter of 3 August 1778 from Salzburg, to Wolfgang in Paris: "You need not send me Vogler's book [*Tonwissenschaft und Tonsetzkunst*] as we can get it here" (Emily Anderson, *The Letters of Mozart and His Family,* 2d ed., ed. A. Hyatt King and Monica Carolan, 2 vols. [London: Macmillan, 1966], 592).

    45. Anderson, *Mozart,* 356, 369, 378, 448–449.

    46. Gustav Nottebohm, *Beethoven's Studien* (Leipzig: Rieter-Biedermann, 1873), 7.

    47. Löhlein, *Clavier-Schule,* 3d ed. (Leipzig: Waisenhaus und Frommann, 1779), 14. The quoted sentence appears right after the description of long appoggiaturas and before the examples. Following the examples we read: "They have their origin in singing, and the syllable is always spoken on the note before the main note [*Vorschlag*]; therefore, the small note also receives more emphasis than the main note" (ibid., 14). This sentence originated in the first edition, which discussed only long appoggiaturas. It does not refer to the newly inserted example of "small notes before eighths or sixteenths," which it follows in the third edition.

Löhlein's section on ornaments remained the same in the fourth edition (1782). Interestingly, J. G. Witthauer, who edited the fifth edition (Leipzig: N. S. Fromanns Erben, 1791) after Löhlein's death, withdrew the example in Fig. 7.14 and the comment pertaining to it. His new section on short appoggiaturas made it very clear that in his opinion those ornaments took their value from the main note (p. 24). The third edition of Löhlein's violin method was edited posthumously by Johann Friedrich Reichardt (1797). As if taking a cue from Witthauer, Reichardt rewrote the realizations of the ornaments in Fig. 7.13, placing the small notes on the beat (*Anweisung zum Violinspielen,* 3d ed., ed. J. F. Reichardt [Leipzig: F. Frommann, 1797], 37).

    48. Georg Friedrich Wolf, *Unterricht im Klavierspielen,* 3d ed. (Halle: Hendel, 1789), 69–70.

    49. Rellstab, *Anleitung,* i, vii. Rellstab was "Berlin's leading music publisher and one of the city's most important impresarios" (Cliff Eisen, "Contributions to a New Mozart Documentary Biography," *JAMS* XXXIX/3 [Fall 1986]:629).

    50. Johann Christian Bach and Francesco Pasquale Ricci, *Méthode . . . pour le forte-piano ou clavecin* (Paris: Le Duc, [ca. 1786]); reissue with new p. n. (Paris: Le Duc, [179?]), 4. This volume was ostensibly written for the Naples Conservatory. See the Selected Bibliography regarding authorship.

    51. Heinrich Christoph Koch, *Musikalisches Lexikon* (Frankfurt: Hermann dem jüngern, 1802; facs., Hildesheim: Olms, 1964), cols. 1725–1726.

    52. Ibid., col. 56. Koch went on to say that there was no widely agreed-upon sign for the acciaccatura, but that ♪ was the most used.

    53. Exponents of the two rhythmic treatments include Alfred Brendel (Murray Hill Records S-3456, [1968] and Daniel Barenboim (Angel S-36491, [1967]). See chap. 10, pp. 370–371, for the rhythmic implications of *con espressione.*

    54. Tromlitz, *Ausführlicher . . . Unterricht die Flöte zu spielen* [n. 34 above], 247–249.

    55. Türk, *Klavierschule,* 201.

    56. Ibid., 223.

57. E. Bach, *Essay*, 92–93.

58. Eva and Paul Badura-Skoda, *Interpreting Mozart on the Piano*, trans. Leo Black (London: Barrie and Rockliff, 1962), 73–75, 80–81.

59. Neumann, *Mozart*, 38–40, 77–78; Peter Serkin, RCA LSC7062, [1969].

60. Johann Samuel Petri, *Anleitung zur Praktischen Musik* (Lauban: Wirthgen, 1767), 30; 2d ed. (Leipzig: Breitkopf, 1782), 151.

61. J. C. Bach and Ricci, *Méthode*, 17.

62. Türk, *Klavierschule*, 238–239.

63. Rellstab, *Anleitung*, vii.

64. Ibid., viii.

65. Milchmeyer, *Pianoforte zu spielen*, 37.

66. Milchmeyer's *Schneller* and short trills indicated by sign are all realized on the beat (ibid., 42).

67. The extant information about Milchmeyer's life must be pieced together from several sources. According to Riemann, Johann Peter Milchmeyer was born in Frankfurt in 1750. He lived for a time in Lyon, then spent ten years in Paris as a teacher of harp and keyboard instruments before going to Mainz in 1783. Subsequently, after a lengthy trip about which there is no specific information, Milchmeyer settled in Dresden in 1797, where his *Pianoforte zu spielen* and other books were published. (In the Preface to that volume Milchmeyer stated that he spent eighteen years in Paris and Lyon.) In 1803 he went to Strasbourg as a piano teacher; he died there in 1813. According to Hugo Riemann, Milchmeyer's teaching works are interesting for their presentation of the "early fortepiano technique" (*Musik Lexikon*, 12th ed., ed. Wilibald Gurlitt [Mainz: Schott, 1961], II, 221).

François-Joseph Fétis, who listed Milchmeyer's given name as Philippe-Jacques, put 1770–1780 as the decade in Paris. Milchmeyer had the reputation of being a good teacher, "particularly for the position of the hand and for fingering" (*Biographie universelle des musiciens*, 2d ed., 8 vols., suppl. 2 vols. [Paris: Firmin Didot, 1861–1870, 1878–1880], VI, 142). A biography in the *Neues Universal-Lexikon der Tonkunst*, compiled and edited by Eduard Bernsdorf, includes Munich as a residence of Milchmeyer for "some time" before 1797. There he was named court musician to the Elector and member of the Musical Academy, the latter supposedly for his much earlier invention of a harpsichord with three keyboards, eleven registers, and 250 possible variations of sound (*Neues Universal-Lexikon . . .* [Dresden: Schaefer, 1857], II, 997–998). Milchmeyer's description of that instrument, which was made with ravens' quills, appears in Cramer's *Magazin der Musik* I (9 November 1783):1024–1028. (This article refers to "P. J." Milchmeyer.)

68. Türk, *Klavierschule*, 2d ed., fn. *, 271–272.

69. Ibid., 1st ed., 200.

70. Beyschlag, *Ornamentik*, 212.

71. Czerny, *Piano Forte*, III, 56. Czerny wrote the same comment for the beginning of Op. 31/2 (*Proper Performance*, 43).

72. The illustrations by Türk are similar (*Klavierschule*, 257, 259, 267, 269), but he did not include any whose main notes fall on the beat, such as Figs. 7.41b and c.

73. Clementi/Rosenblum, *Introduction*, 11.

74. In eighteenth-century terminology a trill was "prepared" (*appuyê*) when it began with a prolonged upper auxiliary. Initial lower auxiliaries to trills, as in Fig. 7.25, did not serve as long appoggiaturas (see Türk, *Klavierschule*, 267).

75. Ibid., 257.

76. E.g., Ignaz Pleyel and Jan Ladislav Dussek, *Méthode pour le piano forte* (Paris: Pleyel, [1797]), 7.

77. Türk, *Klavierschule*, 238, 254; Joseph Nicolas Hüllmandel, *Principles of Music* (London: By the Author, [1796]), 17.

78. Marpurg, *Anleitung*, 57; Hüllmandel, *Principles of Music*, 17; Andreas Streicher, *Brief Remarks*, 6.

79. Türk, *Klavierschule*, 264–265; Viguerie, *L'Art de toucher*, 25; Hummel, *Pianoforte*, Pt. III, 3–4.

80. Türk, *Klavierschule*, 259–260; Hummel, *Pianoforte*, Pt. III, 4; Johann Friedrich Schubert, *Neue Singe-Schule* (Leipzig: Breitkopf & Härtel, [1804]), 64.

81. Türk, *Klavierschule*, 260–261; Viguerie, *L'Art de toucher*, 25; Hummel, *Pianoforte*, Pt. III, 4. Türk and Viguerie offer some examples of the elaborated suffix.

82. E. Bach, *Essay*, 107–108.

83. Emery, *Bach's Ornaments*, 65–66.

84. Cf. the *groppi* and *tremoli* in Girolamo Diruta, *Il Transilvano: Dialogo sopra il vero modo di sonar organi, & istromenti da penna* (Venice: Vincenti, Pt. I, 1593; Pt. II, 1609), 10–11; and the written-out trills in Girolamo Frescobaldi, *Toccate e Partite d'intavolatura di Cimbalo*, 2d ed. (Rome: Borboni, 1616).

85. E.g., Jacques Champion de Chambonnières, *Les pieces [sic] de clavessin*, Livre premier (Paris: chez Jollain, 1670; facs., New York: Broude, 1967), Preface; Johann Caspar Ferdinand Fischer, *Les pièces de clavessin* (Schlakenwerth: Chez l'Auteur, 1696), ed. Ernst Werra (Leipzig: Breitkopf & Härtel, 1901), 5; Henry Purcell, *A Choice Collection of Lessons for the Harpsichord or Spinnet* (London: Printed . . . for Mrs. Frances Purcell, 1696), Rules for Graces. (Not all copies of Purcell's *Choice Collection* dated 1696 contain the Rules for Graces. They may have been inserted in a second edition or state with an unchanged title page.)

86. E. Bach, *Essay*, 100, 110–111.

87. Marpurg, *Anleitung*, 53.

88. Fray Tomás de Santa María described this type of trill start in his remarkable *Libro llamado Arte de tañer fantasía* (Valladolid: Fernández de Córdoba, 1565), 48r–49v. Neumann demonstrates their use in Baroque music (*Ornamentation in Baroque . . . Music*, 280–283, 327–330).

89. J. S. Bach wrote out a main-note trill for this purpose in his Organ Fugue in D minor ("Dorian") BWV 538, mm. 178–184.

90. Emery's survey of Bach's trills discusses the role of the main-note start in a way that is also broadly applicable to other late Baroque and to early Classic music (*Bach's Ornaments*, 37–55, 69–75, 124–141, 146–148). For a more extensive, if somewhat overburdened, discussion see Neumann, *Ornamentation in Baroque . . . Music*, 241–386. David Fuller's review puts Neumann's material into perspective (*JAMS* XXXIII/2 [Summer 1980]:394–402).

91. Galeazzi, *Elementi di musica*, 8–9.

92. Manfredini, *Regole Armoniche*, 26. Galeazzi noted that the differences in the articles on ornamentation by Manfredini and himself "reduce to a question of terms, . . ." (*Elementi di musica*, 193, fn. a); and indeed, there are such differences. But since Galeazzi included only trills beginning on the upper or lower auxiliary, either he interpreted Manfredini's trills as beginning on the initial prolonged E in spite of the written description, or he had not looked carefully at what Manfredini had written, or he chose not to discuss the difference between his trills and Manfredini's.

93. Examples of this mirror-image relationship in the late Baroque are described in the *Rudimenta musices . . . Anweisung zur Singe-Kunst* of Wolfgang Michael Mylius, who termed the trill *tremulus ascendens* and the mordent *tremulus descendens* (under the initials W. M. M. M. T. C. M. G. [Gotha, copy dated 1686], chap. 5 [n.p.]). They are also discussed by Wolfgang Caspar Printz, *Compendium musicae*, 1689; 2d ed. (Dresden: Miethen, 1714; facs., Hildesheim: Olms, 1974), chap. 5 (n.p.); Pablo Nassarre, *Escuela Música*, 2 vols. (Zaragoza: Larumbe, 1724, 1723), II, 470–471; and Francisco Ignacio Solano, *Nova Instrucção Musical* (Lisbon: Costa, 1764), 173–174.

94. Giambattista Mancini, *Practical Reflections on Figured Singing*, trans. and ed. E. Foremann (Champaign, IL: Pro Musica Press, 1967), 49. Mancini's criticism raises

the possibility of a difference of opinion between contemporaries in interpreting Man-fredini's trill (see n. 92).

95. Vincenzio Panerai, *Principi di Musica, Teorico-Pratici* (Florence: Bonini and Pagani [late 1770s to the 1780s?]), 8. This edition of Panerai's volume has up to now been dated variously from ca. 1750 to ca. 1800. The best available clues for dating are the costumes, furniture, and design of the elaborate title page. The bottom scene depicts eleven women and men engaged in domestic music making; the top scene depicts a sacred figure and five cupid-like children engaged in heavenly music making. A later edition of this volume exists with two adaptations of the same title page. One published in Florence by Gius. Volpini has been tentatively dated ca. 1800–1810; another published in Florence by Gregario Chiari may date from ca. 1807 to ca. 1815. I am indebted to Susanne P. Sack, a conservator of Brooklyn, NY; Elaine A. Rose, docent at the Costume Institute, Metropolitan Museum of Art, New York; Helene von Rosenstiel, a costume conservator of Brooklyn, NY; and Barbara Lambert, former keeper, and Catherine Hunter and Michele Wilson, conservators, at the Museum of Fine Arts, Boston, for help in dating these volumes.

Little is known of Panerai, who lived in Florence. He was a composer, keyboard player, and teacher of keyboard instruments (*Enciclopedia della Musica*, ed. Claudio Sartori [Milan: Ricordi, 1964], III, 368). He had published a forerunner to the volume described above, titled simply *Principi di Musica*. This book, with at least three different title pages, is a little shorter than the other and contains no information on ornaments.

96. Johann Georg Albrechtsberger, *Anfangsgründe zur Klavierkunst*, 4. It is not certain whether this fifteen-page manuscript in the Archiv of the Gesellschaft der Musikfreunde, Vienna, is Albrechtsberger's autograph or a copy; nor has it been possible to date this little volume. Peter Riethus of the Gesellschaft der Musikfreunde has suggested that the manuscript may be either a predecessor of Albrechtsberger's *Clavierschule für Anfänger* (Vienna: Artaria, 1800), p.n. 863, which is unlocatable at present, or a copy of that book (personal communication).

Albrechtsberger was born in Klosterneuburg, close to Vienna, in 1736, and died in Vienna in 1809. He was Kapellmeister at St. Stephan's Cathedral from 1793 until his death. Mozart judged other organists against the standard set by his playing (Anderson, *Mozart*, 923–924); and Beethoven studied composition with Albrechtsberger from 1794 to 1795.

97. Albrechtsberger, *Anfangsgründe zur Klavierkunst* [n. 96 above], e.g., 10, 13.

98. Vogler, *Tonschule*, "Clavierschule," 22, Table VI, Fig. 10.

99. Sonja Gerlach, "Haydn's Works for Musical Clocks," in *Haydn Studies*, 126–129; also Joseph Haydn, *Stücke für das Laufwerk (Flötenuhrstücke)*, ed. Sonja Gerlach and George Hill, *JHW*, XXI (1984), ix, and the critical notes for No. B.4, pp. 81–82. (Mozart and Beethoven also wrote pieces for music boxes.)

100. All references to the pinning or performance of works in the musical clocks are to the record *Musik für Spiel- und Flötenuhren*, FSM Vox, 53013, n.d., and to *JHW*, XXI [n. 99 above]. (When the text in Ernst Fritz Schmid's edition of Haydn's *Works for Flute Clock*, "For Keyboard, two hands" [New York: Row, 1965] is accurate, references to that volume are also included because of its ready access.) Trills are clearer than other ornaments in both the Vox record and in the collective evidence available to the flute-clock specialists Sonja Gerlach and George Hill (*JHW*, XXI, 66). Where there is distortion or garbling in the recording of the 1793 clock, I have relied on the ornament realizations in *JHW*, XXI.

101. Milchmeyer, *Pianoforte zu spielen*, 42.

102. Hüllmandel, *Principles of Music*, 16.

103. Viguerie, *L'Art de toucher*, 25.

104. Baillot, Rode, and Kreutzer, *Méthode de violon*, 139–140 (contrary to the report in *NG*, XIII, 845, in which the *Méthode* has "all trills starting on the upper note").

105. Louis Adam, *Méthode de piano du Conservatoire* (Paris: Magasin de Musique du Conservatoire Royal, [1804]), 54.

106. Koch, *Lexikon*, col. 1589.

107. Türk, *Klavierschule*, 2d ed., 289.

108. Starke, *Pianoforte-Schule*, I, Pt. 1, 17–18.

109. *Flötenuhrstücke, JHW*, XXI, No. I.4, m. 4; see also No. A.3, 1792, m. 15.

110. William S. Newman would begin the trill on its main note (personal communication); Martin Canin would do the same and add a turned ending that flows into the F-sharp, obliterating the dotted effect (*PQ* 90 [Summer 1975]:39). Malcolm Bilson begins the trill on its upper auxiliary (Golden Crest CRS-4097, [197?]).

111. *Scarlatti's Chefs-d'oeuvre, for the Harpsichord or PianoForte*, ed. Muzio Clementi (London: The editor, [1791]), 24. (Sonatas II and XII are misattributions.)

112. Tromlitz, *Ausführlicher . . . Unterricht die Flöte zu spielen* [n. 34 above], 271–273. Neumann provides additional evidence for the grace-note trill in *Mozart*, 110, 129–133.

113. See n. 46.

114. Originally cited by Gustav Nottebohm (*Beethoveniana*, 2 vols. [Leipzig: Rieter-Biedermann, 1872, 1887], II, 359), the sketch, S.172, is shown and dated in William S. Newman, "Beethoven's Fingerings as Interpretive Clues," *The Journal of Musicology* I/2 (April 1982): 172–173. Beethoven's annotations to the trills point out their difficulty in one case and impossibility in the other.

115. Date according to Kinsky-Halm, *Beethoven Verz.*, 483.

116. Adam, *Méthode*, 143.

117. The composer's comments about these early "Beethoven trills"—trills that accompany a melodic line played by the same hand—in the postscript of a letter to Eleonore von Breuning in early June 1794 are of more than pianistic interest:

"P.S. The v[ariations] will be rather difficult to play, and particularly the trills in the coda. But this must not intimidate and discourage you. For the composition is so arranged that you need only play the trill and can leave out the other notes, since these appear in the violin part as well. I should never have written down this kind of piece, had I not already noticed fairly often how some people in Vienna after hearing me extemporize of an evening would note down on the following day several peculiarities of my style and palm them off with pride as their own. . . . But there was yet another reason, namely my desire to embarrass those Viennese pianists, some of whom are my sworn enemies. I wanted to revenge myself on them in this way, because I knew beforehand that my variations would here and there be put before the said gentlemen and that they would cut a sorry figure with them." (Emily Anderson, trans. and ed., *The Letters of Beethoven*, 3 vols. [London: Macmillan, 1961], 14–15.)

118. Ludwig van Beethoven, *Autograph Miscellany from circa 1786 to 1799* ("Kafka" Sketchbook), ed. Joseph Kerman, 2 vols. (London: Trustees of the British Museum, 1970), Vol. I, facs., f.132v; Vol. II, transcription, 252.

119. Douglas P. Johnson, *Beethoven's Early Sketches in the "Fischhof Miscellany,"* 2 vols. (Ann Arbor, MI: UMI Research Press, 1980), I, 124–125.

120. William S. Newman, "Second and One-Half Thoughts on the Performance of Beethoven's Trills," *MQ* LXIV/1 (January 1978): 100–101.

121. Robert Winter, "Second Thoughts on Beethoven's Trills," *MQ* LXIII/4 (October 1977): 492–494; Beyschlag, *Ornamentik*, 217; Herbert Grundmann and Paul Mies, *Studien zum Klavierspiel Beethovens und seiner Zeitgenossen* (Bonn: Bouvier, 1966), 125–126. If we include his fingering for the fourths in Op. 2/1/iii/60 and the crossed fingering for the trill in Op. 111, we find that Beethoven tried this fingering on intervals from thirds (Fig. 7.59a) to sixths.

122. Hummel, *Pianoforte*, Pt. III, 3.

123. Recent debate has been carried on in the following articles, prompted primarily in response to William S. Newman's "The Performance of Beethoven's Trills," *JAMS*

XXIX/3 (Fall 1976): 437–462: Robert Winter, "Second Thoughts on Beethoven's Trills" [n. 121 above]; Elfrieda Hiebert, Letter, *JAMS* XXXI/1 (Spring 1978): 173–174; Newman, "Second and One-Half Thoughts on the Performance of Beethoven's Trills" [n. 120 above]; Winter, "And Even More Thoughts on the Beethoven Trill . . . ," *MQ* LXV/1 (January 1979):111–116; Newman, "Beethoven's Fingerings," 192–193.

124. It is widely known that Beethoven was very dissatisfied with Nägeli's first edition of Op. 31/1 and 2 because of the large number of errors and the addition of four measures near the end of the first movement of Op. 31/1. At his behest Simrock published an "Editiou [!] tres Correcte" of those works in 1803 and of Op. 31/3 after Nägeli's edition in 1804. However, as often happens, new typographical errors appeared in the corrected editions. Therefore the slurs shown in Fig. 7.63b, m. 24R and m. 25 in the bass voice are from Nägeli's OE. In both editions the first slur in Fig. 7.64 extends to D; in m. 49 it stops at E-flat, as shown here.

125. For an exhaustive historical and stylistic discussion of the realization of this trill, see William S. Newman, "The Opening Trill in Beethoven's Sonata for Piano and Violin Opus 96," in *Musik: Edition, Interpretation. Gedenkschrift Günter Henle*, ed. Martin Bente (Munich: Henle, 1980), 384–393. I owe my final comment on the addition of trill suffixes (after discussion of Fig. 7.67) in part to evidence suggested in that paper.

126. E. Bach, *Essay*, 110–112. Bach himself called this ornament "Der halbe oder Prall-Triller" (p. 110, fn. 13). Although the tie between the first two notes was accidentally omitted in the original German issue, the text leaves no doubt about the correct rendition of the ornament. The tie was added in the second issue of Pt. I (published by Winter in 1759). Curiously, that tie was also omitted in the first issue of the translated *Essay* and added in a later, unidentified printing.

127. Starke, *Pianoforte-Schule*, I, Pt. 1, 17–18.

128. E. Bach, *Essay*, 142–143 (cf. Türk, *Klavierschule*, 251–252). Bach did not regard the *Schneller* as a trill.

129. Marpurg, *Anleitung*, 1st ed., 56; Table V, Figs. 1–3.

130. Marpurg, *Anleitung*, 1st ed., 57. "Both . . . expressed with notes, and, as in the preceding [paragraph], where it is a foreshortened tied trill and is called a *Pralltriller,* this same [ornament] is nothing but a short mordent in inverted motion. . . . Nevertheless . . . one must always call each ornament by its correct name." For a similar view see also E. Bach, *Essay*, 142, fn. 1.

131. Löhlein, *Violinspielen*, 46–47.

132. Some nineteenth- and twentieth-century writers misapply the name "mordent" to the three-note trill. The reader beware!

133. The references listed in n. 90 include discussion of the short trill and the *Schneller.*

134. Türk, *Klavierschule*, 1st ed., 272–274; 2d ed., 306–307. Cf. also Milchmeyer, *Pianoforte zu spielen*, 42.

135. Louis Adam and Ludwig Menzel Lachnith, *Méthode ou principe général du doigté pour le piano* (Paris: Sieber, [1798]), 142; Adam, *Méthode de piano*, 54; Clementi/Rosenblum, *Introduction*, xii, 11; J. B. Cramer, *Instructions for the Piano Forte*, 31.

136. E. Bach, *Essay*, 105, 114–115; Petschke, *Versuch eines Unterrichts zum Klavierspielen* [n. 34 above], 37; Türk, *Klavierschule*, 285. See also Johann Baptist Lasser, *Vollständige Anleitung zur Singkunst*, 1798; 2d ed. (identical to the 1st; Munich: Hübschmann, 1805), 9.

137. Newman, "Beethoven's Trills," 446–451.

138. The *tr* on the first b^2 of m. 59 in both Artaria and Simrock is an error.

139. Adam and Lachnith, *Méthode du doigté*, 2d ed., 150.

140. Clementi/Rosenblum, *Introduction*, 12.

141. Türk, *Klavierschule*, 275.

142. Ibid., 276–277.

143. Ibid., 282.

144. The basic models (except for Figs. 7.80a, 4, 6, and 7, and 7.80f, 1, 3, and 5) are from Türk, *Klavierschule,* 282–287; Milchmeyer, *Pianoforte zu spielen,* 39–41; and Clementi/Rosenblum, *Introduction,* 10–11. Fig. 7.80a, 4 is from Löhlein, *Clavier-Schule,* 15; Figs. 7.80a, 6 and 7 are from J. F. Schubert, *Neue Singe-Schule,* 67; Fig. 7.80f, 1 is from E. Bach, *Essay,* 119. For Figs. 7.80a, 3 and 5, see n. 164 below.

145. The tempo indications below apply to the absolute length of the ornamented note within the tempo of a piece. Thus, a turn on a very short note in an *adagio* might have to be played in a configuration suited to an *allegro* or a *presto.*

146. This realization (without the triplet sign) from Türk's *Klavierschule,* 283, is congruent with the rest of his turns; only his rhythmization for an *adagio* turn shows the third note longer than the first two. (In E. Bach's *Essay* the triplet sign and the dot are missing from the *moderato* turn; its third note should probably be a sixteenth note [p. 113]. Bach consistently preferred a longer third note in all but *presto* turns; the extra beam is probably an engraver's error. Cf. also Figs. 68 and 128 in the *Essay.*)

147. In Löhlein's realization, the first note is a sixteenth instead of an eighth (*Clavier-Schule,* 43). However, his explanation (following) and the other rhythmic values make it apparent that the sixteenth note was an engraver's error: "This turn is situated between both notes, on the dot; it is also rendered in the value of the dot." Both the realization and the explanation remained unaltered through the fourth edition.

148. Haydn, *Flötenuhrstücke, JHW,* XXI, 66.

149. Joachim Jaenecke of the Staatsbibliothek Preussischer Kulturbesitz, who very kindly read this holograph for me, reports that there is an illegible (perhaps crossed out) ornament sign over the notes in m. 5. Cf. the Commentary in *JHW,* XXI, 72. In Schmid, *Flute Clock,* No. 1, the turn signs are inaccurate.

150. E.g., Clementi/Rosenblum, *Introduction,* xii-xiii, 10–11; Baillot, Rode, and Kreutzer, *Violon,* 142. As early as 1565 Fray Tomás de Santa María had written that the *redoble* and the *quiebro* (two types of turns) with two whole steps were forbidden (*Libro llamado Arte de tañer fantasía* [n. 88 above], 47v).

151. Milchmeyer, *Pianoforte zu spielen,* 39.

152. Ibid., 40; Clementi/Rosenblum, *Introduction,* 10; Löhlein, *Violinspielen,* 48; Adam, *Méthode,* 58.

153. Löhlein, *Violinspielen,* 48.

154. E. Bach, *Essay,* 118; Türk, *Klavierschule,* 284, fn. *.

155. Türk, *Klavierschule,* 284. For rhythmic variants of this realization cf. also Marpurg, *Anleitung,* 53, and Table VI, Fig. 9; and László Somfai, "How to Read and Understand Haydn's Notation in Its Chronologically Changing Concepts," *Joseph Haydn. Proceedings of the International Joseph Haydn Congress,* Vienna, September 1982, ed. Eva Badura-Skoda (Munich: Henle, 1986), 30, 32.

156. Türk, *Klavierschule,* 286.

157. This copy of Op. 2/1 is in a bound, three-volume set of Beethoven's piano sonatas that contains numerous annotations by Nottebohm and Brahms. The annotations include fingerings (some identified as Czerny's), corrections to the score, additional metronomic indications beyond the occasional printed ones, ornament realizations, and other miscellany. Nottebohm signed many of his neatly penciled notes, including that in Figure 7.87b, with " $\mathcal{N}$." These volumes are in the library of the Gesellschaft der Musikfreunde.

158. E. Bach, *Essay,* 120.

159. Türk, *Klavierschule,* 286–287.

160. E. Bach, *Essay,* 119; cf. Türk, *Klavierschule,* 286.

161. Türk, *Klavierschule,* 220, 283.

162. Badura-Skoda, *Mozart,* 78–79; *NMA, Konzerte für Klavier,* V, ed. Eva and Paul Badura-Skoda, e.g., 12, 71. Neumann, *Mozart,* 58–62. However, compare Mozart's written-out turns in K. 376/i/36ff.

163. J. F. Schubert, *Neue Singe-Schule,* 67.

164. Löhlein, *Clavier-Schule,* 43 (Fig. 7.80g); *Violinspielen,* 48 (Fig. 7.80f, 3); *Clavier-Schule,* 5th ed., 30 (Fig. 7.80f, 5). When August Eberhard Müller produced a much expanded sixth edition in 1804, titled *Klavier und Fortepiano-Schule,* he realized all turns after dotted notes in the style of E. Bach and Türk.

165. I. [*sic*] N. Hüllmandel, *Instructions for the Piano Forte,* A New Edition (London: Rt. Birchall, [between 1800 and 1819]), 19; Starke, *Pianoforte-Schule,* I, Pt. 1, 17–18. Starke wrote that when the sign stands "over the dot after a note, then the turn is brought in only shortly before entrance . . . of the dot. . . ." No doubt he recognized both rhythmizations.

Hüllmandel's "New Edition" was not registered at Stationers' Hall. My dating is suggested by a reasonable interval after the first edition (1796) and a change of publisher's imprint during 1819, when Birchall died (Charles Humphries and William Smith, *Music Publishing in the British Isles,* 2d ed. [Oxford: Blackwell, 1970], 74).

166. Koch showed only a turn after a dotted half note in 3/4 time, but wrote that the turn "over the dot of a note . . . should be made on the third part of the note" (*Lexikon,* col. 452).

167. This term is adopted from Raymond Haggh's translation of Türk's *Klavier-schule* (*School of Clavier Playing* [Lincoln: University of Nebraska Press, 1982], 276), in preference to the more usual term, "snapped."

168. E. Bach, *Essay,* 126.

169. Ibid., 125–126.

170. Türk, *Klavierschule,* 288. Türk, too, preferred quick turns played rapidly, rather than with a pause at the start, as appears later in 7.80i, 2 from Clementi/Rosenblum, *Introduction,* 10.

171. Hüllmandel, *Principles of Music,* 27.

172. Lasser, *Vollständige Anleitung zur Singkunst,* 139. This volume came to my attention in Neumann's *Mozart.*

173. Ignaz Pleyel, *Klavierschule,* 3d German ed. (Leipzig: Hoffmeister and Kühnel, [1804]), 8.

174. J. F. Schubert, *Neue Singe-Schule,* 67.

175. Two experienced editors of Haydn's works differ on the placement of the turn signs in this movement, all of which occur in relation to a dotted-eighth and sixteenth-note figure. In HSU Christa Landon placed the signs directly over the dotted eighth notes; in *JHW* and HE Feder placed them between the dotted eighth and sixteenth notes in spite of his statement that "In the sources, the ornament [∞] is uniformly over the first note" (HE, II, v). Feder's decision may have been based on the poor quality of the sources for this sonata—there is not even an authentic first edition—combined with stylistic considerations and Haydn's complaint to Artaria about the placement of turn signs in the same rhythmic figure in other works. (See the excerpt from his letter, p. 270 below.)

176. Neumann, *Mozart,* 144.

177. I am grateful to Sonja Gerlach for detailed information regarding the musical clock pieces.

178. The first edition of Hob. 28 by Hummel is careless in many regards, including the placement of the turn signs. *JHW* is based on several more reliable contemporary manuscript copies. (See n. 199 below.) Somfai also suggests the possibility of quick turns for this movement ("How to Read . . . Haydn's Notation," 31).

179. Tartini, *Traité des agréments,* 88–91, Supplement (Italian ms.), 17–18; L. Mozart, *Violin,* 206–208. Albrechtsberger (*Anfangsgründe zur Klavierkunst,* 4 [n. 96 above]) and Vogler (*Tonschule,* 21–22; *Gründe der . . . Tonschule in Beyspielen* [Mannheim: (1778)], Tables VI, VIII), who did not discuss the traditional mordent at all, gave its name to the turn both over and between notes. See also Sandra P. Rosenblum, "Clementi's Pianoforte Tutor on the Continent," *Fontes Artis Musicae* 27/1 (January–March 1980): 40–41.

180. [Justin Heinrich] *Knechts allgemeiner musikalischer Katechismus* (Biberach: Gebrüder Knecht, 1803), 60.

Knecht (1752–1817), a south German from the town of Biberach, enjoyed a reputation as composer, organist, and musical theorist of the Vogler school. Leopold Mozart's *Violinschule* was a prominent part of his early instruction, but at the Kollegiatstift in Esslingen Knecht became familiar with the writings of Marpurg and probably of Emanuel Bach (*MGG*, VII, 1266–1267). These works provided some balance to his predominantly south German education. Knecht knew intimately both the music and the theoretical writings of Vogler, as witnessed by some of his ornament usage and terminology (e.g., *Schnelzer*) and the title of his first theoretical work, *Erklärung einiger ... missverstandener Grundsätze aus der Voglerschen Theorie* (Ulm: Wagner, 1785). Knecht composed *singspielen* and diverse instrumental and sacred music. He also edited *Die Schlesische Blumenlese* (Landon, *Correspondence*, 215) and wrote articles for other periodicals, including *AMZ* (*NG*, X, 119).

181. L. Mozart, *Violin*, 184, 233.

182. In lieu of an extant holograph or reliable first edition, these copies, both in the Österreichische Nationalbibliothek, Vienna, served Feder (HE, I, vii) and C. Landon (HSU, *Kritische Anmerkungen*, 70), as the primary and third sources for this sonata.

183. Mus. ms. 10119, in the Staatsbibliothek Preussischer Kulturbesitz, Berlin, served me (for an unpublished edition) and C. Landon (in HSU) as the primary source for this sonata. There is no extant holograph or reliable first edition; the first known publication was in an edition with violin accompaniment under Pleyel's name (London: James Cooper, 1787–1795 [according to Humphries and Smith, *Music Publishing ...*, 115, based on the imprint]).

184. Türk, *Klavierschule*, 283–284. (E. Bach had preferred turns on ascending notes; he specified that they "not be applied to rapid, descending notes" [*Essay*, 115].)

185. Türk, *Klavierschule*, 276–277.

186. See also *JHW, Klaviersonaten*, I, x.

187. Neither C. Landon nor Feder considers any of the sources for this sonata, not even the first edition by Beardmore & Birchall (London, [1784]), especially authoritative. There is no holograph.

188. HSU, III, xvii.

189. Christa Landon, *Haydn: Sämtliche Klaviersonaten, Kritische Anmerkungen* (Vienna: Schott/Universal [formerly Universal], 1982), 81.

190. HE, II, iv. Usually in HE (Preface) and in *JHW*, parentheses indicate that something is found in significant secondary sources (*JHW, Klaviersonaten*, I, "Zur Gestaltung der Ausgabe ...," [n.p.]).

191. This problem of misinterpretation may have been compounded by use of the trill sign and sometimes the mordent sign to indicate the turn in music for instruments other than keyboard (E. Bach, *Essay*, 117).

192. *Haydns Werke: Erste kritisch ... Gesamtausgabe, Sonaten*, ed. Karl Päsler (Leipzig: Breitkopf & Härtel, [ca. 1919]), I, x.

193. Landon, *Correspondence*, 31.

194. Ibid., 51–52. Haydn also used "half mordent" to mean the standard mordent in his holograph of the Fuga played by the musical clock of 1793 (Schmid, *Flute Clock* [n. 100 above], No. 24). His note on the manuscript instructed the cylinder engraver that "as often as the theme appears, the following half mordent must appear with each half note," after which he wrote out a standard mordent (*pincé*) for the first entry (Ernst Fritz Schmid, "Neue Funde zu Haydns Flötenuhrstücken," *Haydn-Studien* II/4 [December 1970]:253).

Türk used the terminology "short (half) mordent" to distinguish the usual form from the mordent with five notes (*Klavierschule*, 275).

195. Landon, *Correspondence*, 52, fn. 5.

196. *JHW, Klaviersonaten*, I, x.

197. For further insight into the problems of interpreting Haydn's ornament signs see Christie Tolstoy, "The Identification and Interpretation of Sign Ornaments in Haydn's Instrumental Music," in *Haydn Studies*, 315–325.

198. Somfai, *Haydn,* 62–63; Somfai, "How to Read . . . Haydn's Notation," 33.

199. Unfortunately, there is no extant holograph for this sonata, which was composed "by 1776" (*NG,* VIII, 389). The primary sources for both *JHW* and HSU are manuscript copies from the Viennese copy shops, two of which—in the same hand— are dated 1776 (*JHW, Klaviersonaten,* II, vii; HSU, *Kritische Anmerkungen,* 60). The first printed edition, by J. J. Hummel (1778), may have been issued without Haydn's approval (HSU, II, xvi). In a footnote to the sonata at m. 118 (p. 84), Landon calls attention to "the more precise notation" in m. 22.

200. Somfai, "How to Read . . . Haydn's Notation," 33–34. In his earlier book on Haydn's piano sonatas Somfai had urged consistent realization in the time of the dotted sixteenth note (*Haydn,* 65–67).

201. Sonja Gerlach very kindly sent me the detailed information about these turns.

202. *Flötenuhrstücke, JHW,* XXI, 66.

203. Tartini, *Traité des agréments de la musique,* 88–89; L. Mozart, *Violin,* 206– 207. Quantz's description in *Flute,* 104, 172–173, is not as clear.

204. Neumann, *Mozart,* 148.

205. Hiller, *Violinspielen,* 48–49.

206. E. Bach, *Essay,* 120. Around 1700 the anticipatory turn was well documented by Thomas Balthasar Janowka (*Clavis ad Thesaurum,* 1701; facs. [Amsterdam: Knuf, 1973], 16–17) and Johann Gottfried Walther (*Praecepta der musicalischen Composition,* aut. ms. in Nationale Forschungs- und Gedenkstätten, Weimar, dated 1708; ed. Peter Benary [Leipzig: Breitkopf & Härtel, 1955], 37). Late Baroque keyboard interpretation seems to have favored on-beat rendition.

207. Heinrich Schenker was aware that Haydn had studied E. Bach's *Essay* and compositions as a young man (see Ernst Fritz Schmid, "Joseph Haydn und Carl Philipp Emanuel Bach," *Zeitschrift für Musikwissenschaft* XIV/6 [October 1931–September 1932]:299–312). Building on the differences between Haydn's and Bach's turn usage and notation (e.g., Haydn placed turns on the sixteenth note after a dotted eighth), on what Schenker considered the absolute necessity of a pause on the fourth note of the turn, and on Bach's "turn over the second note," which Schenker considered "the ancestor of Haydn's characteristic turn forms," Schenker reinterpreted Haydn's turn notation to mean that all turns "over a note" become turns "before a note." This sweeping conclusion is without support from any known contemporary source (Schenker, *Ein Beitrag zur Ornamentik* [n. 22 above], German, 57–65; English, 112–127).

208. *Haydns Werke, Sonaten,* I, xi; II, xxv. Päsler listed Milchmeyer's edition as *Kleine Pianoforte-Schule,* Dresden, 1801, and Milchmeyer's given name as Philipp Jacob (II, xxiv), the German equivalent of Fétis's Philippe-Jacques [n. 67 above]. Nevertheless, available information supports the conclusion that Philipp Jacob and Johann Peter are the same person.

209. Neumann, *Mozart,* 140.

210. Based on both recurrences of these measures in OE, Bossler's appoggiatura e-flat^2 in m. 22 and the addition of c^1 on beat 2 in m. 23L must be engravers' errors.

211. Somfai, *Haydn,* 66–67.

212. Beyschlag, *Ornamentik,* 203; Neumann, *Mozart,* 156–157.

213. Cf. Päsler's comment in *Haydns Werke, Sonaten,* I, xi.

214. See n. 160.

215. Gustav Nottebohm, "Zur Reinigung der Werke Beethoven's von Fehlern und fremden Zuthaten" (*AMZ,* 3d series, XI/23 [7 June 1876]): cols. 353–356; Beyschlag, *Ornamentik,* 223–225. Nottebohm printed the turn in Fig. 7.106 from the recapitulation (mm. 129, 131), but with the addition of turn signs between the two notes in the alto part. He did not identify his source, but added "One sign clarifies the other" (cols. 354–

355). A second turn sign does appear in those measures in the first edition of Op. 2/2, published by Artaria in 1796, p.n. 614, and in Pleyel's edition of [1798], p.n. 117, which might have been based in part on Artaria's. (The date of Pleyel's edition is based on the plate numbers in Anik Devriès and François Lesure, *Dictionnaire des éditeurs de musique français* [Geneva: Minkoff, 1979], I, 129. Other dates are from Kinsky-Halm, *Beethoven Verz.*, 8.) Since the lower signs in these editions are actually just under the first soprano eighth notes rather than between the alto notes, they look like a cautionary redundancy or an engraver's error and do not impart any additional information about the placement of the turn. More important, the lower signs do not appear in the Simrock edition of 1798, p.n. 75, for which Beethoven may have supplied additional refinements to the publisher (see chap. 5, n. 50); in the edition that had belonged to Nottebohm (Bureau de Musique de C. F. Peters, 1808), p.n. 646 (see n. 157 above); or in the manuscript copy made by Mathias Swarz under the supervision of Haslinger and with Beethoven's attest to an authoritative version (see chap. 2, n. 40).

216. Beyschlag, *Ornamentik*, 223.

217. Türk, *Klavierschule*, 286. Nottebohm feared that since turns between notes consist of four tones (closing with the main note), placing a turn sign between repeated notes would suggest two main notes at the end (*AMZ* XI/23 [7 June 1876]: cols. 355–356). However, in view of Türk's first Fig. d in his *Klavierschule*, p. 287, and the comment immediately following, musicians must have been quite used to avoiding such redundancy.

218. Max Rudolf, personal communication; Beyschlag, *Ornamentik*, 211.

219. The appearance of this figure so soon after Haydn used it—at least by 1784—may illustrate the fledgling composer's interest in Haydn's works.

220. Hummel, *Pianoforte*, Pt. III, 10.

221. Ibid., Pt. III, e.g., 43, line 2, m. 2; line 3, m. 4; line 4.

222. Date according to *NG*, VIII, 786.

223. Carl Czerny, *Die Schule der Verzierungen, Vorschläge, Mordenten, und Triller*, Op. 355, 6 vols. (Vienna: Diabelli, [ca. 1835]), III, 10.

224. Ibid., 12, 13.

225. Artur Schnabel, ed., Ludwig van Beethoven, *Sonatas for the Pianoforte*, 2 vols. (New York: Simon and Schuster, 1935), I, 36; Claudio Arrau and Lother Hoffmann-Erbrecht, eds., Ludwig van Beethoven, *Sonatas for Piano*, 2 vols. (New York: Peters, ca. 1973–ca. 1978), I, Appendix, n.p. In the same Appendix Arrau writes that "all the grace notes contained in this volume should be played without exception on the beat ... [all trills] starting with the upper note." However, in the case of Op. 22/ii/20, Arrau placed the turn sign between the two B's to achieve anticipation without breaking his rule.

226. E.g., E. Bach, *Essay*, 137–138; Türk, *Klavierschule*, 245–246. Bach and Türk had another form of ascending turn in which a turn proper is preceded by two stepwise rising notes (*Essay*, 127; *Klavierschule*, 289). J. G. Walther had considered both the turn and the inverted turn as types of slides in his *Praecepta der musicalischen Composition* [n. 206 above], 37.

227. Schenker, *Ein Beitrag zur Ornamentik* [n. 22 above], German, 54; English, 107.

228. E.g., Petri, *Anleitung*, 152–153; Clementi/Rosenblum, *Introduction*, 11.

229. Rellstab, *Anleitung*, VII, xi; Löhlein, *Clavier-Schule*, 5th ed., 30, 32.

230. J. C. Bach and Ricci, *Méthode*, 19.

231. Milchmeyer, *Pianoforte zu spielen*, 39.

232. E. Bach, *Essay*, 121; Türk, *Klavierschule*, 290.

233. Türk, *Klavierschule*, 290.

234. Ibid., 292–293.

235. Ibid., 2d ed., 326.

236. Koch, *Lexikon*, col. 453.

237. Türk, *Klavierschule*, 242.

238. Ibid. Türk followed E. Bach here (*Essay,* 132–133).

239. Türk, *Klavierschule,* 243–245.

240. The dynamics in this example are misplaced in the first edition: *f* appears under the chord before the ornament, *p* on the long appoggiatura, and *mf* on the last chord. Figure 7.118 appears as it was corrected in the second edition (p. 277). (In respect to the difference in dynamics between this ornament and the double appoggiatura, Türk appears to have followed E. Bach again [*Essay,* 132, 135].)

241. Hiller, *Violinspielen,* 49.

242. E.g., Michel L'Affilard, *Principes très-facile pour bien apprendre la musique* (Paris: Ballard, 1694), 20–21; Jean-Henri D'Anglebert, *Pieces de clavecin* (Paris: Ballard, 1689), "Marques des Agrements"; Walther, *Praecepta der musicalischen Composition* [n. 206 above], 37.

243. E. Bach, *Essay,* 137–139; Türk, *Klavierschule,* 248.

244. Müller, *Fortepiano-Schule,* 29; Daniel Steibelt, *Méthode de Piano/Pianoforte-Schule* (Leipzig: Breitkopf & Härtel, [ca. 1809]), 59. A diagonal line between chord tones might also indicate an acciaccatura (Türk, *Klavierschule,* 279–280).

245. Türk, *Klavierschule,* 294–295; Müller, *Fortepiano-Schule,* 262; Cramer, *Instructions for the Piano Forte,* 27.

246. Türk, *Klavierschule,* 297.

247. HSU, I, 175.

248. E.g., Girolamo Frescobaldi, *Toccate e Partite* [n. 84 above], Preface, para. 3. This paragraph is translated in Robert Donington, *The Interpretation of Early Music,* New Version (New York: St. Martin's Press, 1974), 278. See also Donington's comments on the broken chord (ibid., 277–278), and François Couperin's on harpsichord style (*The Art of Playing the Harpsichord,* trilingual ed., ed. and German trans. Anna Linde; English trans. Mevanwy Roberts [Leipzig: Breitkopf & Härtel, 1933], 33).

249. Koch, *Lexikon,* col. 567.

250. Ibid., col. 1576.

251. HSU, e.g., I, 163, 176. Rudolf Steglich, "Kadenzen in Haydns Klaviersonaten," *Zeitschrift für Musik* 991/4 (April 1932):295–297.

252. Badura-Skoda, *Mozart,* 214–234; Neumann, *Mozart,* 257–263; Paul Badura-Skoda, *Kadenzen, Eingänge und Auszierungen zu Klavierkonzerten von Wolfgang Amadeus Mozart* (Kassel: Bärenreiter, 1967). Additional information may be found in the articles "Cadenza" and "Improvisation" in *NG;* in the books in the Selected Bibliography by E. Bach, Quantz, Tartini, Türk, and Wolf; and in Michael Sitton, "Mozart's Cadenzas and Improvisations," *PQ* 138 (Summer 1987):40–44.

253. E. Badura-Skoda, "Cadenza," *NG,* III, 586.

254. Mozart differentiated between cadenzas and *Eingänge* in a letter of 15 February 1783 (*Mozart: Briefe und Aufzeichnungen,* ed. Wilhelm A. Bauer and Otto Erich Deutsch, 7 vols. [Kassel: Bärenreiter, 1962–1975], III, 256).

255. For information on improvising lead-ins, with examples, see Badura-Skoda, *Mozart,* 234–241.

256. *NGMI,* "Performing Practice," III, 57.

257. *Haydn Studies,* 220–221; see also 195–197.

258. Neumann offers some sensible guidance for where and where not to introduce lead-ins at *fermatas* in Mozart's works (*Mozart,* 269–270).

259. Hummel, *Pianoforte,* Pt. I, 66, fn. *.

260. Emanuel Bach, *Sechs Sonaten fürs Clavier mit veränderten Reprisen* [with varied reprises] Wq. 50 (Berlin: Winter, 1760), Vorrede (Preface).

261. A. Peter Brown, *Joseph Haydn's Keyboard Music: Sources and Styles* (Bloomington: Indiana University Press, 1986), 220.

262. Türk, *Klavierschule,* 305; examples, pp. 322–331.

263. Ibid., 323, 325.

264. Anderson, *Mozart,* 880.

265. *NMA, Klavierkonzerte,* IV, ed. Marius Flothuis, 208.

266. Badura-Skoda, *Mozart,* 180–196; Neumann, *Mozart,* 240–256.

267. *Thayer's Life of Beethoven,* rev. and ed. Elliot Forbes (Princeton: Princeton University Press, 1967), 350.

268. Ibid., 640.

269. Hiller, *Anweisung zum Violinspielen,* 47.

270. Manuscript copies of this sonata were offered for sale in the Breitkopf Thematic Catalogue of 1767. However, E. Badura-Skoda has pointed out that the opening theme also occurs in an aria from the *singspiel Triumph der Freundschaft,* composed in "the mid seventeen-fifties, presumably by Haydn" ("Haydn, Mozart and their Contemporaries," in *Keyboard Music,* ed. Denis Matthews [New York: Praeger, 1972], 122). See also Brown, *Haydn's Keyboard Music,* 119.

271. I am indebted to the Preface in Etienne Darbellay's edition of these *Sechs Sonaten . . .* Wq. 50 (Winterthur, Switzerland: Amadeus, 1976) for knowledge of this *Handexemplar* in the British Library. See also a facsimile of Fig. 7.126 from Bach's copy in Darbellay, xxx.

272. Johann Adam Hiller, *Anweisung zum musikalisch-zierlichen Gesange* (Leipzig: Junius, 1780; facs., Leipzig: Peters, 1976), chap. VIII, especially 131–133. "*Rubato* ornaments" refers to the various uses of eighteenth-century *tempo rubato* discussed in Hiller's chap. X. Regarding the need for correct harmonic practice, see also Sulzer, *Allgemeine Theorie,* "Vortrag," II, 1257–1258.

8. "Mixed Meters" and Dotted Rhythms

1. Carl Philipp Emanuel Bach, *Essay on the True Art of Playing Keyboard Instruments,* trans. and ed. William J. Mitchell (New York: Norton, 1949), 160. See also Friedrich Wilhelm Marpurg, *Anleitung zum Clavierspielen,* facs. of 2d ed. (New York: Broude, 1969), 24–25, Table I, Figs. 42, 43.

2. E.g., Johann Schobert, Andante cantabile from the Sonata in E-flat major for Violin and Harpsichord, No. 3 in *Denkmäler deutscher Tonkunst,* Ser. 1, Vol. 39, ed. Hugo Reimann (Leipzig: Breitkopf & Härtel, 1909), 28.

3. Johann Abraham Peter Schulz, "Triole," in Sulzer, *Allgemeine Theorie,* II, 1182.

4. Daniel Gottlob Türk, *Klavierschule* (Leipzig and Halle: Schwickert; Hemmerde und Schwetschke, 1789); facs., ed. Erwin R. Jacobi (Kassel: Bärenreiter, 1962), 103–104; Johann Peter Milchmeyer, *Die wahre Art das Pianoforte zu spielen* (Dresden: Meinhold, 1797), 5.

5. Türk, *Klavierschule,* 2d ed. (Leipzig and Halle: Schwickert; Hemmerde und Schwetschke, 1802), 96.

6. George Simon Löhlein, *Clavier-Schule* (Leipzig: Waisenhaus und Frommann, 1765), 70.

7. *The Bach Reader,* ed. Hans David and Arthur Mendel (New York: Norton, 1966), 446. The remainder of the quotation is also interesting: "Otherwise there would be no difference between duple meter, in which such notes occur, and 3/8, 6/8, 9/8 and 12/8 meters. This is what J. S. Bach taught all his pupils; and this is what Quantz says in his Essay."

8. Löhlein, *Clavier-Schule,* 2d ed. (Leipzig: Waisenhaus und Frommann, 1773), 68.

9. Sulzer, *Allgemeine Theorie,* II, 1182.

10. Türk, *Klavierschule,* 104.

11. A very popular aria from the comic opera *La Molinara ossia L'amor contrastato* of 1788.

12. John Wall Callcott, *A Musical Grammar,* 1806; 2d ed. (London: Birchall, 1809), 258.

13. Friedrich Starke, *Wiener Pianoforte-Schule,* 3 vols. (Vol. I, Vienna: Bey dem Verfasser, 1819; Vol. II, Vienna: Sprenger, 1819; Vol. III, Vienna: Berman, 1821), I, Pt. 2, 8.

14. Czerny, *Piano Forte,* I, 92.

15. Czerny, *Proper Performance,* 39; see also chap. 4, n. 100.

16. Leopold Mozart, *A Treatise on the Fundamental Principles of Violin Playing,* trans. Editha Knocker, 2d ed. (London: Oxford University Press, 1951), 41–42; also Marpurg, *Anleitung,* 13.

17. Türk, *Klavierschule,* 361–363. Regarding Türk's "beat division," see ibid., 90, and chap. 3, n.129 above; for his description of heavy and light performance see above, chap. 5, pp. 150–151. Emanuel Bach's similar but less thorough explanation of double-dotting in his *Essay* (157–158) is illustrated by the precise alignment of dotted patterns in the first edition of his *Sechs Sonaten . . . mit veränderten Reprisen* Wq. 50 (Berlin: Winter, 1760), e.g., Sonata V/i/4. These details are retained in an excellent edition of the sonatas prepared by Etienne Darbellay (see the Selected Bibliography).

18. August Leopold Crelle, *Einiges über musicalischen Ausdruck und Vortrag* (Berlin: Maurerschen Buchhandlung, 1823), 76–77, Figs. 25–27.

19. Hummel, *Pianoforte,* Pt. I, 79; German ed., I, 76.

20. The second motive, a "written-out slide," may be "assimilated" by playing its first and third notes with the first two sixteenths of the accompaniment. (Cf. this measure with m. 2 in the Adagio of Haydn's Sonata in E minor, No. 19 in HSU, Hob. 47 in *JHW* [see chap. 3, n. 6 above].)

21. In OE the melody of m. 26 is a whole step too high, perhaps caused in part by a page break between mm. 25 and 26.

22. In the holograph there is no triplet indication for the last three notes in m. 68. However, above the identical rhythmic grouping in m. 70, the upper hook of the *3* and a very short curved line above it are visible. See László Somfai's comment on Haydn's triplet notation in "How to Read and Understand Haydn's Notation in Its Chronologically Changing Concepts," *Joseph Haydn. Proceedings of the International Joseph Haydn Congress,* Vienna, September 1982, ed. Eva Badura-Skoda (Munich: Henle, 1986), 27.

23. Gilbert Kalish, Nonesuch H71344, 1977.

9. Choice of Tempo

1. Leopold Mozart, *A Treatise on the Fundamental Principles of Violin Playing* (Augsburg: In Verlag des Verfassers, 1756); trans. Editha Knocker, 2d ed. (London: Oxford University Press, 1951), 30.

2. Ibid., 33.

3. Emily Anderson, trans. and ed., *The Letters of Mozart and His Family,* 2d ed., ed. A. Hyatt King and Monica Carolan, 2 vols. (London: Macmillan, 1966), 850.

4. Curt Sachs, *Rhythm and Tempo* (New York: Norton, 1953), 321.

5. Papers read by Don O. Franklin and Etienne Darbellay at the Frescobaldi Quadrocentennial Conference at Madison, Wisconsin in 1983 reported that in Frescobaldi's music and perhaps more broadly, the pulse, or "tactus," seems to have been variable to some degree, rather than "fixed," as previously believed. I am indebted to Elfrieda F. Hiebert for bringing this information to my attention.

6. Johann Joachim Quantz, *On Playing the Flute* (Berlin: Voss, 1752); trans. and ed. Edward R. Reilly (London: Faber and Faber, 1966), 284–286. Tempos derived from Quantz's descriptions (ibid., 284–292) are shown in Appendix A to this chapter.

For further information on the relationship of modern time signatures to proportional notation see Robert Donington, *The Interpretation of Early Music,* New Version (New York: St. Martin's Press, 1974), chap. 38. Interestingly, Franz Kullak still referred to proportions in *Beethoven's Piano Playing,* trans. Theodore Baker (New York: Schirmer, 1901), 19–21, 23.

7. These ideas are summarized from J. A. P. Schulz, "Takt," in Sulzer, *Allgemeine Theorie,* II, 1130–1138; and Daniel Gottlob Türk, *Klavierschule* (Leipzig and Halle: Schwickert; Hemmerde und Schwetschke, 1789); facs., ed. Erwin R. Jacobi (Kassel: Bärenreiter, 1962), 359–364. The article "Takt" remained unchanged in the enlarged second edition of Sulzer's encyclopedia.

8. Sulzer, *Allgemeine Theorie,* II, 1134–1136.

9. Alexander Malcolm, *A Treatise of Musick* (Edinburgh: Printed for the Author, 1721), 402. Malcolm's six "Distinctions of *Time,*" from "the slowest . . . and gradually quicker," are "*grave, adagio, largo, vivace, allegro, presto*" (402). In the eighteenth century *vivace* often meant "the mean between quick and slow" (L. Mozart, *Violin,* 50).

10. Malcolm, *A Treatise of Musick* [n. 9 above], 402.

11. Schulz, "Vortrag," in Sulzer, *Allgemeine Theorie,* II, 1253. This article remained unchanged in the enlarged second edition.

12. "Takt," in Sulzer, *Allgemeine Theorie,* II, 1135.

13. Ibid., 1134.

14. The eighteenth-century meaning of *Tempo giusto* was "in the correct and appropriate tempo, that is, not too fast and not too slow" (Georg Friedrich Wolf, *Unterricht im Klavierspielen,* 3d ed. [Halle: Hendel, 1789], 83). Cf. also Johann Gottfried Walther, *Praecepta der musikalischen Composition,* aut. ms. in the Nationale Forschungs- und Gedenkstätten, Weimar, dated 1708; ed. Peter Benary (Leipzig: Breitkopf & Härtel, 1955), 55. In the nineteenth century *giusto* acquired the additional meaning of "exact" or strict time when it was used within a piece or in combination with other tempo words (e.g., Czerny, *Piano Forte School,* I, 156). Thus, according to Hummel, *Allegro giusto* meant "cheerful and lively, but with strict measure" (*Pianoforte,* Pt. I, 69).

15. Schulz, "Takt," in Sulzer, *Allgemeine Theorie,* II, 1133. I am indebted to Max Rudolf for his suggestions regarding this translation.

16. Kirnberger, "Alla Breve," in Sulzer, *Allgemeine Theorie,* I, 27; cf. also Türk, *Klavierschule,* 109; Heinrich Christoph Koch, *Musikalisches Lexikon* (Frankfurt: Hermann dem jüngern, 1802; facs., Hildesheim: Olms, 1964), col. 129.

17. Türk, *Klavierschule,* 2d ed. (Leipzig and Halle: Schwickert; Hemmerde und Schwetschke, 1802), 103.

18. Although many Baroque theorists described the "twice as fast" relationship between *alla breve* and common time, Purcell, among others, recognized that the facts of performance were different. In his *A Choice Collection of Lessons* (London: Frances Purcell, 1696), he explained the relationship among three duple meters, all of which had, according to his description, "one whole note or four quarter notes" to a measure: c, "very slow movement"; ¢, "a little faster"; 𝄵, "brisk and airy time." (These instructions are found in one "state" of Purcell's *Collection of Lessons* dated 1696 [with 𝄵 misprinted as ◐, and not in another of the same year. While Purcell's name is not specifically attached to them in this volume, it is in *The Third Book of the Harpsichord Master* [London: Walsh, 1702], in which they were reprinted. Regarding the use of "state," see n. 162 below.)

Only a few years later Janowka alluded to the fact that signs with meanings supposedly quite distinct were interchanged in different copies of the same piece or even among various parts of the same copy. "But seeing that among lovers of music [*Philomusos*] many various feelings about these symbols [c, 2, ¢] are heard, so that there are as many opinions as there are heads, writers of music [*scripturistae*] occasionally confuse one symbol with another in their musical scores" (Thomas Balthasar Janowka, *Clavis ad Thesaurum . . . ,* facs. [Amsterdam: Knuf, 1973], 16). See also Isidor Saslav,

"Tempos in the String Quartets of Joseph Haydn," D.M. diss., Indiana University, 1969, 23–24.

19. Anderson, *Mozart*, 867.

20. Max Rudolf, "Ein Beitrag zur Geschichte der Temponahme bei Mozart," *Mozart-Jahrbuch* 1976/1977:219.

21. Kirnberger, "Alla breve," in Sulzer, *Allgemeine Theorie*, I, 27.

22. Schulz, "Takt," in Sulzer, *Allgemeine Theorie*, II, 1134.

23. Emily Anderson, trans. and ed., *The Letters of Beethoven*, 3 vols. (London: Macmillan, 1961), 378. For a wide-ranging discussion of Beethoven's choice of time signature and metronomization for the Trio of the Ninth Symphony, see Peter Stadlen, "Beethoven and the Metronome," *Music and Letters* 48/4 (October 1967):330–349.

24. Dates according to *NG*, VIII, 389–390.

25. The Baroque C meter was often subdivided into triplet sixteenth notes and 32d notes, while the smallest value of the Classic 4/4 *allegro* was usually the sixteenth note. For a concise summary of the various uses of C and 4/4 in the eighteenth century, see Saslav, "Tempos in the String Quartets of Joseph Haydn," 24–27.

26. For these aspects of meter-tempo relationships I am indebted to Saslav's study, ibid., 80. See also pp. 313–314 below for confirmation of the *largo-adagio* order.

27. Neal Zaslaw, "Mozart's Tempo Conventions," *Report of the Eleventh Congress of the International Musicological Society, 1972*, 2 vols. (Copenhagen: Hansen, 1974), II, 723.

28. Ibid., 721. Another very helpful section on tempo in Mozart's music is found in Eva and Paul Badura-Skoda, *Interpreting Mozart on the Piano*, trans. Leo Black (London: Barrie and Rockliff, 1962), 30–37.

29. Christoph Eschenbach, Deutsche Grammophon 2720031, [1971]; Walter Gieseking, Angel ANG 35077, [1956]. Ca. 132 for a quarter note in Mozart's K. 485 (in C), close to Quantz's unqualified Allegro (Appendix A), allows the articulation to sound clear and effortless and the sixteenth notes to "flow like oil" (Mozart's letter of 23–24 October 1777; chap. 1, p. 23).

30. Lili Kraus, Odyssey Y3-33220, [1974].

31. Records are the same as those in nn. 29 and 30.

32. Ibid.

33. Malcolm Bilson, Golden Crest CRS-4097, [197?].

34. Kraus, record cited in n. 30; Conrad Hansen, Deutsche Grammophon 18320, [1957]; Gieseking, record cited in n. 29.

35. Richard Kramer, "Notes to Beethoven's Education," *JAMS* XXVIII/1 (Spring 1975):75.

36. L. Mozart, *Violin*, 33.

37. Türk, *Klavierschule*, 110.

38. Ibid., 108; also Sulzer, *Allgemeine Theorie*, enl. 2d ed., I, 139; Ignaz Pleyel and Jan Ladislav Dussek, *Méthode pour le piano forte* (Paris: Pleyel, [1797]), 63; Hummel, *Pianoforte*, 78.

39. Jean-Jacques Rousseau, *Dictionnaire de musique* (Paris: Chez la Veuve Duchesne, 1768), 303.

40. Koch, *Lexikon*, col. 64.

41. Compare also Pierre Baillot, Rodolphe Kreutzer, and Pierre Rode, *Méthode de violon* (Brussels: Weissenbruch, [1803]), 174.

42. Koch, *Lexikon*, col. 890.

43. Ibid., cols. 62, 64–65.

44. Ibid., cols. 142–143.

45. Ibid., cols. 130–131.

46. Ibid., col. 1169.

47. Sébastien de Brossard, *Dictionaire de musique* (Paris: Ballard, 1703), "Adagio," "Largo"; L. Mozart, *Violin*, 51; Rousseau, *Dictionnaire de musique*, 303; Johann Philipp

Kirnberger, *Die Kunst des reinen Satzes in der Musik,* 2 vols. (Vol. II, Berlin and Königsberg: Decker und Hartung, Pt. 1, 1776), 107; Antonio Lorenzoni, *Saggio per ben sonare il flauto traverso* (Vicenza: Modena, 1779), 47; Türk, *Klavierschule,* 108; Francesco Galeazzi, *Elementi di Musica,* Vol. I (Rome: Cracas, 1791), 36; Jan Ladislav Dussek, *Instructions on the Art of Playing the Piano Forte or Harpsichord* (London: Corri, Dussek, [1796]), 44–45; Pleyel and Dussek, *Méthode,* 62; Johann Christian Bach and Francesco Pasquale Ricci, *Méthode . . . pour le forte-piano ou clavecin* (Paris: Le Duc, [ca. 1786]), reissue with new p. n. (Paris: Le Duc, [179?]), 2 (Ricci is supposed to have written the text); Johann Peter Milchmeyer, *Die wahre Art das Pianoforte zu spielen* (Dresden: Meinhold, 1797), 52–53; Koch, *Lexikon,* col. 64; Hummel, *Pianoforte,* Pt. I, 68; Czerny, *Piano Forte School,* I, 156.

48. Galeazzi, *Elementi di Musica,* I, 36.

49. Landon, *Correspondence,* 59–60. In this letter of 8 April 1787, Haydn must have been referring to the original orchestral version, which Forster published later that year. Haydn was allegedly especially fond of this work (Giuseppe Carpani, *Le Haydine* [Milan: Buccinelli, 1812], 105); he arranged it for string quartet and approved and corrected the arrangement for piano (Landon, *Correspondence,* 64–65).

50. Saslav, "Tempos in the String Quartets of Joseph Haydn," 57–58; see also 36–37 and 79.

51. Henry Purcell, Sonnatas [*sic*] of III Parts, (London: John Playford, John Carr, for the author, 1683), Preface; Alexander Malcolm, *A Treatise of Musick* [n. 9 above], 402; James Grassineau, *A Musical Dictionary* (London: Wilcox, 1740), 3, 88, 119; Quantz, *Flute,* 164–165; Emanuel Bach, *Essay on the True Art of Playing Keyboard Instruments,* trans. and ed. William J. Mitchell (New York: Norton, 1949), 414; John Hoyle (pseud. for John Binns), *Dictionarium musica, Being a Complete Dictionary or Treasury of Music* (London: Printed for the Author, 1770), 2, 39; later ed., *A Complete Dictionary of Music* (London: Symonds, 1791), 2, 55; Georg Joseph Vogler, *Kuhrpfälzische Tonschule* (Mannheim: Auf Kosten des Verfassers, in Commission bei Schwan und Götz, [1778]), 11; Thomas Busby, *A Complete Dictionary of Music* (London: R. Phillips, [ca. 1801]), "Adagio," "Largo"; Clementi/Rosenblum, *Introduction,* 13; Charles Mason, *Rules on the Times, Metres, Phrases and Accent of Composition* (London: Printed for the Author, [1801?]), 1; Justin Heinrich Knecht, *Knechts Allgemeiner musikalischer Katechismus* (Biberach: Gebrüder Knecht, 1803), 34; Johann Baptist Cramer, *Instructions for the Piano Forte* (London: Chappell, 1812), 44.

52. Purcell, Sonnatas of III Parts [n. 51 above], Preface.

53. "Vortrag," in Sulzer, *Allgemeine Theorie,* II, 1253.

54. Türk, *Klavierschule,* 108.

55. Koch, *Lexikon,* cols. 130–131.

56. Ibid., col. 890. Max Rudolf points out that in his arrangement of the Second Symphony for piano trio, Beethoven changed the heading of the second movement from Larghetto to Larghetto quasi Andante ("The Metronome Indications in Beethoven's Symphonies," *Journal of the Conductors' Guild* of the American Symphony Orchestra League I/1 [May 1980]:8).

57. Clementi/Rosenblum, *Introduction,* 13.

58. Koch, *Lexikon,* col. 130.

59. Anderson, *Mozart,* 880. If Anderson was correct in including K. 449, Mozart referred to an Andantino among other movements headed Andante.

60. Christian Friedrich Daniel Schubart, *Ideen zu einer Ästhetik der Tonkunst* (Vienna: Degen, 1806), 360. This manuscript, which dates from 1784–1785 (*NG,* XVI, 750), was published posthumously, "edited" by Ludwig Schubart. The book was in Beethoven's library (Anton F. Schindler, *Beethoven As I Knew Him,* trans. Constance Jolly, ed. Donald W. MacArdle [Chapel Hill: University of North Carolina Press, 1966], 366).

61. Busby, *A Complete Dictionary of Music*, n.p. Dussek also described *andante* as "rather slow & distinct" (*Instructions*, 44).

62. Hummel, *Ausführliche theoretisch-praktische Anweisung zum Piano-forte-spiel* (Vienna: Haslinger, 1828), I, 66.

63. Czerny, *Piano Forte*, I, 156.

64. Zaslaw, "Mozart's Tempo Conventions," 723. Regarding minuet tempos see "Beethoven's 'Moderate' Minuets" below.

65. Türk, *Klavierschule*, 109, fn. **.

66. Koch, *Lexikon*, col. 979; cf. Koch's comments about *andante*, p. 313.

67. Rudolf, "Temponahme bei Mozart," 216.

68. E.g., Friedrich Wilhelm Marpurg, *Anleitung zum Clavierspielen*, facs. of 2d ed. (New York: Broude, 1969), 16; Jean-Jacques Rousseau, *Dictionnaire*, 32; J. C. Bach and F. P. Ricci, *Méthode*, 2; *Knechts . . . musikalischer Katechismus*, 34–35; Friedrich Kalkbrenner, *A New Method of Studying the Piano-forte*, 3d ed. (London: D'Almaine, [1837]), "List of Principal Words," n.p.; Ernst Pauer, *The Art of Pianoforte Playing* (London: Novello, [1877]), 80. Pauer wrote that *andantino* is "really slower than Andante, although the term is generally used for 'quicker than andante.'"

69. E.g., Galeazzi, *Elementi di musica*, 36; Jean Baptiste Cartier, *L'art du violon*, 1798; 3d ed. (Paris: Decombe, [1803]), 17; August Eberhard Müller, *Klavier und Fortepiano-Schule* (Jena: Frommann, 1804), 299.

70. Türk, *Klavierschule*, 1st ed., 109, fn.**; 2d ed., 104.

71. Johann Adam Hiller, *Anweisung zum Violinspielen* (Grätz: Trötscher, 1795), 58.

72. Hummel, *Pianoforte*, Pt. I, 69.

73. Gustav Schilling, *Encyclopädie der gesammten musikalischen Wissenschaften*, 7 vols., 1838–1842; 2d ed., Vol. I (Stuttgart: Köhler, 1840), 193.

74. Coincidentally, Haydn's only (and unqualified) use of *andantino* in his string quartets also occurs in one from the 1790s, Hob. III/72/ii (Op. 74/1/ii). (According to Feder, the Quartets Hob. III/13–18 [Op. 3], in which one movement is headed Andantino grazioso, are spurious [*NG*, VIII, 380].)

75. Türk, *Klavierschule*, 109–110.

76. Koch, *Lexikon*, col. 779.

77. Clementi/Rosenblum, *Introduction*, 13.

78. Löhlein lists them as synonyms (*Clavier-Schule*, 66).

79. E.g., Quantz, *Flute*, 130; p. 307 above, 4.; p. 318 below; Schulz, "Vortrag," in Sulzer, *Allgemeine Theorie*, II, 1248.

80. Zaslaw, "Mozart's Tempo Conventions," 727.

81. Rudolf, "Temponahme bei Mozart," 216. In Nardo's aria the successive headings Andantino grazioso, Andante, and Allegretto reflect the increasing intensity of the text. Although the *NMA* reads Andante grazioso at the start, Rudolf has kindly informed me that the holograph (now in Kraków) reads Andantino, as it is in *MGA*.

82. *Thayer's Life of Beethoven*, rev. and ed. Elliot Forbes (Princeton: Princeton University Press, 1967), 555.

83. Surprisingly, taking Koch as his authority and without discussing the matter in relation to any music, Hermann Beck assumes that in Beethoven's works *andantino* is faster than *andante* ("Studien über das Tempoproblem bei Beethoven," Ph.D. diss., Friedrich-Alexander-Universität, 1954, 70, 72, 79).

84. E.g., Wolfgang Michael Mylius, *Rudimenta musices . . . Anweisung zur Singe-Kunst*, under the initials W. M. M. M. T. C. M. G. (Gotha: der Autor, 1686), chap. 5, n.p.; Janowka, *Clavis ad Thesaurum . . .*, 2; Johann Gottfried Walther, *Praecepta der musikalischen Composition* [n. 14 above], 40.

85. Türk, *Klavierschule*, 108.

86. Ibid., 111.

87. Ibid., 2d ed., 106.

88. Quantz, *Flute,* 285.

89. Saslav, "Tempos in the String Quartets of Joseph Haydn," 64–67.

90. Ibid., 15–16, 70–73, 152–160. Examples of minuets marked Allegro in the repertoire for keyboard include the Finale of the Sonata Hob. 38 (comp. mid-1770s [Brown, *Haydn* 123]), the Allegro (last movement) of the Piano Trio Hob. XV/5 (by October 1784 [this and remaining dates from *NG,* VIII, 388]), the Allegro, ma dolce of the Trio Hob. XV/24 (by October 1795), and the Finale of the Trio Hob. XV/28 (by April 1797). The last Piano Trio, Hob. XV/30 (1797), has a scherzo-like movement headed Presto. It is also interesting that Haydn modified *andante,* which already meant "going," only to the faster side (ibid., 90).

91. Landon, *Correspondence,* 9.

92. Ibid., 121, 196.

93. Giuseppe Carpani, *Le Haydine* [n. 49 above], 67. Carpani was "very knowledgeable" about the music of his day (Bruno Cagli, "Carpani," *NG,* III, 818).

94. *AMZ* XIII/44 (30 October 1811), col. 737.

95. Anderson, *Beethoven,* 727. Anderson notes that the year was added to the holograph in another hand (ibid., fn.2).

96. E.g., Friedrich Rochlitz, "Bruchstücke aus Briefen an einen Jungen Tonsetzer," *AMZ* II/4 (23 October 1799), col. 60; Ludwig Spohr, letter from Paris to the *Musikalische Zeitung* in Leipzig, 31 December 1820, reprinted in Spohr, *Autobiography,* trans. anon., 2 vols. (London: Reeves & Turner, 1878), II, 118–119; anonymous review, *Harmonicon* III/29 (May 1825):89; anonymous letter, *Harmonicon* IV/40 (April 1826):84.

97. Brossard, *Dictionaire de Musique* [n. 47 above], "Assai."

98. David Fallows, "Assai," *NG,* I, 659.

99. Johann Gottfried Walther, *Musikalisches Lexikon* (Leipzig: Deer, 1732), 27.

100. Stewart Deas, "Beethoven's 'Allegro assai,' " *Music and Letters* XXXI/4 (October 1950):333–336.

101. Francesco de Alberti di Villanuova, *Nuovo Dizionario Italiano-Francese,* 2 vols. (Marseille: Mossy, 1771, 1772). Beethoven's own Italian-German and French-German dictionaries of 1785 and 1793 respectively are in the collection of the Deutsche Staatsbibliothek (Eve Bartlitz, *Die Beethoven-Sammlung in der Musikabteilung der Deutschen Staatsbibliothek* [Berlin: Staatsbibliothek, 1970], 213–214).

102. Türk, *Klavierschule,* 109.

103. Ibid., 2d ed., 104.

104. Donald F. Tovey and Harold Craxton, eds., Beethoven, *Sonatas for Pianoforte,* 3 vols. (London: Associated Board of the Royal Schools of Music, [1931]), I, 59, 208. Deas discusses the *assai* in all three sonatas ("Beethoven's 'Allegro assai' " [n. 100 above], 333).

105. Quantz, *Flute,* 284; L. Mozart, *Violin,* 50.

106. See Erich Leinsdorf, *The Composer's Advocate* (New Haven: Yale University Press, 1981), 105. Readers will also find much of interest in Leinsdorf's discussion of tempos in *The Marriage of Figaro,* ibid., 102–126.

107. Clementi/Rosenblum, *Introduction,* 14; Hummel, *Pianoforte,* Pt. I, 68; Carl Czerny, *Vollständige theoretisch-praktische Pianoforte-Schule* (Vienna: Diabelli, 1846), I, 118 (*assai* is not in the English volume).

108. Schindler/MacArdle, *Beethoven,* 423, fn. Although the veracity of Schindler's reporting on performance practices is open to serious doubt (see "Schindler and Beethoven" in chap. 3), there is ample evidence in letters, comments to close friends, and in the Conversation Books that realization of his tempo indications was a primary concern of Beethoven.

109. Kirnberger, "Bewegung," in Sulzer, *Allgemeine Theorie,* I, 157. See also Friedrich Blume, *Classic and Romantic Music,* trans. M. D. Herter Norton (New York: Norton, 1970), 36–37.

110. Türk, *Klavierschule,* 114.

111. Anderson, *Beethoven*, 1325.

112. David Fallows writes that like *tempo giusto, tempo ordinario* "was evidently in fairly current use as a concept to describe the ordinary, non-committal tempo that required no tempo designation" ("*Tempo ordinario*," *NG*, XVIII, 685).

113. Anderson, *Beethoven*, 243 (letter of 19 September 1809). For some reason the original heading was printed in *BGA*.

114. Ludwig van Beethoven, holograph of Sonata Op. 111, facs. (Leipzig: Peters, [1952]), n.p.

115. Thayer/Dieters/Riemann, *Beethoven*, III, 347. The chronometer was also described in *AMZ* of 1 December 1813, with Beethoven's previous endorsement noted (unsigned article sent from Vienna, dated November 16; *AMZ* XV/48 [1 December 1813], cols. 784–788).

Maelzel derived the idea for the type of pendulum used in the metronome from the mechanic Winkel of Amsterdam in 1815. By 1816 he was manufacturing metronomes in Paris (*NG*, XI, 485).

116. Nottebohm, *Beethoveniana*, 2 vols. (Leipzig: Rieter-Biedermann, 1872, 1877), I, 126. In this chapter, "Metronomische Bezeichnungen," Nottebohm gave an account of Beethoven's views on the metronome, his relationship with Maelzel, and a list of metronomizations for the miscellaneous works that Beethoven marked, along with an incomplete list for the string quartets.

117. The metronomizations for the Symphonies were reprinted in *AMZ* XIX/51 (17 December 1817), cols. 873–874. They are also included, along with those for Op. 106 and some miscellaneous pieces, in *BGA*. Complete indications for the string quartets are reprinted in Nottebohm, *Beethoveniana*, II, 519–521. A reprinting of all Beethoven's metronomizations and some comparative indications by contemporary and recent Beethoven specialists appear in Rainer Riehn, "Beethovens originale, Czernys und Moscheles' auf Erinnerung gegründete, Kolischs und Leibowitz' durch Vergleiche der Charaktere erschlossene Metronomisierungen," in *Beethoven, Das Problem der Interpretation,* ed. Heinz-Klaus Metzger and Rainer Riehn (Munich: Edition Text & Kritik, 1979), 85–96.

The miscellaneous works with metronomizations by Beethoven are Opp. 112, 121b, and 137 and WoO 148, 149, 104, and 150. Peter Stadlen considers the origin of the indications for the last two questionable ("Beethoven und das Metronom," in *Beethoven Kolloquium, 1977: Documentation und Aufführungspraxis,* ed. Rudolf Klein [Kassel: Bärenreiter, 1978], 12). None are for solo piano.

118. Anderson, *Beethoven*, 1441–1442.

119. Ibid., 1295. The metronomizations referred to in this letter were to have been for the Quartet Op. 131.

120. Ibid., 1314–1315; 1325. Beethoven died before he was able to provide the metronomizations for the *Missa Solemnis*. Schott published the work shortly after his death.

121. Anderson, *Beethoven*, 1343–1345.

122. See n. 117.

123. Schindler/MacArdle, *Beethoven*, 425.

124. Nottebohm, *Beethoveniana*, I, 127. See also Beck, *Tempoproblem*, 39; William S. Newman, "Tempo in Beethoven's Instrumental Music," Pt. I, *PQ* 116 (Winter 1981–82):22.

125. E.g., Anderson, *Beethoven*, 542, 804, 1182.

126. Cf. also Franz Gerhard Wegeler and Ferdinand Ries, *Biographische Notizen über Beethoven* (Coblenz: Bädeker, 1838), 31.

127. Beck, *Tempoproblem*, 56.

128. Anderson, *Beethoven*, 286.

129. Robert Münster, "Authentische Tempi zu den Sechs Letzten Sinfonien W. A. Mozarts?" *Mozart-Jahrbuch* 1962–1963:185–199, especially 198–199. The arrangements are for piano, flute, violin, and cello.

130. William Malloch, "Toward a 'New' (Old) Minuet," *Opus* I/5 (August 1985):17–19. Discussion of metronomizations by Czerny and Moscheles follows below.

131. Thayer/Forbes, *Beethoven,* 808. It would appear from the context in Thayer/Dieters/Riemann (IV, 309), that the source of this report was Anton F. Schindler, *Biographie von Ludwig van Beethoven,* 3d ed., 2 vols. (Münster: Aschendorff, 1860), II, 9.

132. Thayer/Forbes, *Beethoven,* 940–941.

133. H. Bertram Cox and C. L. E. Cox, *Leaves from the Journals of Sir George Smart* (London: Longmans, Green, 1907), 108–109. Two days later Smart heard Beethoven improvise "for about twenty minutes in a most extraordinary manner, sometimes very fortissimo, but full of genius. . . . We all wrote to him by turns, but he can hear a little if you halloo quite close to his left ear" (ibid., 115).

134. Stadlen, "Beethoven and the Metronome," 332–334.

135. Rudolf Kolisch, "Tempo and Character in Beethoven's Music," Pt. I, *MQ* XXIX/2 (April 1943):177.

136. A prime example is Schumann's *Kinderszenen,* Op. 15, for which several of his metronomizations have been considered excessively fast (e.g., $\bd = 138$ for "Hasche-Mann"). Brian Schlotel's article "Schumann and the Metronome" is an interesting discussion of these very problems (in *Robert Schumann, The Man and His Music,* ed. Alan Walker [London: Barrie and Jenkins, 1972], 109–119).

137. Unfortunately, Kolisch's article is not worked out as systematically as Beck's *Studien über das Tempoproblem bei Beethoven,* but Beck does not include as much of the piano repertoire. See also Newman, "Tempo in Beethoven's Instrumental Music."

138. Stadlen, "Beethoven and the Metronome," 333. According to this account it was not always easy for Beethoven to determine with which note value to give the metronomization.

139. David Fallows, "Tempo and expression marks," *NG,* XVIII, 681.

140. Anton Schindler, *The Life of Beethoven,* trans and ed. Moscheles, 2 vols. (London: Colburn, 1841), II, 111, fn.

141. Max Rudolf, *The Grammar of Conducting,* 2d ed. (New York: Schirmer Books, 1980), 329. See also Rudolf, "The Metronome Indications in Beethoven's Symphonies" [n. 56 above], 2–3.

142. Nevertheless, it must be stated that Beethoven's metronomizations are still considered controversial by some. In spite of the many differences in present-day performance circumstances—not the least of which is the difference in the instruments used, Peter Stadlen has taken the point of view that since many of Beethoven's metronomizations have not been precisely met in the recorded performances he has studied, the problem lies with Beethoven's tempo choices rather than the other way around ("Beethoven und das Metronom," *Beethoven Kolloquium 1977,* 57–75). After determining through many resourceful experiments that Beethoven's metronome must have been functioning accurately, Stadlen speculated that some of the "incorrect" tempos resulted from misreading the metronome: specifically, from looking at the numbers from an angle (usually from above) and without pressing the pendulum close to the vertical scale. This speculation not only denigrates Beethoven's intelligence but fails to account for the fact that in one and the same work (e.g., Symphonies Nos. 5 and 9, Quartet Op. 59/3) some metronomizations may be deemed either too fast, too fast though reached, reachable, or even too slow, while others are judged to be fine (ibid., 69–72). As Rainer Riehn points out, had Stadlen included in his study recordings by such eminent Beethoven interpreters as Scherchen, Leibowitz, the Kolisch Quartet, and the LaSalle Quartet, "his metronomic statistics would have been changed significantly" ("Eine musikalische Schlittenfahrt oder Wie man sich um Beethovens Anweisung scherte," in Metzger and Riehn, eds., *Beethoven, Das Problem der Interpretation,* 97, fn. 1).

Herbert Seifert disputes Stadlen's misreading theory on the grounds that the "incorrect" tempos seem to be much more prevalent in first movements, slow movements, and *andantes*, rather than being distributed uniformly throughout the movement types ("Beethovens Metronomisierungen und die Praxis," *Beethoven Kolloquium 1977,* 187). Erich Leinsdorf supports Beethoven's metronomizations in *The Composer's Advocate,* chap. 6.

143. Czerny, *Proper Performance,* 3.

144. Czerny, *Richtigen Vortrag,* 57–59.

145. Schindler/Moscheles, *Beethoven,* II, 252, fn.*. Beethoven instructed Ries to "remove the Assai" in his letter of 16 April 1819, which also had the metronomizations for the first English edition of Op. 106, published by the Regent's Harmonic Institution in October 1819 (Anderson, *Beethoven,* 806).

146. Johann Friedrich Reichardt, *Vertraute Briefe geschrieben auf einer Reise nach Wien, 1808–1809,* 2 vols. (Amsterdam: Im Kunst- und Industrie-Comtoir, 1810), I, 388; *NG,* XII, 599. Although it is clear from his diary that Moscheles preferred pianos with a lighter touch, there is no mention of his having owned a Viennese instrument. In France he played on Pape's pianos; in England he preferred "Clementi's more supple mechanism" until around 1831. From then on the Érards with the double escapement, manufactured in London as well as in Paris, were his favorite instruments (Charlotte Moscheles, *Life of Moscheles,* trans. A. D. Coleridge, 2 vols. [London: Hurst and Blackett, 1873], e.g., I, 40, 51, 65; II, 230–232). See also above chap. 2, n. 2, and p. 47 regarding the relationship between Érard and the English builders.

147. Czerny, *Proper Performance,* Commentary, 6.

148. Artur Schnabel, Angel GRM 4005, recorded in 1935.

149. Paul Badura-Skoda, Musical Heritage Society ORB-375/385, [1970]; Astrée AS 47, 1979.

150. Peter Serkin, Pro Arte PAD 181, 1984; Friedrich Gulda, Amadeo 415 193-2, 1968.

151. E.g., Malcolm Binns, L'Oiseau-Lyre D185 D3, 1981; Alfred Brendel, Murray Hill S-3456 [1968]; Rudolf Serkin, Columbia M 30081, [1971?].

152. Otto Erich Deutsch, "Beethovens gesammelte Werke: Des Meisters Plan und Haslingers Ausgabe," *Zeitschrift für Musikwissenschaft* XIII/2 (November 1930):66.

153. Nottebohm, *Beethoveniana,* II, 357.

154. Ibid., I, 136; this comment refers specifically to Czerny's indications of 1846. Czerny told Nottebohm that he had studied with Beethoven the Sonatas Opp. 13, 14/1 and 2, 31/2, and 101; the Andante from Op. 28; the Piano Concertos Nos. 1, 3, 4, and 5; the Choral Fantasy; the Piano Trio Op. 97; "and many others" (Czerny, *Proper Performance,* Introduction, 3). Paul Badura-Skoda considers this list "probably rather too modest." Czerny's memoirs indicate that he had played the Sonatas Opp. 53 and 57 for Beethoven: "Schindler tells us that Czerny studied Op. 106 with Beethoven 'several times.' Finally a certain internal evidence suggests that Czerny was aware of Beethoven's intentions concerning (at least) the Sonatas Op. 26, Op. 27/2, Op. 31/2 and 3, Op. 81a, the Diabelli Variations and the Kreutzer Sonata, . . . Czerny's extraordinary memory . . . is, together with his irreproachable character, a reasonable guarantee of the reliability of his statements" (ibid.).

155. Czerny, *Proper Performance,* 108.

156. Anderson, *Beethoven,* 231–232.

157. Czerny, *Richtigen Vortrag,* 93.

158. Schindler/MacArdle, *Beethoven,* 426–427.

159. Schindler/Moscheles, *Beethoven,* II, 106–107, fn.†. Readers may judge for themselves, using data in Appendix B, the accuracy of Moscheles's "very slightly" to describe how much his metronomizations in the Cramer edition differed from those of Haslinger 1. Opinions notwithstanding, Moscheles ranks as a knowledgeable devotee of Beethoven's music. (Cf. Schindler/Moscheles, *Beethoven,* I, vi–xxi; Alan Tyson, "Moscheles

and his 'Complete Edition' of Beethoven," *The Music Review* 25/2 [1964]:136–141; and chap. 1, n. 181 above.)

Although it says nothing specific on the topic of tempo, the following excerpt from a review in the London *Times* of 4 May 1841 attests to Moscheles's importance as an interpreter of Beethoven's music: "Artists and amateurs now are glad to own that Beethoven's Ninth Symphony is as much remarkable for majesty and grandeur as for simplicity. For this recognition we are in a great measure indebted to Moscheles, who conducted the work with great care and conscientiousness. As a conductor he surpasses almost all our musicians, for whenever he swings his baton he leads the orchestra, whereas others are led by it.... He is one who inspires the orchestra with a respect due to him, and would always lead it onwards to new successes" (C. Moscheles, *Life*, II, 87).

160. Date according to Newman, "Checklist," 511. "Opp. 2–57 ..., except 22 and 54, were published in 1856; all remaining sonatas through Op. 101 in 1862; and the last 4 in 1868" (ibid.).

161. Deutsch, "Beethoven's gesammelte Werke," 64, 67, 68–69. When permission was granted some time later, Haslinger published Opp. 2 and 7 without metronomizations.

162. "State" is used here as defined by D. W. Krummel in *Guide for Dating Early Published Music* (Hackensack, NJ: Boonin, 1974), 32: "The term *state* (or *variant*) can be applied to any form of musical publication which exhibits variations in content caused by purposeful alteration of the printing surface."

163. The first date is suggested in Newman, "Checklist," 510; the second in Alexander Weinmann, "Tobias Haslingers 'Gesamtausgabe der Werke Beethovens,' " in *Beiträge zur Beethoven Bibliographie*, ed. Kurt Dorfmüller (Munich: Henle, 1978), 271. According to *AMZ*, fourteen sonatas had been issued by January 1831 (XXXIII/2 [12 January 1831], cols. 30–31), and the entire set of 30 is listed in Carl Friedrich Whistling, *Handbuch der musikalischen Literatur*, ed. Adolph Hofmeister (Leipzig: Fr. Hofmeister, 1834), 129. (In the reprint by Olms [Hildesheim, 1975], this reference is II, 129.) Although this catalog is supposed to contain works "newly issued" from January 1829 to the end of 1833, it is possible that the publisher might have submitted the names of some works awaiting publication. This uncertainty arises because Haslinger's catalog of 1837 lists all 30 sonatas in the series, but a review that ran from 23 February to 30 March 1837 in Haslinger's house organ, *Allgemeine Musikalische Anzeiger*, includes only Sonatas Nos. 1 to 22, leaving room for suspicion that the first state may have been completed later than 1837 (Deutsch, "Beethovens gesammelte Werke," 70).

The *terminus ante quem* (latest possible date) for insertion of the new metronomizations in most of the sonatas is 1842, for I have seen all but eight of this second state under the imprint of Tobias Haslinger, who died on 18 June 1842, after which the imprint read *Witwe* (widow) Haslinger. (Date of death from *NG*, VIII, 275.) The only copies I have seen of Opp. 13 and 26 with the later metronomizations were newly engraved and bear the imprint of Carl Haslinger, therefore dating from after March 1848, when Tobias's widow died. However, it is likely that the new indications had been put into earlier issues of those two works under Tobias's name; re-engraving was sometimes necessitated by the wear of the old plates because of the popularity of a work. Unfortunately six Sonatas, Opp. 78, 79, 81, and 109–111, seem to have been issued in both states without imprints, making it more difficult to estimate the dates of their second states.

164. The intervals between adjacent steps on a metronome vary from 3.5 to 5.5 percent of the value. The average difference between adjacent steps is 4.4 percent, between intervals of three steps, 14 percent. (I wish to thank my husband, Louis Rosenblum, for these calculations.) Interestingly, in 1950 N. Garbuzov concluded that "tempo change can be distinguished only when it deviates more than 4 percent from the given or expected tempo" (Joachim Braun, "Beethoven's Fourth Symphony: Com-

parative Analysis of Recorded Performances," *Israel Studies in Musicology* I [1978]:68). Compare Rudolf, *The Grammar of Conducting*, 323.

165. A seventh, the Andante of Op. 49/1, is not included in these percentages since it is not metronomized in all four sets under discussion.

166. Sachs, *Rhythm and Tempo*, 314, 317, 320–324.

167. E. Bach, *Essay*, 148.

168. Joseph Fischhof, "Auffassung von Instrumentalkompositionen in Hinsicht des Zeitmasses, namentlich bei Beethoven'schen Werken," *Caecilia* XXVI (1847):88.

169. Edward Holmes, *A Ramble among the Musicians of Germany*, 2d ed. (London: Whittaker, Treacher, 1830), 180.

170. Fischhof, "Auffassung von Instrumentalkompositionen . . . " [n. 168 above], 87.

171. Adam Carse, *The Orchestra from Beethoven to Berlioz* (Cambridge, England: Heffer, 1948), 351–352. Also Georg Schünemann, *Geschichte des Dirigierens* (Leipzig: Breitkopf & Härtel, 1913), 283–291; and "Beethoven's 'Moderate' Minuets" below.

172. Schünemann, *Geschichte des Dirigierens*, 283–291.

173. G. W. Fink, "Über das Bedürfniss, Mozart's Hauptwerke unserer Zeit so metronomisirt zu liefern, wie der Meister selbst sie ausführen liess," *AMZ* XLI/25 (19 June 1839), col. 477. In the context of the article, "exaggerated" means "too fast."

174. Hector Berlioz, *Selections from his Letters, and Aesthetic, Humorous, and Satirical Writings*, trans. William P. Apthorp (New York: Holt, 1879), 99–100.

175. Carse, *The Orchestra* [n. 171 above], 365.

176. Ottmar Schreiber, *Orchester und Orchesterpraxis in Deutschland zwischen 1780 und 1850* (Berlin: Triltisch & Huther, 1938), 289.

177. *AMZ* XLVI/10 (6 March 1844), col. 164.

178. Braun, "Beethoven's Fourth Symphony" [n. 164 above], 58.

179. Carse, *The Orchestra* [n. 171 above], 372. Pp. 369–373 describe Habeneck's way of working and his influence on the role of the orchestra conductor.

180. "Musikalisches aus Paris," *Neue Zeitschrift für Musik* XXIII/5 (15 July 1845):19.

181. Anton Schindler, *Beethoven in Paris* (Münster: Aschendorff, 1842), 19, 44.

182. Richard Wagner, *On Conducting*, 1869 (in German); trans. Edward Dannreuther (London: Reeves, 1887), 34–37. Schünemann contrasted the "fresh, joyful rendering of the Mendelssohn school" with Wagner's "pathetic, sentimental" interpretation (*Geschichte des Dirigierens* [n. 171 above], 341).

183. C. Moscheles, *Life*, II, 286. Moscheles was born in 1794.

184. Cf. Braun, "Beethoven's Fourth Symphony" [n. 164 above], 58.

185. In a paper that supports Beethoven's metronomizations, Herbert Seifert notes that in Haslinger's *Gesamtausgabe* the String Quartets Op. 18, which were published before December 1833, carry metronomizations of which 63 percent are slower and 23 percent are faster than the composer's own ("Beethovens Metronomisierungen und die Praxis," in *Beethoven Kolloquium, 1977*, 185–186).

Those indications are probably by Ignaz Schuppanzigh or Karl Holz. Schuppanzigh's relationship to Beethoven is described on p. 90. Holz was an able amateur violinist and conductor. He was a member of Joseph Böhm's string quartet and later (1823–1830) of Schuppanzigh's. From 1824 he was a close friend of Beethoven. About 1825 Holz became part-time, and in 1829 regular, conductor of the Concerts spirituels of Vienna.

Both men were from Beethoven's close circle, yet whoever prepared the metronomizations for Haslinger felt compelled—even at that early date—to slow down more than half the movements, with a substantial number from every movement and tempo type. Was this catering to the practical needs of the less-able string players, or was it done out of conviction that Beethoven's tempos were simply too fast for the music? The latter would reflect a difference in tempo ideal between the composer and some of his closest colleagues. Significantly, neither Czerny nor Hummel altered Beethoven's metronomizations; both repeated them on arrangements for piano that they made of the symphonies (ibid., 184).

Emil Platen states that Karl Holz's metronomizations for Beethoven's last five quartets, published in Wilhelm von Lenz, *Beethoven, Eine Kunststudie,* 2d ed., 5 vols. (Hamburg: Hoffmann & Campe, 1860), V, 224–228, are unrealistically slow for the movements that Beethoven wanted performed in a "particularly lively" way ("Zeitgenössische Hinweise zur Aufführungspraxis der letzten Streichquartette Beethovens," in *Beethoven Kolloquium, 1977,* 101).

186. See n. 154 for the list of works Czerny may have studied with Beethoven.

187. Tyson, "Moscheles and his 'Complete Edition' of Beethoven" [n. 159 above], 136–137.

188. Newman "Checklist," 512. Moscheles's third set of metronomizations, different again from those of the Hallberger edition, is in the "second improved edition" of Beethoven's Sonatas published by Holle of Wolfenbüttel. Since "révue par H. W. Stolze" appears over Opp. 2, 7, 106, 109, and 111 in this second edition, and since Stolze died in 1868, it is likely that the edition was properly prepared and published at least in part by that date. Its appearance was not recorded in *Handbuch der musikalischen Literatur* published by Fr. Hofmeister in Leipzig. (Holle's original edition was published in 1857 under the editorship of Franz Liszt, who added relatively little and very few metronomizations [William S. Newman, "Liszt's Interpreting of Beethoven's Piano Sonatas," *MQ* LVIII/2 (April 1972):200–203].) I have not been able to locate a copy of Vol. I of the "second improved edition."

189. I have avoided the term "slow" minuet (Beck, *Tempoproblem,* 166; Rudolf, "Temponahme bei Mozart," 218) because of its possible influence on performance tempos.

The various spelling and forms of the word minuet do not differentiate specific dance types or tempos, as *courante* and *corrente* do. *Menuet* is the French spelling, *Menuett* the German, and *minuetto* the Italian. *Menuetto,* apparently a mixture of *Menuett* and *minuetto,* is used only in non-Italian works (*NG,* XII, 167).

190. Meredith E. Little, "Minuet," *NG,* XII, 356.

191. Rousseau, *Dictionnaire,* 277.

192. *Mozart: Briefe und Aufzeichnungen,* ed. Wilhelm A. Bauer and Otto Erich Deutsch, 7 vols. (Kassel: Bärenreiter, 1962–1975), I, 323.

193. These metronomizations, derived from eighteenth-century measurements that use the pendulum (L'Affilard, La Chapelle, Choquel) and the pulse (Quantz), are from Ralph Kirkpatrick, "Eighteenth-Century Metronomic Indications," *Papers Read at the American Musicological Society Annual Meeting, 1938* (Printed by the Society, 1940), 40–46; and Quantz, *Flute,* 291–292.

194. Münster, "Authentische Tempi" [n. 129 above], 191–196.

195. William Malloch offers additional evidence of appropriate tempos for the Classic minuet from metronomizations by Czerny (in *Proper Performance* and other sources), Hummel, and Antoine Reicha ("Minuet," 14–21, 52). However, the musical clocks cannot provide any absolute tempo information for their minuets, Malloch's statements notwithstanding. Beyond the necessary replacement of the original springs that control the speed, leaving us unsure of the relative speeds of old and new, these mechanical organs were designed with easily adjustable air-brakes that could materially affect their speed. The clock of 1793, for example, can be adjusted sufficiently to play in double or half tempo (Sonja Gerlach and George Hill, eds., *JHW,* XXI, *Flötenuhrstücke,* 62; also Sonja Gerlach, "Haydn's Works for Musical Clock," *Haydn Studies,* 127). Apparently the metronomizations for pieces from the clocks given by several writers and Malloch's statement that these devices "play within a fairly narrow range" ("Minuet," 19) must be viewed guardedly.

196. Rudolf, "Temponahme bei Mozart," 218, 205–206, fn. 6. Wenzel J. Tomášek, Bohemian composer and teacher, came to Prague as a student in 1790, three years after

Mozart had conducted the premiere and several other performances of *Don Giovanni* at the Prague Opera. Mozart was back in Prague at the end of summer 1791 for the premiere of *La clemenza di Tito*. Rudolf has pointed out that Tomášek "could have heard the performance of *Don Giovanni* in September [2 September 1791] that was probably conducted by Mozart himself " (ibid., 205–206, fn. 6). Tomášek was a devotee of Mozart and at the least "he heard the same orchestra and singers trained by Mozart" in so many performances of this opera "that he was able to play the complete opera by ear at the keyboard" (Fink, "Über das Bedürfniss, Mozart's Hauptwerke . . . metronomisirt zu liefern" [n. 173 above], cols. 479–480). Fink implied that Tomášek had prepared the metronomizations in the article not long before its publication in June 1839.

197. Rudolf, *The Grammar of Conducting*, 341.

198. Both the Grumiaux Trio (Philips 6770-159, [1978]) and the Heifetz, Primrose, and Piatagorsky ensemble (RCA Victor LM-2180, [1958]) have recorded the Menuetto, Moderato of Op. 3 at ♩ = ca. 144, which is very close to the Haslinger indication, but the Menuetto, Allegretto at ♩. = 54, which seems too slow to me and which minimizes the intended contrast between the movements.

199. Newman, "Tempo," Pt. I, 26.

200. Compare Newman, "Tempo," Pt. II, 24–26; German, 172–173.

201. Throughout this section a quarter note is implicit wherever the note value is not specified.

202. Bruno Walter, Columbia ML 4696, [1953]; Felix Weingartner, Columbia ML 4508, [1952]; Karl Böhm, DGG 2707 073, [1974]; Wilhelm Furtwängler, Olympic OL 8129, [1974]; Arturo Toscanini, RCA Victor LM-6901, recorded 1952.

203. Richard Wagner, *Mein Leben* (Munich: List Verlag, 1963), 322–323. In his book *On Conducting*, Wagner related a repetition of this incident with Ferdinand Hiller, Mendelssohn's successor at the Gewandhaus Concerts [n. 182 above] (p. 29).

204. Henry Edward Krehbiel, *Review of the New York Musical Season 1888–1889* (New York and London: Novello, Ewer, 1889), 181, 177.

205. Ibid., 176–181; see also the *Review of the . . . Season 1887–1888* (New York and London: Novello, Ewer, 1888), 136–137; and Nottebohm, *Beethoveniana*, I, 135. Von Bülow also considered the Menuetto, Moderato e grazioso of Op. 31/3 and the minuet Allegretto ma non troppo of the Piano Trio Op. 70/2 the slow movements of those works, since these minuets as well were contrasted with "a *Scherzo* (more or less quick) in the rhythm of 2-4" (Krehbiel, *Review . . . 1888–1889* [n. 204 above], 177). However, the tempo unit (note value in which the rhythm moves and to which tempo headings apply) of both the Allegretto (second movement) of the Trio and the Allegretto scherzando (second movement) of the Eighth Symphony is the eighth note, which Beethoven metronomized at ♪ = 88 for the symphony movement. Since speed is perceived as the time between tempo units, these movements—not the "slow" movements of their works. Czerny metronomized Op. 70/2/ii at ♪ = 116 and iii at ♩ = 126. Many modern performers play iii still faster. (Op. 31/3 is discussed below.)

206. Boston Symphony Chamber Players, Nonesuch N-78015, 1982; Members of the Vienna Octet, London LL 1191, [1955]. Beethoven's metronomization for the Scherzo, Allegro molto e vivace in Op. 20 is ♩. = 126. Its rhythm moves in quarter, half, and dotted half notes, with one extended passage of eighth notes for the first violin.

207. Amadeus Quartet, Deutsche Grammophon 2563 258, 1960; Juilliard Quartet, Columbia D3M 34094, [1976].

208. Artur Schnabel, Angel GRM 4005, recorded 1933; Paul Badura-Skoda, Musical Heritage Society ORB-382, [1970]; Angel S-36491, [1967].

209. Czerny, *Richtigen Vortrag*, 40.

210. Friedrich Gulda, Amadeo 415 193-2, 1968.

211. Murray Perahia, Columbia M36695, 1982.

212. Czerny, *Proper Performance*, 45.

213. Friedrich Gulda, Amadeo 415 193-2, 1968; Glenn Gould, Columbia M32349, [1973].

214. It is not known which of the editors of the Haslinger edition metronomized the Sonatas for Violin and Piano.

215. Czerny, *Richtigen Vortrag*, 74.

216. E.g., Arthur Grumiaux and Clara Haskil, Epic LC 3488, [1958]; Henryk Szeryng and Artur Rubinstein, RCA Victor LSC-2620, [1962]; Yehudi Menuhin and Wilhelm Kempff, Deutsche Grammophon 2530-135, [1974?].

217. Czerny, *Proper Performance*, 48. In the Simrock edition, the metronomizations are ♩ = 120 for this movement and ♩ = 108 for the Allegretto. The engraver may have reversed the numbers (not uncommon in the transfer of such indications), for otherwise Czerny's successive indications for the Allegretto would be ♩ = 76, ♩ = 144, and then the surprising ♩ = 108, which reverses his previous slow–fast movement order.

218. Artur Schnabel, Angel GRM 4005, recorded in 1933.

219. Czerny, *Proper Performance*, Commentary, 4; Badura-Skoda, Musical Heritage Society ORB-378, [1970].

220. Wilhelm Backhaus, London CM 9057, [1960].

221. The metronomizations of ♩ = 96 for Op. 34, Var. 4, and ♩ = 92 for Op. 30/3/ii may have some tangential corroborating evidence from Beethoven's "Battle" Symphony Op. 91, which was written for Maelzel's Panharmonikon (a mechanical organ) in 1813, less than a year after the completion of the Eighth Symphony. Nottebohm reported that on both manuscripts of the "Battle" Symphony—the arrangement for Maelzel and the one for orchestra—there are numerical tempo indications probably made with the chronometer and "without doubt from Maelzel's hand." (Nottebohm stated further that measurements made on the chronometer and the later metronome are equivalent.) The amusing "Tempo di Menuetto moderato," based on "God Save the King" and replete with trills for full orchestra and ornamental 32d notes, is marked ♩ = 96. "It is not improbable that these tempos were added according to Beethoven's direction" (Nottebohm, *Beethoveniana*, I, 136–137).

222. Denis Matthews, Vanguard 1032, [1958].

223. E.g., Rudolf Buchbinder, Telefunken SMA 25 081-T/1-3, 1973; Artur Schnabel, Seraphim IC 6067, recorded ca. 1935; Peter Serkin, RCA Red Seal ARL1-4276, 1982.

224. Charles Rosen, Peters Intl. PLE 042, 1977; Leonard Shure, Epic LC 3382, [195?].

225. Cf. interpretations of Paul Badura-Skoda (on both piano, Musical Heritage Society ORB-375/385, [1970] and fortepiano, Pro Arte PAL-1017, recorded 1965, pub. [1981]); Friedrich Gulda (Amadeo 415 193-2, 1968); Malcolm Binns (L'Oiseau-Lyre DSLO 603, 1981); and Malcolm Bilson (Advent E1056, 1977). See also Malloch, "Minuet," 14–21, 52.

226. Arturo Toscanini, RCA Victor LM-1745, [1953].

227. Amadeus Quartet, Deutsche Grammophon 2563 258, 1960; Juilliard Quartet, Columbia D3M 30084, [197?].

228. Friedrich Gulda plays at 120–126 (Amadeo 415 193-2, 1968); Alfred Brendel plays at ca. 104 (Murray Hill S-3456, [1968]); Paul Badura-Skoda starts at 92 (Musical Heritage Society ORB-382, [1970]); Murray Perahia at 88 (Columbia M36695, 1982); and Jörg Demus on fortepiano at ca. 76 (Musical Heritage Society MHS 3038, [1975]).

229. Clementi/Rosenblum, *Introduction*, 13.

230. Ibid., 14.

231. Leon Plantinga, *Clementi, His Life and Music* (London: Oxford University Press, 1977), 283–284. William Crotch was a well-known English composer, organist, and professor of music at Oxford University.

232. Cf. Paul Honigsheim, "Musikformen und Gesellschaftsformen," in *Texte zur Musiksoziologie*, ed. Tiber Kneif (Köln: Volk, 1975), 32; Zaslaw, "Mozart's Tempo Conventions," 723.

10. Flexibility of Rhythm and Tempo

1. Cf. Edward T. Cone, *Musical Form and Musical Performance* (New York: Norton, 1968), 76–82.

2. Carl Philipp Emanuel Bach, *Essay on the True Art of Playing Keyboard Instruments*, trans. and ed. William J. Mitchell (New York: Norton, 1949), 161.

3. Heinrich Christoph Koch, ed., *Journal der Tonkunst*, 2 vols. (Erfurt: Keyser, 1795), I, 112.

4. Hummel, *Pianoforte*, Pt. III, 41.

5. Ibid., 47; the German reads "small ornaments" rather than "graces." Cf. Hummel's examples of tempo change for his Piano Concerto Op. 81, ibid., Pt. III, 43–50.

6. Schulz, "Vortrag," in Sulzer, *Allgemeine Theorie*, II, 1255.

7. Daniel Gottlob Türk, *Klavierschule* (Leipzig and Halle: Schwickert; Hemmerde und Schwetschke, 1789), facs., ed. Erwin R. Jacobi (Kassel: Bärenreiter, 1962), 369.

8. Ibid., 370. The bracketed addition is Türk's explanation from the following paragraph.

9. Czerny, *Proper Performance*, 26.

10. Türk, *Klavierschule*, 334, 338–339.

11. E. Bach, *Essay*, 150.

12. Carl Philipp Emanuel Bach, *Versuch über die wahre Art das Clavier zu spielen*, 2 vols. (Berlin: In Verlegung des Auctoris, 1753, 1762); facs., ed. Lothar Hoffmann-Erbrecht (Leipzig: Breitkopf & Härtel, 1978), 129. In Mitchell's edition of the *Essay*, the crosses in the first example of Fig. 10.1 are mistakenly placed directly over the notes C, E-natural, and F-sharp.

13. E. Bach, *Essay*, 375.

14. Türk, *Klavierschule*, 338; see also p. 90 above.

15. Hugo Riemann, *Musikalische Dynamik und Agogik* (Hamburg: Rahter, 1884).

16. Türk, *Klavierschule*, 338.

17. Ibid., 338–339. Leopold Mozart also described agogic accentuation of the first note under a slur (*A Treatise on the Fundamental Principles of Violin Playing*, trans. Editha Knocker, 2d ed. [London: Oxford University Press, 1951], 220).

18. E.g., Wilhelm Backhaus, London CM 9087, [1960]; Charles Rosen, Nonesuch NC-78010, 1981.

19. For related comments on some agogic aspects of performance, see *Haydn Studies*, 274.

20. The playing of Malcolm Bilson and an article by Vera Schwarz, "Missverständnisse in der Haydn-Interpretation," *Österreichische Musikzeitschrift* XXI/I (January 1976):23–25, brought the importance of the rhetorical rest to my attention. Schwarz introduced the basic ideas from Marpurg. See also "Music and Rhetoric" in chap. 1.

21. Friedrich Wilhelm Marpurg, *Kritische Briefe über die Tonkunst*, 4 vols. (Berlin: Birnsteil, 1760–1764; facs., Hildesheim: Olms, 1974), II (1763), 309–310.

22. Ibid., 4.

23. Ibid., 34.

24. Ibid., 366–367.

25. Ibid., 342, 369–372.

26. Ibid., 373.

27. Ibid., 346, 348, 374.

28. Heinrich Christoph Koch, *Musikalisches Lexikon* (Frankfurt: Hermann dem jüngern, 1802; facs., Hildesheim: Olms, 1964), cols. 562–563.

29. David Fallows suggests that Frescobaldi intended this use of *adagio* in the Preface to the Toccatas of 1615 and in the *Fiori Musicali* of 1635, and that Brossard's definition includes the same implication (*NG*, I, 88). See also Beethoven, Op. 5/1/ii/280–282 (*BNA*).

30. In several piano concertos there are interjections of *adagio* that could be interpreted with varying combinations of immediate tempo change and *ritard:* e.g., K. 246/i/cadenza (*NMA*), K. 413/i/224 (*NMA*).

31. Türk, *Klavierschule,* 1st ed., 371; 2d ed. (Leipzig and Halle: Schwickert; Hemmerde und Schwetschke, 1802), 415. Emanuel Bach pointed out a passage in the Adagio non molto of his "Württemberg" Sonata No. 6 in B minor where "an idea with octaves in the right hand and with rapid notes in the left hand is transposed three times [mm. 44–51]; this can be performed effectively with a gradual gentle acceleration in each transposition, which alternates immediately thereafter with a ritard" (E. Bach, *Versuch,* 129).

32. Türk, *Klavierschule,* 1st ed., 371. In the 1802 edition the paragraph opens, "In passages that are distinguished from the others by an especially tender, languishing, melancholy effect and the like, . . ." (ibid., 2d ed., 415).

33. Türk, *Klavierschule,* 372.

34. Clementi/Rosenblum, *Introduction,* 14.

35. Czerny, *Piano Forte,* III, 34.

36. Czerny, *Proper Performance,* 23.

37. Türk, *Klavierschule,* 304. This advice is in the section on ornamented *fermatas.*

38. *Haydn Studies,* 272–273.

39. E.g., Czerny, *Piano Forte,* III, 33–34.

40. Czerny, *Proper Performance,* e.g., 29 (third musical example), 33, 35, etc. See also p. 391 below.

41. Türk, *Klavierschule,* 372 (end par. 68).

42. Ibid., 373.

43. Ibid., 372; 2d ed., 416. In the 1787 edition of the *Versuch,* Bach had added "when passages in a piece in a major key are repeated in a minor key, the repetition may be a little slower because of the affect" (3d ed. [Leipzig: Schwickert, 1787], 99).

44. Türk, *Klavierschule,* 373.

45. See "Ritenuto," *NG,* XVI, 57; Hans Heinrich Eggebrecht, ed., *Handwörterbuch der Musikalischen Terminologie* (Weisbaden: Steiner, 1972), "Retardatio, ritardando," I, 6–7.

46. Christoph Eschenbach (Deutsche Grammophon 2720031, [1971]), Walter Gieseking (Angel ANG 35068, [1956]), and Lili Kraus (Odyssey Y3-33220, [1974]) alter their tempos; Malcolm Bilson (Golden Crest CRS-4097, [197?]) and Alicia de Larrocha (London CS7008, 1976) maintain their tempos.

47. Czerny, *Richtigen Vortrag,* 87. The B theme actually begins in m. 59.

48. Cf. Alfred Brendel, Murray Hill Records S-3456, [1968].

49. Curt Sachs, *Rhythm and Tempo* (New York: Norton, 1953), 307.

50. Pier Francesco Tosi, *Opinioni de' cantori antichi, e moderni o sieno Osservazioni sopra il canto Figurato* (Bologna: dalla Volpe, 1723); trans. and ed. [Johann Ernst] Galliard, *Observations on the Florid Song; or, Sentiments on the Ancient and Modern Singers* (London: Wilcox, 1742); 2d ed., 1743 (rep., London: Reeves, 1926), 129.

51. Ibid., 156.

52. Ibid., fn. 41. Johann Ernst Galliard (ca. 1687–1749), a north German, went to London in 1706, where until his death he carried on an active musical career, much of it associated with various forms of theater. Apparently he had known Tosi (*NG,* VII, 108), a much-admired *castrato* and singing teacher who spent several periods of time in London.

53. L. Mozart, *Violin,* 224, fn. 1; 223–224.

54. E. Bach, *Versuch,* 3d ed. [n. 43 above], Pt. I, 99–100 (*Essay,* 161–162). Mitchell's translation, "Most keyboard pieces contain rubato passages," is not in the original German, which reads, "In meinen Clavier-Sachen findet man viele Proben von diesem Tempo" (100).

55. Carl Philipp Emanuel Bach, *Sechs Sonaten fürs Clavier mit veränderten Reprisen,* 1760; ed. Etienne Darbellay (Winterthur, Switzerland: Amadeus, 1976), xvii. Darbellay discusses many examples of Bach's *rubato* ornamentation.

56. Heinrich Christoph Koch, "Über den technischen Ausdruck: Tempo rubato," *AMZ* X/33 (11 May 1808), cols. 518-519. Franz Benda (1709-1786) was a virtuoso violinist who served in the musical establishment of Frederick the Great.

57. Charles Burney, *Dr. Burney's Musical Tours in Europe,* 2 vols., 2d ed. (London: Becket, Robson, and Robinson, 1773, 1775); ed. Percy A. Scholes (London: Oxford University Press, 1959), II, 173.

58. Ibid., 177.

59. Koch, *Lexikon,* col. 1503.

60. Johann Friedrich Reichardt, *Briefe eines aufmerksamen Reisenden die Musik betreffend,* 2 vols. (Vol. I, Frankfurt and Leipzig, 1774; Vol. II, Frankfurt and Breslau, 1776), I, 162.

61. Johann Friedrich Agricola, *Anleitung zur Singkunst* (Berlin: Winter, 1757); facs., ed. Erwin R. Jacobi (Celle: Moeck, 1966), 219-220. By 1757, when the translation—with much added information—was published, Agricola was a distinguished singing teacher and composer of opera in the Italian style at the court of Frederick the Great. He had lived in Berlin among Marpurg, Quantz, Bach, and their contemporaries since 1741 (*NG,* I, 165).

62. Friedrich Wilhelm Marpurg, *Anleitung zum Clavierspielen* (Berlin: Haude und Spener, 1755), 40, Table II, Figs. 46, 48. Regarding figures of composition, see Leonard G. Ratner, *Classic Music* (New York: Schirmer Books, 1980), 83-85.

63. Marpurg, *Anleitung,* Index, n.p.

64. Friedrich Wilhelm Marpurg, *Principes de Clavecin* (Berlin: Haude und Spener, 1756), 52, Table II, Fig. 42; 53, Table II, Figs. 46, 50.

65. Johann Adam Hiller, *Anweisung zum musikalisch-zierlichen Gesange* (Leipzig: 1780; facs., Leipzig: Peters, 1976), 88-89, 129; Johann Baptist Lasser, *Vollständige Anleitung zur Singkunst,* 1798; 2d ed. (identical to the 1st; Munich: Hübschmann, 1805), 154, 158. Lucian Kamieński, "Zum 'Tempo rubato'," *Archiv für Musikwissenschaft* I (1918-1919):108-126, surveys this topic.

66. Türk, *Klavierschule,* 374.

67. Ibid., 375.

68. Ibid., 2d ed., 419.

69. Ibid., 1st ed., 375. Türk states that "*tempo rubato* . . . is sometimes understood" to include these effects: i.e., by some musicians (e.g., Johann Samuel Petri, *Anleitung zur Praktischen Musik,* 2d ed. [Leipzig: Breitkopf, 1782], 164).

70. Türk, *Klavierschule,* 375. (See also Friedrich Reichardt's discussion of an aria by Reinhardt Kaiser [*sic*] in Cramer's *Magazin der Musik* I [15 January 1783]:41-42.) The controversy was pursued by Schulz in Sulzer, *Allgemeine Theorie,* 2d enl. ed., "Verrükung" (IV, 653-655); by Carl von Dittersdorf in *AMZ* I/13 (26 December 1798), cols. 203-205; and again by Schulz in *AMZ* II/15 (8 January 1800), cols. 257-265 and II/16 (15 January 1800), cols. 273-280. Türk reported on it in 1802 (*Klavierschule,* 2d ed., 420, fn. *).

71. Koch, "Über . . . Tempo rubato" [n. 56 above], cols. 513-517.

72. Emily Anderson, trans. and ed., *The Letters of Mozart and His Family,* 2d ed., ed. A. Hyatt King and Monica Carolan, 2 vols. (London: Macmillan, 1966), 340.

73. Türk, *Klavierschule,* 2d ed., 418-419. See also Eva and Paul Badura-Skoda, *Interpreting Mozart on the Piano,* trans. Leo Black (London: Barrie and Rockliff, 1962), 43, about adding *rubato* in Mozart's music.

74. Schindler, however, attempted to put the words in his "master's" mouth via a forged conversation (pp. 387-388).

75. Cramer's *Magazin der Musik* I (30 March 1783):387-388.

76. E.g., Charles Rosen, Columbia M3X 30938, [ca. 1975].

77. Louis Adam, *Méthode de piano du Conservatoire* (Paris: Magasin de Musique du Conservatoire Royal, [1804]), 160.

78. Pierre Baillot, *L'Art du violon,* 1834; German ed., *Die Kunst des Violinspieles* (Leipzig: Schubert, [1840]), 182. This book is still considered an important source.

79. Carl Mikuli, ed., Chopin *Mazurkas* (New York: G. Schirmer, 1879), F. F. Chopin," n.p. There is also evidence that Chopin intended this contrametric *rubato* when he wrote "rubato" in some of his early works (e.g., Mazurkas Opp. 6/2/65 and 24/2/29, Nocturne Op. 9/2/26 [OE, Kistner], and Piano Concerto Op. 21/iii/157, 173, piano part only). For example, in Op. 6/2/65, where the completed Mazurka has "rubato," an early holograph version has the repeated melodic motive written in four equal quarter notes in the 3/4 measure. Cf. Fig. 10.7.

80. See quotations in Sachs, *Rhythm and Tempo,* 277–280.

81. Hummel appears to have written "tempo rubato" for both concepts. For "tempo rubato" as tempo flexibility, see *Pianoforte,* Pt. III, 40; for "tempo rubato" in conjunction with the systematic delaying of melody notes, see Sonatina in C major/i/83, attributed to Hummel, in *Complete Piano Sonatas,* ed. Harold Truscott (London: Musica Rara, 1975), II, 84.

82. Thomas Busby, *A Complete Dictionary of Music* (London: Phillips, [ca. 1801]), n.p.

83. Türk, *Klavierschule,* 2d ed., 421.

84. Pierre Baillot, Pierre Rode, and Rodolphe Kreutzer, *Méthode de Violon* (Brussels: Weissenbruch [1803]), 176. An anonymous review of the English translation in *Harmonicon* IV/39 (March 1826):54–55, praised the section on tempo and quoted it extensively.

85. Czerny, *Piano Forte,* III, 8.

86. Ibid., 31–33.

87. Carl Czerny, *Die Kunst des Vortrags* (Vienna: Diabelli, 1846), 31.

88. Ibid.

89. Cf. also L. Mozart's letter to his son in Anderson, *Mozart,* 455; and Badura-Skoda, *Mozart,* 40.

90. See, for example, Czerny's comments on Op. 10/1/iii, Op. 10/3/ii, and the "Moonlight" Sonata Op. 27/1/i and iii in *Proper Performance,* 30, 32, 39. (N.B. In at least one early edition and in *Proper Performance,* the sonatas of Op. 27 are reversed; thus the "Moonlight" Sonata is Op 27/1.) Schindler's stance in this regard is explored in the next section, "Schindler and Czerny on Tempo Flexibility in Beethoven's Piano Music."

91. Paul Badura-Skoda remarks that "the greatest virtuosos" find it "impossible" to play the run in m. 53 in strict tempo, as Czerny recommended. "Czerny probably meant bars 54–56" (*Proper Performance,* Commentary, 3). Czerny was actually writing about the recapitulation (*Proper Performance,* 45), where the unaccompanied run that starts in m. 177 is longer, hence perhaps ordinarily more subject to variation. Would a Viennese fortepiano allow today's virtuosos to play mm. 53 and 177 in strict tempo?

92. Franz Gerhard Wegeler and Ferdinand Ries, *Biographische Notizen über Beethoven* (Koblenz: Bädeker, 1838), 106. The concert in which Ries played took place on 19 July 1804. It was reviewed in the *AMZ* of 15 August: "Herr Ries, who took the solo part, is, at present, Beethoven's only pupil and his most fervent admirer. He had prepared the piece entirely under the direction of his teacher and gave proof of a very smooth expressive execution as well as unusual polish and sureness, overcoming with ease the most extraordinary difficulties" (H. C. Robbins Landon, *Beethoven* [New York: Macmillan, 1970], 131).

93. Oscar Sonneck, ed., *Beethoven: Impressions by His Contemporaries,* facs. (New York: Dover, 1967), 41.

94. Schindler's comment on tempo flexibility in orchestral music is of interest here: "That orchestral music does not admit of such frequent changes of time as chamber

music, is, of course, an understood fact. But it is equally well known that in orchestral performances the greatest and most unexpected effects [*efforts* in Moscheles's translation is an error] may be produced by even slight variations of time" (Anton F. Schindler, *The Life of Beethoven,* trans. and ed. Ignaz Moscheles, 2 vols. [London: Colburn, 1841], II, 140).

95. Johann Friedrich Reichardt, *Vertraute Briefe geschrieben auf einer Reise nach Wien, 1808–1809,* 2 vols. (Amsterdam: Im Kunst- und Industrie-Comtoir, 1810), I, 206.

96. Joseph Schmidt-Görg, "Das Wiener Tagebuch des Mannheimer Hofkapell-meisters Michael Frey," *Beethoven-Jahrbuch* VI (1965–1968):149–150; also 169. The violinist Michael Frey, former pupil of Spohr and an active musician, spent the winter of 1815–1816 in Vienna with the hope of furthering his career. His objective observations are those of a professional who had already received very favorable notices for his own performances in *AMZ* (ibid., 129–132). This article by Schmidt-Görg came to my attention in Bathia Churgin and Joachim Braun, "A Report Concerning the Authentic Performance of Beethoven's Fourth Symphony, Op. 60," research project of the Beethoven Seminar at Bar-Ilan University, Ramat Gan, Israel, 1977, 135.

97. Schmidt-Görg, "Tagebuch Frey" [n. 96 above], 169.

98. Ibid., 138.

99. Theodor von Frimmel also observed that some time after 1802 Beethoven seemed to be moving toward "a freer interpretation of rhythm" (*Beethoven-Studien,* 2 vols. [Munich: Müller, 1905, 1906], II, 270).

100. *Thayer's Life of Beethoven,* rev. and ed. Elliott Forbes (Princeton: Princeton University Press, 1967), 687–688. In her discussion of tempo in Beethoven performance, Bathia Churgin noted that "The examples of a ritard not preceding a fermata [in the symphonies] occur only in the last three symphonies, especially in the Ninth Symphony, and so would seem to reflect the tendency toward a more flexible tempo in Beethoven's later works" (Churgin and Braun, "Authentic Performance of Beethoven's Fourth Symphony, Op. 60" [n. 96 above], 75–76).

101. Schindler/Moscheles, *Beethoven,* II, 129–130; Anton F. Schindler, *Biographie von Ludwig van Beethoven* (Münster: Aschendorff, 1840), 228.

102. Karl-Heinz Köhler, Dagmar Beck, Grita Herre, et al., eds., *Ludwig van Beethovens Konversationshefte,* 8 vols. (Leipzig: Deutscher Verlag für Musik, 1968–), III, 350.

103. Anton F. Schindler, *Beethoven as I Knew Him,* trans. Constance Jolly, ed. Donald W. MacArdle (Chapel Hill: University of North Carolina Press, 1966), 409; in German, Anton Schindler, *Biographie,* 3d ed., 2 vols. (Münster: Aschendorff, 1860), II, 225–226.

104. Schindler/Moscheles, *Beethoven,* II, 123–152. In addition he generalized that the Sonatas Opp. 14, 2/1, 10/1, 13, 27/2, "and some others, are all pictures of feeling; and, in every movement Beethoven varied the time according as the feelings changed" (ibid., 140).

105. Schindler/MacArdle, *Beethoven,* 396.

106. Schindler/Moscheles, *Beethoven,* II, 132, 134. For further comment on the "two principles" see p. 390.

107. See also Köhler, et al., eds. *Konversationshefte,* IV, 285.

108. Czerny, *Proper Performance,* 30.

109. Schindler/MacArdle, *Beethoven,* 417–419.

110. Ibid., 417.

111. Peter Stadlen, "Schindler and the Conversation Books," *Soundings* 7 (1978):8–9; Schindler/MacArdle, *Beethoven,* 446, n. 319. In Köhler et al., eds., *Konversationshefte,* II, 257; III, 102; V, 190.

112. Czerny, *Richtigen Vortrag,* 37.

113. In a brief musical example, Schindler placed a *fermata* over the A-flat three notes from the end of m. 4, as well as over the first chords of mm. 1–3.

114. Schindler/MacArdle, *Beethoven,* 498.

115. Schindler/Moscheles, *Beethoven,* II, 131–136.

116. "Beethoven, in composing, frequently imagined for himself a specific subject. . . ." (Wegeler and Ries, *Biographische Notizen,* 77–78). See Czerny's comments on Opp. 2/3/ii, 27/2/i (misnumbered as 27/1), 31/2/iii, 57/iii, 58/ii, and 73/ii (*Proper Performance,* 26, 39, 44, 50, 100, 103); Karl-Heinz Köhler, "The Conversation Books," *Beethoven, Performers, and Critics,* ed. Robert Winter and Bruce Carr (Detroit: Wayne State University Press, 1980), 157; and, most recently, Owen Jander, "Exploring Sulzer's *Allgemeine Theorie* as a Source Used by Beethoven," *The Beethoven Newsletter* 2/1 (Spring 1987):1–7.

117. E.g., Schindler/Moscheles, *Beethoven,* II, 105ff.; Schindler/MacArdle, *Beethoven,* 421–423, 426–427, 432–433; C. Moscheles, *Life,* II, 247–248. For this self-appointed guardian of Beethoven's "legacy," differing opinions from more-skilled musicians, particularly pianists, were well-nigh intolerable.

118. Czerny, *Proper Performance,* 23.

119. Ibid., 33.

120. Schindler wrote much about this movement in the *Biographie:* it "portrays melancholia in all its phases"; "its pace must be changed fully ten times"; and more (Schindler/MacArdle, *Beethoven,* 421, 406). The numerous forged "conversations" referring to it (Köhler, et al., eds., *Konversationshefte,* II, 200; IV, 285, 320) were presumably intended to provide a measure of authenticity for these remarks.

121. Czerny, *Richtigen Vortrag,* 34.

122. Czerny did not comment on Opp. 49 and 79.

123. Czerny, *Proper Performance,* 45.

124. Ibid., 52; German from *Richtigen Vortrag,* 56.

125. Schindler/Moscheles, *Beethoven,* II, 81.

126. Ibid., 140.

127. Ibid., 151.

128. Schindler/MacArdle, *Beethoven,* 413. This comment, passed on to Schindler in 1827, was supposedly based on Clementi's having heard Beethoven play in 1807.

11. Performing Beethoven's Bagatelle Op. 126, No. 5

1. Ludwig van Beethoven, *Sechs Bagatellen für Klavier Op. 126,* ed. S. Brandenburg, 2 vols. including Aut., sketches, OE, transcription of the sketches, and commentary (Bonn: Beethoven-Haus, 1984), I, 52.

2. Karl-Heinz Köhler, Dagmar Beck, Grita Herre, et al., eds., *Ludwig van Beethovens Konversationshefte,* 8 vols. (Leipzig: Deutscher Verlag für Musik, 1968–), VI, 176; for the dating see also 7–8 and 169.

3. Edward T. Cone, "Beethoven's Experiments in Composition: The Late Bagatelles," *Beethoven Studies,* II, ed. Alan Tyson (London: Oxford University Press, 1977), 84–105.

4. Emily Anderson, trans. and ed., *The Letters of Beethoven,* 3 vols. (London: Macmillan, 1961), 1151.

5. Cone, "Beethoven's Experiments in Composition" [n. 3 above], 92–93.

6. In just such a combination of slur-tie-slur at Var XXI/6 in the "Diabelli" Variations, Beethoven indicated a silent finger change on the second tied note. This allows the legato to continue unbroken to the end of the slur.

7. Sieghard Brandenburg suggests the general importance of repeats to Beethoven in this cycle. Another example is the direction "la seconda parte due volte" in addition to the repeat sign at the end of Op. 126/1 (Ludwig van Beethoven, *Sechs Bagatellen,* ed. Brandenburg [n. 1 above], II, 71).

8. Ibid. This copy is lost.

9. Kinsky-Halm, *Beethoven Verz.,* 382.

10. Ibid.

SELECTED BIBLIOGRAPHY

Some articles and books used for limited reference are not listed here; complete bibliographical information for them is given in the appropriate notes.

When more than one edition of a title is listed, references are to the first edition unless otherwise noted.

For sets of two or more volumes in which the pages are numbered successively, volume numbers are not included in the notes.

Adam, Louis. *Méthode de piano du Conservatoire.* Paris: Magasin de Musique du Conservatoire Royal, [1804].

———, and Ludwig Menzel Lachnith. *Méthode ou principe général du doigté pour le forté-piano.* Paris: Sieber, [1798]. 2d ed. augmentée, Paris: Sieber, [1814].

Adlam, Derek. "The Anatomy of the Piano." In *The Book of the Piano,* edited by Dominic Gill. Ithaca: Cornell University Press, 1981.

Agricola, Johann Friedrich. *Anleitung zur Singkunst.* Berlin: Winter, 1757. Facsimile, edited by Erwin R. Jacobi, Celle: Moeck, 1966. Facsimile includes Pier Francesco Tosi, *Opinioni de'cantori antichi e moderni* (Bologna, 1723), of which Agricola's *Anleitung* is a translation with extensive additions.

Albrecht, Hans, ed. *Die Bedeutung der Zeichen Keil, Strich und Punkt bei Mozart: Fünf Lösungen einer Preisfrage.* Kassel: Bärenreiter, 1957.

Allgemeine musikalische Zeitung (AMZ). Leipzig. 3 series: 1798–1848; Neue Folge, 1863–1865; Leipziger *AMZ,* 1866–1882.

Anderson, Emily, trans. and ed. *The Letters of Beethoven.* 3 vols. London: Macmillan, 1961.

———, trans. and ed. *The Letters of Mozart and His Family.* 2d ed., edited by A. Hyatt King and Monica Carolan. 2 vols. London: Macmillan, 1966.

Bach, Carl Philipp Emanuel. *Essay on the True Art of Playing Keyboard Instruments.* 2 vols., 1753, 1762. Translated and edited by William J. Mitchell. New York: Norton, 1949. Incorporates changes from the eighteenth-century revised editions: Pt. I (Leipzig: Schwickert, 1787); Pt. II (Leipzig: Schwickert, 1797).

———. *Sechs Sonaten fürs Clavier mit veränderten Reprisen,* Wq. 50. Berlin: Winter, 1760. Edited by Etienne Darbellay, Winterthur, Switzerland: Amadeus, 1976.

———. *Versuch über die wahre Art das Clavier zu spielen.* Berlin: In Verlegung des Auctoris, Vol. I, 1753; Vol. II, 1762. Facsimile of 1st ed., edited by Lothar Hoffmann-Erbrecht, Leipzig: Breitkopf & Härtel, 1978. Additions to the "3d" German ed. of 1787 are included in a separate section.

Bach, Johann Christian, and Francesco Pasquale Ricci. *Méthode ou recueil de connoissances [sic] élémentaires pour le forte-piano ou clavecin.* Paris, Le Duc, [ca. 1786]; reissue with new p.n., Paris: Le Duc, [179?]. According to Forkel, Ricci wrote the text and Bach provided the pieces (Carl Parrish, "Criticisms of the Piano When it Was New," *MQ* XXX/4 [October 1944]:432, fn. 1). All references are to the reissue.

Badura-Skoda, Eva. "Prolegomena to a History of the Viennese Fortepiano." *Israel Studies in Musicology,* II (1980): 77–99.

Badura-Skoda, Eva and Paul. *Interpreting Mozart on the Piano.* Translated from German by Leo Black. London: Barrie and Rockliff, 1962.

Baillot, Pierre; Rodolph Kreutzer; and Pierre Rode. *Méthode de violon.* Brussels: Weissenbruch, [1803].

Bamberger, Jeanne. "The Musical Significance of Beethoven's Fingerings in the Piano Sonatas." *The Music Forum* IV (1976):237–280.

Bartlitz, Eve. *Die Beethoven-Sammlung in der Musikabteilung der Deutschen Staatsbibliothek.* Berlin: Deutsche Staatsbibliothek, 1970.

Beck, Dagmar, and Grita Herre. "Einige Zweifel an der Überlieferung der Konversationshefte." In *Bericht über den Internationalen Beethoven-Kongress . . . 1977 in Berlin,* edited by Harry Goldschmidt, Karl-Heinz Köhler, and Konrad Niemann. Leipzig: Deutscher Verlag für Musik, 1978; 257–274.

Beck, Hermann. "Studien über das Tempoproblem bei Beethoven." Ph.D. diss., Friedrich-Alexander Universität, 1954. Summarized under the title "Bemerkungen zu Beethoven's Tempi," *Beethoven-Jahrbuch* II (1955–56):24–54.

Beethoven, Ludwig van. *Autograph Miscellany from circa 1787 to 1799* ("Kafka" Sketchbook). Edited by Joseph Kerman. 2 vols. Facsimile, transcription. London: Trustees of the British Museum, 1970.

———. *Beethovens sämtliche Briefe.* 5 vols. Edited by Alfred C. Kalischer. Berlin: Schuster & Loeffler, 1906–1908.

———. *Kesslersches Skizzenbuch* ("Kessler" Sketchbook). Edited by Sieghard Brandenburg. Vol. I, Transcription (*Übertragung*); Vol. II, Facsimile. Bonn: Beethoven-Haus, 1978, 1976. Facsimile only, edited by Sieghard Brandenburg for Gesellschaft de Musikfreunde, Vienna, Munich: Katzbichler, 1976.

———. *Klaviersonaten.* Edited by Bertha A. Wallner, 2 vols. Munich: Henle, 1952, 1953.

———. *Konversationshefte.* See under Köhler.

———. *L. van Beethoven's Werke: Vollständige kritisch durchgesehene überall berechtigte Ausgabe (BGA).* Leipzig: Breitkopf & Härtel, 1862–1890. Corrections were entered into various volumes reissued within those dates. There are at least three states of Vol. I of the *Sonaten für das Pianoforte* and two states of the *Kleinere Stücke für das Pianoforte,* Ser. 18. The reprint of *BGA* (Ann Arbor: Edwards, 1949) is a mixture of these states.

———. *Letters.* See under Anderson.

———. *Sonatas for the Pianoforte.* Edited by Artur Schnabel. See under Schnabel.

———. *Sonatas for the Pianoforte.* Edited by Donald F. Tovey and Harold Craxton. See under Tovey.

———. *Trios für Klavier, Violine, und Violoncello.* 3 vols. Edited by Günter Raphael. Munich: Henle, 1983.

———. *Werke: neue Ausgabe sämtlicher Werke (BNA).* Edited by Beethoven-Archiv, Bonn, under the direction of Joseph Schmidt-Görg, followed by Martin Staehelin. Munich: Henle, 1961–.

Beethoven-Jahrbuch. 3d series. Bonn: Beethoven-Haus, 1954–.

Beethoven Kolloquium, 1977: Documentation und Aufführungspraxis. Edited by Rudolf Klein for *Österreichische Gesellschaft für Musik, Beiträge '76–'78.* Kassel: Bärenreiter, 1978.

Beethoven, Performers, and Critics: The International Beethoven Congress, Detroit, 1977. Edited by Robert Winter and Bruce Carr. Detroit: Wayne State University Press, 1980.

Beethoven, Das Problem der Interpretation. Edited by Heinz-Klaus Metzger and Rainer Riehn. Munich: Edition Text & Kritik, 1979.

Beethoven Studies. Edited by Alan Tyson. Vol. I, New York: Norton, 1973; Vol. II, London: Oxford University Press, 1977; Vol. III, Cambridge: Cambridge University Press, 1982.

Beyschlag, Adolf. *Die Ornamentik der Musik.* Leipzig: Breitkopf & Härtel, 1908. 2d ed., Leipzig: Breitkopf & Härtel, 1953. References are to the 2d ed.

Broder, Nathan. "Mozart and the 'Clavier.' " In *The Creative World of Mozart,* edited by Paul Henry Lang. New York: Norton, 1963.

Brown, A. Peter. *Joseph Haydn's Keyboard Music: Sources and Style.* Bloomington: Indiana University Press, 1986.

Burney, Charles. *Dr. Burney's Musical Tours in Europe.* 2 vols. 2d ed., London: Becket, Robson, and Robinson, 1773, 1775 (with the titles *The Present State of Music in France and Italy* and *The Present State of Music in Germany, the Netherlands, and United Provinces*). Reprint, edited by Percy A. Scholes, London: Oxford University Press, 1959.

Busby, Thomas. *A Complete Dictionary of Music.* London: R. Phillips, [ca. 1801, according to *NG,* III, 497].

Churgin, Bathia, and Joachim Braun. "A Report Concerning the Authentic Performance of Beethoven's Fourth Symphony, Op. 60." Research Project of the Beethoven Seminar at Bar-Ilan University, Ramat Gan, Israel, 1977.

Clementi, Muzio. *Gradus ad Parnassum,* 3 vols. London: Clementi, Banger, Collard, Davis & Collard, 1817, 1819, 1826; parallel edition by Breitkopf & Härtel. Facsimile of the German edition, edited by Leon Plantinga, New York: Da Capo, 1980.

——. *Introduction to the Art of Playing on the Pianoforte* (Clementi/Rosenblum). London: Clementi, Banger, Hyde, Collard & Davis, [1801]. Facsimile, edited by Sandra P. Rosenblum, New York: Da Capo, 1974.

——. *Klaviersonaten,* Auswahl. 2 vols. Edited by Sonja Gerlach and Alan Tyson. Munich: Henle, 1978, 1982.

——. *Oeuvres complettes.* Leipzig: Breitkopf & Härtel, ca. 1803–1819. Facsimile, New York: Da Capo, 1973. Only the text of Vol. VI, which contains pieces selected and revised by Clementi, can be considered authentic (Tyson, *Clementi Cat.,* 125).

——. *Sonata in F minor, Op. 14/3* (13/6 according to Tyson, *Clementi Cat.*). Composer's previously unpublished revision, edited by Sandra P. Rosenblum. Boston: E. C. Schirmer, 1968.

Couperin, François. *L'Art de toucher le clavecin.* Paris, 1716. Enl. ed., Paris: Chés Mr. Couperin, 1717.

——. *The Art of Playing the Harpsichord,* 1717. Trilingual ed., edited by and German translation by Anna Linde; English translation by Mevanwy Roberts. Leipzig: Breitkopf & Härtel, 1933.

Cramer, Carl Friedrich, ed. *Magazin der Musik.* Hamburg, 1783–1787.

Cramer, Johann Baptist. *Instructions for the Piano Forte.* London: Chappell, 1812.

——. *21 Etüden für Klavier: Nach dem Handexemplar Beethovens aus dem Besitz Anton Schindlers.* See under Kann.

Craw, Howard Allen. "A Biography and Thematic Catalog of the Works of J. L. Dussek (1760–1812)." Ph.D. diss., University of Southern California, 1964; Ann Arbor: University Microfilms 64–9611.

Crelle, August Leopold. *Einiges über musicalischen Ausdruck und Vortrag: für Fortepiano-Spieler....* Berlin: Maurerschen Buchhandlung, 1823.

Czerny, Carl. *Complete Theoretical and Practical Piano Forte School,* Op. 500. 3 vols., 1839. Translated by J. A. Hamilton, London: Cocks, [1839]. Vol. IV, *The Art of Playing the Ancient and Modern Piano Forte Works.* Translator anon. London: Cocks, [1846].

——. *Die Kunst des Vortrags der älteren und neueren Klavierkompositionen,* Vol. IV of *Vollständige ... Pianoforte-Schule,* Op. 500. Vienna: Diabelli, 1846.

——. *On the Proper Performance of all Beethoven's Works for the Piano.* Chapters 2 and 3 of *The Art of Playing the Ancient and Modern Piano Forte Works.* Facsimile, edited by Paul Badura-Skoda, Vienna: Universal, 1970. The volume also includes extracts from Czerny's "Memoirs." Page references in the present book are to those of the Universal Edition (bottom center of each page) rather than to the original numbers.

———. *Über den richtigen Vortrag der sämtlichen Beethoven'schen Klavierwerke.* Chapters 2 and 3 of *Die Kunst des Vortrags.* . . . Facsimile, edited by Paul Badura-Skoda, Vienna: Universal, 1963. The volume includes extracts from Czerny's "Erinnerungen aus meinem Leben."

———. *Vollständige theoretisch-praktische Pianoforte-Schule,* Op. 500. 3 vols. Vienna: Diabelli, 1839. (For Vol. IV, see *Die Kunst des Vortrags.* . . .)

Deutsch, Otto Erich. "Beethovens gesammelte Werke: Des Meisters Plan und Haslingers Ausgabe." *Zeitschrift für Musikwissenschaft* XII/1 (October 1930–1931): 60–79.

———. *Mozart: A Documentary Biography.* Stanford: Stanford University Press, 1965.

———. *Music Publishers' Numbers: A Selection of 40 Dated Lists, 1710–1900.* London: Association of Special Libraries and Information Bureaux, 1946. 2d improved ed., as *Musikverlags Nummern,* Berlin: Merseburger, 1961.

Donington, Robert. *The Interpretation of Early Music.* New Version. New York: St. Martin's Press, 1974.

Dussek, Jan Ladislav. *Instructions on the Art of Playing the Piano Forte or Harpsichord.* London: Corri, Dussek, [1796].

Eggebrecht, Hans Heinrich, ed. *Handwörterbuch der Musikalischen Terminologie.* Wiesbaden: Steiner, 1972.

Eibner, Franz. "Registerpedalisierung bei Haydn und Beethoven." *Österreichische Musikzeitschrift* XX/4 (April 1965):190–196.

Emery, Walter. *Bach's Ornaments.* London: Novello, 1953.

Ferand, Ernest T. *Improvisation in Nine Centuries of Western Music: An Anthology with a Historical Introduction.* Cologne: Arno Volk, 1961.

Ferguson, Howard. *Keyboard Interpretation.* London: Oxford University Press, 1975.

Fétis, François-Joseph. *Biographie universelle des musiciens et bibliographie général de la musique.* 8 vols. Brussels: Meline, Cans, 1837–1844. 2d ed., 8 vols., suppl. 2 vols., Paris: Firmin Didot, 1861–1870, 1878–1880.

"Fischhof" Miscellany. See Johnson, *Beethoven's Early Sketches.*

Forbes, Elliot, ed. *Thayer's Life of Beethoven.* See under Thayer.

Frimmel, Theodor von. *Beethoven-Studien.* 2 vols. Munich: Müller, 1905, 1906 (with the titles *Beethoven's Äussere Erscheinung* and *Bausteine zu einer Lebensgeschichte des Meisters*).

Galeazzi, Francesco. *Elementi di Musica.* Vol. I, Rome: Cracas, 1791; Vol. II, Rome: Puccinelli, 1796. All references are to Vol. 1.

Geiringer, Karl and Irene. *Haydn: A Creative Life in Music.* 3d rev. and enl. ed. Berkeley: University of California Press, 1982.

Gerber, Ernst Ludwig. *Historisch-biographisches Lexicon der Tonkünstler.* 2 vols. Leipzig: Breitkopf, 1790, 1792.

Goldschmidt, Harry. *Die Erscheinung Beethoven.* Leipzig: Deutscher Verlag für Musik, 1974.

Good, Edwin M. *Giraffes, Black Dragons, and Other Pianos: A Technological History from Cristofori to the Modern Concert Grand.* Stanford: Stanford University Press, 1982.

Grundmann, Herbert, and Paul Mies. *Studien zum Klavierspiel Beethovens und seiner Zeitgenossen.* Bonn: Bouvier, 1966.

Harding, Rosamund. *The Pianoforte: Its History Traced to the Great Exhibition of 1851,* 1933. 2d ed., Surrey, England: Gresham Books, 1978.

Harmonicon. 1823–1833.

Haydn, Joseph. *The Collected Correspondence.* . . . See under H. C. Robbins Landon.

———. *The Complete Piano Sonatas (Sämtliche Klaviersonaten)* (HSU). 3 vols. Edited by Christa Landon. Vienna: Schott/Universal (formerly Universal), ca. 1964–1966.

Landon's critical report for this edition is published only in German, as *Haydn: Sämtliche Klaviersonaten, Kritische Anmerkungen,* Vienna: Schott/Universal, 1982.

——. *J. Haydn: Gesammelte Briefe und Aufzeichnungen.* Edited by Dénes Bartha. Kassel: Bärenreiter, 1965.

——. *J. Haydns Werke: Erste kritisch durchgesehene Gesamtausgabe.* Edited by Eusebius Mandyczewski et al. Leipzig: Breitkopf & Härtel, ca. 1907–ca. 1933. The edition remains incomplete, but the four volumes of *Sonaten,* edited by Karl Päsler, contain comprehensive critical reports based on the sources available at the time. These volumes were published ca. 1919.

——. *Klaviersonaten, Auswahl* [Selected keyboard sonatas] (HE). 2 vols. Edited by Georg Feder. Munich: Henle, [ca. 1972]. The text in this edition differs from that in *JHW* (below) only in the addition of fingering; but at the time of writing, limited notes on the sources and text are available only for HE (in each volume), not for the sonatas in *JHW.*

——. *Klaviertrios.* Edited by H. C. Robbins Landon. Vienna: Doblinger, 1970–.

——. *Oeuvres complettes* (OC). 12 vols. Leipzig: Breitkopf & Härtel, [1800–1806].

——. *Sonaten.* Edited by Karl Päsler. See *J. Haydns Werke.*

——. *Werke* (JHW). Edited by the Joseph Haydn-Institut, Cologne, under the direction of Jens Peter Larsen (1958–1961) and Georg Feder (1962–). Munich: Henle, 1958–.

Joseph Haydn. Proceedings of the International Joseph Haydn Congress, Vienna, 1982. Edited by Eva Badura-Skoda. Munich: Henle, 1986.

Haydn-Studien. Cologne: Joseph Haydn-Institut, 1965–.

Haydn Studies. Proceedings of the International Haydn Conference, Washington, DC, 1975. Edited by Jens Peter Larsen, Howard Serwer, and James Webster. New York: Norton, 1981.

Hiller, Johann Adam. *Anweisung zum musikalisch-zierlichen Gesange.* Leipzig: Junius, 1780. Facsimile, Leipzig: Peters, 1976.

——. *Anweisung zum Violinspielen.* Grätz: Trötscher, 1795.

Hirt, Franz Josef. *Meisterwerke des Klavierbaus: Geschichte der Saitenklaviere von 1440 bis 1880.* Olten, Switzerland: Urs Graf, 1955. Bilingual edition, as *Stringed Keyboard Instruments,* German with English translation by M. Boehme-Brown, Dietikon: Urs Graf, 1901.

Hoboken, Anthony van. *Joseph Haydn: Thematisch-bibliographisches Werkverzeichnis.* 3 vols. Mainz: Schott, 1957–1978. All references are to Vol. I.

Hüllmandel, Joseph Nicolas. *Principles of Music, Chiefly Calculated for the Piano Forte or Harpsichord.* London: By the Author, [1796].

Hummel, Johann Nepomuk. *A Complete Theoretical & Practical Course of Instructions on the Art of Playing the Pianoforte,* 1828. Translated, anon., London: Boosey, 1829.

——. *Ausführliche theoretisch-practische Anweisung zum Piano-forte-spiel.* 3 vols. Vienna: Haslinger 1828.

Humphries, Charles, and William Smith. *Music Publishing in the British Isles.* 2d ed. Oxford: Blackwell, 1970.

Jahn, Otto. *W. A. Mozart.* 4 vols. Leipzig: Breitkopf & Härtel, 1856–1859. Translation of 2d German ed., 1867, as *Life of Mozart,* by Pauline D. Townsend, 3 vols., London: Novello, Ewer, 1882.

Janowka, Thomas Balthasar. *Clavis ad Thesaurum. . . .* Prague: Labaun, 1701. Facsimile, Amsterdam: Knuf, 1973.

Jarecki, Gershon. "Die Ausführung der Pedalvorschriften Beethovens auf dem Modernen Klavier." *Österreichische Musikzeitschrift* XX/4 (April 1965):197–200.

Johnson, Douglas P. *Beethoven's Early Sketches in the "Fischhof Miscellany": Berlin Autograph 28.* 2 vols. Ann Arbor: UMI Research Press, 1980.

Journal of the American Musicological Society (JAMS). 1948–.

"Kafka" Sketchbook. See Beethoven, *Autograph Miscellany.*

Kalkbrenner, Friedrich. *A New Method of Studying the Piano-forte.* 3d ed. London: D'Almaine, [1837].

Kann, Hans, ed. Johann Baptist Cramer, *21 Etüden für Klavier: Nach dem Handexemplar Beethovens aus dem Besitz Anton Schindlers.* Vienna: Universal, 1974.

Katalog der Sammlung alter Musikinstrumente. Vol. 1, *Saitenklaviere.* Edited by Victor Luithlen. Vienna: Kunsthistorisches Museum, 1966.

Keller, Hermann. *Phrasing and Articulation.* Translated from German by Leigh Gerdine. New York: Norton, 1965.

Kelly, Michael. *Reminiscences.* 2 vols. London: Colburn, 1826.

"Kessler" Sketchbook. See Beethoven, *Kesslersches Skizzenbuch.*

Kinsky, Georg, and Hans Halm. *Das Werk Beethovens: Thematisch-Bibliographisches Verzeichnis.* Munich: Henle, 1955.

Knecht, [Justin Heinrich]. *Knechts Allgemeiner musikalisher Katechismus.* Biberach: Gebrüder Knecht, 1803.

Koch, Heinrich Christoph. *Musikalisches Lexikon.* Frankfurt: Hermann dem jüngern, 1802. Facsimile, Hildesheim: Olms, 1964.

——. *Versuch einer Anleitung zur Composition.* Vol. I, Rudolstadt: Löwe Erben und Schirach, 1782; Vols. II and III, Leipzig: Böhme, 1787, 1793. Facsimile, Hildesheim: Olms, 1969.

Köchel, Ludwig Ritter von. *Chronologisch-thematisches Verzeichnis sämtlicher Tonwerke W. A. Mozarts.* 7th ed. Edited by Franz Giegling, Alexander Weinmann, and Gerd Sievers. Wiesbaden: Breitkopf & Härtel, 1965.

Köhler, Karl-Heinz; Dagmar Beck; Grita Herre; et al., eds. *Ludwig van Beethovens Konversationshefte.* 8 vols. Leipzig: Deutscher Verlag für Musik, 1968–.

Kolisch, Rudolf. "Tempo and Character in Beethoven's Music," *MQ* XXIX/2 and 3 (April and July 1943):169–187, 291–312.

Kramer, Richard. "On the Dating of Two Aspects in Beethoven's Notation for Piano." In *Beethoven Kolloquium, 1977.* Pp. 160–173.

Krummel, D. W., ed. *Guide for Dating Early Published Music.* Hackensack, NJ: Boonin, 1974.

Kullak, Franz. *Beethoven's Piano Playing, With an Essay on the Execution of the Trill.* (Preface to the Steingräber ed. of Beethoven's Piano Concertos, Leipzig, 1881.) Translated from German by Theodore Baker. New York: G. Schirmer, 1901. Facsimile, New York: Da Capo, 1973.

Landon, Christa. *Kritische Anmerkungen.* See Haydn, *Complete Piano Sonatas.*

Landon, H. C. Robbins. *Haydn: Chronicle and Works.* 5 vols. Bloomington: Indiana University Press, 1976–1980.

——, trans. and ed. *The Collected Correspondence and London Notebooks of Joseph Haydn.* London: Barrie and Rockliff, 1959.

Lasser, Johann Baptist. *Vollständige Anleitung zur Singkunst.* Munich, 1798. 2d ed., Munich: Hübschmann, 1805. All references are to the 2d ed., which is identical to the first, according to Frederick Neumann (*Mozart,* 290).

Leinsdorf, Erich. *The Composer's Advocate: A Radical Orthodoxy for Musicians.* New Haven: Yale University Press, 1981.

Löhlein, George Simon. *Anweisung zum Violinspielen.* Leipzig: Waysenhaus und Frommann, 1774. 3d ed., edited by Johann Friedrich Reichardt, Leipzig: F. Frommann, 1797.

——. *Clavier-Schule, oder kurze und gründliche Anweisung zur melodie und harmonie.* Leipzig: Waisenhaus und Frommann 1765. 2d ed., Leipzig: Waisenhaus und Frommann, 1773. 3d ed., Leipzig: Waisenhaus und Frommann, 1779. 4th ed., 2 vols., Leipzig: Waisenhaus und Frommann, 1782, 1781. 5th ed., edited by Johann Georg Witthauer, Leipzig: N. S. Fromanns Erben, 1791. For a 6th ed., see under Müller.

Lütge, Wilhelm. "Andreas und Nannette Streicher." *Der Bär* (Jahrbuch von Breitkopf & Härtel) IV (1927):53–69.

Malloch, William. "Toward a 'New' (Old) Minuet." *Opus* 1/5 (August 1985):14–21, 52.

Mancini, Giambattista. *Riflessioni Pratiche sul Canto Figurato.* Vienna, 1774. Translated from Italian and edited by Edward Foremann, as *Practical Reflections on Figured Singing,* Champaign, IL: Pro Musica Press, 1967. Translation incorporates additions from 3d ed. (Milan: Galeazzi, 1777).

Manfredini, Vincenzo. *Regole Armoniche o sieno precetti . . . i principi della musica, il portamento della mano, . . . sopra . . . il cembalo, . . .* Venice: Zerletti, 1775.

Marpurg, Friedrich Wilhelm. *Anleitung zum Clavierspielen.* Berlin: Haude und Spener, 1755. 2d ed., Berlin: Haude und Spener, 1765. Facsimile of 2d ed., New York: Broude, 1969. Although the 2d ed. was newly engraved throughout, only changes in the fingerings and ornaments of Tables XV-XVIII and the addition of Tables XIX and XX distinguish the two editions. Their text and pagination are identical.

Mattheson, Johann. *Der vollkommene Capellmeister* [The perfect chapel master]. Hamburg: Herold, 1739. Translated from German and edited by Ernest C. Harriss (retaining the German title), Ann Arbor: UMI Research Press, 1981. All references in the present volume are to the English edition.

Mies, Paul. *Textkritische Untersuchungen bei Beethoven.* Munich: Henle, 1957.

Milchmeyer, Johann Peter. *Die wahre Art das Pianoforte zu Spielen.* Dresden: Meinhold, 1797.

de Momigny, Jérôme-Joseph. *Cours complet d'harmonie et de composition.* 3 vols. [2d ed.], Paris: de Momigny, 1808.

Moscheles, Charlotte. *Life of Moscheles with selections from His Diaries and Correspondence.* Translated from German by A. D. Coleridge. 2 vols. London: Hurst and Blackett, 1873.

Mozart, Leopold. *Versuch einer gründlichen Violinschule.* Augsburg: In Verlag des Verfassers, 1756. Translated by Editha Knocker, as *A Treatise on the Fundamental Principles of Violin Playing.* 2d ed., London: Oxford University Press, 1951. Translation incorporates additions from 3d German ed. (Augsburg: Lotter und Sohn, 1787). All references are to the translation.

Mozart, Wolfgang Amadeus. *Klaviersonaten.* (HE). 2 vols. Edited by Ernst Herttrich. Munich: Henle, 1977.

———. *Letters.* See under Anderson.

———. *Neue Ausgabe sämtlicher Werke* (*NMA*). Edited by Internationale Stiftung Mozarteum, Salzburg. Kassel: Bärenreiter, 1956–.

———. *Piano Sonatas.* 2 vols. Edited by Karl Heinz Füssl and Heinz Scholz. 3d ed., Vienna: Schott/Universal (formerly Universal), 1973.

———. *Sonatas and Fantasies for the Piano* (Bro). Edited by Nathan Broder. Bryn Mawr, PA: Presser, 1956; rev. ed., 1960.

W. A. Mozart: Briefe und Aufzeichnungen. Edited by Wilhelm A. Bauer, Otto Erich Deutsch, and Joseph Heinz Eibl for the Internationale Stiftung Mozarteum, Salzburg. 7 vols. Kassel: Bärenreiter, 1962–1975.

W. A. Mozart's Werke: Kritisch durchgesehene Gesammtausgabe (*MGA*). Edited by Johannes Brahms, . . . Gustav Nottebohm, Carl Reinecke et al. Leipzig: Breitkopf & Härtel, 1876–1905.

Mozart-Jahrbuch. Internationale Stiftung Mozarteum, Salzburg. 1950–.

Müller, August Eberhard. *Klavier und Fortepiano-Schule.* Jena: F. Frommann, 1804. An expanded 6th ed. of Löhlein's *Clavier-Schule,* although it is known under Müller's name.

The Musical Quarterly (*MQ*). 1915–.

Die Musik in Geschichte und Gegenwart (*MGG*). 16 vols. Edited by Friedrich Blume. Kassel: Bärenreiter, 1949–1979.

Neumann, Frederick. *Ornamentation and Improvisation in Mozart.* Princeton: Princeton University Press, 1986.

——. *Ornamentation in Baroque and Post-Baroque Music, with Special Emphasis on J. S. Bach.* Princeton: Princeton University Press, 1978.

The New Grove Dictionary of Music and Musicians (NG). 6th ed., 20 vols. Edited by Stanley J. Sadie. London: Macmillan, 1980.

The New Grove Dictionary of Musical Instruments (NGMI). 3 vols. Edited by Stanley J. Sadie. London: Macmillan, 1984.

Newman, William S. *Beethoven on Beethoven—Playing His Piano Music His Way.* New York: Norton, 1988.

——. "Beethoven's Fingerings as Interpretive Clues." *The Journal of Musicology* I/2 (April 1982):171–197.

——. "Beethoven's Pianos Versus His Piano Ideals." *JAMS* XXIII/3 (Fall 1970):484–504.

——. "A Chronological Checklist of Collected Editions of Beethoven's Solo Piano Sonatas Since His Own Day." *Notes* XXXIII/3 (March 1977):503–530.

——. "On the Problem of Determining Beethoven's Most Authoritative Lifetime Editions." In *Beiträge zur Beethoven-Bibliographie,* edited by Kurt Dorfmüller. Munich: Henle, 1978.

——. "The Performance of Beethoven's Trills." *JAMS* XXIX/3 (Fall 1976):437–462.

——. *The Sonata in the Classic Era.* Chapel Hill: University of North Carolina Press, 1963.

——. "Tempo in Beethoven's Instrumental Music: Its Choice and Its Flexibility." Pt. 1, *PQ* 116 (Winter 1981–1982):22–29; Pt. 2, *PQ* 117 (Spring 1982):22–31. In German, as "Das Tempo in Beethoven's Instrumentalmusik: Tempowahl und Tempoflexibilität." *Die Musikforschung* XXXIII/2 (April-June 1980):161–163.

——. "Yet Another Major Beethoven Forgery by Schindler?" *The Journal of Musicology* III/4 (Fall 1984):397–422.

Nohl, Ludwig. *Beethoven: Nach den Schilderungen seiner Zeitgenossen.* Stuttgart: Cotta, 1877. Translated by Emily Hill, as *Beethoven Depicted by His Contemporaries,* London: Reeves, 1880.

Nottebohm, Gustav. *Beethoveniana.* 2 vols. Leipzig: Rieter-Biedermann, 1872, 1887.

——. "Zur Reinigung der Werke Beethoven's von Fehlern und fremden Zuthaten." *AMZ,* 3d series, XI/21–33 (24 May–16 August 1876). A section of this long article, beginning on the front page, appears in almost every issue between those dates.

Petri, Johann Samuel. *Anleitung zur Praktischen Musik.* Lauban: Wirthgen, 1767. 2d ed., Leipzig: Breitkopf, 1782. Reference is to the 2d ed. unless otherwise noted.

The Piano Quarterly (PQ). Founded as *Piano Quarterly Newsletter.* 1952–.

Plantinga, Leon. *Clementi: His Life and Music.* London: Oxford University Press, 1977.

Pleyel, Ignaz, and Jan Ladislav Dussek. *Méthode pour le piano forte.* Paris: Pleyel, [1797].

Pollini, Francesco. *Metodo per Clavicembalo.* Milan: Ricordi, [1812].

Quantz, Johann Joachim. *On Playing the Flute.* 1752. Translated and edited by Edward R. Reilly. London: Faber and Faber, 1966.

——. *Versuch einer Anweisung die Flöte traversiere zu spielen.* Berlin: Voss, 1752. 3d ed., Breslau: J. F. Korn the elder, 1789. Facsimile of 3d ed., edited by Hans-Peter Schmitz, Kassel: Bärenreiter, 1953. The 3d German ed. is textually identical with the first ed. of 1752.

Ratner, Leonard G. *Classic Music: Expression, Form, and Style.* New York: Schirmer Books, 1980.

Reichardt, Johann Friedrich. *Vertraute Briefe geschrieben auf einer Reise nach Wien . . . , 1808–1809.* 2 vols. Amsterdam: Im Kunst- und Industrie-Comtoir, 1810.

Rellstab, Johann Karl Friedrich. *Anleitung für Clavierspieler.* Berlin: Rellstabschen . . . Musikdruckerey, 1790.

Rimbault, Edward Francis. *The Pianoforte, its Origin, Progress and Construction.* London: Cocks, 1860.

Rosen, Charles. *The Classical Style: Haydn, Mozart, Beethoven.* New York: Norton, 1972.

Rosenblum, Sandra P. "Clementi's Pianoforte Tutor on the Continent." *Fontes Artis Musicae* 27/1 (January–March 1980):37–48.

Rousseau, Jean-Jacques. *Dictionnaire de musique.* Paris: Chez la Veuve Duchesne, 1768.

Rowland, David. "Early Pianoforte Pedalling: The Evidence of the Earliest Printed Markings." *Early Music* XIII/1 (February 1985):5–17.

Rudolf, Max. "Ein Beitrag zur Geschichte der Temponahme bei Mozart." *Mozart-Jahrbuch* 1976/77:204–224.

——. *The Grammar of Conducting.* 2d ed. New York: Schirmer Books, 1980.

——. "Inner Repeats in the Da Capo of Classical Minuets and Scherzos." *Journal of the Conductors' Guild* 3/4 (Fall 1982):145–150.

Rück, Ulrich. "Mozart's Hammerflügel Erbaute Anton Walter, Wien: Technische Studien, Vergleich und Beweise." *Mozart-Jahrbuch* VI (1955):246–262, followed by 26 plates (pages unnumbered).

Sachs, Curt. *Rhythm and Tempo.* New York: Norton, 1953.

Saslav, Isidor. "Tempos in the String Quartets of Joseph Haydn." D.M. diss., Indiana University, 1969.

Schiedermair, Ludwig. *Der junge Beethoven.* Leipzig: Quelle & Meyer, 1925.

Schindler, Anton F. *Biographie von Ludwig van Beethoven.* Münster: Aschendorff, 1840. 3d ed., 2 vols. Münster: Aschendorff, 1860. Translated from the 3d ed. by Constance Jolly and edited by Donald W. MacArdle, as *Beethoven as I Knew Him* (Schindler/MacArdle), Chapel Hill: University of North Carolina Press, 1966. Translated from the 1st ed. and edited by Ignaz Moscheles, as *The Life of Beethoven* (Schindler/Moscheles), 2 vols., London: Colburn, 1841.

Schmid, Ernst Fritz, ed. *Joseph Haydn, Works for Flute Clock.* New York: Row, 1965.

Schnabel, Artur, ed. Ludwig van Beethoven, *Sonatas for the Pianoforte.* 2 vols. New York: Simon and Schuster, 1935.

Schönfeld, Johann Ferdinand von. *Jahrbuch der Tonkunst von Wien und Prag.* Vienna: von Schönfeld, 1796. Facsimile, edited by Otto Biba, Munich: Katzbichler, 1976.

Schubert, Johann Friedrich. *Neue Singe-Schule.* Leipzig: Breitkopf & Härtel, [1804].

Schwarz, Vera. "Missverständnisse in der Haydn-Interpretation." *Österreichische Musikzeitschrift* XXXI/1 (January 1976):25–35.

Solomon, Maynard. *Beethoven.* New York: Schirmer Books, 1977.

Somfai, László. "How to Read and Understand Haydn's Notation in Its Chronologically Changing Concepts." In *Joseph Haydn. Proceedings of the International Joseph Haydn Congress,* Vienna, 1982. Pp. 23–35.

——. *Joseph Haydn zongoraszonátái* [The piano sonatas of Joseph Haydn]. Budapest: Zeneműkaidó, 1979.

Sonneck, Oscar G. T., ed. *Beethoven: Impressions of Contemporaries.* New York: G. Schirmer, 1926. Facsimile, New York: Dover, 1967.

Stadlen, Peter. "Beethoven and the Metronome." *Music and Letters* 48/4 (October 1967):330–349.

——. "Schindler and the Conversation Books." *Soundings* 7 (1978):2–18.

Starke, Friedrich. *Wiener Pianoforte-Schule.* Vol. I, Vienna: Bey dem Verfasser, 1819; Vol. II, Vienna: Sprenger, 1819; Vol. III, Vienna: Bermann, 1821. Vol. I has three sections: Pt. 1, text of the pianoforte tutor, pp. 1–23; Pt. 2, short pieces, pp. 1–56; Pt. 3, a brief singing method, pp. 1–9. Vols. II and III contain more-advanced piano music.

Steibelt, Daniel. *Méthode de piano/Pianoforte-Schule.* Leipzig: Breitkopf & Härtel, [ca. 1809].

Stevens, W.[illiam] S.[eaman]. *A Treatise on Piano-Forte Expression.* London: Jones, 1811.

Streicher, Andreas. *Brief Remarks on the Playing, Tuning, and Care of Fortepianos.* Vienna: Alberti, 1801. Translated from German and edited by Preethi de Silva (Historical Treatises on Musical Instruments, Vol. I), Ann Arbor: Early Music Facsimiles, 1983.

Sulzer, Johann George. *Allgemeine Theorie der Schönen Kunste.* 2 vols. Leipzig: Weidmann, 1771, 1774. Enl. 2d ed., 4 vols., Leipzig: Weidmann, 1792–1794. "Register" in a separate vol., 1799. Facsimile of enl. 2d ed., Hildesheim: Olms, 1967–1970. Unless otherwise noted, references are to the first edition.

    Allgemeine Theorie was also revised in 1778–1779 and 1786–1787. Since the version of 1792–1794 is designated as "Neue vermehrte zweyte Auflage" on the title page of each volume, I refer to it as the enl. 2d ed. I have not seen either of the other revised versions or a 3d rev. ed., published in 1796–1797. (François Lesure, ed., *Écrits imprimés concernant la musique,* RISM B VI [Munich: Henle, 1971], II, 812–813.)

Tartini, Giuseppe. *Traité des agréments de la musique.* The original Italian, written between 1752 and 1756, survives in two manuscript copies. 1st French ed., translated by Pietro Denis, Paris: Chez l'auteur, 1771. Trilingual ed., English translation by Cuthbert Girdlestone, edited by Erwin R. Jacobi, Celle: Moeck, 1961, with facsimile of Italian manuscript included as a Supplement.

Thayer, Alexander Wheelock. *Ludwig van Beethovens Leben.* Translated from the original English by Hermann Dieters, revised by Hugo Riemann. 5 vols. Vol. I, Berlin: Schneider, 1866; Vols. II and III, Berlin: Weber, 1872, 1879; Vols. IV and V, Leipzig: Breitkopf & Härtel, 1907, 1908.

Thayer's Life of Beethoven. Revised and edited by Elliot Forbes. Princeton: Princeton University Press, 1964; rev. ed., 1967. All references are to the revised edition.

Tovey, Donald F., and Harold Craxton, eds. Ludwig van Beethoven, *Sonatas for Pianoforte.* 3 vols. London: Associated Board of the Royal Schools of Music, [1931].

Türk, Daniel Gottlob. *Klavierschule, oder Anweisung zum Klavierspielen für Lehrer und Lernende.* Leipzig and Halle: Schwickert; Hemmerde und Schwetschke, 1789. Facsimile, edited by Erwin R. Jacobi, Kassel: Bärenreiter, 1962. 2d ed., Leipzig and Halle: Schwickert; Hemmerde und Schwetschke, 1802.

————. *School of Clavier Playing,* 1789. Translated and edited by Raymond Haggh. Lincoln: University of Nebraska Press, 1982.

Tyson, Alan. *Thematic Catalogue of the Works of Muzio Clementi.* Tutzing: Schneider, 1967.

Unverricht, Hubert. *Die Eigenschriften und die Originalausgaben von Werken Beethovens in ihrer Bedeutung für die moderne Textkritik.* Kassel: Bärenreiter, 1960.

Viguerie, Bernard. *L'Art de toucher le piano-forte.* Paris: Chez l'Auteur, [1797].

Vinquist, Mary, and Neal Zaslaw. *Performance Practice: A Bibliography.* New York: Norton, 1971.

Vogler, Abbé Georg Joseph. *Kuhrpfälzische Tonschule.* Mannheim: Auf Kosten des Verfassers, in Commission bei Schwan und Götz, [1778]. The musical examples for the *Tonschule* were printed in a separate volume, *Gründe der Kuhrpfälzischen Tonschule in Beyspielen . . .* (Mannheim, [1778]).

Walter, Horst. "Haydns Klaviere." *Haydn-Studien* II/4 (December 1970):256–258.

Wegeler, Franz Gerhard, and Ferdinand Ries. *Biographische Notizen über Beethoven.* Coblenz: Bädeker, 1838.

Wegerer, Kurt. "Beethovens Hammerflügel und ihre Pedale." *Österreichische Musikzeitschrift* XX/4 (April 1965):201–211.

Winter, Robert. "Second Thoughts on the Performance of Beethoven's Trills." *MQ* LXIII/4 (October 1977):483–504.

Wolf, Georg Friedrich. *Unterricht im Klavierspielen.* Göttingen: der Verfasser, 1783. 3d ed., Halle: Hendel, 1789. All references are to the 3d ed.

Zaslaw, Neal. "Mozart's Tempo Conventions." In *Report of the Eleventh Congress of the International Musicological Society, 1972.* 2 vols. Copenhagen: Hansen, 1974; II, 720–733.

INDEX

Musical works are grouped according to the following categories and order: Piano music (Sonatas, Shorter pieces and variations), Concertos, Chamber music, Orchestral music, Vocal music, Pieces for musical clock, Sketchbooks. Within these groups, the order is according to identifying number or alphabetically by title. An asterisk indicates a musical example, bold type a definition, italic a main discussion; capital and lower-case letters indicate major and minor keys respectively. B, C, H, and M are abbreviations of Ludwig van Beethoven, Muzio Clementi, Franz Joseph Haydn, and Wolfgang Amadeus Mozart respectively.